UNMARRIED COUPLES AND THE LAW

By

Graham Douthwaite

Professor of Law
University of Santa Clara School of Law

THE ALLEN SMITH COMPANY
Publishers
Indianapolis, Indiana 46202

Copyright © 1979 by
THE ALLEN SMITH COMPANY
Indianapolis, Indiana

ISBN: O-87473-122-4
Library of Congress Number: 79-63600

The prophecies of what the courts will do in fact, and nothing more pretentious, is what I mean by the law.

Holmes, The Path of the Law,
10 Harv. L. Rev. 457, 461 (1897).

THE AUTHORS

GRAHAM DOUTHWAITE

Born in 1913. B.A. (1934) and LL.B. (1936), Witwatersrand, South Africa. B.C.L., first (1940), Oxford University. Government service, 1946-55. Research Editor, Bancroft Whitney, San Francisco, 1955-59. Assistant Professor of Law, The University of Santa Clara School of Law, 1959-62; Associate Professor, 1962-64; Professor since 1964.

MARY MOERS WENIG (Author of Chapter 5, Marital Status and Taxes)

B.A. (1946), Vassar College. J.D. (1951), Columbia University School of Law. Admitted: New York, Connecticut and Federal Bars. Law practice, New York, 1951-71. Assistant Professor of Law, St. John's University School of Law, 1971-75; Associate Professor, 1975-78. Professor, University of Bridgeport School of Law, since 1978. Visiting Fellow in Law, Yale Law School, since 1978.

ACKNOWLEDGEMENTS

The author wishes to thank Susan N. Norman, Elliot Groffman and Judy Barbour for their able assistance in researching and preparing this work. My deepest thanks also to the editorial staff of The Allen Smith Company for their patience and support in editing and assembling the book.

Graham Douthwaite

Santa Clara, California
May, 1979.

TABLE OF CONTENTS

CHAPTER 1

MARRIAGE AND OTHER LIFE STYLES

Section		Page
1.1	Nature and scope of discussion	1
1.2	Marriage as creating a status	4
1.3	Demerits of cohabitation as an alternative to marriage	6
1.4	Some explanations for preference of the unmarried status	7
1.5	Common-law marriages	10
1.6	Putative marriages	14
1.7	Effect of change of domicile	16

CHAPTER 2

RAMIFICATIONS OF THE UNMARRIED STATUS

2.1	Employment difficulties	21
2.2	Title VII of the Civil Rights Act	24
2.3	Schoolteachers	28
2.4	Students	34
2.5	Unmarried pregnancies in the armed services	35
2.6	Right of privacy	37
2.7	Housing problems	40
2.8	Change of name of female partner	43
2.9	Rights to adopt children	45
2.10	Homestead laws	48
2.11	Welfare benefits	49
2.12	Unemployment benefits	56
2.13	Compensation for death of cohabitant	56
2.14	Immigration and naturalization	61
2.15	Insurance problems generally	63

CONTENTS

Section		Page
2.16	Insurance—Misrepresentation as to marital status in the application	66
2.17	Insurance—Cohabitant as member of "family" or "household"	67
2.18	Insurance—The "family purpose" doctrine	70
2.19	Abortion and contraception	72
2.20	Liability to third persons	80
2.21	Divorced partner's right to alimony	85
2.22	Rights in respect of torts committed against partner	88
2.23	Tort liability of partners inter sese	89
2.24	Homosexual partnerships	92
2.25	Possible criminal liability	94
2.26	Noncohabitation as a condition of probation	107

CHAPTER 3

STATUS OF CHILDREN OF RELATIONSHIP

3.1	Traditional common-law approach to legitimacy	111
3.2	Impact of the Constitution on the common-law approach	117
3.3	Constitutional impact on inheritance and intestacy statutes	122
3.4	Establishment of paternity	129
3.5	Right of illegitimate child to support	132
3.6	Rights to custody and visitation	138
3.7	Legitimation	143
3.8	Adoption and the rights of the biological parents	146

CHAPTER 4

RIGHTS TO ACCUMULATED PROPERTY AND VALUE OF SERVICES RENDERED DURING COHABITATION

4.1	Judicial attitudes where parties believed themselves married, and their applicability absent such belief	153

CONTENTS

Section		Page
4.2	Effect of conveyances to partners as husband and wife	161
4.3	Rights adjusted on analogy of a partnership or joint venture	165
4.4	Agreements to pool earnings	167
4.5	The resulting trust theory	168
4.6	Contract implied-in-fact	171
4.7	Quasi-contract	173
4.8	Constructive trust	174
4.9	Inherent equity powers: the equitable lien	176
4.10	The express contract	177

CHAPTER 5

MARITAL STATUS AND TAXES

5.1	A quick look at taxes	190
5.2	A tax case history of a pair of cohabitants	191
5.3	Marital status and federal income tax rates	202
5.4	Marriage and nonmarriage penalty taxes	206
5.5	"Married," "unmarried," "surviving spouse," "head of household," and "dependent" defined	208
5.6	Gift and estate taxes and the marriage bonus	241
5.7	"Income splitting" by cohabitants	247
5.8	Agreements by cohabitants to share expenses	252
5.9	Cohabitants claiming two households in one	254
5.10	A side-look at social security	255
5.11	Most favored status—Married and divorced in contemplation of cohabitation	257
5.12	Desideratum—Tax reform	259
	Tables	261

CHAPTER 6

STATE-BY-STATE COMMENTARY

6.1	Alabama	274
6.2	Alaska	279

CONTENTS

Section		Page
6.3	Arizona	283
6.4	Arkansas	287
6.5	California	291
6.6	Colorado	299
6.7	Connecticut	305
6.8	Delaware	311
6.9	District of Columbia	317
6.10	Florida	325
6.11	Georgia	334
6.12	Hawaii	342
6.13	Idaho	347
6.14	Illinois	352
6.15	Indiana	362
6.16	Iowa	368
6.17	Kansas	372
6.18	Kentucky	377
6.19	Louisiana	384
6.20	Maine	398
6.21	Maryland	401
6.22	Massachusetts	410
6.23	Michigan	418
6.24	Minnesota	425
6.25	Mississippi	431
6.26	Missouri	436
6.27	Montana	443
6.28	Nebraska	448
6.29	Nevada	453
6.30	New Hampshire	458
6.31	New Jersey	462
6.32	New Mexico	475
6.33	New York	479
6.34	North Carolina	490
6.35	North Dakota	496
6.36	Ohio	501
6.37	Oklahoma	509
6.38	Oregon	518
6.39	Pennsylvania	528
6.40	Rhode Island	537
6.41	South Carolina	542

CONTENTS

Section		Page
6.42	South Dakota	548
6.43	Tennessee	554
6.44	Texas	560
6.45	Utah	570
6.46	Vermont	578
6.47	Virginia	582
6.48	Washington	588
6.49	West Virginia	594
6.50	Wisconsin	598
6.51	Wyoming	604

APPENDICES

A.	Complaint filed by Michelle Marvin against Lee Marvin (February 22, 1972)	609
B.	Opinion of Justice Mathew O. Tobriner, Supreme Court of California, in Marvin v. Marvin, 18 Cal. 3d 660, 134 Cal Rptr. 815, 557 P.2d 106 (December 27, 1976)	617
C.	Memorandum Opinion of Judge Arthur K. Marshall, Superior Court of the State of California for the County of Los Angeles, in Marvin v. Marvin (April 18, 1979)	643

Index 667

CHAPTER 1

MARRIAGE AND OTHER LIFE STYLES

Section
1.1 Nature and scope of discussion
1.2 Marriage as creating a status
1.3 Demerits of cohabitation as an alternative to marriage
1.4 Some explanations for preference of the unmarried status
1.5 Common-law marriages
1.6 Putative marriages
1.7 Effect of change of domicile

1.1. Nature and scope of discussion

The courts are moving away from the often harsh traditional refusal to accord to unmarried couples and their offspring the status and rights which are accorded to lawfully married spouses and their children.

> [T]he prevalence of nonmarital relationships in modern society and the social acceptance of them, marks this as a time when our courts should by no means apply the doctrine of the unlawfulness of the so-called meretricious relationship to the instant case.... The nonenforceability of agreements expressly providing for meretricious conduct rested upon the fact that such conduct, as the word suggests, pertained to and encompassed prostitution. To equate the nonmarital relationship of today to such a subject matter is to do violence to an accepted and wholly different practice.
> We are aware that many young couples live together without the solemnization of marriage, in order to make sure that they can successfully later undertake marriage. This trial period, preliminary to marriage, serves as some assurance that the marriage will not subsequently end in dissolution to the harm of both parties. We are aware ... of the pervasiveness of nonmarital relationships in other situations.
> The mores of the society have indeed changed so radically in regard to cohabitation that we cannot impose a standard based on alleged moral considerations that have apparently been so widely abandoned by so many. Lest we be misunderstood, however, we take this occasion to point out that the structure of society itself largely depends upon the institution of marriage,

1.1 UNMARRIED COUPLES AND THE LAW

and nothing we have said in this opinion should [be taken to] derogate from that institution. The joining of the man and woman in marriage is at once the most socially productive and individually fulfilling relationship that one can enjoy in the course of a lifetime.[1]

The above statement, in a decision holding in substance that unmarried couples who live together are free to make their own contractual arrangements in regard to their mutual rights, duties and responsibilities provided only that sexual favors are not the explicit consideration or the sole consideration supporting the contract,[2] reflects the current change in judicial attitudes.

The purpose of this treatise is to present a contemporary picture of the extent to which the various states, and in some instances the nation as a whole, are adjusting the law to fit the needs of a society in which legal marriage no longer enjoys the prime role it once played in determining the reciprocal rights and duties of cohabiting partners and their offspring.[3]

Many of the legal ramifications of the marital status are clearly inapplicable to couples who cohabit without any belief that they are legally married. For example, the common-law doctrine of coercion (based as it was on the theory of the wife's subjection to her husband's authority and control)[4] which gave to married women a defense to many criminal charges[5] has no application to unwed partners. A fortiori any presumption that a woman committing a crime in the presence of her husband was acting under his coercion (a presumption which by now should be relegated to the museum) would have no place in this discussion.[6]

Other aspects of the marriage relation not applicable to unwed partners include: the liability of a surety on the obligation of a

---

[1] Marvin v. Marvin, 18 Cal. 3d 660, 683, 134 Cal. Rptr. 815, 831, 557 P.2d 106, 122 (1976) (Tobriner, J.).
[2] The decision receives more consideration in sections 4.10 and 6.5, herein.
[3] See Glendon, Marriage and the State: The Withering Away of Marriage, 62 Va. L. Rev. 663, 686 (1976); Weitzman, Legal Regulation of Marriage: Tradition and Change, 62 Calif. L. Rev. 1169 (1974).
[4] Perkins, *Criminal Law,* ch. 10, § 2 (2d ed., 1969). A husband even had a limited right of chastisement in case of his wife's disobedience, id., ch. 8, § 4.
[5] Id., ch. 8, § 4.
[6] Id., at p. 915, wherein the author lists the states that have abolished the presumption, either by statute or judicial decision.

woman incurred while under the disability of coverture;[7] the reciprocal common-law rights of husband and wife to dower and curtesy[8] (now for the most part replaced by statutes which provide for a forced share on the death of one or the other); competency to testify for or against the other spouse;[9] and the possible incapacity of a married woman to act as an executor or administrator.[10]

As to other ramifications of the marriage relationship, the extent of their application to unmarried cohabitants can present a legion of legal questions.[11] The problems related to the couple's accumulations and mutual services rendered during the existence of the relationship,[12] and to the status of any offspring of such a union, will be treated separately.[13] In the final chapter,[14] attention is drawn to miscellaneous areas where the laws of the state under consideration confirm, add to, or differ from the discussion in the preceding chapters. No attempt is there made to cover the law of each state in its entirety.

As will be seen, the Supreme Court has, in the name of equal protection, gone far to erode distinctions between legitimate and illegitimate children, and, in the name of equal protection and a constitutional right of privacy, recently created a significant impact on many concepts associated with marriage which have long been regarded as traditional.[15] Further, modern courts have shown an increasing tendency to accord to the extramarital

---

[7]See 74 Am. Jur. 2d, Suretyship, § 25.
[8]See 25 Am. Jur. 2d, Dower and Curtesy.
[9]See 81 Am. Jur. 2d, Witnesses, §§ 111–133. As to a cohabitant as a competent witness, see id., § 131. The doctrine may still apply, however, where a common-law marriage is involved. See United States v. White, 545 F. 2d 1129 (C.A.-8 Ark., 1976) where the attempt by an alleged common-law wife to assert marital privilege failed because Arkansas does not recognize such marriages. Also see State v. Durham, 49 Ohio App. 2d 231, 360 N.E.2d 743 (1976) where the requirements for a common-law marriage not having been found, the alleged wife could testify against the defendant in a criminal case.
[10]See 31 Am. Jur. 2d, Executors and Administrators, § 70.
[11]See Chapter 2, herein.
[12]Chapter 4, herein.
[13]Chapter 3, herein.
[14]Chapter 6, herein.
[15]See Noonan, Family and the Supreme Court, 23 Catholic U. L. Rev. 255 (1973).

cohabitant the status hitherto accorded to the relation of husband and wife.[16]

1.2. Marriage as creating a status

A marriage, which is of course the legal union of two people of the opposite sex[17] resulting from more than mere cohabitation,[18] has its origin in a contract[19] — a status-creating contract.[20] In the development of our law the legal family has long been regarded as the basic foundation of a civilized society.[21] For this reason, our domestic relations law, in which the state obviously has a vital interest,[22] has striven to foster and encourage this status.[23] In 1888, the Supreme Court of the United States said:

> [W]hen the contract to marry is executed by marriage, a relation between the parties is created which they cannot change.

---

[16] It has been suggested somewhat cynically that marriage be redefined as "some sort of relationship between two individuals of indeterminate duration, involving some kind of sexual conduct, entailing vague mutual property and support obligations, that may be formed by consent of both parties and dissolved at the will of either." Comment, New Marriage, 12 Willamette L. J. 441, 451 (1976). For a provocative discussion of the rights of extramarital cohabitants, see also Comment, Domestic Partnership, A Proposal for Dividing the Property of Unmarried Families, 12 Willamette L. J. 453 (1976).

[17] Hooks v. State, 197 So. 2d 238, 240 (Miss., 1967); Singer v. Hara, 11 Wash. App. 247, 522 P.2d 1187 (1974).

[18] Reger v. Reger, 242 Ind. 302, 177 N.E.2d 901, 905 (1961).

[19] State v. Lard, 86 N.M. 71, 519 P.2d 307 (1974).

[20] Buchholz v. Buchholz, 197 Neb. 180, 248 N.W.2d 21 (1976); B v. B, 78 Misc. 2d 112, 355 N.Y.S.2d 712 (1974); Washington Statewide Organization of Stepparents v. Smith, 85 Wash. 2d 564, 536 P.2d 1202, 75 A.L.R.3d 1119 (1975).

[21] Morris v. Morris, 31 Misc. 2d 548, 220 N.Y.S.2d 590 (1961); Garlock v. Garlock, 279 N.Y. 337, 18 N.E.2d 521, 120 A.L.R. 1331 (1939). "Marriage is a device intended to perpetuate family groups within the larger social entities of which each marital unit is a part." Coleman v. Coleman, 32 Ohio St. 2d 155, 291 N.E.2d 530, 57 A.L.R.3d 213 (1972). "[N]ever has there been a greater need for the courts to maintain a high level of moral conduct than exists today. This court intends to give more than lip service to the principle that the fabric of our society is composed of the family unit and when the family unit is damaged, the fabric of society suffers. Our courts will continue to insist upon a high level of moral conduct . . . and will never succumb to the 'Hollywood' type of morality so popular today. . . ." In re Anonymous, 37 Misc. 2d 411, 412–413, 238 N.Y.S.2d 422, 423 (1962).

[22] Rothman v. Rothman, 65 N.J. 219, 320 A.2d 496 (1974); Trask v. Trask, 85 Misc. 2d 980, 381 N.Y.S.2d 584 (1976); State v. Austin, —— W. Va. ——, 234 S.E. 2d 657 (1977).

[23] State v. Austin, ——W. Va. ——, 234 S.E.2d 657 (1977).

Other contracts may be modified, restricted or enlarged, or entirely released upon the consent of the parties. Not so with marriage. The relation once formed, the law steps in and holds the parties to various obligations and liabilities. It is an institution, in the maintenance of which in its purity the public is deeply interested, for it is the foundation of the family and society, without which there would be neither civilization nor progress.[24]

Though utterances of this nature may well provoke a raised eyebrow in American society today, where "swinging couples," homosexual or lesbian cohabitants and in particular heterosexuals who cohabit without the sanction of marriage are not regarded with the puritanical horror of earlier days, they nonetheless go far to explain many of the potential hazards which unmarried partners are likely to encounter. The law cannot be immutable; it must and does change with a change in social mores. But even if the courts and legislatures were of a mind to sweep away the whole institution of marriage and the rights and responsibilities that accompany membership of a legal familial group, they could not do so; public confidence in the stability, certainty and predictability of the law would be dynamited.

Hence this book. In many of the areas discussed, the law is in a state of flux. And it is the attorney's responsibility to his client to advise him, as far as is possible, where he stands in this fluid situation.

The statutes, the decisions, and an enormous body of legal documents frequently contain the ambiguous words "family," "household," "spouse," "widow" and "child."[25] It is hoped that this treatise will shed some light on the extent to which, if at all, such words embrace extramarital cohabitants and their offspring.

---

[24]Maynard v. Hill, 125 U.S. 190, 211, 31 L. Ed. 654, 659, 8 Sup. Ct. 723, 729 (1888).
[25]See, e.g., Comment, Legal Family: A Definitional Analysis, 13 J. Family L. 781 (1973–74); Annotations, Who included in term "family" in bequest or devise, 154 A.L.R. 1411 (1945); Who is member of family within statute relating to service of process by leaving copy with member of family, 136 A.L.R. 1505 (1942); What constitutes a "family" within meaning of zoning regulation or restrictive covenant, 71 A.L.R.3d 693 (1976).

1.3. Demerits of cohabitation as an alternative to marriage

In addition to the possible pitfalls and the legal disadvantages to which the unmarried cohabitant is subjected, which will be discussed later, there are obvious factors which help to weigh the scales in favor of entering into the married status.

Firstly, our Western civilization grew up and was nurtured in the Judeo-Christian ethic. Christianity regards sex outside of marriage as sinful. Whatever may be one's personal views in this area, there remain many who adhere to this belief. Extramarital cohabitation does expose the participant to a form of discrimination, social if not economic, which can be embarrassing.

Secondly, whether or not an employer, a landlord, or an institution offering facilities to the public can constitutionally base its lack of co-operation on a style of living which it finds to be offensive, a matter which receives later consideration,[26] it is all too clear that this does happen.

Last but by no means least, the married status carries with it manifold advantages. The state has always made its voice heard in the ownership and disposition of the assets of married partners both during the marriage and on its dissolution; as between unmarried cohabitants the voice, if voice there be, is seldom heard or understood.[27] In states whose law orginated in part at least from the civil law, the protection accorded a spouse lies in the doctrine of community property.[28] Though the rules controlling this institution are far from identical in such states, the general concept is that assets acquired by the spouses during the marriage are commonly owned, and that one spouse cannot by will dispose of more than his or her half share. In general, too, the testamentary capacity of either spouse is restricted to ensure that the children are not left destitute.

In the "common law" states (as distinguished from community property states), if the old common-law rights of dower and curtesy no longer survive, they are replaced by legislation which ensures that a surviving spouse is not left without an interest in

---

[26] See Chapter 2, herein.
[27] See Chapter 4, herein.
[28] See 15A Am. Jur. 2d, Community Property.

the property of the decedent spouse.[29] On a termination of the marriage other than by death of a spouse, the protection of the law extends to such matters as support, separate maintenance, and custody of the children. During the marriage, a legal wife, or in many states, a legal spouse, has an enforceable right to support. A wife's right to be supported by her husband takes precedence over any right of his parents to his earnings, even if he is a minor.[30]

A majority of the states today permit a divorce without any showing of fault on either side.[31] But the right to alimony is seldom affected by the presence or absence of fault, the prime consideration being the relative earning power of the divorcing spouses.[32]

In addition, the law recognizes a legal right to consortium, from which can flow a right to damages for a tortious deprivation by a spouse of the services, companionship and sexual favors of the other. It is doubtful whether any such right would be recognized in the unmarried cohabitant who is so deprived.[33]

1.4. Some explanations for preference of the unmarried status

Notwithstanding the strong advantages the law has to offer in favor of the married state, current attitudes disfavoring marriage as against a less formal union are readily explainable.

There was a time—and the time may yet to an extent be with us—when the lot of the married woman, like that of W. S. Gilbert's policeman, was not a happy one. In the early law she was incapable of entering into a contract of her own, of acquiring or disposing of property without her husband's consent, or of

---

[29]See 25 Am. Jur. 2d, Dower and Curtesy.
[30]Generally, see 41 Am. Jur. 2d, Husband and Wife, § 329 et seq.
[31]Proof of fault is still required in more than a dozen states. See Annotation, Validity, construction and effect of "no-fault" divorce statutes providing for dissolution of marriage upon finding that relationship is no longer viable, 55 A.L.R. 3d 581 (1974).
[32]See Freed and Foster, Economic Effects of Divorce, 7 Family L. Q. 275 (1973). As to the constitutionality of a statute which permits alimony to be paid to women but not to men, see section 2.21, herein.
[33]See section 2.22, herein.

suing or being sued in her own right. Any premarital debts owed by the one spouse to the other were extinguished by the mere fact of the marriage. She was relegated to the status of a servant of her husband, to whom she was almost entirely subject. Her legal existence was virtually merged into that of the husband. This status, described as "coverture," carried with it the duty to perform, without compensation, whatever household duties were appropriate to their station in life. The husband, who had the duty of support, had the right to such services.[34] Though the Married Women's Property Acts[35] have for the most part eliminated these disabilities, her right to validly contract for compensation for her domestic services remains unsettled.[36]

The husband probably still retains the right to determine their mode and standard of living as long as the home is maintained and the parties live together,[37] and to determine their place of abode.[38] Except insofar as the wife can obtain a separate domicile for divorce purposes,[39] she is generally held to have adopted the domicile of her husband.[40] This can operate to her disadvantage in such matters as the right to run for public office, voting place, the duty to serve on a jury, tax liabilities, school tuition rates, to name but a few.[41]

Additionally, though a woman who is married can today earn

---

[34]Weitzman, To Love, Honor and Obey? Traditional Legal Marriage and Alternative Family Forms, 1975 Family Co-ordinator 531. Weitzman is fiercely critical of the traditional concept of the wife's status as subordinate to the "head of the family" and without hope of compensation for domestic and child care services. Her comments in the above article, and in her article, Legal Regulation of Marriage: Tradition and Change, 62 Calif. L. Rev. 1169 (1974), undoubtedly influenced the Supreme Court of California in Marvin v. Marvin, 18 Cal. 3d 660, 134 Cal. Rptr. 815, 557 P.2d 106 (1976).
[35]See 41 Am. Jur. 2d, Husband and Wife, § 56.
[36]See Comment, Marriage Contracts for Support and Services: Constitutionality Begins at Home, 49 N.Y.U. L. Rev. 1161 (1974). See also Krauskopf and Thomas, Partnership Marriage: The Solution to an Ineffective and Inequitable Law of Support, 35 Ohio St. L. J. 558 (1974). In a critical survey of the existing common law, these authors suggest statutory revision substituting a model that would bring the marital status more into line with a partnership status.
[37]See McGuire v. McGuire, 157 Neb. 226, 59 N.W.2d 336 (1953).
[38]See Carlson v. Carlson, 75 Ariz. 308, 256 P.2d 249 (1953).
[39]See, e.g., Goodrich and Scoles, *Conflict of Laws*, § 36 (1964).
[40]E.g., Langlais v. Langlais, 90 Misc. 2d 29, 393 N.Y.S.2d 292 (1977).
[41]See Brown, et al., Equal Rights Amendment: A Constitutional Basis for Equal Rights for Women, 80 Yale L. J. 871 (1971).

her own money, hold title to property, and become a creditor in her own right, lending institutions and creditors not infrequently expect her to seek credit in her husband's name.[42] Also, a marriage has, at any rate in the not too distant past, operated to deprive a wife of governmental benefits.[43]

The husband's legal duty to support his wife in a style appropriate to his means is seldom capable of realistic enforcement; if he chooses to be parsimonious, she would have scant hope of holding the marriage together if she pressures him unduly, and few courts, if any, would come to her aid in a domestic difficulty of such a nature.

Over and above these legal or quasi-legal considerations, there are psychological or temperamental explanations for the choice to live together outside of marriage. Persons of both sexes often feel a natural reluctance to be bound by legal ties when the desire to remain together has vanished. It is sometimes thought that love is more likely to endure when the parties to a relationship are completely free to break up when they like, without the need for a formal severance of the relationship. Though the social stigma once associated with divorce has been largely eroded, it can still be a traumatic experience and, especially if rights to property, support and custody are contested, an expensive proceeding.

The wage earner, or the wealthier of the two partners, may be reluctant to endow the other "with all his worldly goods," or even to agree to a sharing of assets. He (or she)[44] may balk at the thought of liability for alimony in the event their relationship goes sour.

Finally, whether or not society as a whole continues to be outraged by the concept of "living in sin,"[45] nonmarital cohabitation

---

[42]See Brown, Discredited American Woman: Sex Discrimination in Consumer Credit, 6 U.C.D. L. Rev. 61 (1973).

[43]See, e.g., Beckman v. Mayhew, 49 Cal. App. 3d 529, 122 Cal. Rptr. 604 (1974) (government pension). See Foster, Marriage and Divorce in the Twilight Zone, 17 Ariz. L. Rev. 462 (1975).

[44]As to the right of a husband, in a proper case, to seek alimony from his ex-wife, see, e.g., Thaler v. Thaler, 89 Misc. 2d 315, 391 N.Y.S.2d 331 (1977), revd. on other grounds 58 App. Div. 2d 890, 396 N.Y.S.2d 815 (1977).

[45]See Seidenberg, Myth of the "Evil" Female as Embodied in the Law, 2 Env. L. 218 (1971). But the fact of an illicit relationship has been held admissible in evidence to impeach the credibility of a witness. See State v. Bland, 353 S.W. 2d 584 (Mo., 1962).

is often favored as being in the nature of a "dry run"; the argument being that many unhappy permanent unions could have been avoided had the parties lived together for a time before entering into a commitment from which they can be relieved only at considerable trouble and expense.

1.5. Common-law marriages

There is a popular tendency to regard unmarried cohabitants as "common-law spouses." It need hardly be stated that whether such cohabitants qualify as common-law spouses, putative[46] spouses, or are merely living in "illicit relations," can have a profound impact on their status and mutual rights and obligations.

Despite the name given to the practice, it is doubtful whether the common law of England ever recognized such a union. It achieved a footing in this country in the early days of its development, when travel between remote settlements was difficult, and there were few places where marriage licenses could be obtained.[47] Because present conditions are such that one can no longer find much excuse for resorting to so dubious a means of entering into the married state, many of the states which once recognized the common-law marriage have since abolished it either by statute or judicial legislation.[48] The current judicial attitude is well illustrated by a court of the District of Columbia. In ruling on a complex dispute resulting in an action for alienation of affections, the court, while holding that the District of Columbia does recognize the common-law marriage, expressed doubts as to whether it today merits such recognition, and commended to the legislature the question whether such an "informal and almost uniformly misunderstood status" should not be abolished. The historical considerations which gave it birth no longer exist. "Cost is certainly not prohibitory, and a plethora of public and quasi-public officials are available to solemnize such

---

[46] As to "putative" marriages, see section 1.6, herein.
[47] See Middlebrook v. Wideman, 203 S.W.2d 686 (Tex., 1947).
[48] See Kirkpatrick, Common Law Marriages: Their Common Law Basis and Present Need, 6 St. Louis U. L. J. 30 (1960); Annotation, Validity of common-law marriage in American jurisdictions, 133 A.L.R. 758 (1941).

an important and socially significant occasion." No one would contend that facilities for recordation are unavailable today.[49]

The Uniform Marriage and Divorce Act,[50] while it does not validate common-law marriages, has an optional provision whereby an adopting state could invalidate such marriages as of the effective date of its adoption.[51]

Among the few jurisdictions which continue to recognize the common-law marriage,[52] (excluding states which recognize them in respect of unions entered into before the date of their statutory abolition),[53] are Alabama, Colorado, District of Columbia, Georgia, Idaho, Iowa, Kansas, Montana, Ohio, Pennsylvania, Rhode Island, South Carolina and Texas.

As long as the state's requirements for declaratory relief are present, the validity or otherwise of an alleged common-law marriage can properly be brought before a court by seeking a declaratory judgment.[54]

Requisites of a common-law marriage

States are not uniformly agreed as to the nature of the conduct and the formalities which can result in the status of common-law spouses.[55] (For an examination of the requirements of any particular state, reference should be made to Chapter 6, herein.) Among the generally accepted requirements, however, are the following:

---

[49] Johnson v. Young, 372 A.2d 992, 996 (D.C. App., 1977).
[50] Uniform Marriage and Divorce Act, 9 U.L.A. Matr., Fam., & Health Laws (1973).
[51] Id., section 211.
[52] See the state-by-state commentary in Chapter 6, herein.
[53] See, e.g., Carlson v. Olson, —— Minn. ——, 256 N.W.2d 249 (1977), holding that only common-law marriages contracted before April, 1941 are recognized.
[54] Annotation, Judicial declaration of validity of existence of common-law marriage, 92 A.L.R.2d 1102 (1963).
[55] "A valid definition of common law marriage without infinite qualifications can hardly be found. All we have are approximations which demonstrate ambiguous and vacillating notions of some more or less informal kind of marital status. Whatever hazy notions we have vary not only from jurisdiction to jurisdiction but from case to case within a recognizing jurisdiction.... Again, the shades of nonrecognition may vary from case to case. A good deal may depend on how the issue comes up." Weyrauch, Informal and Formal Marriage—An Appraisal of Trends in Family Organization, 28 U. Chi. L. Rev. 88, 91 (1960).

1.5 UNMARRIED COUPLES AND THE LAW

(1) An agreement to be married (in some states it can be inferred from the circumstances;[56] usually, it must be *per verba de praesenti*);[57]
(2) A reasonable period of open cohabitation;[58]
(3) Reputation of marriage in the community;[59] and
(4) Capacity of the parties to enter into a valid marriage.[60]

Failure of the female partner to adopt the surname of the male would certainly militate against the likelihood that a marriage was intended.[61]

Jurisdictions are not agreed as to whether, if during the initial cohabitation (in a state recognizing common-law marriage) some impediment existed to the validity of the marriage, a continued cohabitation after the impediment was removed results in a common-law marriage in the absence of clear and convincing proof of a change of status.[62] A marriage ceremony would of course furnish such proof,[63] as would a renewed agreement to live together as husband and wife.[64]

If the parties reside in a state which does not recognize common-law marriages, the mere fact that in the course of a visit to a state which does recognize them the parties held themselves

---

[56]See In re Marriage of Winegard, 257 N.W.2d 609 (Iowa, 1977). Annotation, Validity of marriage as affected by intention of the parties that it should be only a matter of form or jest, 14 A.L.R.2d 624 (1950).

[57]See, e.g., In re Estate of McClelland, 168 Mont. 160, 541 P.2d 780 (1975); Kiska v. Ziegenfuss Co., 154 Pa. Super. 100, 35 A.2d 532 (1944) (denying workers' compensation benefits to one whom decedent workman had merely promised to marry at a future date); Rager v. Johnstown Traction Co., 184 Pa. Super. 474, 134 A.2d 918 (1957).

[58]Annotations, Habit and repute as essential to common-law marriage, 33 A.L.R. 27 (1924); Proxy marriages, 170 A.L.R. 947 (1947).

[59]In re Peters' Estate, 73 Colo. 271, 215 Pac. 128, 33 A.L.R. 24 (1923); Huard v. McTeigh, 113 Ore. 279, 232 Pac. 658, 39 A.L.R. 528 (1925).

[60]Anderson v. Anderson, 235 Ind. 113, 131 N.E.2d 301 (1956).

[61]See State v. Durham, 49 Ohio App. 2d 231, 360 N.E.2d 743 (1976).

[62]See In re Marriage of Grother, 242 N.W. 2d 1 (Iowa, 1976); In re Estate of Garges, 474 Pa. 237, 378 A.2d 307 (1977); Annotations, Continued cohabitation between parties to ceremonial marriage contracted when one of them was insane as creating presumption of common-law marriage, 85 A.L.R. 1302 (1933); Inference or presumption of marriage from continued cohabitation following removal of impediment, 104 A.L.R. 6 (1936); Common-law marriage between parties previously divorced, 82 A.L.R.2d 688 (1962).

[63]See Hodge v. Conley, 543 S.W.2d 326 (Mo. App., 1976).

[64]Byers v. Mount Vernon Mills, Inc., 268 S.C. 68, 231 S.E.2d 699 (1977).

out as husband and wife would not bring the status into existence.[65] From the language used in the cases so holding, however, it seems implicitly recognized that if they *take up residence* in a state recognizing common-law marriage, the mere fact that their cohabitation prior to the change of residence was without legal sanction would be immaterial.

Dissolution of a common-law marriage

Once the status has come into existence, a common-law marriage can only be terminated by death or divorce.[66] A later ceremonial marriage to another will not effect a dissolution;[67] a fortiori is this so where the second relationship is kept secret.[68]

After the parties to a common-law marriage have been divorced, a mere resumption of cohabitation is not enough to reinstate the marriage, whether or not the state recognizes common-law marriage.[69]

Validity as affected by place of cohabitation

If a common-law marriage is recognized in the state where the requirements are met, and one spouse has been forbidden to marry by a court of a sister state, which decree has no extraterritorial effect, it would not affect the validity of the common-law marriage.[70] However, it would seem that if the parties comply with the requisites of such a union simply to avoid the consequences of the fact that such unions receive no recognition in the state where they intend to live, and to which they move immediately thereafter, no common-law marriage results.[71] The

---

[65]See Walker v. Yarbrough, 257 Ark. 300, 516 S.W.2d 390 (1974); In re Binger's Estate, 158 Neb. 444, 63 N.W.2d 784 (1954); State ex rel. Smith v. Superior Court for King County, 23 Wash. 2d 357, 161 P.2d 188 (1945).
[66]Catlett v. Chestnut, 107 Fla. 498, 146 So. 241 (1941). State ex rel. Bailey v. Powers, 566 P.2d 454 (Okla., 1977).
[67]Evans v. Marbut, 140 Ga. App. 329, 231 S.E.2d 94 (1976).
[68]Catlett v. Chestnut, 107 Fla. 498, 146 So. 241 (1941).
[69]See Duey v. Duey, 343 So. 2d 896 (Fla. App., 1977). See also Annotation, Common-law marriage between parties previously divorced, 82 A.L.R.2d 688 (1962).
[70]See Smallwood v. Bickers, 139 Ga. App. 720, 229 S.E.2d 525 (1976).
[71]See Huard v. McTeigh, 113 Ore. 279, 232 Pac. 658, 39 A.L.R. 528 (1925).

good faith of the parties seems to be a controlling factor. If they enter into a common-law marriage in a state where such receives recognition, and then immediately move to a state which does not recognize such marriages, where they cohabit as spouses, the state of the marriage should allow evidence of the cohabitation out of state to establish their status as lawful spouses.[72]

It should be noted that even in states which do not recognize common-law marriages, the mere fact that a required license was not obtained, or was defective or improperly obtained, does not necessarily invalidate the marriage.[73]

1.6. Putative marriages

States which derive their marriage laws from civil law origins recognize that where the parties have solemnized their marriage in due form and in good faith,[74] but the marriage is void or voidable due to some legal infirmity, the parties qualify as "putative spouses."[75] The effect of the doctrine is, in general, to confer on the mistaken party all the rights of a true spouse.[76] The mistake

---

[72] In Franzen v. Equitable Life Assur. Soc. of United States, 130 N.J.L. 457, 33 A.2d 599 (1943), the parties entered into a common-law marriage in New Jersey (prior to the abolition of the status in that state). They immediately moved to Louisiana due to the husband's employment. It was held that evidence of their cohabitation and repute in Louisiana should be admitted not to show a putative marriage in that state, but to show that the common-law marriage was valid in New Jersey where it had been entered into. By accepted principles, Louisiana too should recognize such a common-law marriage. See section 1.7, herein.

[73] Annotation, Validity of solemnized marriage as affected by absence of license required by statute, 61 A.L.R.2d 847 (1958).

[74] As to the test of good faith for a California putative marriage, see Spearman v. Spearman, 482 F.2d 1203 (C.A.-5 Ala., 1973), applying Cal. Evidence Code, § 604 et seq. See also Tucker v. Joseph, 292 So. 2d 357 (La. App., 1974) (no putative community absent good faith); Miller v. Johnson, 214 Cal. App. 2d 123, 29 Cal. Rptr. 251 (1963) (no putative marriage where "divorce" and subsequent "marriage" merely "farcical").

[75] Annotations, Validity of marriage celebrated while spouse by former marriage of one of the parties was living and undivorced, in reliance upon presumption from lapse of time of death of such spouse, 93 A.L.R. 345 (1934), 144 A.L.R. 747 (1943); Cohabitation of persons ceremonially married after learning of facts negativing dissolution of previous marriage of one, as affecting right to annulment, 4 A.L.R. 2d 542 (1949).

[76] One who enters into a marriage ceremony with knowledge that the man is already married is not entitled to a widow's social security benefits as a putative wife. Hunter v. Richardson, 346 F. Supp. 123 (M.D. La., 1972) (applying Louisiana

might, for example, be a belief in the validity of a Mexican divorce[77] or even, it has been held, a belief that common-law marriages are good in the state where the relationship existed.[78]

The term "putative spouse" is at times used to denote any person who has conferred benefits in the good faith belief in a valid marriage.[79] In fact an optional section of the Uniform Marriage and Divorce Act[80] suggests a general legislative adoption of this doctrine. The section would confer on a good faith cohabitant all the rights of a legal spouse, including the right to maintenance following termination of the relationship. The Commissioners suggest:

> If there is a legal spouse or other putative spouses, rights acquired by a putative spouse do not supersede rights of the legal spouse or those acquired by other putative spouses, but the court shall apportion property, maintenance and support rights among the claimants as appropriate in the circumstances and in the interests of justice.[81]

Although few states have developed a workable alternative,[82] this provision has so far received little recognition by states adopting the Uniform Act, probably because it hardly seems an adequate formula for the solution of problems that can become frightening in their complexity.[83]

---

law). A putative wife may qualify for permanent alimony. Cortes v. Fleming, 307 So. 2d 611, 81 A.L.R.3d 267 (La., 1973). She may sue for his wrongful death. King v. Cancienne, 316 So. 2d 366 (La., 1975).

[77]Dean v. Goldwire, 480 S.W.2d 494 (Tex. Civ. App., 1972).

[78]Sancha v. Arnold, 114 Cal. App. 2d 772, 251 P.2d 67 (1952), reh. den. 114 Cal. App. 2d 772, 252 P.2d 55 (1953).

[79]See, e.g., Rakestraw v. City of Cincinnati, 69 Ohio App. 504, 44 N.E.2d 278 (1942).

[80]Uniform Marriage and Divorce Act (U.L.A.), § 209.

[81]Id. An example of the adjustment of the rights between a legal spouse and a putative spouse is presented in Estate of Ricci, 201 Cal. App. 2d 146, 19 Cal. Rptr. 739 (1962).

[82]See Chapter 6, herein.

[83]See, generally, Comment, Competitive Rights of Legal and Putative Wives, 1 Loyola U. L. Rev. (L.A.) 99 (1968); Annotations, Right to attack validity of marriage after death of party thereto, 47 A.L.R.2d 1393 (1956); Rights in decedent's estate as between lawful and putative spouses, 81 A.L.R.3d 6 (1977); Estoppel or laches precluding lawful spouse from asserting rights in decedent's estate as against putative spouse, 81 A.L.R.3d 110 (1977).

1.7. Effect of change of domicile

The traditional rule of conflicts of laws, that the formal validity of a marriage is controlled by the laws of the place of celebration,[84] is for the most part honored by the courts of today. Further, if the parties initiated a common-law marriage in a state where such unions are still recognized,[85] it will receive recognition by the state to which they have moved.[86] Conversely, if the union does not qualify as a valid marriage in the state where the relationship had its origins, it will receive recognition nowhere.[87]

However, concerning the essential validity, as distinguished from the mere rules controlling the necessary formalities for a valid marriage, the "significant contacts" test which pervades the modern Restatement approach to conflict of laws is of obvious relevance.[88] If a couple, whose marriage is not only compliant with the ceremonial forms required by the state where it is con-

---

[84]Bronislawa K. v. Tadeusz K., 90 Misc. 2d 183, 393 N.Y.S.2d 534 (1977).

[85]See section 1.5, herein.

[86]E.g., Mission Ins. Co. v. Industrial Comm., 114 Ariz. 170, 559 P. 2d 1085 (1976); Grant v. Superior Court In and For County of Pima, 27 Ariz. App. 427, 555 P.2d 895 (1976); Jennings v. Jennings, 20 Md. App. 369, 315 A.2d 816 (1974); Hodge v. Conley, 543 S.W.2d 326 (Mo. App., 1976); Merritt v. Chevrolet Tonawanda Division, General Motors Corp., 50 App. Div. 2d 1018, 377 N.Y.S.2d 663 (1975); In re Estate of Macklin, 82 Misc. 2d 376, 371 N.Y.S.2d 238 (1975); Estate of Booker, 27 Ore. App. 779, 557 P.2d 248 (1976); Old Republic Ins. Co. v. Christian, 389 F. Supp. 335 (E.D. Tenn., 1975). But compare In re Vetas' Estate, 110 Utah 187, 170 P.2d 183 (1946), holding that because common-law marriage is not recognized in Utah, and because by statute Utah recognizes only those marriages "solemnized" in another state, persons domiciled in Utah cannot go to another state and enter into a common-law marriage that will on their return be recognized in Utah.

[87]See Spearman v. Spearman, 482 F.2d 1203 (C.A.-5 Ala., 1973). See also Bronislawa K. v. Tadeusz K., 90 Misc. 2d 183, 393 N.Y.S.2d 534 (1977) (denying validity of a marriage contracted in a foreign state which required, in addition to a religious ritual or in the place thereof, a civil ceremony); In re Marriage of Reed, 226 N.W.2d 795 (Iowa, 1975) (denying jurisdiction to "dissolve" or adjudicate property rights under a common-law marriage allegedly contracted in California, since that state does not recognize such marriages).

[88]See Annotation, Recognition by forum state of marriage which, although invalid where contracted, would have been valid if contracted within forum state, 82 A.L.R.3d 1240 (1978). Restatement (Second), *Conflict of Laws,* § 283(1) states that the validity of a marriage should be determined by the local law of the state which, with respect to the particular issue, has the most significant relationship to the spouses and the marriage. Protection of the justified expectations of the parties and the relevant policies of the forum are significant factors.

tracted but is in every way recognized by that state as a valid union, transfer their domicile to another state, can such state, by reason of the significant contacts it has acquired as a result, properly decline to recognize the validity of the marriage? A qualification to the rule that the law of the place of celebration controls has long been recognized when such recognition would go contra to a strong policy of the forum state,[89] as for example when the union is incestuous by the laws of the domicile of either party.[90] Such qualifications no longer invalidate a marriage which is prohibited because it involves miscegenation.[91]

The major problem for the purposes of this discussion, of course, is the question "to what extent will the fact that an informal union between unmarried partners is frowned upon by a state to which the partners move justify it in declining on policy grounds to give it the effect accorded to it by the state where the relationship originated?" No doubt due to the relative recency of judicial attitudes which decline to condemn such relationships as "meretricious," authority is slight.[92] The discussion of Goodrich

---

[89]See State v. Austin, —— W. Va. ——, 234 S.E.2d 657 (1977). A statute providing that a marriage contracted in another state by residents of West Virginia with intention of evading the marriage laws will be governed by the law of West Virginia, is merely a statutory extension of the common-law rule that a state is not required to recognize a marriage performed in another state which is repugnant to the forum state's statutes or public policy.

[90]See Annotation, Recognition of foreign marriage as affected by policy in respect of incestuous marriages, 117 A.L.R. 186 (1938). Where the marriage is prohibited by the laws of the place of celebration, though valid in the forum state (parties were first cousins), a California court has held the marriage to be invalid, and that the woman enjoys the status of a putative spouse and not that of a surviving spouse, thus limiting her award to property acquired during the putative marriage. Estate of Levie, 50 Cal. App. 3d 572, 123 Cal. Rptr. 445, 82 A.L.R. 3d 1234 (1975).

[91]See Loving v. Virginia, 388 U.S. 1, 18 L. Ed. 2d 1010, 87 Sup. Ct. 1817 (1967); Annotations, Recognition of foreign marriage as affected by local miscegenation law, 3 A.L.R.2d 240 (1949); Marriage recognized as valid because valid by law of another state where it was celebrated, as subject to annulment under law of forum for reasons which would have subjected it thereto if celebrated at forum, 104 A.L.R. 1294 (1936).

[92]In In re Estate of Dauenhauer, 167 Mont. 183, 535 P.2d 1005 (1975), a purported father died a resident of Montana but had lived unwed with mother of their children in California. It was held that the question of their legitimacy would depend on whether California would recognize a "de facto" marriage or whether the father had legitimized them by compliance with Cal. Civil Code, § 230 (receiving them into his home, etc.).

and Scoles,[93] relating to a limited recognition accorded by our courts to foreign unions which would not qualify as marriage in any American state, is relevant.

It may well be doubted whether a Mohammedan visitor would be permitted to cohabit here with his four wives. Children of the union could, and probably would, be recognized as legitimate, as they are in the Indian cases. If the case involved devolution of personalty, it most probably would be referred to the domiciliary law of the deceased and distribution made accordingly. Even a question concerning the devolution of real property, or a claim by four bereft spouses under a Workmen's Compensation Act, while more difficult should, and seems likely would, be disposed of by according the foreign marriage limited recognition in order that the reasonable expectations of the family members arising out of their relationships based on their personal law could be given the maximum effect possible under forum law.[94]

To what extent, if any, would a court today regard an informal union between unmarrieds as repugnant to a strong social policy?

---

[93]Goodrich and Scoles, *Conflict of Laws*, pp. 240–243 (1964).

[94]Id., at p. 243. Generally, see Annotations, Effect in third state of marriage valid where celebrated but void by law of domicil of parties, 51 A.L.R. 1412 (1927); Marriage recognized as valid because valid by law of another state where it was celebrated, as subject to annulment under law of forum for reasons which would have subjected it thereto if celebrated at forum, 104 A.L.R. 1294 (1936); Public policy of forum against recognition of marriage valid (or voidable only) by the law of the place where it was celebrated, as affected by the fact that neither of the parties was domiciled at the forum at the time of the marriage, 127 A.L.R. 437 (1940); Right to attack validity of marriage after death of party thereto, 47 A.L.R. 2d 1393 (1956); Conflict of laws as to validity of marriage attacked because of nonage, 71 A.L.R.2d 687 (1960); Change of domicil as affecting character of property previously acquired as separate or community property, 14 A.L.R.3d 404 (1967); Recognition of foreign marriage as affected by the conditions or manner of dissolving it under the foreign law, or the toleration of polygamous marriages, 74 A.L.R. 1533 (1931); Conflict of laws as to legitimacy or legitimation or as to rights of illegitimates, as affecting descent and distribution of decedent's estate, 87 A.L.R.2d 1274 (1963).

As of collateral interest, it has been held that where a Texas divorce decree incorporated as part of a property settlement agreement a provision that "if . . . either party desires to claim that some community property has not been divided, he or she shall be free to do so . . ." a Florida court is precluded by the doctrine of res judicata from entertaining a suit to adjudicate the wife's claim to mineral rights in Florida real property; the court holding that Florida not being a community property state was not required to recognize rights predicated on a sister state's community property law. Estabrook v. Wise, 348 So. 2d 355 (Fla. App., 1977). The decision seems to contradict the traditional rule that the lex situs

was a homosexual, but rather on the fact that following his application for employment he had publicized his homosexuality and his views on equal rights for homosexuals through the media. The court concluded that the board could reasonably have decided that to hire him would be giving "tacit approval" to his conduct. (Policies related to the employment of schoolteachers are somewhat less likely to be held unconstitutional due to the nature of their employment and the obvious interest of the school authorities in the morality of those instructing the young.)[7]

In Hollenbaugh v. Carnegie Free Library,[8] the court held that the discharge of employees hired "at will" without a pretermination hearing did not violate the due process clause of the Fourteenth Amendment. The motivating factor behind their discharges was that they were living together in a state of "open adultery." In answer to the contention that there was no rational connection between their conduct and their fitness to perform their jobs, and that they had thus been denied equal protection, the court noted that the library's board of trustees were charged with representing what they perceived to be the library's best interest. "As employees of a library in a relatively small community, plaintiffs were frequently called on to deal directly with that community. Under these circumstances, any rights plaintiffs have to live together must be balanced against the state's interest ... in being able to properly perform its function in the community...."[9] The court was unwilling to call the board's decision to dismiss an arbitrary, unreasonable or capricious one, or to conclude that it violated the equal protection clause, but expressly stated that it did not regard it as the court's function to impose its own views of morality on the defendant board of trustees.

In summary, then, it would seem that if a hiring or firing policy were simply based on the fact of cohabitation outside of marriage, without any showing as to any possible adverse impact on the employee's job performance or on the employer's interest in the public image held by the employee, the policy can be successfully attacked as discriminatory. But on such a showing, the policy will

---

[7]See section 2.3, herein.
[8]436 F. Supp. 1328 (W.D. Pa., 1977).
[9]Id., at 1333.

be defended. It need hardly be added that the mere fact that a public employee has married would be highly unlikely to have any adverse impact on job performance;[10] nor, absent special circumstances, the fact that the employee has an extramarital relationship. Gross immorality, for the purpose of justifying removal from office, refers to willful, flagrant or shameless immorality,[11] as, for example, where an official whose duty it is to prosecute brothel-keepers frequents such an institution.[12]

2.2. Title VII of the Civil Rights Act

Title VII of the Civil Rights Act of 1964 forbids an employer to discriminate against any individual on the basis of sex,[13] unless sex is a bona fide occupational qualification reasonably necessary to the operation of the employer's business.[14]

Employers not uncommonly have policies against the hiring of, or requiring the termination of, persons on the basis of their marital status.[15] Some such policies are aimed at ensuring the employment of single persons exclusively.[16] Others, though less frequent, are aimed at ensuring the employment of married per-

---

[10] Annotation, Marriage as ground for discharge of one employed in public service other than as teacher, 135 A.L.R. 1346 (1941).
[11] See 63 Am. Jur. 2d, Public Officers and Employees, § 192.
[12] Moore v. Strickling, 46 W. Va. 515, 33 S.E. 274 (1899).
See also Mindel v. United States Civil Service Comm., 312 F. Supp. 485 (N.D. Cal., 1970), holding the dismissal of a postal clerk for living with a woman not his wife to be violative of due process where no reasonable connection between this conduct and his work was demonstrated. Board of Trustees of Compton Junior College Dist. of Los Angeles County v. Stubblefield, 16 Cal. App. 3d 820, 94 Cal. Rptr. 318 (1971).
[13] 42 U.S.C. § 2000e-2(a). See Annotation, Construction and application of provisions of Title VII of Civil Rights Act of 1964 (42 U.S.C. §§ 2000e et seq.) making sex discrimination in employment unlawful, 12 A.L.R. Fed. 15 (1972).
[14] 42 U.S.C. § 2000e-2(e).
[15] See Binder, Sex Discrimination in the Airline Industry: Title VII Flying High, 59 Calif. L. Rev. 1091 (1971); Comment, Sex-Plus: Failure of the Attempt to Subvert the Sex Provision of the Civil Rights Act of 1964, 7 Gonzaga L. Rev. 83 (1971); Note, Employment Discrimination and Title VII of the Civil Rights Act of 1964, 84 Harv. L. Rev. 1109 (1971).
[16] E.g., Phillips v. Martin Marietta Corp., 400 U.S. 542, 27 L. Ed. 2d 613, 91 Sup. Ct. 496 (1971); Stroud v. Delta Air Lines, Inc., 544 F.2d 892 (C.A.-5 Ga., 1977), cert. den. 434 U.S. 844, 98 Sup. Ct. 146 (1977).

sons exclusively.[17] Yet other policies have the objective of disenabling a married couple from both being in the employ of the employer.[18] Or such a policy can be aimed at ensuring that no one is employed whose spouse is employed by a competitor;[19] or that his or her occupation does not present a potential conflict of interest in a person seeking employment.[20]

Controversy rages as to the extent to which policies of this nature are violative of Title VII, especially in the airline industry.[21] The practice of disenabling a married couple from both being in the employ of the employer, or at least in the same department of the organization, is generally ruled unobjectionable since the employer is virtually always able to show that such a restriction bears a rational relation to job performance.[22] Of importance to unmarried partners is Espinoza v. Thoma,[23] in which it was held that not only is a "no spouse" policy a reasonable classification, bearing a substantial relation to an employer's policy to eliminate the potential for serious conflicts that might affect job performance, but also that "no spouse" rules and policies of this nature can properly be extended to embrace persons who live together without the benefit of a legal marriage.

---

[17]See C.C.H. E.E.O.C. Decisions (1973) ¶ 6244, where the Commission declined to decide whether, as a general matter, an employer's private standards of morality or public standards of morality are a proper basis for invoking the good faith occupational qualification to Title VII.

[18]See Harper v. Trans World Airlines, Inc., 525 F.2d 409, 34 A.L.R. Fed. 639 (C.A.-8 Mo., 1975); Yuhas v. Libbey-Owens-Ford Co., 562 F.2d 496 (C.A.-7 Ill., 1977), cert. den. —— U.S. ——, 98 Sup. Ct. 1510 (1978) (an employer's rule prohibiting hiring hourly employees when the applicant's spouse is already employed in the same capacity does not violate Title VII where the no-spouse rule is job-related. Such a rule does not penalize women on the basis of their environmental or genetic background).

[19]E.g., Emory v. Georgia Hosp. Serv. Assn., 446 F.2d 897 (C.A.-5 Ga., 1971).

[20]E.g., Satterwhite v. Greenville, Texas, 395 F. Supp. 698 (N.D. Tex., 1975).

[21]E.g., Lansdale v. Air Line Pilots Assn. Internat., 430 F.2d 1341 (C.A.-5 Fla., 1970); Sprogis v. United Air Lines, Inc., 444 F.2d 1194 (C.A.-7 Ill., 1971), cert. den. 404 U.S. 991, 30 L.Ed. 2d 543, 92 Sup. Ct. 536 (1971); In re National Airlines, Inc., 434 F. Supp. 266 (S.D. Fla., 1977). See 15 Am. Jur. 2d, Civil Rights, §§ 176–183. As to disqualification based solely on pregnancy, see id., § 177.

[22]Siegel, "No Spouse" Rule and Changing Lifestyles, 1 Nat. Law J. 23 (Jan. 22, 1979).

[23]580 F.2d 346 (C.A.-8 Neb., 1978).

Though the problem has no direct bearing on the legal status of unwed cohabitants, it is worth noting that if such a policy of this nature is applicable only to females, and not to males in the same situation, it is virtually certain to be condemned as a "sex-plus" violation of the statute.[24]

An EEOC decision involved an employer's policy of hiring only married couples to work as residential apartment managers. The commission ruled that refusal of employment to a single female applicant was not discriminatory because two individuals are required for the position. However, it added that by limiting the two employees filling such positions to married couples, the employer was discriminating against potential applicants of both sexes who may apply in pairs of persons of the same sex.[25] It could be urged, however, that marriage is a bona fide occupational qualification for a job of this nature. If the decision is sound in holding that it would violate Title VII to withhold the employment from a couple of homosexuals or lesbians due solely to their sexual preferences, a fortiori a refusal to hire an unmarried heterosexual couple for the reason that they are not married would be discriminatory.

A denial of maternity leave to a pregnant employee, wed or unwed, is a violation of Title VII.[26] But the transfer of an unmarried teacher to a nonteaching position by reason of pregnancy has been held not so violative. The court noted that an unmarried male teacher who made no secret of the fact that he was respon-

---

[24]See Harper v. Trans World Airlines, Inc., 525 F.2d 409, 34 A.L.R. Fed. 639 (C.A.-8 Mo., 1975), where no "disparate effect" upon women due to a "no-spouse" employment policy was established. A "no-spouse" policy which plausibly improves work environment and does not penalize women on the basis of their environmental or genetical background has been considered to be job-related and not violative of Title VII. See Yuhas v. Libbey-Owens-Ford Co., 562 F.2d 496 (C.A.-7 Ill., 1977), cert. den. —— U.S. ——, 98 Sup. Ct. 1510 (1978). Decisions of the Equal Employment Opportunity Commission (EEOC) are collected in the Annotation, Distinctions based on marital status as constituting sex discrimination under § 703 (a) of Civil Rights Act of 1964 (42 U.S.C.S. § 2000e-2(a)), 34 A.L.R. Fed. 648 (1977).

[25]C.C.H. E.E.O.C. Decisions (1973) ¶ 6302; 4 F.E.P. Cases 253 (1972).

[26]Annotation, Pregnancy leave or maternity leave policy, or lack thereof, as unlawful employment practice violative of Title VII of the Civil Rights Act of 1964, 27 A.L.R. Fed. 537 (1976).

sible for such a pregnancy would presumably receive the same treatment.[27]

Of more direct interest is a ruling that a policy of refusing to hire unwed mothers is a violation of Title VII. Even if an employer attempted to apply this standard to males as well as females, it would be difficult, if not impossible, to determine to which males it would apply.[28] Similarly, termination of an unmarried employee by reason of her pregnancy is a violation of her Title VII rights. Such an artificial, arbitrary and unnecessary barrier to employment cannot be sustained where the Act removes such barriers in cases of pregnancy of a married woman and where there is no evidence that a classification based on marriage has a rational relationship to the normal operation of the employer's business.[29]

The commission has also held that an employer's maternity leave policy that limits benefits to married female employees is unlawful sex discrimination against unwed mothers in the absence of a similar provision for unwed fathers.[30] The employer in that case was a government contractor, and it was noted that the sex discrimination guidelines issued by the Office of Federal Contract Compliance provided that any distinction between married and unmarried persons of the same sex that is not made between married and unmarried persons of the opposite sex will be considered to be distinction made on the basis of sex. Since a maternity leave policy for fathers, whether wed or unwed, would be an absurdity, it would seem that the unmarried female employee must share whatever rights the married female enjoys in regard to maternity leave.

When company rules leave it to the partners to decide which one is to leave the job, attacks, often sponsored by women's rights organizations, based on the argument that the end result is a

---

[27] Wardlaw v. Austin Independent School Dist., 9 C.C.H. E.P.D. ¶ 10,222 (1975).
[28] C.C.H. E.E.O.C. Decisions (1973) ¶ 6164.
[29] Jacobs v. Martin Sweets Co., 550 F.2d 364 (C.A.-6 Ky., 1977), cert. den. 431 U.S. 917, 97 Sup. Ct. 2180 (1977), 13 C.C.H. E.P.D. ¶ 11,537. But an airline's policy of requiring flight attendants to take unpaid maternity leave on discovery of pregnancy does not violate the Civil Rights Act. Harriss v. Pan Amer. World Airways, Inc., 437 F. Supp. 413 (N.D. Cal., 1977).
[30] C.C.H. E.E.O.C. Decisions (1973) ¶ 6184.

discriminatory impact on the female partner (who is usually the one to quit) have met with little success.[31]

2.3. Schoolteachers

The right of an employee to engage in extramarital cohabitation, without fear that such conduct will affect his or her employment, merits a closer examination in the area of schoolteachers.

> A teacher works in a sensitive area in a schoolroom. There (s)he shapes the attitude of young minds toward the society in which they live. In this, the state has a vital concern. It must preserve the integrity of the schools. That the school authorities have the right and the duty to screen the officials, teachers, and employees as to their fitness to maintain the integrity of the schools as a part of ordered society, can not be doubted.[32]

In a Nebraska decision quoting these words, the teacher had developed a good relationship with the students and was considered likely to be a model to them in wide-ranging aspects, including personal values. Many of the students knew her to be unmarried and probably pregnant. Though she had not been shown to have given any definite answers to their questions about this, the board of education was held to have acted properly in deciding that to permit this teacher to continue to teach would be viewed as a condonation of pregnancy out of wedlock. For this reason, the action of the board in terminating the teacher's employment was held to bear a relationship to its legitimate educational function. On appeal, the court, without reaching the question whether the school had declined to renew her contract for constitutionally permissible reasons, reversed the decision because the teacher's post-termination hearing, conducted some two years

---

[31]Siegel, note 22 supra. See also C.C.H. E.E.O.C. Decisions (1973) ¶ 6103. Generally, see Annotation, Construction and application of provisions of Title VII of Civil Rights Act of 1964 (42 U.S.C. §§ 2000e et seq.) making sex discrimination in employment unlawful, 12 A.L.R. Fed. 15 (1972). See also Note, Love's Labors Lost: New Conceptions of Maternity Leaves, 7 Harv. Civ. Rights & Civ. Lib. L. Rev. 260 (1972).

[32]Adler v. Board of Education of City of New York, 342 U.S. 485, 493, 96 L. Ed. 517, 72 Sup. Ct. 380, 385 (1952). Generally, see Annotation, Sexual conduct as grounds for dismissal of teacher or denial or revocation of teaching certificate, 78 A.L.R.3d 19 (1978).

after the termination, denied her the right to procedural due process.[33]

That is not to say that extramarital cohabitation per se is grounds for dismissal. In Fisher v. Snyder,[34] for example, a mere showing of facts which might raise a question as to a teacher's good judgment in her personal affairs, without any evidence even pointing to a community reaction against her conduct, was held insufficient to warrant her termination; such a dismissal was considered arbitrary and capricious, and in violation of her right to substantive due process under the Fourteenth Amendment.

But the schoolteacher who cohabits without benefit of clergy is, to say the least, skating on thin ice. In Sullivan v. Meade County Independent School District No. 101,[35] it was shown simply that the teacher lived with her boyfriend. She was notified by a representative of the school that if she did not discontinue this conduct there was a strong possibility that she could lose her job. At a hearing before the school board, a petition with approximately 140 signatures was presented showing a strong community reaction to her conduct. The court held that her dismissal was related to the proper functioning of the educational system, was not "arbitrary and capricious," and did not violate due process in that, vague though the statutory authority may have been, she had received admonition from the school authorities as to their view of her conduct and their intended action.

Statutes commonly provide that a conviction of sex offenses

---

[33]Brown v. Bathke, 416 F. Supp. 1194 (D. Neb., 1976), revd. 566 F.2d 588 (CA-8 Neb., 1977).
[34]476 F.2d 375 (CA-8 Neb., 1973).
[35]387 F. Supp. 1237 (D. S.D., 1975), affd. 530 F.2d 799 (C.A.-8 S.D., 1976). The doctrine that a dismissal is constitutionally permissible only if there is a nexus between the allegedly immoral conduct and the workings of the educational process or the working relationships within the educational institution was also applied in Morrison v. State Bd. of Education, 1 Cal. 3d 214, 82 Cal. Rptr. 175, 461 P.2d 375 (1969), where a teacher's diplomas were revoked because he had engaged in private consensual homosexual activity. In Pettit v. State Bd. of Education, 10 Cal. 3d 29, 109 Cal. Rptr. 665, 513 P.2d 889, 78 A.L.R.3d 1 (1973), the court, requiring the same nexus between the conduct and the teaching performance, said "an unqualified proscription against immoral conduct would raise serious constitutional problems."

requires denial of any application for teaching credentials, revocation of existing credentials, and termination of employment.[36] However, such statutes are usually construed to apply only when the offenses involved demonstrate that the defendant cannot be a suitable behavior model for students, or is unfit to teach.[37] A statute which permits revocation of teaching credentials for "immoral" conduct per se, conduct which has no relation to teaching performance, has been strongly criticized.[38]

Although extramarital cohabitation has in a proper case justified termination,[39] and although it is undoubtedly within the power of the school authorities to establish the requisites of moral character for teachers,[40] few states would today be likely to regard mere extramarital cohabitation, absent any showing of an adverse effect on fitness to teach[41] or some notoriety which impairs the teacher's on-campus relations,[42] as enough to affect his or her employment.

School boards often have a policy of not permitting spouses to teach in the same school.[43] At least one attack on such a policy as violative of the Civil Rights Act,[44] where the complainant had left

---

[36] E.g., Cal. Educ. Code, § 12910 et seq.

[37] Under the provisions of California's statute (Cal. Educ. Code, § 13202) requiring the state board of education to revoke or suspend a teaching credential for "immoral conduct . . . or for evident unfitness for service," the determinative test is fitness to teach. Id., § 13403 (a, e). An arrest for homosexual solicitation did not per se demonstrate unfitness to teach. Board of Education of Long Beach Unified School Dist. of Los Angeles County v. Jack M., 19 Cal. 3d 691, 139 Cal. Rptr. 700, 566 P.2d 602 (1977).

[38] See Comment, Unfitness to Teach: Credential Revocation and Dismissal for Sexual Conduct, 61 Calif. L. Rev. 1442 (1973); Willemsen, Sex and the School Teacher, 14 Santa Clara Law. 839 (1974); Fleming, Teacher Dismissal for Cause: Public and Private Morality, 7 J. L. & Educ. 423 (1978).

[39] E.g., Board of Trustees of Mount San Antonio Junior College Dist. of Los Angeles County v. Hartman, 246 Cal. App. 2d 756, 55 Cal. Rptr. 144 (1966).

[40] See 68 Am. Jur. 2d, Schools, §§ 133, 176.

[41] See, e.g., Erb v. Iowa State Bd. of Public Instruction, 216 N.W.2d 339 (Iowa, 1974).

[42] See Board of Trustees of Compton Junior College Dist. of Los Angeles County v. Stubblefield, 16 Cal. App. 3d 820, 94 Cal. Rptr. 318 (1971); Jerry v. Board of Education of City School Dist. of Syracuse, 35 N.Y.2d 534, 364 N.Y.S.2d 440, 324 N.E.2d 106 (1974).

[43] See Annotation, Distinctions based on marital status as constituting sex discrimination under § 703 (a) of Civil Rights Act of 1964 (42 U.S.C. § 2000e-2(a)), 34 A.L.R. Fed. 648, 679 (1977).

[44] As to Title VII rights, see section 2.2, herein.

the decision to the employer as to which spouse should be transferred,[45] has failed. As to unwed teachers, transfer to a nonteaching position was held not to violate Title VII where a pregnant teacher told the school of her intentions to inform her classes of her unwed pregnancy.[46] No doubt the same treatment would be accorded to an expectant father in the same situation.[47]

Motherhood as such, in the context of the discharge of an unwed mother from a teaching position, has been described as "an area in which the need to reflect rapidly changing norms affecting important interests in liberty compels an individualized determination, one not bound by any pre-existing rule of thumb, within the zone of moral change."[48]

In view of the somewhat precarious status of the teacher engaging in extramarital cohabitation, it seems proper to inquire as to whether marriage can be a ground for the dismissal of a female teacher. Where there have existed valid regulations of the school board providing against the employment of married women, or where the contract of employment provided for a termination in the event of marriage, such provisions have been upheld. (But such a provision or regulation may well today be regarded as an invidious discrimination on the basis of sex.) If, on the other hand, the regulations or the contract merely provide for termination for "good cause," it is hardly conceivable that a mere marriage could be regarded as "cause." Pregnancy can present a more difficult question. Many school districts make provision for maternity leaves based on pregnancy. Where there is no such provision, at least one state has held a decision to terminate a female teacher's contract solely because of her refusal to resign in accordance with a regulation requiring resignation by the end of the fifth month of

---

[45]Meier v. Evansville-Vanderburgh School Corp., 416 F. Supp. 748 (S.D. Ind., 1975), affd. without opinion 539 F.2d 713 (C.A.-7 Ind., 1976).

[46]Wardlaw v. Austin Independent School Dist., 9 C.C.H. E.P.D. ¶ 10,222 (1975).

[47]Id. See Case of the Pregnant School Teachers: An Equal Protection Analysis, 34 Md. L. Rev. 287 (1974). Annotation, Mandatory maternity leave rules or policies for public school teachers as constituting violation of equal protection clause of Fourteenth Amendment to Federal Constitution, 17 A.L.R. Fed. 768 (1973).

[48]Tribe, Structural Due Process, 10 Harv. Civ. Rights & Civ. Lib. L. Rev. 269 (1975). See New Mexico State Bd. of Education v. Stoudt, 91 N.M. 183, 571 P.2d 1186 (1977).

pregnancy to be illegal. Such temporary lack of physical fitness does not constitute "incompetency" which could be a valid cause for termination. Further, absent any evidence that a male teacher would receive similar treatment for temporary disabilities due to illness, the termination was held violative of the Human Rights Act of the state involved.[49]

It is probable that most states would frown upon mere marriage as a ground for refusal to hire or for dismissal, and the validity of a school regulation or a contractual provision for termination on the ground of pregnancy ought to turn on a more pragmatic test: e.g., is it likely that the pregnancy would adversely affect her performance in the classroom or would she be unlikely to return to her duties if the situation is taken care of by a grant of maternity leave?[50] In fact, a regulation or policy which mandates leave, and a fortiori discharge, of a teacher by reason of pregnancy (wed or unwed) has been held unconstitutional, inter alia, as violative of equal protection.[51] In Cleveland Board of Education v. La Fleur,[52] the Supreme Court of the United States has held that arbitrary mandatory maternity leaves are violative of the due process clause of the Fourteenth Amendment, even though most of the lower courts had used an equal protection analysis. Noting that irrebuttable presumptions have "long been disfavored" under the due process clause, the Court held a regulation, mandating maternity leave five months before the child was due, conclusively to presume physical inability to work, to create a presumption neither necessarily nor universally true—and that administrative convenience alone is not enough to validate such a violation of due process.[53]

---

[49]Cerra v. East Stroudsberg Area School Dist., 450 Pa. 207, 299 A.2d 277 (1973).
[50]See Annotations, Marriage of teacher as ground of removal or discharge, 81 A.L.R. 1033 (1932), 118 A.L.R. 1092 (1939); Temporary inability of teacher without fault of school authorities to perform duty as justifying termination of contract, 72 A.L.R. 283 (1931). Generally, see 68 Am. Jur. 2d, Schools, § 172.
[51]Green v. Waterford Bd. of Education, 473 F.2d 629 (C.A.-2 Conn., 1973). See Mandatory Maternity Leave of Absence Policies—An Equal Protection Analysis, 45 Temple L. Q. 240 (1972).
[52]414 U.S. 632, 39 L. Ed. 2d 52, 94 Sup. Ct. 791 (1974).
[53]See also Vlandis v. Kline, 412 U.S. 441, 37 L. Ed. 2d 63, 93 Sup. Ct. 2230 (1973).

In New Mexico State Bd. of Education v. Stoudt, 91 N.M. 183, 571 P.2d 1186 (1977), it was held that a certified teacher's dismissal for unwed pregnancy was

RAMIFICATIONS 2.3

Of related interest is the question whether unwed pregnancy is sufficient "cause" to justify termination of a school employee acting in an administrative, nonteaching capacity. In Lewis v. Delaware State College[54] a plaintiff employed as director of residence halls for women at a state college sought a preliminary injunction against such action. The injunction issued. Her claim that the school's action violated both substantive due process and equal protection was considered so strong as to make it "virtually a foregone conclusion" that the school would not be able to establish a compelling state interest sufficient to justify the intrusion on her right to decide to bear her child.

Due process was violated in that (1) the defendants had no basis in fact for discharging her. The only basis it purported to furnish was that her condition rendered her presumptively unfit to counsel students effectively by reason of her unorthodox lifestyle. But she was not responsible for counselling students on personal matters; hence this reason was rejected. (2) She had received no warning that bearing an illegitimate child would be a ground for termination. (3) The refusal to renew her contract infringed her constitutional right of privacy. As illustrated, inter alia, by the abortion decisions,[55] the Supreme Court of the United States has left no room for dispute that the decision whether to bear a child is one in which no state interference will be tolerated absent a showing of a compelling state interest.

Equal protection guaranties of the Constitution were regarded as violated in that the school had taken no action against other members of the nonteaching staff who had borne children out of wedlock.

Of interest is the court's view that interference with constitutional rights cannot be justified solely on the ground that the

---

arbitrary, unreasonable and not supported by substantial evidence. There was a showing that five other unwed mothers had been retained by the school board involved, and that the teacher in question was fit to perform her duties. The court, however, declined to promote guidelines as to what constitutes immoral conduct such as would be sufficient cause for discharge.

[54]455 F. Supp. 239 (D. Del., 1978). For an affirmation of the termination of a transsexual teacher, see In re Grossman, 127 N.J. Super. 13, 316 A.2d 39 (1974), cert. den. 65 N.J. 292, 321 A.2d 253 (1974), discussed 1976 Wis. L. Rev. 670.

[55]See section 2.19, herein.

community is hostile to their exercise and vigorous in its demonstration of its feelings. Such a view may well require qualification where a "classroom image" is involved.

2.4. Students

In Hollenbaugh v. Carnegie Free Library,[56] it is suggested that an expulsion by a state university based on the living arrangements of the students involved could be an irrational classification violative of the equal protection provisions of the United States Constitution.

It is well recognized that regulations for the administration of schools and the control of students are primarily a matter for the school authorities concerned, and will not be subject to judicial attack unless they constitute an unreasonable or arbitrary exercise of the school's undisputed authority.[57] On this basis, the restriction of married high school students in respect of extracurricular activities has been upheld as not unreasonable.[58] It is argued that such a rule discourages student marriages, and where students do marry, the rule helps preserve the marriage by reducing the amount of time devoted to school activities.[59] At least one state, however, has held that such a restriction is irrational discrimination, not based on any compelling state interest, and violative of a declared policy of the state to promote the marriage relationship.[60]

The question whether a public school has the right to expel a student on the grounds of extramarital cohabitation seems yet to

---

[56]436 F. Supp. 1328, 1333 (W.D. Pa., 1977).
[57]See, generally, 68 Am. Jur. 2d, Schools, § 242.
[58]Board of Directors of Independent School Dist. of Waterloo v. Green, 259 Iowa 1260, 147 N.W.2d 854 (1967).
[59]Id. See also Cochrane v. Board of Education of Mesick Consol. School Dist., 360 Mich. 390, 103 N.W.2d 569 (1960) (divided court); Estay v. Lafourche Parish School Bd., 230 So. 2d 443 (La. App., 1969); State ex rel. Baker v. Stevenson, 27 Ohio Ops. 2d 223, 189 N.E.2d 181 (1962); Kissick v. Garland Independent School Dist., 330 S.W.2d 708 (Tex. Civ. App., 1959); Starkey v. Board of Education of Davis County School Dist., 14 Utah 2d 227, 381 P.2d 718 (1963).
[60]Beeson v. Kiowa County School Dist. RE-1,——Colo. App.——, 567 P.2d 801 (1977), reasoning that the acknowledged intent to discourage eligible persons from marriage obviously contravenes the declared public policy of the state "to promote and foster the marriage relationship." It was also argued that family

be presented. Where a student marries or becomes pregnant, some courts have upheld as reasonable school regulations calling for expulsion; others have held the other way.[61]

It seems unlikely that a school regulation authorizing the exclusion or expulsion of a high school student who openly admits to his or her classmates that he or she is cohabiting outside of marriage would be vulnerable to an attack on constitutional grounds. Social mores have not yet been demolished to an extent that would make this classifiable as an "irrational" discrimination.

Concerning students at the university level, however, it would seem outrageous even to regard the question as an open one.

2.5. Unmarried pregnancies in the armed services

Traditionally, the courts have been highly reluctant to interfere in reviewing decisions of the military.[62] Of late, however, there has been a tendency to find that such regulations and policies are as much open to judicial review on constitutional grounds as are any employment policies. In Crawford v. Cushman,[63] for example, it was held that not only do the courts have a right to review a Marine Corps regulation which mandated the dismissal of a pregnant marine, but also that a

---

responsibilities often require a higher education, and that a potential deprivation of married students from participating in extracurricular activities could prevent their obtaining (via scholarships, for example) a much needed source of funds for this purpose. See also Moran v. School Dist. # 7, Yellowstone County, 350 F. Supp. 1180 (D. Mont., 1972); Indiana High School Athletic Assn. v. Raike,——Ind. App.——, 329 N.E.2d 66 (1975).

[61] See Annotation, Marriage or pregnancy of public school student as ground for expulsion or exclusion, or of restriction of activities, 11 A.L.R.3d 996 (1967), annotating a decision (Board of Education of Harrodsburg, Kentucky v. Bentley, 383 S.W.2d 677, 11 A.L.R.3d 990 (Ky., 1964)) invalidating a school regulation providing that a student who married must withdraw from school, subject to readmittance after one full year as a special student with the principal's permission. As to pregnancy as a ground for exclusion from public school, see 68 Am. Jur. 2d, Schools, § 226. As to the fact that the unwed mother would be compelled to attend night school as an alternative, an economically less viable alternative, as rendering the school policy unconstitutional, see Houston v. Prosser, 361 F. Supp. 295 (N.D. Ga., 1973).

[62] See Annotation, Judicial review of military action with respect to type of discharge given serviceman, 4 A.L.R. Fed. 343 (1970).

[63] 531 F.2d 1114 (C.A.-2 Vt., 1976).

classification based on sex "must rest on some ground . . . having a fair and substantial relation to the object[ive] of the legislation, so that all persons similarly circumstanced should be treated alike."[64] The regulation under attack was held "irrationally underinclusive" since it did not apply to personnel with any other temporary disabilities, and "overinclusive" because it operated to discharge pregnant marines automatically without any individualized determination of their fitness to serve. The ability of any particular pregnant woman in the military to continue to work past any fixed time in her pregnancy is as much an individual matter as it is in the case of a schoolteacher.[65]

This notwithstanding, West v. Brown[66] presented a constitutional challenge to a nonwaivable regulation of the Secretary of the Army which barred the enlistment of unwed parents of minor children. This was held nonreviewable. Rational restrictions on noncontractual government benefits and services are valid in the absence of affirmative governmental action which curtails important constitutional liberties, since such benefits do not in themselves enjoy constitutionally protected status. There is no right to join the armed services, and the regulation was not regarded as affirmatively curtailing marriage or childbearing. Further, experience with an earlier form of the regulation which permitted waiver by the military authorities of the restriction had shown that singles with dependent children had caused embarrassment in the management of a military force and created problems of morale.

From an article discussing the litigious adventures of three Air Force employees who were dismissed for unwed pregnancy (which actions had become moot by reason of waivers), it becomes clear that the courts no longer regard terminations of military employment by reason of pregnancy as not open to review on con-

---

[64]Id., at 1122, quoting Royster Guano Co. v. Virginia, 253 U.S. 412, 415, 64 L. Ed. 989, 990, 40 Sup. Ct. 560, 561 (1920).
[65]Cleveland Bd. of Education v. La Fleur, 414 U.S. 632, 645, 39 L. Ed. 2d 52, 94 Sup. Ct. 791, 799 (1974).
[66]558 F.2d 757 (C.A.-5 Fla., 1977), cert. den.——U.S.——, 98 Sup. Ct. 1493 (1978). See also Note, Marriage, Pregnancy, and the Right to Go to School, 50 Tex. L. Rev. 1196 (1972).

stitutional grounds.[67] But it is hard to avoid the conclusion that regulations of the kind under consideration, the needs of the military being as they are, will likely withstand constitutional attack, especially if the authorities have the discretion to waive their application in a proper case.

2.6. Right of privacy

In the landmark case of Griswold v. Connecticut,[68] holding unconstitutional a statute prohibiting the use of contraceptives, the Supreme Court of the United States made some pronouncements which have significant bearing on the nature and scope of this constitutional right. After noting a number of constitutional amendments (first, third, fourth, fifth and ninth) which guarantee by implication certain zones of privacy, one of which is the marriage relationship, the court held that the statute had a maximum destructive impact on that relationship. Justice Goldberg, concurring in the judgment, said:

> To hold that a right so basic and fundamental and so deep-rooted in our society as the right of privacy in marriage may be infringed because that right is not guaranteed in so many words by the first eight amendments to the Constitution is to ignore the Ninth Amendment and to give it no effect whatsoever.[69]

Since the Griswold decision, there have been attempts to invoke this constitutional right of privacy, which was specifically ruled to encompass the marital relationship, in respect of sexual behavior outside the marital relationship. The extent to which the right protects state intrusion into the private sexual activities of consenting adults has become a matter of much debate. For example, in Hollenbaugh v. Carnegie Free Library,[70] discussed

---

[67]Note, Pregnancy Discharges in the Military: The Air Force Experience, 86 Harv. L. Rev. 568 (1973), wherein it is suggested that armed services must revise their policies regarding pregnancy "to safeguard the procreative interests of female personnel and to afford them equal protection of the laws."

[68]381 U.S. 479, 14 L. Ed. 2d 510, 85 Sup. Ct. 1678 (1965). As to contraceptives, see section 2.19, herein.

[69]Id., 381 U.S. at 491, 85 Sup. Ct. at 1685.

[70]436 F. Supp. 1328 (W.D. Pa., 1977).

earlier,[71] the plaintiffs, contesting their discharge as library employees because they lived in adultery, also argued that their discharge constituted an unwarranted intrusion into a matter fundamentally affecting their own personal lives and was thus in violation of a constitutionally guaranteed right of privacy under the first, fourth, ninth and fourteenth amendments of the Constitution.

This right of privacy has at times been premised on the individual's right under the declaration of rights to the pursuit of happiness.[72] However, the notion that it has a basis in any of the constitutional guaranties mentioned has been criticized.[73] Only in the sense that the Constitution protects against certain kinds of governmental intrusion (as for example the fourth amendment) can the "right to be let alone" properly be said to have a constitutional basis.[74]

Although this right has been extended to some areas that have traditionally been categorized as "immoral," the court in the Hollenbaugh case did not consider that there was any "fundamental" privacy right "implicit in the concept of ordered liberty" that could be harnessed to impeach the decision of the library trustees to discharge them on the grounds of their adulterous cohabitation.[75] However, the Supreme court has held that denying an unmarried woman[76] the right to an abortion,[77] can be characterized as a violation of this right to privacy.

---

[71]See section 2.1, herein.

[72]See 16 Am. Jur. 2d, Constitutional Law, § 351.

[73]See Clark, Constitutional Sources of the Penumbral Right to Privacy, 19 Villanova L. Rev. 833 (1974); Lusky, Invasion of Privacy: A Clarification of Concepts, 72 Colum. L. Rev. 693 (1972).

[74]See Annotation, Right of privacy, 14 A.L.R.2d 750 (1950). See also Annotation, Waiver or loss of right of privacy, 57 A.L.R.3d 16 (1974).

[75]To the same effect, see Sullivan v. Meade County Independent School Dist. No. 101, 387 F. Supp. 1237 (D. S.D., 1975), affd. 530 F.2d 799 (C.A.-8 S.D., 1976).

[76]Griswold v. Connecticut, 381 U.S. 479, 14 L. Ed. 2d 510, 85 Sup. Ct. 1678 (1965). See also Eisenstadt v. Baird, 405 U.S. 438, 31 L. Ed. 2d 349, 92 Sup. Ct. 1029 (1972), invalidating a statute which made the exhibition of contraceptives and the giving of contraceptives to an unmarried person criminal acts.

[77]Roe v. Wade, 410 U.S. 113, 35 L. Ed. 2d 147, 93 Sup. Ct. 705 (1973), reh. den. 410 U.S. 959, 35 L. Ed. 2d 694, 93 Sup. Ct. 1409 (1973); Doe v. Bolton, 410 U.S. 179, 35 L. Ed. 2d 201, 93 Sup. Ct. 739 (1973), reh. den. 410 U.S. 959, 35 L. Ed. 2d 694, 93 Sup. Ct. 1410 (1973).

The personal intimacies of marriage, the home, procreation, motherhood, childbearing and the family are held "fundamental" and protected by the right of privacy, but it has been held that once a couple admits strangers into the marital bedchamber to witness illegal marital intimacies "they may not exclude the state as a constitutionally forbidden intruder."[78]

In short, though there are certain rights which can be asserted by unwed couples, violation of which could constitute an invasion of their right to "do their own thing," any constitutional right of privacy cannot be regarded as a shield against all the possible problems which unmarried cohabitants face. To pose an extreme example, would such a right to privacy be a defense to a charge of rape if the male partner had forcible intercourse with the female?

"[T]he protection of a person's *general* right to privacy—his right to be let alone by other people—is, like the protection of his property and of his very life, left largely to the law of the individual States."[79] A California court has regarded the constitutional right of privacy as buttressing its holding that a regulation of public housing which automatically excludes unmarried couples cannot be sustained.[80] The Supreme Court of the United States has made it clear that the right of an individual to bear or not to bear children cannot constitutionally be controlled by state legislation.[81]

---

[78]Lovisi v. Slayton, 539 F.2d 349, 351 (C.A.-4 Va., 1976), cert. den. 429 U.S. 977, 97 Sup. Ct. 485 (1976), affirming a conviction of a married couple of a crime against nature where they had waived any constitutional right to privacy by admitting third party to their bedroom. See also People v. Parker, 33 Cal. App. 3d 842, 109 Cal. Rptr. 354 (1973), holding that Cal. Penal Code, § 288 proscribing oral copulation, while it may be violative of the Constitution when applied to consenting adults in private, is not unconstitutional as applied to such acts performed before an audience; Chesebrough v. State, 255 So. 2d 675 (Fla., 1971), holding sexual intercourse between a married couple in their own home in the presence of their immature child to be punishable as lewd and lascivious conduct and not protected by any right of privacy.

[79]Katz v. United States, 389 U.S. 347, 350–351, 19 L. Ed. 2d 576, 88 Sup. Ct. 507, 510–511 (1967).

[80]Atkisson v. Kern County Housing Authority, 59 Cal. App. 3d 89, 97, 130 Cal. Rptr. 375, 389 (1976), discussed in section 2.7, herein.

[81]See notes 76 and 77, supra. See also section 2.19, herein.

These somewhat random observations, tending as they do to show that the constitutional source and the exact scope of this penumbral right to privacy is as yet undetermined, are by no means the end of the matter. It is well recognized that rights associated with the status of marriage are deemed fundamental or implicit in the concept of ordered liberty, and that any state regulation of privacy within the marriage relationship must be justified by a compelling state interest.[82] Beyond that, the impact of this relatively recent extension of constitutional guarantees, insofar as concerns not only heterosexual unmarried couples but also lesbians and homosexuals, has become a matter of the greatest interest. It is for this reason that, throughout this work, statutes and decisions bearing on the constitutional rights of those who indulge in sexual activities which deviate from normal sexual behavior are of constant concern. Insofar as they are protected by rights of privacy, ordinary extramarital cohabitants are surely protected; insofar as they are not so protected, a threat, albeit oblique, to the nonmarital status of any cohabitants is presented.[83]

2.7. Housing problems

Outside of the guaranties of the Constitution and of the Civil Rights Act, discussed later in this section, a landowner is entitled to sell or rent to whomsoever he chooses, and unmarried partners who are rejected have no legal recourse.

Further, it is possible that a hotel or motel operator has the legal right to refuse accommodation to a couple when he has

---

[82]See section 2.25, herein.
[83]On right to privacy generally, see Barnett, Population Growth, Population Organization Participants, and the Right to Privacy, 12 Family L.Q. 37 (1978); Craven, Personhood: The Right to be Let Alone, 1976 Duke L.J. 699; Freedom of Choice; Personal Autonomy and the Right to Privacy, 14 Idaho L. Rev. 447 (1978); Constitutional Law—Minors' Access to Contraceptives—The Right to Privacy, Due Process and the First Amendment, 23 N.Y. L. S. L. Rev. 777 (1978); Abortion and Privacy: A Woman's Right to Self Determination, 10 S. U. L. Rev. 173 (1978); Toward a Constitutional Theory of Individuality: The Privacy Opinions of Justice Douglas, 87 Yale L.J. 1579 (1978); Doss and Doss, On Morals, Privacy and the Constitution, 25 U. Miami L. Rev. 395 (1971).

RAMIFICATIONS 2.7

reason to believe that their purpose is extramarital cohabitation;[84] at any rate he may do so if he is able to show that their relationship is offensive to other guests.[85] In an early annotation discussing whether an improper motive or purpose in going to a hotel affects one's status as a guest for the purposes of the tort liability of the proprietor, writers are quoted as saying that an innkeeper would have a right to eject such a guest on a showing that he was there for purposes of prostitution.[86]

Today, a federal statute (the "Fair Housing Act")[87] exists to eliminate discrimination in the selling or leasing of housing based on race, color, religion, national origins or sex. The Act covers many dwellings which do not come within the purview of the housing and urban development laws.[88] Although a refusal to sell or rent to an unmarried couple could hardly be classed as discrimination based on sex, regulations of local housing authorities administering these public housing units may well be open to attack on constitutional grounds.[89] An Arkansas regulation to the effect that a family shall not be eligible for admission or continued occupation if anyone residing regularly with the family has a child or children born out of wedlock was so attacked.[90] The object of the regulation was to discourage prostitution. Single unwed mothers of illegitimate children charged that

---

[84]40 Am. Jur. 2d, Hotels, Motels, and Restaurants, § 65. See also Annotations, Validity, construction, and application of § 201(b)(1) and related provisions of Civil Rights Act of 1964 (42 U.S.C. § 2000a(b)(1), prohibiting discrimination or segregation in inns, hotels, motels, or other establishments providing lodging to transient guests, 7 A.L.R. Fed. 450 (1974); Hotel or innkeeper's liability for refusal to honor reservation, 58 A.L.R.3d 369 (1974).

[85]Id.

[86]Annotation, Improper motive or purpose in going to hotel as affecting one's status as guest, or invitee of a guest, for purpose of determining degree of care owed by proprietor, 16 A.L.R. 1388 (1922). The weight of authority is to place him as an invitee and not a mere trespasser. See Cramer v. Tarr, 165 F. Supp. 130 (D. Me., 1958). An innkeeper may be liable for personal injury to guests even if the room is being used for improper purposes, as where they register as husband and wife, if no causal relation exists between improper registration and injury. 40 Am. Jur. 2d, Hotels, Motels, and Restaurants, §§ 21, 86.

[87]42 U.S.C. §§ 3601–3619, 3631 (Titles VIII & IX of Civil Rights Act).

[88]See 15 Am. Jur. 2d, Civil Rights, § 249; 42 U.S.C. §§ 3603(b), 3604(c).

[89]See, e.g., Hills v. Gautreaux, 425 U.S. 284, 47 L. Ed. 2d 792, 96 Sup. Ct. 1538 (1976).

[90]Thomas v. Housing Authority of City of Little Rock, 282 F. Supp. 575 (E.D. Ark., 1967).

the regulation violated the equal protection and due process clauses of the Constitution. The court found the regulation overly broad because it made no distinction between unwed mothers with one illegitimate child and one with ten, nor did it take into account the circumstances of the illegitimate birth, age and training of the mothers and the likelihood of further illegitimate births. It also found the regulation out of harmony with the aim and spirit of the low-rent housing program. Though not saying that an unwed mother cannot be denied public housing, the court felt the criteria for denial must be tighter. It suggested that a policy giving evidentiary or presumptive effect to the presence of illegitimate children as indicating criminal activity (prostitution) is undefensible.

That mere cohabitation outside of marriage can be a factor influencing denial of low-income housing privileges appears from a more recent California decision.[91] The housing authority involved based the policy on the view that such cohabitation is immoral; that it results in a continuous turnover of cohabitants which results in management problems such as computation of rents; and that, inter alia, such a tenant becomes or is less responsible to the authority, is a poor influence on the other tenants, and the result could be a situation where the number of cohabitants could not be controlled. The court held that HUD regulations forbid the establishment of policies which *automatically* deny admission or continued occupancy to a *particular class,* such as unmarried mothers or families having one or more children born out of wedlock. A policy automatically excluding all unmarried cohabiting adults violates this regulation. Citing a number of cases from other jurisdictions[92] in support of the proposition that the classification in issue cannot be rationally justified under the applicable statutory purposes, the court commented that each of them involved an *inflexible* policy based on a

---

[91] Atkisson v. Kern County Housing Authority, 59 Cal. App. 3d 89, 130 Cal. Rptr. 375 (1976).

[92] United States Dept. of Agriculture v. Moreno, 413 U.S. 528, 37 L. Ed. 2d 782, 93 Sup. Ct. 2821 (1973); Tyson v. New York City Housing Authority, 369 F. Supp. 513 (S.D. N.Y., 1974); Neddo v. Housing Authority of City of Milwaukee, 335 F. Supp. 1397 (E.D. Wis., 1971); Thomas v. Housing Authority of City of Little Rock, 282 F. Supp. 575 (E.D. Ark., 1967).

classification with no *rational* connection between the undesirable conduct associated with a group, and the actions of an individual.

> The policy regulation ... clearly contains an *inflexible* policy which places plaintiff in a definable class of unmarried adults living together. Such a classification improperly assumes a connection with undesirable conduct associated with the class (e.g. demoralizing tenancy relations) and the conduct of the individual. The classification thus lacks the required rational basis, possesses the fatal flaw of "inflexibility," and must be held to be in violation of equal protection.[93]

Incidentally, perhaps as a makeweight argument, the court drew attention to a provision of the state health and safety code which proscribed the withholding of a sale or rental of publicly assisted housing accommodation because of the race, color, religion, sex, *marital status,* etc., of such persons. Though the amendment to include marital status was enacted after the issue was presented to the trial court, the reviewing court regarded it as an expression of the state's legislative intent which may well have rendered moot the broad constitutional questions on which it had ruled.

However, outside of publicly assisted housing, the conclusion remains: in the absence of controlling local legislation,[94] a private owner cannot be forced to rent or to sell to persons of whose lifestyle he or she does not approve.

2.8. Change of name of female partner

The right of a married woman to retain her maiden name has received some judicial attention.[95] Is the married woman's taking of the surname of her husband a rule of law, or merely based on

---

[93] Atkisson v. Kern County Housing Authority, 59 Cal. App. 3d 89, 97–98, 130 Cal. Rptr. 375, 380 (1976).
[94] For example, a New York statute makes it unlawful to discriminate against those seeking housing on the basis of their marital status. See section 6.33, herein.
[95] See Annotation, Right of married woman to use maiden surname, 67 A.L.R.3d 1266 (1975), and the articles cited therein.

custom?[96] The trend seems to be toward a recognition that it is merely a matter of custom, and the common-law principle that one is free to adopt (or retain) whatever name one chooses[97] should control. Statutes which authorize a judicial declaration of a name change are commonly construed as merely furnishing an alternative, nonexclusive means of securing judicial recognition of a right everyone has to merely adopt a new name, provided this is done for an honest purpose.[98]

Typically, when couples decide to embark on an extramarital cohabitation, the adoption by the female partner of the other's name would not be seriously considered; the woman would not encounter the disadvantages, such as having an automobile not registered under her "legal name,"[99] or in running for public office, or the like[1] to which a legally married woman who retains her maiden name can be exposed.

If, however, the partners are in a state recognizing common-law marriages,[2] or there is a possibility that they might subsequently be deemed common-law spouses by reason of a change of domicil,[3] a change of name might be proper for consideration. There can be no doubt that a woman's adoption of her partner's surname would be evidence of a common-law marriage, a "holding-out" of herself

---

[96]See Lamber, A Married Woman's Surname: Is Custom Law?, 1973 Wash. U. L. Q. 779. In re Erickson, 547 S.W.2d 357 (Tex. Civ. App., 1977), holding that to establish good cause for the change, it was enough for the applicant to feel a necessity for being known by her previous name. To deny this right would violate the guarantee of equal protection by creating an invalid classification based on sex. This was notwithstanding the trial court's view that such a change would give an appearance of illicit cohabitation against the morals of society and would not be in the best interests of the children, but detrimental to the institution of the home and family life and contrary to the common law and customs of Texas.

[97]See Secretary of Commonwealth v. City Clerk of Lowell,——Mass.——, 366 N.E.2d 717 (1977). See also Recording of Surnames—Clerks Have No Authority to Inhibit the Rights of Individuals to Choose Their Own and Their Children's Surnames, 13 New England L. Rev. 588 (1978).

[98]See 57 Am. Jur. 2d, Name, §§ 10, 11.

[99]E.g., Bacon v. Boston Elevated Ry. Co., 256 Mass. 30, 152 N.E. 35, 47 A.L.R. 1100 (1926).

[1]For a discussion of problems a married woman can encounter by retention of her maiden name, see Weitzman, Legal Regulation of Marriage: Tradition and Change, 62 Calif. L. Rev. 1169, 1175 (1974).

[2]Discussed in section 1.5, herein.

[3]See section 1.7, herein.

as his legal wife. She may or may not desire such a consequence. If she does so desire, evidence that she continued to use her maiden name is not necessarily fatal to her claim to be a common-law spouse.[4] In Estate of Greenfield v. Greenfield,[5] for example, a woman (who did desire this consequence) was held to be the common-law widow of one with whom she had apparently shared a happy marital life and to whom the local community believed her to be married. The fact that in business transactions she used her maiden name, as in employment applications, tax records and social security information, was accounted for by the fact that they shared apprehensions that his Jewish surname might have adverse repercussions on her career.

The possibility of being "trapped" into a common-law marriage, which could be a very real one when the partners seek to avoid social opprobrium by appearing to the public as spouses, and particularly so when one of them has died, could best be avoided by executing a writing (whether or not as a part of some contractual arrangement as to their mutual rights and obligations) declaring their nonmarital status. Such a declaration need not be publicized but, for obvious reasons, should be witnessed. An alternative sometimes resorted to is for each partner officially to change his or her name to a common surname.

2.9. Rights to adopt children

There is no state which by statute expressly forbids the adoption of a child by single persons or by unmarried couples. The statutory procedures, which almost invariably require a petition to court and the consent of any parent whose parental rights have not been judicially terminated by reason of neglect or unfitness,

---

[4]E.g., Chaachou v. Chaachou, 73 So. 2d 830 (Fla., 1954).
[5]245 S.C. 595, 141 S.E.2d 916 (1965).
In Forbush v. Wallace, 341 F. Supp. 217 (M.D. Ala., 1971), affd. without opinion 405 U.S. 970, 31 L. Ed. 2d 246, 92 Sup. Ct. 1197 (1972), a statute precluding a married woman from obtaining a driver's license except under her married name was upheld based on a legitimate state interest. Generally, see Note, Married Women and the Name Game, 11 U. Richmond L. Rev. 121 (1976).

or voluntary relinquishment, follow a fairly consistent pattern.[6] However, if resort is had to the usual procedure of approaching a licensed adoption agency, whose responsibility it is to secure for the child a good home, such an agency might well have its doubts as to the stability of the home environment of such parents.[7] As to whether a prospective adopter can go over the head of the adoption agency and secure a judicial decree without its consent, there is a surprising lack of uniformity both in the statutory and case law.[8]

It is of course possible for a couple, faced with a situation where they cannot obtain the approval of a licensed agency and are unlikely to secure judicial approval without such a recommendation, to go outside the normal channels to acquire a child.[9] This is sometimes called the "black" or "gray" baby market. The difference between these two terms is not hard and fast. In general, the black market, which has been well described as a "taint on civilized society,"[10] involves a marketeer who is simply trafficking

---

[6]At one time Florida limited the right to adopt to a married couple or survivor thereof. See Tsilidis v. Pedakis, 132 So. 2d 9 (Fla. App., 1961), where a court construes its statute to exclude right of single persons to adopt. A few states require that the adopter be of the same religious upbringing as the adoptive child. Such requirements are open to the criticism that they might drive unwed mothers into the black market to avoid having social workers prying into their religious background; they might also be an oblique invasion of the policy of noninterference by the arm of the state in matters of religion. At any rate, they should, if present at all, be discretionary and not mandatory. See Hauser, Adoption and Religious Control, 54 A.B.A. J. 771 (1968); Religious Factors in Adoption, 28 Ind. L. J. 401 (1952–53). On adoption generally, see also Annotations, Right of presumptive heir to object to adoption, 16 A.L.R. 1020 (1922); Change of child's name in adoption proceedings, 53 A.L.R.2d 927 (1957); Requirements as to residence or domicil of adoptee or adoptive parent for purposes of adoption, 33 A.L.R.3d 176 (1970); Race as factor in adoption proceedings, 54 A.L.R.2d 909 (1957).

[7]Though many administrative agencies have rules of thumb as to the respective ages of adoptive parents and those to be adopted, in the absence of a statute such guidelines should not be regarded as conclusive. See In re Adoption of Tachick, 60 Wis. 2d 540, 210 N.W.2d 865 (1973); Annotations, Age of prospective adopting parent as factor in adoption proceedings, 56 A.L.R.2d 823 (1957); Religion as factor in adoption proceedings, 48 A.L.R.3d 383 (1973).

[8]See Annotation, Adoption of child in absence of statutorily required consent of public or private agency or institution, 83 A.L.R.3d 373 (1978).

[9]Due to the increase in abortions, the declining birth rate, and the widespread use of contraceptives, adoptable white infants are becoming hard to find.

[10]Black Market Adoptions, 22 Catholic Law. 48 (1976). See also Moppets on the Market: The Problem of Unregulated Adoptions, 59 Yale L. J. 715 (1950).

in babies. The welfare of the child is subordinated to the profit and the chances of securing a judicial decree of adoption in respect of a child so procured are slight indeed. In contrast, a gray market situation is presented where the intermediary, perhaps an attorney, a physician or a well-meaning friend of the parties, receives no fee, though perhaps the adopting couple pay the expenses of the mother's confinement and delivery.[11] Most states, though not actually prohibiting this form of transaction, regulate it in some way, for example by requiring a disclosure to the court of the expenses involved in securing the baby or by requiring a state agency to report on the domestic situation of the prospective foster parents before its decree.[12] A major drawback to this procedure is the danger of future interference from the child's biological parents, who usually know who has the child. Further, since the ascertainment of the best interests of the child, which is always the paramount consideration,[13] involves considerable expertise, the likelihood of judicial approval by a decree of adoption without a recommendation from some authorized agency is greatly reduced. However, at least one writer thinks that, in this age of state paternalism, there is little justification for abolishing private placement in toto if the possibility of unsatisfactory matching can be made as minimal as that found in an agency placement.[14]

If, for whatever reason, adoption is found to be impracticable, consideration might be given to approaching the appropriate

---

[11] This is sometimes also known as a "private-placement adoption." It involves a private transaction between adoptive parents and the natural mother in which the attorney serves as an adviser, usually charging the adoptive parents for his services, and processes the adoption papers.

[12] Report of Committee on Adoptions: Attorney's Role in Independent Adoptions, 36 Calif. S.B. J. 970 (1961).

[13] E.g., Watson v. Shepard, 217 Va. 538, 229 S.E.2d 897 (1976) where, though the evidence sustained a finding that it would not be in the child's best interest to return custody to the mother, it did not sustain a finding that such interests would best be served by its adoption by her aunt, who was involved in a marital dispute.

[14] See Grove, Independent Adoption: The Case for the Gray Market, 13 Villanova L. Rev. 116 (1967).

As to the inheritance rights of an adopted child, see Annotations, Right of adopted child to inherit from intestate natural grandparent, 60 A.L.R.3d 631 (1974); Adoption as affecting right of inheritance through or from natural parent or other natural kin, 37 A.L.R.2d 333 (1954); Conflict of laws as to adoption as affecting descent and distribution of decedent's estate, 87 A.L.R.2d 1240 (1963).

agency with a view to becoming a foster parent. The difference between this and an adoption is that the placing agency is free to terminate the relationship at will. A foster home is usually an emergency means of caring for an abandoned child until a permanent home for it can be found. Whether or not the foster parent stands in loco parentis to the child seems to be a matter of semantics; for some purposes, he or she surely does.[15]

The rights of the biological parents, when the child sought to be adopted is illegitimate, receive later consideration.[16]

2.10. Homestead laws

Most states have statutes designed to protect from execution real property which the owner has registered as a homestead and occupies as a home. Under the typical statute (such a process has no common-law recognition) the homeowner seeking this protection must have residing with him someone to whom he owes a natural or a moral obligation to support. He must be the "head of the family," but he can qualify as such without actually being married. A wife, too, can qualify as "head of the family" for such protection if she is in fact the supporter of the group.[17]

A few states allow a single adult to protect himself from his creditors by the same process,[18] but of course such an extension would not permit two unmarried adults to protect the same property as "heads of the household."[19]

Statutes of this nature, precluding the seizure and forced sale of

---

[15] See 59 Am. Jur. 2d, Parent and Child, § 90.

[16] See section 3.8, herein.

[17] Annotation, Wife as head of family within homestead or other property exemption provision, 67 A.L.R.2d 779 (1959). Even if the wife does not own any part of the lands impressed by her husband with the homestead character, she does have an estate in such lands, to wit, the homestead, of which she cannot be deprived except by alienation by her own consent, and by which on the death of her spouse becomes a life estate. Norman v. First Bank & Trust, Bryan, 557 S.W.2d 797 (Tex. Civ. App., 1977), where homestead rights were denied to a common-law wife, by reason not of the fact of invalidity of such status but because she could not establish that the land had been homesteaded.

[18] See, e.g., Ariz. Rev. Stat. Ann., § 33-1101.

[19] First Nat. Bank of Dona Ana County v. Boyd, 378 F. Supp. 961 (D. Ariz., 1974). Comment, Effects of Extending the Homestead Exemption to Single Adults, 26 Baylor L. Rev. 658 (1974).

property under legal process, are applicable to the father of illegitimate children who maintains a household and supports them there.[20] Though it is stated that one engaged in an adulterous union would not qualify as "head of a household,"[21] there could be room for doubt in the situation of a couple who are simply living together without any adultery being involved. Florida, for one, requires that the applicant for homestead protection must either have a legal duty toward others in his home, or be regarded as the person in charge of a continued communal living situation.[22]

If the controlling statute affords no guidance, it seems unlikely that an extramarital cohabitant would qualify to homestead his and his partner's place of abode. If he has a common-law wife or a putative spouse, he would qualify because he owes a moral duty to protect his "family," but a mere contractual duty is a dubious basis on which to predicate a moral duty, and it is on this moral duty that the homestead exemptions are basically predicated.[23]

2.11. Welfare benefits

In an effort to combat the depression of the thirties, Congress enacted the Social Security Act.[24] Its objective is the provision of public assistance to needy citizens. Programs were set up to include child welfare, food supplies to the needy, aid to the aged, blind and others in need of medical assistance. The general pattern of this federal legislation, in which all states of the union to a great extent participate, is to provide uniform standards for the

---

[20]Lane v. Phillips, 69 Tex. 240, 6 S.W. 610 (1887).
[21]40 Am. Jur. 2d, Homestead, § 71 (presumably unless the support of illegitimate children is involved).
[22]See Heard v. Mathis, 344 So. 2d 651 (Fla. App., 1977); Comment, Our Legal Chameleon, The Florida Homestead Exemptions, 2 U. Fla. L. Rev. 12 (1949).
[23]See, generally, 40 Am. Jur. 2d, Homestead. But as the trend to substitute some nuclear stable unit other than the licensed marriage relationship progresses, if it does, the moral duty of a committed partner to support his "household" may come to be recognized as a basis on which a claim for homestead exemption can be predicated.
[24]42 U.S.C. § 301 et seq.

distribution, by the states, of funds for these purposes. If the standards furnished by the statute are met, federal funds are usually made available to help the state on a matching basis.[25]

If a state, in determining who is in need, ignores the uniform standards set forth in the statute, federal funds are withheld. For example, Congress has required that, as a condition for receiving federal funds under the aid for dependent children portions of the statute, the state must require the applicant for such assistance to assign to it any rights the applicant has against any other person in establishing paternity of an illegitimate child, unless the applicant has "good cause" for not so co-operating.[26] State regulations purporting to define what are the "best interests of the child" for the purpose of excusing an applicant from co-operating have been held invalid, this being a responsibility of the federal authorities.[27]

In addition to the federally sponsored programs, the states have their own provisions for the care of the poor and needy.[28]

---

[25]Generally, see 79 Am. Jur. 2d, Welfare Laws.

[26]42 U.S.C. § 602(a)(26). As to the present status of this requirement, see Maher v. Doe, 432 U.S. 526, 53 L. Ed. 2d 534, 97 Sup. Ct. 2474 (1977), holding valid a Connecticut statute requiring mothers of illegitimate children, as a condition of receiving AFDC benefits, to disclose the name of the child's father providing the state authorities have first determined the mother did not have good cause for refusal. See also Annotation, Validity of state action imposing sanctions on AFDC mother failing to name or seek support from putative father of illegitimate child, 45 L. Ed. 2d 268 (1975).

In Requiring an AFDC Applicant to Name Her Child's Father: Are the Rights of the Putative Fathers Being Protected?, 23 S.D. L. Rev. 379 (1978), the writer observes that requirements of this nature put pressure on the mother to name someone at the cost of foregoing benefits. She may well name a person for reasons of the heart (or avarice); if he denies paternity and goes to trial, judges and juries tend to favor the claimant, often on slim evidence. The contention is that if policy goals mandate a naming of the father, the rights of one so named should be far more carefully protected; e.g., the mother's unsupported testimony should never suffice; more extensive blood tests and polygraph testing should be used, lest the interests of mother, child and taxpayer be furthered at the expense of an alleged father's rights.

[27]Martella v. Commonwealth, Dept. of Public Welfare, 31 Pa. Cmwlth. 144, 375 A.2d 869 (1977).

[28]Generally, see 70 Am. Jur. 2d, Social Security and Medicare.

The social security fund

As a part of this general federal program, provision is made whereunder self-employed persons, employers and their employees are required to contribute to a fund which is designed to ensure that they, and their dependents on their death, are not left destitute on retirement or disablement.[29] A cohabitant as such cannot of course qualify as a survivor under this part of the statute. But if the contributor to this fund died domiciled in a jurisdiction which recognizes common-law marriage, and the survivor qualifies as such, the surviving partner would so qualify.[30] Conversely, if the survivor is not a common-law spouse, he or she would not qualify.[31]

As to the offspring of an extramarital cohabitation: if there was a good faith belief in the validity of the marriage[32] there can be no doubt that they would qualify as "children" of the decedent contributor.[33] As to other biological children, the test to be applied is, broadly speaking, the law that would be applied in determining the distribution of *intestate* personal property by the courts of the state in which the decedent was domiciled at the time of his death.[34] This test has been soundly criticized in that a state's

---

[29] 26 U.S.C. §§ 3101 et seq., 1401 et seq.

[30] See Sanabria v. Secretary of Health, Education & Welfare, 390 F. Supp. 538 (D. Puerto Rico, 1975), affd. without opinion 530 F.2d 961 (C.A.-1 Puerto Rico, 1976).

[31] See McSweeney v. Celebrezze, 253 F. Supp. 100 (S.D. N.Y., 1966); Moots v. Secretary, United States Dept. of Health, Education & Welfare, Social Security Administration, 349 F.2d 518 (C.A.-4 Va., 1965), cert. den. 382 U.S. 996, 15 L. Ed. 2d 483, 86 Sup. Ct. 582 (1966); Annotations, Who qualifies as "widow" or "widower" under § 216 of the Social Security Act [42 U.S.C. § 416], pertaining to survivor's benefits, where two or more alleged spouses survive decedent, 31 A.L.R. Fed. 300 (1977); Effect of divorce, remarriage, or annulment, on widow's pension or bonus rights or social security benefits, 85 A.L.R.2d 242 (1962).

[32] E.g., Polotti v. Flemming, 277 F.2d 864 (C.A.-2 N.Y., 1960). As to putative spouses, see section 1.6, herein.

[33] See, e.g., Arcand v. Flemming, 185 F. Supp. 22 (D. Conn., 1960).

[34] See, e.g., Moots v. Secretary, United States Dept. of Health, Education & Welfare, Social Security Administration, 349 F.2d 518 (C.A.-4 Va., 1965); McDaniel v. Flemming, 172 F. Supp. 153 (S.D. Cal., 1959); Semmel, Social Security Benefits for Illegitimate Children After Levy v. Louisiana, 19 Buffalo L. Rev. 289 (1970).

policies on intestate succession may be quite different from its policies in regard to areas such as support of dependents.[35] However, the federal statute goes on to provide for recognition of such child as a dependent (i) if the decedent (I) had acknowledged in writing that the applicant is his child, (II) had been decreed by a court to be the father of the applicant, or (III) had been ordered by a court to contribute to the support of the applicant because the applicant was his son or daughter, and such acknowledgment, court decree, or court order was made before the death of the individual involved, or (ii) if the decedent is shown by satisfactory evidence to have been the father of the applicant, and such insured individual was living with or contributing to the support of the applicant at the time of death.[36] There is not entire agreement as to whether dependency of the applicant, coupled with his or her living with the decedent, qualifies a child regardless of the "inheritance law of the domicil" test first enunciated.[37] Posthumous illegitimate children have often been held entitled to social security benefits, even though they cannot literally be said to have been "living with" the decedent at the time of his death.[38]

Mindful as the courts are of the injustice of a classification based on legitimacy or otherwise as tending to visit upon the children the sins of their parents,[39] the statute, as will be seen

---

[35]See Rights of Illegitimates Under Federal Statutes, 76 Harv. L. Rev. 337 (1962).

[36]42 U.S.C. § 416(h)(2)(A), (h)(3)(C). In Massey v. Weinberger, 397 F. Supp. 817 (D. Md., 1975) it was held that, even assuming arguendo that, in respect to a Maryland statute pertaining to legitimation of a child openly and notoriously recognized by the father to be his child, legitimation does not occur for all purposes, such statute, being sufficient to establish a right to support from the father, was likewise broad enough to entitle the minor to social insurance benefits provided through her father under the scheme of the Social Security Act which equates legitimacy with dependency.

[37]Annotation, Who qualifies as "child" within survivor benefit provisions of Federal Social Security Act, § 216(h)(2) [42 U.S.C. § 416(h)(2)], 60 A.L.R.2d 1070 (1958).

[38]Annotations, Who qualifies as widow "living with," within survivor or insurance benefit provisions of Federal Social Security Act, 60 A.L.R.2d 1082 (1958); Posthumous illegitimate child as "child" entitled to survivor's benefits under § 216 of the Social Security Act [42 U.S.C. § 416], 36 A.L.R. Fed. 166 (1978).

[39]Annotation, Discrimination on basis of illegitimacy as denial of constitutional rights, 38 A.L.R.3d 613 (1971). Generally, see section 3.2 et seq., herein.

RAMIFICATIONS 2.11

later,[40] has been the subject of various constitutional attacks.[41] But it can be explained by a need to ensure that the authorities entrusted with the dispensing of social security funds are not to be forced to disburse them without being clearly satisfied that the recipient is in reality a child of the contributing wage earner, and one to whom the latter owed a legal duty to support, and not a spurious claimant or windfall recipient of benefits he does not need.[42]

Aid for dependent children (A.F.D.C.)

An important part of the federally sponsored program for the alleviation of poverty through federal and state aid is aimed specifically to assist children in need.[43] Again, the question is raised, to what extent can illegitimate children qualify under this aspect of the program? The statute gives the states considerable latitude in their determination as to who is a "needy" child. Thus a state statute which requires home visits by caseworkers for the purpose of investigating a recipient's continuing need for assistance has withstood objections that it authorizes an unlawful search and is

---

[40]See section 3.2, herein.

[41]E.g., Jimenez v. Weinberger, 417 U.S. 628, 41 L. Ed. 2d 363, 94 Sup. Ct. 2496 (1974); Tanner v. Weinberger, 525 F.2d 51 (C.A.-6 Ohio, 1975).

Statutes in this area which provide for a presumption of dependency in respect of legitimate children and do not so provide in respect of posthumous illegitimate children are not necessarily unconstitutional. See, e.g., Kimbrell v. Mathews, 429 F. Supp. 440 (M.D. La., 1977).

[42]Annotations, Supreme Court's view as to the status and the rights of illegitimate children, 41 L. Ed. 2d 1228 (1975); What amounts to recognition within statutes affecting the status or rights of illegitimates, 33 A.L.R.2d 705 (1954). See also Weinberger v. Salfi, 422 U.S. 749, 45 L. Ed. 2d 522, 95 Sup. Ct. 2457 (1975), involving the constitutionality of a statute which deprived some widows with dependent children of social security benefits unless they had been married to the decedent for nine months prior to his death. It was clearly aimed at preventing sham marriages for the purpose of securing such benefits, but it did not permit the widow to establish that the marriage was in good faith. The Supreme Court held the provision to be rationally related to a legitimate state objective, therein (in fact), authorizing a conclusive presumption of improper motives. The "strict scrutiny" test (since classifications based on race, sex or religion were not involved) was not applied.

[43]Annotation, Who is "dependent child" within meaning of § 406(a), 407(a), and 408(a) of the Social Security Act [42 U.S.C. § 606(a), 607(a), and 608(a)], entitling families to aid for dependent children (AFDC), 23 A.L.R. Fed. 232 (1975).

thus unconstitutional.[44] It is a reasonable administrative measure. The recipient is not being charged with crime, and the only consequence of a refusal to permit such a visit would be a cessation of such aid.

Notwithstanding this latitude, a state program which includes as a "substitute father" one who merely cohabits with the mother and owes no duty to support her children is objectionable. Though there are indications that at one time states participating in A.F.D.C. were free to impose eligibility requirements relating to the moral character of the applicants,[45] the Supreme Court has now ruled that a state plan may not impose an eligibility condition that would deny assistance to a needy child on the basis that the home conditions are unsuitable, while the child continues to reside in the house.[46] Immorality should be dealt with through rehabilitative measures rather than measures that punish dependent children. "[T]he immorality of the mother has no rational connection with the need of her children under any welfare program."[47] The situation would probably be otherwise if there were proof that the cohabitant actually did set the bread on the table, whether or not he had this obligation, because "need" would be pro tanto eliminated.[48]

Where the state laws require one who lives in the same residence to contribute, such contributions are obviously relevant to determine whether the child of a cohabitant is in need. California, for example, provides that an unmarried adult male in residence must contribute a sum not less than it would cost him to provide himself with an independent living arrangement.[49] He does not meet this obligation by merely furnishing his share of the household expenses.[50] Further, when he does in fact contribute, and the

---

[44]Wyman v. James, 400 U.S. 309, 27 L. Ed. 2d 408, 91 Sup. Ct. 381 (1971).
[45]See King v. Smith, 392 U.S. 309, 321, 20 L. Ed. 2d 1118, 88 Sup. Ct. 2128 (1968).
[46]Id.
[47]Id., 392 U.S. at 336, 88 Sup. Ct. at 2143 (concurring opinion of Douglas, J.).
[48]See Lewis v. Martin, 397 U.S. 552, 25 L. Ed. 2d 561, 90 Sup. Ct. 1282 (1970).
[49]Cal. Welf. & Inst. Code, § 11351.5. See Note, AFDC Income Attribution: The Man-in-the-House and Welfare Grant Reductions, 83 Harv. L. Rev. 1370 (1970).
[50]Russell v. Carleson, 36 Cal. App. 3d 334, 111 Cal. Rptr, 497 (1973), wherein the constitutionality of this provision was upheld.

mother fails to inform the authorities, she can be convicted of obtaining money by false pretenses.[51]

A state regulation which allows full shelter allowance portion of A.F.D.C. when heads of a family unit are of the same sex, but not where they are unmarried and not of the same sex, has no rational justification in the eyes of the Oregon courts and is unconstitutional.[52] Of a similar nature is a holding that an amendment to the Food Stamp Act which denies food stamps to persons otherwise eligible because their households contain one or more unrelated individuals (an attempted blow at communes) violates the equal protection clauses as an irrational classification.[53]

The message seems clear enough. Any denial of welfare benefits based solely on a state's reluctance to subsidize living units which offend its own notions of morality, or even violate its criminal laws as adultery or fornication,[54] is of dubious constitutionality. Welfare programs are to take care of the needy, not to promote good morals.

The constitutionality of state statutes wherein legitimacy and illegitimacy is made a basis of discrimination receives later general consideration.[55] Decisions relating to particular state statutes pertaining specifically to welfare assistance are to be found in the final chapter of this work.

---

[51]E.g., People v. Shirley, 55 Cal. 2d 521, 11 Cal. Rptr, 537, 360 P.2d 33, 92 A.L.R.2d 413 (1961). See Annotation, Criminal liability in connection with application for, or receipt of, public relief or welfare payments, 92 A.L.R.2d 421 (1963).

[52]See Sawhney v. Public Welfare Div., 24 Ore. App. 685, 546 P.2d 768 (1976). (It might be observed that such a classification, while certainly tending to discourage extramarital cohabitation, might also tend to encourage lesbianism or homosexuality.)

[53]United States Dept. of Agriculture v. Moreno, 413 U.S. 528, 37 L. Ed. 2d 782, 93 Sup. Ct. 2821 (1973).

[54]See New Jersey Welfare Rights Organization v. Cahill, 349 F. Supp. 491 (D. N.J., 1972), revd. 411 U.S. 619, 36 L. Ed. 2d 543, 93 Sup. Ct. 1700 (1973) on the basis that a state has no compelling interest in refusing to subsidize a living unit which violates its laws against fornication and adultery.

[55]See section 3.2 et seq., herein. Generally, see also Rombauer, Marital Status and Eligibility for Federal Statutory Income Benefits: A Historical Survey, 52 Wash. L. Rev. 227 (1977); Seidelson and Bowler, Determination of Family Status in the Administration of Federal Acts: A Choice of Law Problem for Federal Agencies and Courts, 33 Geo. Wash. L. Rev. 863 (1965); Lewis and Levy, Family Law and Welfare Policies: The Case for "Dual Systems," 54 Calif. L. Rev. 748 (1966).

2.12. Unemployment benefits

The Federal Unemployment Tax Act[56] requires, in effect, that every employer who pays out wages of any significant amount pay a tax to ensure that his employees, if he cannot or will not continue to employ them, are not left destitute. The states are required to enact substantially similar legislation.[57] A question of interest to the extramarital cohabitant is whether, if she becomes pregnant and quits her job as a result, she forfeits any right to the unemployment benefits that are payable from such funds. At one time there was little unanimity in the state statute law on this point.[58] Today, however, the statute requires that state laws must not deny compensation solely on the basis of pregnancy.[59]

2.13. Compensation for death of cohabitant

Federal statutes

Congress has many provisions controlling the recovery of compensation on behalf of survivors and dependents of employees in governmental occupations and in occupations not covered by state workers' compensation laws. Among these are the Federal Employers' Liability Act, which concerns mainly carriers in interstate commerce,[60] and the Federal Employees Compensation Act.[61] There are indications of reluctance to recognize as a "wife" one who in good faith believes in the existence of a valid marriage.[62] If the employee died domiciled in a state which does

---

[56] 26 U.S.C. § 3301 et seq.

[57] Generally, see 76 Am. Jur. 2d, Unemployment Compensation, § 64 et seq.

[58] See, e.g., Geduldig v. Aiello, 417 U.S. 484, 41 L. Ed. 2d 256, 94 Sup. Ct. 2485 (1974). Annotation, Termination of employment because of pregnancy as affecting right to unemployment compensation, 51 A.L.R.3d 254 (1973).

[59] 26 U.S.C. § 3304(a)(12).

[60] 45 U.S.C. § 51. As to the Safety Appliance Acts, see 45 U.S.C. § 1 et seq. Generally, see 32 Am. Jur. 2d, Federal Employers' Liability and Compensation Acts.

[61] 5 U.S.C. § 8133(a)(3). As to the Jones Act (merchant seamen), see 46 U.S.C. § 688.

[62] See McPherson v. Steamship South African Pioneer, 321 F. Supp. 42 (E.D. Va., 1971); Beebe v. Moormack Gulf Lines Inc., 59 F.2d 319 (C.A.-5 La., 1932).

not recognize common-law marriage, the cohabitant could not qualify.[63]

As to illegitimates, courts have held that the appropriate state law controlling succession on intestacy is the test of their qualification to recover.[64] For policy reasons, for example the need for expeditious liquidation and distribution of decedents' estates, states have had, and sometimes still do have, rather stricter tests of qualification of illegitimates to succeed on intestacy than those that determine legitimacy for other purposes.[65] Since these policy reasons have little relevance where deprivation of support as a result of industrial death is involved, the more enlightened view is that, once parenthood and an obligation to support are established, the illegitimate child should qualify.[66]

Under the Longshoremen's and Harbor Workers' Compensation Act,[67] the term "widow" includes only the decedent's wife living with him or dependent on him for support at the time of his death, or one living apart for justifiable cause or by reason of his desertion at such time.[68] In Turnbull v. Cyr[69] the claimant had been living with the decedent as man and wife in Colorado when the decedent was killed. Since that state recognizes common-law marriage, the court had no difficulty in allowing recovery under the Harbor Workers' Compensation Act as extended by section 1 of the Defense Base Compensation Act.[70] But a mere showing of dependency with no claim of marriage would not qualify an applicant.[71] Even a dependent claiming as a common-law wife would fail if the parties were not domiciled in a state recognizing this type of union at the time of decedent's death.[72] A "child," under this statute, includes an acknowledged illegitimate child who was

---

[63] See Bell v. Tug Shrike, 215 F. Supp. 377 (E.D. Va., 1963) (under 46 U.S.C. § 699).
[64] See Note, Rights of Illegitimates Under Federal Statutes, 76 Harv. L. Rev. 337 (1962).
[65] See section 3.2, herein.
[66] See Hammond v. Pennsylvania R. Co., 31 N.J. 244, 156 A.2d 689 (1959).
[67] 33 U.S.C. § 901 et. seq.
[68] 33 U.S.C. § 902(16).
[69] 188 F.2d 455 (C.A.-9 Cal., 1951).
[70] 42 U.S.C. § 1651.
[71] See Powell v. Rogers, 496 F.2d 1248 (C.A.-9 Cal., 1974).
[72] See Bolin v. Marshall, 76 F.2d 668 (C.A.-9 Ore., 1935).

dependent on the decedent; such acknowledgment does not have to be in writing.[73]

Under the Copyright Act,[74] in the context of a copyright holder's right of renewal, such a right being more analogous to a right of property than to a right of support, whether an illegitimate child would qualify ought logically to depend on whether such child qualifies to succeed on the holder's death intestate.[75]

Under the Death on the High Seas Act[76] it is held that one who innocently entered into a bigamous marriage with the decedent cannot qualify as a "wife" for compensation.[77] But a common-law marriage, if recognized by the state of the domicil of the spouses at the time of death, would qualify the survivor as a wife.[78]

Where a widow or child can recover death benefits under the Veterans' Administration Act,[79] a "widow" is restricted to mean a wife who had lived with the decedent continuously between marriage and death.[80] As to illegitimate children, the requirements to establish paternity are as much the same as those claiming social security benefits.[81] But an illegitimate child can claim under the National Service Life Insurance Act only if named as a beneficiary.[82]

In short, a mere extramarital cohabitant has little if any chance of recovering under any of these federal enactments. An illegitimate child would have a strong claim whenever the federal legislation is designed to ensure his continued support.

---

[73]33 U.S.C. § 902(14). Weyerhaeuser Timber Co. v. Marshall, 102 F.2d 78 (C.A.-9 Wash., 1939).

[74]17 U.S.C. § 101 et seq.

[75]See De Sylva v. Ballentine, 351 U.S. 570, 100 L. Ed. 1415, 76 Sup. Ct. 974 (1956).

[76]46 U.S.C. § 761. Annotation, Who constitutes decedent's "wife, husband, parent, child, or dependent relative" for whose benefit damage suit by decedent's personal representative is authorized under § 761 of Death on the High Seas Act [46 U.S.C. § 761], 15 A.L.R. Fed. 834 (1973).

[77]Lawson v. United States, 192 F.2d 479 (C.A.-2 N.Y., 1951).

[78]See Tetterton v. Arctic Tankers, Inc., 116 F. Supp. 429 (E.D. Pa., 1953).

As to the rights of illegitimate children, see Middleton v. Luckenbach S.S., 70 F.2d 326 (C.A.-2 N.Y., 1934). The Jones Act overlaps with the Death on the High Seas Act where death occurs more than one marine league from United States shores.

[79]38 U.S.C. § 101 et seq.

[80]38 U.S.C. § 101(3).

[81]See 38 U.S.C. § 101(4). As to social security benefits, see section 2.11, herein.

[82]38 U.S.C. § 701(3).

State workers' compensation statutes

In Weber v. Aetna Casualty & Surety Company[83] the Supreme Court held that a state statute which denied the right of dependent, unacknowledged illegitimates to recover workers' compensation benefits on an equal footing with dependent, legitimate children of the decedent violates the equal protection clauses of the Constitution. The statute under attack relegated unacknowledged illegitimates to a lesser status of "other dependents" who could recover only if there were not enough surviving dependents in preceding statutory classification to exhaust the maximum allowable benefits. The court reasoned that persons would not shun illicit sex merely because of a possibility that the offspring of such a union might not reap workers' compensation benefits. It saw in this classification no significant relation to the purpose of such statutes, which is to make provision for those on whom the decedent owed a duty of support. It considered such a visitation of society's condemnation of irresponsible liaisons on the heads of innocent infants as illogical and unjust, and not justified by any legitimate state interest.

Since that decision the states construe their statutes to recognize the rights of illegitimates.[84] Some indicate that actual dependency on the decedent is not material.[85] Some require a showing of dependency.[86] Paternity must of course be established.[87]

At least one state has extended the rule of the Weber case, invalidating statutes which restrict the eligibility of illegitimates to acknowledged illegitimate children, to cover illegitimates who are born subsequent to the death of the father. The court reasoned that, since the controlling statute conclusively presumes dependency of posthumous children and acknowledged illegitimate children, and since the requirement that they have been acknowledged is unconstitutional, unacknowledged posthumous children qualify for workers' compensation.[88] A dissenting judge

---

[83]406 U.S. 164, 31 L. Ed. 2d 768, 92 Sup. Ct. 1400 (1972).

[84]See state-by-state commentary, Chapter 6, herein.

[85]E.g., section 6.43, herein (Tennessee).

[86]E.g., section 6.44, herein (Texas).

[87]See Hagley v. Browns of Bellport, 45 App. Div. 2d 546, 360 N.Y.S.2d 103 (1974).

[88]Anonymous Child v. Deceased Father's Employer,——Ind. App.——, 377 N.E.2d 407 (1978).

2.13 UNMARRIED COUPLES AND THE LAW

took the position that, in the Weber holding, the Supreme Court of the United States had in mind only the plight of the illegitimate who could not, under the laws of Louisiana, have been acknowledged even had the father desired to do so. He states that lines "must be drawn somewhere. To allow recovery to an unacknowledged, posthumous illegitimate child creates a class of recipients never contemplated by the legislature."[89]

There is much to be said for the dissent. In the fact situation involved, it was reasonably clear that the decedent was the father. The couple had made plans to marry. The industrial board had found that he was indeed the father, and the mother was not dating or having sexual relations with anyone else. It would appear sounder to state the rule as follows: an unacknowledged posthumous illegitimate child can qualify for workers' compensation benefits when, and only when, the authority entrusted with the allocation of benefits is satisfied, on clear and convincing proof, that the decedent worker was indeed the father of such child.

The general trend is to deny recovery to an extramarital cohabitant. Even if the controlling statute uses the word "family," the courts will usually require some showing of (at least) a moral obligation to support existing between the component individuals.[90] As will appear from the final chapter of this work, however, some states recognize the claim of a good faith putative[91] spouse.

---

[89]Id., 377 N.E.2d at 414.

[90]See Utah Fuel Co. v. Industrial Comm. of Utah, 64 Utah 328, 230 Pac. 681 (1924); Annotations, Children of one with whom deceased workman was living in illicit relations as dependents within workmen's compensation act, 154 A.L.R. 698 (1945); "Dependency" within Workmen's Compensation Act, 13 A.L.R. 686 (1921), 100 A.L.R. 1090 (1936); Right of woman who marries injured workman to compensation as his widow or surviving wife under Workmen's Compensation Act, 98 A.L.R. 993 (1935); Survival of right to compensation under workmen's compensation acts upon the death of the person entitled to the award, 15 A.L.R. 821 (1921), 95 A.L.R. 254 (1935); Bigamous character of marriage as affecting right of one party thereto to compensation for death of other under workmen's compensation act, 80 A.L.R. 1428 (1932).

[91]E.g., Holland America Ins. Co. v. Rogers, 313 F. Supp. 314 (N.D. Cal., 1970); Neureither v. Workmen's Compensation Appeals Bd., 15 Cal. App. 3d 429, 93 Cal. Rptr. 162 (1971); Parkinson v. J & S Tool Co., 64 N.J. 159, 313 A.2d 609 (1974) (where a priest had told a reconciled couple after divorce that they were still married "in the eyes of God.")

An Oregon statute which draws a distinction between unmarried cohabitants of one year or more duration who have children and such cohabitants who do not have children has been held to pass the test of "minimum rationality," in that the former class of cohabitant is more likely to be financially dependent than the latter.[92]

2.14. Immigration and naturalization

Where an extramarital cohabitant is an alien, the relationship may have an adverse effect on his rights to enter, or to remain in, the United States as well as on any petition for naturalization.[93] A provision of the Immigration and Nationality Act,[94] for example, excludes from admission to this country persons coming in for an "immoral purpose."[95] Other provisions relate to the exclusion or deportation of aliens because of immoral character.[96] But as early as 1934 it was held that merely reentering the United States to continue "illicit relations" does not render an alien subject to deportation for immorality.[97]

The above provisions can present a problem as to what is "moral turpitude" such as can justify exclusion or deportation of aliens.[98] Crimes such as rape — even statutory rape — do involve moral turpitude.[99] As to adultery, the early decisions indicate a lack of unanimity, though it seems settled that intercourse

---

[92] In re Lacey, 34 Ore. App. 877, 580 P.2d 1032 (1978).
[93] For a more detailed analysis of these provisions, see Danilov, Criminal Law and the Foreign Born, Case and Comment, Vol. 83, No. 2 (1978).
[94] 8 U.S.C. § 1182(a)(12).
[95] See 3 Am. Jur. 2d, Aliens and Citizens, § 61.
[96] Annotation, Construction and application of provisions relating to exclusion or deportation of aliens because of immoral character or immoral purpose, 78 L. Ed. 973 (1934).
[97] Hansen v. Haff, 291 U.S. 559, 78 L. Ed. 968, 54 Sup. Ct. 494 (1934).
[98] Annotation, What constitutes "crime involving moral turpitude" within meaning of §§ 212(a)(9) and 214(a)(4) of Immigration and Nationality Act (8 U.S.C. §§ 1182(a)(9), 1251(a)(4)), and similar predecessor statutes providing for exclusion or deportation of aliens convicted of such crime, 23 A.L.R. Fed. 480 (1975).
[99] Marciano v. Immigration and Naturalization Service, 450 F.2d 1022, 23 A.L.R. Fed. 466 (C.A.-8 Minn., 1971), cert. den. 405 U.S. 997, 31 L. Ed. 2d 466, 92 Sup. Ct. 1260 (1972).

between two unmarried persons does not amount to moral turpitude.[1] Perhaps due to the disparity in state laws as to exactly what constitutes adultery,[2] this lack of unanimity continues, and the sheer volume of decisions on the matter indicate that this type of sexual misconduct is not a matter that can be lightly brushed over.[3]

Similarly, cohabitation outside of marriage can have an adverse impact on a petition for naturalization.[4] In Petition of De Leo,[5] however, where the court granted such a petition, the government having offered no evidence to disprove the petitioner's denial of any illicit relation with a woman with whom he lived, along with two other roomers, the judge (perhaps prophetically)[6] observed that the standard of "good moral character" may vary from one generation to the other.[7]

For the purposes of the provision of the Immigration and Nationality Act requiring a shorter waiting period for the naturalization of an alien married to an American citizen, it seems that a putative marriage will not suffice.[8] Special preference is

---

[1] Annotation, What constitutes a crime involving moral turpitude within meaning of immigration acts—federal cases, 95 L. Ed. 899 (1951).

[2] See section 2.26, herein.

[3] See Annotation, Definition of "adultery" within meaning of § 101(f)(2) of the Immigration and Nationality Act of 1952 (8 U.S.C. § 1101(f)(2)), 33 A.L.R. Fed. 120 (1977); What constitutes "convicted" within meaning of § 241(a) (4, 11, 14–16, 18) of Immigration and Nationality Act (8 U.S.C. § 1251(a) (4, 11, 14–16, 18) providing that alien shall be deported who has been convicted of certain offenses, 26 A.L.R. Fed. 709 (1976).

[4] E.g., Petition of Pacora, 96 F. Supp. 594 (S.D. N.Y., 1951) (petition was denied where petitioner knew his paramour would not marry him and had no intention of marrying him). See Annotation, What constitutes showing of "good moral character" on the part of an applicant for naturalization, 22 A.L.R.2d 244 (1952).

[5] 75 F. Supp. 896 (W.D. Pa., 1948).

[6] See also In re Labady, 326 F. Supp. 924 (S.D. N.Y., 1971), granting the naturalization petition of a male homosexual who participated in purely private, consensual acts of sodomy. "[P]rivate conduct which is not harmful to others, even though it may violate the personal moral code of most of us, does not violate public morality which is the only proper concern of [the naturalization statute]." Id., at 927–928. Compare In re Petition of Schmidt, 56 Misc. 2d 456, 289 N.Y.S.2d 89 (1968) (lesbian denied).

[7] A more recent trend disfavors extramarital cohabitation as a bar to naturalization. See, e.g., Posusta v. United States, 285 F.2d 533 (C.A.-2 N.Y., 1961); In re Mortyr, 320 F. Supp. 1222 (D. Ore., 1970).

[8] Annotation, Construction and application of § 319(a) of Immigration and Nationality Act (8 U.S.C. 1430(a)), making special provisions for naturalization of aliens married to United States citizens, 24 A.L.R. Fed. 339 (1975).

accorded, too, to a child of an American citizen who seeks to be naturalized.[9] There is held to be no unconstitutionality in denying this preference to the child of a biological father while allowing it to the mother of the child.[10] The act provides, inter alia, that a parent or child of a citizen of the United States may enter the country without regard to a numerical quota or labor certificate. A "child," for these purposes, does not include the illegitimate child who claims preferential status through the biological father, though it does include those who claim such status through the biological mother. The Supreme Court of the United States took the position that the conditions of entry for every alien, the particular classes of aliens that can be denied entry, the basis for determining such classification, the right to terminate hospitality toward aliens, and the grounds on which such determination can be based, are matters solely for Congress and outside the power of the courts to control.[11] Notwithstanding the modern trend in the direction of striking as violative of equal protection statutes which arbitrarily discriminate between children who are legitimate and those who are not,[12] the court felt that in this area it had no power to "probe and test" the justifications for such a legislative decision.[13]

2.15. Insurance problems generally

State laws at times regard it as violative of the Constitution for an insurer to cancel[14] or to refuse to issue or renew an insurance

---

[9]Immigration and Nationality Act, 8 U.S.C. § 1101(b)(1).
[10]Fiallo v. Bell, 430 U.S. 787, 52 L. Ed. 2d 50, 97 Sup. Ct. 1473 (1977). For a critical discussion of this decision, see Discrimination Based on Sex and Illegitimacy Is Permissible in the Immigration Area, 27 De Paul L. Rev. 515 (1978).
[11]Fiallo v. Bell, 430 U.S. 787, 52 L. Ed. 2d 50, 97 Sup. Ct 1473 (1977).
[12]See sections 3.2, 3.3, herein.
[13]The Fiallo decision is criticized in Note, "Legitimate" Discrimination Against Illegitimates: A Look at Trimble v. Gordon and Fiallo v. Bell, 16 J. Family L. 57 (1977), mainly on the ground that the historical rule that the courts do not discipline congressional legislation regarding immigration policies no longer has any good reason; alien immigration no longer poses a threat to national security.
[14]Cancellation of insurance policies because of the insureds' "mode of living," i.e., insureds living with persons to whom they are not married, is discrimination based on marital status and violates McKinney's N.Y. Insurance Law, § 40-e. 1976, Op. Atty. Gen. 58.

policy[15] on the basis, inter alia, of the applicant's cohabitation outside of marriage.

It is a well settled policy of insurance law that a person cannot take out insurance against a contingency in respect of which he has no insurable interest. Insofar as concerns *property insurance,* any person who would suffer loss from its destruction or derives a benefit from the existence of the property is regarded as having an insurable interest. There are situations where this test cannot even be met by lawful spouses in respect of the property of the other.[16] Thus, in the case of extramarital cohabitants, if there is any real question as to the nonexistence of a pecuniary interest in the subject matter, it would be wise for the partner holding title to take care of the insurance.

Insofar as concerns *life insurance,* it is clear that a legal spouse has an insurable interest in the life of the other. This ceases, however, on divorce.[17] Most courts agree that a fiancé or fiancée has an insurable interest in the life of the other.[18] It does not necessarily follow that, absent a firm commitment on the part of the would-be insured to support the applicant, the same would apply to unmarried partners. There are holdings that one with whom the insured lives as his spouse, and is so recognized by the community, has an insurable interest.[19] Also a woman who lived with a man as his wife knowing there was no valid marriage, but who had joint liability with him on a promissory note, had such interest.[20] The court in that case declined to pass on the claim of a meretricious cohabitant who predicated her claim alone on such a relationship. In Washington State Public Employees Board v. Cook,[21] neighbors chosen by the decedent to receive his accumulated

---

[15]S.D. Codified Laws Ann. § 58-11-55.
[16]Annotation, Insurable interest of husband or wife in other's property, 27 A.L.R.2d 1059 (1953).
[17]Denton v. Travelers Ins. Co., 555 S.W.2d 825 (Ky. App., 1977); Kentucky Cent. Life Ins. Co. v. Willett, 557 S.W.2d 222 (Ky. App., 1977); Annotation, Divorce of insured and beneficiary as affecting the latter's right in life insurance, 175 A.L.R. 1220 (1948).
[18]Annotation, Insurable interest of fiancé or fiancée, 17 A.L.R. 580 (1922).
[19]See 43 Am. Jur. 2d, Insurance, § 506.
[20]Rakestraw v. Cincinnati, 69 Ohio App. 504, 44 N.E.2d 278 (1942), where the beneficiary was required to have an insurable interest to qualify as named beneficiary.
[21]88 Wash. 2d 200, 559 P.2d 991 (1977).

contributions in a public employees retirement system were held not to have an insurable interest as required by statute to qualify as beneficiaries. The court, however, recognized the term "insurable interest," in the context of procuring insurance, to be extendable to anyone having an economic interest in the continuation of the life of the insured. The reason for the requirement of an insurable interest was said to be to prevent wagering, to assure the beneficiary has an interest in protecting and prolonging the life of the insured. On this rationale, even if an unmarried partner could show no direct pecuniary interest in the other partner's life, an argument could be made that the unwed relation is a tie of sufficient strength to qualify as an insurable interest, being a substantial interest engendered by love and affection, or even, if the interest has to be "pecuniary," that it is so by reason of reciprocal obligations the partners have assumed.

Immoral relations between the insured and the named beneficiary of his life insurance do not affect the insurer's obligations to pay the proceeds. Just as a person may give his property to unworthy causes during his lifetime as an exercise of his right of ownership, so too may he name his mistress as beneficiary of such life insurance.[22] Some early reluctance on the part of the courts of Louisiana can be ascribed to a provision of the civil code of that state restricting or limiting donations to a concubine. In the case of fraternal or benefit societies which issue insurance, however, a cohabitant may fail to fall within the "eligible" class which is often spelled out in the provisions of the society as necessary to qualify as a named beneficiary.[23] But outside of such qualifications, for a court to award life insurance proceeds to the widow when a paramour is the named beneficiary would be to do extreme violence to the sanctity of contract.[24]

When an insured has changed the named beneficiary of his or her life insurance from the legal spouse to another, that other is

---

[22] Annotation, Immoral relations between insured and beneficiary as affecting liability of insurer or rights in respect of proceeds of policy, 173 A.L.R. 716 (1948).

[23] See 36 Am. Jur. 2d, Fraternal Orders and Benefit Societies, §§ 142, 145–148. In Metropolitan Life Ins. Co. v. Spearman, 344 F. Supp. 665 (M.D. Ala., 1972), "widow" in the Federal Employees Group Life Insurance Act of 1954 was held to mean lawful widow.

[24] See Alexander, Meretricious Relations with Respect to Life Insurance, 44 Ins. Counsel J. 321 (1977).

held to bear the burden of proving that the change was not a result of undue influence brought to bear.[25] This heavy burden (of proving a negative fact) is not applicable where the insured's paramour is the initially named beneficiary.[26]

A mere erroneous designation by the applicant for insurance of the named beneficiary as his "wife," absent fraud, does not affect the latter's right; it is mere *descriptio personae*.[27] If, however, the beneficiary is not named but is designated merely by status, for example "wife" or "husband," in a contest between the legal spouse and a cohabitant, the former would succeed.[28]

2.16. Insurance—Misrepresentation as to marital status in the application

Although a mere erroneous description of the named beneficiary of insurance proceeds as a "spouse" or "wife" does not afford ground for a repudiation of liability on the part of the insurer,[29] this can be otherwise if such a representation is a material one.[30] Much could depend on whether either the insured or the named beneficiary was known to be married to someone else.[31] Where the insured had deserted his wife and children and was living in adultery with the named beneficiary, the deserted wife may perhaps argue her claim to the proceeds.[32] Where the

---

[25] Beatty v. Strickland, 136 Fla. 330, 186 So. 542 (1939).
[26] Hill v. Hill, 222 So. 2d 454 (Fla. App., 1969).
[27] See Annotation, Effect of erroneous designation of beneficiary of insurance as "wife," 32 A.L.R. 1481 (1924).
[28] Annotation, Right of second wife to take under policy designating "wife" or "widow" as beneficiary, issued during life of first wife, 20 A.L.R. 959 (1922).
[29] See section 2.15, herein. Also see, e.g., Strachan v. Prudential Ins. Co. of America, 321 Mass. 507, 73 N.E.2d 840, 173 A.L.R. 711 (1947); Service Life Ins. Co. of Fort Worth v. Davis, 466 S.W.2d 190 (Mo. App., 1971) (holding the description of beneficiary as a fiancée was mere descriptio personae and did not control over specific designation of individual intended to receive proceeds); Annotation, Misrepresentation or misstatement as to insured's marital status, or as to his relationship to beneficiary, as ground for avoiding liability under life insurance policy, 14 A.L.R.3d 931 (1967).
[30] E.g., Chitwood v. Prudential Ins. Co. of America, 206 Va. 314, 143 S.E.2d 915, 14 A.L.R.3d 923 (1965).
[31] See 43 Am. Jur. 2d, Insurance, § 825.
[32] See dissent in Mutual Benefit Life Ins. Co. of Newark, N.J. v. Cummings, 66 Ore. 272, 133 Pac. 1169 (1913), opining that to allow the mistress to recover would be "contrary to public policy and good morals."

insurer would not have issued the policy had it known of the meretricious relation, some courts have held the insured's misrepresentation of his relationship to the named beneficiary to be sufficiently material to warrant the avoidance of the policy.[33] Though the ordinary cohabitant named beneficiary is not likely to encounter objections of this nature, there are situations, especially where someone other than the claimant has more pressing claims on the insurance proceeds, where courts have denied recovery to the named beneficiary, for example on the basis of undue influence, breach of warranty or simply public policy.[34] In respect of accident insurance, an early decision suggests that the misrepresentation as to the marital status of the parties is more likely to be regarded as material, on the theory that a man who, in violation of law, is living in cohabitation with a woman is a less desirable risk than one who is leading a "regular and clean life."[35] In another early case, a representation by a man, in his application for accident insurance, that his habits were correct and temperate, was held to justify avoidance of the policy when at the time he was living with a woman not his wife, "if for no other reason because he may become at any time the subject of the vengeance of his deserted wife or her insulted kinsmen."[36]

It seems unlikely that such attitudes would receive any resounding affirmation in modern times.[37]

2.17. Insurance—Cohabitant as member of "family" or "household"

It is common for insurance policies to provide for the inclusion (or exclusion) of coverage of members of the insured's "family" or "household." Whether an unmarried partner does or does not

---

[33]See Alexander, Meretricious Relations with Respect to Life Insurance, 44 Ins. Counsel J. 321 (1977).

[34]Id.

[35]Continental Cas. Co. v. Lindsay, 111 Va. 389, 392, 69 S.E. 344 (1910).

[36]Elliott v. Frankfort Marine, Accident & Plate Glass Ins. Co. of Frankfort on the Main, Germany, 172 Cal. 261, 156 Pac. 481, 483 (1916).

[37]See Annotation, Insured's misrepresentation or misstatement as to his name or marital status as ground for avoiding liability insurance, 27 A.L.R.3d 849 (1969).

qualify under such a provision admits of no unqualified answer. The problem is presented in a variety of situations. Much depends on the type of insurance, the wording of the provision and the context in which it is used. The word "family" is ambiguous.[38] It could, for example, mean a group of persons who reside under the same roof, or it could mean persons who are of the same lineage or are descended from a common progenitor.

Automobile insurance contracts often exclude liability for bodily injury to the insured or any member of his family, or a spouse of the insured, or to a member of his household. For the purposes of "family exclusion clauses" of this nature, the trend is against regarding an unmarried cohabitant as a "spouse"; thus the insurer is liable for injuries to such a person notwithstanding the exclusionary clause.[39] But where an exclusionary clause used the term "family" to include persons habitually residing under one roof and forming one domestic circle, a woman who lived under the same roof with the insured, adulterously, as his wife, for about six years, and bore him children, was held a member of his family,[40] and therefore within the exclusion.

The same construction applies where a policy extends coverage to the spouse of the insured. A cohabitant who does not qualify as a legal spouse under the law of the state controlling the construction of the policy is not within its coverage.[41] Similarly, where the applicable state statute defined "the insured" to include, inter alia, his "spouse," a cohabitant of the insured was held not to fall within a policy provision insuring against injury to the insured by an uninsured motorist.[42] This was notwithstanding the fact that

---

[38]See Henderson v. State Farm Mut. Auto Ins. Co., 59 Wis. 2d 451, 208 N.W.2d 423 (1973).

[39]State Farm Mut. Auto Ins. Co. v. Oliver, 406 F.2d 409 (C.A.-6 Tenn., 1969); State Farm Mut. Auto Ins. Co. v. Thompson, 372 F.2d 256 (C.A.-9 Ariz., 1967); Hicks v. Hatem, 265 Md. 260, 289 A.2d 325 (1972); Crilley v. Allstate Ins. Co., 18 App. Div. 2d 1012, 239 N.Y.S.2d 27 (1963), affd. 15 N.Y.2d 821, 257 N.Y.S.2d 939, 205 N.E.2d 863 (1965).

[40]Hunter v. Southern Farm Bureau Cas. Ins. Co., 241 S.C. 446, 129 S.E.2d 59 (1962); Annotation, Validity, construction, and application of provision of automobile liability policy excluding from coverage injury or death of member of family or household of insured, 46 A.L.R.3d 1024 (1972).

[41]E.g., Harleysville Mut. Cas. Ins. Co. v. Carroll, 50 Del. Super. 67, 123 A.2d 128 (1956).

[42]Menchaca v. Hiatt, 59 Cal. App. 3d 117, 130 Cal. Rptr. 607 (1976).

the state involved (California) entertains liberal notions regarding the property rights of extramarital partners. "[W]e are not dealing with the division of jointly acquired property between two equally guilty parties, but rather with the rights of one meretricious spouse against a third party with whom the other spouse has dealt at arm's length."[43]

The problem appears in another form when the automobile insurer's liability excludes damage resulting from the driving of other cars "when the other car is regularly used by a member of his household." Such a provision usually extends coverage to a casual driving by the insured of a stranger's car, but not to the driving of a car owned by others of his household. In view of the tendency to construe insurance contracts strictly, resolving ambiguities in favor of the insured, it is entirely possible that an insured driving the car of an unmarried partner would be covered.[44]

In Fisher v. Hodge,[45] the words "immediate family," in an automobile lease provision so restricting the use of a rented car, were construed to include a brother of the insured, the court acknowledging, obiter, that a spouse would come under the broader definition of "family" as a person living under the same roof. This being so, it could well be that an unmarried partner would be regarded as "family" for the purposes of such a restriction.

Automobile insurance policies often contain an "omnibus clause." This extends coverage in respect of persons coming within a defined class: a general example would be "those driving with the insured's consent."[46] Where such a clause extends coverage

---

[43]Id., 59 Cal. App. 3d at 127, 130 Cal. Rptr. at 613.

[44]Annotation, Exclusion from "drive other cars" provision of automobile liability insurance policy of other automobile owned, hired, or regularly used by insured or member of his household, 86 A.L.R.2d 937 (1962). See Defining "Relative," "Member of the Household," "Member of the Family" or "Resident" Within the Meaning of Homeowner's and Automobile Liability Policies, 26 Drake L. Rev. 824 (1976–77). The writer suggests that, the courts construing such instruments as they do against the draftsman, the insured may have "the best of both worlds" when a policy inclusion or exclusion provision is involved.

[45]162 Conn. 363, 294 A.2d 577, 80 A.L.R.3d 1164 (1972).

[46]Annotations, "Omnibus" clauses of automobile insurance extending liability of insurer to "household," 126 A.L.R. 544 (1940); Who is "relative" or "member" or "resident" of same family or household, within liability insurance provision defining additional insureds, 78 A.L.R.2d 1404 (1961).

in respect of persons driving with the insured's consent, or with the consent of any adult member of his family or household, other than a domestic servant or chauffeur, it is likely that the consent of an unmarried partner would be regarded as extending the coverage.[47]

When insurance in respect of fire or property damage purports to cover the belongings of an insured's "family" or "household," it by no means follows that the goods of a cohabitant are necessarily within the coverage. If the partners have an agreement as to what goods belong to which partner, it is questionable whether the coverage would extend beyond the insured's own goods. Much depends on the wording of the policy. For example, even a legal wife's property was not covered under a policy in which the coverage related to household members "living with" the insured where she had ejected the insured from the house.[48] A Missouri court has held that a man living in illicit cohabitation with the insured is not a member of her family within the meaning of a fire policy covering belongings of the insured's "family."[49]

2.18. Insurance—The "family purpose" doctrine

When an automobile is owned, provided or maintained by a parent for the customary conveyance of family members and other family business, and at the time of an accident the automobile is being driven by a member of the family for whom the car is maintained, some states hold the owner to be liable for the driver's negligence under the "family purpose" or "family car" doctrine.[50] The liability, which the courts often predicate on a somewhat strained[51] basis of agency, probably had its origins in

---

[47]Id.

[48]Kohner v. National Surety Co., 105 Cal. App. 430, 287 Pac. 510 (1930).

[49]Brown v. Shield Fire Ins. Co., 260 S.W.2d 337 (Mo. App., 1953); Annotation, Who is member of insured's "family" or "household" within coverage of property insurance policy, 1 A.L.R.2d 561 (1948).

[50]E.g., Coffman v. McFadden, 68 Wash. 2d 954, 416 P.2d 99 (1966), holding that the burden is on the plaintiff to show the car was for the general use, pleasure and convenience of the family. See 8 Am. Jur. 2d, Automobiles and Highway Traffic, §§ 588–594.

[51]See Phillips v. Dixon, 135 Ga. App. 161, 217 S.E.2d 331 (1975), affd. 236 Ga. 271, 223 S.E.2d 678 (1976), holding the doctrine applicable where a son of the

the notion that it would be against public policy not to allow the victim of some financially irresponsible driver, for example a child, to be without a remedy where a parent is not liable for the torts of his minor child.[52] The word "family," for this purpose, is construed to embrace those who live in the same household and are subject to the general management and control of the head thereof, dependence being on the head of the household[53] and the rendition of mutual gratuitous services.[54] The doctrine has been rejected in most states, but still applies in some jurisdictions.[55]

In those states still espousing the doctrine, the question whether the owner of an automobile would be liable thereunder for the negligent driving of an unmarried partner or a child of the unwed pair admits of no definitive answer. Where the owner is not by statute made strictly liable for the operator's fault, liability cannot ordinarily be predicated on a theory of implied consent.[56] But, since at least one state regards implied consent as a basis of the doctrine,[57] it would seem unnecessary and unjust to harness the doctrine as a basis for liability of a car owner whose

---

owner permits a third party to drive the car; Hawes v. Taylor, 246 Ore. 32, 423 P.2d 775 (1967), holding where the owner gave his son and his son's girlfriend permission to use the car but instructed the girl was to drive, owner had consented for family purpose and was liable for injuries when son was driving; Heenan v. Perkins, 278 Ore. 583, 564 P.2d 1354 (1977), applying the doctrine to a stepson, a part of the family, when a truck was for farming purposes but not being used by the stepson for such authorized purposes at the time; Driver v. Smith, 47 Tenn. App. 505, 339 S.W.2d 135 (1959), holding where daughter had permission to use the car and asked friend to drive, and the daughter kissed the driver who lost control of car, doctrine applied to impute negligence to the parent owner.

[52]Annotation, Liability of owner under "family-purpose" doctrine, for injuries by automobile while being used by member of his family, 132 A.L.R. 981 (1941).

[53]See Keeney v. Smith, 521 S.W.2d 242 (Ky. App., 1975), holding the doctrine inapplicable where there is no duty to support.

[54]Manning v. Hart, 255 N.C. 368, 121 S.E.2d 721 (1961). One not of kin may be considered as a member of the family for the purposes of the doctrine, provided he is a bona fide household member. Smith v. Simpson, 260 N.C. 601, 133 S.E.2d 474 (1963).

[55]See Note, Modern status of family purpose doctrine with respect to motor vehicles, 8 A.L.R.3d 1191 (1966).

[56]Liability could of course be predicated on agency or employment. See 8 Am. Jur. 2d, Automobiles and Highway Traffic, § 571 et seq. A co-owner as such is not liable for the other owner's negligence. Id., § 562.

[57]See Gotcher v. Rowell, 2 Wash. App. 615, 468 P.2d 1004 (1970). Compare Duckworth v. Oliver, 112 Ga. App. 371, 145 S.E.2d 115 (1965), holding doctrine not applicable where parent merely gave special permission for a specific use.

car is used by a cohabitant without his consent.[58] However, if the living together is on a firmly established basis, consent of the insured may readily be implied.[59]

2.19. Abortion and contraception

Abortion

Prior to the decisions of the Supreme Court in Roe v. Wade[60] and Doe v. Bolton,[61] in most states abortions were permitted, if at all, only to save the health or life of the potential mother.[62] The question as to whether a potential mother had any rights superior to the asserted right of a state to criminalize abortions or to impose conditions on exercising the right to an abortion was, however, the subject of considerable discussion and controversy.[63]

---

[58]At least one state so holds: the court in Hiter v. Shelp, 129 Ga. App. 401, 199 S.E.2d 832 (1973) declined to apply the doctrine where the owner and operator lived together as husband and wife but owner lacked capacity to establish a common-law marriage due to a prior undissolved marriage.

[59]See State Farm Mut. Auto Ins. Co. v. Williamson, 331 F.2d 517 (C.A.-9 Ariz., 1964) (where insured parents permitted twenty-year-old son to use car, the issue of whether operation by son's girlfriend was with implied permission of insured presented jury question); Protective Fire & Cas. Co. v. Cornelius, 176 Neb. 75, 125 N.W.2d 179 (1963) (used car dealer's employee was an additional insured; insurer liable though car was operated by employee's girlfriend where employee had permission from dealer to use it and was passenger at time of accident); Hanover Ins. Co. v. Miesemer, 42 Misc. 2d 881, 249 N.Y.S.2d 87 (1964) (where named insured gave minor daughter unlimited possession and use of automobile, but instructed her to allow no one else to use it, and accident occurred while her boyfriend, in her company, was driving, driver was insured under the omnibus clause); Hardware Mut. Cas. Co. v. Shelby Mut. Ins. Co., 213 F. Supp. 669 (N.D. Ohio, 1962). Compare Selected Risk Ins. Co. v. Travelers Ins. Co., —— Del. ——, 287 A.2d 675 (1972) (under omnibus clause of policy, fact that use of car by insured's daughter on date was within scope of named insured's permission did not result in extension of coverage to daughter's boyfriend while he was driving car unless such actual operation was within scope of permission).

[60]410 U.S. 113, 35 L. Ed. 2d 147, 93 Sup. Ct. 705 (1973), reh. den. 410 U.S. 959, 35 L. Ed. 2d 694, 93 Sup. Ct. 1409 (1973).

[61]410 U.S. 179, 35 L. Ed. 2d 201, 93 Sup. Ct. 739 (1973), reh. den. 410 U.S. 959, 35 L. Ed. 2d 694, 93 Sup. Ct. 1410 (1973).

[62]See, e.g., Planned Parenthood of New York City, Inc. v. State, Dept. of Institutions and Agencies, 75 N.J. 49, 379 A.2d 841 (1977).

[63]See, e.g., Lamm, Reproductive Revolution, 56 A.B.A. J. 41 (1970); Kummer, Criminal Abortion: A Failure of Law, 50 A.B.A. J. 52 (1964); Mietus, Criminal Abortion: "A Failure of Law" or a Challenge to Society, 51 A.B.A. J. 924 (1965);

Many states had statutes providing for consent of some person, often the husband if the woman was married, or the parents if she was not, as a prerequisite to a lawful abortion.[64] In a decision preceding Roe v. Wade, a California court held that a hospital committee must decide an unwed pregnant woman's request for a therapeutic abortion on its merits, without requiring her to obtain parental consent.[65]

In Roe v. Wade, the court held that the woman's right of privacy has a vitally important bearing on her right to make her own decision as to whether or not to have a pregnancy terminated without the consent of any others. In the words of Mr. Justice Blackmun:

> [T]he detriment that the State would impose upon the pregnant woman by denying this choice altogether is apparent. Specific and direct harm, medically diagnosable, even in early pregnancy, may be involved. Maternity, or additional offspring, may force upon the woman a distressful life and future. Psychological harm may be imminent. Mental and physical health may be taxed by child care. There is also the distress, for all concerned, associated with the unwanted child, and there is the problem of bringing a child into a family already unable, psychologically and otherwise, to care for it. In other cases, as in this one, the additional difficulties and continuing stigma of unwed motherhood may be involved. All these are factors the woman and her responsible physician necessarily will consider in consultation.

The effect of the decision is that the woman's right to privacy gives way to state power to regulate as the embryo or fetus develops. As the case outlines:

Fox, Abortion: A Question of Right or Wrong?, 57 A.B.A. J. 667 (1971); Law and the Unborn Child: The Legal and Logical Inconsistencies, 46 Notre Dame Law. 349 (1971); New Approach to Old Crimes: The Model Penal Code, 39 Notre Dame Law. 310 (1964); Byrn, Abortion-on-demand: Whose Morality?, 46 Notre Dame Law. 5 (1970); Shaffer, Abortion, The Law and Human Life, 2 Val. U. L. Rev. 94 (1967); Note, Constitutional Aspects of Present Criminal Abortion Law, 3 Val. U. L. Rev. 102 (1968).

[64] Annotation, Right of minor to have abortion performed without parental consent, 42 A.L.R.3d 1406 (1972). See Minor's Right to Abortion and the Requirement of Parental Consent, 60 Va. L. Rev. 305 (1974).

[65] Ballard v. Anderson, 4 Cal. 3d 873, 95 Cal. Rptr. 1, 484 P.2d 1345, 42 A.L.R.3d 1392 (1971).

(a) For the stage prior to approximately the end of the first trimester, the abortion decision and its effectuation must be left to the medical judgment of the pregnant woman's attending physician. [He, in consultation with his patient, is free to determine, without regulation by the state, that in his medical judgment the patient's pregnancy should be terminated. The initial decision, then, is one that is purely personal to the mother and the physician, and any unreasonable governmental interference must yield to the mother's right of privacy.]
(b) For the stage subsequent to approximately the end of the first trimester, the State, in promoting its interest in the health of the mother, may, if it chooses, regulate the abortion procedure in ways that are reasonably related to maternal health.
(c) For the stage subsequent to viability, the State, in promoting its interest in the potentiality of human life may, if it chooses, regulate, or even proscribe, abortion except where it is necessary, in appropriate medical judgment, for the preservation of the life or health of the mother.[66]

Viability of a fetus cannot be determined by statute; it has to be on a fetus-by-fetus basis.[67] Since it has now been shown that an ovum, fertilized *outside* the uterus in a test tube and transplanted into the uterus of another woman, can result in the birth of a human being, is there any stage at which any physician can honestly say that any embryo, at whatever stage of development, is not "viable"? Insofar as concerns the health of the mother, with our present knowledge of psychiatry is there any physician who could not at any time certify that in his judgment the mental health of the mother would be endangered by childbirth?

In Doe v. Bolton,[68] the Court struck down, as unconstitutionally burdening the right of a woman to choose abortion, a statute requiring that abortions be performed only in accredited hospitals, in the absence of proof that the requirement was substantially related to the state's interest in protecting the patient's health.

In the light of these decisions, the state statutes referred to above, insofar as they place consensual restrictions on the right of

---

[66]Roe v. Wade, 410 U.S. 113, 164-165, 35 L. Ed. 2d 147, 93 Sup. Ct. 705, 732 (1973), reh. den. 410 U.S. 959, 35 L. Ed. 2d 694, 93 Sup. Ct. 1409 (1973).
[67]Floyd v. Anders, 440 F. Supp. 535 (D. S.C., 1977).
[68]410 U.S. 179, 35 L. Ed. 2d 201, 93 Sup. Ct. 739 (1973), reh. den. 410 U.S. 959, 35 L. Ed. 2d 694, 93 Sup. Ct. 1410 (1973).

the woman to abort her child during the initial period of pregnancy, are of dubious constitutionality.[69] During this period, it may be that the most a statute can do is regulate the formalities for the woman's valid consent.[70] But the decisions do not mean that the state does not have a valid and important interest in encouraging childbirth, or an important and legitimate interest in the potentiality of human life. Thus, it is within the competence of a state to withhold medicaid to indigent women who cannot establish a medical need for an abortion.[71]

As a result of the above decisions, the Commissioners on Uniform State Laws have drafted a uniform statute which delineates the respective interests of the state and the pregnant woman, and sets forth the varying degrees of requirements that can be imposed in abortion cases. The uniform act makes provision for the consent of the potential mother (even if a minor). If she is incapable of consenting, the consent can be that of the parent or guardian or of the appropriate court. If, in the medical judgment of the physician, abortion is immediately necessary to preserve the life of the woman it may be performed anywhere, and if she is unable to consent, without such consent. But in no event can it be done without her consent unless necessary to preserve her life or health. The draft contains an optional clause to the effect that no one involved can be required to participate in this operation, or be discriminated against in any way for lack of co-operation. In the penal provisions of the draft, the use of the word "knowingly" precludes criminal liability for inadvertent violation.

Though most of the states have amended their abortion laws to conform to the mandates of the Supreme Court, to date no state has adopted the uniform law in its entirety.

---

[69]See, e.g., Planned Parenthood of Central Missouri v. Danforth, 428 U.S. 52, 49 L. Ed. 2d 788, 96 Sup. Ct. 2831 (1976).
[70]Framingham Clinic, Inc. v. Board of Selectmen of Southborough, —— Mass. ——, 367 N.E.2d 606 (1977).
[71]Beal v. Doe, 432 U.S. 438, 53 L. Ed. 2d 464, 97 Sup. Ct. 2366 (1977), reh. den. 434 U.S. 880, 97 Sup. Ct. 2394 (1977). As to the right to medicaid payment for abortions, see Butler, Right to Medicaid Payment for Abortion, 28 Hastings L. J. 931 (1977). Perry, Abortion Funding Cases: A Comment on the Supreme Court's Role in American Government, 66 Georgetown L. J. 1191 (1978); Medicaid Funding for Abortions: The Medicaid Statute and the Equal Protection Clause, 6 Hofstra L. Rev. 421 (1978).

2.19 UNMARRIED COUPLES AND THE LAW

Turning now to the rights of the male partner: from the language used in the decisions relating to the requirement of parental consent[72] and from the few direct holdings on this issue,[73] a lawful male spouse would appear to have no rights whatever to control the mother's decision in the matter. A fortiori, an unwed male partner would have no such rights. In Jones v. Smith,[74] a potential putative father's attempt to restrain the mother from obtaining an abortion failed. (Apparently to bring the case within the rationale of Roe v. Wade, the court granted an emergency hearing since the mother was reaching the end of the first trimester of pregnancy, but there seems no reason to believe the result would be different if the mother's pregnancy was more advanced.) The appellant furnished some ingenious arguments to support his position. First, he contended that any right of privacy the woman might have had was waived by her participation in the sex act. This argument the court rejected as "somewhat tenuous," adding a suggestion that a rapist could not claim that his victim's right of privacy was vitiated by participation in the sex act. (This is of course true, but a rape victim's "participation" is not voluntary). Second, he contended that by indicating her desire for abortion, the woman had demonstrated her unfitness as a parent, thereby giving him, as putative father, the legal right to custody and control. This argument was dismissed as equally tenuous. Third, he contended that his earlier agreement to support a child if she became pregnant, and her agreement to marry him if this occurred, formed the basis of an implied contract. As to this the court observed that his agreement to support such child would fail

---

[72]E.g., State v. Koome, 84 Wash. 2d 901, 530 P.2d 260 (1975), where the court rejected arguments that the consent requirement was justified by the state's interest in supporting parental authority, strengthening the family unit and ensuring informed and considered decision-making by minors. See also Poe v. Gerstein, 517 F.2d 787 (C.A.-5 Fla., 1975), affd. 428 U.S. 901, 49 L. Ed. 2d 1205, 96 Sup. Ct. 3202 (1976).

[73]See Doe v. Doe, 365 Mass. 556, 314 N.E.2d 128, 62 A.L.R.3d 1082 (1974); Planned Parenthood of Central Missouri v. Danforth, 428 U.S. 52, 49 L. Ed. 2d 788, 96 Sup. Ct. 2831 (1976); Annotation, Woman's right to have abortion without consent of, or against objections of, child's father, 62 A.L.R.3d 1097 (1975); Constitutional Law: Abortion, Parental and Spousal Consent Requirements, Right to Privacy, 10 Akron L. Rev. 367 (1976).

[74]278 So. 2d 339 (Fla. App., 1973), cert. den. 415 U.S. 958, 39 L. Ed. 2d 573, 94 Sup. Ct. 1486 (1974).

for want of consideration, since he has this obligation as a matter of law. In a final observation, the court said that if such a male partner had standing to prevent the abortion, would he also not have standing to compel an abortion against her wishes? Citing Young Women's Christian Association of Princeton, N.J. v. Kugler,[75] the court concluded that the decision to terminate a pregnancy is a personal decision to be made by the mother and her physician.[76]

A few states, in their new statutes, require that notice of a proposed abortion be given either to the spouse or, if the potential mother is a minor, to her parents. Whether such provisions can withstand a challenge of unconstitutionality, it now seems clear that, unless they are such as to make it very clear to the parents that their wishes are, in the final analysis, subordinated to those of the mother herself, they are vulnerable to attack.[77] In a footnote, the Court in Planned Parenthood of Central Missouri v. Danforth[78] indicates that a state might properly provide for some spousal (or presumably parental) input regarding the mother's decision without requiring spousal or parental consent as a prerequisite. But a notice provision does mean that the mother would, if unmarried, be indirectly affected in her decision; she would be influenced to avoid abortion, or to resort to self help or to illegal operators, if she did not want her parents to know of her pregnancy.

Other states provide for notice to be given by the performing

---

[75]342 F. Supp. 1048 (D. N.J., 1972), affd. 493 F.2d 1402 (C.A.-3 N.J., 1974), cert. den. 415 U.S. 989, 39 L. Ed. 2d 885, 94 Sup. Ct. 1587 (1974).

[76]See, generally, Perry, Abortion, the Public Morals, and the Police Power: The Ethical Function of Substantive Due Process, 23 U.C.L.A. L. Rev. 689 (1976); Towards a Practical Implementation of the Abortion Decision: The Interests of the Physician, the Woman and the Fetus, 25 De Paul L. Rev. 676 (1976). Since the court in Planned Parenthood of Central Missouri v. Danforth, 428 U.S. 52, 49 L. Ed. 2d 788, 96 Sup. Ct. 2831 (1976) did not find the possible adverse effect on the marital relationship to be so compelling as to outweigh the woman's right to make her own decision, it follows a fortiori that an unmarried male's interest in a nonmarital relationship would be even less compelling. See Right to Abortion: The End of Parental and Spousal Consent Requirements, 31 Ark. L. Rev. 122 (1977); Schwartz, Rights of a Father with Regard to His Illegitimate Child, 36 Ohio S. L. J. 1 (1975); Abortion: The Father's Rights, 42 U. Cin. L. Rev. 441 (1973).

[77]See Bellotti v. Baird, 428 U.S. 132, 49 L. Ed. 2d 844, 96 Sup. Ct. 2857 (1976), discussed in section 6.22, herein.

[78]428 U.S. 52, 49 L. Ed. 2d 788, 96 Sup. Ct. 2831 (1976).

physician to appropriate authorities. The Danforth court held such requirements constitutional so long as, in furthering its legitimate concerns for maternal health, the state properly respects a patient's confidentiality and privacy. Such a reporting statute would not as such have any legally significant impact on the abortion decision.[79]

Access to contraceptives

Federal legislation, once known as the Comstock Act,[80] aimed at preventing interstate or foreign traffic in contraceptives, is no longer applicable to contraceptive devices.[81]

Though state legislation aimed at controlling contraceptives was at one time held to be within the police power of the state,[82] the law has changed. In 1965 the Supreme Court of the United States struck down a state prohibition of the use of contraceptives as having "a maximum destructive impact" on privacy rights.[83] It has since held that, whatever the rights of the individual in this respect may be, the rights must be the same for the unmarried and the married alike.[84]

In the area of sexual mores, as in other areas, the court has conceded that the scope of permissible state regulation is broader as to minors than as to adults.[85] Nevertheless, it is held that a blanket prohibition, or even a blanket requirement of parental consent, on the choice of an unwed mother to terminate her

---

[79]Id. See Note, Due Process and Equal Protection: Constitutional Implications of Abortion Notice and Reporting Requirements, 56 B. U. L. Rev. 522 (1976).

[80]18 U.S.C. §§ 1461, 1462; 19 U.S.C. § 1305.

[81]P.L. 91–662, p. 2318 (1971).

[82]See Annotation, Validity of regulations as to contraceptives or the dissemination of birth control information, 96 A.L.R.2d 955 (1964).

[83]Griswold v. Connecticut, 381 U.S. 479, 14 L. Ed. 2d 510, 85 Sup. Ct. 1678 (1965).

[84]Eisenstadt v. Baird, 405 U.S. 438, 453, 31 L. Ed. 2d 349, 92 Sup. Ct. 1029, 1038 (1972). "If the right of privacy means anything, it is the right of the *individual*, married or single, to be free from unwarranted governmental intrusion into matters so fundamentally affecting a person as the decision whether to bear or beget a child."

[85]Prince v. Massachusetts, 321 U.S. 158, 88 L. Ed. 645, 64 Sup. Ct. 438 (1944); Ginsberg v. New York, 390 U.S. 629, 20 L. Ed. 2d 195, 88 Sup. Ct. 1274 (1968), reh. den. 391 U. S. 971, 88 Sup. Ct. 2029 (1968).

RAMIFICATIONS   2.19

pregnancy being unconstitutional,[86] the same reasoning invalidates a statute forbidding, without qualification, the distribution of contraceptives to minors.[87]

By reason of these decisions, many of the state statutes in this area have been held unconstitutional. Thus, a court has enjoined enforcement of a Wisconsin statute criminalizing those who make contraceptives available for use in a nonmarital situation, saying that the state's interest in deterring extramarital sex is not sufficiently compelling to justify a denial or impairment of the fundamental interest of unmarried women in preventing pregnancy.[88] Similarly, a New York statute forbidding *anyone* from distributing such devices to persons under the age of sixteen, and anyone but licensed pharmacists from making them available to persons over sixteen, and forbidding the advertisement or display of such devices, was held unconstitutional as to the portion relating to those under sixteen. The constitutionality of the remainder of the statute was not conclusively adjudicated.[89]

In those states which retain legislation of this nature—and

---

[86]Planned Parenthood of Central Missouri v. Danforth, 428 U.S. 52, 49 L. Ed. 2d 788, 96 Sup. Ct. 2831 (1976).

[87]Carey v. Population Services Internat., 431 U.S. 678, 52 L. Ed. 2d 675, 97 Sup. Ct. 2010 (1977). Stevens, J., concurring in part, would not "leave open the question whether there is a significant state interest in discouraging sexual activity among unmarried persons under 16 years of age." Id., 97 Sup. Ct. at 2031. Rehnquist, J., dissenting, finds it "difficult to imagine" the possible reaction to the stalwart defenders of Bunker Hill, those valiants who made possible the constitutional amendments, to a holding that "their efforts had enshrined in the Constitution the right of commercial vendors of contraceptives to peddle them to unmarried minors through such means as window displays and vending machines located in the men's room of truck stops, notwithstanding the considered judgment of the New York Legislature to the contrary." Id., 97 Sup. Ct. at 2033. See also Annotations, Legality of voluntary nontherapeutic sterilization, 35 A.L.R.3d 1444 (1971); Validity of regulations as to contraceptives or the dissemination of birth control information, 96 A.L.R.2d 955 (1964); Validity of statute or ordinance forbidding pharmacist to advertise prices of drugs or medicines, 44 A.L.R.3d 1301 (1972); Note, Parental Consent Requirements and Privacy Rights of Minors: The Contraceptive Controversy, 88 Harv. L. Rev. 1001 (1975).

[88]Baird v. Lynch, 390 F. Supp. 740 (W.D. Wis., 1974).

[89]Population Services Internat. v. Wilson, 398 F. Supp. 321 (S.D. N.Y., 1975), affd. 431 U.S. 678, 52 L. Ed. 2d 675, 97 Sup. Ct. 2010 (1977). See Note, Parental Consent Requirements and Privacy Rights of Minors: The Contraceptive Controversy, 88 Harv. L. Rev. 1001 (1975); Annotation, Legality of voluntary nontherapeutic sterilization, 35 A.L.R.3d 1444 (1971).

this is no rarity—challenge to its constitutionality can always be anticipated.

The Social Security Act requires that state plans for the federally funded Aid to Families of Dependent Children Program include provisions for family planning services for members of families receiving aid, "including minors who can be considered to be sexually active."[90]

2.20. Liability to third persons

Contract liability

Under modern rules, authority to act for one's spouse is not implied from the married relation; one seeking to hold a spouse for the contractual liabilities of the other must at least establish implied authority. However, a presumption of a wife's authority to pledge her husband's credit for household necessaries is commonly recognized, and in a known living-together situation, whether or not the parties hold themselves out as married, a liability based on ostensible authority or agency by estoppel cannot safely be ignored.[91]

Tort liability

If one of the cohabitants is married to someone else, in some states there is a possibility of the other partner being faced with a tort action for *alienation of affections* or for *criminal conversation*. Many states have abolished one or both of these torts by statute.[92] The plaintiff in such an action is usually the legal spouse of the one whose affections are alienated, albeit a mere common-law spouse.[93] Actions by a child of the latter are a rarity, and actions by a parent even rarer.[94]

Though the two torts are separate and distinct there is no reason why, in a state which has not abolished one or the other, a

---

[90] 42 U.S.C. § 602(a)(15).
[91] See 41 Am. Jur. 2d, Husband and Wife, § 341 et seq.
[92] See, generally, 41 Am. Jur. 2d, Husband and Wife, § 463 et seq.
[93] See 41 Am. Jur. 2d, Husband and Wife, § 509.
[94] Annotation, Right of child or parent to recover for alienation of other's affections, 60 A.L.R.3d 931 (1974).

cause of action cannot be based on both torts.[95] Criminal conversation is simply adultery in the aspect of a tort.[96] The gist of the action is the adulterous intercourse, and if the action is based on that alone the resultant alienation of affections is merely a matter of aggravation.[97] The action, which has ancient roots, was, at the time of Blackstone, available only to a husband, when adultery as a crime was left to the ecclesiastical courts.[98] Today, however, a married woman can sue where the tort action has not been abolished.[99] Alienation of affections is a tortious deprivation of a person's right to the comfort, society, assistance and services of a spouse whose affections have been alienated.[1] Abolition of these two torts does not mean that a claim based on interference with a spouse's right to support would be outlawed.[2]

The constitutionality of statutes abolishing these torts has generally been sustained,[3] as has the constitutionality of statutes abolishing civil actions for seduction and breach of promise to marry.[4] A statute making it unlawful to file such actions has, however, been invalidated, inter alia as tending to put a premium on violation of the moral law, making violators a privileged class, free to pursue such conduct without fear even of liability in damages.[5] A Pennsylvania court, on the other hand, has opined that

---

[95]E.g., Bailey v. Huling, —— R.I. ——, 377 A.2d 220 (1977) ($75,000 awarded for alienation of affections, $1,000 for criminal conversation); Roberts v. Berry, 541 F.2d 607 (C.A.-6 Tenn., 1976).

[96]See 41 Am. Jur. 2d, Husband and Wife, § 477.

[97]Roberts v. Berry, 541 F.2d 607 (C.A.-6 Tenn., 1976).

[98]Criminal Conversation: Civil Action for Adultery, 25 Baylor L. Rev. 495 (1973).

[99]E.g., Kromm v. Kromm, 31 Md. App. 635, 358 A.2d 247 (1976); Bailey v. Huling, —— R.I. ——, 377 A.2d 220 (1977); Annotation, Wife's right of action for criminal conversation, 28 A.L.R. 327 (1924).

[1]See Hafner v. Hafner, 135 N.J. Super. 328, 343 A.2d 166 (1975). A married woman living apart from her husband can sue for alienation of his affections, even though the statute gives a right of action to a husband for criminal conversation or adultery with wife. Emerson v. Fleming, 127 Ga. App., 296, 193 S.E.2d 249 (1972).

[2]See Hafner v. Hafner, supra.

[3]E.g., Langdon v. Sayre, 74 Cal. App. 2d 41, 168 P.2d 57 (1946). See Note, Case for Retention of Causes of Action for Intentional Interference with the Marital Relationship, 48 Notre Dame Law. 426 (1972).

[4]Annotation, Constitutionality, construction, and application of statutes abolishing civil actions for alienation of affections, criminal conversation, seduction, and breach of promise to marry, 167 A.L.R. 235 (1947).

[5]Id. Wyoming has statutes which denounce as a felony the mere filing of a complaint for relief of this nature. Wyo. Stat., §§ 1-23-101 to 1-23-104.

that state's former action for criminal conversation was an "anachronism," and that it would be unreasonable to impose harsh results without affording the defendant any real opportunity to interject logically valid defenses such as the role of plaintiff's spouse in the adulterous relationship or the quality of the plaintiff's marriage prior to the commission of the tort.[6]

Liability for criminal conversation can flow from a single act of sex. No malice need be shown. Plaintiff can qualify for nominal damages without any showing of pecuniary damages;[7] although, as stated, alienation of affections may be an element of the damages proven.

The gist of the action for alienation of affections is the alienation of one spouse from another. Damages flow from loss of consortium and affection. Adultery need not be proven. As to the mental element, however, states vary. Some require that the conduct of the defendant must have been "malicious," or "intentional." In one such state, there could be no recovery against church officials simply for disseminating to wives a belief that they should leave a spouse who does not subscribe to their religious views.[8] Such a requirement is sometimes found to have been established on rather slight evidence, as where a defendant told the plaintiff that he was in love with the plaintiff's wife and was "going to win her."[9] Other courts have used the terms "malice or improper motives" as the requisite mental element.[10]

It seems likely that legislative abolition of either of, or both of, these torts is prompted by the commonsense reason that a home so easily broken up is barely worth maintaining, and that the existence of such causes of action has proved a ready instrument for blackmailers and extortionists.[11] Moreover, the requirement

---

[6]Fadgen v. Lenkner, 469 Pa. 272, 365 A.2d 147 (1976).
[7]Swartz v. Steele, 42 Ohio App. 2d 1, 325 N.E.2d 910 (1974).
[8]Radecki v. Schuckardt, 50 Ohio App. 2d 92, 361 N.E.2d 543 (1976). See Annotation, Action for alienation of affections based on exercise of religious influences, 31 A.L.R. 1115 (1924).
[9]Gorder v. Sims, 306 Minn. 275, 237 N.W.2d 67 (1975).
[10]Roberts v. Berry, 541 F.2d 607 (C.A.-6 Tenn., 1976).
[11]See Alienation of Affections: Flourishing Anachronism, 13 Wake Forest L. Rev. 585 (1977).

that the alienation of affections resulted from defendant's "malicious," "intentional" or "wilful" conduct[12] is hard to establish. In view of the difficulty of showing that the "victim's" change of heart was so induced, it seems surprising that such actions are ever successful, the authorities usually holding that there is no liability if the conduct of the "alienated" spouse was voluntary.[13] Some explanation is to be found when the court merely instructs the jury that a contribution to the alienation is enough, and that defendant need not be the controlling cause.[14]

Few states, if any, recognize the existence of any cause of action for a minor against one who entices a parent from the home and deprives the child of care and attention or affection.[15]

The damages that can flow from either criminal conversation or alienation of affections are only such as are natural and probable consequences, or direct probable consequences, of the act. For example, where an employee confronted his employer with the latter's adultery with his wife, and as a result was dismissed from his employment, the employee's claim for wages earned could not properly be regarded as resulting from the employer's criminal conversation.[16] The defendant's present financial situation is a relevant factor in determining the amount of punitive damages that may be awarded.[17] Also material to the question of damages is the fact that plaintiff's spouse consented to the criminal conversation. Plaintiff's own consent is an absolute defense.[18] So, too, the fact that the spouse whose affections were alienated had little

---

[12]See Wheeler v. Fox, 16 Ill. App. 3d 1089, 307 N.E.2d 633 (1974).

[13]See Annotation, Element of causation in alienation of affections action, 19 A.L.R.2d 471 (1951).

[14]In Bailey v. Huling, —— R.I. ——, 377 A.2d 220 (1977), the jury instruction required a finding that defendant's conduct was "the procuring or contributing cause." See Annotation, Element of causation in alienation of affections action, 19 A.L.R.2d 471 (1951).

[15]See Wallace v. Wallace, 155 W. Va. 569, 184 S.E.2d 327 (1971).

[16]Breiner v. Olson, 195 Neb. 120, 237 N.W.2d 118 (1975).

[17]Williamson v. Weeks, 142 Ga. App. 149, 235 S.E.2d 587 (1977). See also Annotations, Punitive or exemplary damages in action by spouse for alienation of affections or criminal conversation, 31 A.L.R.2d 713 (1953); Excessiveness or inadequacy of damages for alienation of affections, criminal conversation or seduction, 36 A.L.R.2d 548 (1954).

[18]Fadgen v. Lenkner, 469 Pa. 272, 365 A.2d 147 (1976).

2.20 UNMARRIED COUPLES AND THE LAW

affection for the plaintiff, though not ordinarily regarded as a defense,[19] is material on the issue of damages.

If the partnership is with a minor, and without parental consent, there is authority to support a tort action against the other partner.[20]

Should there be offspring of the unwed union, courts have generally resisted attempts to recover damages against the parents for a tortious causing of birth (*wrongful birth*).[21] Among explanations for this reluctance are the lack of precedent, the possibility of opening doors to a floodgate of litigation, and policies disfavoring actions between family members.[22] Probably the most cogent reason is the virtual impossibility of determining damages. Who can tell whether "nonexistence" is preferable to life as an illegitimate child?

On the other hand, the Supreme Court of Illinois has ruled (prospectively) that an infant could maintain a cause of action for damages resulting from a negligent transfusion of Rh-negative blood into a mother whose blood was Rh-positive, this act being

---

[19]Gorder v. Sims, 306 Minn. 275, 237 N.W.2d 67 (1975); Moranz v. Schiller, 525 S.W.2d 785 (Mo. App., 1975). Compare Wheeler v. Fox, 16 Ill. App. 3d 1089, 307 N.E.2d 633 (1974), holding that plaintiff must plead and prove love and affection of spouse for plaintiff.

Generally, as to defenses, see Husband and Wife—Statute of Limitations Period Applicable to a Civil Action for Alienation of Affections Brought in Concert with an Action for Criminal Conversation, 15 J. Family L. 838 (1976–77). See also 46 A.L.R.2d 1086 (1956). Annotation, Condonation or forgiveness of spouse as affecting liability for alienation of affections or criminal conversation, 38 A.L.R.2d 1234 (1954); Divorce or separation decree as res judicata or estoppel, or as evidence, in alienation of affections or criminal conversation action, 96 A.L.R.2d 903 (1964); Survival of action or cause of action for alienation of affections or criminal conversation, 14 A.L.R. 693 (1921), 57 A.L.R. 351 (1928); Liability of parent, relative, or person in loco parentis in action by husband or wife for alienation of affection, 108 A.L.R. 408 (1937).

[20]See Annotation, Civil liability for carnal knowledge with actual consent of girl under age of consent, 45 A.L.R. 780 (1926), 79 A.L.R. 1229 (1932).

[21]See Kashi, Case of the Unwanted Blessing: Wrongful Life, 31 U. Miami L. Rev. 1409 (1977); Liability to Bastard for Negligence Resulting in His Conception, 18 Stan. L. Rev. 530 (1966), where it is suggested that, if courts were to permit a bastard to sue his biological father in tort, they might be implicitly approving "shotgun" marriages.

[22]Annotation, Tort liability for wrongfully causing one to be born, 83 A.L.R.3d 15 (1978). But for an example of an action against a physician (by parents) for "wrongful conception" (negligent performance of a sterilization), see Sherlock v. Stillwater Clinic, —— Minn. ——, 260 N.W.2d 169 (1977).

performed long before the infant's conception.[23] If this decision is viewed as sound, it seems a short step away from permitting an action by the infant for wrongful causing of birth.

2.21. Divorced partner's right to alimony

When a divorced person, male or female,[24] lives with another without marriage, consideration should be given to the question whether, and if so to what extent, this can have repercussions on an award of alimony which accompanied the decree. Though there is some authority to the contrary,[25] the mere fact of a divorced wife's sexual immorality is not usually today regarded as affecting her rights in this respect; since it is usually the husband who owes this responsibility, to hold otherwise would be to penalize the ex-wife for her sexual activities while no penalty is imposed on the husband if he participates in similar sexual activities.[26]

A Kentucky court, without ruling on the trial court's authority to condition an award of alimony on a proper demeanor of the recipient wives, declined to modify the award saying that it could not have been intended that the women must "emulate St. Simeon Stylites" if they wanted alimony to continue.[27] It is believed by some that the whole question of attempting to control

---

[23]Renslow v. Mennonite Hosp., 67 Ill. 2d 348, 10 Ill. Dec. 484, 367 N.E.2d 1250 (1977).

[24]See Thaler v. Thaler, 89 Misc. 2d 315, 391 N.Y.S.2d 331 (1977), revd. on other grounds 58 App. Div. 2d 890, 396 N.Y.S.2d 815 (1977), holding a statute which permits an award of alimony to women but not to men denies equal protection and involves a suspect differentiation which serves no compelling state interest. Harnett, J., described the sex distinction as an "anachronism rooted in sexist soil which must be pulled out," and awarded both support pendente lite and attorney's fees to a husband who, being a nonresident alien, could not support himself while defending his wife's divorce suit.

[25]See Glendon, Marriage and the State: The Withering Away of Marriage, 62 Va. L. Rev. 663 (1976). See also Cal. Civil Code, § 485 (presumption of lack of need for support when former spouse is living with another).

[26]See In re Anonymous, 90 Misc. 2d 801, 395 N.Y.S.2d 1000 (1977) (discussed in section 6.33, herein). A New York court could not eliminate a wife's alimony without proof of (1) habitual living with another man *and* (2) holding herself out as his wife. Northrup v. Northrup, 43 N.Y.2d 566, 402 N.Y.S.2d 997, 373 N.E.2d 1221 (1978).

[27]Blakely v. Blakely, 261 Ky. 318, 87 S.W.2d 628 (1935).

the moral behavior of the population through provisions dealing with alimony or divorce defenses needs re-evaluation.[28]

However, almost all if not all states allow the divorcing court discretion to modify permanent awards of alimony.[29] Where a wife has brought property into the marriage or has earned a right to marital accumulations and the court, instead of ordering a clear-cut property settlement, merely grants the wife lump sum alimony, albeit payable in installments, it would seem clear that not even her remarriage should affect the husband's liability.[30] But if the award merely reflects the husband's duty to care for her in the manner to which she has grown accustomed, no firm rule can be stated as to whether her subsequent living with a partner who can and does furnish her needs will influence a court's discretion to modify the alimony award. As to this, local authorities should be consulted.[31] If the unmarried partnership does not involve any support commitments on the part of the other partner, any statute or case law which puts her in a worse position than the divorcee who is occasionally unchaste (and whose right to alimony is not thereby affected) would have the illogical result of making it safer for her to "play the field" with different men for short periods of time.[32]

In short, though the states are far from uniform in their attitudes on this question, it is likely that any judicial discretion to terminate or modify alimony awards by reason of living together will be restricted to situations where a really firm and stable relationship exists between the alimony claimant and her partner who is committed to, and well able to, care for her financial needs.[33]

---

[28] Wadlington, Sexual Relations After Separation or Divorce: The New Morality and the Old and New Divorce Laws, 63 Va. L. Rev. 249 (1977).

[29] See 24 Am. Jur. 2d, Divorce and Separation, § 646 et seq.

[30] See 24 Am. Jur. 2d, Divorce and Separation, § 912; Annotation, Divorced wife's subsequent misconduct as authorizing or affecting modification of decree of alimony, 6 A.L.R.2d 859 (1949).

[31] See Jones v. Jones,——Nev.——, 571 P.2d 103 (1977) (where a property settlement agreement stipulated that alimony would cease if the wife cohabited with another, proof of such cohabitation relieved her former husband of his alimony obligations).

[32] See In re Anonymous, 90 Misc. 2d 801, 395 N.Y.S.2d 1000 (1977).

[33] See, e.g., Kent v. Kent, 28 Utah 2d 34, 497 P.2d 652 (1972); Fleming v. Fleming, 221 Kan. 290, 559 P.2d 329 (1977); Hazelwood v. Hazelwood, 89 N.M.

RAMIFICATIONS 2.21

Most courts hold that, absent a statute, an award of alimony cannot accompany a decree annulling a marriage. The rationale is that, since there has never been a marriage, there is nothing on which such an obligation could be based.[34] When, however, there is a valid award of alimony by its terms terminable on a remarriage, and the second marriage is annulled, there is some authority for the proposition that the initial alimony award can be revived if the second marriage was "void" as distinguished from merely "voidable."[35] This, coupled with the view that a remarriage as such at best only affords "strong ground" for a modification of the alimony award where there is a showing that the second husband can provide for her in the manner to which she is accustomed,[36] compels the conclusion that the right to alimony would not be affected by cohabitation after divorce without a very strong showing that her needs are being, and will continue to be, adequately cared for.

In some states, a wife is able to seek support (separate maintenance) without obtaining a divorce. Usually, of course, such a right is recognized only where the husband, either by his desertion or "constructive desertion" (making life with him unendurable) has justified her leaving him. In these situations, a

---

659, 556 P.2d 345 (1976); Stern v. Stern, 88 Misc. 2d 860, 389 N.Y.S.2d 265 (1976); Wadlington, Sexual Relations After Separation or Divorce: The New Morality and the Old and New Divorce Laws, 63 Va. L. Rev. 249 (1977).

[34] See Annotation, Right to allowance of permanent alimony in connection with decree of annulment, 81 A.L.R.3d 281 (1977); Contra: Cortes v. Fleming, 307 So. 2d 611, 81 A.L.R.3d 267 (La., 1973) (in the case of good faith spouse).

[35] See Annotation, Annulment of later marriage as reviving prior husband's obligations under alimony decree or separation agreement, 45 A.L.R.3d 1033 (1972).

[36] See Annotation, Remarriage of wife as affecting husband's obligation under separation agreement to support her or to make other money payments to her, 48 A.L.R.2d 318 (1956). See also Ballew v. Ballew, 187 Neb. 397, 191 N.W.2d 462 (1971), where the right of a divorced wife to alimony was terminated on her remarriage and was not revived by subsequent annulment of her remarriage, the provision for termination on remarriage having been a part of the divorce settlement and incorporated in the divorce decree. Annotations, Retrospective modification of, or refusal to enforce, decree for alimony, separate maintenance, or support, 6 A.L.R.2d 1277 (1949); Change in financial condition or needs of husband or wife as ground for modification of decree for alimony or maintenance, 18 A.L.R.2d 10 (1951).

resumption of spousal cohabitation is ordinarily ground for the termination of a support decree.[37]

In at least one case,[38] a husband was held not to be relieved from this responsibility by reason of the wife's living with another man where the support received from that source was inadequate for her needs. From this decision it seems permissible to infer that, if she is receiving her support needs from a cohabitant other than her husband, a court would readily terminate a support decree.[39]

2.22. Rights in respect of torts committed against partner

In most states, when a spouse can recover for damages tortiously caused to the other spouse, recovery can be had for loss of consortium as an element of such damages.[40] In California, where the right to so recover is of relatively recent recognition,[41] courts have indicated that such recovery must be narrowly circumscribed and cannot be extended to all foreseeable relationships.[42] That state has held that there is no cause of action for loss of consortium arising from a wife's injuries incurred before marriage while the couple was living together.[43] Thus it would appear that even in a state which recognizes and honors obligations, expressly or impliedly incurred, between cohabitants, it would be difficult if not impossible for the cohabitant to state a cause of

---

[37]See 41 Am. Jur. 2d, Husband and Wife, § 397.
[38]Germer v. Germer, 167 Misc. 882, 4 N.Y.S.2d 747 (1938); Compare Houg v. Houg, 159 Misc. 894, 289 N.Y.S. 27 (1936), terminating support where the wife had been convicted of prostitution, thereafter contracting a bigamous marriage, and was also afflicted with syphilis. (This last aspect seems of little relevance.)
[39]Generally, see Annotation, Defenses available to husband in civil suit by wife for support, 10 A.L.R.2d 466 (1950).
[40]See, e.g., Mann v. Golden, 428 F. Supp. 560 (D. Kan., 1977), holding a statutory denial of the right to sue for loss of consortium when applied to a wife but not to a husband to be violative of equal protection.
[41]Rodriguez v. Bethlehem Steel Corp., 12 Cal. 3d 382, 115 Cal. Rptr. 765, 525 P.2d 669 (1974).
[42]Borer v. American Airlines, Inc., 19 Cal. 3d 441, 138 Cal. Rptr. 302, 563 P.2d 858 (1977).
[43]Tong v. Jocson, 76 Cal. App. 3d 603, 142 Cal. Rptr. 726 (1977).

action. Even if the tort was an intentional one, any damage would probably be regarded as too remote.[44]

Where the wrong consisted in the tortious causing of the death of the cohabitant, any claim would have to be based on the controlling wrongful death statute. The rights of an illegitimate child under such statutes are commonly recognized.[45] The rights of a putative spouse are likely to receive recognition.[46] It would be difficult, to say the least, to predicate a recovery by a mere cohabitant on any of the controlling statutes even if general words such as "other dependents" are used in the eligibility provision.[47]

2.23. Tort liability of partners inter sese

Under the early common law, there could be no tort action by one spouse against the other, or by a parent against a child, or vice versa.[48] This rule, though far from receiving universal approval,[49] continues to receive recognition in most states. Some have abolished it by statute, and some have construed the Married Women's Property Act to have negated it.[50] But whatever may be the status of the rule in any particular state, very few courts extend it to disenable a relative more distant than that of

---

[44] As to damages for intentional interference with contract relations, see Dobbs, *Handbook on the Law of Remedies,* p. 459 et seq. (1973).

[45] See state-by-state commentary, Chapter 6, herein.

[46] See Wrongful Death by a Surviving Putative Spouse—How Large an Extension?, 22 Loyola L. Rev. 359 (1975–76); 22 Am. Jur. 2d, Death, §§ 29, 49.

[47] Generally, see Annotations, Child adopted by another as beneficiary of action or settlement for wrongful death of natural parent, 67 A.L.R.2d 745 (1959); Damages for wrongful death of spouse as affected by personal relations of the spouses, or the marital misconduct of either spouse, 90 A.L.R. 920 (1934); Judgment in spouse's action for personal injuries as binding, as regards loss of consortium and similar resulting damage, upon other spouse not a party to the action, 12 A.L.R.3d 933 (1967); Spouse's or parent's right to recover punitive damages in connection with recovery of damages for medical expenses or loss of services or consortium arising from personal injury to other spouse or to child, 25 A.L.R.3d 1416 (1969); Wife's right of action for loss of consortium, 36 A.L.R.3d 900 (1971).

[48] See Annotation, Right of one spouse to maintain action against the other for personal injury, 43 A.L.R.2d 632, 660 (1955).

[49] See United States v. Jones, 542 F.2d 661 (C.A.-6 Tenn., 1976), discussing a possible interspousal exception to the wiretap act (18 U.S.C. § 2511 et seq.).

[50] See 41 Am. Jur. 2d, Husband and Wife, § 524.

husband and wife, or parent and child.[51] For this reason it is unlikely in the extreme that any court would harness the doctrine to bar a tort action by one unmarried cohabitant against the other.

Thus, in addition to the rights to restitutionary relief, to compensation for services or to some equitable division of the accumulations of the partnership,[52] actions by a putative spouse (that is, one who was misled into believing in the validity of a marriage) are no rarity. The fraud may, for example, consist in having misrepresented a marital status, or in having arranged a fake wedding ceremony or the like. There is no reason why the defrauded plaintiff cannot be the male partner, though damages in such a situation would likely be more difficult to establish.[53] Continuance of cohabitation after learning of the deceit ought to go in mitigation of damages, though it is conceivable that a long continued cohabitation with knowledge that the factor vitiating the purported marriage no longer exists could result in a common-law marriage.[54]

Seduction under promise to marry

A more difficult question is presented when, the relationship having gone sour, the female partner seeks to recover tort damages for seduction based on a promise of marriage.

Under the early common law, the civil action for seduction was exclusively an action brought by a father to recover damages for the loss of the services of his daughter; the "services" could be of a nominal nature, this requirement being a mere fiction to establish his cause of action. Damages could also be predicated on his own loss of honor and on the disgrace to himself and his family. As time went by, some courts denied the action unless he could

---

[51]Tort Actions Between Members of the Family— Husband and Wife—Parent and Child, 26 Mo. L. Rev. 152 (1961). Annotation, Family relationship other than that of parent and child or husband and wife between tortfeasor and person injured or killed as affecting right to maintain action, 81 A.L.R.2d 1155 (1962).

[52]See Chapter 4, herein.

[53]See Annotation, Liability of one putative spouse to other for wrongfully inducing entry into or cohabitation under illegal, void, or nonexistent marriage, 72 A.L.R.2d 956 (1960).

[54]See section 1.5, herein.

truly show a loss of services.[55] The female who was allegedly seduced was regarded as barred by the doctrines of *volenti non fit injuria* and *in pari delicto*.[56] At a later date, some courts permitted the female to sue in her own right, usually requiring in such a case that she establish a promise to marry and its breach.[57] Today, though a few states continue to permit an action by the female, many have abolished it by the so-called "Heart Balm Statutes."[58] These statutes are prompted by a realization that such actions have failed to accomplish their original social purpose, that they tend to create embarrassment and damage to persons who may be wholly innocent of wrongdoing, and that they can afford a fruitful opportunity for blackmail and extortion.[59]

Where such an action does lie, the fact that a woman has already been married does not preclude her from suing as having "surrendered her chastity" (an essential element of the tort).[60]

The Supreme Court of Washington, though recognizing that state policies should not encourage marriage when a person has "second thoughts" about it, held that there should be an avenue of redress where the victim has suffered, even merely emotionally, as a result, but that she cannot recover for loss of expected social and financial position, marriage being "no longer" considered to be a property transaction.[61] There is no reason why her damages could not include payments for her trousseau, or for wedding expenses, but they should not include payments for the defendant's rent, food and clothing.[62]

---

[55] Prosser, *Torts*, pp. 885–886 (4th ed., 1971).

[56] See Annotations, Right of seduced female to maintain action for seduction, 121 A.L.R. 1487 (1939); Constitutionality, construction, and application of statutes abolishing civil actions for alienation of affections, criminal conversation, seduction, and breach of promise to marry, 167 A.L.R. 235 (1947).

[57] E.g., Colly v. Thomas, 99 Misc. 158, 163 N.Y.S. 432 (1917). See also Annotations, Promise of marriage as a condition of civil action for seduction, 21 A.L.R. 303 (1922); Right of seduced female to maintain action for seduction, 121 A.L.R. 1487 (1939).

[58] The action for seduction under breach of promise to marry has been modified or abolished in Alabama, California, Colorado, Connecticut, Florida, Indiana, Maine, Maryland, Massachusetts, Michigan, New Jersey, New York, Pennsylvania, West Virginia, Wisconsin and Wyoming.

[59] Feinsinger, Legislative Attack on "Heart Balm," 33 Mich. L. Rev. 979 (1935). See also Heck v. Schupp, 394 Ill. 296, 68 N.E.2d 464, 167 A.L.R. 232 (1946).

[60] See Breece v. Jett, 556 S.W.2d 696 (Mo. App., 1977).

[61] Stanard v. Bolin, 88 Wash. 2d 614, 565 P.2d 94 (1977).

[62] See Worthy v. Major, 275 A.2d 244 (D.C. App., 1971).

It is perhaps superfluous to comment that, absent clear proof of a promise to marry, the chances of an action of this nature succeeding might be compared to those of an action in tort by a ball player for assault as a result of an injury received on the playing field.[63]

Guest statutes

Many states have statutes providing in effect that, before a passenger can recover for the negligence of one driving an automobile in which he is riding as the "guest" of the driver, there must be a showing of "gross" and not mere "simple" negligence. The general view is the fact that the injured passenger is a member of the driver's family does not exclude him from being considered as a "guest."[64] It follows a fortiori that an unmarried partner, even though he or she may qualify as "family" for some purposes of the law, would almost surely be regarded as a "guest" for this purpose.

2.24. Homosexual partnerships

A few of the problems presented in this chapter can have an impact on the homosexual relationship. For example, in the area of employment difficulties,[65] a conviction of homosexual acts has furnished grounds for termination of employment in the civil service.[66] Also, a partnership of a "gay" nature might for some

---

[63] See Breece v. Jett, 556 S.W.2d 696 (Mo. App., 1977), reversing judgment for plaintiff, jury not having been instructed to find promise knowingly false when made and made with intent to seduce, and plaintiff's reliance on such promise in consenting to intercourse.

[64] Annotation, Guest statute as applicable to member of family riding in car driven by another member, 2 A.L.R.2d 932 (1948). Where passenger and uninsured driver were not married, although passenger was mother of four children by him and used his name, she was held not to be his "spouse" and not barred from recovery from an Unsatisfied Claim and Judgment Fund. Lopez v. Santiago, 125 N.J. Super. 268, 310 A.2d 500 (1973).

[65] See section 2.1 et seq., herein.

[66] Taylor v. United States Civil Service Comm., 374 F.2d 466 (C.A.-9 Cal., 1967). But see Morrison v. State Bd. of Education, 1 Cal. 3d 214, 82 Cal. Rptr. 175, 461 P.2d 375 (1969), holding that some showing of detriment to fellow employees or to the public is a prerequisite to termination.

purposes be considered as a "household," or a "family."[67] But for the most part the ramifications that accompany the unmarried status of a heterosexual couple have little application. For example, it would be an absurdity to regard a partner of the same sex as a "spouse" for any purposes.[68] Thus, a person who is not biologically a female at the time of celebrating a "marriage," notwithstanding a change of sex subsequent to the ceremony, cannot get an annulment. There is nothing to annul.[69]

A dilemma of homosexual couples is that they cannot marry each other. Attempts to assert such a right on constitutional grounds have consistently failed.[70] The Supreme Court has found no irrational or invidious discrimination in a state's classification of persons authorized to marry as being persons of different sexes.[71] Whether a couple can or intends to raise children, marriage is an institution protected by the law primarily because of the societal values associated with the propagation of the human race.[72] Yet, there are states that take a highly liberal stance in adjusting the equities between unwed heterosexual partners when their relationship comes to an end.[73] To what extent will the courts adopt the same attitudes in adjusting the rights of cohabitants of the same sex?

The Supreme Court of the United States, in overturning a New York statute banning the sale of contraceptives, has left open the question of how far states can go in regulating private sex acts of

---

[67] See, e.g., section 2.17, herein.
[68] "Marriage" is founded on the distinction of sex. B v. B, 78 Misc. 2d 112, 355 N.Y.S.2d 712 (1974). A marriage ceremony between two of the same sex would not result in a "marriage." Jones v. Hallahan, 501 S.W.2d 588, 589, 63 A.L.R.3d 1195 (Ky. App., 1973).
[69] Anonymous v. Anonymous, 67 Misc. 2d 982, 325 N.Y.S.2d 499 (1971). Compare B v. B, 78 Misc. 2d 112, 355 N.Y.S.2d 712 (1974), annulling a marriage where the husband, who had undergone a hysterectomy and a mastectomy, was incapable of performing the functions of a male in the marriage role.
[70] See Jones v. Hallahan, 501 S.W.2d 588, 63 A.L.R.3d 1195 (Ky. App., 1973); Annotation, Marriage between persons of the same sex, 63 A.L.R.3d 1199 (1975).
[71] Baker v. Nelson, 291 Minn. 310, 191 N.W.2d 185 (1971), appeal dismissed 409 U.S. 810, 34 L. Ed. 2d 65, 93 Sup. Ct. 37 (1972).
[72] Singer v. Hara, 11 Wash. App. 247, 522 P.2d 1187 (1974); Same Sex Marriage and the Constitution, 6 U.C.D. L. Rev. 275 (1973); Note, Legalities of Homosexual Marriage, 82 Yale L. J. 573 (1973); Constitutional Aspects of the Homosexual's Right to a Marriage License, 12 J. Family L. 607 (1973).
[73] See Chapter 4, herein.

consenting adults.[74] But the same court has frequently let stand convictions of sodomy under state laws forbidding consenting adults to commit private homosexual acts.[75]

A probable answer is that, unless there is clear evidence of sexual misconduct of a criminal nature, partnerships between persons of the same sex will receive the same treatment accorded heterosexual extramarital partnerships. If the parties acknowledge a criminal association, only the future will tell whether courts will ignore this factor in adjusting the mutual equities of the partners.

2.25. Possible criminal liability

The varieties of sexual misconduct by unmarried cohabitants which might invite criminal prosecution, if only for the reason that the authorities might use them as a weapon where more serious offenses are suspected but cannot be substantiated, deserve consideration.

Crimes that could be involved are multifarious. They embrace, for example, statutory rape (sexual intercourse with a person declared by statute to be beneath the age at which an effective consent can be given), rape by fraud (intercourse obtained under pretense of a marriage), and contributing to the sexual delinquency of a minor.[76] Some states denounce the concealment of a birth or of the death of an illegitimate. There is also feticide (destruction of a fetus), infanticide and, of course, abortion.

Statutes denouncing sodomy, sometimes as "deviate sexual intercourse," or an "abominable and detestable crime against nature," or in even more obscure terms, commonly withstand a challenge of unconstitutionality for vagueness.

---

[74]Eisenstadt v. Baird, 405 U.S. 438, 31 L. Ed. 2d 349, 92 Sup. Ct. 1029 (1972); Griswold v. Connecticut, 381 U.S. 479, 14 L. Ed. 2d 510, 85 Sup. Ct. 1678 (1965). See section 2.25, herein.

[75]E.g., Doe v. Commonwealth's Attorney for City of Richmond, 425 U.S. 901, 47 L. Ed. 2d 751, 96 Sup. Ct. 1489 (1976). See also Cyr v. Walls, 439 F. Supp. 697 (N.D. Tex., 1977).

[76]The crime of *forcible* rape is omitted as being of too collateral a nature.

Statutes denouncing sexual conduct when perpetrated by a male on a female, but which are silent as to female criminality, have thus far withstood challenge. People v. Clark, 85 Mich. App. 96, 270 N.W.2d 717 (1978); State v. Thompson, 162 N.J. Super. 302, 392 A.2d 678 (1978).

RAMIFICATIONS

Other offenses frequently appearing on the statute books are lewd and lascivious cohabitation, fornication, adultery, bigamy, incest, abduction, and seduction under promise of marriage. Statutes denouncing miscegenation, which may or may not involve marriage, although unconstitutional,[77] have not all been repealed.

In the light of recent decisions reflecting a change in the social mores regarding sexual behavior, many of these statutes are of dubious constitutionality. Time and again, it has been argued that it is beyond the function of the state to use the criminal process as a means of legislating the private morals of its inhabitants; that private sexual activity between consenting adults causes no public harm. To this, some have answered that the public harm is indeed there. For example, when two persons of opposite sex live together it would be naive to ignore the likelihood that they share more than the television and the dinner table. This fact cannot but reach the knowledge of impressionable youth. Further, the likelihood of offspring whom an irresponsible couple cannot or will not support places an additional load on the taxpayers. (The response that there are many tax liabilities imposed to finance objectives of which the taxpayer actively disapproves seems hardly adequate.)

Strong as those arguments may appear, they are not universally shared. From across the Atlantic emanates a totally different viewpoint: "Unless a deliberate attempt is made by society, acting through the agency of the law, to equate the sphere of crime with that of sin, there must remain a realm of private morality and immorality which is, in brief and crude terms, not the law's business . . ."[78]

Those responsible for the framing of our own Model Penal Code agree, having deemed it "inappropriate for the government to attempt to control behavior that has no substantial significance except as to the morality of the actor."[79]

---

[77]Loving v. Virginia, 388 U. S. 1, 18 L. Ed. 2d 1010, 87 Sup. Ct. 1817 (1967).
[78]The Wolfenden Report, Report of the Great Britain Committee on Homosexual Offenses and Prostitution, § 61 (1963).
[79]Model Penal Code, Tent. Draft Nos. 1 through 4 (1953), p. 207. (The commissioners did not recommend criminalization of private consensual relations between adults in the final draft of the Code.)

Such matters are best left to religious, educational and other social influences. Apart from the question of constitutionality which might be raised against legislation avowedly commanding adherence to a particular religious or moral tenet, it must be recognized, as a practical matter, that in a heterogeneous community such as ours, different individuals and groups have widely divergent views of the seriousness of various moral derelictions.[80]

The topic has been a matter of voluminous discussion in law reviews.[81] It has already been indicated that recognition of a constitutional right of privacy has had a significant impact on the criminal law, for example in the area of abortion and contraception.[82] California, a state which takes the lead in liberalizing doctrines which have their roots in Christian or Judeo-Christian ethic, has removed criminal sanctions from adultery, and deviate sexual behavior is not punishable except when committed with a minor, or when force is used, or when the participants are confined in specified detention facilities.[83]

A further argument against legislation criminalizing sexual immorality where no public harm is evident is the difficulty of enforcement of such laws. The sheer number of violators stands in the way. This, as it was with the Volstead Act, serves only to engender disrespect for the law. It may well be that, since the existence of penal sanctions can well discourage persons from seeking psychiatric help for their problems, if that is needed, such forms of behavior are better left to religious, educational and other social influences. Moreover, the states have their family courts, their departments of health, welfare and of social services, which are usually better equipped to cope with possible evils from

---

[80]Id.
[81]See, e.g., Cohen, Moral Aspects of the Criminal Law, 49 Yale L. J. 987 (1940); Dworkin, Lord Devlin and the Enforcement of Morals, 75 Yale L. J. 986 (1966); Bedroom Should Not Be Within the Province of the Law, 4 Calif. Western L. Rev. 115 (1968); Hart, Social Solidarity and the Enforcement of Morality, 35 U. Chi. L. Rev. 1 (1967); Raz, Legal Principles and the Limits of Law, 81 Yale L. J. 799, 837 (1972); Sartorius, Enforcement of Morality, 81 Yale L. J. 799, 891 (1972); Skolnick, Coercion to Virtue: The Enforcement of Morals, 41 So. Calif. L. Rev. 588 (1968).
[82]See section 2.19, herein.
[83]See Cal. Penal Code, § 286.

adult sexual behavior which pose an indirect threat to the welfare of the community.

Nevertheless, the statutes are there. They cannot be ignored. Further, by reason of the close association between unmarried partners, the possibility of one incurring criminal liability for the misconduct of the other, totally unrelated to sexual mores, based on theories of accomplice liability or conspiracy cannot be overlooked.

Fornication

Under the common law of England, fornication, like adultery, was regarded as a matter for the ecclesiastical courts and not punishable at law. But many states denounce intercourse outside of marriage. The marital status of the offender depends on the wording of the controlling statute. Examples of the more modern-day judicial approach in these matters are to be found in decisions from New Jersey[84] and New York.[85]

Cohabitation

Illicit cohabitation, too, was not a crime at common law unless open and notorious.[86] As to crimes of this nature, usually punishable as misdemeanor, Perkins comments that the statutes are so poorly enforced that their principal influence seems to be to breed disrespect for law while their chief accomplishment is to furnish opportunities for blackmail.[87] Though the Supreme Court of the United States has indicated that such statutes are not violative of the constitutional right of privacy,[88] this question cannot yet be

---

[84]State v. Saunders, 75 N.J. 200, 381 A.2d 333 (1977), discussed section 6.31, herein.

[85]In re P., 92 Misc. 2d 62, 400 N.Y.S.2d 455 (1977), discussed section 6.33, herein.

[86]See Clark and Marshall, *A Treatise on the Law of Crimes,* p. 766 (7th ed., 1967). An early Kentucky case holds that illicit cohabitation, if known by the community to be taking place, is punishable as a public nuisance. Adams v. Commonwealth, 162 Ky. 76, 171 S.W. 1006 (1915).

[87]Perkins, *Criminal Law,* p. 379 (2d ed., 1969).

[88]Goldberg, J., in Griswold v. Connecticut, 381 U.S. 479, 498, 14 L. Ed. 2d 510, 523, 85 Sup. Ct. 1678, 1689 (1965).

said to have been conclusively resolved.[89] At any rate, such adjectives as "immoral," "lewd," "lascivious" or "indecent" should be eschewed by legislatures as calling for too subjective a standard of application and rendering the statute vulnerable to a challenge of being void for vagueness.[90] The early judicial attitude, that the objective of fornication or cohabitation laws is to prohibit the public scandal of persons of opposite sex living together, an "illicit intimacy" which outrages public decency and can only have a demoralizing and debasing influence,[91] seems on the way out, if not already a museum piece. Yet for the crimes to be punishable, the statutes usually require that the conduct be open and notorious; cohabitation, for example, under an honest belief in the existence of a marriage, even under the older view, would not be punishable unless the behavior is such as scandalizes the public.[92]

The crime against nature

At least seventeen of the states have repealed their consensual sodomy statutes. In those that remain, there is little uniformity as to what types of deviate sexual behavior are denounced and as to the severity of the resulting punishment. Statutes denouncing "the abominable and detestable crime against nature" (an emotionally charged rubric) usually withstand a challenge of unconstitutionality for vagueness if some specific reference is made to oral or anal sex.[93] However, the question as to the extent to which the legislature can constitutionally denounce deviate sexual behavior outside the privacy of a marriage still awaits a definitive answer.[94] In Doe v. Commonwealth's Attorney for

---

[89]See section 2.6, herein.
[90]See Note, Function of Law in the Regulation of Sexual Conduct, 29 Ind. L. Rev. 539 (1954).
[91]See People v. Bright, 77 Colo. 563, 238 Pac. 71 (1925); Landrum v. State, 96 Okla. Crim. 356, 255 P.2d 525 (1953).
[92]See, e.g., Campbell v. State, 331 So. 2d 289 (Fla., 1976); State v. Brooks, 215 Wis. 134, 254 N.W. 374, 94 A.L.R. 401 (1934).
[93]See Wainwright v. Stone, 414 U.S. 21, 38 L. Ed. 2d 179, 94 Sup. Ct. 190 (1973).
[94]See Richards, Unnatural Acts and the Constitutional Right to Privacy: A Moral Theory, 45 Fordham L. Rev. 1281 (1977); Wilkinson and White, Constitutional Protection for Personal Life-styles, 62 Cornell L. Rev. 563 (1977); Comment,

Richmond,[95] a three-judge District Court divided two to one in rejecting a challenge to the state sodomy statute. Justice Bryan declined to express an opinion as to the wisdom or policy of state legislation of this character. At the same time he declined to rule that it offends any constitutional guarantee. He considered that Griswold v. Connecticut,[96] striking down a state statute forbidding the use of contraceptives, was based on the rights of marital privacy. The same rationale, he opined, does not extend to sexual conduct outside of the marital bedchamber. (Virginia has since held that the marital right of privacy does not extend to acts of fellatio by married persons in the presence of spectators.)[97] Quoting from an earlier decision, "adultery, homosexuality and the like," he says, "are sexual intimacies which the State forbids ... but the intimacy of husband and wife is necessarily an essential and accepted feature of the institution of marriage, an institution which the State not only must allow, but which always and in every age it has fostered and protected. It is one thing when the State exerts its power either to forbid extramarital sexuality ... or to say who may marry, but it is quite another when, having acknowledged a marriage and the intimacies inherent in it, it undertakes to regulate by means of the criminal law the details of that intimacy...."

Equally forceful, he added, are the words of Justice Harlan

> ... even though the State has determined that the use of contraceptives is as iniquitous as any act of extramarital sexual immorality, the intrusion of the whole machinery of the criminal law into the very heart of marital privacy, requiring husband and wife to render account before a criminal tribunal of their uses of that intimacy is surely a very different thing indeed from punishing those who establish intimacies which the

---

Constitutionality of Sodomy Statutes, 45 Fordham L. Rev. 553, 592 (1976); Constitutionality of Laws Forbidding Private Homosexual Conduct, 72 Mich. L. Rev. 1613 (1974).

[95] 403 F. Supp. 1199 (E.D. Va., 1975), affd. 425 U.S. 901, 47 L. Ed. 2d 751, 96 Sup. Ct. 1489 (1976), reh. den. 425 U.S. 985, 48 L. Ed. 2d 810, 96 Sup. Ct. 2192 (1976).

[96] 381 U.S. 479, 14 L. Ed. 2d 510, 85 Sup. Ct. 1678 (1965).

[97] Lovisi v. Slayton, 539 F.2d 349 (C.A.-4 Va., 1976), cert. den. 429 U.S. 977, 97 Sup. Ct. 485 (1976).

law has always forbidden and which can have no claim to social protection.[98]

As to homosexual activity, Justice Bryan's view is that if a state determines that punishment therefor, when committed in the home, is appropriate in the promotion of morality and decency, it is not for the courts to say that the state is not free to do so. The state need not show that moral delinquency actually results—a burden virtually impractical to discharge; it is enough to show that such conduct is likely to end in a contribution to moral delinquency.

The inevitable dissent takes the position that private consensual acts between adults are matters, absent evidence that they are harmful, in which the state has no legitimate interest. Illustrative of the dilemma with which all states having statutes denouncing deviate sexual conduct are confronted are decisions from New York,[99] which receive later discussion.[1]

Without hearing argument or giving any reasons, the Supreme Court of the United States summarily affirmed the dismissal of a challenge to the Virginia law.[2] This disposition of the appeal may well lead one to conclude that the Supreme Court has ruled that a state's sodomy laws cannot be attacked as a constitutional violation of one's right to privacy. However, a reading of a later decision of that Court in a contest as to the constitutionality of a state statute restricting the distribution of contraceptives[3] indicates that the justices of the Supreme Court retain their own doubts as to whether indeed such a conclusion must be drawn from the decision.

---

[98] Doe v. Commonwealth's Attorney for City of Richmond, 403 F. Supp. 1199, 1201 (E.D. Va., 1975), affd. 425 U.S. 901, 47 L. Ed. 2d 751, 96 Sup. Ct. 1489 (1976), reh. den. 425 U.S. 985, 48 L. Ed. 2d 810, 96 Sup. Ct. 2192 (1976).

[99] People v. Rice, 87 Misc. 2d 257, 383 N.Y.S.2d 798 (1976), affd. 41 N.Y.2d 1018, 395 N.Y.S.2d 626, 363 N.E.2d 1371 (1977); compare In re P., 92 Misc. 2d 62, 400 N.Y.S.2d 455 (1977).

[1] See section 6.33, herein.

[2] Doe v. Commonwealth's Attorney for City of Richmond, 425 U.S. 901, 47 L. Ed. 2d 751, 96 Sup. Ct. 1489 (1976).

[3] Carey v. Population Services Internat., 431 U.S. 678, 52 L. Ed. 2d 67, 97 Sup. Ct. 2010 (1977).

The debate has excited voluminous attention in the law reviews.[4]

Adultery

In the early law of England, adultery, like fornication, was not a crime.[5] A once accepted view in this country, however, was to the contrary, if the acts were committed so openly and notoriously as to constitute a public scandal or nuisance.[6] (Insofar as concerns civil liability, in addition to affording grounds for divorce, this form of conduct is more commonly actionable as a tortious alienation of affections.)[7] Adultery, unlike fornication, involves an affront to a specific marriage relationship. There is the added danger in that the aggrieved partner may create a breach of the peace in seeking private vengeance. It is common to denounce the crime in terms of open and notorious conduct,[8] due no doubt to a reluctance to denounce as criminal conduct a matter which is largely of private morality.

In some states, a crime is committed only if the female is married, in which case both parties are guilty. In others, only the married participant can be convicted; though the other could be chargeable with fornication. In still other states, both can be convicted of adultery if either of them is married to another.[9]

---

[4]See, in addition to the articles and notes cited in section 2.6, herein, Bernstein, Sexual Freedom v. The People of the State of California, 2 U.S.F.V. L. Rev. 1 (1972); Cantor, Deviation and the Criminal Law, 55 J. Crim. L. 441 (1964); Crimes Against Nature, 16 J. Public L. 159 (1967); Bedroom Should Not Be Within the Province of the Law, 4 Calif. Western L. Rev. 115 (1968); Private Consensual Adult Behavior: The Requirement of Harm to Others in the Enforcement of Morality, 14 U.C.L.A. L. Rev. 581 (1967); Sodomy Statutes—A Need for Change, 13 S.D. L. Rev. 384 (1968); Sodomy—Crime or Sin?, 12 U. Fla. L. Rev. 83 (1959); Notes, Deviate Sexual Behavior: The Desirability of Legislative Proscription, 30 Albany L. Rev. 291 (1966); Criminal Law—Consensual Homosexual Behavior—The Need for Legislative Reform, 57 Ky. L. J. 591 (1969); Criminal Law—Sexual Offenses—Sodomy—Cunnilingus, 8 Natural Resources J. 531 (1968); Constitutional Law—Sodomy Statutes: The Question of Constitutionality, 50 Neb. L. Rev. 567 (1971); Victimless Sex Crimes: To the Devil, Not the Dungeon, 25 U. Fla. L. Rev. 139 (1972).
[5]See Perkins, *Criminal Law*, p. 377 (2d ed., 1969).
[6]See Clark and Marshall, *A Treatise on the Law of Crimes*, p. 768 (7th ed., 1967).
[7]See section 2.20, herein.
[8]See Perkins, *Criminal Law*, pp. 378–379 (2d ed., 1969).
[9]See Chapter 6, herein.

There is also variance as to the nature of the conduct involved. For example, a problem is presented when the parties to a divorce continue to cohabit and the decree is later set aside,[10] and when there is an isolated act of sex, without a continuing course of conduct.[11] Also, there is a question as to whether one who has intercourse with a married person, and his conduct does not constitute adultery, can be guilty of aiding and abetting adultery.[12]

Statutes denouncing adultery as criminal have withstood a variety of constitutional attacks.[13] Among these is the argument that a provision in some of the statutes that only the offended spouse can institute a prosecution is an unlawful delegation by the legislature of executive functions.[14] It seems clear, however, that objections based on rights of privacy, so hotly disputed in the case of cohabitation and fornication, have little merit here. The potential for disruption of the institution of marriage presents an additional factor.

Bigamy

Unless a marriage is entered into by the cohabitants, the crime of bigamy, which ordinarily involves a second marriage by one already married, is not pertinent for consideration. However, in a state where common-law marriages are recognized, a subsequent marriage by one who is already a common-law spouse could present a basis for prosecution.[15]

If a person cohabits with another in the mistaken belief that he

---

[10]See Annotation, Cohabitation under marriage contracted after divorce decree as adultery, where decree is later reversed or set aside, 63 A.L.R.2d 816 (1959).

[11]See Annotation, Isolated acts of sexual intercourse as constituting criminal offense of adultery or fornication or illicit cohabitation, 74 A.L.R. 1361 (1931).

[12]See Annotations, Criminal responsibility of one co-operating in offense which he is incapable of committing personally, 131 A.L.R. 1322 (1941). As to conspiracy to commit adultery—a "concerted action" crime—see 104 A.L.R. 1430 (1936).

[13]See Annotation, Validity of statute making adultery and fornication criminal offenses, 41 A.L.R.3d 1338 (1972). As to an objection that the statute contains less severe penalties for women than for men, see section 6.12, herein.

[14]See State v. Ronek, 176 N.W.2d 153, 41 A.L.R.3d 1329 (Iowa, 1970), upholding the provision on the ground that the purpose was to make allowance for the possibility of a spousal reconciliation, which might be thwarted if the authorities could proceed against the wishes of the aggrieved spouse. As to the right of the injured spouse to discontinue prosecutions for adultery, see 61 A.L.R. 973 (1929).

[15]See 10 Am. Jur. 2d, Bigamy, § 10.

or she is properly divorced (mistake of law) or in the mistaken belief that a former spouse is no longer living (mistake of fact), the question whether that person commits bigamy is one on which courts are divided.[16] Since a similar question could be presented in prosecutions for fornication, lewd cohabitation or adultery, it is worth noting, as the better view, that absent a criminal state of mind such a mistake ought to be a good defense.[17]

Incest

Incest, where statutes have not modified its meaning, is sexual commerce, whether habitual or in a single instance, and either under a form of marriage or without it, between persons too nearly related in consanguinity or affinity to be entitled to intermarry.[18] The forbidden degrees are a matter of statute; they usually apply to illegitimate as well as legitimate relatives.[19] Though statutes dispensing with proof of knowledge of the prohibited relationship have been upheld,[20] it is likely that any legislative attempt to impose strict liability in this area is of dubious constitutionality.

The Model Penal Code follows the prevailing trend by including those related by blood more closely than first cousins. But a relationship of parent and child created by adoption is included.[21] If the rationale for punishing incest is the danger of biological mutations which might occur in the offspring, such inclusion seems

---

[16]Annotations, Mistaken belief in existence, validity, or effect of divorce or separation as defense to prosecution for bigamy or allied offense, 56 A.L.R.2d 915 (1957); Construction and application of statutes which in effect, under prescribed conditions, validate, after removal of impediment, marriage celebrated while a former spouse of one of the parties was living and undivorced, 95 A.L.R. 1292 (1935); Religious belief as affecting crime of bigamy, 24 A.L.R. 1237 (1923); Bigamy as affected by place where second or later marriage is celebrated, 70 A.L.R. 1036 (1931); Conviction or acquittal on charge which includes element of illicit sexual intercourse as bar to prosecution for adultery, 94 A.L.R. 405 (1935).

[17]See, generally, Perkins, *Criminal Law*, pp. 919-948 (2d ed., 1969).

[18]Martin v. State, 266 Ala. 290, 96 So. 2d 298 (1957).

[19]See Annotation, Sexual intercourse between persons related by half blood as incest, 72 A.L.R.2d 706, 707 (1960).

[20]See 41 Am. Jur. 2d, Incest, § 9.

[21]Model Penal Code (U.L.A.), § 230.2 (1974). See also Annotation, Relationship created by adoption as within statute prohibiting marriage between parties in specified relationships, or statute regarding incest, 151 A.L.R. 1146 (1944).

unsound. But if the rationale is the protection of children from abuse of parental authority,[22] or the promotion of domestic peace and cultural traditions,[23] it is justifiable.

Seduction

In addition to possible civil liability,[24] an extramarital cohabitant could face prosecution for seduction. The Model Penal Code does not require that the female be unmarried or chaste but does require a false promise of marriage. It does not provide that a subsequent intermarriage of the parties bars a prosecution.[25]

Statutory rape and related offenses

Important among the criminal statutes relating to offenses against minors of a specified age (which includes the offense of contributing to the delinquency of a minor), is the crime commonly known as statutory rape. This crime is not really "rape," but merely an act of sex with a female other than the defendant's spouse who, by reason of nonage, or in some states mental incapacity of some other sort,[26] is legally incapable of giving consent to the act.[27] The age of consent is a matter for local statute; some states have degrees of severity of the offense determinable by

---

[22] See People v. York, 29 Ill. App. 3d 113, 329 N.E.2d 845 (1975).
[23] See People v. Boyer, 24 Ill. App. 3d 671, 321 N.E.2d 312 (1974), revd. 63 Ill. 2d 433, 349 N.E.2d 50 (1976), cert. den. 429 U.S. 1063, 97 Sup. Ct. 789 (1977).
[24] See sections 2.20, 2.23, herein.
[25] Model Penal Code (U.L.A.), § 213.3 (1974). See Annotations, Presumption and burden of proof as to chastity of prosecutrix in a prosecution for seduction, 64 A.L.R. 265 (1929); Subsequent intermarriage of parties, forgiveness, compromise, etc., as defense to prosecution for seduction, 80 A.L.R. 833 (1932); Facts preventing valid marriage between prosecutrix and defendant as defense in criminal or civil action for seduction, 85 A.L.R. 123 (1933).
[26] Annotation, Rape or similar offense based on intercourse with woman who is allegedly mentally deficient, 31 A.L.R.3d 1227 (1970).
[27] The elements of force, consent and resistance are irrelevant to statutory rape. Drake v. State, 239 Ga. 232, 236 S.E.2d 748 (1977). By the weight of authority, the fact that the female is or was married does not affect her want of capacity as a minor to consent. See Annotations, Statutory rape of female who is or has been married, 32 A.L.R.3d 1030 (1970); Criminal liability for contributing to delinquency of minor by sexually immoral acts as affected by fact that minor was married at time of acts charged, 84 A.L.R.2d 1254 (1962).

reference to the victim's age.[28] When the statute designates the age of consent with the addition of the words "or under," most courts hold the statute to be inapplicable to a victim who has passed the birthday on which such age was arrived at; but when it merely proscribes the act on a victim "between" designated ages, there is little agreement as to its applicability to one who has passed the anniversary date of such age.[29]

Most courts decline to recognize that an honest, reasonable mistake as to the age of the victim is a defense.[30]

Some states have a rape-by-fraud type of statute, covering the situation where the victim is deceived into a valid marriage.

In the light of Meloon v. Helgemoe,[31] very real doubt is cast on the constitutionality of statutes (which are common) which proscribe intercourse with a consenting female below a stated age and are silent as to the criminality of similar conduct where a female is the defendant and the victim is a male. That decision, while acknowledging that under a minimum rationality test a suggestion that there were more potential male than female offenders would justify such a gender-based classification,[32] held that a more stringent test is required where a criminal statute is involved. It requires a state, to justify such a statute notwithstanding the guarantees of equal protection, to show that by concentrating its enforcement resources on the gender class with more potential offenders it is likely to achieve some greater measure of protection for minors than a gender-neutral law would achieve or

---

[28]At least one state raises the age of consent where the actor is the victim's guardian or otherwise responsible for her welfare. See section 6.7, herein (Connecticut).

[29]Annotation, Applicability of criminal statutes relating to offenses against children of a specified age with respect to a child who has passed the anniversary date of such age, 73 A.L.R.2d 874 (1960).

[30]See Annotation, Mistake or lack of information as to victim's age as defense to statutory rape, 8 A.L.R.3d 1100 (1966).

[31]564 F.2d 602 (C.A.-1 N.H., 1977), cert. den.——U.S.——, 98 Sup. Ct. 2858 (1978).

[32]See State v. Elmore, 24 Ore. App. 651, 546 P.2d 1117 (1976). Compare Hall v. McKenzie, 537 F.2d 1232 (C.A.-4 W. Va., 1976). See also Commonwealth v. MacKenzie, —— Mass. ——, 334 N.E.2d 613 (1975), holding that finding father but not mother criminally responsible for birth of illegitimate child violates equal protection; In re Interest of J.D.G., 498 S.W.2d 786 (Mo., 1973), wherein the objection that a statutory rape law discriminates against males on the basis of age and sex withstood objection.

that by protecting a class disproportionately vulnerable to attack it was maximizing its over-all objective of protecting all children from sexual exploitation. (Far from taking judicial notice of the fact that in matters of sex, human as well as animal, it is usually the male who takes the initiative, the court was disposed to think that young boys are just as likely to be victimized by older females on the prowl for sex partners as are young girls by older men.)[33]

The Mann Act

The Mann Act (White Slave Traffic Act)[34] makes criminally punishable a person "who knowingly transports in interstate or foreign commerce . . . any female for the purpose of prostitution or debauchery or for any other immoral purpose . . . or with the intent to induce such female . . . to engage in any other immoral practice."

The primary purpose of the act was to eliminate the traffic in women for commercial vice.[35] However, cases decided thereunder up until the late 1960's show that there were numerous convictions where the interstate transportation was not for commercial purposes. Most of these are of early vintage, or involve situations where there was something more than a mere exchange of personal intimacies.[36] In one of the more recent decisions,[37] involving a casual affair with an unattached and willing woman, the court declined to convict a defendant under this statute. Was this,

---

[33]People v. Mackey, 46 Cal. App. 3d 755, 120 Cal. Rptr. 157 (1975), cert. den. 423 U.S. 951, 46 L. Ed. 2d 287, 96 Sup. Ct. 372 (1975).

[34]18 U.S.C. § 2421.

[35]See Annotation, Construction and application of the word "cause" in provision of White Slave Traffic Act which declares that one who shall knowingly cause a woman or girl to be transported in interstate commerce for purposes of prostitution shall be guilty of an offense, 156 A.L.R. 971 (1945); White Slave Traffic Act (Mann Act) as affecting constitutionality or application of state statutes dealing with prostitution, 161 A.L.R. 356 (1946).

[36]See Annotation, Prosecution under White Slave Traffic Act (18 U.S.C. § 2421) based on interstate transportation not involving commercial vice, 23 A.L.R.3d 423 (1969). See, e.g., Whitt v. United States, 261 F.2d 907 (C.A.-6 Ky., 1959) (conviction upheld for living in marriage relationship, defendant being married to another).

[37]United States v. McClung, 187 F. Supp. 254 (E.D. La., 1960).

the court asks, the evil trafficking the act condemns? Was the girl the "white slave" the act was designed to protect? It is improbable that, whatever the early applications of this statute may have been, a mere crossing of state lines by unmarried cohabitants would render them open to prosecution.[38]

A contention that the statute denies equal protection because it denounces only the transportation of females, and not of males, lacks validity. The Mann Act may be violated by either males or females, and is thus sexually neutral. The fact that the possible victims can only be females does not affect its constitutionality.[39]

2.26. Noncohabitation as a condition of probation

When a person has been convicted of crime, can a court properly condition probation on his or her not living with another person of the opposite sex?

It is firmly recognized that a grant of probation is aimed at re-education or rehabilitation of one convicted of crime, and that its objective should thus be to promote such goals.[40] This being so, it follows that, though a trial court is invested with considerable discretion in determining the terms of probation,[41] a condition which has no connection with the crime of which defendant was convicted can be vacated by a higher court as arbitrary or capricious. The limitations on a court's authority in this respect were fully spelled out by the California Supreme Court in People v. Lent.[42] A condition of probation will be invalid if (i) it has no relationship to the crime of which the offender was convicted, (ii)

---

[38] But see United States v. Bennett, 364 F.2d 77, 23 A.L.R.3d 418 (C.A.-4 S.C., 1966), upholding a conviction where the defendant's intent was only to have intercourse with the woman if she would respond to his advances.

[39] United States v. Green, 554 F.2d 372 (C.A.-9 Wash., 1977) (also holding that the mere fact that an interstate transportation ends in prostitution is not enough to convict a defendant of causing a female to be transported for the "purpose" of prostitution).

[40] 21 Am. Jur. 2d, Criminal Law, § 565.

[41] See United States v. Smith, 414 F.2d 630 (C.A.-5 Tex., 1969), revd. sub. nom. Schacht v. United States, 398 U.S. 58, 26 L. Ed. 2d 44, 90 Sup. Ct. 1555 (1970); United States v. Consuelo-Gonzales, 521 F.2d 259 (C.A.-9 Cal., 1975); In re Schoengarth, 66 Cal. 2d 295, 57 Cal. Rptr. 600, 425 P.2d 200 (1967).

[42] 15 Cal. 3d 481, 124 Cal. Rptr. 905, 541 P.2d 545 (1975).

it relates to conduct which is not in itself criminal, and (iii) it requires or forbids conduct which is not reasonably related to future criminality.[43]

In line with this reasoning, if a defendant's relationship with another is viewed by the trial court as clearly a factor in misbehavior that has resulted in his or her conviction of assault, a condition of probation that defendant stay away from that person would in all likelihood be sustained even though associating with that other person is not in itself criminal.[44] Similarly, if the crime was committed in close concert with some other individual a condition that defendant refrain from consorting further with that person could well be unobjectionable.[45]

In People v. Dominguez,[46] on the other hand, an appellate court rejected a probationary condition prohibiting a woman convicted of second degree robbery from cohabiting or becoming pregnant until she was married. The court found no rational basis to believe that cohabitation, or pregnancy out of wedlock, led to future crimes and declared that "becoming pregnant while unmarried is a misfortune, not a crime."[47]

An Ohio Appellate Court viewed a similar probationary condition as an impermissible burden on constitutional rights and privileges. In State v. Livingston[48] a twenty-year-old unmarried woman was convicted of child abuse and, as a condition of probation, was prohibited from becoming pregnant for five years. That court recognized the broad discretion reposed in a trial court in the matter, but emphasized that a court "is not free to impose arbitrary conditions that significantly burden the defendant in the exercise of her liberty."[49] The condition was struck down as an invasion of her constitutional right to privacy.

In Mays v. State[50] a Florida court upheld, as a condition of

---

[43] Id., 15 Cal. 3d at 486, 124 Cal. Rptr. at 908, 541 P.2d at 548.
[44] See Willis v. United States, 250 A.2d 569 (D.C. App., 1969).
[45] See Edwards v. State, 74 Wis. 2d 79, 246 N.W.2d 109 (1976). Annotation, Propriety of conditioning probation or suspended sentence on defendant's refraining from political activity, protest or the like, 45 A.L.R.3d 1022 (1972).
[46] 256 Cal. App. 2d 623, 64 Cal. Rptr. 290 (1967).
[47] Id., 256 Cal. App. 2d at 627, 64 Cal. Rptr. at 293.
[48] 53 Ohio App. 2d 195, 372 N.E.2d 1335 (1976).
[49] Id., 372 N.E.2d at 1337.
[50] 349 So. 2d 792 (Fla. App., 1977).

probation for a person convicted of second degree burglary, a requirement that he not live with a female unless married. Although the court modified the decree to allow the probationer to reside with female relatives, the general prohibition against cohabitation was deemed valid despite the fact that this condition bore no relationship to the crime of which he was convicted. This decision can only be condemned as completely out of line with the established doctrine and inconsistent with the avowed objectives of the institution of probation. Such a condition of probation, if ever it can be proper, could not reasonably be so regarded where the crime of which a defendant has been convicted has no conceivable relation to his or her sexual activities.

CHAPTER 3

STATUS OF CHILDREN OF RELATIONSHIP

Section
3.1 Traditional common-law approach to legitimacy
3.2 Impact of the Constitution on the common-law approach
3.3 Constitutional impact on inheritance and intestacy statutes
3.4 Establishment of paternity
3.5 Right of illegitimate child to support
3.6 Rights to custody and visitation
3.7 Legitimation
3.8 Adoption and the rights of the biological parents

3.1. Traditional common-law approach to legitimacy

Of old, it was said that the "bastard, like the prostitute, thief, and beggar, belongs to that motley crowd of disreputable social types which society has generally resented, always endured. He is a living symbol of social irregularity, and undeniable evidence of contra-moral forces; in short, a problem—a problem as old and unsolved as human existence itself."[1]

An Ohio judge, in ruling on the claim of a father of an illegitimate child for custody, saw fit to discuss, as a matter of historical interest, "one of the most cherished privileges of males of the upper socio-economic classes," namely, "the time honored pastime of 'wenching'."[2]

The participants in this sport have traditionally been protected by both the common law and statute law. In essence, the law has traditionally denigrated the mother of an illegitimate child; branded and banished the child from any claim of birthrights from and through the father including name and fortune. The pattern is woven throughout recorded history from ancient Rome to Kent to South Africa to Natchez.

In preserving and protecting this practice for men of the upper socio-economic classes, the law also fostered and indeed

---

[1] Davis, Illegitimacy and the Social Structure, 45 Am. J. Soc. 215 (1939).
[2] In re Wright, 52 Ohio Misc. 4, 367 N.E.2d 931, 933 (1977).

encouraged bastardy among the poor. Recent reexamination of this question tends to recognize the inequities as well as social detriment caused such legal treatment of children born out of wedlock.[3]

The judge then quoted from two law review articles[4] which are critical of a tendency in modern states to permit a biological[5] father little say in the matter of the custody of his progeny. As will be seen, decisions of the Supreme Court of the United States have done much to alleviate this situation.[6]

The judge's observations serve as an appropriate introduction to the traditional doctrines espoused by early Anglo-American courts controlling the status of the illegitimate child. Such a child was a *filius nullius,* a child of no one. Its parents owed it no obligation of support.[7] It had no inheritance rights from either parent. Only the issue of its body could inherit from it. There were no statutes providing for its legitimation, either by establishing paternity, by acknowledgment, or by subsequent marriage of its parents. Adoption was unknown.[8]

Since those early days, state statutes have done much to better the lot of the illegitimate, and the Supreme Court of the United States, mainly through application of the equal protection provisions of the Constitution, has made gigantic strides in the direction of equating the status of illegitimates with that of

---

[3]Id. The rationale against the granting of any title of nobility by the United States would equally prohibit a badge of ignobility by reason of birth out of wedlock. Eskra v. Morton, 524 F.2d 9 (C.A.-7 Wis., 1975).

[4]Marcus, Equal Protection: The Custody of the Illegitimate Child, 11 J. Family L. 1, 47 (1971); Tabler, Paternal Rights in the Illegitimate Child: Some Legitimate Complaints on Behalf of the Unwed Father, 11 J. Family L. 231, 252, 254 (1971).

[5]The term "biological" is preferred to the term "natural" parent because it is more precise. Natural parent is sometimes used to denote the legal parent of a child who has been adopted out.

[6]See section 3.6, herein. See also Note, Constitutional Law—Equal Protection of Illegitimate Children, 17 Loyola L. Rev. 170 (1970–71).

[7]Baby X. v. Misiano, —— Mass. ——, 366 N.E.2d 755 (1977), holding that an illegitimate child has no common-law right to support from its putative father; any right the mother has to recover for pregnancy and confinement expenses is purely statutory.

[8]See Helmholz, Support Orders, Church Courts, and the Rule of *Filius Nullius:* A Reassessment of Common Law, 63 Va. L. Rev. 431 (1977).

legitimates. In addition to the rights to succession on the intestacy of the parents, which has been the subject of numerous rulings of the Supreme Court over the past decade, the Court has had occasion to pronounce on the constitutionality, inter alia, of state laws denying support obligations of a biological parent,[9] laws denying workers' compensation and similar benefits to illegitimates,[10] and laws denying a remedy for wrongful death to illegitimates.[11]

Indirectly, these developments have a bearing on a more basic question, namely, to what extent does the law regard an illegitimate child as a "child" when that term is used in instruments which the courts are required to construe. The word "child," in its most general sense, denotes the biological progeny of human parents. Whether or not it embraces illegitimate children depends on the context in which the word is used. When the term "children" is used to denote the beneficiaries of a life insurance policy, there is a want of consensus as to whether illegitimate children are to be included.[12] If, to pose an extreme example, a bachelor were to bequeath all his goods to his "children," and he dies leaving only illegitimate children, it is, to say the least, unlikely that the courts will construe the term to embrace only legitimate children. However, when used in a will or deed, the usual construction is that illegitimate children were not intended by the testator or

---

[9]See section 3.5, herein.
[10]See section 2.13, herein.
[11]Levy v. Louisiana, 391 U.S. 68, 20 L. Ed. 2d 436, 88 Sup. Ct. 1509 (1968), reh. den. 393 U.S. 898, 21 L. Ed. 2d 185, 89 Sup. Ct. 65 (1968).
[12]See, e.g., Cooper v. Melvin, 223 Ga. 239, 154 S.E.2d 373 (1967), holding the word "children" not to embrace illegitimates as included in a group life insurance policy covering the distribution of the proceeds in the absence of designated beneficiaries; Unborn Child v. Evans, —— Minn. ——, 245 N.W.2d 600 (1976) (illegitimates not within group life policy's substitute beneficiary clause); Compare Green v. Green, 365 A.2d 610 (D.C. App., 1976) (illegitimates within definition of "children" in substitute beneficiary clause of Federal Group Life Insurance Act); In re Estate of R.L.B., 259 So. 2d 206 (Fla. App., 1972) (fact that insured's acknowledgment of paternity was not written did not preclude illegitimate from taking proceeds payable to his estate); Samuels v. Aetna Life Ins. Co., 48 Mich. App. 761, 211 N.W.2d 104 (1973) ("unmarried child" within group life policy embraced illegitimate child raised by employee); Annotation, Insurance: Term "children" as used in beneficiary clause of life insurance policy as including illegitimate child, 62 A.L.R.3d 1329 (1975); Haley v. Metropolitan Life Ins. Co., 434 S.W.2d 7 (Mo. App., 1968), holding an illegitimate to be a "child" within Federal Employees Life Insurance Act.

grantor.[13] A fortiori, if for example the words "children lawfully begotten of their bodies" are employed, illegitimates would be excluded.[14] Similarly, when the words "child" or "children" appear in a statute, such words are usually interpreted in the sense in which they are used in legal and common parlance, and refer to children begotten in lawful wedlock, whether born before or after the death of the father, or begotten out of wedlock but subsequently legitimized by some method known to the law of the state involved.[15] Thus, it was at one time held that illegitimate children are not beneficiaries of a decedent entitled under the Federal Employers Liability Act to any recovery for the death of a decedent so employed.[16] On some occasions, the courts have used as a test the question "would such a person qualify under the controlling laws of intestacy?"[17]

---

[13]See Byers v. Womack, 367 F.2d 816, 818 (C.A.-7 Ind., 1966); McManus v. Lollar, 36 Misc. 2d 1046, 235 N.Y.S.2d 61 (1962); Pasley v. State, 215 Ga. 768, 113 S.E.2d 454 (1960); but compare Uniform Parentage Act of 1973 (U.L.A.), which gives to illegitimates equal parity to legitimates when a gift is made to a class, such as "my children." If a state has not enacted this statute it may well have achieved a qualified but similar result by having adopted § 2–611 of the Uniform Probate Code (U.L.A.), whereunder a person born out of wedlock is treated as legitimate for the purposes of class gift terminology if, inter alia, such person is openly and notoriously treated by the male progenitor as his child. See Annotations, Right of illegitimate child to take under testamentary gift to "children," 34 A.L.R.2d 4 (1954); Right of illegitimate to take under testamentary gift to "heirs," 27 A.L.R.2d 1232 (1953).

Often the word "child," as used in a will, is not construed to include adopted children absent clear indications of a contrary testamentary intent. See, e.g., Baker v. Giffrow, 257 Iowa 929, 135 N.W.2d 629 (1965); a fortiori is this so if the child was adopted after the death of the testator. See In re Uihlein's Estate, 269 Wis. 170, 68 N.W.2d 816 (1955). Compare Prince v. Nugent, 93 R.I. 149, 172 A.2d 743 (1961), construing a trust instrument to include adopted child of beneficiary and as such entitled to benefits on beneficiary's death.

[14]E.g., Byers v. Womack, 367 F.2d 816 (C.A.-7 Ind., 1966).

[15]See Cruz v. Gardner, 375 F.2d 453 (C.A.-7 Wis., 1967), cert. den. 389 U.S. 886, 88 Sup. Ct. 160 (1967); Hunt v. United States Steel Corp., 274 Ala. 328, 148 So. 2d 618 (1963).

[16]See Bowen v. New York Cent. R. Co., 179 F. Supp. 225 (D. Mass., 1959); but compare Hebert v. Petroleum Pipe Inspectors, Inc., 396 F.2d 237 (C.A.-5 La., 1968); Smith v. Clark Sherwood Oil Field Contractors, 457 F.2d 1339 (C.A.-5 La., 1972), cert. den. 409 U.S. 980, 34 L. Ed. 2d 243, 93 Sup. Ct. 308 (1972), holding (since Levy v. Louisiana, discussed in section 3.2, herein) "children" to embrace illegitimates.

[17]Where an illegitimate child had been acknowledged in writing by his father pursuant to statute and was entitled to inherit his father's estate, he fell within the term for the purposes of a statute giving a deceased author's child the right to

When "child" is used in a statute to denote a class of persons the law is designed to protect from harm, a more enlightened construction (which, as will become evident, is likely to be adopted more and more as time goes by) embraces all persons below a particular age, regardless of legitimacy. Thus, "children," used in a statute conferring jurisdiction on a court to enforce support obligations owed to minors, includes illegitimate children.[18] Under similar reasoning, a statute providing that the issue of parents whose marriage is null in law shall nevertheless be legitimate has a "benign and benevolent purpose," and must be liberally construed; the word "marriage" as used therein is interpreted to mean a de facto marriage, a purported marriage or an informal marriage.[19]

The presumption that a child born to a woman who is married at the time of conception or birth is legitimate[20] may well have its impact in the area of unwed cohabitations. A child who cannot prove a marriage, either legal or putative, between the mother and the person claimed to be the father, or facts creating a presumption of marriage, is not entitled to the benefit of such presumption and has the burden of proving legitimacy.[21] However,

---

renew or extend copyrights. De Sylva v. Ballentine, 351 U.S. 570, 100 L. Ed. 1415, 76 Sup. Ct. 974 (1956).

It has been held that a child of employee, within the meaning of the Railroad Retirement Act providing for annuities to child or to widow having child in her care, must be one who would inherit employee's property if he died intestate. Minefield v. Railroad Retirement Bd., 217 F.2d 786 (C.A.-5 La., 1954). But this is of dubious authority. See section 3.2, herein.

[18]Johnson v. Johnson, 117 App. D.C. 6, 324 F.2d 884 (1963).

[19]Santill v. Rossetti, 87 Ohio Abs. 400, 178 N.E.2d 633, 640 (1961).

[20]See, e.g., People ex rel. Smith v. Cobb, 33 Ill. App. 3d 68, 337 N.E.2d 313 (1975); Schenectady County Dept. of Social Services v. Hilvan R. R., 57 App. Div. 2d 688, 394 N.Y.S.2d 71 (1977), holding that the fact that petitioner's husband had briefly visited his children and brought them baskets on Easter Sunday did not constitute a "possibility of access," and thus a finding of nonaccess in a paternity suit could be made and the presumption of legitimacy rebutted.

[21]See Succession of Matte, 346 So. 2d 1345 (La. App., 1977), holding that absent evidence that the child's mother had any kind of intimate relationship with the putative father shortly before or after the child's birth, evidence that at the time of the birth the mother began living with another man and used his last name, as did the child, that the child retained the name of that man even after she and the mother began living with the putative father, and that the child decided to take the name of the putative father only when she sought a marriage license and obtained a baptism certificate was insufficient to show the child to be the acknowledged daughter of the putative father.

the children of a marriage which is not regarded as void, but which can be or has been annulled, are not generally regarded as illegitimate.[22] The policy of the law is to favor legitimacy; thus children born of a putative marriage[23] or of a common-law marriage in a state recognizing this institution,[24] are not illegitimate.

In the light of the modern uprootings of ice-age dogma in the area of choice of law, there is vast disharmony on the question as to what law governs (as precluding, permitting or creating) the attainment of the full status of legitimacy. Support can be found for at least five different theories: (1) the law of the domicile of the father at the time of the birth of the child; (2) the law of the domicile of the father at the time of his legitimating acts; (3) the law of the domicile of the father at the place where the legitimating acts occurred; (4) the law of the domicile of the child (ordinarily that of its custodial parent) at birth; and (5) the law of the situs of property, succession to which depends on the status of legitimacy in that jurisdiction.[25] In view of the recent tendency of the courts to resolve all such problems in favor of equality for the illegitimate, it is likely that the courts will adopt whichever of these theories achieves that result.

Problems can arise where some policy of the forum is contrary to the law of the jurisdiction where the child allegedly acquired legitimacy; or where the foreign law confers on the child only a right to inherit and not a full status of legitimacy; or where the child has become a recognized natural child (in a civil law state such as Louisiana) so that he can inherit from the father but is

---

[22]See, e.g., Gibson v. Gibson, 207 Va. 821, 153 S.E.2d 189 (1967); Annotation, Presumption of legitimacy of child born after annulment, divorce or separation, 46 A.L.R.3d 158 (1972).

[23]See section 1.6, herein.

[24]See section 1.5, herein.

[25]In re Lund's Estate, 26 Cal. 2d 472, 159 P.2d 643, 162 A.L.R. 606 (1945); Succession of Goss, 304 So. 2d 704 (La. App., 1974), cert. den. 423 U.S. 869, 46 L. Ed. 2d 99, 96 Sup. Ct. 133 (1975); Fuss v. Fuss, —— Mass. ——, 368 N.E.2d 271 (1977); In re Estate of Sherman, 76 Misc. 2d 551, 351 N.Y.S.2d 570 (1974); Shelby County v. Williams, 510 S.W.2d 73 (Tenn., 1974); Annotations, What law, in point of time, governs inheritance from or through adopted person, 52 A.L.R.2d 1228 (1957); Conflict of laws as to contract to adopt, 81 A.L.R.2d 1128 (1962); Conflict of laws as to legitimacy or legitimation or as to rights of illegitimates, as affecting descent and distribution of decedents' estates, 73 A.L.R. 941 (1931), 87 A.L.R.2d 1274 (1963).

not fully legitimated. Here again, modern judicial attitudes are likely to favor an answer which gives the child the full status of legitimacy, no matter how such status may be qualified in the state where it was allegedly legitimated.[26]

3.2. Impact of the Constitution on the common-law approach

The Supreme Court of the United States has recently done much under the equal protection clause of the Fourteenth Amendment to invalidate the arbitrary distinctions once drawn between legitimate and illegitimate children.[27] There is also some suggestion that a denial of rights based purely on a status (illegitimacy) would be a denial of due process.[28]

Classifications based on illegitimacy, though not subject to the "strictest scrutiny" test,[29] where in the state must show a compelling state interest before it can constitutionally discriminate between persons,[30] are nonetheless subject to a scrutiny which is

---

[26] Ester, Illegitimate Children and Conflict of Laws, 36 Ind. L. J. 163 (1961).

[27] As to the rights of unwed partners and their progeny in respect of social security and akin welfare benefits, see section 2.11, herein. See also Gray and Rudovsky, Court Acknowledges the Illegitimate: Levy v. Louisiana and Glona v. American Guarantee & Liability Insurance Co., 181 U. Pa. L. Rev. 1 (1969); Krause, Legitimate and Illegitimate Offspring of Levy v. Louisiana—First Decisions on Equal Protection and Paternity, 36 U. Chi. L. Rev. 338 (1969); Krause, Equal Protection for the Illegitimate, 65 Mich. L. Rev. 477 (1967); Rights of Illegitimates Under Federal Statutes, 76 Harv. L. Rev. 337 (1962); Equal Protection, 82 Harv. L. Rev. 1065 (1969); Annotation, Discrimination on basis of illegitimacy as denial of constitutional rights, 38 A.L.R.3d 613 (1971).

[28] See Miller v. Laird, 349 F. Supp. 1034 (D. D.C., 1972), holding a provision of the Dependents' Medical Care Act denying medical care to dependent illegitimate children of military personnel to be a denial of due process. See also Gray and Rudovsky, note 27, supra; Note, Constitutional Law—Due Process and Equal Protection—Classifications Based on Illegitimacy, 1973 Wis. L. Rev. 908.

[29] Underlying all suspect classifications, as to which the "strictest scrutiny" test is applied, is the stigma of inferiority and second-class citizenship association with them. See Tyrrell v. City & County of San Francisco, 69 Cal. App. 3d 876, 138 Cal. Rptr. 504 (1977).

[30] See Notes, Constitutional Law—A Less Than Most Exacting Scrutiny for Illegitimates, 42 Mo. L. Rev. 444 (1977); Constitutional Law—Equal Protection and the Inheritance Rights of Illegitimates Under Intestate Succession Laws, 43 Mo. L. Rev. 116 (1978).

by no means "toothless."[31] The most widely accepted doctrine is that such a classification is vulnerable on equal protection grounds if it does not demonstrate that the legislation has a rational relationship to a legitimate state objective.[32] The objective need not constitute a "compelling" state interest.[33] However, as will be seen from the discussion of statutes restricting the inheritance rights of illegitimates[34] it is not always easy to say whether a statute does have this magical "rational relationship" to a legitimate governmental objective. In the landmark case, Jimenez v. Weinberger,[35] a provision of the federal Social Security Act which, for the purpose of determining a child's eligibility for benefits, divided illegitimates born after the wage earner's disability into two classes, one of which could qualify for benefits without any showing of dependency and the other of which was conclusively denied benefits, was held constitutionally infirm as having no rational relation to the legitimate governmental interest in preventing spurious claims. On the other hand, provisions of the same statute requiring certain classes of illegitimates to prove dependency as a prerequisite to recovery for such benefits, while others were presumed to be dependent, have been upheld.[36] It is true that by reasons of the statutory

---

[31]See Secretary of Commonwealth v. City Clerk of Lowell, —— Mass. ——, 366 N.E.2d 717 (1977); In re Minor of Martin, 51 Ohio App. 2d 21, 365 N.E.2d 892 (1977), holding that a statute which denies an opportunity to be legitimated to some because the father does not choose to initiate such procedures denies equal protection.
[32]Levy v. Louisiana, 391 U.S. 68, 20 L. Ed. 2d 436, 88 Sup. Ct. 1509 (1968), reh. den. 393 U.S. 898, 21 L. Ed. 2d 185, 89 Sup. Ct. 65 (1968); Labine v. Vincent, 401 U.S. 532, 28 L. Ed. 2d 288, 91 Sup. Ct. 1017 (1971), reh. den. 402 U.S. 990, 29 L. Ed. 2d 156, 91 Sup. Ct. 1672 (1971); Weber v. Aetna Cas. & Surety Co., 406 U.S. 164, 31 L. Ed. 2d 768, 92 Sup. Ct. 1400 (1972); Gomez v. Perez, 409 U.S. 535, 35 L. Ed. 2d 56, 93 Sup. Ct. 872 (1973); New Jersey Welfare Rights Organization v. Cahill, 411 U.S. 619, 36 L. Ed. 2d 543, 93 Sup. Ct. 1700 (1973); Jimenez v. Weinberger, 417 U.S. 628, 41 L. Ed. 2d 363, 94 Sup. Ct. 2496 (1974); Annotation, Supreme Court's view as to the status and rights of illegitimate children, 41 L. Ed. 2d 1228 (1975).
[33]Weber v. Aetna Cas. & Surety Co., 406 U.S. 164, 31 L. Ed. 2d 768, 92 Sup. Ct. 1400 (1972).
[34]See section 3.3, herein.
[35]417 U.S. 628, 41 L. Ed. 2d 363, 94 Sup. Ct. 2496 (1974). See also section 2.11, herein; Annotation, Social Security Act scheme denying illegitimate children benefits from parents' disability insurance, 41 L. Ed. 2d 363 (1975).
[36]Mathews v. Lucas, 427 U.S. 495, 49 L. Ed. 2d 651, 96 Sup. Ct. 2755 (1976).

presumptions of dependency set forth it is possible that some persons who are not in fact dependent might qualify for benefits, but the Court felt the likelihood is the other way.

> Such presumptions in aid of administrative functions, though they may approximate, rather than precisely mirror, the results that case-by-case adjudication would show, are permissible under the Fifth Amendment, so long as that lack of precise equivalence does not exceed the bounds of substantiality tolerated by the applicable level of scrutiny.[37]

The Court reasoned that the dollars lost to any such overincluded recipients (because they fell within one of the presumptions though not actually dependents) might well be exceeded by administrative expenses if each claim had to be examined separately and proof of actual dependency furnished. In other words, the Court was not particularly concerned as to whether the statutory presumptions, relieving certain classes of illegitimates from the burden of establishing their dependency on the wage earner, were wise. It held that the government had a legitimate objective in enacting them (cutting administrative costs); therefore, even though the net result was to place those illegitimates who did not fall within the presumptions under a slight disadvantage, the statute was not unconstitutional. The dissent, expressed by Justice Stevens, would seem to indicate that the "scrutiny" classifications based on illegitimacy should be as "exacting" as where discrimination based on race and sex are involved.[38]

Applicability of wrongful death statutes to illegitimates

Not very long ago there was little unanimity among the states as to whether an illegitimate child could claim the right under a wrongful death statute to recover for the death of its mother. For the wrongful causing of the death of its father, most courts denied

---

[37] Id., Blackmun, J., 427 U.S. at 509, 96 Sup. Ct. at 2764.
[38] Id., 427 U.S. at 516 et seq. See Note, Mathews v. Lucas: A Setback in the Illegitimate's Quest for Equality Under the Law, 16 J. Family L. 37 (1977), criticizing the decision as ill-conceived "and a result of a tradition of considering illegitimates as less than full-fledged citizens."

any such right.[39] But times have changed. In 1968 a Washington court construed its statute to permit such a child to recover,[40] suggesting that there could be no valid social reason for construing the statute in a discriminatory fashion. Virginia, too, has so construed its wrongful death statute.[41]

In Levy v. Louisiana,[42] the Supreme Court of the United States took the same position. The legitimacy of a plaintiff victim has no relevance to the nature of the injury resulting in the death of its parent. To permit a legitimate child an action, and to deny it to an illegitimate, would be an invidious discrimination and violative of the equal protection clause of the Constitution. (However, since the state of Louisiana recognizes different types of illegitimates, reference should be made to section 6.19 herein for more detailed consideration of the status of children born out of wedlock in that state.)[43] In Glona v. American Guarantee & Liability Insurance Company,[44] the Supreme Court applied the same rule to permit a mother an action under the wrongful death statute for the death of her child, notwithstanding the latter's illegitimacy. The Court could find no possible rational basis for assuming that illegitimacy would be encouraged by a recognition of such right.

A year later, a New York court held unconstitutional a statute which permitted recovery by an illegitimate for the wrongful death of its mother but denied such recovery for the father's death.[45] The court conceded that it might be possible to find some rational purpose in excluding illegitimates in a statute controlling succession on intestacy, but held that to make the qualification for recovery for the wrongful death of a putative father

---

[39]Annotation, Right of recovery, under wrongful death statute, for benefit of illegitimate child or children of decedent, 72 A.L.R.2d 1235 (1960).
[40]Armijo v. Wesselius, 73 Wash. 2d 716, 440 P.2d 471 (1968).
[41]See section 6.50, herein.
[42]391 U.S. 68, 20 L. Ed. 2d 436, 88 Sup. Ct. 1509 (1968), reh. den. 393 U.S. 898, 21 L. Ed. 2d 185, 89 Sup. Ct. 65 (1968).
[43]In Succession of Vincent, 229 So. 2d 449 (La. App., 1969), affd. 401 U.S. 532, 28 L. Ed. 2d 288, 91 Sup. Ct. 1017 (1971), reh. den. 402 U.S. 990, 91 Sup. Ct. 1672 (1971), the court stated that it did not accept Levy and Glona as deciding more than that wrongful death statutes should be construed to permit illegitimates to recover.
[44]391 U.S. 73, 20 L. Ed. 2d 441, 88 Sup. Ct. 1515 (1968), reh. den. 393 U.S. 898, 21 L. Ed. 2d 185, 89 Sup. Ct. 66 (1968).
[45]In re Estate of Ortiz, 60 Misc. 2d 756, 303 N.Y.S.2d 806 (1969).

depend on whether plaintiff was qualified to succeed to such person on intestacy would be an irrational discrimination. New Jersey has taken the same position.[46]

Would a statute which denies to a parent the right to recover for the wrongful death of its illegitimate child be unconstitutional? Since much of the judicial reasoning behind the decisions invalidating laws that discriminate against illegitimates, expressly or implicitly, rests on the fact that the illegitimate had no say in the matter of his coming into existence, it could be argued that discrimination of this nature between married and unmarried parents is not "invidious." But Glona holds that the mother can sue. Another Louisiana case holds that the father cannot recover where, at the time of conception and birth, the mother was living with the father but remained married to another.[47] On the other hand, a Florida court has held that to recognize the right of a mother to sue in these cases and to deny it to the biological father would be unconstitutional.[48] Probably an action by the latter would be a rarity because the wrongful death statutes usually purport to cover pecuniary loss sustained by the plaintiff, and such persons are more likely to sustain pecuniary liabilities than losses.

Incidentally, there is no irrational denial of equal protection in construing a wrongful death statute, where it applies to parents, to be restricted to the parents of *born* children, whether or not legitimate.[49]

---

[46] Schmoll v. Creecy, 54 N.J. 194, 254 A.2d 525, 38 A.L.R.3d 605 (1969). See Annotation, Right of illegitimate child, after Levy v. Louisiana, to recover under wrongful death statute for death of putative father, 78 A.L.R.3d 1230 (1977).

[47] George v. Bertrand, 217 So. 2d 47 (La. App., 1968), writ refused 253 La. 647, 219 So. 2d 177 (1969), cert. den. 396 U.S. 974, 24 L. Ed. 2d 443, 90 Sup. Ct. 439 (1969).

[48] Wilcox v. Jones, 346 So. 2d 1037 (Fla. App., 1977). See Note, Domestic Relations—State Statute May Not Forbid a Putative Father from Suing for the Wrongful Death of His Illegitimate Child, 22 Buffalo L. Rev. 1111 (1973).

[49] Tyrrell v. City & County of San Francisco, 69 Cal. App. 3d 876, 138 Cal. Rptr. 504 (1977), wherein the court observes that California's Code of Civil Procedure, § 377 gives a cause of action to survivors for pecuniary loss only. Mental anguish is not an element of damages, and the likelihood of pecuniary loss prior to birth is sufficiently minimal to justify a rational drawing of the line to exclude prebirth losses.

As to the status of illegitimate children under state workers' compensation laws, see section 2.13, herein.

3.3. Constitutional impact on inheritance and intestacy statutes

Under the early English common law, an illegitimate child could not be the heir of anyone.[50] In this country, this disability to inherit from its biological parents has been relaxed or removed by various state statutes. It is common, for example, for a statute to permit an illegitimate child to inherit by intestacy if its parents have since married (even if the attempted marriage is void), or if the father's paternity has been judicially established or acknowledged.[51] Such statutes have at times been regarded as derogatory of the common law and hence strictly construed.[52] Other courts, concerned with the public policy disfavoring discrimination against an innocent class, have construed the statutes liberally.[53]

It has long been recognized that a statute which, in plain, unambiguous language, *qualifies* an illegitimate to succeed on intestacy will encounter no difficulty of application. Though in derogation of the common law, this is a matter exclusively of state cognizance, and the courts, whatever their views as to the social desirability of such legislation, will not interfere.[54] The difficulty is that statutes of this nature usually condition the right of the illegitimate to succeed on intestacy on some such factor as legitimation, or written acknowledgment of paternity, or the like. As

---

[50]See, e.g., Jones v. Jones, 234 U.S. 615, 58 L. Ed. 1500, 34 Sup. Ct. 937 (1914). Annotation, Inheritance by, from, or through illegitimate, 24 A.L.R. 570 (1923), 60 A.L.R.2d 1182 (1958).

[51]See Annotation, What amounts to recognition within statutes affecting the status or rights of illegitimates, 33 A.L.R.2d 705 (1954).

[52]Annotation, Inheritance from illegitimate, 48 A.L.R.2d 759 (1956).

[53]American courts tend to construe a testamentary gift to "children," if there is no statutory limitation on the amounts a testator can bequeath, to embrace illegitimates. See Annotation, Right of illegitimate child to take under testamentary gift to "children," 34 A.L.R.2d 4 (1954). Some states restrict the right of a parent to devise or bequeath property to illegitimate children, at least where there are legitimate descendants or a lawful spouse. See id., at 48. A statute which prohibits natural parents from bequeathing property to an adulterously conceived illegitimate child has been held unconstitutional. Succession of Robins, 349 So. 2d 276 (La., 1977). See also Note, From Levy to Robins: Equal Protection for Adulterous Illegitimates, 3 So. U. L. Rev. 287 (1977). In the final analysis, whether a gift to "heirs," "blood relations" or the like embraces illegitimates is a question of construction. See Annotation, Right of illegitimate to take under testamentary gift to "heirs," 27 A.L.R.2d 1232 (1953).

[54]See Cope v. Cope, 137 U.S. 682, 34 L. Ed. 832, 11 Sup. Ct. 222 (1891).

indicated in the preceding section, the Supreme Court of the United States, in its concern for equal protection when rights involve social security benefits, or the right to sue for wrongful death or for workers' compensation benefits, have required at least a showing that conditions imposed on an illegitimate claimant bear some rational relationship to a legitimate state objective. In Mathews v. Lucas[55] the Court considered and rejected an argument that classifications based on illegitimacy are "suspect" so that any state justification for difference in treatment must survive "strict scrutiny."[56] The Court concluded such classifications to be in a realm of less than strict scrutiny. This newer middle scrutiny would require a state to articulate its legislative purpose. Then the burden is on those challenging such a statute to show that it bears no rational relationship to a legitimate governmental interest.

When, however, the condition is a prerequisite to a child's recovery as an intestate successor, this "scrutiny" appears to have been less strict.[57] For example, in Labine v. Vincent[58] the Supreme Court held it not unconstitutional to provide that illegitimate children can only take in the absence of legitimate heirs, thus barring an illegitimate who has not been legitimated. Such a classification had a rational basis in view of the state's interest in promoting family life and of directing the disposition of property left in the state. The father could have resorted to a variety of other methods to ensure that the child recovered from his estate; hence the statute did not unequivocally bar the child from succession; and the Court found nothing in the vague generalities of the equal protection clauses which empowered it to nullify the deliberate choice of the elected representatives of the people of the

---

[55]427 U.S. 495, 49 L. Ed. 2d 651, 96 Sup. Ct. 2755 (1976).
[56]See section 3.2, herein.
[57]Examples are to be found in Chapter 6, herein. See, e.g., sections 6.31 (New Jersey); 6.33 (New York); 6.36 (Ohio).
[58]401 U.S. 532, 28 L. Ed. 2d 288, 91 Sup. Ct. 1017 (1971), reh. den. 402 U.S. 990, 29 L. Ed. 2d 156, 91 Sup. Ct. 1672 (1971). See Petrillo, Labine v. Vincent: Illegitimates, Inheritance, and the Fourteenth Amendment, 75 Dick. L. Rev. 377 (1971).

Levy v. Louisiana (see section 3.2, herein), the landmark decision invalidating a statute barring an illegitimate from an action for wrongful death of its mother, "did not say and cannot fairly be read to say that a State can never treat an illegitimate child differently from legitimate offspring." Id., 401 U.S. at 535-536, 91 Sup. Ct. at 1019.

state. State courts, too, have sanctioned the use by the legislature of its inheritance laws as a method of encouraging the institution of marriage and discouraging sexual promiscuity. Thus, in In re Estate of Ginochio,[59] a California court held constitutional a statute providing that an illegitimate takes only from and through its mother, in the absence of acknowledgment by the intestate father. The thinking is often that, there being no vested right to succession, the matter is subject to such conditions and limitations as the legislature may prescribe.[60]

Another reason sometimes given for this lax attitude in ruling on the constitutionality of statutes imposing conditions on the right of an illegitimate to succeed on intestacy is of a less moralistic nature. To permit such progeny to assert claims, without there being existing cogent evidence of the paternity of the decedent, would tend to hold up the expeditious administration of estates while the issue of paternity is being litigated.[61]

Other courts have reasoned that statutes requiring some form of acknowledgment by the decedent father, since a person is constitutionally free to dispose of his property as he or she likes, reflect the probable intent of the decedent and thus cannot be held to be an invidious discrimination.[62]

The stricter scrutiny given to provisions restricting the rights of illegitimates to recover for the wrongful death of a parent[63] has also been accounted for by reasoning that in the wrongful death

---

[59] 43 Cal. App. 3d 412, 117 Cal. Rptr. 565 (1974).

[60] See Farmers & Merchants Nat. Bank of Los Angeles v. Superior Court of Los Angeles County, 25 Cal. 2d 842, 155 P.2d 823 (1945); In re Perkins' Estate, 21 Cal. 2d 561, 134 P.2d 231 (1943).

[61] See, e.g., Strahan v. Strahan, 304 F. Supp. 40 (W.D. La., 1969), affd. 444 F.2d 528 (C.A.-5 La., 1971), cert den. 404 U.S. 949, 30 L. Ed. 2d 265, 92 Sup. Ct. 284 (1971), holding the rationale of decisions permitting illegitimate children to sue for wrongful death does not extend to a state's succession laws. Succession of Captain, 341 So. 2d 1291 (La. App., 1977), justifies such discrimination, inter alia, as "contributing to the stability of land titles."

[62] E.g., In re Estate of Pakarinen, 287 Minn. 330, 178 N.W.2d 714 (1970), appeal dismissed 402 U.S. 903, 28 L. Ed. 2d 644, 91 Sup. Ct. 1384 (1971). Compare Eskra v. Morton, 524 F.2d 9 (C.A.-7 Wis., 1975), holding that even though it is not irrational to assume that most decedents would discriminate against persons born out of wedlock, the state may not for that reason alone, make comparable discriminatory choices by prohibiting illegitimates from inheriting in all or certain circumstances.

[63] See section 3.2, herein.

cases, recovery by the legitimate children is in no way jeopardized; whereas with recognition of claims by illegitimates in the area of intestate succession this is likely to be the case.[64]

Another reason to justify the imposition of more rigid requirements of proof of parentage when the illegitimate is seeking to recover against an alleged father's estate than when the claim is made against an intestate mother's estate carries with it a lot of common sense. Though admittedly it places a greater burden on an (innocent) illegitimate, if the alleged father has denied paternity, or even pleaded guilty in a paternity action, or even been adjudicated the father, there is not the same element of certainty of parentage as in the case of the mother.[65]

However, notwithstanding all such explanations, there are indications that the Supreme Court does recognize that there is a line beyond which statutory preconditions cannot go. In Trimble v. Gordon,[66] that court ruled on an Illinois statute which denied illegitimates the right to inherit from their fathers. The statute did make provision for succession by all "legitimate" children, and embraced as legitimate children the offspring of parents who have intermarried and who were acknowledged by the father as his children. This could well be regarded as a rational legislative precaution against spurious claims, which Illinois had hitherto regarded as a proper state interest.[67] In fact, in Labine the Supreme Court of the United States had indicated that the state interest in establishing an accurate and efficient method of disposing of property at death was enough to enable a statute to

---

[64]E.g., In re Estate of Ortiz, 60 Misc. 2d 756, 303 N.Y.S.2d 806 (1969).

[65]See In re Estate of Pakarinen, 287 Minn. 330, 178 N.W.2d 714 (1970), appeal dismissed 402 U.S. 903, 28 L. Ed. 2d 644, 91 Sup. Ct. 1384 (1971), where the court recognized the likelihood of the mother of an illegitimate as standing in a closer relationship to the child than does the alleged male parent, and that thus more stringent preconditions of succession to the latter are constitutionally permissible where the child's claim is based on paternity and not maternity. See also Burnett v. Camden, 253 Ind. 354, 254 N.E.2d 199 (1970), cert. den. 399 U.S. 901, 90 Sup. Ct. 2202 (1970), pointing out that the Levy decision and Glona v. American Guarantee & Liability Ins. Co. (see section 3.2, herein) involved situations where there appeared to be no question as to the relationship of mother and child in the wrongful death actions. And see Annotation, Eligibility of illegitimate child to receive family allowance out of estate of his deceased father, 12 A.L.R.3d 1140 (1967).

[66]430 U.S. 762, 52 L. Ed. 2d 31, 97 Sup. Ct. 1459 (1977).

[67]In re Estate of Karas, 61 Ill. 2d 40, 329 N.E.2d 234 (1975).

withstand the challenge of unconstitutionality.[68] But the Supreme Court found the Illinois statute defective in that it did not give adequate consideration to a possible middle ground between complete exclusion and a case-by-case determination of paternity.[69] The Court was well aware of the problems involving proof of paternity. But, it said, such problems cannot be made "into an impenetrable barrier" that shields otherwise invidious discrimination. The statute, it said, was not carefully attuned to alternative considerations.[70] (The decedent in Trimble had been adjudicated parent of the claimant and ordered to pay support.)

The Trimble decision may well throw into limbo the constitutionality of a great many of the state statutes relating to succession on intestacy by illegitimates.[71] The fears expressed in Trimble in a dissent by Justice Rehnquist that the vague standards the Court purports to set up will create much confusion appear justified. "Without any [antecedent] constitutional mandate," he

---

[68] The court in Trimble used language to indicate that, if its decision was inconsistent with the ruling in Labine, the Trimble analysis is to control.

[69] In Gomez v. Perez, 409 U.S. 535, 35 L. Ed. 2d 56, 93 Sup. Ct. 872 (1973), the Court had said that once a state posits a judicially enforceable right on behalf of children to needed support from their natural fathers, there is no sufficient justification for denying such a right merely because the natural father has not married the mother. It is suggested that the middle ground might be covered in a statute which embraces, as qualified to succeed to the father, illegitimate children with whom (irrespective of judicial establishment of paternity or acknowledgment by the deceased parent) the court is clearly satisfied as to parentage. (Or is this a "case-by-case" determination?)

[70] Trimble v. Gordon, 430 U.S. 762, 52 L. Ed. 2d 31, 97 Sup. Ct. 1459 (1977).

[71] See "Legitimate" Discrimination Against Illegitimates: A Look at Trimble v. Gordon and Fiallo v. Bell, 16 J. Family L. 57 (1977); Illegitimate Succession—Illinois Statute Denying the Rights of Illegitimate Children to Inherit from Father's Estates Is Unconstitutional, 13 Tulsa L. J. 178 (1977); Constitutional Law—Equal Protection and the Inheritance Rights of Illegitimates Under Intestate Succession Laws, 43 Mo. L. Rev. 116 (1978); Constitutional Law—Right of an Illegitimate Child to Inherit Under Intestacy Statutes, 22 N.Y. L. S. L. Rev. 103 (1976) (discusses the implications for New York of a case which was decided before Trimble reached the Supreme Court). Indeed, the Uniform Probate Code, which requires proof of paternity and the father's acknowledgment, might well be suspect. See also Constitutional Law—Equal Protection—Denial of Illegitimate Child's Right of Inheritance from Father Who Had Acknowledged but Not Legitimated Heir Does Not Constitute a Violation of Child's Equal Protection Rights Under the Fourteenth Amendment, 47 Notre Dame Law. 392 (1971); Lee, Changing American Law Relating to Illegitimate Children, 11 Wake Forest L. Rev. 415 (1975); Illegitimacy and Equal Protection: Two Tiers or an Analytical Grab-Bag?, 7 Loyola U. L. J. (Chicago) 754 (1976).

says, "we have created on the premise[s] of the equal protection clause a school for legislators whereby opinions of this Court are written to instruct them in a better understanding of how to accomplish their ordinary legislative tasks."[72] Since Trimble, New Jersey has invalidated its statute providing that an illegitimate cannot qualify for succession unless his parents marry.[73] Wisconsin, on the other hand, regards its requirements as meeting the mandate of Trimble v. Gordon. The statute conditions inheritance rights on either adjudication, or admission by the father in open court of paternity, or an acknowledgment by the father in a writing signed by him. "To permit paternity to be established after the death of the putative father, on the basis of his alleged informal, verbal statements, would be to place his estate at an unreasonable disadvantage in defending against spurious claims."[74]

Since the decision in Trimble, the matter has again come to the attention of the Supreme Court. Whereas the Illinois statute, condemned in Trimble, required intermarriage of the parents plus acknowledgment by the intestate father, the New York statute in effect restricted the right of the illegitimate to inherit from the father to the situation where the father had been adjudicated as such. This was, in a 5–4 decision, upheld as constitutional. Justice Powell considered that the Illinois statute faltered in that it effected a total statutory disinheritance of those who were not legitimated by a subsequent marriage of the parents. The reach of the statute was thus far in excess of its justifiable purposes. Though far from lauding the New York statute as the ideal solution to the problem (he concedes that it might operate unfairly as to a child who can produce ample proof of his paternal origins but does not have the magic document), he concludes that the statute is substantially related to the important state interests it is designed to promote and does not violate the equal protection clause.[75]

The main objection of the dissenters has its basis in the fact that

---

[72]Trimble v. Gordon, 430 U.S. 762, 784, 52 L. Ed. 2d 31, 97 Sup. Ct. 1459, 1472 (1977).
[73]See section 6.31, herein.
[74]In re Estate of Blumreich, 84 Wis. 2d 545, 267 N.W.2d 870, 877 (1978).
[75]Lalli v. Lalli, ——U.S.——, ——L. Ed. 2d——, 99 Sup. Ct. 518 (1978).

there are obviously situations where, the father having acknowledged his paternity and being perfectly willing to perform his obligations, no one has ever seen any need for, or desirability of, litigating the matter of parentage, and to bar the child from inheritance when, as in the Lalli situation, paternity has never been seriously disputed is an invidious discrimination not substantially related to any legitimate state interests.

An excellent example of a more thorough legislative attempt to meet the mandates of Trimble is to be found in the Virginia statute.[76]

The eligibility of illegitimates to succeed on intestacy to persons other than their parents, for example the mother's other legitimate or illegitimate children, as also their rights to inherit from or through the mother's ancestors or collateral kindred, must perforce rest on a controlling statute.[77] Few courts have given a liberal construction to statutes which have not dealt expressly with such aspects.[78] However there is some indication that denying to an illegitimate child the same rights to inherit from his ancestors and collateral relatives as if he were legitimate is constitutionally infirm.[79]

As to inheritance *from* an illegitimate child, the common law was that it had no heirs except the heirs of its body, that is, its lineal descendants, and its spouse, if any. Hence, in the absence of statute, neither its mother nor father, nor their children, legitimate or otherwise, can qualify to succeed. If the illegitimate died unmarried, without lineal descendants, his or her estate became subject to escheat.[80] However, the harshness of the common law

---

[76] See section 6.47, herein.

[77] Annotations, Inheritance by illegitimate from mother's legitimate children, 60 A.L.R.2d 1182 (1958); Illegitimate child as "lineal descendant" and "child" within the provisions of inheritance, succession, or estate tax statutes respecting exemption and tax rates, 3 A.L.R.2d 166 (1949); Inheritance by illegitimate from mother's other illegitimate children, 7 A.L.R.3d 677 (1966); see also 41 L. Ed. 2d 1228, 1238; Inheritance by illegitimate from or through mother's ancestors or collateral kindred, 97 A.L.R.2d 1101 (1964).

[78] See, e.g., section 6.21, herein (Maryland).

[79] Annotation, Discrimination on basis of illegitimacy as denial of constitutional rights, 38 A.L.R.3d 613, 631 (1971).

[80] Annotation, Inheritance from illegitimate, 48 A.L.R.2d 759 (1956) (indicates an exception in the case of Connecticut, where mutual rights of succession on intestacy have always been recognized between mother and child; also discusses

has been almost alleviated throughout the country by statutes. Some of these, for example if they allow the mother of an illegitimate to succeed on intestacy but deny such right to the established father, are of course of vulnerable constitutionality.[81]

3.4. Establishment of paternity

In the typical unwed partnership of any degree of stability, the paternity of any offspring is not likely to be a matter of serious dispute. Hence, the discussion that follows is of a cursory nature. It can, if necessary, be supplemented by reference to the appropriate section in the final chapter of this work.

At common law, the father of an illegitimate child had no duty to provide support. Thus, a mother's remedy against a putative father rests entirely on the controlling statutory provisions.[82] Suits to establish paternity, which are mostly regarded as civil, and not criminal, in nature,[83] may take a variety of forms. The typical statute makes provision for a "filiation" proceeding, but the issue of paternity can be litigated in a suit for the annulment of a putative marriage[84] or, by the alleged father, for declaratory relief.[85]

---

the dual nature of the status of illegitimacy in Louisiana, either as "true" illegitimates (not acknowledged by either parent) or "natural children" (acknowledged by one or both parents)).

[81] Generally, see Annotation, Conflict of laws as to legitimacy or legitimation, or as to rights of illegitimates, as affecting descent and distribution of decedents' estates, 73 A.L.R. 941 (1931), 87 A.L.R.2d 1274 (1963).

[82] E.g., Ehorn v. Podraza, 51 Ill. App. 3d 816, 9 Ill. Dec. 866, 367 N.E.2d 300 (1977).

[83] See Annotation, Right to jury trial in bastardy proceedings, 94 A.L.R.2d 1128 (1964). Bastardy statutes have withstood a challenge of unconstitutionality as being discriminatory against the male sex. See, e.g., Salas v. Cortez, 80 Cal. App. 3d 427, 145 Cal. Rptr. 727 (1978).

[84] Annotation, Determination of paternity, legitimacy, or legitimation in action for divorce, separation, or annulment, 65 A.L.R.2d 1381 (1959).

[85] A —— B —— v. C —— D ——, 150 Ind. App. 535, 277 N.E.2d 599 (1971); Thomas v. Solis, 263 Md. 536, 283 A.2d 777 (1971). On jurisdiction to determine paternity under the Uniform Reciprocal Enforcement of Support Act, see 23 Am. Jur. 2d, Desertion and Nonsupport, § 142; Annotation, Maintainability of bastardy proceedings against infant defendent without appointment of guardian ad litem, 69 A.L.R.2d 1379 (1960).

3.4 UNMARRIED COUPLES AND THE LAW

The usual party plaintiff in such actions is the mother of the child.[86] Though in at least one state the child cannot sue unless the mother is dead or disabled,[87] statutes commonly permit the child an independent action.[88] Often, provision is made for the conduct of the trial, and many of the statutes prescribe what evidence can be admitted; for example, blood grouping tests[89] and related matters.[90] It is not uncommon for provision to be made limiting the time within which actions of this nature can be

---

[86] See Annotations, Effect of marriage of woman to one other than defendant upon her right to institute or maintain bastardy proceeding, 98 A.L.R.2d 256 (1964); Right of mother of illegitimate child to appeal from order or judgment entered in bastardy proceedings, 18 A.L.R.2d 948 (1951); Right of nonresident mother to maintain bastardy proceedings, 57 A.L.R.2d 689 (1958); Effect of death of child prior to institution of bastardy proceedings by mother, 7 A.L.R.2d 1397 (1949). As to who are indispensable parties in such an action, see Perez v. Department of Health, 71 Cal. App. 3d 923, 138 Cal. Rptr. 32 (1977).

[87] C.L.W. v. M. J., 254 N.W.2d 446 (N.D., 1977).

[88] Annotation, Maintainability of bastardy proceedings by infant prosecutrix in her own name and right, 50 A.L.R.2d 1029 (1956).

[89] See Harris, Some Observations on the Un-Uniform Act on Blood Tests to Determine Paternity, 9 Vill. L. Rev. 59 (1963). See also Commonwealth v. D'Avella, 339 Mass. 642, 162 N.E.2d 19 (1959); State ex rel. Walker v. Clark, 144 Ohio St. 305, 58 N.E.2d 773 (1944); State ex rel. Freeman v. Morris, 156 Ohio St. 333, 102 N.E.2d 450 (1951). The constitutionality of a statute providing that when blood tests show by clear and convincing evidence that the alleged father is not the father, the court shall dismiss the paternity suit with prejudice, has been upheld in the face of arguments that it violates the equal protection and the due process guaranties. Such a test provides a method for accurately determining parentage and the prevention of invalid claims of paternity and, as such, achieves a valid governmental interest. In the Interest of B——M——N——, 570 S.W.2d 493 (Tex. Civ. App., 1978).

[90] See Annotations, Right to jury trial in bastardy proceedings, 94 A.L.R.2d 1128 (1964); Right of mother of illegitimate child to appeal from order or judgment entered in bastardy proceedings, 18 A.L.R.2d 948 (1951); Effect of death of child prior to institution of bastardy proceedings by mother, 7 A.L.R.2d 1397 (1949); Death of putative father as precluding action for determination of paternity of for child support, 58 A.L.R.3d 188 (1974); Avoidance of lump-sum settlement or release of bastardy claim on grounds of fraud, mistake, or duress, 84 A.L.R.2d 593 (1962); Lump-sum compromise and settlement, or release, of bastardy claim or of bastardy or paternity proceedings, 84 A.L.R.2d 524 (1962); Admissibility, on issue of child's legitimacy or parentage, of declarations of parents, relatives, or the child, deceased or unavailable, 31 A.L.R.2d 989 (1953); Who may dispute presumption of legitimacy of child conceived or born during wedlock, 53 A.L.R.2d 572 (1957); Allowance of attorneys' fees in bastardy proceedings, 40 A.L.R.2d 961 (1955); Effect of marriage of woman to one other than defendant upon her right to institute or maintain bastardy proceeding, 98 A.L.R.2d 256 (1964); Race or color of child as admissible in evidence on issue of legitimacy or paternity, or as basis for

brought.[91] Statutes safeguarding information in vital statistics records relating to such children are common.

Since much of the statutory law relating to the rights of succession of illegitimates is open to attack on constitutional grounds, the provisions of the Uniform Parentage Act[92] merit consideration. This legislation establishes the principle that, regardless of the marital status of the parents, children share equal rights. In setting out how the parent-child relation can be established, the Act sets up a network of presumptions, most of which are based on common-law presumptions of legitimacy, to cover situations where paternity is probable. When these presumptions do not apply, or are inadequate to establish paternity, pretrial procedures are spelled out which are designed to reduce the cost and inefficiency of paternity litigation, and to facilitate settlement without litigation.

The Act also contains provisions for setting the level of support and the enforcement of support decrees. It provides for a three-year limitation period, running from the date of the child's birth,

---

rebuttal or exception to presumption of legitimacy, 32 A.L.R.3d 1303 (1970); Presumption of legitimacy of children born after annulment, divorce or separation, 46 A.L.R.3d 158 (1972).

[91] See Annotation, Statute of limitations in illegitimacy or bastardy proceedings, 59 A.L.R.3d 685 (1974). In State ex rel. Krupke v. Witkowski, 256 N.W.2d 216 (Iowa, 1977), it was held that a statute which provides that proceedings to enforce the obligation of a father shall not be brought more than two years after birth of the child unless paternity has been judicially established or has been acknowledged by the father is not constitutionally infirm and cannot be circumvented by first bringing an action to establish paternity and then suing to enforce the father's support obligation. No decision of the Supreme Court of the United States has required that illegitimates be given an unrestricted right throughout their minority to bring a paternity action.

[92] The Uniform Parentage Act of 1973 (U.L.A.) has been adopted, with a few variations, in California, Hawaii, Montana, North Dakota, Washington and Wyoming. The earlier Uniform Act on Paternity of 1960 (U.L.A.) established a simple and effective civil action to replace the antiquated "bastardy" proceeding with its preliminary examination and other quasi-criminal features. This Act was adopted in Kentucky, Maine, Mississippi, Montana, New Hampshire and Utah. The more recent Uniform Parentage Act brings the law more into line with the mandates of the Supreme Court of the United States with regard to the substantive legal equality of children, whether or not legitimate. The latter Act also carries provisions for setting the level of support, enforcement of judgments, and resolution of custody disputes, including a procedure whereby a court may ascertain the identity of the father and permit a speedy termination of his potential rights if he shows no interest.

in respect of an action to establish paternity; but an action brought on behalf of the child is not barred until three years have elapsed after the child has reached the age of majority. It also contains provisions for jurisdiction, which can be acquired by an extension of the "long arm" concept to include one who has had sexual intercourse in the state where the child was allegedly conceived. It emphasizes that the illegitimate is a necessary party to any such action and must be properly represented. It makes provision as to what evidence is admissible to prove paternity (including blood tests). It also makes provision for a wide range of orders permissible regarding the support, custody, guardianship, visitation privileges and the like, and sets forth guidelines to assist the court in setting support obligations.

Probably the most significant contribution of the Uniform Parentage Act toward the development of the law in a uniform fashion lies in the provisions to ensure that a biological parent's rights (except on a showing of unfitness for parenthood) to consent to the illegitimate's adoption are not ignored. The male parent is presumed to be the father if the parties entered into marriage (albeit an invalid marriage) before or after the birth of the child, or if he has received the child into his home and openly held out the child as his.[93]

3.5. Right of illegitimate child to support

The old rule was that the mother of an illegitimate child, being presumptively entitled to its custody,[94] was exclusively responsible for its support.[95] This rule has been almost totally eroded by statute. Statutes imposing on the father the duty of supporting his children usually include illegitimates.[96] The Supreme Court

---

[93]See Krause, Bringing the Bastard into the Great Society—A Proposed Uniform Act on Legitimacy, 44 Tex. L. Rev. 829 (1966); Wallach and Tenoso, Vindication of the Rights of Unmarried Mothers and Their Children: An Analysis of the Institution of Legitimacy, Equal Protection, and the Uniform Parentage Act, 23 Kan. L. Rev. 23 (1974).

[94]See section 3.6, herein.

[95]See Ehorn v. Podraza, 51 Ill. App. 3d 816, 9 Ill. Dec. 866, 367 N.E.2d 300 (1977); Annotation, Nonstatutory duty of father to support illegitimate child, 30 A.L.R. 1069 (1924).

[96]See Clark, *Law of Domestic Relations,* p. 162 (1968).

of the United States has held that a statute which grants to legitimate children an enforceable right to support from their biological fathers and denies the same right to illegitimate children violates the Constitution.[97] Though well aware that problems relating to proof of paternity can constitute a difficulty, to permit such problems to create an impenetrable barrier constitutes invidious discrimination.[98] Though some state courts prior to this decision had held the same way,[99] a reluctance on the part of other states to so hold can perhaps be explained by the fact that, where a child falls under the presumption of legitimacy, to compel its support from the biological father, though it enlarges its rights, also saddles it with the stigma of illegitimacy.[1]

This right to support can be enforced after the death of the father against his estate.[2]

Statutes which "freeze" this liability of the natural father, while leaving modifiable the obligations respecting his legitimate children, also deny equal protection.[3] However, in at least one respect, illegitimates have not been regarded as on an exactly equal footing with legitimates. A father, seeking modification of a

---

[97] Gomez v. Perez, 409 U.S. 535, 35 L. Ed. 2d 56, 93 Sup. Ct. 872 (1973).

[98] Id., followed in In Interest of R——V——M——, 530 S.W.2d 921 (Tex. Civ. App., 1975). Compare Baston v. Sears, 15 Ohio St. 2d 166, 239 N.E.2d 62 (1968), where the court said the state action complained of can only be its recognition of the nature of the voluntary contract which is undertaken with marriage, which contract includes, by tradition and custom, the husband's promise to support his legitimate children. It considered the extension of liability to an unmarried father to be a dramatic change in social pattern which should only be made by the legislature. Generally, see Krause, Equal Protection for the Illegitimate, 65 Mich. L. Rev. 477 (1967); Shaw and Kass, Illegitimacy, Child Support, and Paternity Testing, 13 Houston L. Rev. 41 (1975).

[99] See Munn v. Munn, 168 Colo. 76, 450 P.2d 68 (1969); R——v. R——, 431 S.W.2d 152 (Mo., 1968).

[1] See Kennelly v. Davis, 221 So. 2d 415 (Fla., 1969), cert. den. 396 U.S. 916, 90 Sup. Ct. 237 (1969); George v. Bertrand, 217 So. 2d 47 (La. App., 1968), writ refused 253 La. 647, 219 So. 2d 177 (1969), cert. den. 396 U.S. 974, 24 L. Ed. 2d 443, 90 Sup. Ct. 439 (1969).

[2] In re Estate of Holley, 44 Ohio Misc. 78, 337 N.E.2d 675 (1975); see also Annotation, Eligibility of illegitimate child to receive family allowance out of estate of his deceased father, 12 A.L.R.3d 1140 (1967); as to whether it is constitutionally permissible to deny support to an illegitimate whose biological father has died prior to the completion of bastardy proceedings, see Annotation, Death of putative father as precluding action for determination of paternity or for child support, 58 A.L.R.3d 188 (1974).

[3] Munn v. Munn, 168 Colo. 76, 450 P.2d 68 (1969).

support decree in respect of his legitimate children, asked the court to consider payments he was making for the support of a later-born illegitimate child. This the court refused to do. It said that the father's primary obligation, to support his legitimate children, cannot be affected by this subsequent obligation.[4]

As between the male and the female parent today, at any rate in states that have adopted the Equal Rights Amendment, the support obligation should be shared on a sexless basis, the test being on which parent the financial burden can better be carried.[5]

If the mother marries another between the conception and the birth of the child, the duty of support is often regarded as having shifted to the new husband.[6] But if the mother marries after the birth of the child, and if her husband has not in some way assumed parental obligations, for example by treating it as his own,[7] the liability for its support remains on the biological father.[8]

Most of the states have statutes whereunder a father can be prosecuted for the nonsupport of his illegitimate child. Whether or not bastardy or filiation proceedings are to be regarded as criminal in nature—a matter of some disagreement[9]—prosecutions for noncompliance with a support decree are clearly

---

[4]Mitchell v. Mitchell, 257 A.2d 496 (D.C. App., 1969). This decision, in the light of Gomez, note 97, supra, may well be open to criticism.

[5]See Rand v. Rand, 280 Md. 508, 374 A.2d 900 (1977); State v. Unterseher, 255 N.W.2d 882 (N.D., 1977); Conway v. Dana, 456 Pa. 536, 318 A.2d 324 (1974); Smith v. Smith, 13 Wash. App. 381, 534 P.2d 1033 (1975). See also State v. Wood, 89 Wash. 2d 97, 569 P.2d 1148 (1977), holding, obiter, that under the statutory law of Washington a biological father with custody of the child could have an action against the mother for support. Annotation, Financial status of defendant in bastardy proceeding as affecting amount of award for support and maintenance, 74 A.L.R. 763 (1931).

[6]See Hall v. Rosen, 50 Ohio St. 2d 135, 363 N.E.2d 725 (1977), holding that he who marries with full knowledge of the woman's pregnancy thereby consents to stand in loco parentis to the child and to being its father.

[7]See Clevenger v. Clevenger, 189 Cal. App. 2d 658, 11 Cal. Rptr. 707, 90 A.L.R.2d 569 (1961); T——v. T——, 216 Va. 867, 224 S.E.2d 148 (1976) (husband's promise to treat wife's illegitimate child as his own enforced).

[8]Annotations, Validity, construction, and application of statute imposing upon stepparent obligation to support child, 75 A.L.R.3d 1129 (1977); Liability of mother's husband, not the father of her illegitimate child, for its support, 90 A.L.R.2d 583 (1963).

[9]See, e.g., Robertson v. Apuzzo, 170 Conn. 367, 365 A.2d 824 (1976) (paternity actions are civil, not criminal); G. L. v. S. D., —— Del. Super.——, 382 A.2d 252

criminal.[10] The Uniform Reciprocal Enforcement of Support Act (U.L.A.), either in its original form (1950) or as amended in 1952, 1958 and 1968, has been substantially adopted in all the states, including District of Columbia, Puerto Rico and most other areas subject to the jurisdiction of the United States. The Act makes specific provision conferring jurisdiction on the state called upon to enforce support obligations, and to hear the issues if the alleged obligor disputes liability.[11] In view of the dearth of statutory law as to who actually owes the duty of support, the Commissioners have also produced the Uniform Civil Liability for Support Act.[12]

An earlier Uniform Illegitimacy Act, which placed the obligation to support on both parents as well as on the father's estate, if he is dead, was placed on the inactive list of uniform acts in 1943. However, that act was adopted in Iowa, Nevada, New Mexico, New York, North Dakota, South Dakota and Wyoming. It contains provisions, inter alia, for a limitation, absent prior notice to him, on recovery from the father to two years' support furnished prior to the bringing of suit; for recovery of support furnished by persons other than the mother; for the discharge of the father's obligations of support by the child's adoption; for the liability of the father's estate once paternity has been established; and for the conduct of proceedings to establish paternity. Such proceedings may be instituted during pregnancy of the mother or after

---

(1977) (actions are quasi-criminal when paternity is an issue); State v. Clay,—— W. Va.——, 236 S.E.2d 230 (1977) (actions are criminal even where paternity is an issue).

[10]Commonwealth v. Parrish,——Pa. Super.——, 378 A.2d 884 (1977). As to provability and dischargeability in bankruptcy of claims for support of illegitimate children, see 9 Am. Jur. 2d, Bankruptcy, §§ 417, 794. Annotations, Determination of paternity of child as within scope of proceeding under Uniform Reciprocal Enforcement of Support Act, 81 A.L.R.3d 1175 (1977); Long-arm statutes: Obtaining jurisdiction over nonresident parent in filiation or support proceeding, 76 A.L.R.3d 708 (1977).

[11]Annotations, Foreign filiation or support order in bastardy proceedings, requiring periodic payments, as extraterritorially enforceable, 16 A.L.R.2d 1098 (1951); Determination of paternity of child as within scope of proceeding under Uniform Reciprocal Enforcement of Support Act, 81 A.L.R.3d 1175 (1977).

[12]Though the Act does not in terms embrace illegitimate children, it is applied to them. See Watts v. Watts, 115 N.H. 186, 337 A.2d 350 (1975). This Act was aimed to rectify the rather chaotic situation where state laws, if any, are unclear as to who owes this duty of support. Though it does not specifically so provide, the effect of the statute is to establish liability for support of an illegitimate even if the statutory time for paternity proceedings has elapsed.

the birth of the child; but, except with his consent, the action cannot be tried until after the birth. The judgment may provide for the payment of the necessary expenses of childbirth. This liability of the father can be discharged by compromise only when the compromise consideration is paid or adequately secured and approved by the court. There is a two-year limitation period for actions for support unless paternity has been judicially established or has been acknowledged by the father in writing or by the furnishing of support.

A contract of a putative father to support his child is generally sustained if supported by adequate consideration.[13] Most courts, far from regarding the agreement as violative of public policy, consider it as furthering the policy of the law, especially where a biological father owes a statutory duty of support.[14] The mother's agreement to refrain from instituting proceedings to which the law entitles her is sufficient consideration, but if the consideration lies in her promise to forbear from pressing criminal charges, or to continue sexual relations with him, there is more doubt.[15] There is not entire agreement as to whether a mere moral obligation to pay for past support or provide for future support is sufficient.[16] In view of the ubiquity of statutes imposing this obligation on the established father, the question is of little importance. Such a contract must of course conform to any statutory provisions covering settlement agreements of this nature.[17] Some states require a writing, this being a contract not to be performed within a year. Others take the position that it may or may not be performed within a year, and an oral agreement can suffice.[18] If

---

[13] See C——S——v. J——W——, 514 S.W.2d 848 (Mo. App., 1974); Tuttle v. Palmer,——N.H.——, 374 A.2d 661 (1977); Peterson v. Eritsland, 69 Wash. 2d 588, 419 P.2d 332 (1966); Annotation, What law governs validity and enforceability of contract made for support of illegitimate children, 87 A.L.R.2d 1306 (1963).

[14] See 10 Am. Jur. 2d, Bastards, § 70.

[15] Annotation, Validity and construction of putative father's promise to support or provide for illegitimate child, 20 A.L.R.3d 500 (1968).

[16] Annotation, Moral obligation as consideration for contract——Modern trend, 8 A.L.R.2d 787 (1949).

[17] See Smazal v. Dassow's Estate, 23 Wis. 2d 336, 127 N.W.2d 234, 20 A.L.R.3d 493 (1964).

[18] See Annotation, Contract to support, maintain, or educate a child as within provision of statute of frauds relating to contracts not to be performed within a year, 49 A.L.R.2d 1293 (1956).

STATUS OF CHILDREN 3.5

the contract makes provision for judicial modification in the event of the father's income being reduced, it should contain similar provision for the event of an increase in his income; otherwise the court might decline to review it on the ground that the clause constitutes an invidious discrimination between legitimate and illegitimate children.[19] Some states require judicial approval of such contracts.[20]

A more difficult question is presented when the mother, instead of exacting an agreement to support the child, accepts consideration for a release of the putative father from any future claims based on his illegitimate parenthood. Several states hold that an illegitimate's right to support from its putative father cannot be contracted away by its mother, and that any release executed by her is invalid to the extent that it purports to affect the rights of the child.[21] However, in the light of Roe v. Wade,[22] wherein the Supreme Court has given the mother the exclusive right, during the earlier period of pregnancy, to decide whether or not to destroy the embryo, it can well be argued that she has exactly the same right to bargain away any potential rights to support.[23] Hence, state laws or decisions invalidating such releases, if they predate the year 1973, may well be suspect.

---

[19]See Storm v. None, 57 Misc. 2d 342, 291 N.Y.S.2d 515 (1968).

[20]See Ferrer v. Ferrer, 58 App. Div. 2d 529, 395 N.Y.S.2d 197 (1977), holding the New York Family Court Act provision requiring court approval of agreements or compromises in paternity cases not to be unconstitutional, in that providing for support by putative fathers of children born out of wedlock presents sufficiently different practical problems from those involving the support of children born in wedlock, so as to justify different statutory treatment for the two classes of children.

As to who may enforce such contracts, and the nature of the relief available, see 10 Am. Jur. 2d, Bastards, § 73.

[21]See Walker v. Walker, 266 So. 2d 385 (Fla. App., 1972); Fox v. Hohenshelt, 19 Ore. App. 617, 528 P.2d 1376 (1974); Reynolds v. Richardson, 483 S.W.2d 747 (Tenn. App., 1971).

If, of course, there is a statute authorizing such compromise, and its provisions are complied with, the mother herself is barred. But there is no unanimity among the states as to whether such an agreement bars an action by the public body on whom the burden of support may have fallen. Annotations, Lump-sum compromise and settlement, or release, of bastardy claim or of bastardy or paternity proceedings, 84 A.L.R.2d 524 (1962); Avoidance of lump sum settlement or release of bastardy claim on grounds of fraud, mistake, or duress, 84 A.L.R.2d 593 (1962).

[22]410 U.S. 113, 35 L. Ed. 2d 147, 93 Sup. Ct. 705 (1973), reh. den. 410 U.S. 959, 35 L. Ed. 2d 694, 93 Sup. Ct. 1409 (1973). See section 2.19, herein.

[23]See dissent in Shinall v. Pergeorelis, 325 So. 2d 431 (Fla. App., 1975).

3.6. Rights to custody and visitation

In the very early law of England, the custody of an illegitimate child was the responsibility of the parish in which it was born. The rule in this country today is that, *all else being equal*, it is the mother who is entitled to the custody of the child.[24] This is logical. There is no doubt, as there can be with the father, as to the mother's identity, and her natural feelings for the child almost invariably are stronger than those of anyone else.[25] However, absent special considerations, the father is often regarded as having a claim superior to that of anyone other than the mother.[26]

The Uniform Child Custody Jurisdiction Act (U.L.A.),[27] which has been adopted in a substantial number of states, was proposed

---

[24] See Jones v. Smith, 278 So. 2d 339 (Fla. App., 1973), cert. den. 415 U.S. 958, 39 L. Ed. 2d 573, 94 Sup. Ct. 1486 (1974); Behn v. Timmons, 345 So. 2d 388 (Fla. App., 1977).

This proposition, if the Equal Rights Amendment becomes law, will become open to dispute. For example, in Commonwealth ex rel. Scott v. Martin, —— Pa. Super. ——, 381 A.2d 173 (1977), the court, in holding that the mother does not have a greater right to custody than does the father of the illegitimate, questions the legitimacy of a doctrine that is predicated on the traditional roles of men and women in a marital union, as offensive to the concept of equality of the sexes. See also Annotation, Right of mother to custody of illegitimate child, 98 A.L.R.2d 417 (1964). As to the Uniform Child Custody Jurisdiction Act (9 U.L.A. 99) (1968), see Bodenheimer, Uniform Child Custody Jurisdiction Act: A Legislative Remedy for Children Caught in the Conflict of Laws, 22 Vand. L. Rev. 1207 (1969).

[25] See 10 Am. Jur. 2d, Bastards, § 60; Annotation, Modern status or maternal preference rule or presumption in child custody cases, 70 A.L.R.3d 262 (1976). A bargain by one entitled to the custody of a minor child to transfer the custody to another, or not to reclaim custody already transferred, is illegal unless authorized by statute. Restatement, *Contracts*, § 583 (1932). See also, e.g., Rainer v. Rowlett, 255 Ark. 794, 502 S.W.2d 617 (1973), noted in section 6.4, herein.

[26] See In re Adoption of Child by A.R., 152 N.J. Super. 541, 378 A.2d 87 (1977); Barry W. v. Barbara K., 55 App. Div. 2d 607, 389 N.Y.S.2d 624 (1976) (though stating that prima facie the mother is entitled to custody, court held that the rule of paramount importance is the child's welfare and granted custody to the father); People ex rel. Blake v. Charger, 76 Misc. 2d 577, 351 N.Y.S.2d 322 (1974) (custody granted to putative father after death of mother).

In Carle v. Carle, 503 P.2d 1050 (Alaska, 1972) a custody decree was remanded because of the trial court's apparent prejudice against the father's unique Indian lifestyle and extended family situation. See Foster and Freed, Child Snatching and Custodial Fights: The Case for the Uniform Child Custody Jurisdiction Act, 28 Hastings L. J. 1011 (1977); Annotation, Right of putative father to custody of illegitimate child, 45 A.L.R.3d 216 (1972).

[27] See Hudak, Seize, Run and Sue: The Ignominy of Interstate Child Custody Litigation in American Courts, 39 Mo. L. Rev. 521, 547 (1974).

STATUS OF CHILDREN 3.6

with a view to clearing up the chaotic situation existing where virtually any state which had a child within its borders regarded itself as having jurisdiction to make determinations as to that child's custody, thereby encouraging "seize and run" tactics by parents confronted with a custody dispute.

Where, in a custody dispute, the court is asked to determine a mother's fitness to raise a child, the law will not hold her "to the morality of saints and seers." The criterion is not whether the court condones her mode of living or considers it to be contrary to good morals, but whether the child is best located with her, and will it be well-behaved and cared for.[28] The lodestar is the best interests of the child.[29] This standard has been held not unconstitutionally vague. Given the variety of fact situations involved, it must contain a degree of imprecision. But to argue that it lacks precise meaning is not to say that it is without content. Such content has been articulated over the years. The "best interests of the child" standard requires the judge to make an informed and rational judgment, free of bias, as to the least detrimental alternative. No more precision appears possible. No more is constitutionally required.[30]

Each case is decided on its facts[31] without the harnessing of any *conclusive*[32] presumption favoring the mother. The court, representing the state as *parens patriae,* should put itself in the position of a "wise, affectionate and careful parent."[33] Proof that the

---

[28]S. v. J., 81 Misc. 2d 828, 367 N.Y.S.2d 405 (1975). See In re Cager, 251 Md. 473, 248 A.2d 384 (1968) (fact that mother has more than one illegitimate child does not necessarily render the home environment "unstable," so as to deprive her of the right to custody); Johnson v. Lloyd, 211 A.2d 764 (D.C. App., 1965) (custody awarded to mother although she had five children by four different men, none of whom had married her).

[29]When the "best interests" test becomes applicable by reason of circumstances that would drastically affect the child's welfare, the court must weigh all relevant factors which include the parent's and child's "rights." State ex rel. Wilson v. Wilson, 56 App. Div. 2d 794, 392 N.Y.S.2d 639 (1977).

[30]In re Adoption of J.S.R., 374 A.2d 860 (D.C. App., 1977).

[31]Casale v. Casale, 549 S.W.2d 805 (Ky., 1977).

[32]In re Marriage of Tweeten, —— Mont. ——, 563 P.2d 1141 (1977) (presumption but not conclusive); Waagen v. R.J.B., 248 N.W.2d 815 (N.D., 1976); Smith v. Smith, 564 P.2d 307 (Utah, 1977) (no statutory presumption).

[33]Sovereign v. Sovereign, 354 Mich. 65, 92 N.W.2d 585 (1958).

mother has abused or grossly neglected a child obviously should disqualify her for custody.[34]

The mere fact that the mother is cohabiting with the putative father is not usually regarded as affecting her right to custody of their child.[35] But if she has abandoned the child and is cohabiting with a new paramour, custody will be awarded to the father, if he is qualified.[36] If not, the court will heed the recommendations of the appropriate welfare authority.[37] Proof of a mother's lesbian preferences should not, without more, be a ground for deprivation of her custodial rights. If no connection with the child's interests is shown, "the specter of child custody based largely on unfounded societal and judicial preferences" should be eliminated.[38]

The natural right of a parent to the custody of her or his offspring, legitimate or otherwise, is not of course absolute.[39] The state being *parens patriae,* its authority to wrest custody from a parent in the best interests of the child, usually on the recommendation of some welfare administrative agency, is unquestioned.[40] As to the putative father, though he certainly has legal standing to seek custody against all the world, including even the mother,[41] the logical considerations that weigh in a determination of a mother's right to custody are weaker. It would not be fair to say more than that his claim to custody of the child should be

---

[34] E.g., In re Paul X, 57 App. Div. 2d 216, 393 N.Y.S.2d 1005 (1977); Annotation, Sexual abuse of child by parent as ground for termination of parent's right to child, 58 A.L.R.3d 1074 (1974). See also Annotation, Alienation of child's affections as affecting custody award, 32 A.L.R.2d 1005 (1953).

[35] See Turner v. Head, 236 Ga. 483, 224 S.E.2d 360 (1976); Greenfield v. Greenfield, 199 Neb. 648, 260 N.W.2d 493 (1977); Snegirev v. Samoilov, 26 Ore. App. 687, 554 P.2d 595 (1976). Lauerman, Nonmarital Sexual Conduct and Child Custody, 46 U. Cin. L. Rev. 647 (1977).

[36] See Boatwright v. Otero, 91 Misc. 2d 653, 398 N.Y.S.2d 391 (1977).

[37] E.g., In re Wright, 52 Ohio Misc. 4, 367 N.E.2d 931 (1977).

[38] Hunter and Polikoff, Custody Rights of Lesbian Mothers: Legal Theory and Litigation Strategy, 25 Buffalo L. Rev. 691 (1976).

[39] Rejda v. Rejda, 198 Neb. 465, 253 N.W.2d 295 (1977).

[40] E.g., Matter of Barlow, 78 Mich. App. 707, 260 N.W.2d 896 (1977); In re R.F., ——Vt.——, 376 A.2d 38 (1977); Annotations, Consideration of investigation by welfare agency or the like in making or modifying award as between parents of custody of children, 35 A.L.R.2d 629 (1954); Right of indigent parent to appointed counsel in proceeding for involuntary termination of parental rights, 80 A.L.R.3d 1141 (1977).

[41] Boatwright v. Otero, 91 Misc. 2d 653, 398 N.Y.S.2d 391 (1977); In re Wright, 52 Ohio Misc. 4, 367 N.E.2d 931 (1977).

accorded serious consideration before custody is awarded to a stranger.[42] There are no absolute rights here.

A statute which permits a noncustodial father to be deprived of parental rights if he willfully fails to support his child for one year, but which allows a noncustodial mother to preserve her parental rights merely by communicating with the child, without the need to contribute to its support, has been upheld.[43] It did not violate the equal protection rights of the father, since the gender-based distinction was rational in that it was premised on a difference in parental earning capacity. Such a difference usually leads a court to order that the father pay for support of minor children whose custody has been awarded to the mother.[44]

One right, however, is clearly established: all parents have a constitutional right to a hearing on their fitness before a child can be taken from them. Hence, it was held in Stanley v. Illinois[45] that a state's statutory procedure whereunder an unmarried father is presumed unfit to take custody of his illegitimate child on the mother's death, and may be deprived of custody of the child without a hearing, when a hearing is extended to all parents of legitimate children before the state can deprive them of custody, violates the Constitution. This rule has been extended to a situation where the children are up for adoption and the father has had no subsisting relation with them.[46] It is, of course, possible that any attempt to give such notice to the biological father would be futile; in that case a court could in its discretion hear the matter

---

[42]See In re Guardianship and Estate of Arias, 21 Ariz. App. 568, 521 P.2d 1146 (1974); In re Reyna, 55 Cal. App. 3d 288, 126 Cal. Rptr. 138 (1976); In re Doe, 52 Haw. 448, 478 P.2d 844 (1970); In re Zink, 269 Minn. 535, 132 N.W.2d 795 (1964); In re Guardianship of C., 98 N.J. Super. 474, 237 A.2d 652 (1967); Schwartz, Rights of a Father with Regard to His Illegitimate Child, 36 Ohio S. L. J. 1 (1975); Tabler, Paternal Rights in the Illegitimate Child: Some Legitimate Complaints on Behalf of the Unwed Father, 11 J. Family L. 231 (1971); Note, Paternal Custody of Minor Children, 5 Memphis St. U. L. Rev. 223 (1975); Annotation, Right of putative father to custody of illegitimate child, 45 A.L.R.3d 216 (1972).

[43]Adoption of Coffee, 59 Cal. App. 3d 593, 130 Cal. Rptr. 887 (1976). See Putative Father—The Evolving Constitutional Concepts of Due Process and Equal Protection, 2 West. St. U. L. Rev. 261 (1975).

[44]Adoption of Coffee, supra.

[45]405 U.S. 645, 31 L. Ed. 2d 551, 92 Sup. Ct. 1208 (1972).

[46]Rothstein v. Lutheran Social Services of Wisconsin and Upper Michigan, 405 U.S. 1051, 31 L. Ed. 2d 786, 92 Sup. Ct. 1488 (1972). See also Vanderlaan v. Vanderlaan, 405 U.S. 1051, 31 L. Ed. 2d 787, 92 Sup. Ct. 1488 (1972).

without such notice.[47] The Stanley decision has brought problems.[48] Some states, preoccupied with the mother's right of privacy, have responded to it by providing that notice to the father is not required unless he is known and is identified by the mother, or has acknowledged paternity.[49]

In determining whether a putative father should have the right to visit his child, and when and how often, the courts look not to the interests of the parents, but to those of the child; a denial of such a right without giving the father a right to a hearing on this question is a violation of due process.[50] A judge of long ago expressed his opinion that, in the case before him, such visits would help an illegitimate child "more lightly to bear the ignominy of his origin" if he knew the father held him in as much affection as he did his legitimate child.[51] In short, where the child's custodian shows opposition, the matter is entirely for the discretion of the court.[52]

To state as a matter of law that the visits of a putative father are always detrimental to the illegitimate child's best interests is to exalt rule over reality. This approach ignores the growing recognition in our courts, and in courts throughout the nation, of the need to determine the welfare of each child in light of his own particular needs and circumstances. The putative father may, in many instances, instill in the child a sense of stability. He may develop qualities in the child which the mother is

---

[47] See Rogers v. Lowry, 546 S.W.2d 881 (Tex. Civ. App., 1977).

[48] See Barron, Notice to the Unwed Father and Termination of Parental Rights: Implementing Stanley v. Illinois, 9 Family L. Q. 527 (1975); Plight of the Putative Father in California Child Custody Proceedings: A Problem of Equal Protection, 6 U.C.D. L. Rev. 1 (1973); Protecting the Putative Father's Rights After Stanley v. Illinois: Problems in Implementation, 13 J. Family L. 115 (1973–74); Father of an Illegitimate Child—His Right to Be Heard, 50 Minn. L. Rev. 1071 (1966); "Strange Boundaries" of Stanley: Providing Notice of Adoption to the Unknown Putative Father, 59 Va. L. Rev. 517 (1973).

[49] The Uniform Parentage Act (U.L.A.), while providing for notice to be given to the putative father where he is known, leaves it open to the court to determine whether, in the light of possible embarrassment for the mother or of other circumstances such as the improbability of publication leading to any successful identification of the father, notice by publication or public posting should be required in proceedings to determine custodial rights of such children. See Schafrick, Emerging Constitutional Protection of the Putative Father's Parental Rights, 7 Family L. Q. 75 (1973).

[50] In re One Minor Child,——Del.——, 295 A.2d 727 (1972).

[51] Baker v. Baker, 81 N.J. Eq. 135, 85 Atl. 816 (1913).

[52] See Sullivan v. Bonafonte, 172 Conn. 612, 376 A.2d 69 (1977).

uninterested, unwilling or incapable of developing. To the extent that he can perform such a valuable service, his presence becomes exceedingly important. Certainly, to the illegitimate child, the father is never putative.[53]

For reasons such as these, the courts almost invariably exercise their discretion in favor of the putative father,[54] sometimes to the extent of appearing to elevate the right of visitation into a legal right,[55] which it is not.[56]

3.7. Legitimation

The harsh rule of the early common law that a bastard was doomed to that status for life has today yielded to a more enlightened view. The "sins" of the parents are no longer visited in this manner upon their children.

It is realized that to permit a child to be legitimated, to have a right to his father's name and to inherit from him, tends, if not to deter the potential father from irresponsible liaisons, to conform more closely to current notions of justice.[57] In at least two states

---

[53] Commonwealth v. Rozanski, 206 Pa. Super. 397, 213 A.2d 155, 157, 15 A.L.R.3d 880 (1965).

[54] Annotation, Right of putative father to visit illegitimate child, 15 A.L.R.3d 887 (1967), wherein it is indicated that the chances of the child making a satisfactory adjustment to the mother's marriage to another can at times be jeopardized if the child forms a too close attachment to its putative father. The reluctance to further a renewal of meretricious relations between the parents might also influence a court.

[55] E.g., Phillips v. Horlander, 535 S.W.2d 72 (Ky. App., 1975), which seems to place the burden of showing that such visits would be detrimental to the child on the opposing parent.

In vacating a decree of adoption because the biological father had no opportunity to be heard, a Hawaii court affirmed that the father was not devoid of parental rights. But the decision clearly means that he has a constitutional right to be heard on his right or privilege to visit, and no more. Willmott v. Decker, 56 Haw. 462, 541 P.2d 13 (1975).

[56] See Sullivan v. Bonafonte, 172 Conn. 612, 376 A.2d 69 (1977); Baehr v. Baehr, 56 Ill. App. 3d 624, 14 Ill. Dec. 401, 372 N.E.2d 412 (1978); In Interest of K., 535 S.W.2d 168 (Tex., 1976), cert. den. 429 U.S. 907, 97 Sup. Ct. 273 (1976).

Generally, as to visitation privileges, see Domestic Relations—Illegitimate Child—Visitation Rights Granted to Putative Father, 26 Albany L. Rev. 335 (1962); Father's Right to Visit His Illegitimate Child, 27 Ohio S. L. J. 738 (1966).

[57] See In re Lund's Estate, 26 Cal. 2d 472, 159 P.2d 643, 162 A.L.R. 606 (1945).

the status of illegitimacy has been eliminated.[58] The Uniform Parentage Act of 1973,[59] which has been adopted in five states and is likely, in view of recent constitutional pronouncements, to receive further adoption, sets forth presumptions of paternity flowing from a marriage of the biological parents, or from conduct whereunder the male parent has substantially acknowledged his paternity. Statutory provisions of a similar nature, which vary from state to state, are common; as are statutes permitting legitimation by a court adjudication of paternity irrespective of the male parent's acknowledgment.[60]

Illustrative of current judicial attitudes is an Ohio decision which holds that a legitimation statute which denies an opportunity to be legitimated to some illegitimate children only because their fathers choose not to initiate procedures violates the equal protection provisions of the Constitution.[61] It requires the statute to be expanded in its application to afford all such children an opportunity to become legitimated. Neither acknowledgment by the biological father nor consent of the mother is a necessary prerequisite.

However, whether it is the child or the alleged father who has a statutory right to bring a legitimation proceeding, it would seem that due process requires that the mother receive notice and an opportunity to be heard. This is so because legitimation would confer on the male parent the rights of a natural father. He could withhold consent to the adoption of the child. It would put him in a strong position to claim custody and to change the name of the child.[62]

In view of the diversity of statutory and case law in the various states, more than a general survey of legitimation would at this stage be inappropriate. For example, a Louisiana statute providing that only those natural children can be legitimated who are

---

[58]See herein, sections 6.3 (Arizona); 6.38 (Oregon).
[59]See section 3.4 herein, note 92.
[60]See Note, Illegitimacy, 26 Brooklyn L. Rev. 45 (1959).
[61]In re Minor of Martin, 51 Ohio App. 2d 21, 365 N.E.2d 892 (1977).
[62]See Roe v. Conn, 417 F. Supp. 769 (M.D. Ala., 1976), also holding that giving preference to the wishes of the father in permitting him to control the child's name does not serve a legitimate state interest in administrative convenience, has no rational basis, and violates the equal protection clause.

the offspring of parents who at the time of conception could legally have married has withstood a challenge of unconstitutionality.[63]

Nearly all the states have statutes which legitimate children by the subsequent marriage of their biological parents, but the phraseology and construction of such laws are by no means uniform.[64] Especially is this so if inheritance rights are conditioned on legitimacy,[65] or if the subsequent marriage was for some reason invalid.[66] Again, authority is not uniform as to whether, when a statute provides for legitimation by subsequent marriage of the biological parents, a child born to a married woman by a man not her husband can be so legitimated. Logic would dictate that, by reason of the presumption of legitimacy, the child is already the legitimate child of the woman's husband at time of

---

[63]Succession of Bush, 222 So. 2d 642 (La. App., 1969). The mandate of Levy v. Louisiana, Glona v. American Guarantee & Liability Ins. Co., and similar Supreme Court decisions (see section 3.2, herein) could well dispose other states to reach a contrary conclusion.

[64]Annotations, Legitimating effect of intermarriage of parents as affected by father's failure to acknowledge paternity, 175 A.L.R. 375 (1948); Legitimation by subsequent marriage annulled under a statute declaring that certain marriages shall be void from the time their nullity is declared, 27 A.L.R. 1121 (1923).

[65]E.g., Olmsted v. Olmsted, 216 U.S. 386, 54 L. Ed. 530, 30 Sup. Ct. 292 (1910), holding there to be nothing in the full faith and credit clause of the federal Constitution which would require the courts of New York to give effect to a Michigan statute legitimizing children born prior to the marriage of their parents, so as to control the devolution of land in New York; State v. Bragg, 152 W. Va. 372, 163 S.E.2d 685 (1968), holding that, though under certain conditions an illegitimate can inherit from its father, there is no way it can be made legitimate. See also Annotations, Illegitimate child as within contemplation of statute regarding rights of child pretermitted by will, or statute preventing disinheritance of child, 142 A.L.R. 1447 (1943); Inheritance from illegitimate, 48 A.L.R.2d 759 (1956); Inheritance by illegitimate from mother's legitimate children, 60 A.L.R.2d 1182 (1958); What amounts to recognition within statutes affecting the status or rights of illegitimates, 33 A.L.R.2d 705 (1954).

[66]See Estate of Dussell, 145 N.J. Super. 363, 367 A.2d 1188 (1976), construing the New Jersey statute to mean that a child is legitimated by the common-law marriage of his parents, notwithstanding that such marriage is void as bigamous and even if the law of the place where such marriage takes place does not recognize as valid a bigamous common-law marriage; Home of Holy Infancy v. Kaska, 397 S.W.2d 208 (Tex., 1965), holding the marriage of the parents to be effective for all purposes notwithstanding that the intermarriage and its subsequent annulment both occur prior to the child's birth; Annotation, What constitutes a "marriage" within meaning of a statute legitimating issue of all marriages null in law, 84 A.L.R. 499 (1933).

conception. But the decisions often resolve the issue of legitimation in favor of the child.[67]

Similarly, the statutes which enable a child to be legitimated by an acknowledgment of paternity differ in their form and construction. Typically, such a statute requires a public acknowledgment by the father, a reception of the child into his family, with the consent of his wife, if married.[68] Is a living-together situation a "family" for this purpose?[69] How "public" must the acknowledgment be? These and a host of similar questions must, perforce, depend on the wording of the statute and its judicial construction.[70] In general, such statutes are construed quite liberally in order to spare a child, innocent of any wrongdoing, from being stigmatized as illegitimate.[71]

3.8. Adoption and the rights of the biological parents

All the states have some statutory provisions controlling the rights of parents to put a child out for adoption. It is universally recognized that, once this has been knowingly and voluntarily done, the decree is irrevocable. All legal rights of the natural parents are terminated.[72]

Ordinarily, whether or not the child is legitimate, parental

---

[67] Annotation, Legitimation by marriage to natural father of child born during mother's marriage to another, 80 A.L.R.3d 219 (1977).

[68] E.g., In re Swarer, 566 P.2d 126 (Okla., 1977), construing the child of an unmarried father, publicly acknowledged and received into his "family," to have assumed the status of an adopted child from moment of birth upon legitimation and was for all purposes legitimate from time of birth.

[69] The "family" for this purpose may consist only of the father and unmarried mother. Darwin v. Ganger, 174 Cal. App. 2d 63, 344 P.2d 353 (1959). See In re Reyna, 55 Cal. App. 3d 288, 126 Cal. Rptr. 138 (1976) so holding at any rate where the biological parents intended marriage.

[70] See Annotation, What amounts to recognition within statutes affecting the status or rights of illegitimates, 33 A.L.R.2d 705 (1954). Generally, see 10 Am. Jur. 2d, Bastards, § 51 et seq.

[71] Estate of Dussell, 145 N.J. Super. 363, 367 A.2d 1188 (1976).

[72] In Interest of Jones, 34 Ill. App. 3d 603, 340 N.E.2d 269 (1975); In Interest of Konczak, 55 Ill. App. 3d 217, 13 Ill. Dec. 441, 371 N.E.2d 136 (1977); Blanchard v. Nevada State Welfare Dept., 91 Nev. 749, 542 P.2d 737 (1975); In re Adoption of T.W.C., 38 N.Y.2d 128, 379 N.Y.S.2d 1, 341 N.E.2d 526 (1975) (infancy of mother no ground for revocation); Harry v. Fisher, 216 Va. 530, 221 S.E.2d 118 (1976).

rights cannot be terminated without their consent.[73] The exception is where the parents have forsaken their parental rights by a course of conduct which amounts either to a substantial abandonment of the child or a very substantial neglect of parental duties, with no expectation of any reversal of such conduct.[74] In that situation, the courts will terminate their parental rights and dispense with the necessity of their consent for adoption.[75] Parents are constitutionally entitled to a hearing on their fitness before such an adjudication.[76]

The courts do not readily find the necessary "substantial abandonment" which can justify involuntary termination of parental rights. The quantum of proof usually required is "clear and convincing" or a "substantial preponderance" of evidence.[77] The mere fact that the person seeking to adopt is able to give the child superior advantages over those of the natural parents is not enough.[78] In fact, in an adoption hearing where the parent's consent is being dispensed with on the ground of unfitness, evidence as to the domestic situation of the prospective parents should not be admitted until such a determination of unfitness has been

---

[73]Annotations, Sufficiency of parent's consent to adoption of child, 24 A.L.R.2d 1127 (1952); Consent of natural parents as essential to adoption where parents are divorced, 47 A.L.R.2d 824 (1956); Consent by public authority or by person other than parent having control of child, as necessary to valid adoption, 104 A.L.R. 1464 (1936); Necessity of securing consent of parents of illegitimate child to its adoption, 51 A.L.R.2d 497 (1957).

[74]Sorentino v. Family & Childrens Soc. of Elizabeth, 74 N.J. 313, 378 A.2d 18 (1977).

[75]In re Patricia Ann W., 89 Misc. 2d 368, 392 N.Y.S.2d 180 (1977).

[76]Phillips v. Horlander, 535 S.W.2d 72 (Ky. App., 1975); Annotation, Right of indigent parent to appointed counsel in proceeding for involuntary termination of parental rights, 80 A.L.R.3d 1141 (1977).

[77]In re Adoption of J.S.R., 374 A.2d 860 (D.C. App., 1977); Durden v. Henry, 343 So. 2d 1361 (Fla. App., 1977); In re Ladewig, 34 Ill. App. 3d 393, 340 N.E.2d 150 (1975); Robertson v. Hutchison, 560 P.2d 1110 (Utah, 1977). See Annotations, Failure to provide medical attention for child as criminal neglect, 12 A.L.R.2d 1047 (1950); What constitutes abandonment or desertion of child by its parent or parents within purview of adoption laws, 35 A.L.R.2d 662 (1954); Mental illness and the like of parents as ground for adoption of their children, 45 A.L.R.2d 1379 (1956); Application, to illegitimate children, of criminal statutes relating to abandonment, neglect, and nonsupport of children, 99 A.L.R.2d 746 (1965); Sexual abuse of child by parent as ground for termination of parent's right to child, 58 A.L.R.3d 1074 (1974).

[78]In re Adoption of D., 28 Ore. App. 887, 561 P.2d 1038 (1977).

arrived at.[79] The fact that a mother has other illegitimate children cannot be automatically applied to mean that she is an unfit custodian.[80]

In the absence of a showing of unfitness and an involuntary termination of her parental rights, the mother of an illegitimate cannot be divested of her rights by the adoptive process without her consent.[81] As to the putative father, the statutes vary. Some dispense with the need for his consent. Some require his consent, at any rate where the child has been acknowledged by and is being supported by him.[82] In Stanley v. Illinois,[83] discussed earlier,[84] the Supreme Court held that a state was barred, both as a matter of due process and of equal protection, from taking custody of the children of an unmarried father without a hearing and a finding of his unfitness. The Court concluded that a father's interest in the companionship, care, custody and management of his children is a substantial one, and that a state's interest in caring for the children is *de minimis* if the father is in fact a fit person. Soon after this decision, the same Court, in Rothstein v. Lutheran Social Services of Wisconsin and Upper Michigan,[85] remanded an adoption case for reconsideration by the state court in the light of Stanley, suggesting that it extends to adoption proceedings. Since then, the states have rather consistently recognized the right of a biological father to notice and an opportunity to be heard before an adoption is decreed.[86] The decision, however, carries with it its problems. Both the interests of the child itself and the placement agency, if involved, demand that adoption be completed as

---

[79]In re Adoption of Burton, 43 Ill. App. 3d 294, 1 Ill. Dec. 946, 356 N.E.2d 1279 (1976).
[80]In re Cager, 251 Md. 473, 248 A.2d 384 (1968).
[81]Franklin v. Biggs, 14 Ore. App. 450, 513 P.2d 1216 (1973).
[82]Annotation, Necessity of securing consent of parents of illegitimate child to its adoption, 51 A.L.R.2d 497 (1957).
[83]405 U.S. 645, 31 L. Ed. 2d 551, 92 Sup. Ct. 1208 (1972).
[84]See section 3.6, herein.
[85]405 U.S. 1051, 31 L. Ed. 2d 786, 92 Sup. Ct. 1488 (1972). See Comment, Emerging Constitutional Protection of the Putative Father's Parental Rights, 70 Mich. L. Rev. 1581 (1972); Hession, Adoptions After "Stanley"—Rights for Fathers of Illegitimate Children, 61 Ill. B. J. 350 (1973).
[86]E.g., In Interest of Baby Boy S., 349 So. 2d 774 (Fla. App., 1977), holding failure to apprise a putative father of agency's report as to his fitness violates due process. Adoption of Male Minor Child, 56 Haw. 543, 544 P.2d 728 (1975).

expeditiously as possible after the birth. As the baby grows older, its attractiveness as a candidate for adoption usually decreases. The longer it stays with the mother, the more likely it is that the experience of separation can prove traumatic to both mother and child. If the whereabouts of the putative father are unknown, notice by publication could result in embarrassment and humiliation to the mother.[87] Hence, it is likely that some form of constructive service of process, where the father's whereabouts are unknown, would withstand any challenge of unconstitutionality.[88] In view of these problems, however, an unwed mother would do well to advise the appropriate welfare authorities of her pregnancy well in advance of her intention to put the baby out for adoption, giving them whatever information she can to assist them in locating the putative father.

It is clear, then, that notice to the putative father, and an opportunity of a hearing as to his fitness or otherwise to be a parent, is ordinarily required.[89] If he does not appear, or if the court is satisfied that he is unfit as a parent, his consent is not required.[90] Such unfitness requires a showing that he failed to use his available resources to preserve his parental relationship.[91] Failure to support and visit the child would not constitute abandonment where he simply lacks the means to support, or where, for example, the mother has obstructed his attempts to visit the child.[92] There must be a willful substantial lack of regard for his parental obligations.[93]

In the light of the Stanley and Rothstein decisions, many states have amended their adoption statutes to make provision for the consent of the putative father as a prerequisite.[94] However, the

---

[87] See "Strange Boundaries" of Stanley: Providing Notice of Adoption to the Unknown Putative Father, 59 Va. L. Rev. 517 (1973).

[88] In re Kerr, 547 S.W.2d 837 (Mo. App., 1977); see Rogers v. Lowry, 546 S.W.2d 881 (Tex. Civ. App., 1977); See Barron, Notice to the Unwed Father and Termination of His Parental Rights: Implementing Stanley v. Illinois, 9 Family L. Q. 527 (1975).

[89] In re Sean B. W., 86 Misc. 2d 16, 381 N.Y.S.2d 656 (1976).

[90] Adoption of Rebecca B., 68 Cal. App. 3d 193, 137 Cal. Rptr. 100 (1977); Adoption of Doe, 89 N.M. 606, 555 P.2d 906 (1976).

[91] Adoption of M.T.T., 467 Pa. 88, 354 A.2d 564 (1976).

[92] Adoption of Bantsari, 29 Ore. App. 747, 564 P.2d 1371 (1977).

[93] Adoption of Webb, 14 Wash. App. 651, 544 P.2d 130 (1975).

[94] See Chapter 6, herein.

constitutionality of statutes which *dispense* with the need for paternal consent has at times received judicial attention.[95] In In re Adoption of Malpica-Orsini[96] a statute requiring the consent of all natural parents except that of the father of an illegitimate was held not unconstitutional. Orsini had been adjudicated father of the child, directed to pay support and granted visitation rights. When one Blasi, who had subsequently married the mother, filed for adoption, Orsini moved for an order dismissing the petition for adoption. When the adoption was approved he appealed, contending that the statute, which required only the consent of the mother of a child born out of wedlock, was unconstitutional. He lost. The Court appears to read Stanley v. Illinois to mean that only procedural due process is required to be accorded to the father.

However, in Adoption of Walker[97] the Supreme Court of Pennsylvania declared unconstitutional the portion of that state's adoption act which required only the consent of the mother for the adoption of an illegitimate. One difference between this and the Malpica case is that in Walker the mother could readily have ascertained the putative father's current address and did not do so; hence the adoption proceeding was infirm for reasons other than the unconstitutionality of the statute. Another significant difference is that Pennsylvania has adopted the Equal Rights Amendment, and the statute discriminates against unwed fathers vis-a-vis unwed mothers.[98]

In Wojciechowski v. Allen[99] the court, notwithstanding that the

---

[95] See, e.g., In re Adoption of B., 152 N.J. Super. 546, 378 A.2d 90 (1977) (no adoption without consent of biological father where he has not forsaken his parental obligations, even if mother is dead). See also Schwartz, Rights of a Father With Regard to His Illegitimate Child, 36 Ohio S. L. J. 1 (1975); Constitutional Law—Right of Putative Father to Consent to Proposed Adoption of His Child, 21 N.Y. L. F. 646 (1976).

[96] 36 N.Y.2d 568, 370 N.Y.S.2d 511, 331 N.E.2d 486 (1975), appeal dismissed sub nom. Orsini v. Blasi, 423 U.S. 1042, 46 L. Ed. 2d 631, 96 Sup. Ct. 765 (1976). See Note, Constitutional Law—Fourteenth Amendment Equal Protection—Rights of the Unwed Father—Consent to Adoption, 61 Cornell L. Rev. 312 (1976).

[97] 468 Pa. 165, 360 A.2d 603 (1976).

[98] The case is discussed in Adoption—Equal Rights Amendment—Pennsylvania Law Permitting Adoption of Illegitimate Child Without Consent of Unwed Father Held Unconstitutional, 81 Dick. L. Rev. 857 (1977).

[99] 238 Ga. 556, 234 S.E.2d 325 (1977) (the decision makes no reference whatever to Stanley v. Illinois). See also In Interest of V——M——B——, 559 S.W.2d 901

statute law of Georgia had been changed to require the consent of a natural father to adoption, a change not to take effect until 1978, held that its then applicable statute, which did not require consent other than that of the mother, was constitutional.

These differences of judicial opinion have been at least partially laid to rest by the Supreme Court of the United States in Quilloin v. Walcott.[1] In a contest involving the same Georgia statute approved in Wojciechowski, the Court declined to find that the father had been denied due process and equal protection of the laws:

> ... this is not a case in which the unwed father at any time had, or sought, actual or legal custody of his child. Nor is this a case in which the proposed adoption would place the child with a new set of parents with whom the child had never before lived. Rather, the result of the adoption in this case is to give full recognition to a family unit already in existence, a result desired by all concerned, except appellant. *Whatever might be required in other situations,* we cannot say that the State was required in this situation to find anything more than that the adoption, and denial of legitimation, was in the "best interests of the child." (Emphasis added.)[2]

Perhaps, then, the ideal statute would be one which vests the court with a discretion to determine whether the situation is such that the consent of the putative father is a prerequisite, the best interests of the child here, as always, being the paramount determinative factor.[3]

(Tex. Civ. App., 1977), holding that where an unwed father, though through no fault of his own, had established no relationship with the child, and the mother had consented to its adoption, the father could not assert parental rights in absence of legitimation.

[1] ——U.S.——, — L. Ed. 2d —, 98 Sup. Ct. 549 (1978).

[2] Id., 98 Sup. Ct. at 555 (emphasis by author).

[3] Florida requires the consent of the father, inter alia, if he has provided the child with support in a repetitive, customary manner. In Lovell v. Mason, 347 So. 2d 144 (Fla. App., 1977), an adoption granted over the objection of a father who had overwhelmingly established his fitness to continue the responsibilities of parenthood was reversed. The test of this statute, though undoubtedly an effort to implement the Stanley decision, seems a little mechanical. Such a parent, though budget-wise impeccable, does not necessarily qualify as matching the best interests of the child. As to the provisions of the Uniform Adoption Act (U.L.A.) relating to whose consent is required, see § 5 of that Act; as to when consent and notice to a putative parent can be dispensed with, see § 6.

CHAPTER 4

RIGHTS TO ACCUMULATED PROPERTY AND VALUE OF SERVICES RENDERED DURING COHABITATION

Section
4.1 Judicial attitudes where parties believed themselves married, and their applicability absent such belief
4.2 Effect of conveyances to partners as husband and wife
4.3 Rights adjusted on analogy of a partnership or joint venture
4.4 Agreements to pool earnings
4.5 The resulting trust theory
4.6 Contract implied-in-fact
4.7 Quasi-contract
4.8 Constructive trust
4.9 Inherent equity powers: the equitable lien
4.10 The express contract

4.1. Judicial attitudes where parties believed themselves married, and their applicability absent such belief

Accumulated property

Every state of the union has, absent recognition of common-law marriage, recognized that when property has been accumulated during the existence of what was mistakenly believed to be a valid marriage, justice demands some kind of equitable division of such property.[1] This division, however, may not exactly coincide with the distribution that would take place had the marriage

---

[1] Annotation, Rights of parties to void marriage in respect of transfers or gifts to other in mistaken belief marriage was valid, 14 A.L.R.2d 918 (1950). See Evans, Property Interests Arising from Quasi-marital Relations, 9 Cornell L. Q. 246 (1924); Weyrauch, Informal and Formal Marriage—An Appraisal of Trends in Family Organization, 28 U. Chi. L. Rev. 88 (1960).

actually been valid.[2] When only one of the parties was mistaken, the other knowing of the meretricious nature of the relation, courts may be disposed to treat the innocent participant, vis-a-vis the nonmistaken partner, as they would have done had the marriage been valid.[3] The element of fraud here strengthens an argument for the imposition of a constructive trust on the deceiver.[4]

To arrive at this equitable division of property, when the relationship is terminated by death or dispute, the courts have resorted to a variety of theories, including partnership, joint ventures, agreements to pool earnings, or restitutionary theories. At times the harnessing of such theories seems a little strained.[5] Frequently, too, these doctrinal "pigeonholes" are avoided, and the courts simply rely on the inherent jurisdiction of equity to achieve a just result.[6]

The sections which follow will serve as an introduction to the

---

[2]See Estate of Ricci, 201 Cal. App. 2d 146, 19 Cal. Rptr. 739 (1962), upholding an award of one-half of a decedent's estate to a good faith putative wife and the other half to his true wife, rejecting the former's contention that on his death she qualified for the entire estate. In a community property state, a putative spouse, i.e., one who in good faith believes in the existence of a valid marriage, is entitled to the same share in acquisitions of the couple during the relationship as would be a de jure spouse. In California, the test of good faith here is an objective one. An unreasonable belief in the validity of the marriage would not be sufficient. Spearman v. Spearman, 482 F.2d 1203 (C.A.-5 Ala., 1973) (applying California law). See Comment, Effect of Invalid Marriage on Property Rights, 20 Wash. & Lee L. Rev. 91 (1963).
[3]See Spearman v. Spearman, 482 F.2d 1203 (C.A.-5 Ala., 1973); Sousa v. Freitas, 10 Cal. App. 3d 660, 89 Cal. Rptr. 485 (1970); Estate of Goldberg, 203 Cal. App. 2d 402, 21 Cal. Rptr. 626 (1962); Texas Co. v. Stewart, 101 So. 2d 222 (La. App., 1958); Davis v. Davis, 521 S.W.2d 603 (Tex., 1975); Buck v. Buck, 19 Utah 2d 161, 427 P.2d 954 (1967); Annotation, Liability of one putative spouse to other for wrongfully inducing entry into or cohabitation under illegal, void, or nonexistent marriage, 72 A.L.R.2d 956 (1960).
[4]See section 4.8, herein.
[5]E.g., In re Estate of Thornton, 81 Wash. 2d 72, 499 P.2d 864 (1972), affd. 14 Wash. App. 397, 541 P.2d 1243 (1975), wherein the equities of the parties were adjusted on a partnership analogy by reason of their joint contribution of labor to a farming enterprise and a sharing of the decision making, notwithstanding no belief in the existence of a marriage.
[6]See, e.g., Fung Dai Kim Ah Leong v. Lau Ah Leong, 27 F.2d 582 (C.A.-9 Haw., 1928), cert. den. 278 U.S. 636, 73 L. Ed. 552, 49 Sup. Ct. 33 (1928); Carlson v. Olson, —— Minn. ——, 256 N.W.2d 249 (1977). Generally, see section 4.10, herein; also Foster and Freed, Marital Property and the Chancellor's Foot, 10 Family L. Q. 55 (1976).

PROPERTY RIGHTS—VALUE OF SERVICES 4.1

aforementioned theories. However, this chapter is not primarily concerned with the so-called putative marriage situation. Decisions from the various states involving rights arising from the putative marriage receive consideration in a state-by-state commentary in Chapter 6. The concern in this chapter is more with the application of such doctrines to the unwed partnership where there was not the slightest belief in an existing marriage.

Notwithstanding some support for the proposition that modern cohabitants, neither of whom had any belief in the existence of a marriage, are not automatically deprived of the aid of the courts, it is wise, if a theory of contract cannot be established, to base the cause of action on a partnership analogy, or an agreement to pool earnings, or on circumstances sufficient to establish a resulting or constructive trust. Many courts do not recognize any equities arising from mere cohabitation without marriage,[7] especially where the parties knew their relationship to be one actively condemned as bigamous, adulterous or the like.[8]

Aside from the moral issue, living together without marriage ordinarily involves no more than a mutual exchange of domestic services and support, the extent of the contribution in respect of either aspect being a variable. Do not such cohabitants simply intend that what is his shall remain his, and what is hers shall remain hers? Even if the exchange appears uneven, should not the presumption of gratuity, which controls such exchanges in the legal marriage, take care of this?

Early in the development of our law, where neither cohabitant believed in the existence of a valid marriage, the courts would leave the parties where they stood.[9] *Ex turpi causa non oritur actio.*[10] Later, however, some courts, moved by the injustice that

---

[7]See, e.g., Rehak v. Mathis, 239 Ga. 541, 238 S.E.2d 81 (1977) (section 6.11, herein); Humphries v. Riveland, 67 Wash. 2d 376, 407 P.2d 967 (1965) (section 6.48, herein).

[8]E.g., Meador v. Ivy, 390 S.W.2d 391 (Tex. Civ. App., 1965) (section 6.44, herein).

[9]See Schmitt v. Schneider, 109 Ga. 628, 35 S.E. 145 (1900); De France v. Johnson, 26 Fed. 891 (C.C. Minn., 1886); Abramson v. Abramson, 161 Neb. 782, 74 N.W.2d 919 (1956); Meador v. Ivy, 390 S.W.2d 391 (Tex. Civ. App., 1965); West v. Knowles, 50 Wash. 2d 311, 311 P.2d 689 (1957).

[10](No action can arise out of an immoral cause). E.g., Wellmaker v. Roberts, 213 Ga. 740, 101 S.E.2d 712 (1958), denying relief to either party in respect of an agreement to purchase land jointly and build thereon, the agreement being a part of an agreement for illicit cohabitation.

could result to persons whose only sin was living together without benefit of clergy, showed a readiness to analogize their relationship to that of partners or joint venturers where the parties, in addition to sharing a household, embarked on a business venture. And where one had clearly contributed to the acquisition of an asset to which the other had taken legal title, it was held that a resulting trust could arise.[11] Further, where it appeared unconscionable to permit one party to retain all the benefits of the association (notwithstanding the parties' knowledge of the nonexistence of a marriage), a case for a constructive trust could be found.[12]

In the light of what might be called the sexual revolution, living together without marriage is no longer regarded with the puritanical horror of earlier times.[13] With this change of judicial attitude, a willingness to adjust the property rights of unwed cohabitants is becoming increasingly apparent.[14] One could get the impression that we are moving toward an age where, given a reasonably substantial period of cohabitation in a "family-type" situation, the whole concept of marriage will be supplanted by a "domestic partnership," on dissolution of which the concepts of partnership rather than of marriage dissolution will prevail.[15]

---

[11] See section 4.5, herein.
[12] See section 4.8, herein.
[13] See section 1.1, herein.
[14] See Warner v. Warner, 76 Idaho 399, 283 P.2d 931 (1955) (fact that the relationship was meretricious in its inception did not defeat a spouse's rights in property accumulated during the relationship); Hyman v. Hyman, 275 S.W.2d 149 (Tex. Civ. App., 1954) (want of good faith did not preclude recovery of a share in joint accumulations during cohabitation); Bruch, Property Rights of De Facto Spouses Including Thoughts on the Value of Homemakers' Services, 10 Family L. Q. 101 (1976).
[15] See Folberg and Buren, Domestic Partnership: A Proposal for Dividing the Property of Unmarried Families, 12 Willamette L. J. 453 (1976); Bissett-Johnson, Mistress's Right to a Share in the "Matrimonial Home," 125 New L. J. 614 (1975); Note, Family Law—Property Rights of Unmarried Cohabitants—California Affords Contract and Equitable Remedies to Meretricious Spouses, 23 Wayne L. Rev. 1305 (1977); Property Rights Between Unmarried Cohabitants, 50 Ind. L. J. 389 (1975) (suggesting, after a discussion of pooling agreements, partnerships and joint venture analogies, and the equitable remedies, that the courts could eliminate a lot of confusion and uncertainty as to their rights by treating illicit cohabitation as essentially an economic venture). See also Prager, Sharing Principles and the Future of Marital Property Law, 25 U.C.L.A. L. Rev. 1 (1977). For a

That age is not yet with us.[16] Nonetheless, as will appear from the discussion which follows, it seems predictable that: (a) all but the most puritanical of the states will honor an express contract between extramarital partners as long as illicit intercourse does not form an element of the consideration; (b) if a contract implied-in-fact can be established in regard to their joint accumulations, its terms will be enforced; and (c) even absent proof as to any agreement, express or tacit, where there is an actual and ostensible family relationship and a union that has been in existence for a substantial period, the courts will regard both of the parties, no matter where the legal title lies, as having an equity in some portion of the accumulated assets.

Value of services rendered

A distinction between the good faith putative spouse and the ordinary unwed cohabitant retains much of its early vitality when a claim is in respect of services contributed to the household. The courts are almost unanimous in holding that when a woman voluntarily and knowingly lives in illicit relations with a man, she cannot recover on a basis of implied contract for her services.[17] The reasons given are twofold. Not only is the nature of the relation so completely intertwined with the rendition of services as to be indistinguishable therefrom,[18] but also the presumption of gratuity applicable when services are rendered in

---

discussion of the various matrimonial property arrangements in the United States, see Foote, Levy and Sander, *Cases and Materials on Family Law*, p. 749 (1976).

[16]See Latham v. Hennessey, 13 Wash. App. 518, 535 P.2d 838 (1975), affd. 87 Wash. 2d 550, 554 P.2d 1057 (1976) (possible doctrines for division of property held inapplicable); Humphries v. Riveland, 67 Wash. 2d 376, 407 P.2d 967 (1965) (unsuccessful effort to recover a half interest in paramour's estate on a basis of agreement to pool earnings, joint venture or constructive trust); Annotation, Rights and remedies in respect of property accumulated by man and woman living together in illicit relations or under void marriage, 31 A.L.R.2d 1255 (1953).

[17]See Emmerson v. Botkin, 26 Okla. 218, 109 Pac. 531 (1910); Willis v. Willis, 48 Wyo. 403, 49 P.2d 670 (1935) (not only does the relationship as husband and wife negate that of a master and servant, but such cohabitation, being in violation of principles of morality and chastity, and against public policy, no promise to pay implied).

[18]Guerin v. Bonaventure, 212 So. 2d 459 (La. App., 1968).

a familial situation[19] rules out such a claim. However, when the claimant for compensation in good faith believes in the existence of a valid marriage, there is strong authority to support a claim in quantum meruit to the extent that the services exceed the value of the support, if any, that has been received.[20]

As early as 1962, however, a dissenting California judge, in Keene v. Keene,[21] expressed disapproval, as an immoral double standard, of a decision which punished a female meretricious cohabitant by depriving her of compensation for services rendered during her and her male partner's common venture while, in a sense, rewarding the male partner by permitting him to retain the fruits of the venture. Then, in Marvin v. Marvin,[22] the court said: "There is no more reason to presume that services are contributed as a gift than to presume that funds are contributed as a gift; in any event the better approach is to presume ... that the parties intended to deal fairly with each other."[23]

The Marvin decision has been criticized in that, where no contract exists between cohabitants, the vague possibility that courts might utilize "quasi partnership," quasi-contract, implied-in-fact contract, or other such fictions leaves no guidelines as to when such doctrines are to be harnessed.[24]

Such criticisms are justified. It is suggested that much difficulty, confusion and possible litigation could be avoided by maintaining a clear distinction between the mere exchange of support and services and the accumulations acquired during the cohabitation period.

---

[19]See Kirby v. Kirby, —— S.C. ——, 241 S.E.2d 415 (1978); Douthwaite, *Attorney's Guide to Restitution,* § 9.1, p. 365 (1977).

"It is not essential that there be [a] kinship or meretricious cohabitation between an unmarried man and woman residing in the same dwelling to have a family relationship. But the relationship must be established by evidence before the presumption that services rendered must be gratuitous" [comes into play]. Schanz v. Estate of Terry, 504 S.W.2d 653, 657 (Mo. App., 1974).

[20]Annotations, Right of woman who lives with man in the mistaken belief that they are lawfully married to recover for services, 31 A.L.R. 424 (1924).

[21]57 Cal. 2d 657, 21 Cal. Rptr. 593, 371 P.2d 329 (1962).

[22]18 Cal. 3d 660, 134 Cal. Rptr. 815, 557 P.2d 106 (1976).

[23]Id., 18 Cal. 3d at 683, 134 Cal. Rptr. at 831, 557 P.2d at 121.

[24]See Comment, Property Rights upon Termination of Unmarried Cohabitation: Marvin v. Marvin, 90 Harv. L. Rev. 1708 (1977); see also Family Law—Property Rights of Unmarried Cohabitants—California Affords Contract and Equitable Remedies to Meretricious Spouses, 23 Wayne L. Rev. 1305 (1977).

Possible distinction between accumulations and services

Though there is some doubt where the claimant cohabitant had a good faith belief in the validity of a marriage, the courts rather consistently decline to imply a promise to compensate a claimant for the value of services where he or she clearly knew of the nonexistence of a married relationship.[25] "It would appear unusual to say the least to demand rental and/or board from a person with whom one shares an apartment for a period of eighteen years in a meretricious relation. Because of the intimacy resulting in such relationship, in the absence of any demand for payment, there is strong indication that such services were rendered gratuitously."[26] No matter how great the disparity of value between the support furnished and the services rendered, the presumption of gratuity should control in the absence of circumstances justifying the use of the "escape mechanisms" discussed in the sections which follow.

As far as concerns tangible accumulations, however, there seems no reason why any presumption of gratuity should be invoked. Whether or not the partners live in a community property state, the fact is they are not married. If the male wage earner acquires a Porsche with his earnings, or the female wage earner a mink coat, what logic is there in invoking a presumption that a gift of these items, or a half of them, was intended? A presumption that the parties intend to "deal fairly with each other" could hardly be said to extend this far.

More difficult is the problem where the acquisition is of household goods. But here again it seems not unreasonable, absent agreement, to assume that they belong exclusively to the one who paid for them. The statement that "the parties may well expect that property will be divided in accord[ance] with the parties' own tacit understanding and that in the absence of such understanding the courts will fairly apportion property accumulated through

---

[25] Annotation, Recovery for services rendered by member of household or family other than spouse without express agreement for compensation, 7 A.L.R.2d 8 (1949).

[26] In re Klemow's Estate, 411 Pa. 136, 191 A.2d 365, 368 (1963). See also In re Thompson's Estate, 337 Ill. App. 290, 85 N.E.2d 840 (1949); In re Ballard's Estate, 252 Iowa 548, 107 N.W.2d 436 (1961); Jenkins v. Prevost, 140 So. 2d 238 (La. App., 1962).

mutual effort"[27] seems disputable. If the parties get into court, it is probably because their understanding as to the ownership of these assets was not mutual. If it was not mutual, to saddle a court with the responsibility of an enlightened paternalism in determining "what is fair" seems itself unfair to the court. Unless there has been some element of chicanery in their relations, it could be argued that cohabitants who do not have the foresight to make express provision as to what is to become of such assets in the event of a termination of their relationship have only themselves to blame. On this basis, title to the refrigerator, the stereo or the waterbed should remain in the partner who bought and took delivery, without any allowance to the one who shared in its enjoyment without paying.

Such an argument is in no way weakened by the fact that, if it is not clear which of the parties paid for the property, or how much of the price was paid by each, an equal division can be decreed.[28] In this situation, the parallel between a joint venture or an agreement to pool earnings is too close to be ignored. Nevertheless, it remains only a suggestion. "Unless it can be argued that a woman's services as cook, housekeeper, and home-maker are valueless, it would seem logical that if, when she contributes money to the purchase of property, her interest will be protected, then when she contributes her services in the home, her interest in property accumulated should be protected."[29] In Carlson v. Olson,[30] where the female partner had contributed nothing beyond services, the Supreme Court of Minnesota held a trial court justified in finding that the parties intended that their accumulations were to be divided equally on the theory of irrevocable gifts: of money on the one side and of services on the other.

Perhaps there is a compromise solution. In Carlson, the parties had cohabited for twenty-one years without marriage. In Marvin,

---

[27]Marvin v. Marvin, 18 Cal. 3d 660, 682, 134 Cal. Rptr. 815, 830, 557 P.2d 106, 121 (1976).
[28]See King v. Jackson, 196 Okla. 327, 164 P.2d 974 (1945) (section 6.37, herein); Poole v. Schrichte, 39 Wash. 2d 558, 236 P.2d 1044 (1951) (section 6.48, herein).
[29]Curtis, J. in Vallera v. Vallera, 21 Cal. 2d 681, 686–687, 134 P.2d 761, 764 (1943).
[30]——Minn.——, 256 N.W.2d 249 (1977).

the period was six years. Could not the "justified expectations" of the parties be determined by reference to the length of the duration of the relationship? To pose an extreme hypothetical: if the wage earner (whatever sex) expended some $5,000 on the purchase of household appliances while the other cohabitant, though warming up an occasional TV dinner, mixing martinis and ensuring that the doors were locked at night, did little more, and the relationship broke up after six months, would it be a fair expectation of the parties that their mutual contributions should be divided on a fifty-fifty basis?

Justice Clark, concurring in the Marvin decision because the situation did present issues of fact as to whether express or implied contract could be established, raises some provocative questions. Will not the application of equitable principles reimpose on trial courts the unmanageable burden of arbitrating domestic disputes? Will not a quantum meruit system of compensation for services—discounted by benefits received—place meretricious spouses in a better position than lawful spouses? If a quantum meruit system is to be allowed, does fairness not require inclusion of all services and all benefits regardless of how difficult the evaluation?[31]

4.2. Effect of conveyances to partners as husband and wife

In the absence of a statute changing the common-law concept of the unity of spouses,[32] a conveyance to persons legally married as husband and wife creates an estate by the entireties.[33] But if the

---

[31] Prior to the Marvin decision, California courts had held that, absent express contract, the cohabitant who had no belief in a marriage could share in the accumulations only in proportion to the funds contributed. Services were not included. See Vallera v. Vallera, 21 Cal. 2d 681, 134 P.2d 761 (1943); Keene v. Keene, 57 Cal. 2d 657, 21 Cal. Rptr. 593, 371 P.2d 329 (1962). Admittedly, this could operate to the grave prejudice of the woman, who usually is the one who contributes services, but the Marvin opinion, which is that services should always enter into consideration, could equally operate to the prejudice of the wage earner.

[32] See Annotation, Estates by entireties as affected by statute declaring nature of tenancy under grant or devise to two or more persons, 32 A.L.R.3d 570 (1970).

[33] Annotation, Character and incidents of estate created by a deed to persons as husband and wife who are not legally married, 83 A.L.R.2d 1051 (1962).

grantees are not legally married, no such estate can come into existence.[34] Ordinarily, the favored rule today is that such a conveyance operates to create a tenancy in common, and not a joint tenancy.[35] If this is the result, there is no right of survivorship, and on termination of the relationship each grantee, or his or her successor in title, will receive an undivided one-half interest.[36]

The mere use of the phrase "tenants by the entirety" in a deed ordinarily is not enough to support an adjudication of joint tenancy.[37] However, the language of the deed plus the circumstances surrounding the transaction have at times resulted in a construction that the parties hold as joint tenants,[38] especially where

---

[34]See Young v. Young, 37 Md. App. 211, 376 A.2d 1151 (1977); Beaton v. LaFord, 79 Mich. App. 373, 261 N.W.2d 327 (1977); In re Will of Imp, 68 Misc. 2d 911, 328 N.Y.S.2d 595 (1972); Vlcek v. Vlcek, 42 App. Div. 2d 308, 346 N.Y.S.2d 893 (1973); In re Estate of Kolodji, 85 Misc. 2d 946, 380 N.Y.S.2d 610 (1976) (a statute whereby joint tenancy is created when persons not legally married take real property as husband and wife cannot be applied retroactively); Masgai v. Masgai, 460 Pa. 453, 333 A.2d 861 (1975); Cavanagh v. Cavanagh, ——R.I.——, 375 A.2d 911 (1977); Knight v. Knight, 62 Tenn. App. 70, 458 S.W.2d 803 (1970).

A fortiori, a claimed second wife, who married a decedent who had been previously married, is not entitled to assert a tenancy by entirety despite her innocence, where the property was acquired in their joint names before a ceremonial marriage. Jablonski v. Caputo, 297 So. 2d 310 (Fla. App., 1974).

[35]Fuss v. Fuss,——Mass.——, 368 N.E.2d 276 (1977); In re Meyron's Estate, 6 Misc. 2d 673, 164 N.Y.S.2d 443 (1957); Hildebrand v. Hildebrand, 25 App. Div. 2d 698, 268 N.Y.S.2d 44 (1966); Thurmond v. McGrath, 70 Misc. 2d 849, 334 N.Y.S.2d 917 (1972). Compare Coleman v. Jackson, 109 App. D.C. 242, 286 F.2d 98, 83 A.L.R.2d 1043 (1960), cert. den. 366 U.S. 933, 6 L. Ed. 2d 391, 81 Sup. Ct. 1656 (1961), discussed in section 6.9, herein.

Joint tenancies are not favored in courts of equity. McKissick v. McKissick, —— Nev. ——, 560 P.2d 1366 (1977).

[36]Reed v. Reed, 516 S.W.2d 568 (Mo. App., 1974); Place v. Cundaro, 34 App. Div. 2d 698, 309 N.Y.S.2d 714 (1970); Annotation, Division of property upon annulment of marriage, 11 A.L.R. 1394 (1921).

[37]See Place v. Cundaro, supra.

[38]See In re Jackson's Estate, 112 Cal. App. 2d 16, 245 P.2d 684 (1952); Horton v. Estate of Elmore, 420 S.W.2d 48 (Mo. App., 1967) (note payable to man or woman as tenants by the entirety created ambiguity as to unmarried payees; intention of parties must be drawn from instrument and surrounding circumstances).

Where grantees are not husband and wife, unless terms of agreement expressly or by necessary implication call for a joint tenancy, tenancy in common will be presumed. Margarite v. Ewald, —— Pa. Super. ——, 381 A.2d 480 (1977). See also Maxwell v. Saylor, 359 Pa. 94, 58 A.2d 355 (1948), where the conveyance was

the partners were simply mistaken as to their marital status and the rights of innocent third parties were involved, or where there was additional language evincing an intent to provide for a right of survivorship.[39]

Whatever the nature of the estate created, the "meretricious" nature of the parties' relationship should not automatically deprive them of their legal rights as tenants of some description, no matter to what extent the "righteous indignation of the neighborhood" is aroused.[40]

If, as is usual, unmarried partners hold title as tenants in common, their subsequent marriage cannot convert the estate into a tenancy by the entireties or into a joint tenancy.[41]

It should be borne in mind that the courts, when adjusting or determining the rights of unmarried partners who took title as husband and wife, are almost always if not always exercising jurisdiction of an *equitable nature*.[42] Equity is truly elastic in its

---

to a couple living in illicit relations "as tenants by the entireties," and the evidence showed that the entire price was paid by the woman, the court found it inconceivable that the parties could have intended that on the death of the man she should be deprived of any part of the title acquired solely by the fruits of her own labor.

[39]Pennsylvania seems unusually ready to find a joint tenancy. See Estate of Whiteman v. Whiteman, 466 Pa. 343, 353 A.2d 386 (1976). See also Duke v. Hopper, 486 S.W.2d 744 (Tenn. App., 1972) (where grantee had himself and his cohabitant falsely designated as husband and wife in deed, grantee would have been estopped to show facts contrary to deed as against person assuming truth of that fact, and grantee's heirs were estopped from denying tenancy by the entireties as against innocent purchaser from surviving spouse).

[40]Casini v. Lupone, 8 N.J. Super. 362, 72 A.2d 907 (1950). See also Hynes v. Hynes, 28 Wash. 2d 660, 184 P.2d 68 (1947), where the court honored the agreement that all assets should be held in both names though both knew the male partner was undivorced.

[41]Young v. Young, 37 Md. App. 211, 376 A.2d 1151 (1977), where, though at the time of taking title the grantees were not legally married, the court thought that the fact that they were named in the deed as "tenants by the entireties, their assigns, the survivor of them and the survivor's personal representatives and assigns ..." was enough to warrant a finding of a joint tenancy.

[42]Divorce actions, probate proceedings, actions to quiet title, declaratory relief, and marriage annulments are all equitable in origin.

employment of remedial devices.[43] Thus, neither the determination of a joint tenancy nor that of a tenancy in common necessarily means that the proceeds of the property may not be apportioned on a basis of the couple's respective contributions toward its acquisition or improvement.[44] At times the courts, finding one partner to be sole owner by right of survivorship, will impress the property with an equitable lien in favor of the other partner to compensate for contributions of this nature.[45] At times the presumption of a gift will come into play. When a party who pays for the property causes title to be placed in the name of another to whom he or she is under a natural or moral obligation to provide, the law ordinarily presumes a gift was intended.[46] A resulting trust for the payor[47] would only arise on rebuttal of this presumption.[48] This presumption of a gift has been found where a putative husband pays for the property and title is taken in his and his putative wife's joint names.[49]

---

[43]In granting relief a court of equity may adapt its orders and decrees so as to meet the needs of the particular case, and preserve, so far as possible, the equities of all of the parties. McClintock, *Equity,* ch. 2, § 14 (1948). Specific performance could be had of a promise made by one partner to the other, who in good faith believed in their common-law marriage, to leave that partner all his property when he died. Sancha v. Arnold, 114 Cal. App. 2d 772, 251 P.2d 67 (1952), reh. den. 114 Cal. App. 2d 772, 252 P.2d 55 (1953). A decedent's oral promise to his paramour to convey her a home, toward the cost of which she had contributed, could be enforced against the decedent's estate. Tyranski v. Piggins, 44 Mich. App. 570, 205 N.W.2d 595 (1973). Generally as to the inherent power of the court to grant equitable relief, see section 4.10, herein. Annotation, Enforcement of antenuptial contract or settlement conditioned upon marriage, where the marriage was subsequently declared void, 46 A.L.R.3d 1403 (1972).

[44]For a decree quieting title in the male partner with adjustment for advancements made by the female for repairs, see Anderson v. Stacker, 317 S.W.2d 417 (Mo., 1958).

[45]See, e.g., Conkling v. Conkling, 126 N.J. Eq. 142, 8 A.2d 298 (1936). Generally, see section 4.10, herein. In Trecot v. Taxter, 69 Misc. 2d 248, 329 N.Y.S.2d 139 (1972), where defendant wife had not told plaintiff husband of a prior marriage, plaintiff was entitled to reformation of a deed granting tenancy by the entirety, but the property was impressed with an equitable lien for the sum paid by defendant.

[46]Mountford v. Mountford, 181 Md. 212, 29 A.2d 258 (1942); Yohe v. Yohe, 466 Pa. 405, 353 A.2d 417 (1976); Galvan v. Galvan, 534 S.W.2d 398 (Tex. Civ. App., 1976).

[47]See section 4.4, herein.

[48]Galvan v. Galvan, 534 S.W.2d 398 (Tex. Civ. App., 1976).

[49]E.g., Brandt v. Brandt, 215 Ore. 423, 333 P.2d 887 (1958). See Annotations, Effect of annulment of marriage on rights arising out of acts of or transactions

PROPERTY RIGHTS—VALUE OF SERVICES 4.3

Especially evident is this flexibility of approach where the rights of the legal spouse vis-a-vis a putative spouse or an extramarital partner fall for adjudication.[50] This notwithstanding the suggestion of the proponents of the Uniform Marriage and Divorce Act, to the effect that in the event of a conflict between the asserted rights of a legal spouse and those of a putative spouse, the court shall do whatever is appropriate to achieve justice,[51] is unlikely to receive a standing ovation from those who strive for certainty in the law.

4.3. Rights adjusted on analogy of a partnership or joint venture

In their effort to achieve an equitable adjustment of the property rights on the termination of an unwed cohabitation the courts, whether or not the cohabitants believed in the existence of a valid marriage, frequently analogize their arrangement to that of a partnership or joint venture.[52] The analogy is not of course an

---

between parties during the marriage, 2 A.L.R.2d 637 (1948); Rights of party to void marriage in respect of transfers or gifts of other in mistaken belief marriage was valid, 14 A.L.R.2d 918 (1950).

As to restitution to the nonbreaching partner of land purchased with his funds (with title taken as joint tenants) of a gift made in contemplation of marriage, without allowance to the breaching partner for her services during their cohabitation, see Shaw v. Shaw, 227 Cal. App. 2d 159, 38 Cal. Rptr. 520 (1964). See also Gaden v. Gaden, 29 N.Y.2d 80, 323 N.Y.S.2d 955, 272 N.E.2d 471 (1971). See also Douthwaite, *Attorney's Guide To Restitution*, § 2.7 (1977).

[50] See Comment, Competitive Rights of Legal and Putative Wives, 1 Loyola U. L. Rev. (L.A.) 99 (1968); Annotations, Rights in decedent's estate as between lawful and putative spouses, 81 A.L.R.3d 6 (1977); Estoppel or laches precluding lawful spouse from asserting rights in decedent's estate as against putative spouse, 81 A.L.R.3d 110 (1977). See also Annotations, Person entitled to devise or bequest to "husband," "wife," or "widow," 75 A.L.R.2d 1413 (1961); Presumption as to validity of second marriage, 14 A.L.R.2d 7 (1950); Who qualifies as "widow" or "widower" under § 216 of the Social Security Act (42 U.S.C. § 416), pertaining to survivor's benefits, where two or more alleged spouses survive decedent, 31 A.L.R. Fed. 300 (1977).

[51] See section 1.6, herein.

[52] See Meretricious Relationships—Property Rights: A Meretricious Relationship May Create an Implied Partnership—In re Estate of Thornton, 81 Wash. 2d 72, 499 P.2d 864 (1972), 48 Wash. L. Rev. 635 (1973). That the partnership theory is at best an analogy, at least where the relationship is not for profit-making purposes, is supported by the commentators under the Uniform Partnership Act (U.L.A.), § 6, wherein they state that it is essential for the operation of that Act that it should be confined to associations organized for profit.

exact one. As a general rule, one who contributes only services to a partnership, and no money, shares in the profits only, and not in the capital assets.[53] Applied to the situation under consideration, one who contributes services only can share only in the *jointly acquired* accumulations.[54] No actual business transactions need necessarily be involved,[55] if there is enough evidence to show that a cohabitant has by his or her efforts contributed to the business success of the other.[56] However, if the parties merely lent their mutual efforts toward earning a livelihood and acquiring real or personal property (which is what virtually all cohabitants do), any housewife might be labeled as implied partner in her husband's business, and any unemployed cohabitant who performs household duties could invoke the theory of a quasi-partnership[57] as a means of achieving an equitable property division in states which do not recognize common-law marriage.[58] Reasoning of this nature has indeed been resorted to, especially in situations of an innocent putative spouse whose partner is threatening to deprive her of all interest in the property to which he acquired title during the relationship.[59] However, in such a situation the theory of partnership has often been rejected;[60] there is no need for any fiction of a partnership to award to the injured good faith believer

---

[53] See Hunter v. Allen, 174 Ore. 261, 147 P.2d 213 (1944), mod. 174 Ore. 261, 148 P.2d 936 (1944).

[54] See, e.g., In re Estate of Thornton, 81 Wash. 2d 72, 499 P.2d 864 (1972), affd. 14 Wash. App. 397, 541 P.2d 1243 (1975).

[55] E.g., Colwell v. Zolkosky, 29 App. Div. 2d 720, 286 N.Y.S.2d 422 (1968).

[56] See, e.g., Hyman v. Hyman, 275 S.W.2d 149 (Tex. Civ. App., 1954).

[57] See Implied Partnerships: Equitable Alternative to Contemporary Methods of Postmarital Property Distribution, 26 U. Fla. L. Rev. 221 (1974).

[58] If a common-law marriage is found, such a cohabitant has the status of and shares the rights of a legal wife. See section 1.5, herein.

[59] See In re Brenchley's Estate, 96 Wash. 223, 164 Pac. 913 (1917).

In applying the partnership analogy the courts are not of course committing themselves to award an equal division of property accumulated. See Poole v. Schrichte, 39 Wash. 2d 558, 236 P.2d 1044 (1951).

[60] See Schmitt v. Schneider, 109 Ga. 628, 35 S.E. 145 (1900) (a very harsh early decision, virtually relegating the innocent victim of a fraudulently induced marriage to the status of a creditor with a right of action at law for damages); Latham v. Hennessey, 13 Wash. App. 518, 535 P.2d 838 (1975), affd. 87 Wash. 2d 550, 554 P.2d 1057 (1976), holding parties not to have intended a business relationship in connection with residential property acquired by the woman during a meretricious relationship.

in a valid marriage such proportion of the property as, under all the circumstances, would be just.[61]

An apt illustration of the working of the doctrine is where a couple each contributes rental residential property to their venture, live on the rentals and acquire additional property with the receipts, without any actual agreement as to a sharing of the profits.[62]

There is some logic to support this partnership or joint venture analogy. If living together is considered immoral, it is unreasonable to permit a defendant to assert his own immorality as a defense to an action on a business arrangement; if it is considered amoral, the social relations of the parties should have no bearing on their rights under the arrangement. It was long ago stated that rights accruing out of labor and property embarked in a joint venture are not destroyed by the existence of unchaste sexual relations between the venturers.[63]

In In re Estate of Thornton[64] the court, conceding that an implied partnership can be found even though title to the alleged partnership property is held in the name of one of the partners only, rejected the partnership theory where a woman had worked hard alongside a farmer in a cattle-raising operation over a period of sixteen years, thereby contributing significantly to the success of the farmer's venture. It found the evidence to be as consistent with a finding that the woman was a managerial employee as it was that she was a partner. The court declined to answer whether a long-term, stable meretricious relationship in which the partners appear to hold themselves out as husband and wife would give rise to a property interest because the facts simply refuted any such situation.

4.4. Agreements to pool earnings

Some states have long recognized that, even if the cohabitants have no belief in the existence of a marriage, if they have agreed

---

[61]See Buckley v. Buckley, 50 Wash. 213, 96 Pac. 1079 (1908).
[62]Fernandez v. Garza, 88 Ariz. 214, 354 P.2d 260 (1960).
[63]Morales v. Velez, 18 F.2d 519 (C.A.-1 Puerto Rico, 1927) (dissenting opinion).
[64]81 Wash. 2d 72, 499 P.2d 864 (1972), affd. 14 Wash. App. 397, 541 P.2d 1243 (1975).

to pool their earnings and share equally in the joint accumulations, equity will protect the interests of each in such property.[65] A view commonly taken is that if the unlawful cohabitation is merely incidental to or separate from a contract concerning the ownership of property, the courts will give effect to the agreement.[66] Another view is that if the cohabitants have specifically agreed to share equally the accumulations derived from their pooled earnings, this will be enforced, but that if there was no express agreement, the property will be divided on a basis proportionate to their respective contributions.[67] A difficulty here is that if no express agreement need be shown, the mere fact that the partners operated a joint bank account ought to be enough from which an agreement to pool earnings can be inferred. Furthermore, in the event of termination of the relationship, the task of determining whose money was used for what purpose would simply be impossible.

In view of the divergent attitudes of the courts in regard to pooling of earnings as a justification for apportioning the property interests of cohabitants when no express agreement can be established, such pooling should only be used as a makeweight. The decisions which discuss this aspect frequently blend it into the partnership concept.[68] Moreover, when purchases are made from a joint bank account, an implied-in-fact contract to share equally in such acquisitions could readily be assumed.

4.5. The resulting trust theory

It is a well established rule of the law of trusts that when one person takes title to land and another person has paid, or as-

---

[65]E.g., Vallera v. Vallera, 21 Cal. 2d 681, 134 P.2d 761 (1943).
[66]See Mitchell v. Fish, 97 Ark. 444, 134 S.W. 940 (1911); Bracken v. Bracken, 52 S.D. 252, 217 N.W. 192 (1927).
[67]Fancher v. Brunger, 94 Cal. App. 2d 727, 211 P.2d 633 (1949); Vallera v. Vallera, 21 Cal. 2d 681, 134 P.2d 761 (1943). In Barlow v. Collins, 166 Cal. App. 2d 274, 333 P.2d 64 (1958), where one cohabitant absconded with the proceeds of a joint bank account, the amount of the deposit was held equally divisible between the parties.
[68]In Stevens v. Anderson, 75 Ariz. 331, 256 P.2d 712 (1953), a woman had cohabited with a decedent for over thirty years. She had lent him $318. He had told her that he would "care for" her on his death. He did. He left her $5,000 and a

sumed liability for, the purchase price, the presumption is that the parties intended the title holder to hold the land as a trustee for the one responsible for payment.[69] This is known as the purchase money resulting trust.[70] This doctrine is frequently applied by the courts in adjudicating the interests in acquisitions by persons living in a nonmarital relationship.[71] Although the application of the doctrine in the various states is not entirely inflexible, a good deal more predictability is possible than, for example, in the case of the constructive trust or the equitable lien.

It is also a settled rule of law that when the payor of the purchase price is the husband of the grantee, the presumption is that the conveyance was by way of gift or advancement, and not of a resulting trust.[72] This presumption of a gift would ordinarily extend to a situation where the male partner pays the purchase price and title is taken in the names of both good faith putative spouses.[73] It is inferred that the payor intended a gift if the grantee is a natural object of his bounty.[74] But the same presumption of a gift does not ordinarily apply to unmarried persons unlawfully cohabiting.[75] This could have the result that if a lawful spouse pays the purchase price and has title taken in the name of the other, the other has all rights, but if a meretricious cohabitant so acts, the payor of the purchase price can assert a resulting trust,[76] provided the deed was not for the purpose of inducing or

---

life estate in a furnished home. In the course of dismissing her claim for a share in his estate, the court quoted from the Vallera judgment but declined to find any "pooling" involved in the situation.

[69] Restatement (Second), *Trusts*, § 440 (1959).

[70] See Bogert and Bogert, *Handbook of the Law of Trusts*, p. 261 et seq. (5th ed. 1973).

[71] See, e.g., Akers v. Stamper, 410 S.W.2d 710 (Ky. App., 1966) (where title to land was taken in the name of the female partner, neither being apparently greatly concerned as to the legality of their "marriage," which was in fact invalid, the male was awarded one half on a theory of joint venture).

[72] Bogert and Bogert, note 70, supra, at p. 278.

[73] E.g., Brandt v. Brandt, 215 Ore. 423, 333 P.2d 887 (1958); Buck v. Buck, 19 Utah 2d 161, 427 P.2d 954 (1967).

[74] Restatement (Second), *Trusts*, § 442 (1959).

[75] "No case has been cited ... holding that a resulting trust between persons living in illicit cohabitation *ipso facto* fails for illegality." Walberg v. Mattson, 38 Wash. 2d 808, 232 P.2d 827, 831 (1951).

[76] See Evans v. Evans, 301 P.2d 232 (Okla., 1956); Hall v. Bone, 210 Ore. 98, 309 P.2d 997 (1957).

prolonging illicit cohabitation.[77] But any such presumption of a resulting trust can always be rebutted by proof that a gift was intended.[78] Thus, where a male cohabitant paid over all his earnings to the female, who bought properties in her name alone, the court, on a showing that the couple had agreed to hold one half each, held that the properties were owned by them as tenants in common.[79]

The theory of a resulting trust has been rejected where the alleged payor is unable to establish the precise amount contributed by the claimant.[80] But if the precise amount can be shown, at times the only basis on which a meretricious cohabitant can assert a claim to any judicial division of property held in the other cohabitant's name is this pro tanto resulting trust.[81] Courts often rigidly insist that a mere "pooling" of a couple's resources to pay familial obligations, including the payments on a mortgage, is not enough on which to predicate a resulting trust. Such courts require that the price, or the aliquot portion on which the claim for a resulting trust pro tanto is based, have been paid at the time the purchase was made.[82]

Historically, the resulting trust doctrine related to land. It is doubtful whether it could be extended to assets which constitute personal property.[83] The contribution made by a claimant for a

---

[77] Williams v. Bullington, 159 Fla. 618, 32 So. 2d 273 (1947); Walberg v. Mattson, 38 Wash. 2d 808, 232 P.2d 827 (1951). See also Yeiser v. Rogers, 19 N.J. 284, 116 A.2d 3 (1955), denying a resulting trust in favor of a gambler who had title to his land vested in a paramour to prevent its seizure for fines and unpaid income taxes.

[78] See Orth v. Wood, 354 Pa. 121, 47 A.2d 140 (1946).

[79] See Ross v. Sampson, 4 N.C. App. 270, 166 S.E.2d 499 (1969).

[80] E.g., McQuin v. Price, 88 Cal. App. 2d 914, 199 P.2d 742 (1948). In Anderson v. Stacker, 317 S.W.2d 417 (Mo., 1958), land purchased by a male cohabitant was put in the name of the partners as husband and wife. Absent convincing proof of the amount which each had contributed to the purchase price, the court quieted title in the male ordering an adjustment to the female in respect of money she had advanced for repairs.

[81] See Sugg v. Morris, 392 P.2d 313 (Alaska, 1964).

[82] See Smith v. Smith, 108 So. 2d 761 (Fla., 1959); Glover v. Glover, 268 S.C. 433, 234 S.E.2d 488 (1977).

[83] See Keene v. Keene, 57 Cal. 2d 657, 21 Cal. Rptr. 593, 371 P.2d 329 (1962) (Peters, J., dissenting opinion). In Williams v. Teachers Ins. & Annuity Assn., 15 Ill. App. 3d 542, 304 N.E.2d 656 (1973), an attempt to impose a resulting trust on life insurance proceeds failed, but there is no suggestion that it could not apply to personal property.

PROPERTY RIGHTS—VALUE OF SERVICES 4.6

resulting trust need not necessarily be pecuniary. Services can suffice if they were rewarded by the acquisition of property;[84] services rendered toward the improvement of property, once acquired, do not constitute consideration for an interest in such property on which a resulting trust can be predicated.[85]

In states which have abolished the purchase money resulting trust,[86] the unwed cohabitant, seeking an equitable adjudication as to the accumulations of the partners, need not despair: the resulting trust theory is only one of several escape mechanisms from the harsh rule that one who forms an illicit alliance has no claim to a share in the "acquets and gains of her paramour accumulated during the years of her debasement."[87]

4.6. Contract implied-in-fact

Modern authority supports the proposition that, as long as sexual favors are not an explicit part of the consideration, the courts will honor an express contract between unmarried cohabitants as to their respective rights in property accumulated, during the period of their cohabitation.[88] Since the only difference between an express contract and a contract implied-in-fact is in the manner in which it is established, it follows that an implied-in-fact contract can form a basis of recovery of a share in these accumulations.[89] As often as not, such a cause of action is intertwined with a claim based on the analogy of a partnership or joint venture.[90]

Once again, a major stumbling block is the presumption of

---

[84]See Dean v. Goldwire, 480 S.W.2d 494 (Tex. Civ. App., 1972).

[85]Keene v. Keene, 57 Cal. 2d 657, 21 Cal. Rptr. 593, 371 P.2d 329 (1962).

[86]Among states which have for most purposes abolished the doctrine are Kentucky, Michigan, Minnesota, New York, and Wisconsin.

[87]The quoted language is from Vallera v. Vallera, 126 P.2d 638, 639 (1942), affd. 21 Cal. 2d 681, 134 P.2d 761 (1943). For a full review of the equitable remedies that can be used when the facts surrounding the unwed cohabitation warrant their application, see Marvin v. Marvin, 18 Cal. 3d 660, 134 Cal. Rptr. 815, 557 P.2d 106 (1976), discussed in section 4.10, herein.

[88]See sections 4.1 and 4.10, herein.

[89]See Latham v. Hennessey, 13 Wash. App. 518, 535 P.2d 838 (1975), affd. 87 Wash. 2d 550, 554 P.2d 1057 (1976).

[90]See Garza v. Fernandez, 74 Ariz. 312, 248 P.2d 869 (1952).

gratuity that ordinarily accompanies the knowing living-together-without-marriage relationship.[91] To overcome this presumption, the claimant would have to show that his or her contribution went well beyond the ordinary give-and-take exchanges that occur while living together: in the purchase of groceries, performance of domestic chores, entertainment of occasional guests and dining out. An example of the kind of situation where it can readily be shown, by their conduct, that the parties tacitly agreed that some form of reward would be forthcoming may be seen in Roznowski v. Bozyk.[92] Here, when the couple began cohabiting, the defendant owned a resort consisting of four cabins and a bar. The plaintiff, who had previously worked as a cocktail waitress, helped him run his resort. Her work included painting and cleaning the cabins and tending bar. In addition, she performed most of the domestic chores in the home. In return, the defendant paid all of their expenses, including upkeep of the home, the plaintiff's insurance premiums, car payments, clothing, food and medical bills. The parties had a joint checking account.

This case could well have been decided for the plaintiff on a basis of joint venture, or on a basis of contract implied-in-fact. It was remanded for a new trial because the trial judge had found for the plaintiff on a basis of quantum meruit, a theory that had not been pleaded. (In so doing, the Court of Appeals may have been misguided. Implied-in-fact contract was pleaded, and the trial court, in granting relief in quantum meruit may have simply meant "plaintiff is entitled to whatever her services were worth." The term quantum meruit is ambiguous; it may mean (1) that there is a contract "implied-in-fact" to pay the reasonable value of the services, or (2) that, to prevent unjust enrichment, the claimant may recover on a quasi-contract (an "as if" contract) for that reasonable value.)[93]

It is for the fact trier to determine whether a cohabitant, knowing of the nonexistence of a marriage, has overcome the

---

[91]See section 4.1, herein.
[92]73 Mich. App. 405, 251 N.W.2d 606 (1977).
[93]See Martin v. Campanaro, 156 F.2d 127, 130 (C.A.-2 N.Y., 1946), cert. den. 329 U.S. 759, 91 L. Ed. 654, 67 Sup. Ct. 112 (1947); Costigan, Implied-in-Fact Contracts, 33 Harv. L. Rev. 376, 387 (1920).

presumption of gratuity and can establish an implied contract. Circumstances such as the remoteness of the operation from the domestic regime, and the nature of the services performed, are of crucial importance.[94] Of obvious relevance too is the nature and extent of the other cohabitant's participation, and his or her station in life and occupation.

4.7. Quasi-contract

In the days when courts of law and chancery operated separately, quasi-contract was introduced as a means whereby a court of common law could prevent unjust enrichment. Since in disputes involving the property rights of cohabitants on a termination of their relationship the appeal is usually addressed to the "equity" side of the court, quasi-contract does not often appear as a possibility. It can so appear, however, when one cohabitant is seeking a money judgment reflecting the fair value of services contributed to the domestic menage. Historically, such an action would be an action in *indebitatus assumpsit,* or general assumpsit on the common counts, the count being for work and labor. A good faith putative spouse, having rendered services solely because of belief in the marriage, will have caused the other spouse to be unjustly enriched by the amount by which the reasonable value of such services exceed the amount devoted by the other to the good faith putative spouse's support and maintenance.[95] Such an issue does not involve an equitable division of their joint accumulations. Most states today would allow quasi-contractual relief in this situation.[96]

Where there was no belief in a marriage, however, the difficulty of establishing any expectation of payment, by reason of the presumption of gratuity which can bar a recovery on a theory of contract implied-in-fact,[97] is again presented.[98] The decisions to

---

[94]See Keene v. Keene, 57 Cal. 2d 657, 21 Cal. Rptr. 593, 371 P.2d 329 (1962); Fancher v. Brunger, 94 Cal. App. 2d 727, 211 P.2d 633 (1949).

[95]E.g., Lazzarevich v. Lazzarevich, 88 Cal. App. 2d 708, 200 P.2d 49 (1948), discussed in section 6.5, herein.

[96]See Fung Dai Kim Ah Leong v. Lau Ah Leong, 27 F.2d 582 (C.A.-9 Haw., 1928), cert. den. 278 U.S. 636, 73 L. Ed. 552, 49 Sup. Ct. 33 (1928) (section 6.12, herein).

[97]See section 4.6, herein.

[98]See Hill v. Westbrook's Estate, 95 Cal. App. 2d 599, 213 P.2d 727 (1950).

the effect that an express contract between the cohabitants will be honored by the courts[99] are of relatively recent origin. Theoretically, in states which so hold, there seems no reason why quasi-contract, as an alternative remedy for breach of contract,[1] could not be pleaded. But, as mentioned, most of the litigation in this field to date has involved relief of an equitable, as distinguished from common law, nature.[2]

Nevertheless, there are decisions long predating the modern sexual revolution which recognize that, where sexual relations between the parties is merely a coincidental and collateral occurrence and not the consideration for, or motive inducing, a payment or transfer, such collateral immorality does not bar restitutionary relief.[3] A theory of quasi-contract would not be objectionable as such.[4]

4.8. Constructive trust

The constructive trust, known in this country as "the formula through which the conscience of equity finds expression"[5] by reason of its complete elasticity of application, can rank prominent in importance among the various doctrines on which a claim by a cohabitant for an adjustment of the equities in respect of their joint accumulations can be predicated. The theory underlying this remedy is that where property had been acquired in such circumstances that the holder of legal title may not in good conscience retain the beneficial interest, equity converts him into a trustee.

---

[99]See section 4.10, herein.

[1]See Dobbs, *Handbook on the Law of Remedies*, p. 791 (1973).

[2]E.g., Annotation, Right, on annulment of marriage, to allowance for services, 111 A.L.R. 348 (1937).

[3]Annotation, Illicit sexual relations between man and woman as affecting right of either to recover money paid or property transferred to other, 120 A.L.R. 475 (1939). Zytka v. Dmochowski, 302 Mass. 63, 18 N.E.2d 332, 120 A.L.R. 470 (1938), to which this annotation is appended, however, was a bill for an accounting and not an action in quasi-contract.

[4]As to criminal or wrongful conduct as a bar to restitution, an area in which the courts, perhaps consciously (see Dobbs, *Remedies,* p. 1003 (1973)) preserve remarkable flexibility, see Restatement, *Restitution*, § 140 (1936).

[5]Cardozo, J., in Beatty v. Guggenheim Exploration Co., 225 N.Y. 380, 122 N.E. 378, 380 (1919). See Restatement, *Restitution*, § 160 (1936).

PROPERTY RIGHTS—VALUE OF SERVICES   4.8

Only a few examples need be presented to illustrate the potential range of this device.

In Kuhlman v. Cargile,[6] an elderly divorced man lived with one Molly, also advanced in years. At the suggestion of a mutual friend, he built a house on the friend's land, and had the title placed in Molly's name. She contributed three or four thousand dollars, and the plaintiff, her male cohabitant, over $24,000. The court, without even adverting to the possible presumption of gratuity, and without so much as a reference to illicit relations, regarded this as a straightforward case of unjust enrichment and decreed Molly a constructive trustee of the land for the benefit of the plaintiff with an allowance (a "setoff") in respect of her contribution.

A mere breach of a promise, absent other factors, does not warrant the imposition of a constructive trust on what was promised.[7] Usually, though not necessarily, the remedy is not invoked absent a showing, if not of fraud,[8] of the breach of a confidence reposed in the defendant. Thus, where the parties had cohabited for twenty years, albeit in adultery, when land was purchased for their common ownership, and title was taken in the name of one only, proof that the other contributed cash for the purchase and subsequent maintenance, as well as having made improvements on it, was enough to warrant a decree impressing a trust on the land and directing a conveyance of an undivided one-half interest in the fee thereof.[9]

A constructive trust was again the remedy for a situation

---

[6]200 Neb. 150, 262 N.W.2d 454 (1978).
[7]See Franklin v. Phoenix, 294 A.2d 483 (D.C. App., 1972) (section 6.9, herein).
[8]See Schwarz v. United States, 191 F.2d 618 (C.A.-4 Md., 1951) (constructive trust where wife defrauded as to marital status of husband).
[9]Muller v. Sobol, 277 App. Div. 884, 97 N.Y.S.2d 905 (1950), appeal den. 277 App. Div. 951, 99 N.Y.S.2d 757 (1950). As to the argument that since the agreement was not in writing, it was unenforceable, the court held the part performance was "unequivocally referable" to the agreement. It could have contented itself with a statement that, a constructive trust being a trust which arises by operation of law, the statute of frauds is not applicable. Compare Wirth v. Wirth, 38 App. Div. 2d 611, 326 N.Y.S.2d 308 (1971) (not a cohabitation situation) where, by mutual agreement, the wife's earnings were used for family support and the husband's were set aside "for our latter days." The husband used his earnings to acquire land to which he took title. On their divorce the court declined to hold him as a constructive trustee, apparently considering that the alimony award was enough to satisfy the "conscience of equity."

where a putative wife, with the object of avoiding claims by a prior wife of the putative husband, induced him to convey land to her with the understanding that she would reconvey it to him on request.[10] The confidential nature of the interspousal relation beyond a doubt extends to the putative marriage.[11] Though it seems there is no presumption of a confidential relation where the parties do not purport to be spouses or believe in a marriage, such a relation can readily be established.[12]

When the situation would have called for a constructive trust against a cohabitant, putative or meretricious, had he or she been alive, there is no reason why the same remedy cannot avail against his or her heirs.[13]

When land is conveyed to grantees as tenants by the entirety, and in fact their marriage is invalid, the usual rule is that the parties hold as tenants in common.[14] However, in a situation where only one of the grantees knows of the invalidity of the marriage and induces the other, who has paid the purchase price, to have the deed so drawn, this is fraud; a constructive trust can be decreed to vest the title entirely in the innocent grantee along with an annulment of the "marriage."[15]

4.9. Inherent equity powers: the equitable lien

There is almost no limit on the inherent power of courts, in the exercise of their equitable jurisdiction, to decree what is fitting to adjust the property rights of couples who have accumulated property while living together unwedded.[16] If the parties themselves have come to some agreement prior to litigating their dispute, the courts will, absent a showing of unconscionability, undue influence or the like, give effect to it.[17] Frequently, the court simply

---

[10] Mathews v. Mathews, 310 S.W.2d 629 (Tex. Civ. App., 1958).
[11] Id.
[12] See Comment, Rights of the Putative and Meretricious Spouse in California, 50 Calif. L. Rev. 866 (1962).
[13] See Patrick v. Simon, 237 Ga. 742, 229 S.E.2d 746 (1976).
[14] See section 4.2, herein.
[15] Randolph v. Randolph, 28 Misc. 2d 66, 212 N.Y.S.2d 468 (1961).
[16] See Omer v. Omer, 11 Wash. App. 386, 391, 523 P.2d 957, 960 (1974).
[17] See Karoley v. Reid, 223 Ark. 737, 269 S.W.2d 322 (1954); Whitney v. Whitney, 192 Okla. 174, 134 P.2d 357 (1942) (discussed in section 6.37, herein).

orders an accounting as on the dissolution of a partnership.[18] It may order the payment of a fixed sum of money to the innocent partner in such a relationship in whatever amount it considers reasonable;[19] this amount could of course reflect a reimbursement of contributions plus sums needed for child support.[20]

Commonly, when the circumstances are not such as to warrant the imposition of a constructive trust, a court will permit one of the partners to retain the accumulations, but impose, for the benefit of the other partner, an equitable lien to secure that partner's claim to reimbursement of contributions to the regime.[21] This was the result in a case where one cohabitant had procured the other's signature on a note for funds to buy building materials for a house to which he took title, the lien being to protect her against the contingency that the note might be enforced against her.[22] Since a lien does no more than secure the enforcement of an award,[23] if the property acquired by the partners has greatly enhanced in value since its acquisition, a partner who has been misled by the other as to the validity of the marriage would do well to press hard for a constructive trust, if only for a partial interest in such property.[24]

4.10. The express contract

The preceding discussion surveys the extent to which, notwithstanding a meretricious relationship between the partners, courts resort to various remedies to achieve a just result in

---

[18] E.g., Reese v. Reese, 132 Kan. 438, 295 Pac. 690, 75 A.L.R. 728 (1931).
[19] See Maple v. Maple, 566 P.2d 1229 (Utah, 1977) (discussed in section 6.45, herein).
[20] E.g., Snegirev v. Samoilov, 26 Ore. App. 687, 554 P.2d 595 (1976).
[21] E.g., Walker v. Walker, 330 Mich. 332, 47 N.W.2d 633, 31 A.L.R.2d 1250 (1951); Marum v. Marum, 21 Misc. 2d 474, 194 N.Y.S.2d 327 (1959); Colwell v. Zolkosky, 29 App. Div. 2d 720, 286 N.Y.S.2d 422 (1968).
[22] Beckman v. Mayhew, 49 Cal. App. 3d 529, 122 Cal. Rptr. 604 (1974) (wherein the court indicated reluctance to follow earlier cases, since overruled by implication, which declined to allow a meretricious contributor credit for domestic services).
[23] Merit v. Losey, 194 Ore. 89, 240 P.2d 933 (1952).
[24] Restatement, *Restitution,* § 161, comment a (1936).

adjudicating the equities of unmarried partners on a termination of their relationship.[25] Remaining for consideration is the question of the extent to which such cohabitants, prior to or during the relationship, can resolve this problem by an express agreement.

The idea of such an agreement had the backing of judicial dicta long before the current revolution in sexual mores. In 1937 a Maryland judge said: "the mere fact that a man and a woman are living together in an unlawful relation does not disable them from making an enforceable contract with each other, if it has no reference to continuation of the relation, or is only incidentally connected with it and may be supported independently of it."[26] Of more modern times, the states are moving toward a recognition that substantial rights very much akin to, if not identical with, those of married partners can flow from any relationship, of whatever intended duration, involving sexual conduct of a more or less permanent, or more than merely sporadic, duration. Corbin writes that: "A bargain between two persons is not made illegal by the mere fact of an illicit relationship between them, so long as that relationship constitutes no part of the consideration bargained for and no promise in the bargain is conditioned upon it."[27] The enforceability, via a division of the accumulations of the meretricious cohabitants, of an agreement to pool earnings has already been mentioned.[28] In that situation, the fact that the parties, at the time of the agreement, were living in, or contemplating, an immoral relationship has long been held not to disqualify them from entering into such a contract, as long as

---

[25]This approach by the courts has been described as a "patchwork attempt to stretch ... old law to deal with modern realities." Weitzman, Legal Regulation of Marriage: Tradition and Change, 62 Calif. L. Rev. 1169 (1974).

[26]Baxter v. Wilburn, 172 Md. 160, 190 Atl. 773, 774 (1937) (dictum). Weitzman questions whether the state has any legitimate interest in interfering with such contracts between consenting adults, and expresses doubt as to whether it would be possible to write a contract that would be made more disadvantageous to the woman than the traditional marriage contract. Weitzman, note 25, supra.

[27]Corbin, *Contracts*, § 1476, p. 622 (1962); Williston, *Contracts*, § 1745 (3d ed., 1972) is to the same effect. See also Krauskopf and Thomas, Partnership Marriage: The Solution to an Ineffective and Inequitable Law of Support, 35 Ohio S. L. J. 558 (1974); Poulter, Cohabitation Contracts and Public Policy, 124 New L. J. 999 (1974).

[28]Section 4.4, herein.

PROPERTY RIGHTS—VALUE OF SERVICES 4.10

such immoral relation is not made a consideration of their agreement.[29] So, too, an agreement by one cohabitant to build a house in return for the other's promise to convey land has been upheld.[30]

However, it was not until Marvin v. Marvin[31] that a court explicitly and unequivocally applied to the extramarital situation the proposition of Professor Corbin.[32]

Michelle Triola Marvin (having adopted the surname of movie actor Lee Marvin) averred, in an action against the actor, that she and he had entered into an oral agreement that while they lived together they would combine their efforts and earnings and would share equally any property accumulated as a result of their efforts; further that they agreed to hold themselves out to the general public as husband and wife, and that she would render her services as a companion, homemaker and the like to Lee. She also alleged that she agreed to give up her "lucrative" career as an entertainer and singer to devote full time to her domestic duties; and that in return Lee agreed to provide for all of her financial support and needs for the rest of her life. They lived together for over five years, and she alleged her fulfillment of all her obligations under the agreement. Then Lee compelled her to leave his household and, after continuing to support her for a year and a half, refused to provide further support. She asked for declaratory relief with respect to her contract and for a constructive trust on half the property acquired during the course of the relationship. She appealed a judgment on the pleadings, and the Supreme Court of California held that the complaint stated a cause of action for breach of contract.

Although the Marvin decision is far-reaching in its implications, and has received much attention,[33] it is really no more than

---

[29]Trutalli v. Meraviglia, 215 Cal. 698, 701–702, 12 P.2d 430, 431 (1932); Bridges v. Bridges, 125 Cal. App. 2d 359, 270 P.2d 69 (1954).
[30]Croslin v. Scott, 154 Cal. App. 2d 767, 316 P.2d 755 (1957).
[31]18 Cal. 3d 660, 134 Cal. Rptr. 815, 557 P.2d 106 (1976).
[32]See note 27, supra, and related text.
[33]See Clark, New Marriage, 12 Willamette L. J. 441 (1976); Kay and Amyx, Marvin v. Marvin: Preserving the Options, 65 Calif. L. Rev. 937 (1977); Marvin v. Marvin: The Scope of Equity with Respect to Non-Marital Relationships, 5 Pepperdine L. Rev. 49 (1977); Note, Oral Agreement Between Nonmarital Partners to Hold Joint Property and Pool Earnings Is Enforceable in Equity But Not Under Family Law Act, 1977 Calif. Family L. Rep. 1002.

4.10   UNMARRIED COUPLES AND THE LAW

a judicial acknowledgment of what has long been recognized: that extramarital partners can make a valid and enforceable contract as to their property rights in their accumulations if sex is not made an explicit part of the consideration. The decision compels the conclusion that any such agreement, even if only implied in fact, will be recognized and enforced provided it falls short of calling for prostitution. (It has been suggested that, on termination of a union which is "functionally marital" in structure, much the same reasoning as is applied to support an equitable division of the accumulations of the partners could be harnessed, in a proper case, to ensure that a partner who is left in need receive "quasi-spousal" support.)[34]

Perhaps, however, no court previous to Marvin has been so forthright in its sanctioning of unmarried relationships. In Green v. Richmond,[35] for example, a decedent had orally promised to bequeath all his assets to the plaintiff if she would "stay with him." She complied, and it was clear that there was a sexual relationship between them. The court, holding an oral promise to make a will not to be enforceable under Massachusetts statute law, allowed her a quantum meruit recovery for her services. It held her to be so entitled unless the agreement was based on a sexual relationship; and that whether sexual favors are a part of the consideration for such a contract is a question for the fact trier. The distinction between this and Marvin may well be more than mere semantics. The principle announced in Marvin is that such a contract will be enforced "unless expressly and inseparably based upon an illicit consideration."[36] The Massachusetts court thought was that the fact trier must look at the surrounding circumstances to determine whether the agreement was "based on a sexual relationship." But if, as was the case in Green, the fact trier chooses to close his eyes to the facts, the net result is the same. The Marvin approach negates any taint of hypocrisy in the matter. Theoretically, however, the Green attitude precludes a plaintiff from circumventing the morality issue by merely

---

[34]Beyond Marvin: A Proposal for Quasi-Spousal Support, 30 Stan. L. Rev. 359 (1978).
[35]—— Mass. ——, 337 N.E.2d 691 (1975).
[36]Marvin v. Marvin, 18 Cal. 3d 660, 672, 134 Cal. Rptr. 815, 823, 557 P.2d 106, 114 (1976).

refraining to state sexual services as an essential term of the bargain.[37]

Michigan, too, has held that, while bargains in whole or in part in consideration of an illicit relationship are unenforceable, agreements between parties to such relationships with respect to money or property will be enforced if the agreement is independent of the illicit relationship.[38] Thus, one who illicitly cohabited with and performed services for a decedent, also contributing to the price of a home he purchased, could enforce the agreement. And this result was notwithstanding Michigan's denunciation, as criminal, lewd and lascivious cohabitation.[39] According to the Michigan court, "Where a meretricious relationship has already been entered upon, to penalize one of the parties by striking down their otherwise lawful promises, will not undo the relationship, nor is it likely to discourage from entering upon such relationships."[40] (However, to attempt a distinction between those who make a commitment prior to embarking on an illicit relationship and those who are already immersed in it would present unimaginable difficulties of proof.)

In Carlson v. Olson[41] the Supreme Court of Minnesota, relying heavily on the Marvin decision, affirmed a decree equally dividing personal and real property accumulated during a 21-year unwed union. As discussed earlier,[42] such a solution, crediting wifely services as a contribution that justifies a fifty-fifty division, on a basis of contract implied-in-fact, seems worthy of recognition when the relationship has stood the test of time. It has little to commend it when the rendition of services is of a short-term nature; in fact, it could do much to encourage liaisons entered into by predators.

The spirit of the Marvin case received recognition in an Oregon decision.[43] The court upheld a contract whereby the plaintiff was to receive one-half of all of the defendant's property, real and

---

[37] See Robbins, Domestic Relations—Expansion of the Property Rights of Non-marital Partners; 11 Suffolk U. L. Rev. 1327 (1977).
[38] Tyranski v. Piggins, 44 Mich. App. 570, 205 N.W.2d 595 (1973).
[39] Mich. Comp. Laws, § 750.335.
[40] Tyranski v. Piggins, 44 Mich. App. 570, 205 N.W.2d 595, 598 (1973).
[41] —— Minn. ——, 256 N.W.2d 249 (1977).
[42] See section 4.1, herein.
[43] Latham v. Latham, 274 Ore. 421, 547 P.2d 144 (1976).

personal, accumulated by them during the agreement. This was regarded as not void as against public policy, despite allegations that the primary consideration was future illicit cohabitation. The consideration, the court felt, was not restricted to sexual relations but contemplated "all of the burdens and other amenities of married life." The case differs from the Michigan situation[44] in that the Oregon statute denouncing as criminal lewd and lascivious cohabitation was repealed with the objective of removing all criminal sanctions from private consensual activity between consenting adults.[45]

Whatever the jurisdiction, it can today safely be said that where each of the partners has made some tangible contribution to the accumulation of property, the judicial "hands-off" attitude, a harsh refusal to adjust the equities in any way with a resultant deprivation by one of any share because of the "meretricious" nature of the relationship, should belong in the past.[46] Even the courts of England, traditionally opposed to the notion of cohabitation contracts as a substitute for marriage, may well be on the way to a change of viewpoint.[47]

Whether a contract between cohabitants must be in writing rests on state statutes. Some states, prompted no doubt by the uncertainty of the property rights of such persons engendered by decisions of the Marvin type, are actively considering legislation of this nature. In Marvin, the statute provision requiring writing for a contract for a marriage settlement was not applicable because marriage was not even contemplated. But if the agreement is to make a will bequeathing assets to the co-cohabitant, a statute of frauds may bar enforceability,[48] though not necessarily restitutionary relief such as quantum meruit.[49] Even if there are

---

[44]See note 40, supra, and related text.
[45]See Yturri, Three Rs of Penal Law Reform, 51 Ore. L. Rev. 427, 435 (1972).
[46]But see Wellmaker v. Roberts, 213 Ga. 740, 101 S.E.2d 712 (1958), declining relief on an agreement to buy land jointly and build thereon because it was part of an agreement for illicit cohabitation. The sounder qualification would restrict this ostrich-like attitude to contracts where the cohabitation is of the essence of the contract. See Updeck v. Samuel, 123 Cal. App. 2d 264, 266 P.2d 822 (1954).
[47]See Poulter, Cohabitation Contracts and Public Policy, 124 New L. J. 999 (1974).
[48]See Bridgman v. Stout, 10 Ore. App. 474, 500 P.2d 731 (1972).
[49]Douthwaite, *Attorney's Guide to Restitution*, § 7.5 (1977).

no statutory requirements of a writing, the so-called Dead Man's Statutes may present difficulties of proof of an oral agreement of this nature. Typically, such statutes provide that in proceedings in which an executor or personal representative of a decedent is a party, involving matters that occurred during the decedent's lifetime, one who is a party to the issue, whose interest is adverse to the estate, is not competent to testify as to such matters.

The traditional view that a bargain between married persons, or those contemplating marriage, to change the essential incidents of marriage is illegal has met with a good deal of criticism.[50] Some writers argue that childless couples ought to have the right to regulate the terms of their marriage by contract; that the relationship is within the zone of protection afforded by the right of privacy decisions, Griswold v. Connecticut, Roe v. Wade and the like.[51] The traditional position may at times operate as an incentive to persons who wish to live together, but to avoid the trappings the law places on spouses, to embark on extramarital cohabitation. "To the proposition that marriage contracts are contrary to public policy, one might sensibly respond that it is against public policy to *refuse* to enforce marriage contracts. Like the existence of contracts which subject workers to inhumane working conditions, the absence of marriage contracts is in effect oppressive to housewives, since without the right to contract with their husbands, housewives have no right to bargain for their services in the home."[52] "Since a disappointment of reasonable expectations offends the most basic principles of equity, asserted state action constituting an invalidation [of a marriage contract] should demand at least as much, if not more, scrutiny than state action constituting an enforcement."[53]

---

[50]See Foster, Marriage and Divorce in the Twilight Zone, 17 Ariz. L. Rev. 462 (1975).

[51]As to the impact of the right of privacy on unmarried couples, see section 2.6, herein. See also Fleischmann, Marriage by Contract: Defining the Terms of Relationship, 8 Family L. Q. 27 (1974).

[52]See Note, Marriage Contracts for Support and Services: Constitutionality Begins at Home, 49 N.Y.U. L. Rev. 1161, 1204 (1974).

[53]Id., at 1212.

4.10 UNMARRIED COUPLES AND THE LAW

Some states have statutes allowing contracts between husband and wife just as freely as if they were not married.[54]

Suggested provisions for a contract in lieu of marriage

Whether the judicial approach to contracts in lieu of marriage will throughout the states become as liberal as that evidenced in the Marvin decision, it is likely that the approach of Professor Corbin,[55] to the effect that an illicit relation does not invalidate a bargain between the parties as long as sexual relations form no part of the consideration, is of general acceptance. In Kozlowski v. Kozlowski,[56] for example, which receives later attention,[57] the court stated that persons involved in immoral acts are not automatically barred from contracting amongst themselves regarding those aspects of their behavior or property which are severable from their immoral acts. "The court will not assist them in the advancement of immoral intentions, but they are not denied all access to judicial intervention where the rights asserted do not directly depend on such illicit behavior. Thus, one who expressly contracts to receive compensation for domestic services such as housekeeping, cleaning and cooking should not be denied the right to enforce that contract even though the parties may also engage in a meretricious relationship.... Any other result would reward one of the parties thereto by relieving him of an otherwise enforceable obligation at the expense of the party providing the services."[58] Hence, no matter in what state the partners are domiciled, it is wise for persons contemplating an extramarital relationship to commit themselves to a written agreement, signed and, if not notarized, attested to by two witnesses, defining the partners' mutual rights and obligations. Such a writing can obviate the need for litigation in the event of a breakdown in the relationship, and, if the worst befalls, the agreement itself would

---

[54]E.g., Cal. Civil Code, § 5103.

For illustrations of a trend recognizing the validity of antenuptial contracts which contemplate divorce, see Posner v. Posner, 233 So. 2d 381 (Fla., 1970); Volid v. Volid, 6 Ill. App. 3d 386, 286 N.E.2d 42 (1972); Buettner v. Buettner, 89 Nev. 39, 505 P.2d 600 (1973); Unander v. Unander, 265 Ore. 102, 506 P.2d 719 (1973).

[55]See note 27, supra, and related text.

[56]164 N.J. Super. 162, 395 A.2d 913 (1978).

[57]See section 6.31, herein.

[58]Kozlowski v. Kozlowski, 395 A.2d at 918.

in all probability be admissible in evidence to assist a court in adjudicating the equities of the situation.

No standard form of contract would serve any useful purpose, because too much depends on the circumstances of the partners and the nature of their wishes. Such an agreement could, for example, provide:

(1) That the parties agree to live together in an unmarried state, until such time, if ever, as they decide to become married, or, unilaterally or by mutual consent, decide to separate.

(2) That the parties have made this choice and this agreement freely and voluntarily, without any element of duress or undue influence on the part of either or of anyone else.

(3) That, no matter to which state they may decide to move, the parties do not desire to be regarded as husband and wife. (They can stipulate as they choose regarding the names by which they are to be known; the fact that they are known to the world as "Mr. and Mrs. Jones" would not of itself create a common-law marriage.)

(4) That the parties attach, as a part of the agreement, an inventory of their present belongings, real as well as personal, stating the ownership of each item. That such property, and the proceeds or fruits thereof, shall forever remain the property of the party in whose name it is recorded. (Alternatively, they might choose to provide for joint ownership of some or all of their assets, but such a provision is not recommended, since the economic entanglements accompanying the division of such assets may tend to act as a brake on the partners' complete freedom to sever the relationship.)

(5) That all acquisitions by each or either party subsequent to this agreement shall be owned solely by the acquiring party. Checking and savings accounts will be separately owned and operated. (Joint bank accounts, and purchases made therefrom, can present embarrassing problems of ownership, but, if the parties anticipate making joint purchases, there is no objection to a provision that in such case a written agreement, to provide for the ownership, e.g., in proportion to the share of the price contributed, shall be annexed to the contract.)

(6) That —————— shall be responsible for all household expenses, including repairs, taxes, rentals, and domestic supplies. (Alternatively, that the parties shall be equally responsible for such; itemized accounts to be kept of all such disbursements and a settlement made on the final day of each month.)

(7) That the parties shall be, as far as practicable, equally responsible for the performance of household duties. (If only one party is earning an income, a provision that the items in (6)

shall be considered offset by the contribution of the other by way of household services would be acceptable.)

(8) That, in the event either or both parties incur legal responsibility for a child (state how the financial and custodial responsibility is to be allocated). Unless the parties are in a state where there is no serious possibility that a sexual involvement could taint the contract, it would be wise not to make any explicit reference to such matters as sexual relations, birth control or illegitimate offspring. (If the child is not the biological child of both parties, and the nonparent objects to the application of their agreement to such child, a termination of the relationship presents a way out.)

(9) That, if either party becomes ill, disabled or laid off work, the parties agree (e.g., that the other party shall for that period assume the following duties of such disabled party).

(10) That either party is free to terminate this arrangement without assigning any reasons and without any liability for damages resulting to the other. (A provision for liquidated damages in the event of a breach seems ill-advised. It would tend to detract from the voluntary nature of the relationship and might generate unnecessary ill feeling.)

(11) That should any provision of this contract be found contrary to the law or policy of any state, the parties intend the remaining provisions to remain in force; they further intend that the provisions of the contract be binding on them without regard to their legal enforceability.

(12) (Optional.) That in the event of a dispute over the interpretation of this agreement, the parties shall agree to defer the decision to three informal arbitrators to be selected by (a mutual friend).

(13) (Optional, if there are existing children of one or the other party.) That the responsibility for the care, support and education of (names of children) shall be shared in exactly the same way as if the parties had been the legal parents of such child. (Or John Jones shall carry such responsibility, or Mary Jones shall carry such responsibility).

(14) (Optional.) That each party is free to take (an evening a week) (a week-long vacation) (a month-long vacation) without the other at his or her choice as long as the relationship continues.

(15) (Optional, if the contract provides for joint ownership of any assets.) That any gifts received by one of the parties, whether by inheritance or otherwise, shall be the sole property of such donee.

(16) (Optional.) That any amendments to this contract shall be signed in writing by the parties, witnessed and annexed to this agreement.

PROPERTY RIGHTS—VALUE OF SERVICES 4.10

The foregoing provisions do not purport to exhaust the possibilities of what could be included. For example, provisions could cover the partners' respective right and obligations regarding children in the event of a termination.[59] But since the law cannot readily be supplanted by agreement in this area (the state being a *parens patriae*) such provisions would, if enforceable, likely be redundant.

An explicit statement that "sexual relations in no way constitute a consideration for this agreement," though probably not objectionable, might present a danger; if a court, in judging the validity of the agreement, looks at the realities of the situation, such a statement, akin to "protesting too much," might sway it to find the facts to be exactly the other way.

---

[59] If the contract should contain any provision relating to the devolution of property on death, care should be taken to comply with the formalities required by the controlling statutes on wills.

CHAPTER 5

MARITAL STATUS AND TAXES

By Mary Moers Wenig*

Section
5.1 A quick look at taxes
5.2 A tax case history of a pair of cohabitants
5.3 Marital status and federal income tax rates
5.4 Marriage and nonmarriage penalty taxes
5.5 "Married," "unmarried," "surviving spouse," "head of household," and "dependent" defined
   (A) Married or unmarried under state law
   (B) Married or unmarried under federal tax law
   (C) Surviving spouse
   (D) Head of household
   (E) Dependent
5.6 Gift and estate taxes and the marriage bonus
5.7 "Income splitting" by cohabitants
5.8 Agreements by cohabitants to share expenses
5.9 Cohabitants claiming two households in one
5.10 A side-look at social security
5.11 Most favored status—Married and divorced in contemplation of cohabitation
5.12 Desideratum—Tax reform

Tables

I.   Income tax consequences of marriage and divorce
II.   Taxable income brackets for individuals: comparison of the four rate tables
III. Max-tax table
IV.   Tax cost of marriage and nonmarriage: comparison of joint return tax and tax on two unmarried individuals
IV-A. Tax cost of marriage and nonmarriage: dollar amount of marriage penalty tax—Comparison of joint return tax and tax on two unmarried individuals
V.   Tax cost of marriage exacerbated by filing separate returns
V-A. Tax cost of marriage: dollar cost of filing separate returns rather than joint return
VI.   Tax cost of marriage and nonmarriage: comparison of joint return tax and tax on two unmarried individuals where one taxed as head of household

*Professor of Law, University of Bridgeport School of Law.

5.1 UNMARRIED COUPLES AND THE LAW

VI-A. Tax cost of marriage and nonmarriage: dollar amount of marriage penalty tax—Comparison of joint return tax and tax on two unmarried individuals where one taxed as head of household

VII. Tax cost of marriage and nonmarriage: comparison of joint return tax and tax on two unmarried individuals where both taxed as head of household

VII-A. Tax cost of marriage and nonmarriage: dollar amount of marriage penalty tax—Comparison of joint return tax and tax on two unmarried individuals where both taxed as head of household

VIII. Marriage status definitions—Requirements

5.1. A quick look at taxes

Intentionally or unintentionally, consistently or inconsistently, taxes which we pay have an impact upon us in different ways and amounts, depending upon whether we are married or unmarried.

The United States demands income taxes from those of us whose annual income exceeds a threshold amount,[1] plus the $1,000 for each personal exemption allowed us.[2] The threshold amount, the tax rates, and a number of tax credits, exclusions and deductions will vary, depending upon our marital status. And for the Internal Revenue Code, there are more definitions of marital status than the two of "married" and "unmarried."

The social security tax is imposed on each worker's first $22,900 of annual earned income. While marital status does not affect the tax rate, marriage or remarriage may affect benefits.[3]

There is a federal tax cost of dying for a small percentage of

---

[1] I.R.C. § 63(d). This is the "zero bracket amount" or ZBA, the amount at which the applicable tax rate schedule starts to assess the tax. The ZBA is Congress' 1977 substitute for the standard deduction, and is determined as follows:

	Z.B.A.
Married couple filing joint return	$3,400
Unmarried individual characterized as a surviving spouse	3,400
Unmarried individual who is not a surviving spouse	2,300
Married individual filing a separate return	1,700

[2] I.R.C. § 151.
[3] See section 5.10, herein.

decedents.[4] There is a roughly parallel tax cost of generosity during a taxpayer's lifetime. These costs may vary depending upon the marital status of the deceased or donor taxpayer.

What this chapter deals with is a considerable portion of the Internal Revenue Code.[5] More than forty sections of the Code produce different consequences for taxpayers who are friendly and married, for taxpayers who are unfriendly and married, for taxpayers who are unfriendly and divorced, and for taxpayers who are friendly and unmarried.[6]

5.2. A tax case history of a pair of cohabitants

For an overview of the impact of the Internal Revenue Code on married couples versus unmarried cohabitants, let us take a hypothetical pair of marvinizers, Robert Roe and Jane Doe, and follow them through several tax years.

As the story unfolds, Robert is married, but not to Jane. As such, Robert can file a joint return with his wife,[7] even though

---

[4]Prior to the Tax Reform Act of 1976, only seven per cent of individuals dying each year incurred any federal estate tax liability, and less than two per cent will be subject to the tax as a result of the 1976 Act. Surrey, et al., *Federal Wealth Transfer Taxation*, p. 11 (1977).

[5]Discussion of state taxes will not be attempted, not because their burden falls alike on all taxpayers, but because of the variety of these laws. Generally, state death and gift taxes do differentiate, as does the federal law, among taxpayers on the basis of marital status. On the other hand, the majority of the state laws imposing income taxes are unlike the federal system, which pays considerable attention to marital status. Some of the states do provide benefits or burdens based on marital status, but not necessarily the same as imposed by the Internal Revenue Code.

Sales, duty, excise and property taxes, which generally, but not always, are unaffected by marital status (whether federal, state or local), are also outside the scope of this chapter.

[6]A LEXIS scan of the Internal Revenue Code of 1954, as amended through 1978, using the search words joint return, separate return, spouse, wife, husband, married, unmarried, living apart, living separately, and separated, produced 284 references to Code sections and subsections. Definitional, repetitive, obsolete and irrelevant references, and references to attribution rules which were not limited to spouses, but also included familial and other relationships, were winnowed out and references to provisions outside of Subtitle A—Income Taxes were also eliminated. The remaining income tax sections which turn on these marital status words are: §§ 1, 37, 41, 42, 43, 44, 44A, 46, 48, 50A, 58, 63, 101, 105, 120, 151, 163, 170, 179, 213, 217, 280, 401, 408, 505, 672, 674, 677, 913, 1034, 1211, 1233, 1244, 1251, 1302, 1303, 1304, 1348, 1371, 1402.

[7]I.R.C. § 6013(a).

he is living with Jane,[8] as long as (a) Robert and his wife are husband and wife, rather than ex-husband and ex-wife, and are not legally separated on December 31 of the tax year,[9] and (b) his wife consents to the filing of a joint return.[10]

It will be worth Robert's while to obtain his wife's consent to the joint return. If their taxable income for the year is $300,000, all of it earned income, and all of it earned by Robert, and if Robert is not a resident of one of the community property states (Arizona, California, Idaho, Louisiana, New Mexico, Nevada, Texas or Washington), the tax computed on the joint return will be $138,678, some $54,000 less than Robert's tax of $192,662 if he must file a separate return.[11] This $54,000 tax penalty is imposed because he is now taxed as a married individual filing a separate return and, in addition, because as such he is not entitled to take advantage of the 50% maximum tax (max-tax) on personal service income.[12]

Robert's wife, though married to him in the eyes of both state law and federal tax law, does not have to sign the joint return, and she may not want to do so. The Code says that although not one penny of the income shown on the joint return is hers, she herself is liable for the tax thereon.[13]

If Robert is a resident of one of the community property states, half of his $300,000 of taxable income will be deemed his wife's.[14] If they file separate tax returns, reporting, as they must, half of the income in each return, the tax on each is $87,662 or a total of $175,324, some $36,000 more than if they filed a joint return.[15] As beneficiary of the automatic split income rule arising from the community property status of the earned income, Robert's wife, whether friendly or unfriendly, will want to sign the joint return in order to avoid her separate obligation of the $87,662 tax. This is her obligation, so far as the

---

[8] I.R.C. § 6013(d).
[9] Id. See section 5.5(B), herein.
[10] Treas. Reg. § 1.6013–1(a)(2).
[11] See column A, lines 1 and 2(b) of Table I, infra.
[12] I.R.C. § 1348(c). See section 5.3, herein.
[13] I.R.C. § 6013(d)(3). For the "innocent spouse" exception, see I.R.C. § 6013(e).
[14] Poe v. Seaborn, 282 U.S. 101, 75 L. Ed. 239, 51 Sup. Ct. 58 (1930).
[15] See column A, line 2(a) of Table I, infra.

IRS is concerned, even if she never receives any of her $150,000 share of the earned income.[16]

If by the end of the second tax year, Robert is divorced or legally separated from his wife, the tax on his $300,000 would be $142,142.[17] He is now an unmarried individual filing a separate return and, unlike a married individual filing separately, is entitled to the 50% maximum tax ceiling on personal service income.[18]

Robert pays some $3,000 for his bachelordom, as compared to his married/joint return status, but he prefers being a bachelor to being unhappily married since he would be charged $175,374 on his $300,000 income if he were married, filed a separate return, and lived in a community property state. This tax would be increased to $192,662 if he were married filing separately in a noncommunity property state.[19]

The tax cost of Robert's unhappy marriage can diminish if he and his wife are legally separated or divorced. Any periodic amounts he has agreed or is required to pay for her support are taxed to her and not to him.[20] His remaining taxable income is subject to the ceiling tax of the 50% max-tax on earned income.[21] The periodic payments to his ex-wife are taxed to her as alimony income. Even though paid out of Robert's earned income, and deductible by him, this alimony income will not have the benefit of the 50% max-tax rate.[22] To the extent that the ex-wife's alimony income exceeds $41,500, it will be subject to progressive income tax rates of 55% to 70%, rather than the 50% max-tax ceiling that benefits Robert. If she is taxed as head of household, however, rather than as an unmarried individual, her alimony income in excess of $44,700 will be taxed at the over 50% tax rates of 54% to 70%.[23]

See Table I, at the end of this chapter, for the income tax con-

---

[16] United States v. Mitchell, 403 U.S. 190, 29 L. Ed. 2d 406, 91 Sup. Ct. 1763 (1971).
[17] See column A, line 3 of Table I, infra.
[18] I.R.C. § 1348. See also section 5.3, herein.
[19] See column A, lines 2(a) and 2(b) of Table I, infra.
[20] I.R.C. §§ 71(a), 215(a).
[21] I.R.C. § 1348. See section 5.3, herein.
[22] I.R.C. § 1348(b)(1); Treas. Reg. § 1.1348–3(a).
[23] See section 5.3, herein.

sequences of Robert's marriage and divorce, determined both on the basis of an income of (A) $300,000 and (B) $30,000. Note from this table the tax advantages accruing to divorce or legal separation, with income splitting via deductible alimony or separate maintenance.

If Robert lives in a community property state, a transfer to his ex-wife of her share of their community property will not be subject to taxation.[24] However, if she receives cash rather than her half interest in the community assets, she will be deemed to have sold her half interest in the community assets and will be taxed on her gain, that is, on the excess of the fair market value, which she receives in cash, over the cost or basis of her half interest in the community assets.[25]

If Robert lives in a noncommunity property state and transfers his cash or property to his wife, what she receives will not be subject to income tax, unless she receives it in periodic payments or in installments payable over a period of more than ten years.[26] Robert's transfer of property may, however, trigger an income tax for him, if the property has a fair market value which exceeds Robert's cost or basis.[27] His transfer of property because of the divorce will not, however, be deemed a transfer by gift subject to the gift tax.[28]

---

[24] Property settlements fall outside the alimony tax rules of I.R.C. §§ 71 and 215. See, e.g., Rev. Rul. 69–471, 1969–2 C.B. 10; John Sydner Thompson, 22 T.C. 275 (1954) *acq.* 1954–2 C.B. 6. No gain or loss will be realized by either spouse when there is an approximately equal division of the aggregate fair market value of community property, even when some of the assets go in their entirety to one spouse and some to the other. Rev. Rul. 76–83, 1976–1 C.B. 213.
[25] Carrieres v. Commissioner, 552 F.2d 1350 (C.A.-9 Cal., 1977); aff'g. per curiam, 64 TC 959 (1975); Deyoe v. Commissioner, 66 T.C. 904 (1976). See Rev. Rul. 76–83, 1976–1 C.B. 213.
[26] I.R.C. § 71.
[27] United States v. Davis, 370 U.S. 65, 8 L. Ed. 2d 335, 82 Sup. Ct. 1190 (1962); Wiles v. Commissioner, 499 F.2d 255 (C.A.-10 Kan., 1974); Wallace v. United States, 439 F.2d 757 (C.A.-8 Iowa, 1971); Pulliam v. Commissioner, 329 F.2d 97 (C.A.-10 Colo., 1964); Rev. Rul. 74–347, 1974–2 C.B. 26. But see Imel v. United States, 523 F.2d 853 (C.A.-10 Colo., 1975); Collins v. Commissioner, 412 F.2d 211 (C.A.-10 Okla., 1969), holding that in the equitable division states of Oklahoma and Colorado, wife's interest in husband's property was a new "species of common ownership"; hence transfer was akin to division of community or jointly held property, triggering no tax to husband on gain.
[28] I.R.C. § 2516.

Let us look now at the unmarried pair of this triangle. After Robert and his wife are legally separated or divorced, and regardless of whatever agreement he and Jane have, the tax law says that Robert is unmarried.[29] If he pays nothing by way of deductible alimony or separate maintenance to his ex-wife, all of his income is taxable to him, even if he and Jane have a "share and share alike" agreement.[30]

Income splitting, brought about by the joint returns of married couples or the payment of alimony, cannot be availed of by an unmarried cohabiting couple.

Only if, and to the extent that, Robert makes payments to Jane in money or money's worth by way of reasonable compensation for services actually rendered by her in a trade or business carried on by him, or as ordinary and necessary expenses in the production or collection of his taxable income, will these payments be taxable to Jane and deductible by Robert.[31] For example, if Jane is paid for services rendered as business manager or secretary to Robert, these payments are income to her and deductible by him, a form of income splitting that will reduce the overall federal income tax burden. That Robert's payments to Jane for her services may be made in a form other than cash does not change the tax consequence. The fair market value of goods or services received by way of compensation is taxable income to the recipient.[32] Thus, if instead of receiving cash for her services, Jane charges her clothing bills to Robert or receives plane tickets and resort hotel reservations for her vacations, the value of these benefits is taxable to her. There is, however, an important exception—"meals and lodging"—which may be applicable.[33] If Jane is a live-in business manager or secretary, the value of the room and board she receives is not includable in her gross income if three conditions are met: (1) the live-in arrange-

---

[29] See section 5.5(A), (B), herein.
[30] Lucas v. Earl, 281 U.S. 111, 74 L. Ed. 731, 50 Sup. Ct. 241 (1930). See section 5.8, herein.
[31] I.R.C. §§ 61, 162(a), 212.
[32] I.R.C. § 83; Treas. Reg. §§ 1.61-1(a), 1.61-2(d). See, e.g., Rev. Rul. 79-24, I.R.B. 1979-4, 6 (exchange of services and goods for rent-free use of apartment results in income).
[33] I.R.C. § 119.

ment is for Robert's convenience as Jane's employer; (2) Jane is required to accept the live-in arrangement as a condition of her employment; and (3) the living-in is on Robert's business premises or at Jane's place of employment.[34]

The IRS can scrutinize the amount of compensation Jane receives for "reasonableness." If the IRS thinks Jane is being paid too much for her services, it can deny Robert the right to deduct the excessive portion.[35] At the same time, Jane will be taxed on both the reasonable and the excessive portion of compensation she receives in cash or in kind.[36]

This "double taxation" also results to the extent that Jane's services are of a domestic or personal nature, and not rendered in connection with a trade or business of Robert's, or in connection with the production or collection of his taxable income. But this occurs, however, only with respect to cash or benefits other than room and board. The "meals and lodging" exception referred to above is more likely, under the circumstances of Jane's rendering domestic or personal services, to permit the exclusion of the fair market value of such benefits from her taxable income.[37]

If the cash or other benefits which Jane receives is not by way of compensation for services, whether business or nonbusiness, but is because of her personal relationship as Robert's friendly live-in companion, Jane is not taxed,[38] but Robert might be.[39]

---

[34]Treas. Reg. § 1.119–1(b) and (c)(1): "For purposes of this section, the term 'business premises of the employer' generally means the place of employment of the employee. For example, meals and lodging furnished in the employer's home to a domestic servant would constitute meals and lodging furnished on the business premises of the employer."

[35]I.R.C. § 162(a)(1); Treas. Reg. § 1.162–7(b)(3).

[36]Smith v. Manning, 189 F.2d 345 (C.A.-3 N.J., 1951).

[37]See Treas. Reg. § 1.119–1(b) and (c)(1).

[38]I.R.C. § 102(a).

[39]See section 5.7, herein. See also Lillian Pascarelli, 55 T.C. 1082 (1971), discussed in section 5.8, herein.

Gifts, in excess of $3,000 a year,[40] may be subject to the federal gift tax.[41]

Termination of the relationship

The alimony and property settlement tax consequences on divorce are inapplicable to cohabitants who terminate their relationship. Periodic payments required by agreement or decree to be made to an ex-wife are taxable to the ex-wife and deductible by the ex-husband.[42] Payments which are fixed in amount and not contingent, and which are payable in a lump sum or over a period of less than ten years, are not deductible by the ex-husband, but neither are they taxable to the ex-wife.[43] And no gift tax is required to be paid.[44]

Since Robert and Jane were never married to each other, once they separate they are not, for tax purposes, legally separated by decree or agreement, nor are they divorced. Therefore, any payments made by Robert to Jane, whether voluntarily, or by negotiated agreement, or on account of any judgment against Robert in a lawsuit brought by Jane, will be treated for tax purposes in accordance with the characteristics of the payments, to be determined by the underlying reason therefor.

If the payments are for past services rendered to Robert in a trade or business of his or, in connection with his production or collection of taxable income, he can deduct them.[45] Again, the reasonableness of the amount of the payments can be examined

---

[40] I.R.C. § 2503(b) provides a gift tax exclusion of $3,000 per donee per annum.

[41] I.R.C. § 2505 provides a phased-in credit against the gift tax which results in the following exemption equivalency:

Year of gift	Credit against tax	Exemption equivalency
1st half of 1977	$ 6,000	$ 33,333
2nd half of 1977	30,000	120,677
1978	34,000	134,000
1979	38,000	147,333
1980	42,500	161,563
1981	47,000	175,625

[42] I.R.C. §§ 71(a), 215.
[43] I.R.C. §§ 71(c), 215.
[44] I.R.C. § 2516.
[45] I.R.C. §§ 162(a)(1), 212.

5.2 UNMARRIED COUPLES AND THE LAW

by the IRS, which can disallow the deduction of excessive compensation.[46] If the services rendered were of a personal or domestic nature, he cannot deduct the payments.[47]

If the payments were of a mixed nature, in part for business services and in part for personal or domestic services, the IRS can make its own determination of the allocation between deductible and nondeductible compensation.

Even if Robert can deduct no part of the payments which constitute compensation for past services rendered by Jane, she will be taxed on every penny of these payments. She may be able to make use of income averaging[48] or, unlike an ex-wife receiving alimony, the 50% max-tax ceiling on personal service or earned income.[49] If she obtains these payments with an attorney's aid, the attorney's fees and any other costs of litigation paid by her are deductible.[50]

Unless the nature of Jane's claim for payments from Robert rests on services rendered in connection with a trade or business of his or in connection with production or collection of his taxable income, Robert cannot deduct any legal expenses incurred in resisting, compromising, or arranging for the method of payment.[51]

The tax law which specifically states that transfers to an ex-wife pursuant to agreement, followed by a divorce, are not deemed to be gifts and are not subject to the gift tax,[52] is not so kind to the paying ex-cohabitant. To the extent that payments by Robert are founded upon an agreement of support, or upon an agreement to share assets acquired during cohabitation, *without regard to Jane's services as the quid pro quo*, the payments will be characterized for tax purposes as gifts.[53] This is so whether,

---

[46]I.R.C. § 162(a)(1); Treas. Reg. § 1.162-7.
[47]I.R.C. § 262.
[48]I.R.C. §§ 1301-1305.
[49]I.R.C. § 1348. See section 5.3, herein.
[50]I.R.C. § 212 (3). Cf. R. K. Wild, 42 T.C. 706 (1964), acq. 1967-2 C.B. 4.
[51]I.R.C. § 212(3). Cf. United States v. Gilmore, 372 U.S. 39, 9 L. Ed. 2d 570, 83 Sup. Ct. 623 (1963); United States v. Patrick, 372 U.S. 53, 9 L. Ed. 2d 580, 83 Sup. Ct. 618 (1963).
[52]I.R.C. § 2516.
[53]See Lillian Pascarelli, 55 T.C. 1082 (1971), discussed in section 5.8, herein. Cf. Commissioner v. Wemyss, 324 U.S. 303, 89 L. Ed. 958, 65 Sup. Ct. 652 (1945).

after cohabitation ceases, Robert makes these payments voluntarily or because of a post-cohabitation negotiated settlement or court order.[54]

Therefore Jane benefits: the recipient of gifts is not required to pay tax on them.[55] However, any legal or other costs incurred in the collection of gifts are not deductible.[56]

The gift tax can be expensive to the paying ex-cohabitant or to his heirs. Payments made by Robert to Jane which are characterized as gifts for tax purposes and which exceed $3,000 a year may or may not incur an immediate gift tax liability, depending on the aggregate amount of the payments, and on whether Robert has made other gifts in 1977, 1978 or 1979.[57] Whether Robert's payments to Jane incur an immediate gift tax liability,[58] and whether Jane, by agreement, assumes any such gift tax liability, these payments will increase the gift tax cost to Robert of any subsequent taxable gifts made by him to anyone at all,[59] and will increase the estate tax burden on his estate.[60] And any legal or other costs incurred by Robert in connection with Jane's attempt to enforce his agreement to make such gift payments will not be deductible by him.[61]

A Marvin-type award

Robert may be required to make payments to Jane pursuant to judgment of a court which finds the basis for Robert's obligation not to rest on contract or agreement, nor on the right of Jane to

---

[54]Commissioner v. Greene, 119 F.2d 383 (C.A.-9 Cal., 1941), cert. den. 314 U.S. 641, 62 Sup. Ct. 80 (1941); Stokowska v. Pedrick, 10 F.R.D. 259 (S.D. N.Y., 1952).

[55]Gifts are not taxable income to the donee, I.R.C., § 702(a). The donor is primarily liable for the gift tax, I.R.C. § 2502(d); Treas. Reg. 25.2502-2. For the transferee liability of the donee, see I.R.C. § 6324(b); Treas. Reg. § 301.6324-1(b); Lillian Pascarelli, 55 T.C. 1082 (1971), discussed in section 5.8, herein.

[56]I.R.C. § 212(3).

[57]I.R.C. § 2505.

[58]Where the donee assumes liability, the gift tax paid is deductible from the value of the gift. Rev. Rul. 75-72, 1975-1 C.B. 310; Rev. Rul. 71-232, 1971-1 C.B. 275.

[59]The gift tax is cumulatively progressive over the donor's lifetime. I.R.C. § 2502.

[60]Post-1976 taxable gifts are added to the taxable estate to determine the amount with respect to which the estate tax is to be computed. I.R.C. § 2001(b).

[61]I.R.C. § 212(3).

recover in quantum meruit for the reasonable value of her services rendered less the reasonable value of support received. The California Supreme Court suggested in the Marvin decision in 1976 that its enumeration of those bases for recovery "does not preclude the evolution of additional equitable remedies to protect the expectations of the parties to a nonmarital relationship in cases in which existing remedies prove inadequate."[62] By way of pointing the direction such evolution might take, the Court commented that: "In some instances a confidential relationship may arise between nonmarital partners, and economic transactions between them should be governed by the principles applicable to such relationship."[63]

A monetary award in Jane's favor, granted by way of an equitable remedy and determined, in amount, by the highest weekly paycheck (e.g., $1,000) ever received by Jane in the course of employment by someone other than Robert, multiplied by the number of weeks in a reasonable post-cohabitation period (e.g., 104 weeks), may be made "for rehabilitation purposes, so that she may have the economic means to re-educate herself and to learn new, employable skills or to refurbish those utilized, for example, during her most recent employment."[63a] Such a rehabilitation award may be characterized for tax purposes in several different ways. Each characterization may have different tax consequences to Jane and to Robert.

If the award is compensation for Jane's forbearance from paid employment during the period of cohabitation, the award constitutes taxable income to her.[64] Her attorney's fees and other costs of litigation would then be deductible by her.[65] She should be able to make use of income averaging[66] but she cannot use the

---

[62]Marvin v. Marvin, 18 Cal. 3d 660, 134 Cal. Rptr. 815, 557 P.2d 106, 123, n. 25 (1976).

[63]Id., 557 P.2d at 121, n. 22.

[63a]Marvin v. Marvin, 5 Fam. L. Rep. 3077, 3085 (1979). This trial court opinion awarding Michelle Triola Marvin $104,000 for "rehabilitation purposes" is set out in its entirety as Appendix C following Chapter 6, herein.

[64]I.R.C. § 61(a)(1).

[65]I.R.C. § 212.

[66]I.R.C. §§ 1301 to 1305.

50% max-tax ceiling rate on personal service income to reduce her tax for the year of payment.[67]

Neither Robert's payment to Jane of the award, nor the payment of his litigation costs, are deductible by him. A payment for such forbearance is not a "trade or business expense"[68] or an expense incurred in connection with the "production or collection of [taxable] income" or "for the management, conservation, or maintenance of property held for the production of income."[69]

If the award stems from Robert's obligation, arising out of the relationship, to provide support for Jane for a limited period of time following termination of the relationship, the payment is neither income to Jane nor deductible by Robert. Until the alimony tax provisions of the Code were enacted in 1942, support payments to ex-wives were not income to them nor deductible by the paying ex-husbands.[70] Even today, the provisions which require payments in the nature of alimony or separate maintenance to be taxed to the recipient, and which permit such payments to be deductible by the payor, apply only if the payor and payee had been married to each other, and only if other prescribed conditions, none of which are present here, have been met.[71]

Although made involuntarily, without "donative intent" and pursuant to court order, the award, if for support, may, nonetheless, be treated under the Code as a gift by Robert, subject to the gift tax.[72] If a gift for tax purposes, the amount of the gift is $104,000 ($1,000 × 104 weeks) minus the annual per donee exclusion of $3,000,[73] or a gift of $101,000. If Robert has made no other taxable gifts since 1976 to anyone at all, he will not have to pay a gift tax on the award.[74] His payment of the award, however, will increase the rate of a gift tax on any subsequent tax-

---

[67]"The term . . . [earned income, now personal service income] does not include amounts received for refraining from rendering personal services." Treas. Reg. § 1.1348–3(a).
[68]I.R.C. § 162(a).
[69]I.R.C. § 212(1).
[70]Gould v. Gould, 245 U.S. 151, 62 L. Ed. 211, 38 Sup. Ct. 53 (1917).
[71]I.R.C. § 2503.
[72]See notes 53 and 54, supra.
[73]I.R.C. § 2503.
[74]See the gift tax credit at note 41, supra.

able gifts which he makes to anyone at all[75] and will increase the rate of his estate tax.[76]

Another possibility is that Jane's award may be a "make whole" award, arising out of the termination of the personal and confidential relationship. The award may then be treated for tax purposes like a judgment for damages for personal injuries, whether physical or psychic, such as an award for pain and suffering or for loss of consortium. Or the award may be treated like a judgment for damages on account of alienation of affections. Payment of such damages is not taxable income to the recipient,[77] nor deductible for tax purposes by the payor, since it is not a cost of doing business, nor treated as a gift by the payor for gift tax purposes.

5.3. Marital status and federal income tax rates

To move beyond the tax treatment of Robert Roe and Jane Doe, our hypothetical pair of marvinizers, toward a more general look at marriage, cohabitation, and taxes, it is necessary to identify the various marital, semi-marital and nonmarital classifications of taxpayers under the federal tax law.

The four income tax rate schedules

The federal income tax rate tables identify five kinds of individual taxpayers and classify them by marital status.

1. Married, filing joint return[78]
2. Surviving spouse (unmarried)[79]
3. Head of household (unmarried)[80]

---

[75]I.R.C. § 2502.
[76]I.R.C. § 2001(b).
[77]I.R.C. § 104(a)(2); Rev. Rul. 74–77, 1974–1 C.B. 33. Damages received on account of personal injuries, excluded from gross income by I.R.C. § 104(a)(2), are defined as damages received "through prosecution of a legal suit or action based upon tort or tort type rights." Treas. Reg. § 1.104–1(d). This exclusion is available even though the damages may have been determined on the basis of lost earnings.
[78]I.R.C. §§ 1(a)(1), 143, 6013.
[79]I.R.C. §§ 1(a)(2), 2(a).
[80]I.R.C. §§ 1(b), 2(b).

4. Unmarried individual who is not a surviving spouse or head of household[81]
5. Married, filing separate return[82]

There are four separate tables setting the rate of income taxes applicable to these five kinds of taxpayers.[83] Married taxpayers who file joint returns and surviving spouses use the same rate table to determine their income tax liability.[84] Married taxpayers must combine their separate incomes if they file a joint return.[85] Except for the year in which a surviving spouse's deceased spouse has died, however, there need be no aggregation of the two incomes on a surviving spouse's return.

The four rate tables would appear at first glance to tax married taxpayers filing joint returns and surviving spouses the most favorably, and deal less kindly with the remaining three kinds of taxpayers, in ascending order of harshness.[86]

For instance, the lowest tax rate, 14%, is assessed on the first dollar of taxable income over $3,400 of married couples filing joint returns and of surviving spouses, but applies sooner for other taxpayers:[87]

	Marrieds filing joint & surviving spouses	Heads of Household	Unmarrieds	Marrieds filing separate returns
Tax starts at 14% of first dollars over:	$3,400	$2,300	$2,300	$1,700

The highest tax rate, 70%, is assessed on the first dollar of income over $215,400 for the most favored taxpayers but strikes sooner for the other taxpayers:[88]

---

[81]I.R.C. §§ 1(c), 143.
[82]I.R.C. §§ 1(d), 143.
[83]See I.R.C. § 1(a) through (d).
[84]I.R.C. § 1(a).
[85]I.R.C. § 6013(d)(3).
[86]See Table II infra, for a side-by-side view of the four rate schedules.
[87]I.R.C. § 63(d).
[88]I.R.C. § 1.

5.3 UNMARRIED COUPLES AND THE LAW

	Marrieds filing joint & surviving spouses	Heads of Household	Unmarrieds	Marrieds filing separate returns
Highest tax rate is 70% of all dollars over:	$215,400	$161,300	$108,300	$107,700

The 50% max-tax

The 50% max-tax ceiling rate, applicable to personal service or "earned" income, as distinguished from "unearned" income such as dividends, interest and rents,[89] does not apply to diminish the tax of the most favored taxpayers until the taxable income level hits $60,000, because the taxable income of such taxpayers below that amount is taxed at rates less than 50%.[90] Other less favored taxpayers reach the 50% max-tax ceiling rate relief at lower levels of taxable income.

	Marrieds filing joint & surviving spouses	Heads of Household	Unmarrieds
50% max-tax ceiling provides relief for taxable income over.......	$60,000	$44,700	$41,500
because the rate of tax on income below this amount is................	49%	46%	49%
and the rate of tax on income in excess of this amount is............	54%	54%	55%

---

[89]I.R.C. § 1348. For definition of personal service income, see I.R.C. § 1348(b); Treas. Reg. § 1.1348–3.
[90]I.R.C. § 1(a), applicable to taxable years beginning after 12/31/78.

Married taxpayers who file separate returns are not shown on this 50% max-tax schedule because the Code prohibits their use of the 50% max-tax.[91] Therefore, when the personal service or earned income of such a taxpayer exceeds $30,000, his next dollars of personal service or earned income will be taxed at 54%, until the rate jumps to 59% for the next dollars over $42,800.

See Table III, infra, for application of the 50% max-tax ceiling rate on personal service or earned income.

The additional tax on tax preference items

As a result of special deductions and deferrals of tax liability, Congress believed that some taxpayers were permitted tax advantages which were not available to others. To redistribute the tax burden, Congress enacted a 15% tax to be imposed, in addition to other taxes, on certain tax preference items.[92]

In figuring this 15% tax for an individual, the total of tax preference items is reduced by an exemption of the greater of $10,000 or one half of the regular income tax for the year. This $10,000 exemption amount is reduced to $5,000 for a married person filing separately.[93]

In addition to this add-on tax of 15%, the tax law now imposes an alternative minimum tax in graduated rates of 10%, 20%, and 25% on an individual taxpayer's alternative minimum taxable income, i.e., his taxable income plus the amount of the capital gains deduction and certain itemized deductions.[94] The tax so computed is assessed only if it exceeds the regular tax. A married taxpayer who files a separate return is required to compute this alternative minimum tax by doubling his alternative minimum taxable income and then dividing the resulting alternative minimum tax in half.[95] The effect of this requirement is to impose a more steeply progressive rate of alternative minimum tax on this taxpayer than would be imposed on him if he were single.[96]

---

[91] I.R.C. § 1348(c).
[92] I.R.C. § 56.
[93] I.R.C. § 58(a).
[94] I.R.C. § 55.
[95] I.R.C. § 58(a).
[96] McCaffrey, "Income Taxation of Husband and Wife and the Marriage Penalty Tax," *10th National Conference on Women and the Law Sourcebook*, p. 27 (1979).

5.4. Marriage and nonmarriage penalty taxes

Tax rate penalties based on marital status

Married taxpayers who file joint returns are referred to in section 5.3 herein as the taxpayers who, together with surviving spouses, are treated most favorably by the Internal Revenue Code tax rate schedules. In fact, only the traditional married couple is treated kindly by the Code, i.e., where one spouse works for pay and the other has no or little income.

Tables IV and IV A at the end of this chapter show the tax cost of marriage by comparing the tax due on a joint return with tax due on separate returns filed by paired but unmarried taxpayers with the same combined income. As these Tables show, almost whatever the income, if 90% or more of it is earned by one married partner, the couple saves taxes by being married. This is the circumstance in which the tax law imposes a penalty on unmarried taxpayers because of their unmarried state.

On the other hand, if one partner earns from 25% to 50% of the couple's income, in all income brackets except the lowest, the couple, for tax purposes, is better off unmarried. Even where one partner earns as little as 20% of the couple's total income, at most tax brackets, being married costs more than being unmarried.

The larger tax, shown in Tables IV and IV-A, imposed because a couple is married (the marriage penalty tax), may be reduced for some couples if, instead of filing joint returns, they stay married but file separate returns. This is not a function of the rate tables, as Table V at the end of this chapter shows, but of the floor that adjusted gross income imposes on the deduction of medical expenses. But even married taxpayers who lower their taxes by filing separate returns pay more than singles, and thus pay a marriage penalty tax.

The amount of the marriage penalty tax is even larger if one or both of the cohabitants can qualify as an (unmarried) surviving spouse or an (unmarried) head of household. See Tables VI, VII and VIII.

Credit, deduction and exclusion penalties based on marital status

The "zero bracket amount," or ZBA, (see note 1, section 5.1 herein) is built into the tax tables. An unmarried taxpayer has a

ZBA of $2,300. Two taxpayers therefore have two ZBA's of $2,300 apiece or $4,600. If they marry, their ZBA is only $3,400.

The earned income credit[97] is equal to 10% of earned income up to $5,000, or $500. This credit is phased out gradually above $6,000 of income by a reduction of 12.5% of adjusted gross income in excess of $6,000. Therefore a taxpayer with adjusted gross income of $10,000 or more cannot claim this credit.

The earned income credit cannot be claimed by married taxpayers unless they file a joint return. If both spouses are otherwise eligible for the credit and if each has $6,000 of earned income (which would give each a $500 credit) they cannot claim their credits on separate returns. And if they file a joint return their income totals $12,000 and they have therefore lost $1,000 worth of refundable tax credit and, in addition, must pay a tax.[98]

Married taxpayers must also file a joint return to claim the child and dependent care credit[99] which can reduce their tax by as much as $800. This credit is 20% of certain household services and child and dependent care expenses, up to a maximum of $2,000 of expenses if there is one qualifying child (dependent under 15) or other dependent (physically or mentally incapacitated), and up to a maximum of $4,000 if there are two or more such dependents. The household and dependent care expenses cannot exceed the amount of the taxpayer's earned income. If the taxpayer is married, the expenses which produce the credit cannot exceed the earned income of the lesser earner spouse unless he or she is a full-time student or physically or mentally incapacitated.

A taxpayer who is 55 years or older can exclude from taxable income up to $100,000 of gain realized on the sale of a residence, if it has been the taxpayer's home for three years or more.[1] If the

---

[97] I.R.C. § 43.
[98] Taxpayer A is unmarried, has one dependent child, and an annual adjusted gross income of $6,000. Taxpayer B is in an identical situation. Each of them, after taking into account the earned income credit, will pay no tax and will receive $262 from the Federal Treasury each year. If A and B were to marry, they would receive no credit, and would owe an annual tax of $702. Their annual tax cost of marriage would amount to $1,226, about 10% of their combined annual income. McCaffrey, "Income Taxation of Husband and Wife and the Marriage Penalty Tax," *10th National Conference on Women and the Law Sourcebook,* p. 30 (1979).
[99] I.R.C. § 44A.
[1] I.R.C. § 121.

taxpayer and spouse own the property jointly, only one of them need satisfy the age and home requirement. But even if the home is owned by one of the spouses only, and that spouse qualifies for the exclusion, if he or she files a separate return the $100,000 exclusion is cut in half. And this is a once in a lifetime exclusion: if one spouse has used the election the other cannot.

Some deductions have ceilings. These ceilings are halved for a married taxpayer who fails to file a joint return. The $10,000 ceiling on deduction for excess interest on investment indebtedness is cut down to $5,000 if a married taxpayer files separately, even if all the investment interest is his.[2] The ceiling on certain moving expenses is halved for a married taxpayer who files a separate return.[3] The $3,000 ceiling on deduction of capital losses against ordinary income is also cut in half if a married taxpayer files separately, even though he or she may have incurred every penny of the capital loss.[4]

On the other hand, some benefits or deductions are doubled. A taxpayer can treat up to $50,000 of loss on small business stock as an ordinary loss and deduct it against his ordinary income. There is no requirement that he file a joint return but if he is married and does file a joint return, he can deduct as much as $100,000 without regard to whether his wife incurred any portion of the loss or whether the income sheltered by the loss is all his.[5]

5.5. "Married," "unmarried," "surviving spouse," "head of household," and "dependent" defined

There are some tax rules of thumb to be drawn from the marriage and nonmarriage penalty tax tables.

Generally speaking, if one partner is going to stay home and not work for pay, the couple should probably get married. If both are to work for pay or have other income, and one will produce from 20% to 50% of the combined income, they should, for tax purposes, stay unmarried.

---

[2] I.R.C. § 163.
[3] I.R.C. § 217.
[4] I.R.C. § 1211.
[5] I.R.C. § 1244.

If a widow or widower would be taxed as a surviving spouse if not married, she or he should cohabit rather than marry until the third year after the year in which the spouse died.

A single parent who, because of his or her children, would be taxed as a head of household if not married, should live with his or her partner and not marry until the children grow up and move out on their own.

Single taxpayers who support their mother or father, whether or not the parent lives with them, should cohabit rather than marry unless the partner has little income.

The import of the above generalizations can be made clearer by an examination of the law's definition of the various married, semi-married and unmarried characterizations of taxpayers.

(A) MARRIED OR UNMARRIED UNDER STATE LAW

The Internal Revenue Code states that the determination as to whether a taxpayer is married is to be made the last day of the taxable year in question.[6] If the taxpayer's wedding is on December 31, 1979, he and his wife are married taxpayers for all of 1979 and entitled to file a joint return. If they file separate returns each is taxed as a married taxpayer filing separately. Even though each has been unmarried for 364 days out of the 365 days of 1979, neither can file as an unmarried taxpayer.

Death provides an exception to this rule. If one spouse dies during the year, the determination of marital status is made as of the date of the death.[7] The surviving spouse can, if he or she has not remarried at any time during the remainder of the year, elect to file a joint return. This return must include all of the surviving spouse's income for the year and all of deceased spouse's income from the beginning of the year to date of death.

With some few exceptions, which will be discussed later, whether or not taxpayers are married for federal tax purposes will be determined in accordance with state law,[8] although not

---

[6] I.R.C. § 143(a)(1).
[7] Id.
[8] Rev. Rul. 58–66, 1958–1 C.B. 60. See Alfred L. Von Tersch, Jr., 47 T.C. 415, 419 (1967).

necessarily in accordance with the state courts' determination of that law.[9]

Common-law marriage

If a couple cohabits without a formal marriage ceremony in a state which does not recognize common-law marriage, they are not married for federal tax purposes.[10] If applicable state law recognizes common-law marriages, individuals who are living in such a relationship that the state would treat them as husband and wife are, for federal income tax purposes, husband and wife.[11]

The conflicts of law principle that recognizes a common-law marriage if valid in the jurisdiction where entered into, although not valid if entered into in the state in which the couple live,[12] has been adopted for federal tax law. The IRS recognizes that even if a man and woman are living in a common-law marriage relationship in a state which does not recognize such a relationship, the couple are nonetheless married for tax purposes if their relationship commenced in, and would be characterized as a common-law marriage in, another state in which they had previously resided.[13]

Both the IRS and the courts will scrutinize the law of the state in which the common-law marriage is asserted to have been created, and the circumstances of the relationship.

Miscegenation

State laws which prohibited marriage between persons of different races were declared unconstitutional by the Supreme Court in 1967.[14] Therefore a husband and wife of different races

---

[9]See Stark v. United States, 351 F.2d 160 (C.A.-6 Mich., 1965), where a woman paid some $70,000 of her cohabitant's medical bills through his last illness, and the probate court found a common-law marriage, she was nonetheless found not to be married and not permitted to file joint returns for the three years prior to his death, nor to deduct his medical expenses.
[10]Joseph F. Amaro, 29 T.C.M. (CCH) 914 (1970).
[11]James M. Ross, 31 T.C.M. (CCH) 489 (1972).
[12]See section 1.7, herein.
[13]Rev. Rul. 58–66, 1958–1 C.B. 60. See Alfred L. Von Tersch, Jr., 47 T.C. 415, 419 (1967). Cf. Rev. Rul. 29, 1953–1 C.B. 67.
[14]Loving v. Virginia, 388 U.S. 1, 18 L. Ed. 2d 1010, 87 Sup. Ct. 1817 (1967).

who reside in a state still having a miscegenation statute are married for the purpose of filing joint returns.[15]

Homosexual marriages

The highest court of no state has sanctioned the attempted marriage of homosexuals. The Supreme Court of the United States is unlikely to hold that state denial of the validity of a marriage entered into by homosexuals is unconstitutional. Therefore, whatever trappings of legality appear to surround a homosexual couple's marriage ceremony, and even if, for whatever reasons, their marriage certificate is on file with the appropriate municipal or state bureau, they are unmarried for federal tax purposes.[16]

Effect of annulment

An annulment can be obtained on the ground that a marriage is void or voidable. Where a marriage is annulled because it was void from its inception, the IRS says that the taxpayers not only are unmarried for the year in which the annulment was granted, but for all previous years. Such taxpayers must file amended returns claiming unmarried status for all tax years not barred by the statute of limitations, in which their filing status was determined by their annulled marriage.[17]

The IRS will reopen as many prior years as the statute of limitations permits, in order to assert deficiencies on the ground that a taxpayer filed joint returns with an individual subsequently determined not to be his or her spouse. In the Harry J. Chap case,[18] Harry had married Grace in 1955. Nine years later, in 1964, the government successfully pursued Harry for $200 of deficiencies for 1957 and 1958 because of a 1961 decree annulling his marriage. A tax bill for misstating marital status was assessed against Harry despite the fact that he had married, and

---

[15]Rev. Rul. 68–277, 1968–1 C.B. 526.
[16]See VII Tax Notes 551 (11/6/78).
[17]Rev. Rul. 76–255, 1976–2 C.B. 40; Tax Information for Divorced or Separated Individuals, I.R.S. Pub. 904, p. 1 (1979).
[18]Harry J. Chap, 23 T.C.M. (CCH) 132 (1964). But see Wondsel v. Commissioner, 350 F.2d 339, 340 (C.A.-2 N.Y., 1965).

thereafter had filed joint returns, in all innocence of an impediment to his marriage. Grace had a former husband whom she mistakenly thought had divorced her and who, himself, had remarried and raised a family, believing Grace to be dead.

What's sauce for the goose is sauce for the gander. Linda obtained a 1971 annulment of her 1962 marriage on the ground that her husband, Bob, was still married to his former wife, apparently because of an invalid out-of-state divorce. Because Linda was held not to be married in 1966 and 1967, she was able to avoid the consequences of an earlier Tax Court determination, to which she had been a party, that she and Bob owed $20,000 in taxes for those two years.[19] The earlier deficiency had resulted from the couple's $30,000 a year overstatement in their 1966 and 1967 joint returns of their travel and entertainment deductions.

The IRS and the taxpayer, when the tables are turned, are successful in asserting that if an annulment is based on a void, rather than a voidable marriage, the "spouses" have never been husband and wife for joint return purposes. Nonetheless, the Tax Court has held that periodic payments made pursuant to a decree of annulment based on a void marriage are taxable to the "wife" and deductible by the "husband" because they were made "in discharge of . . . a legal obligation which, because of the marital or family relationship, is imposed on . . . the husband under the decree [of divorce or of separate maintenance.]"[20]

Thus, some decisions treat a void marriage ended by annulment as no marriage for joint return purposes and others treat it as creating "husbands and wives" for taxable/deductible alimony purposes. Odd consequences ensue. For instance, suppose in 1976, John, believing himself divorced from Jill, though in fact he is not, marries Josephine. Later that year Jill dies. In 1978, Josephine obtains a decree of annulment and separate mainte-

---

[19]William R. (Bob) Wilson and Linda F. Wilson, 35 T.C.M. (CCH) 1276 (1976).
[20]Andrew Newburger, 61 T.C. 457 (1974). See also Denny C. Williamson, P.H. Memo T.C. ¶ 78,279 (court denied taxpayer the right to deduct what it found to be a principal sum payable in installments of less than ten years, but stated: "Initially, we put aside any considerations based upon any argument that North Carolina law may require the conclusion that the payments herein were related to a void marriage [because bigamous] and therefore not based upon a marital relationship as required by section 71 and therefore a condition of section 215.") Cf. Newburger, supra.

nance. John, who has filed joint returns with Josephine, aggregating her income with his for 1976 and 1977, now disavows those joint returns. And because he has had a dependent child living with him during these years, he files amended returns as head of household for 1976. For 1977 and 1978 he files as surviving spouse, using the joint return table and zero bracket amount of $3,400, but excludes Josephine's income from the income shown on his amended returns. For his 1978 return, he further reduces his income by his deduction for alimony paid to Josephine. Josephine now discovers that she is liable for the tax on returns which she must file for 1976, 1977 and 1978 as an unmarried individual.

Effect of invalid divorce and subsequent marriage

Suppose a husband and wife No. 1 live in state A. The husband obtains an out-of-state divorce in an ex parte proceeding or on grounds not recognized in state A. The husband then marries wife No. 2. To whom is the husband married for federal income and estate tax purposes?

Or, if the husband, after obtaining such a divorce from wife No. 1, does not marry, is he married or unmarried for federal income tax purposes?

This second question has not been answered or even raised in a decided case. The answer should presumably be determined on the basis of the answer to the first question. Unfortunately, the answer to the first question may depend on the court to which the question is put.

If the jurisdiction in which the divorce is obtained declares the divorce a nullity, all courts which have spoken on the subject agree that the husband is still married to wife No. 1.[21]

If the home state declares that the out-of-state divorce is a nullity, the IRS takes the position that the husband is still married to wife No. 1.[22] All courts which have spoken on the subject,

---

[21] Estate of Daniel Buckley, 37 T.C. 664 (1962), *Acq.*, 1964-2 C.B. 4. See also Estate of Borax v. Commissioner, 349 F.2d 666, 672 (C.A.-2 N.Y., 1965), cert. den. 383 U.S. 935, 86 Sup. Ct. 1064 (1966); Wondsel v. Commissioner, 350 F.2d 339, 341 (C.A.-2 N.Y., 1965).

[22] Rev. Rul. 67-442, 1967-2 C.B. 65.

except the Second Circuit, agree that the husband is still married to wife No. 1.[23] The Second Circuit appears to be of two minds about this question, depending on whether the issue is raised in an estate tax case, where the question is whether wife No. 2 is the deceased husband's "surviving spouse," for the purpose of permitting his estate the estate tax marital deduction, or on whether the issue is raised in an income tax case, where the issue is whether husband and wife No. 2 may file joint income tax returns.

In an estate tax case, if the state which declares the out-of-state divorce a nullity is the state where the deceased husband's estate is being administered, the Second Circuit will abide by that state's determination.[24] However, if the state where the deceased husband's estate is being administered has not ruled on the validity of the divorce, the Second Circuit assumes the divorce valid for the purpose of validating the second marriage and permitting the estate tax marital deduction for second spouse's share of the estate.[25]

Where the issue is whether husband and wife No. 2 can file joint returns, the Second Circuit appears still to prefer a "rule of validation" by which "the living marriage and not the atrophied one is recognized."[26] Therefore, if the home state declares the out-of-state divorce a nullity, but the divorcing jurisdiction has not invalidated its own decree, the Second Circuit treats husband and wife No. 2 as married for federal income tax purposes.[27]

If the Second Circuit were faced only with the husband who had divorced wife No. 1, via an invalid out-of-state divorce, but who had not married anyone else, would the Second Circuit's dislike of upholding "atrophied" marriages for tax purposes continue, where there is no "living marriage" to protect?

Even if no state at all has intervened to invalidate the out-of-state divorce, the Ninth Circuit and Tax Court both appear to insist on providing a federal declaration with respect to this state question and will hold the out-of-state divorce and remarriage a

---

[23]Lee v. Commissioner, 550 F.2d 1201 (C.A.-9 Cal., 1977); Estate of Steffke v. Commissioner, 538 F.2d 730 (C.A.-7 Wis., 1976).
[24]Estate of Goldwater v. Commissioner, 539 F.2d 878 (C.A.-2 N.Y., 1976).
[25]Estate of Spalding v. Commissioner, 537 F.2d 666 (C.A.-2 N.Y., 1976).
[26]See id. at 669.
[27]Wondsel v. Commissioner, 350 F.2d 339 (C.A.-2 N.Y., 1965); Estate of Borax v. Commissioner, 349 F.2d 666 (C.A.-2 N.Y., 1965).

nullity[28] even, possibly, where the courts of the state of the first marriage would not.[29] The IRS has issued several rulings in which it has said that if no state has made a finding of invalidity, the IRS will not.[30] Despite these "hands-off" proclamations, however, the IRS pressed on against the unfortunate husband in the Ninth Circuit decisions in Lee v. Commissioner[31] and Gersten v. Commissioner[32] where there had been no state declaration of invalidity.

If the issue is not whether a second marriage is valid but only whether the first marriage continues for tax purposes, despite a spouse's attempts to discontinue that marriage, will the IRS insist that there is still tax life in the atrophied marriage, although no state court has so held? The answer appears to be yes, if the IRS can exact a marriage penalty tax by insisting that the couple is still married. One couple, in a move designed to bring attention to the marriage penalty tax, obtained a foreign divorce late in December so that as of December 31 they would be unmarried individuals, and thus able to benefit from lower taxes (see section 5.4, herein). They remarried in January. The consequence was not the hoped-for legislative reform. Instead, they prompted an IRS proclamation. Whether or not the divorce was valid where granted or under the laws of the couple's marital domicile, the IRS stated that, since the divorce was obtained for tax avoidance purposes and remarriage was contemplated, the IRS could borrow from the corporate and business tax field the doctrines of sham or step transaction and ignore the divorce for tax purposes.[33]

Will the IRS be successful in obtaining a judicial determination that divorce and remarriage to save taxes doesn't? This is yet to be decided.

What about a divorce for tax purposes, but no remarriage?

---

[28]Lee v. Commissioner, 550 F.2d 1201 (C.A.-9 Cal., 1977); Gersten v. Commissioner, 267 F.2d 195 (C.A.-9 Cal., 1959); Ruth Borax, 40 T.C. 1001 (1963), revd. 349 F.2d 666 (C.A.-2 N.Y., 1965); Harold E. Wondsel, 23 T.C.M. (CCH) 1278 (1964), revd. 350 F.2d 339 (C.A.-2 N.Y., 1965).
[29]Cf. Alfred Von Tersch, 47 T.C. 405 (1967).
[30]Rev. Rul. 71-390, 1971-2 C.B. 82; Rev. Rul. 67-442, 1967-2 C.B. 65.
[31]Note 28, supra.
[32]Id.
[33]Rev. Rul. 76-255, 1976-2 C.B. 40; Tax Information for Divorced or Separated Individuals, I.R.S. Pub. 904, p. 1 (1979).

Here, the IRS treads a little more cautiously. A divorce by December 31, in contemplation of continued *cohabitation* rather than remarriage, is effective, the IRS admits, to produce an unmarried individual tax status for each of the couple and, hence, to save taxes for both of them.[34]

(B) MARRIED OR UNMARRIED UNDER FEDERAL TAX LAW

Legally separated under decree

The Internal Revenue Code states that "an individual legally separated from his spouse under a decree of divorce or of separate maintenance shall not be considered as married."[35] If a couple obtained such a decree on or before the last day of the year, they are considered unmarried for the entire year.[36]

Although periodic payments made pursuant to an order of temporary support or a written separation agreement not "incident to" a decree of divorce or separate maintenance qualify as alimony, taxable to the payee spouse and deductible by the payor spouse,[37] the couple is still considered married for income tax purposes.[38] Hence they may elect, annually, either to file a joint return or to split income, via taxable/deductible alimony, on their separate returns and be taxed as married individuals filing separate returns.[39]

The "decree of separate maintenance" which "legally separates" married couples and therefore changes them into unmar-

---

[34] Letter Ruling 7835076 (6/1/78) (replying to married taxpayers' 2/27/78 inquiry that they intend to divorce and not remarry but to live "together much of the time after the divorce," I.R.S. stated that "if a couple obtains a divorce that is not declared invalid by a court of competent jurisdiction and there are no factors present to indicate that the couple should not be considered as unmarried individuals, the Internal Revenue Service will recognize the divorce").

[35] I.R.C. §§ 143(a)(2), 6013(d)(2).

[36] I.R.C. §§ 143(a)(1), 6013(d)(1).

[37] I.R.C. § 71(a)(2), (3).

[38] Treas. Reg. § 1.143-1(a) Example (1) (written separation agreement); § 1.6013-4(a) (interlocutory decree).

[39] I.R.C. § 71(a)(2) and (3), which provide for alimony treatment of periodic payments made under a written separation agreement or decree of support (to be distinguished from I.R.C. § 71(a)(1) which refers to decree of support or separate maintenance), state that these paragraphs (2) and (3) "shall not apply if the husband and wife make a single return jointly."

ried individuals for the purpose of the federal income tax must be something more than a "decree for support."

Temporary support orders and orders for support *pendente lite* do not "legally separate" a married couple.[40] Nor even does a New Jersey "decree of separate maintenance" based on extreme cruelty.[41] The distinction is ecclesiastical: divorce *a vinculo matrimonii* (from bond of matrimony) and divorce *a mensa et thoro* (from bed and board) do "legally separate." Other matrimonial decrees do not.[42]

The phrase "divorced or legally separated . . . under a decree of divorce or separate maintenance" came into the Internal Revenue Code not by way of definition of married/unmarried, but by the 1941 amendment which changed alimony to its present taxable/deductible status. Judge Harron's two decisions in 1946, the first of any to deal with the question of what is a decree of separate maintenance for alimony purposes, held that an order of support obtained by a wife against a husband who had abandoned her and an order of alimony *pendente lite* awarded a wife upon her initiation of her divorce action, although decrees of separate maintenance, were not decrees of separate maintenance which "legally separated" the couples.[43] Only by insisting on "legal separation" by decree, thought Judge Harron, could the thin line between nondeductible "personal, living, or family expenses" and deductible alimony be drawn.[44]

The distinction between decrees which legally separate and those which merely recognize that in fact a husband and wife are living separately was obliterated for the purpose of alimony in 1954. This distinction nonetheless continues for the purpose of characterizing taxpayers as married or unmarried, to the shock

---

[40]Stanley A. Dunn, 70 T.C. 361 (1978), taxpayer's appeal to Seventh Circuit pending; Gene Forrest, 37 T.C.M. (CCH) 1033 (1978).
[41]R. T. Capodanno, 69 T.C. 638 (1978).
[42]See Legget v. Commissioner, 329 F.2d 509 (C.A.-2 Fla., 1964) for discussion of modern replacements, in Florida's Statutes §§ 65.08 and 65.09, for divorce *a mensa et thoro,* a divorce which, the Second Circuit holds, is divorce for purpose of I.R.C. § 71(a)(1) (and therefore for § 143(a)(2) and § 6013(d)(2)), and divorce of (separate) maintenance (Fla. Stat., § 65.10) which, apparently, is not a "divorce or separate maintenance" for I.R.C. § 71(a)(1) or § 143(a)(2) or § 6013(d)(2).
[43]Frank J. Kalchthaler, 7 T.C. 625 (1946); George D. Wick, 7 T.C. 723 (1946), affd. per curiam 161 F.2d 732 (C.A.-3, 1947).
[44]See Frank J. Kalchthaler, 7 T.C. 625, 627 (1946).

5.5(B) UNMARRIED COUPLES AND THE LAW

and sorrow of some taxpayers who find that neither they,[45] nor the IRS agents[46] are able to make this distinction. The Wall Street Journal reported this experience of one unhappy taxpayer.

Gene lived apart from his wife pending their divorce. He asked the IRS how to file. Jointly with his wife, or as single head of household, the IRS advised. He used head of household, for it meant less tax. Later, the IRS said he didn't qualify as head of a household and owed $215 based on rates for single taxpayers. He agreed to pay. But then the IRS said he wasn't legally separated so he couldn't file as "single" and owed $812 based on rates for married filing a separate return.

However, he appealed to an IRS conferee who cut the amount to $142. Gene gave him a check. The IRS returned the check and demanded the $812. The IRS didn't tell Gene he could amend his return and file a joint one with his estranged wife to avoid the added tax. Nor did it tell him that if he appealed the matter to the Tax Court that would bar him from amending his return. He appealed to the court but didn't get any relief there.

"Misrepresentations of law were consistently made" by the

---

[45]See Stanley A. Dunn, 70 T.C. 361 (1978):
"Petitioner argues that by a layman the temporary order entered March 29, 1974, would be considered to constitute a legal separation since it provided that 'defendant shall be responsible for the debts of the parties incurred prior to the *separation* of the parties [Emphasis supplied].' He states this argument as follows:

'4. Petitioner was *separated* from his then wife during 1974, the tax year in question by documents which were *legal* and which were backed up by legally constituted Wisconsin State authority, a *legal separation****.
'5. C. F. Kading, Judge, who issued the legal orders, indicated in the preceding Item No. 4, referred to the resulting status existing between Petitioner and his then wife as "separation,"***.'

"Petitioner argues that the explanation of 'filing status' supplied with the Form 1040 would lead an ordinary layman to conclude that he was entitled to file as an unmarried individual when an order such as that of March 29, 1974, had been entered. The portion of the instructions accompanying the return to which petitioner specifically refers states as follows:

'Were you Married or Single?—If you were married on December 31, consider yourself married for the whole year. If you were single, divorced, or legally separated on December 31, consider yourself single for the whole year.***'

"While it may be that some individuals would not understand the difference between being 'separated' from their spouse and being 'legally separated' from their spouse, the law itself is clear that in order to be considered an unmarried individual, a taxpayer must be 'legally separated' from his spouse 'under a decree of divorce or of separate maintenance.' Certainly petitioner in this case was not unaware that he and his wife were still married under Wisconsin law at the end of 1974." [as they would have been even if the court had issued the kind of decree of separate maintenance that results in their being unmarried for federal income tax purposes. Ed. comment]
[46]Gene Forrest, 37 T.C.M. (CCH) 1033 (1978).

IRS, but that didn't block the agency from collecting the $812, the court said.[47]

Still another distinction has been made. A decree of divorce "legally separates" the couple at least as much as does a decree of legal separation, whether or not the divorce decree is final or becomes final only after a statutory waiting period, or whether or not the divorce decree is final, despite the possibility of appeal, or under state law becomes final only after appeal. That such legal niceties should be ignored seems to have been intended by Congress, and so the Tax Court in one case, but in few others, understood:

> Congress was legislating with respect to State court decrees, and the range of unmarried status for the purpose of the statutes was to extend from the separation by decrees of divorce to separate maintenance. ... It is somewhat logical to assume Congress meant the types of divorce decrees that are granted by most States. But the most convincing argument ... is found in the language of the Senate report with respect to section 25(b)(2). See S. Rept. No. 1013, 80th Cong., 2d Sess., 1948–1, C.B. 285, 324, as follows:
>
>> Section 25(b)(2) of the [1939] Code ... relates to the determination of marital status for the purposes of the credits provided with respect to a spouse in section 25(b) ... [A]n individual *legally separated (although not absolutely divorced)* from his spouse under a decree of divorce or of separate maintenance shall not be considered as married.*** [Emphasis added.]
>
> The intent of Congress appears to be that any separation by a divorce decree that is less than an absolute divorce ... will suffice to render the parties unmarried for the purpose of the statute.[48]

The IRS, however, conceded[49] to a long line of cases which held,

---

[47]Wall Street Journal, July 19, 1978.
[48]Marcel Garsaud, 28 T.C. 1086, 1088 (1957).
[49]Treas. Reg. § 1.6013-4(a); Rev. Rul. 75–536, 1975–2 C.B. 462 (couples divorced under Wisconsin interlocutory decree which becomes final in six months or upon the sooner death of either can file joint return for the year which ends within the six-month waiting period unless either has died within that period) (Comment: If the decree is entered December 31, 1978, joint tax returns are filed April 15, 1979, and one "spouse" dies 6/29/79, the return therefore turns out, retroactively, to have been improperly filed on a joint return basis); superseding Rev. Rul. 59–266, 1959–2 C.B. 377; Rev. Rul. 57–368, 1957–2 C.B. 896, withdrawing nonacquiescence to Eccles (see note 50, infra) and revoking Rev. Rul. 55–178, 1955–1 C.B. 322.

5.5(B) UNMARRIED COUPLES AND THE LAW

in favor of taxpayers who were then better off with joint returns, that a couple who was divorced was nonetheless married until after the "divorce became final" under state law.[50] As so often happens, what begins as a victory for taxpayers in possibly ill-considered opinions ends up as the misfortune of other taxpayers. Marriner Eccles[51] succeeded in getting the Tax Court to hold that he and his wife, who had obtained a Utah divorce which made no provision for support or maintenance of Mrs. Eccles, and which under state law became absolute six months later, were not legally separated under decree of divorce or of separate maintenance and hence could file a joint return for the year which ended after the entry of the divorce decree but before the six months had run. Although the Eccles case turned on a misplaced reliance on the intricacies of the local divorce law, this case was followed by many others.[52]

The Eccles holding resulted in misfortune for subsequent taxpayers. Mrs. Seaman, who was divorced under a California interlocutory decree in 1967 and was supporting herself and her children, could not deduct child care expenses under I.R.C. § 214 since she was not, as § 214(d)(5) then required, "legally separated from spouse under decree of divorce or separate maintenance."[53]

Since the Deyoes, a California couple, were still husband and wife after entry of an interlocutory decree of divorce, sale by the wife of her share of the community ranch to the husband before

---

[50]Commissioner v. Ostler, 237 F.2d 501 (C.A.-9 Cal., 1956) (California interlocutory decree); United States v. Holcomb, 237 F.2d 502 (C.A.-9 Cal., 1956) (California interlocutory decree); Boyar v. United States, 56–2 U.S.T.C. ¶ 9765 (S.D. Cal., 1956) (California interlocutory decree); Ellik v. United States, 56–1 U.S.T.C. ¶ 9184 (S.D. Cal., 1955) (California interlocutory decree); J. R. Calhoun, Jr., 27 T.C. 115 (1956), *Acq.* 1957–2 C.B. 4 (California interlocutory decree); Joyce Primrose Lane, 26 T.C. 405 (1956), *Acq.* 1956–2 C.B. 7, 1957–2 C.B. 5 (California interlocutory decree); Marriner S. Eccles, 19 T.C. 1049 (1953), affd. per curiam on Tax Court opinion, 208 F.2d 796 (C.A.-4 Utah, 1953), *Acq.* 1957–2 C.B. 4, withdrawing *Nonacq.* 1953–2 C.B. 8. Fred F. Davis, 15 T.C.M. (CCH) 1235 (1956) (Colorado interlocutory decree). Compare Sullivan v. Commissioner, 256 F.2d 664 (C.A.-4 Md., 1958) (husband and wife could not file joint return in 1951 while wife's appeal from Maryland decree of divorce *a mensa et thoro* was undecided; the appeal did not suspend the decree and therefore the Commissioner's $7,000 deficiency against the husband was upheld). See also 8 CCH 1979 Fed. Tax Rep. ¶ 5020.6355.

[51]Marriner S. Eccles, note 50, supra.

[52]See note 50, supra.

[53]Seaman v. Commissioner, 479 F.2d 336 (C.A.-9 Cal., 1973).

entry of the final decree of divorce resulted in characterization of her gain with respect to the high value-low basis depreciable assets, including orchard trees, buildings and equipment, as ordinary income under I.R.C. § 1239, rather than capital gain.[54]

Merle Johnson, divorced under a California decree in 1964, which became final in 1965, could not file a separate return for 1964 claiming benefit of head of household rate although he supported his mother and maintained the household which was her principal place of abode.[55]

Written separation agreement

Whatever the status and consequence of decrees, one thing is certain. A husband and wife who are legally separated only by written separation agreement are still married. A Mr. Donigan, who had been separated since 1964 from his wife under a written separation agreement, under which he had been dutifully paying alimony, was hit with a $1,000 deficiency in 1977 because he was required to use the tax rate schedule for married taxpayers filing separately, rather than the schedule for unmarried taxpayers.[56]

"Legally separated"—Living apart?

"Legally separated,"[57] or, in the words of the alimony regulations, "separated and living apart,"[58] does not necessarily require that the couple live in separate residences. In two cases, Sydnes and Del Vecchio, the Tax Court required separate roofs,[59] but in Sydnes, the Tax Court was reversed.[60]

In the Sydnes matter, an Iowa court, on Mrs. Sydnes' application for temporary support, required Mr. Sydnes to make periodic payments and ordered the spouse "to continue to live separately but in the same house." The couple occupied separate bedrooms,

---

[54]Elizabeth L. Deyoe, 66 T.C. 904 (1976).
[55]Merle Johnson, 50 T.C. 723 (1968).
[56]James F. Donigan, 68 T.C. 632 (1977).
[57]I.R.C. §§ 143(a)(2), 6013(d)(2).
[58]Treas. Reg. § 1.71–1(b)(3)(i); § 1.71–1(c)(1)(ii).
[59]Richard J. Sydnes, 68 T.C. 170 (1977); Marion S. Del Vecchio, 32 T.C.M. (CCH) 1153 (1973).
[60]Sydnes v. Commissioner, 577 F.2d 60 (C.A.-8 Iowa, 1978).

rarely saw one another, and never shared meals. The Tax Court nonetheless did not permit Mr. Sydnes to deduct the periodic payments.

In Del Vecchio, because of reduced economic circumstances, Mr. Del Vecchio could not maintain his separate residence and, against his wife's wishes, moved back into their jointly owned home. Although they did not live as man and wife, and Mr. Del Vecchio was directed by the local court to continue making payments to his wife under a prior order, after he moved back, the Tax Court held that the payments were not deductible since husband and wife were not "separated and living apart."

Although the Tax Court said in Sydnes that it should not be required to delve into the intimate question of whether husband and wife are in fact living apart while residing in the same house, the Eighth Circuit reversed, disagreeing with the Tax Court holding "that under no facts and circumstances can husband and wife live separately in the same residence." The Eighth Circuit found, on the basis of the trial record, that the Sydnes couple, while living in the same house, were living separately and apart.

Death of a spouse

If John Smith dies on December 1, 1979 (or at any other time during the year), Mrs. Smith can file a joint return or a separate return as she wishes. If she files a joint return, it will include all of her 1979 income and Mr. Smith's income up to December 1, the date of his death. She can file a joint return because the Code says that the determination of whether she is married for 1979 shall be made as of the time of her husband's death.[61]

If Mrs. Smith wants to file a separate return, must she be taxed as married individual filing separate return? She is in fact not married on December 31. But the regulations appear to take the position that the Code's determination of married status not on the last day of the year but as of the date of Mr. Smith's death is not elective but mandatory for Mrs. Smith.[62] Therefore, if Mrs. Smith files her own separate return she will be subject to what-

---

[61] I.R.C. § 6013(d)(1)(B).
[62] I.R.C. § 1.143–1(a).

ever disadvantages may accrue to her from her tax characterization as married filing separately.

The Code says that if Mrs. Smith remarries in 1979, she can't file a joint return with deceased Mr. Smith[63] (though the regulations concede that she can with her new husband).[64] If Mrs. Smith remarries in 1979, the deceased Mr. Smith's return must be filed for him on the basis of married filing separately. If Mrs. Smith does not remarry in 1979 but elects to file a separate return, even if her characterization as married can be said not to be mandatory, the deceased Mr. Smith is, for the purpose of his final return, married, and therefore taxed as married filing separately.

"Living apart a full taxable year"

Because of the anomalous effect of a portion of the marital status definition of the Code, if a husband and wife have lived apart for the full taxable year, one of the two may be considered married, while the other may be considered unmarried. Although Mrs. Smith is married under the state law or federal tax law definitions, she is nonetheless considered unmarried (a) if she lives in and maintains and pays over half the cost of a household for more than half of the taxable year; (b) that household is the home of her dependent child or dependent stepchild; and (c) during the entire taxable year her husband, Mr. Smith, was not a member of that household.[65]

If Mr. Smith's absence from the household was not temporary nor for a nonpermanent reason of illness, education, business, vacation or military service,[66] Mrs. Smith is "unmarried," but Mr. Smith is "married."

This provision was enacted in 1969 to protect the "abandoned spouse."[67] But it is not just the abandoned spouse who benefits from being able to be treated as unmarried although married and not legally separated by divorce or separation decree. If Mr. and Mrs. Smith have more than one dependent child, and both set up

---

[63]I.R.C. § 6013(a)(2).
[64]Treas. Reg. § 1.6013–1(d)(2).
[65]I.R.C. § 143(b).
[66]Treas. Reg. § 1.143–1(b)(5).
[67]Mertens, *Law of Federal Income Taxation, Code Commentary*, § 143:2.

independent housekeeping with one or more of the children, both can claim not to be married.

What is more likely is that the one Smith child or all the Smith children live with Mrs. Smith. In this case, she is unmarried, but Mr. Smith is nonetheless married.

It is not just the abandoning spouse who is penalized by being treated as married and having to file a separate return. Poor Mr. Donigan[68] again, who paid every penny of alimony due under his 1964 separation agreement with Mrs. Donigan, finds himself hit with the higher tax applicable to married individuals filing separately while Mrs. Donigan, if the support payments she receives are taxable to her and if she has a dependent child at home, may file as unmarried.

The one spouse who is considered married endures not only the disadvantageous consequences of higher tax rates,[69] but also reduced or denied credits and deductions,[70] when he files his separate return. And if his "unmarried" spouse itemizes her deductions on her return, he must also, even if his itemized deductions are less than his zero bracket amount.[71] But if he itemizes, his "unmarried" spouse is not forced to itemize her deductions, as she would be if she were a married individual filing a separate return, and she can take full advantage of her zero bracket amount. The "unmarried" spouse of the married couple enjoys the advantage of qualifying for the lower tax rate tables applicable to heads of households[72] and otherwise being treated as unmarried for the purpose of credits, deductions and benefits reduced or denied to the "married" spouse of this anomalous twosome.

Two sections of the Code use a "living apart" test which is

---

[68]See James F. Donigan, 68 T.C. 632 (1977).

[69]See section 5.4, herein.

[70]Id.

[71]I.R.C. § 63(e) requires that "a married individual filing a separate return where either spouse itemizes deductions," for the purpose of determining his taxable income, add to his adjusted gross income his "unused zero bracket amount" or the excess (if any) of his Z.B.A. over his itemized deductions. And I.R.C. § 63(b) says that for the "purpose of this section marital status shall be determined under section 143." The "married individual" is still married under § 143 and his spouse is still his spouse even if she is "unmarried" under § 143. Therefore, although § 63(b) doesn't say whose marital status is to be determined under § 143 for the purpose of § 63(e), the unfortunate but logical conclusion to be drawn is that the command of § 63(e) is directed at the spouse who is married.

[72]See section 5.4, herein, and subsec. (D) of this section.

different from the marital status of "abandoned spouse" test, which requires that a dependent child be a member of the household for more than half of the year and that the other spouse not be a member of the household for the *entire* year.

The credit for child care and dependent care expenses is available to a taxpayer who meets the dependency and maintenance of household tests required for that credit and who, although married, does not file a joint return, as long as the taxpayer's spouse is not a member of the household for the *last six months* of the year.[73]

The credit for the elderly can be claimed only on a joint return, by taxpayers who are married, under the tax definitions, unless they live apart *at all times during the year*.[74]

Nonresident alien spouse

A taxpayer subject to the federal income tax who is married to a nonresident alien is married for almost all purposes of the Code,[75] but, except under special circumstances, he may not file a joint return.[76] He must be taxed as a married individual filing a separate return[77] or, if he qualifies, as head of household.[78] The highest tax rate table applies if he doesn't qualify as a head of household.[79] The zero bracket amount, i.e., the amount over which income is subject to tax, starts at $1,700, rather than $2,300 for unmarried taxpayers or heads of household or $3,400 for married taxpayers filing a joint return.[80]

---

[73] I.R.C. § 44A(f)(4)(B).
[74] I.R.C. § 37(d)(1).
[75] I.R.C. § 143. This marriage definition section is cited in IRC §§ 1, 2, 37, 42, 43, 63, 85, 105, 151, 152, 153, 219, 220, 879, 1302, 1304, 3402, 6012, 6362, 6428 and Treas. Reg. §§ 1.2.2-2, 1.4-3, 1.42A-1, 1.43-1, 1.46-1, 1.48-3, 1.50A-1, 1.141-1, 1.214A-4, 1.304-3, 1.6012-1, 301.6362-7.
[76] I.R.C. § 6013(a)(1). Although marital status is otherwise determined on the last day of the taxable year (I.R.C. § 6013(d)(1), § 143(a)(1)) except for a widow or widower whose spouse dies during the year (I.R.C. § 6013(d)(1)(B), § 143(a)(1)), if either spouse is a nonresident alien "at any time during the taxable year" (I.R.C. § 6013(a)(1)), the couple is denied the right to file a joint return for the year. For the special circumstances under which taxpayer with nonresident spouse may file joint return, see text at note 81, infra.
[77] I.R.C. § 1(d).
[78] I.R.C. § 2(b). See subsection (D) of this section.
[79] I.R.C. § 1(d). See section 5.3, herein.
[80] I.R.C. § 63(d). See section 5.3, herein.

The taxpayer who has a nonresident alien spouse can file a joint return only if they agree to subject all of the nonresident alien spouse's income to taxation by the United States.[81] However, if the taxpayer married to a nonresident alien at any time during the year otherwise qualifies as "head of household," he is deemed unmarried for the purpose of using the head of household tax rate table,[82] but only for that purpose.[83] Since the taxpayer is married for most purposes of the Code and since the filing of joint returns is prohibited unless the nonresident alien spouse's foreign income is included, the taxpayer cannot claim the elderly tax credit,[84] the child or dependent care credit[85] or the 50% max-tax ceiling rate on personal service income.[86] The taxpayer must reduce from $100,000 to $50,000 the maximum of any gain on the sale of a residence excludable from gross income if the taxpayer is over age 55,[87] reduce from $3,000 to $1,500 any otherwise deductible excess capital losses,[88] and cut in half any otherwise deductible moving expenses.[89]

Hence, a taxpayer married to a nonresident alien may be subject to increased taxes because of the marriage. The taxpayer can avoid these increased taxes only if he (1) becomes unmarried by end of year, by divorce or by being legally separated by decree, or (2) becomes unmarried by living apart from his nonresident alien spouse for the entire year, as long as he pays more than half the cost of his home which is also the home of his dependent child or stepchild for more than half of the year, or (3)

---

[81] I.R.C. § 6013(g). This subsection was enacted by the Tax Reform Act of 1976. Unlike most of the amendments in that Act, this provision applies to taxable years ending on December 31, 1975, which provides a year's worth of retroactive relief, especially for those highly paid corporate executives stationed abroad who married or remarried without seeking advice of tax counsel and discovered that romance legitimatized by marriage increased their marginal tax bracket from the 50% max-tax ceiling rate provided by I.R.C. § 1348 to the 70% maximum tax bracket which starts at $101,600 of taxable income under I.R.C. § 1(d) tax rate table.
[82] I.R.C. § 2(b)(2)(C).
[83] I.R.C. § 143.
[84] I.R.C. § 37(d).
[85] I.R.C. § 44A(f)(2).
[86] I.R.C. § 1348(c).
[87] I.R.C. § 121(b)(1).
[88] I.R.C. § 1211(b)(2).
[89] I.R.C. § 217(b)(3)(B), (h)(i)(C).

the taxpayer and nonresident spouse elect to include in their joint return not only taxpayer's income but all of spouse's income even though that income would not otherwise be subject to the federal income tax because spouse's income was earned or otherwise derived outside of the United States.

What the Code is saying is that if a taxpayer wants to marry a nonresident alien he should make sure she is poor.

(C) SURVIVING SPOUSE

Widows and widowers may want to consider the impact of income taxes before they remarry. Both a deceased spouse and the surviving spouse are deemed married for the year in which the spouse dies.[90] A joint return must be filed, aggregating their income for that year, or they will be taxed as married individuals filing separately.[91] If a surviving spouse remarries by year end, the deceased spouse's return will be that of a married individual filing separately.[92]

For the next two years following the year in which a spouse dies, however, the surviving spouse is treated more kindly than any other taxpayer if he or she meets the Code definition of "surviving spouse."[93] A widow or widower is a "surviving spouse" only for the two years following the spouse's death.[94] If, for instance, the husband dies in 1978, the widow can be a surviving spouse for 1979 and 1980. Also, a widow or widower can be a "surviving spouse" only if he or she: (1) does not remarry,[95] and (2) could have filed a joint return with deceased spouse for the year of the spouse's death,[96] i.e., they were "married" as of

---

[90] I.R.C. §§ 143(a)(2), 6013(d)(1)(B).
[91] Cf. I.R.C. § 2(b)(2)(D).
[92] Treas. Reg. § 1.6013–1(d)(2) states that in the year of the death of one spouse, a joint return can be filed for the deceased spouse and surviving spouse only if the surviving spouse does not remarry before the close of his taxable year. The remarriage of the surviving spouse does not, however, turn the deceased spouse into an unmarried individual as of the date of his death, the close of his taxable year. I.R.C. § 143(a)(1).
[93] I.R.C. §§ 1(a), 2(a).
[94] I.R.C. § 2(a)(1)(A).
[95] I.R.C. § 2(a)(2)(A).
[96] I.R.C. § 2(a)(2)(B).

date of spouse's death[97] and neither were nonresident aliens,[98] and (3) pays over half the costs of maintaining the home in which he or she lives,[99] and (4) has a child or stepchild who lives with him or her for the entire year,[1] and (5) is deemed, under the support test for dependents, to have supplied over half of the support of this child or stepchild for the year,[2] and (6) the child or stepchild is either under age nineteen by the end of the year or is a full-time student for at least five months of the year or has a gross income of under $1,000.[3]

If the taxpayer satisfies these conditions, the taxpayer's income tax is computed under the tax rate table applicable to married individuals filing joint returns, which provides the lowest tax rates.[4]

The surviving spouse is in a better tax position than married taxpayers filing jointly since no other income need be aggregated with the surviving spouse's income. A surviving spouse gets the full benefit of the $3,400 zero bracket amount applied against a married couple's aggregated income.[5] Since the surviving spouse is not married, he or she can use the 50% max-tax ceiling rate available to a married couple only if they file a joint return and aggregate their income.[6] A surviving spouse can also use the child-care credit which can reduce a taxpayer's tax by as much as $400 for one child or other qualifying dependent and $800 for two or more qualifying dependents,[7] or the credit for elderly, which can reduce a taxpayer's tax by as much as $375.[8] Married couples

---

[97] I.R.C. § 143.
[98] I.R.C. § 6013(a)(1). See subsection (B) of this section.
[99] I.R.C. § 2(a).
[1] I.R.C. § 2(a)(1)(B).
[2] I.R.C. § 152(a), (c), (d), (e). I.R.C. § 152(e) deals with the "support test in case of child of divorced parent, et cetera." The "et cetera" includes parents separated under a written separation agreement. These separated parents are considered married (if so under local law) for tax purposes (I.R.C. § 143(a)), unless one of them meets the "abandoned spouse" test. That spouse is, therefore, mandatorily not married for tax purposes while the other, if not an "abandoned" spouse in his own right, is married for tax purposes. (I.R.C. § 143(b)). See subsection (B) of this section.
[3] I.R.C. § 151(e).
[4] I.R.C. § 1(a).
[5] I.R.C. §§ 63(d)(1), 6013(d)(3).
[6] I.R.C. § 1348(c).
[7] I.R.C. § 44A.
[8] I.R.C. § 37.

who do not live apart obtain the benefit of these tax credits only if they file joint returns.[9]

(D) HEAD OF HOUSEHOLD

The two individuals treated most kindly by the Internal Revenue Code are the surviving spouse and the married taxpayer whose spouse has no income subject to tax. The Code permits use of the lowest tax rate table by such a married taxpayer however many thousands of dollars of tax-exempt income his spouse may have,[10] and without regard to need. The separate income of a widow (or widower) who, in the first two full years of widowhood, is supporting a child is also taxed for those two years at the lowest rates provided by the Code. This benefit is available to a widow or widower even without regard to the amount of her or his income and if the child's own sizeable income is being invested and reinvested for future use.[11]

The next lowest tax rate table applies to "heads of households."[12]

An individual can be taxed at the head of household rate if he or she is not married and meets other requirements.[13] Marital status is determined as of December 31,[14] with two exceptions: (1) a widow or widower whose spouse has died during the year is a married taxpayer,[15] unless considered unmarried under the "legally separated under decree" rule[16] or because of meeting the "living apart for the full year," child dependency and household maintenance tests for "abandoned spouse" characterization,[17] and (2) an individual whose spouse is a nonresident alien at any time during the year is considered unmarried but only for the

---

[9] I.R.C. §§ 37(d), 44A(f)(2).

[10] State and municipal bond interest, tax-exempt under I.R.C. § 103, is not a tax preference item (I.R.C. § 57) subject to the minimum tax on tax preference items (I.R.C. § 56) or the alternative minimum tax (I.R.C. § 55).

[11] The child whose dependency status qualifies his widowed or widowered parent as surviving spouse may have income of any amount as long as he is under nineteen or a full-time student. I.R.C. § 151(e)(1)(B).

[12] I.R.C. § 1(b).
[13] I.R.C. § 2(b).
[14] I.R.C. § 143(a)(1).
[15] Id.
[16] I.R.C. § 143(a)(2).
[17] I.R.C. § 143(b).

5.5(D) UNMARRIED COUPLES AND THE LAW

purpose of the head of household rate table.[18] For all other purposes the taxpayer is married.[19]

If, as of December 31, the taxpayer has been a widow or widower for more than twelve months and has not remarried, the taxpayer is unmarried. Or, if the taxpayer is legally separated by decree as of December 31, he or she is unmarried.[20] If the taxpayer, though married, meets the "living apart for the full year," child dependency and household maintenance tests for the "abandoned spouse" characterization, the taxpayer is unmarried.[21]

If the taxpayer satisfies the tests for the "abandoned spouse" characterization, the taxpayer may also, but not necessarily, satisfy the requirements for use of the head of household rate table.[22]

To satisfy the requirements for use of the head of household tax rate table, rather than the somewhat more costly unmarried individuals (other than heads of households and surviving spouses) tax rate table, the taxpayer must not only be "unmarried" but must meet other requirements. The taxpayer must furnish over half the costs of maintaining a household for the full year.[23] The household need not be the taxpayer's home if it is the home of the taxpayer's parent and that parent is the taxpayer's dependent.[24]

If the household which the taxpayer maintains is the taxpayer's home, and it is also the home of a child, stepchild or grandchild of the taxpayer, the taxpayer qualifies as head of household. The child, stepchild or grandchild, need not be taxpayer's dependent, as long as such child, stepchild or grandchild

---

[18] I.R.C. § 2(b)(2)(C).
[19] I.R.C. § 143.
[20] I.R.C. § 143(a)(2).
[21] I.R.C. § 143(b).
[22] Compare I.R.C. § 143(b)(1) with I.R.C. § 2(b)(1)(A). Both "head of household" and "abandoned spouse" must furnish over half the cost of maintaining the household for the full year, but that household could be the principal place of abode for the dependent child or stepchild who qualifies the taxpayer as an abandoned spouse, and therefore as unmarried, for only "more than one-half of the taxable year" but must be the principal place of abode of the person who qualifies the taxpayer as a head of household.
[23] I.R.C. § 2(b)(1).
[24] I.R.C. § 2(b)(1)(B).

is not married by December 31.[25] Thus a multimillionaire taxpayer, with an unmarried child, of any age, who also is a multimillionaire, receives the benefit of the head of household rate table, if the child resides in the taxpayer's home more than 50% of the costs of which the taxpayer pays.[26]

If the household which the taxpayer maintains is the taxpayer's home and is also the home for the full year of a dependent of taxpayer's, the taxpayer also qualifies as a head of household.[27] The dependency test, for the purpose of qualifying the taxpayer as a head of household, is almost the same as, but is somewhat more restrictive than, the dependency test (see subsection (E) below) for the purpose of the $1,000 personal exemption deduction. The dependent supported by a taxpayer must be related as a child or a descendant of a child; stepchild; parent, stepparent or grandparent; brother, sister or stepbrother or stepsister; niece or nephew; aunt or uncle; son-in-law, daughter-in-law, father-in-law, mother-in-law, brother-in-law or sister-in-law.[28] An individual who is defined as the taxpayer's dependent for the purpose of the $1,000 personal exemption deduction because of a multiple support agreement[29] does not permit the taxpayer to be characterized as a head of household,[30] even if that individual lives with the taxpayer in a home all of the costs of which are furnished by the taxpayer.

In addition, an unrelated individual who resides with a tax-

---

[25]I.R.C. § 2(b)(1)(A)(i).
[26]See Estate of Jean Foster Fleming, 33 T.C.M. (CCH) 619, 621 (1974) (the Tax Court dismissed the Commissioner's argument that the taxpayer, who failed to demonstrate the necessity for her to maintain a home for her independently wealthy adult daughter, should not be permitted to claim head of household treatment, and quoted House Ways & Means and Senate Finance Committee Reports and House Discussion to show that Congress was aware that for head of household treatment it is immaterial how much gross income an unmarried child or grandchild may have.) A taxpayer should not only pay more than half the costs of maintaining the household but the IRS might assert in addition that the household should be owned or rented by the taxpayer. Cf. Zelta J. Bombarger, 31 T.C. 473 (1958), which denied a § 152(a)(9) dependency relationship since the person supported by the taxpayer was the one who owned the house and therefore was not a member of "taxpayer's household." This phrase does not appear in I.R.C. § 2.
[27]I.R.C. § 2(b)(1)(A)(ii), (b)(3)(B).
[28]I.R.C. § 152(a)(1) through (8).
[29]I.R.C. § 152(c). See text at note 44, infra.
[30]I.R.C. § 2(b)(3)(B)(ii).

payer may be the taxpayer's dependent,[31] but this fact does not permit the taxpayer to claim the benefit of the head of household tax rate table.[32]

Since "child" is defined as including a legally adopted child,[33] what the Internal Revenue Code is saying is this. If one of a pair of unmarried cohabitants can legally adopt the other, no matter how wealthy either or both may be, as long as the adopting cohabitant pays 51% of the cost of the home in which they both live, the adopting cohabitant can claim the lower tax rates applicable to heads of households.

(E) DEPENDENT

Personal exemption deduction

Each individual is born with his or her own deduction for personal exemption. This deduction has increased, with inflation, over the years to $1,000 for 1979.[34] The $1,000 exemption is increased to $2,000 if the taxpayer is age 65 or over by December 31.[35] A taxpayer who is blind has an additional $1,000 exemption.[36]

Sometimes a taxpayer can use not only his or her own personal exemption deduction for the purpose of determining his taxable income, but can also use another person's exemption deduction. If a taxpayer and spouse file a joint return, both of their personal exemption deductions, $1,000 apiece, plus an additional $1,000 for either if over 65, plus another $1,000 for either if blind (within the Code's definition), can be used in computing the aggregate joint return taxable income.

Even if the taxpayer and spouse do not file a joint return, the taxpayer can use his or her spouse's $1,000 exemption deduction (or $2,000 if the spouse is over 65 or blind, or $3,000 if the spouse is over 65 and blind) on the taxpayer's separate return.[37]

---

[31] I.R.C. § 152(a)(9). See text at note 50, infra.
[32] I.R.C. § 2(b)(3)(B)(i).
[33] I.R.C. § 2(b)(2)(A).
[34] I.R.C. § 151(b).
[35] I.R.C. § 151(c)(1).
[36] I.R.C. § 151(d).
[37] I.R.C. § 151(b), (c)(2), (d)(2).

The taxpayer can use the spouse's personal exemption deduction, however, only if the spouse has no gross income for the year and is not a dependent of another taxpayer.[38] The test is gross income, not support. The spouse can have $100,000 annual tax-exempt municipal bond interest[39] or $50,000 yearly installment payments of a lump-sum amount payable by an ex-spouse,[40] or $5,000 a year of social security payments[41] and use these funds for support. But since these items are not includable in gross income and need not be reported on the spouse's separate return or the couple's joint return, her or his personal exemption deduction can be used by the taxpaying spouse on his or her own separate return.

In addition, the taxpayer can claim another $1,000 exemption deduction, but not an over age 65 nor a blindness exemption deduction, for each of taxpayer's dependents.[42]

Dependent defined

A person qualifies as another taxpayer's dependent only if the dependent receives over half of his support from the taxpayer.[43] There are two exceptions, the multiple support agreement exception and the divorced parents exception.

A person who otherwise qualifies as a dependent may receive support from the taxpayer and one or more other persons. As long as those who contribute support together contribute more than 50% of the support, but each contributes no more than 50% and no less than 10% of the support, they can agree, in writing, that one of them is entitled to claim the dependent's exemption deduction.[44]

One of a pair of divorced or legally separated parents can use

---

[38]Id.

[39]I.R.C. § 103 excludes interest on state and municipal bonds from gross income.

[40]I.R.C. § 71(c) excludes from gross income the full amount of installment payments of a principal sum payable pursuant to decree or agreement, unless the period for payment exceeds ten years.

[41]Social security benefits are excluded from gross income. Rev. Rul. 70-217, 1970-1 C.B. 12, superseding I.T. 3447, 1941-1 C.B. 191.

[42]I.R.C. § 151(e). Note, a spouse is never a dependent. See note 53, infra.

[43]I.R.C. § 152(a).

[44]I.R.C. § 152(c).

the personal exemption deduction for their child without providing more than half of the support of the child as long as the parents together provided more than 50% of the child's support,[45] and the child lives with one or both of his parents for more than half the year. The parent with custody of the child is deemed to provide over half the support of the child for any year in which the noncustodial parent does not provide $1,200 or more for the child's support. If the noncustodial parent provides the required $1,200, the custodial parent must prove that he provided more for the child's support than did the noncustodial parent.

The noncustodial parent who provides less than half of a child's support can claim the child as a dependent if the parents together provide more than 50% of the child's support and if the child otherwise qualifies as a dependent. The noncustodial parent can use the child's $1,000 personal exemption deduction, without regard to that parent's having supplied less than 50% of the child's support, if the parents' agreement or the decree of divorce or separate maintenance prohibits the custodial parent from claiming the child's personal exemption deduction and the noncustodial parent provides $600 (or more) for the child.[46]

In addition to the over 50% support test, other tests must be met.

A person cannot be claimed as another's dependent unless the dependent has a gross income of less than $1,000.[47] The only exception to this "gross income test" is a child under age nineteen on December 31 or over age nineteen but a full-time student for each of five months during the year.[48] Thus, as long as a parent pays more than 50% of a child's support, or falls within the multiple support agreement or divorced parents exceptions to

---

[45]I.R.C. § 152(e).
[46]Note that by agreement, an expenditure of $600 can produce a $1,000 deduction for the noncustodial parent. This $600 was pegged to the old dependency exemption deduction of $600 and has not kept pace with the increase in that exemption which is now $1,000. I.R.C. § 151(d).

Scholarships received by the child or stepchild are not taken into account for the purpose of determining whether the 50% plus support test has been met. I.R.C. § 152(d).
[47]I.R.C. § 151(e)(1)(A).
[48]I.R.C. § 151(e)(1)(B).

the support test, the child who is under nineteen or a student can be independently wealthy and still be the parent's dependent.

The third test that must be met is the relationship test. A person cannot be a taxpayer's dependent unless he is related to the taxpayer as the taxpayer's child (including legally adopted child) or child's descendant; stepchild; parent, stepparent or grandparent; sibling, stepsibling or sibling by the half blood; niece or nephew; aunt or uncle; child-in-law, parent-in-law, or sibling-in-law. With the exception of the legally adopted child who is a nonresident alien and a child placed by an authorized adoption placement agency for adoption by the taxpayer, those who meet the relationship test need not live with the taxpayer in order for the taxpayer to claim their dependency exemption deduction.[49]

The member of household test is required for others. Any individual who meets the under $1,000 gross income test and with respect to whom the taxpayer meets the over 50% support test can be the taxpayer's dependent but only if that individual "has as his principal place of abode the home of the taxpayer and is a member of the taxpayer's household."[50] The taxpayer must both maintain and occupy the household.[51] Moreover, it must be the taxpayer who owns or rents the household, as well as pays its expenses, in order for it to be the "taxpayer's household."[52]

---

[49] I.R.C. § 152(a)(1) through (8). I.R.C. § 152(b)(1), (2). Except for a legally adopted child who resides with the taxpayer, a nonresident alien cannot be a dependent unless he resides in the Canal Zone, Panama, Canada or Mexico, and a legally adopted child cannot be claimed by a taxpayer as a dependent unless the taxpayer himself is a citizen or national of the United States. I.R.C. § 152(b)(3); Treas. Reg. § 1.152-2(a).

[50] I.R.C. § 152(a)(9).

[51] Treas. Reg. § 1.152-1(b). Neither I.R.C. § 152 nor Treas. Reg. § 1.152 define "maintain," but presumably reference must be made to I.R.C. § 2(a) and (b)(1) which state: "For the purposes of this paragraph, an individual shall be considered as maintaining a household only if over half of the cost of maintaining the household during the taxable year is furnished by such individual."

[52] Zelta J. Bombarger, 31 T.C. 473 (1958) (taxpayer and her young son lived in the home owned by a widowed friend whose relationship with the taxpayer was "like mother and daughter," and taxpayer, the only wage earner in the household, contributed most of the cash to maintain the household while the friend did the major share of the household chores; the court denied the taxpayer the "member of household" dependency deduction for the friend since she did not live in the taxpayer's household, but the taxpayer and her son lived in the friend's household).

Two categories of individuals cannot be "member of the household" dependents. One is a person who was the taxpayer's spouse at any time during the year under the local law and not the tax law definition of married.[53] The other is a person whose relationship with the taxpayer is "in violation of local law" at any time during the year.[54]

Cohabitant as dependent?

The Code provision which denies a taxpayer a personal exemption deduction for a person who meets the under $1,000 gross income test, the over 50% support test and the member of household test, because their relationship "is in violation of local law," was enacted in 1958,[55] four years after the member of the household test was added to the Code.

The year before, the Tax Court had considered the claim of one Leon Turnipseed for a dependency exemption for one Tina Johnson for 1954.[56] Since 1949 Tina had been separated but not divorced from her husband, David, who, except for $52 in 1950, never paid anything for her support or the support of their two children. In 1953 Tina moved into Leon Turnipseed's home and in all of 1954 "they lived openly together as man and wife." In April 1954 Tina gave birth to a child. Tina had no income of her own and received her entire support from Leon.

The Tax Court was shocked and said so:

> The uncontroverted facts disclose that petitioner in the taxable year in question was living in adulterous cohabitation with Tina Johnson, the undivorced wife of David Johnson. The support which petitioner furnished Tina was voluntarily assumed and not legally imposed.

---

[53] I.R.C. § 152(9) excludes from member of household dependents "an individual who at any time during the taxable year was the spouse, determined without regard to section 143, of the taxpayer." A spouse is also not listed as a relationship dependent. The reason for and result of these omissions is that a taxpayer is not entitled to deduct $1,000 for his spouse because he supports her but only if they file a joint return or, if they do not file a joint return, only if she has not one penny of gross income and is not another taxpayer's dependent. I.R.C. § 151(b); S. Rep. No. 1983, 85th Cong., 2nd Sess., 1958–3 C.B. 936.

[54] I.R.C. § 152(b)(5).

[55] Technical Amendments Act of 1958, Pub. L. No. 85–866, § 4(c).

[56] Leon Turnipseed, 27 T.C. 758 (1957).

The question presented is one of first impression. Is the language used in section 152 (a) (9) to be construed literally so as to embrace an individual living in illicit intimacy with a taxpayer?

The 1954 Code retains the eight provisions of the 1939 Code, all of which are based on relationship by blood or marriage, and to which have been added two new classifications. Paragraph (9) of section 152 (a), with which we are concerned, permits greater flexibility in that it provides a new concept to the tests for dependency in which no such relationship is required. ...

In our opinion Congress never intended the specific paragraph in question to be construed so literally as to permit a dependency exemption for an individual whom the taxpayer is maintaining in an illicit relationship in conscious violation of the criminal law of the jurisdiction of his abode.

We are of the opinion that to so construe the statute would in effect ascribe to the Congress an intent to countenance, if not to aid and encourage, a condition not only universally regarded as against good public morals, but also constituting a continuing, willful, open, and deliberate violation of the laws of the State of Alabama. Ala. Code tit. 14, sec. 16 (1940). [Living in adultery or fornication.] This we are unable to do.[57]

Congress agreed with the Tax Court's rewriting of the member of the household test. When Congress enacted the "relationship ... in violation of local law" amendment in 1958, Congress made it retroactive to 1954, the effective date of the member of household provision.[58]

Today, Leon Turnipseed's and Tina's cohabitation may not be "universally regarded as against good public morals" nor "a continuing, willful, open and deliberate violation of the laws." Nonetheless, the supporting cohabitant may be denied the personal exemption deduction for the supported cohabitant.

Congress explained its retroactive illegal relationship amendment in House and Senate Reports which stated that the purpose of the amendment is to "make it clear that an individual who is a 'common-law wife' where the applicable State law does not recognize common-law marriages would not qualify as a de-

---

[57] Id., at 760–761.
[58] Pub. L. No. 85–866, § 1(c), § 4.

pendent of the taxpayer."[59] Some twenty years later, it is not so obvious that a relationship which approaches that of common-law marriage, but is not a common-law marriage, is in violation of local law.[60] Nonetheless, the Tax Court still seems shocked by the Leon Turnipseeds or marvinizers of today.

Some Tax Court decisions have denied a taxpayer the personal exemption deduction for his dependent cohabitant without examining local law to determine if in fact the relationship was illegal.[61] Another Tax Court decision presumed from the fact that a man and woman lived together that their relationship was of the sort forbidden by the criminal laws of the states in which they lived.[62] Still other Tax Court decisions have put the burden on the taxpayers of proving that their relationships were not "open and notorious cohabitation"[63] or that they were not "lewdly and lasciviously"[64] or "lewdly and viciously"[65] cohabiting, or that their relationship was not otherwise in violation of local law. The Tax Court found each taxpayer to have failed in his burden of proof even where the community in which the cohabiting couple resided accepted them as husband and wife.

In some cases the Tax Court has not asserted illegality of relationship to deny the dependency deduction for the taxpayer's cohabitant. Instead, the Tax Court has used a *quid pro quo* argument, asserting that the taxpayer did not support his cohabitant but instead remunerated her for her services by providing her support.[66]

---

[59]H.R. Rep. No. 775, 85th Cong., 1st Sess., 1958–3 C.B. 819; S. Rep. No. 1983, 85th Cong., 2nd Sess., 1958–3 C.B. 936.
[60]The trend is toward the repeal of statutes which criminalize private sexual acts of consenting adults. See section 2.25, herein.
[61]See John J. Untermann, 38 T.C. 93 (1962); Estate of Daniel Buckley, 37 T.C. 664 (1962); Alfred Davis, 23 T.C.M. (CCH) 1099 (1964).
[62]See Sheral Jackson Martin, 32 T.C.M. (CCH) 656 (1973).
[63]See Cassius L. Peacock III, T.C.M. (P-H) ¶78,029 at 78,188 (1978).
[64]See Nevett F. Emsinger, 36 T.C.M. (CCH) 934 (1977).
[65]See Leonard J. Eichbauer, 30 T.C.M. (CCH) 581 (1971).
[66]William Thomas Hamilton, 37 T.C. 927 (1960); D. L. Angstadt, 27 T.C.M. (CCH) 693 (1968); See Leon Turnipseed, 27 T.C. 758 (1957) (concurring opinion). Compare Dorothy H. Limpert, 37 T.C. 447 (1961) (support provided by a taxpayer for her mother who lived with taxpayer and took care of taxpayer's young son was held to be support provided for the son; the taxpayer could take the child-care deduction under former I.R.C. § 214 but could not take a dependency deduction for her mother); Zelta J. Bombarger, 31 T.C. 473 (1958) (taxpayer paid

MARITAL STATUS AND TAXES 5.5(E)

A taxpayer may be denied the personal exemption deduction for his dependent cohabitant on the ground of the presumed illegality of their relationship. But, nonetheless, if the taxpayer's cohabitant's children or mother meet all the dependency tests (under $1,000 gross income, more than 50% of support from taxpayer, and member of taxpayer's household for the full year) the taxpayer can claim these children and his "mother-in-law" as dependents.[67]

Other tax uses of dependent

The $1,000 personal exemption deduction is of greatest benefit to the highest income taxpayer. The $1,000 deduction for a taxpayer in the 70% income tax bracket reduces his tax by $700.

---

the expenses of the household owned by a widowed friend who did the major share of the household chores; the taxpayer was denied dependency deduction for the friend, the Tax Court stating that "[t]hese parties are mutually dependent upon one another. Each contributes something to the other (sic) needs and each receives a benefit from a mutually satisfactory arrangement. It is not necessary to attempt to weigh the comparative worth of the contributions and say which is the greater."); Massey v. Commissioner, 51 F.2d 76, 77 (C.A.-6 Ky., 1931) (petitioner claimed personal exemption as "head of family"; he was single and owned a home in which his forty-year-old widowed sister lived; she had no income or property of her own; the Board of Tax Appeals' view was accepted that the sister (who supervised the running of the household) "had the status of an employee rather than a dependent, and that contributions to her support were in return for the performance of the duties of a housekeeper, rather than by reason of any legal or moral obligation of support." But in Alfred E. Fuhlage, 32 B.T.A. 222 (1935), the taxpayer was allowed the personal exemption as head of family where he owned and paid all the expenses of his home in which his unmarried 55-year-old sister lived. He was her sole support; she had no trade or occupation, and no income, and acted as the taxpayer's housekeeper. The taxpayer also employed a servant. The Board, finding the Massey case distinguishable, stated that the sister "was not employed by the petitioner . . . under the circumstances we consider it only natural that a feeling of gratitude or interest in the household would prompt the sister to act as housekeeper. The only inference to be drawn . . . is that what she did in this respect was done gratuitously." See also GCM 10431, XI–1 CB 37 (1932).

[67]Estate of Daniel Buckley, 37 T.C. 664 (1962); Sheral Jackson Martin, 32 T.C.M. (CCH) 656 (1973); Alfred Davis, 23 T.C.M. (CCH) 1099 (1964) (IRS concession, in each case). But see James D. Protiva, 29 T.C.M. (CCH) 1318 (1970) (taxpayer could not claim dependency exemptions for the two children of his live-in babysitter where she received food, lodging and incidental items, such as utilities, for herself and the children, as well as $100 per month, from the taxpayer in exchange for her services as babysitter for the taxpayer's own three children).

5.5(E)   UNMARRIED COUPLES AND THE LAW

The same deduction reduces the tax of a taxpayer in the 20% income tax bracket by only $200. Other deductions and credits, a dollar-for-dollar reduction of tax, are available to a taxpayer because of expenditures for his dependents.

A taxpayer's rate of tax may be reduced if he has certain specified dependents.[68] However, a "member of a household" dependent does not permit use of the lower tax rate schedules available to abandoned spouses,[69] surviving spouses,[70] and heads of households.[71] Similarly, the dependent who may qualify a taxpayer for the earned income credit cannot be a "member of the household" dependent.[72]

The credit for household and dependent care services expenses, however, is available for any dependent, including a "member of the household" dependent, but only if the dependent is under age fifteen or physically or mentally incapable of caring for himself.[73]

A taxpayer may deduct medical expenses he pays for a dependent, including a "member of the household" dependent.[74] Under the Tax Court's Turnipseed series of cases, a taxpayer cannot de-

---

[68] I.R.C. §§ 2(a),(b), 143. See Table VIII at the end of this chapter.
[69] I.R.C. § 143(b). See Table VIII and subsection (B) of this section.
[70] I.R.C. § 2(a). See subsection (C) of this section.
[71] I.R.C. § 2(b). See subsection (D) of this section.
[72] I.R.C. § 43(c)(1). The following relationships permit a taxpayer to claim earned income credit:

Taxpayer's status	Dependent	Nondependent	Other requirements
Married, filing joint	Child	—	Child must live with taxpayer, and in U.S.
Surviving spouse	Child	—	Child must live with taxpayer, and in U.S.
Head of household	Any dependent other than member of household dependent	Unmarried child or descendant of child	Dependent or nondependent must live with taxpayer, and in U.S.
Married, filing separate	No earned income credit available		
Unmarried, other than surviving spouse and head of household	No earned income credit available		

[73] I.R.C. § 44A(c)(1).
[74] I.R.C. § 213(a). A taxpayer can also deduct medical expenses he pays for his spouse, including his "abandoned spouse." I.R.C. § 213(e)(4) refers to I.R.C.

duct medical expenses he pays for his cohabitant. The taxpayer can, however, deduct medical expenses he pays for his cohabitant's children or mother, if they are members of the taxpayer's household and otherwise qualify as his dependents.

Some employment fringe benefits, such as medical care premium costs or payments,[75] group legal services costs or benefits,[76] and certain meals and lodgings provided by an employer for a taxpayer's dependents[77] are not taxable to the taxpayer or his dependents. Here "dependents" include, for tax purposes, unrelated but member-of-the-household dependents.[78] It is likely, however, that employers' fringe benefit plans do not include a taxpayer's unrelated dependents as permissible beneficiaries of these plans.

5.6. Gift and estate taxes and the marriage bonus

The Internal Revenue Code subjects transfers by gift to the possibility of a gift tax.[79] A taxable gift can be made in cash or in property,[80] but not by the lending, for free, of cash or property[81] or by the rendering of services.[82]

---

§ 6013(d) for the definition of marital status. I.R.C. § 6013(d) copies the I.R.C. § 143(a) definition but not the unmarried "abandoned spouse" definition of I.R.C. § 143(b).

[75] I.R.C. § 105. Treas. Reg. § 1.106–1 refers to employee's spouse or dependents, although I.R.C. § 106 refers only to employee.

[76] I.R.C. § 120.

[77] I.R.C. § 119.

[78] I.R.C. § 120(e)(5) and Treas. Reg. § 1.106–1 refer to I.R.C. § 152 for definition of dependent. I.R.C. §§ 105 and 119 contain no definition of dependent. Compare Treas. Reg. § 1.61–2(d)(2)(ii)(b) which excludes from gross income the cost of group term life insurance on the life of an employee's spouse or children paid by the employer which is "merely incidental," that is, not in excess of $2,000.

[79] I.R.C. §§ 2501–2524.

[80] I.R.C. § 2501(a)(1) states that a tax is imposed "on the transfer of property by gift." See Treas. Reg. § 25.2511–1(a) for an example of "transfer[s] by way of gift ... whether the gift is direct or indirect, and whether the property is real or personal tangible or intangible." See Crown v. Commissioner, 585 F.2d 234 (C.A.–7 Ill., 1978).

[81] Interest-free loans: Crown v. Commissioner, 585 F.2d 234 (C.A.–7 Ill., 1978), Nonacq., 1978–20 I.R.B., at 6; Johnson v. United States, 254 F. Supp. 73 (N.D. Tex., 1966). Contra, Rev. Rul. 73–61, 1973–1 C.B. 408.

While rent-free use of apartment has been held a gift under I.R.C. § 102(a) and therefore excludable from a taxpayers' gross income (Emil Mesinger, 31 T.C.M. (CCH) 1127 (1972)), there is no indication that, in that case or others, the IRS has

The closest the Code gets to defining gift is a statement that, where property is transferred for less than an adequate and full consideration in money or money's worth, the amount by which the value of the property exceeds the value of the consideration shall be deemed a gift.[83]

Gift tax marital deduction and donee spouse vs. donee cohabitant

The tax regulations state that donative intent on the part of the transferor is not an essential element in the application of the gift tax for the transfer.[84] Transfers reached by the gift tax, say the regulations, are not confined only to those which, being without a valuable consideration, are in accord with the common-law concept of gifts, but embrace as well sales, exchanges, and other dispositions of property for a consideration to the extent that the value of the property transferred by the donor exceeds the value in money or money's worth of the consideration given therefor. However, a sale, exchange, or other transfer of property made in the ordinary course of business (a transaction which is bona fide, at arm's length, and free from any donative intent), will be considered as made for an adequate and full consideration in money or money's worth. A consideration not reducible to a value in money or money's worth, as love and affection, promise of marriage, etc., is to be wholly disregarded, and the entire value of the property transferred constitutes the amount of the gift.[85]

A transfer in satisfaction of a legal obligation of support is deemed a transfer for consideration and not a gift.[86] However,

---

sought to tax as a gift the economic value of the free use of property other than interest-free loans. See Crown v. Commissioner, 585 F.2d 234, text at n. 18 (C.A.-7 Ill., 1978).

[82]Cf. Commissioner v. Hogle, 165 F.2d 352 (C.A.-10 Utah, 1947); Rev. Rul. 66–167, 1966–1 C.B. 20; Rev. Rul. 64–225, 1964–2 C.B. 15, amending Rev. Rul. 56–472, 1956–2 C.B. 21. See Crown v. Commissioner, 585 F.2d 234, n. 6 ("[T]he IRS has apparently made an administrative determination that a donor's free offering of his personal services is not subject to the gift tax.").

[83]I.R.C. § 2512(b).

[84]Treas. Reg. § 25.2511–1(g)(1).

[85]Treas. Reg. § 25.2512–8.

[86]Rev. Rul. 68–379, 1968–2 C.B. 414. Cf. I.R.C. § 2516(2); Rev. Rul. 71–67, 1971–1 C.B. 271.

possibly by way of a striving toward uniform application of the federal tax law, the IRS has insisted, and the courts and Congress have decreed or implied, that the only persons a taxpayer is deemed obligated to support, so that payments or transfers made for their support do not constitute gifts, are his spouse and ex-spouse, and his children under the age of twenty-one.[87] Transfers or payments even to these persons may incur a gift tax to the extent that such transfers or payments exceed support needs.

Gifts to any one donee of no more than $3,000 a year are not transfers subject to the gift tax.[88] Gifts which exceed the $3,000 per donee per year exclusion are transfers subject to the gift tax; however, not until such transfers, aggregated for all donees and all years, exceed $175,625 will the donor be required to pay the tax. A donor is entitled to a credit of $47,000 against his gift tax, effectively wiping out his gift tax liability until the tax on the aggregated gifts exceeds the amount of the credit. The gift tax on $175,625 is $47,000, equal to the amount of the credit against the tax.[89]

Once the taxable gifts, in the aggregate over the years, exceed $175,625, the gift tax rate bracket commences at 32%.[90]

The sheltering of a taxable gift by the tax credit may be only a deferment of the tax, since these taxable gifts must be added to a taxpayer's estate for the purpose of computing his estate tax.[91]

If a taxpayer's taxable estate plus any taxable gifts made by him after 1976, including those taxable gifts on which no gift tax

---

[87]Id. For cases and rulings holding that support payments, even though made pursuant to court decree, are transfers subject to the gift tax, see Commissioner v. Greene, 119 F.2d 383 (C.A.-9 Cal., 1941), cert. den. 314 U.S. 641, 86 L. Ed. 514, 62 Sup. Ct. 80 (1941) (payments directed by a California court to be made from the income of the $2,000,000 estate of an incompetent for support of her two adult daughters, neither of whom were able to engage in any gainful occupation, were held to be subject to the gift tax); Stokowski v. Pedrick, 52-2 U.S.T.C. ¶ 10,861 (S.D. N.Y., 1952) (payments pursuant to a court order from an infant's substantial estate for the support of the infant's mother, with whom the infant neither lived nor visited, were held to be subject to the gift tax); Rev. Rul. 73-612; 1973-2 C.B. 322; Rev. Rul. 67-280, 1967-2 C.B. 349. See Rev. Rul. 54-343, 1954-2 C.B. 318 (medical and hospital bills paid by a father for his adult son and living expenses paid for his son's family constitute transfers subject to gift tax).

[88]I.R.C. § 2503(b).

[89]I.R.C. §§ 2502, 2505, referring to I.R.C. § 2001(c) rate schedule. In place of the $60,000 estate tax exemption deduction (repealed I.R.C. § 2052) and in place of the $30,000 lifetime gift tax exemption deduction (repealed I.R.C. § 2521) the Tax

had to be paid because the tax did not exceed the credit, exceeds $175,625, his estate will have to pay an estate tax. The same credit of $47,000 is available to wipe out the estate tax on the first $175,625 of the combined taxable estate and taxable gifts.[92] The estate tax, like the gift tax, starts at 32% on the first bracket of the sum of the taxable estate and taxable gifts in excess of $175,625.[93]

It is the taxable gift and the taxable estate, i.e., the gift or estate minus allowable deductions, which is subject to tax.

Here is where being married pays off.

A donor spouse or the estate of a deceased spouse can reduce the gift or the estate by the *marital deduction*. The marital deduction, for lifetime gifts, is the larger of $100,000 or 50% of the aggregate of all gifts (after the $3,000 per donee per year exclusion) to the donee spouse.[94]

Thus if a wife, in addition to making gifts of $3,000 a year to her husband, also gives him a cumulative total of $300,000, her aggregate taxable gift to him will be only $150,000, the gift tax on which will be wiped out by her $47,000 credit. If a donor gives this same amount to someone to whom she is not married, there

---

Reform Act of 1976 enacted one unified credit in various phased-in amounts (I.R.C. §§ 2010, 2505):

	Unified Credit	Exemption Equivalency
In case of gifts made 1/1/77–6/30/77	$ 6,000	$ 33,333
In case of decedents dying 1/1/77–6/30/77	30,000	120,667
In case of gifts made and		
In case of decedents dying		
7/1/77–12/31/77	30,000	120,667
in 1978	34,000	134,000
in 1979	38,000	147,333
in 1980	42,500	161,563
after 1980	47,000	175,625

[90] I.R.C. § 2502, referring to I.R.C. § 2001(c) rate schedule.
[91] I.R.C. § 2001(b).
[92] See note 89, supra.
[93] I.R.C. §2001(c).
[94] I.R.C. § 2523.

is no deduction; the taxable gift is $300,000 and a gift tax of $87,800 minus the $47,000 credit, or $40,800, is due.

Estate tax marital deduction and surviving spouse vs. surviving cohabitant

Because of the estate tax marital deduction, which is the larger of $250,000 or 50% of the adjusted gross estate,[95] an estate can be as large as $425,625, after deductions for debts, funeral and administration expenses, and no federal estate tax will be due if the decedent leaves a surviving spouse who gets at least $250,000.

If it is a surviving unmarried *cohabitant* rather than a surviving spouse who inherits, there is no marital deduction to reduce the estate and there will be an estate tax of $83,512 after the $47,000 credit.

The status of the spouse for purpose of the estate tax marital deduction is determined as of the date of the decedent's death. Hence, marriage by cohabitants in contemplation of death of one of them makes sense if there might otherwise be an estate tax. And even if there is likely to be no estate in excess of $175,625, and therefore no estate tax to save, marriage in contemplation of death can enable the surviving partner in the subsequent two years to qualify as a surviving spouse, if the other qualifying conditions can be met, and therefore to be taxed at the lowest income tax rate.[96]

Other transfer tax costs of cohabiting

In addition to the gift and estate tax marital deductions, a donee spouse and surviving spouse are treated more kindly in other ways by the gift and estate tax law than the donee and surviving cohabitant.

If a spouse receives cash or property from a donor spouse in what would otherwise be a gift transfer, but the transfer is made pursuant to a written agreement followed, within two years, by divorce, the transfer is not deemed a gift.[97] There is therefore no

---

[95] I.R.C. § 2056.
[96] I.R.C. §§ 1(a), 2(a). See subsection (C) of this section.
[97] I.R.C. § 2516.

gift tax or deferred gift tax, by way of an estate tax on the estate plus the gift, to worry about. There is no way an unmarried pair of donor and donee can benefit from this exception to the gift tax law except by getting married in order to get divorced.

The creation of a joint interest without consideration is an immediate transfer by gift of one half of the value of the property.[98] However, if a spouse creates a joint interest in his or her spouse in real property, whether it is their home or the Empire State Building, there is deemed to be no gift unless the couple files a gift tax return electing to treat the transfer of the half interest as a gift.[99] If the couple have not made this election, however, when they sell the real property and divide the proceeds there will then be a gift with respect to half the proceeds,[1] unless a divorce follows.[2] This deferred gift rule with respect to a donee's interest in jointly held property does not apply if the donor and donee are not married to each other.

If an unmarried couple own property jointly, when one of them dies the entire value of the jointly held property will be included in the deceased's estate except for that portion which the surviving joint owner is able to prove stemmed from his or her contribution in money or money's worth. That the creation of the joint interest was a transfer by gift by the deceased, even at the cost of a gift tax, will not keep the jointly held property from being included, at 100% of its value, in the deceased's estate.[3]

The reverse is true for married couples. If the creation of the joint interest was a transfer by gift, only one half of the value of the jointly held property will be included in the deceased's estate for estate tax purposes.[4]

With the gift and estate tax marital deduction, the no-gift-if-divorce rule and the estate-taxation-of-only-half-of-spouse's-joint-property rule, if a taxpayer is wealthy and thinking of

---

[98] Treas. Reg. § 25.2511–1(h)(5).
[99] I.R.C. § 2515.
[1] I.R.C. § 2515(b).
[2] I.R.C. § 2516.
[3] I.R.C. § 2040(a).
[4] I.R.C. §2040(b), applicable to joint interests created after December 31, 1976. Pub. L. No. 94–455, § 2002(d)(3). See also I.R.C. § 2040(c), enacted by the Revenue Act of 1978.

being generous, or of dying and not taking it all with him, he is better off married than single.

5.7. "Income splitting" by cohabitants

Cohabitants may be "playmates, grandmothers, or other sinners."[4a] They may be a couple who live together as if married, except for the fact that they don't want to be married or for the fact that, because they are of the same sex, the law says they cannot marry. They may be brother and sister, parent and grown child, or unrelated senior citizens who, unmarried or formerly married to others, now make their home together.

The important thing these cohabitants or marvinizers have in common is that they are more than roommates. They have a common household and a life in common on a long-term or indefinite duration basis. They usually do not segregate assets and expenses the way roommates do, with the yogurt on the top shelf of the refrigerator "mine" and the pie on the bottom shelf "yours." These cohabitants, unmarried though they may be, live the way married couples live. Although one may have more income and more assets than the other, the good fortune of the one benefits the other. They have, formally or informally, expressly, impliedly or merely as a way of life, entered into an "LTA," or "living together arrangement."[5]

However much like a marriage their LTA may be, unless they are married via the required ceremony or hold themselves out as married in a state which recognizes their relationship as a common-law marriage, they cannot file a joint income tax return.[6] If the taxable income of one is more than 20% of the taxable income of both, the fact that they must file separate returns may be advantageous.[7]

[4a]Cantwell, "Estate Planning for Playmates, Grandmothers and Other Sinners," New York State Bar Association Trusts & Estates Section Program (1978).

[5]See Gutierrez, "Estate Planning for the Unmarried Cohabitant," *13th Miami Institute on Estate Planning,* ¶ 1502.2 (1979).

[6]For a couple whose joint returns should be protected by the court's alternative finding of common-law marriage, see McCullon v. McCullon, 410 N.Y.S.2d 226 (1978).

[7]See section 5.4, herein, and Tables IV–VII at the end of this chapter.

By agreement

Because of the progressive rate structure of the tax law, the splitting of income or the allocating of deductions so that each of two taxpayers would be taxed on 50% of their combined taxable income, rather than one taxed on 30% and the other 70%, may reduce the total tax payable. Splitting of earned income by way of a share-and-share-alike agreement, however, is ineffective for income tax purposes. The Supreme Court held in 1930, in Lucas v. Earl,[8] that earned income is taxable to the one who earns it, despite a long-standing share-and-share-alike agreement of a taxpayer and his (married) cohabitant. In Poe v. Seaborn,[9] the Supreme Court carved out an exception to the Lucas rule for married couples whose earned income is split between them by operation of community property law. The Marvin case, which gave one cohabitant the right to assert a claim to half of the other's earnings during their cohabitation did not do so because of the community property law of California, but because of an alleged share-and-share-alike agreement.[10] Therefore, even if one cohabitant obtains a judgment for some portion of the other's income under such an agreement, that income will still be taxable to the cohabitant who earned it.

If cohabitants join as partners in a business or income-producing venture, partnership law splits the income from their venture between them. The split is automatically 50–50, unless they agree to some other division, and without regard to how much, by way of cash or property, one has contributed more than the other.[11]

This splitting of income from the cohabitants' business venture is recognized for income tax purposes[12] unless a disproportionate rendition of services to the business permits the IRS to ignore the

---

[8]Lucas v. Earl, 281 U.S. 111, 74 L. Ed. 731, 50 Sup. Ct. 241 (1930).

[9]Poe v. Seaborn, 282 U.S. 101, 75 L. Ed. 239, 51 Sup. Ct. 58 (1930). For Internal Revenue Code provisions which apply Lucas v. Earl, note 8, supra, to attribute income to the person who earns it, rather than split such income because of community property law, see I.R.C. § 879(a)(1); § 911(c)(3); § 1303(c)(2); § 1304(c)(3); § 1402(a)(5)(A).

[10]Marvin v. Marvin, 18 Cal. 3d 660, 134 Cal. Rptr. 815, 557 P.2d 106 (1976). See also section 4.10, herein.

[11]Uniform Partnership Act, § 18.

[12]See Claire A. Ryza, 36 T.C.M. (CCH) 269 (1977).

50–50 split.[13] In that case, the IRS can require an apportioning of the partnership income on some basis that gives adequate recognition to the greater productivity of one of the partners.

By transfer of assets

A taxpayer may have assets which themselves produce income: stock certificates; savings accounts; rental property; or an interest in a business. While earned income cannot be split for income tax purposes except by married couples living in community property states, the "unearned" income from assets can be moved around.

If a cohabitant has $100,000 of earned income and another $60,000 from income-producing assets, he cannot file a joint return, and he cannot, by agreement, attribute half of his income to his co-cohabitant so that it will be taxed to her. He can, however, by transferring the assets themselves, cause the income from them to be taxed to a cohabitant in a lower tax bracket.

The transfer can be a transfer of a life estate or term interest. The simplest way to effect the transfer is by the creation of a trust. The Supreme Court has said that income from property is taxed to the one who owns the property.[14] A cohabiting taxpayer who transfers property into a trust for his cohabitant is not deemed the owner of the property, the income from which is being paid or accumulated for the cohabitant, if the taxpayer gives a term interest of more than ten years and does not retain other powers over the trust.[15]

If the income from the trust is distributed, or held for distribution, to the taxpayer's cohabitant, it will be taxed to the cohabitant. At the end of the trust's term, ten years plus, or at the termination of the life estate if the transfer is for the life of the cohabitant, the trust fund can, under the terms of the trust agreement, revert to the taxpayer.[16]

This kind of income splitting cannot be accomplished by a spouse since income distributed or held for distribution to a donee

---

[13] See I.R.C. § 704(e).
[14] Helvering v. Horst, 311 U.S. 112, 85 L. Ed. 75, 61 Sup. Ct. 144 (1940).
[15] I.R.C. § 673.
[16] Id.

spouse from a trust created by the donor spouse will be taxed to the donor spouse.[17]

The donor cohabitant considering a trust must be reminded that should the relationship with his cohabitant end, the income from the trust the donor has created must still continue to be paid to his ex-cohabitant for the term of the trust. If the donor cohabitant gives himself or anyone else, other than the donee cohabitant, the power to revoke the trust, so that the trust fund will revert to the donor earlier than ten years and a day, the donor will be taxed on all of the income.[18] If the donor gives himself or anyone else, other than the donee, the power to direct that the income be paid to someone else, during the term of the trust, the donor will be taxed on all of the income.[19]

Gift tax consequence

A taxpayer may have succeeded in diverting, for income tax purposes, income from assets of his to his cohabitant, but he must file a gift tax return and he may have to pay a gift tax. The gift tax value of the right to income from a ten-year trust is 44.16% of the value of the assets that have funded the trust.[20] If a taxpayer funds a ten-year-and-a-day trust with $100,000, he has made a taxable gift, after the $3,000 exclusion, of $42,835 (44.16% of $97,000). This taxable gift will not incur a gift tax if the taxpayer has not used up his gift tax credit.[21] But the trust fund itself, plus the taxable gift of the life estate, will be part of the base for computing his estate tax.[22]

For this reason, and because the trust must last at least ten years, even if the cohabiting relationship does not, the taxpayer may prefer to invest the $100,000 in tax-exempt bonds rather than divert the income from that fund, for tax purposes, to his cohabitant.

The Marvin case says that if one of a pair of cohabitants, married or unmarried, can prove the existence and terms of a share-

---

[17] I.R.C. § 677(a).
[18] I.R.C. § 676(a).
[19] I.R.C. § 674.
[20] Treas. Reg. § 25.2512–9(f), Table B.
[21] See note 89, supra.
[22] I.R.C. § 2001(b).

and-share-alike agreement, it will be enforced. Thus, such an agreement may be effective in its economic consequences of dividing earned income so that, although X earns 80% of the total income and Y earns 20%, nonetheless X owns 50% and Y 50%. However, 80% of this earned income will continue to be taxed to X.[23]

In addition, says the IRS, for gift tax purposes one must look, year by year, to see which of the two taxpayers has come out the winner and which the loser under such an agreement.[24] If the loser ends up handing over more than $3,000 to the winner, the loser must file a gift tax return and, once he's used up his credit against the gift tax, start paying a gift tax. Thus, if X earns $48,000 and Y $12,000 of their combined $60,000 income, but because of the agreement, X actually ends up with $30,000 and Y with $30,000, Y is $18,000 ahead and X must file a gift tax return showing $15,000, or $18,000 minus the $3,000 exclusion, as a taxable gift he has made to Y.

If, in a subsequent year, the tables are turned and it is Y who earns more than X, it is Y who may now have to file a gift tax return.

The IRS issued this gift tax ruling with respect to a married couple's share-and-share-alike agreement. If the agreement, however, were made "in the ordinary course of business (a transaction which is bona fide, at arm's length and free from any donative intent)," the IRS would not attempt to determine whether one party to the agreement was giving in value more than what he was receiving. The IRS would assume that market place bargaining would produce equivalency of consideration.[25]

Because the share-and-share-alike married couple are assumed not to be arm's length bargainers, the IRS insists on examining the value of the *quid pro quo* and then, finding each promise not susceptible of valuation, postpones the determination of whether a gift has been made and who has made it. Perhaps the determination should be made not on an annual basis but only on the termination of the agreement.[26] Perhaps also unmarried cohabi-

---

[23]Lucas v. Earl, 281 U.S. 111, 74 L. Ed. 731, 50 Sup. Ct. 241 (1930).
[24]Rev. Rul. 77–359, 1977–2 C.B. 24.
[25]Treas. Reg. § 25.2512–8.
[26]See Macris, Open Valuation and the Completed Transfer: A Problem Area in Federal Gift Taxation, 34 Tax L. Rev. 273 (1979).

tants are closer to arm's length bargainers and the value of their mutual promises should be assumed to be equal.[27]

5.8. Agreements by cohabitants to share expenses

The share-and-share-alike agreement or the living together arrangement may not apply to what's left over after the couple's living expenses. Instead the agreement may concern itself only with allocation of shared personal expenses and of each cohabitant's services within the household.

If each cohabitant pays half of the costs of the household, neither realizes any income from such payments nor has made any gifts. There should also be no tax consequences even if the expenses are allocated on some basis other than equally. The IRS car-pool ruling describes the automobile owner who does all the driving and receives from his fellow employees and car-pool members unspecified payments toward the transportation costs. These payments, a sharing of personal expenses, are not taxable to the owner-driver unless he has "established a trade or business of transporting workers for hire from which a profit is derived."[28]

By the express or implied terms of their living together arrangement one cohabitant may bear all the out-of-pocket costs, taking on the traditional role of the provider. The other, playing the traditional role of the "house spouse," may provide the household services. Is the cohabitant who assumes the role of "house spouse" working for pay so that the fair market value of the benefits he or she receives is subject to income tax? The answer is no.

The Tax Court cohabitant cases in this area are those where a taxpayer claimed his cohabitant as his dependent and, in some cases, filed joint returns and, in other cases, filed as head of

---

[27]See Zelta J. Bombarger, 31 T.C. 473 (1958) (in denying the dependency exemption to the taxpayer, who paid the household expenses for a widowed friend who performed the household chores, the Tax Court stated: "These parties are mutually dependent upon one another. Each contributes something the other needs and each receives a benefit from a mutually satisfactory arrangement. It is not necessary to attempt to weigh the comparative worth of the contributions and say which is greater.").

[28]Rev. Rul. 55–555, 1955–2 C.B. 20.

household. A few Tax Court decisions found that the cohabitant claimed as dependent did not receive her living expenditures as support from the taxpayer but instead as "remuneration for the services she rendered to him as a member of his household." These cases did not suggest that the remuneration was taxable income.[29]

To the extent that the "remuneration" consisted of meals and lodging furnished in kind by a taxpayer on the premises where the services were rendered, the Code treats such remuneration as nontaxable.[30]

The issue of whether remuneration constitutes income arises primarily in Tax Court cases dealing with "living out" rather than "living in" arrangements. Without explicitly saying so, the Tax Court nonetheless clearly holds that where the "living out" mistress is or had been a "professional," the payments (but not clothing or jewelry) she receives from her steady admirer constitute income to her.[31] Where there appeared to be no hint of professionalism in the payee's present life or past, and the relationship between the payee and payor was characterized by the Court as a "very personal relationship," the payments were held not to be taxable because of the Code provision which excludes gifts from gross income.[32]

The one "living together" case which dealt with the question of taxation of the recipient involved the transfer of substantial funds in excess of living expenses.[33] Anthony and Lillian had a "close personal relationship" for twenty-five years. He transferred amounts to her which averaged over $40,000 a year for the five years in question. He also paid for substantial capital improvements on the home she owned and in which he lived until disaster hit: his corporation filed for bankruptcy; he himself was adjudged a bankrupt; he was convicted of interstate transportation of forged documents and was sentenced to a twenty-year jail term. Anthony's payments to Lillian were held to be gifts for

---

[29]See cases cited in note 66, supra.
[30]I.R.C. § 119. See also section 5.2, note 34, herein.
[31]Lyna Kathryn Jones, 36 T.C.M. (CCH) 1323 (1977); Everett W. Brizendine, 16 T.C.M. (CCH) 149 (1957); Thelma Blevins, 14 T.C.M. (CCH) 840 (1955).
[32]Louis B. Libby, 28 T.C.M. (CCH) 915 (1969); Greta Starks, 25 T.C.M. (CCH) 676 (1966).
[33]Lillian Pascarelli, 55 T.C. 1082 (1971).

income tax purposes and therefore not income to Lillian. These payments were also held to be gifts for gift tax purposes and Lillian, as transferee, was held liable for the gift taxes which Anthony should have, but did not, pay.

Even though one cohabitant pays all the household and living expenses, he may not be able to deduct certain ordinarily deductible expenditures because they are not "his" expenses. If the other cohabitant owns the home in which they live, the real estate taxes and the mortgage payments are her obligation and therefore her expenses. These taxes and the interest on the mortgage are deductible for income tax purposes but only by the owner of the property.[34]

If the property is owned by the cohabitants as joint owners with right of survivorship, the obligation to pay the taxes and the mortgage is a joint and several obligation. If one cohabitant pays all of these expenses, he can deduct them in toto. His right to deduct 100% should not be affected by the fact that, as a matter of property law, he may have a right, which he does not assert, to be reimbursed for 50% of his payments.[35]

If one cohabitant pays the other's medical expenses, these expenses are deductible only if the cohabitant who has incurred them is the dependent of the one who pays them.[36]

5.9. Cohabitants claiming two households in one

In order for an unmarried taxpayer to qualify for the more favorable tax rates applicable to surviving spouses or heads of households, he or she must meet certain requirements, including the requirement of furnishing over half the cost of maintaining his household for the full year.

Suppose a recent widower, his child, and a woman—divorced, long widowed, or otherwise unmarried—and her child (dependent or not), share joint living quarters. Each, on his or her own,

---

[34]See, e.g., Cooper v. Commissioner, 264 F.2d 889 (C.A.-4 D.C., 1959); Acker v. Commissioner, 258 F.2d 568 (C.A.-6 Ohio, 1958); Kathleen Marie Emmons, 20 T.C.M. (CCH) 1513 (1961).

[35]Commissioner v. Whitcomb, 103 F.2d 1009 (C.A.-6 Mich., 1939); Thomas D. Conroy, 17 T.C.M. (CCH) 21 (1958); F. C. Nicodemus, Jr., 26 B.T.A. 125 (1932); William R. Tracy, 25 B.T.A. 1055 (1932).

[36]I.R.C. § 213.

would have qualified, respectively, as surviving spouse and head of household. Can each claim his or her separate households under the one roof?

The answer is yes, if they are as careful as Mrs. Fleming and her daughters were.[37] Mrs. Fleming, a widow, had lived with her unmarried adult daughter, Jean. They gave up this home and moved in with Mrs. Fleming's married daughter, Louise, and her family. When Mrs. Fleming attempted to retain her prior head of household status, the IRS insisted that the one roof meant one household and that Mrs. Fleming did not pay over half of the costs of that household. The Tax Court, however, said that "the extent of a 'household' is not determined solely by physical or tangible boundaries."

The court's finding of separate households under the same roof resulted from the taxpayer's careful planning and record keeping. Mrs. Fleming and Jean had four rooms of their own (an office, bedroom, bathroom and sitting room) on one floor and Louise's family had its "private quarters" on another floor. Each had access to the others' floors and all shared the rest of the house in common. The court was impressed that Mrs. Fleming and Jean paid for the furnishings of their own quarters, maintained a separate telephone for which they paid the bills, subscribed to their own magazines, gave Christmas presents, Christmas cards, wedding gifts and charitable contributions by themselves and not with Louise and her family. Mrs. Fleming and Jean contributed 50% of the deposits in a joint account established by all the occupants for household expenses and, as to that half, Mrs. Fleming carefully contributed 51% and Jean 49%.

5.10. A side-look at social security

The social security and medicare (FICA) tax of 6.13% for employed persons and 8.10% for self-employed persons is imposed on each worker's first $22,900 of annual earned income.[38] This is a regressive tax, since it is a flat rate and starts on the first penny of earned income without regard to exemptions or deductions. The

---

[37]Estate of Jean Foster Fleming, 33 T.C.M. (CCH) 619 (1974).
[38]I.R.C. § 3101(a), (b).

FICA tax of $613 a $10,000 wage earner pays is at the full rate of 6.13%, while the tax of $1,368 (6.13% of $22,900) a $100,000 salaried employee pays is an effective tax rate to him of 1.368%.

This tax penalizes the second earner of a married couple since the social security protection she or he earns as a worker may duplicate, rather than add to, the protection she or he already has as a spouse. Moreover, benefits are often higher for the couple where one spouse earns all or most of the income than for the couple where both spouses have earnings, even though both couples have the same total family income. Nonetheless, social security favors married workers over single workers. Both compute their tax in the same way, but the married worker's social security tax "buys" benefits not only for himself but also for his lower-earner spouse.[39] For the purpose of the social security benefits "bought" by the earnings of one cohabitant, therefore, the cohabitants should consider marriage in contemplation of retirement or death of the covered cohabitant.

The social security law, however, encourages cohabitation in a few situations. For example, children of a deceased worker who receive benefits because they are under eighteen, or under 22 and going to school full time, lose these benefits if they marry.[40] And remarriage of a divorced wife who would otherwise be entitled to benefits on her ex-husband's account, when he becomes eligible for benefits, terminates her rights to benefits[41] unless her new husband is receiving benefits as a widower or parent of a covered worker.[42] Remarriage of a widow or surviving divorced wife, the analogue of the widow entitled to widow's benefits, does not terminate her benefits based on her husband's or deceased ex-husband's earnings record, but if she remarries before age sixty, her benefits may be reduced.[43] A widower must never have remarried if he is to obtain benefits on his deceased wife's earnings record, even if he is unmarried at the time he applies for these benefits.[44]

---

[39] *Social Security and the Changing Roles of Men and Women*, U.S. Dept. of Health, Education, and Welfare, p. 11 (1979).
[40] 42 U.S.C. § 403(d)(1)(D).
[41] 42 U.S.C. § 402(b)(1)(C), (H).
[42] 42 U.S.C. § 402(b)(3).
[43] 42 U.S.C. § 402(e)(3), (4).
[44] 42 U.S.C. § 402(f)(1)(A).

5.11. Most favored status—Married and divorced in contemplation of cohabitation

Married couples have obtained year-end divorces in order to be taxed as unmarried taxpayers. If they remarry, the IRS says that it will refuse to recognize the divorce.[45] If they divorce and cohabit instead, the IRS says it will recognize the divorce and the unmarried status of each of the former spouses.[46]

Unmarried cohabitants who want share-and-share-alike living arrangements may find these arrangements ineffective in splitting income for income tax purposes.[47] In addition, these arrangements may incur a gift tax and an increased estate tax, unalleviated by the marital deduction.[48] But the Code provides an effective substitute, with the application of a little foresight. Get married, and then get divorced.

The solution for the couple whom the income tax laws would render asunder is to "enter into a written agreement relative to their marital and property rights."[49] If the agreement provides for the division of their assets and divorce follows within two years there will be no gift tax due on any transfer from the have to the have-not ex-spouse.[50] If the transfer is made not to satisfy the obligation of support but by way of the split-up of jointly held or community property,[51] or in a state whose equitable division of property on dissolution of marriage is recognized as a "new spe-

---

[45]Rev. Rul. 76–255, 1976–2 C.B. 40.
[46]Letter Ruling 7835076 (6/1/78).
[47]See section 5.7, herein.
[48]See section 5.6, herein.
[49]I.R.C. § 2516.
[50]Id. There may, however, be an estate tax if a quirk caused by absence of an estate tax provision parallel to gift tax provision I.R.C. § 2516 is not cured by amendment of the estate tax law. Before 1977, gratuitous transfers made within three years of the donor's death were includable in his gross estate if made in contemplation of death. The Tax Reform Act of 1976 amended I.R.C. § 2035 to eliminate the contemplation of death test. Therefore, with the automatic inclusion in a decedent's estate of transfers made without adequate and full consideration in money or money's worth and the fact that transfers made in exchange for relinquishment of marital rights "shall not be considered to any extent a consideration 'in money or money's worth'" (I.R.C. § 2043(b)), if the transferor ex-spouse dies within three years of the date of a transfer which is not a gift for gift tax purposes because of I.R.C. § 2516, his transfer is nonetheless a gratuitous transfer for estate tax purposes and includable in his gross estate because of I.R.C. § 2035.
[51]See section 5.2, note 24, herein.

cies of common ownership,"[52] the transferor may transfer appreciated property without being taxed on the gain. Otherwise the transfer should be of cash and property with value no greater than basis.

By way of future income, gift and estate tax planning, the couple can agree that each has a continuing obligation to support the other, and that, therefore, the ex-spouse whose income for any taxable year exceeds 50% of the aggregate income of both in that year should pay that excess to the other ex-spouse.[53] This income splitting by agreement, because of the alimony provisions of the Code, and because of the progressive income tax rates, reduces the overall tax on both incomes, unless the fact that the 50% max-tax ceiling rate on personal service income does not apply to alimony intervenes. No gift or estate tax marital deduction is available but no such deduction is needed. These payments are not gifts and, because of them, the equal division of the ex-spouses' estates is continued.

If there is one child, careful structuring of the support obligation under the separation agreement can give the dependent's personal exemption deduction to one of the ex-spouses and the advantage of the head of household tax rate to the other, as long as that other furnishes over half of the cost of his and the child's common household.[54] If the child is under the age of fifteen and there are child-care expenses which will provide a tax credit, the couple can agree that the parent who is entitled to claim the child as a dependent should have the custody of the child.[55] The fact that one parent may then have all of the tax advantages of the child-care expense credit, the personal exemption deduction for the child, the head of household rate and the deduction for the child's medical expenses can be taken into account in splitting the couple's taxable income between them. If there are two or more children, each parent may be entitled to all of these tax advantages. Even if the divorced couple, now unmarried cohabitants, live together under the same roof, it may be possible, with careful

---

[52]See section 5.2, note 27, herein.
[53]Orr v. Orr, —— U.S. ——, —— L. Ed. 2d ——, —— Sup. Ct. —— (1979) holds that alimony laws must be sex-neutral.
[54]I.R.C. § 2(b). See section 5.5(D), herein.
[55]I.R.C. § 44A.

planning and record keeping, to assert that there are two separate households.[56]

One of the cohabiting pair can now itemize deductions without depriving the other of his right to his full $2,300 zero bracket amount. And the payor of alimony or separate maintenance can deduct his payments from his gross income and also be entitled to his full $2,300 zero bracket amount. Therefore it may make sense and save tax dollars if the pair plan for the other to be obligated to pay and therefore to be able to deduct items like real estate taxes and mortgage interest.

5.12. Desideratum—Tax reform

When the Revenue Act of 1913 was enacted, there was only one rate schedule. The individual was the sole taxation unit. It was not until 1948, to staunch the flow of states adopting community property law, that Congress enacted the provision permitting spouses to split their income and reduce their effective tax rate by filing joint returns.

With differentiation among taxpayers came the request for further differentiation. In 1951 the head of household rate was enacted, its benefits admittedly not limited to those in need of kinder tax treatment. In 1954, the surviving spouse categorization was devised, again, as available to the wealthiest of recent widows and widowers as to the poor. In 1969 the new rate table for single taxpayers was enacted to reduce the maximum tax differential between married and single taxpayers to 20%. The companion enactment was the new and highest rate table for married taxpayers filing separately to prevent married taxpayers from being able to choose between aggregating income and filing jointly or dividing income and filing separately. While the discrimination against single taxpayers in favor of one-earner married couples was alleviated but not abolished, the discrimination against two-earner married couples was exacerbated.[57]

With the differentiation among taxpayers by the rate schedule

---

[56]See section 5.9, herein.
[57]For this tax history, see, e.g., Klein, *Policy Analysis of the Federal Income Tax*, pp. 569–605 (1976).

came a proliferation of credits, exclusions and deductions, the allowance or amount of which turn on the taxpayers' marital status and whether they file joint or separate returns. With such decisions playing an increasingly important role in the determination of an individual's income tax liability, the IRS and the Tax Court have breached the privacy of the bedroom.

There are reasons to marry and reasons to cohabit unmarried. Certain consequences ensue from the marriage relationship and others from the unmarried cohabitants' relationship. That taxes should assume such a substantial place among these reasons and consequences appears no less distasteful than the concomitant invasion of privacy of intimates by the taxing authorities.

The answer is surely not to complicate the Code further by additional distinctions and differentiations and new credits or deductions. Marriage and nonmarriage should be tax-neutral events. An Internal Revenue Code designed for such neutrality will be an easier one for every taxpayer and tax collector to live with.

TABLE I
Income Tax Consequences of Marriage and Divorce

Taxable income,* all earned, and all earned by husband	A $300,000 Tax	Effective tax rate	B $30,000 Tax	Effective tax rate
1) Married, filing joint return	$138,678	46.2%	$5,593	18.6%
2) Married, filing separate returns				
a) Community property state	$175,324	58.4%	$5,593	18.6%
b) Noncommunity property state	$192,662	64.2%	$9,349	31.2%
3) Unmarried	$142,142	47.4%	$7,522	25.1%
4) Divorced or legally separated and splitting income, 2/3–1/3 via alimony	$141,515	47.2%	$5,014	16.7%
5) Unmarried and head of household	$141,111	47.0%	$6,943	23.1%
6) Divorced or legally separated and head of household (husband, only) and splitting income, 2/3–1/3 via alimony	$140,484	46.8%	$4,733	15.8%
7) Divorced or legally separated and head of household (ex-wife, only) and splitting income, 2/3–1/3 via alimony	$138,033	46.0%	$4,929	16.4%
8) Divorced and legally separated and heads of household (husband, and ex-wife, both) and splitting income, 2/3–1/3 via alimony	$137,002	45.7%	$4,648	15.5%

*Before deductions for personal exemptions. The 1979 tax rates are used in this table. Head of household computations are made on the basis of only one personal exemption for the taxpayer. The 50% max-tax rate is used where applicable. See section 5.5(D), herein, for a discussion of the head of household classification, and section 5.3, for the 50% max-tax.

TABLE II
Taxable Income Brackets for Individuals:
Some Comparisons of the Four Rate Tables.

Taxable income brackets	(a) Married Individuals Filing Joint Returns & Surviving Spouses	(b) Heads of Households	(c) Unmarried Individuals (other than Surviving Spouses & Heads of Households)	(d) Married Individuals Filing Separate Returns
$ 1,700	0	0	0	14% over $1,700
2,300	0	14% over $2,300	14% over $2,300	
2,750	0			$147+16%
3,400	14% over $3,400		$154+16%	
3,800				$315+18%
4,400		$294+16%	$314+18%	
5,500	$294+16%			
5,950				$702+21%
6,500		$630+18%	$692+19%	
7,600	$630+18%			
8,000				$1,133+24%
8,500			$1,072+21%	
8,700		$1,026+22%		
10,100				$1,637+28%
10,800			$1,555+24%	
11,800		$1,708+24%		
11,900	$1,404+21%			
12,300				$2,253+32%
12,900			$2,059+26%	
14,950				$3,101+37%
15,000		$2,476+26%	$2,605+30%	
16,000	$2,265+24%			
17,600				$4,081+43%
18,200		$3,308+31%	$3,565+34%	
20,200	$3,273+28%			
22,900				$6,360+49%
23,500		$4,951+36%	$5,367+39%	
28,800		$6,859+42%	$7,434+44%	
29,900	$4,505+32%			
30,000				$9,839+54%
34,100		$9,085+46%	$9,766+49%	
35,200	$6,201+37%			
41,500			$13,392+55%*	
42,800				$16,757+59%
44,700		$13,961+54%*		
45,800	$12,720+49%			
54,700				$23,772+64%
55,300			$20,982+63%	
60,000	$19,678+54%*			
60,600		$22,547+59%		
81,200				$40,732+68%
81,800		$35,055+63%	$37,677+68%	
85,600	$33,502+59%			
107,700				$58,752+70%
108,300		$51,750+68%	$58,752+70%	
109,400	$47,544+64%			
161,300		$87,790+70%		
215,400	$117,504+70%			

The tax at each bracket is the dollar amount plus the percentage of taxable income in excess of the taxable income bracket. The 1979 tax rate tables are used.
*The bracket at which the 50% max-tax ceiling rate on personal service income is applicable.

MARITAL STATUS AND TAXES Table III

TABLE III
Max-Tax Table

Taxable income[a] (all "earned")	Marrieds filing joint, & surviving spouses Tax	Effective tax rate	Marginal tax rate[b]	Heads of Household Tax	Effective tax rate	Marginal tax rate[b]	Unmarrieds Tax	Effective tax rate	Marginal tax rate[b]	Marrieds filing separate returns Tax	Effective tax rate	Marginal tax rate[b]
$ 30,001	$ 6,239	20.8%	37%	$ 7,364	24.5%	42%	$ 7,963	26.5%	44%–50%[e]	$ 9,840	32.8%	54%
42,801	11,431	26.7%	43%	13,088	32.6%	46%–50%[d]	14,083	32.9%	50%	16,752	39.1%	59%
54,701	17,082	31.2%	49%–50%[c]	18,962	34.7%	50%	19,993	36.5%	50%	23,773	43.2%	64%
81,201	30,279	37.3%	50%	32,212	39.7%	50%	33,243	40.9%	50%	40,733	50.2%	68%
107,701	43,529	40.4%	50%	45,462	42.2%	50%	46,493	43.2%	50%	58,753	54.6%	70%

(a) The income jumps are taken from the tax rate table for married individuals filing separate returns. IRC § 1(d). The 1979 tables are used.
(b) "Marginal tax rate" means the highest tax rate on all dollars of taxable income up to the next level of taxable income.
(c) The 49% marginal tax rate starts at taxable income of $45,800; the 50% max-tax ceiling rate starts at $60,000.
(d) The 46% marginal tax rate starts at taxable income of $34,100; the 50% max-tax ceiling rate starts at $44,700.
(e) The 44% marginal tax rate starts at taxable income of $28,800; the 50% max-tax ceiling rate starts at $41,500.

263

TABLE IV
Tax Cost of Marriage (Shaded Area) and Nonmarriage

Tax when couple not married to each other or anyone else and each is taxed on rate table applicable to unmarried individuals (other than surviving spouses and heads of households), and share of income earned by lower-earning cohabitant is:

Couple's total taxable income (before personal exemptions)	Tax when couple is married and files joint return	0%	5%	10%	15%	20%	25%	30%	35%	40%	45%	50%
$ 5,000	$ 0	$ 250	$ 209	$ 169	$ 132	$ 97	$ 62	$ 27	$ 0	$ 0	$ 0	$ 0
10,000	702	1,176	1,071	976	881	786	692	601	539	519	501	500
15,000	1,635	2,344	2,149	1,962	1,782	1,602	1,502	1,451	1,414	1,398	1,391	1,384
20,000	2,745	3,836	3,504	3,204	2,904	2,702	2,594	2,506	2,444	2,390	2,363	2,353
25,000	4,057	5,562	5,111	4,686	4,324	4,086	3,896	3,746	3,609	3,521	3,462	3,446
30,000	5,593	7,521	6,926	6,341	5,926	5,618	5,378	5,153	4,948	4,808	4,718	4,689
35,000	7,348	9,721	8,951	8,209	7,704	7,333	6,979	6,648	6,434	6,261	6,121	6,110
40,000	9,366	12,167	11,186	10,304	9,703	9,188	8,698	8,334	8,036	7,801	7,721	7,673
45,000	11,516	14,642	13,516	12,581	11,866	11,183	10,611	10,144	9,759	9,547	9,386	9,373
50,000	13,798	17,142	15,891	14,891	14,083	13,343	12,665	12,066	11,676	11,358	11,223	11,124
55,000	16,248	19,642	18,266	17,223	16,351	15,528	14,802	14,186	13,366	13,358	13,096	13,074
60,000	18,698	22,142	20,641	19,563	18,618	17,744	16,986	16,351	15,853	15,403	15,183	15,043
65,000	21,178	24,642	23,016	21,903	20,891	19,984	19,197	18,558	18,041	17,629	17,303	17,243
70,000	23,678	27,142	25,419	24,243	23,173	22,226	21,447	20,818	20,258	19,879	19,613	19,443
75,000	26,178	29,642	27,829	26,583	25,456	24,486	23,697	23,078	22,566	22,163	21,951	21,884
80,000	28,678	32,142	30,239	28,928	27,744	26,746	25,978	25,338	24,873	24,543	24,348	24,334
85,000	31,178	34,642	32,649	31,273	30,049	29,046	28,278	27,648	27,181	26,923	26,826	26,784
90,000	33,678	37,142	35,061	33,618	32,354	31,346	30,578	29,983	29,573	29,349	29,303	29,284
95,000	36,178	39,642	37,476	35,963	34,666	33,646	32,878	32,318	31,968	31,829	31,784	31,784
100,000	38,678	42,142	39,891	38,318	36,986	35,978	35,204	34,663	34,363	34,309	34,283	34,283

Tax is computed on basis of 1979 rates. The taxable income in column 1 is before deductions for personal exemptions. For computation of tax on joint return (column 2), taxable income is reduced by $2,000 for two personal exemptions. For all other columns, each taxpayer's share of the total taxable income is reduced by $1,000 for one personal exemption. The 50% max-tax on personal service income is used where applicable.

TABLE IV-A
Tax Cost of Marriage (Shaded Area) and Nonmarriage

Dollar amount of marriage penalty tax: comparison of joint return tax and tax when couple not married to each other or anyone else and each is taxed as unmarried individual, and share of income earned by lower-earning cohabitant is:

Couple's total taxable income (before personal exemptions)	0%	5%	10%	15%	20%	25%	30%	35%	40%	45%	50%
$ 5,000	$ −250	$ −209	$ −169	$ −132	$ −97	$ −62	$ −27	$ 0	$ 0	$ 0	$ 0
10,000	−474	−369	−274	−179	−84	+9	+100	+162	+182	+200	+201
15,000	−709	−514	−327	−147	+32	+132	+183	+220	+236	+243	+250
20,000	−1,091	−759	−459	−159	+43	+151	+239	+301	+355	+382	+392
25,000	−1,505	−1,054	−629	−267	−29	+160	+310	+447	+535	+594	+610
30,000	−1,928	−1,333	−748	−333	−25	+215	+440	+645	+785	+875	+904
35,000	−2,373	−1,603	−861	−356	+14	+368	+699	+913	+1,086	+1,226	+1,237
40,000	−2,801	−1,820	−938	−337	+177	+667	+1,031	+1,329	+1,564	+1,644	+1,692
45,000	−3,126	−2,000	−1,065	−350	+332	+904	+1,371	+1,756	+1,968	+2,129	+2,142
50,000	−3,344	−2,093	−1,093	−285	+455	+1,133	+1,732	+2,122	+2,440	+2,575	+2,674
55,000	−3,394	−2,018	−975	−103	+720	+1,446	+2,062	+2,582	+2,890	+3,152	+3,174
60,000	−3,444	−1,943	−865	+80	+954	+1,712	+2,347	+2,845	+3,295	+3,515	+3,655
65,000	−3,464	−1,838	−725	+287	+1,194	+1,981	+2,620	+3,137	+3,549	+3,875	+3,935
70,000	−3,464	−1,741	−565	+505	+1,452	+2,231	+2,860	+3,420	+3,799	+4,065	+4,235
75,000	−3,464	−1,651	−405	+722	+1,692	+2,481	+3,100	+3,612	+4,015	+4,227	+4,294
80,000	−3,464	−1,561	−250	+934	+1,932	+2,700	+3,340	+3,805	+4,135	+4,330	+4,344
85,000	−3,464	−1,471	−95	+1,129	+2,132	+2,900	+3,530	+3,997	+4,255	+4,352	+4,394
90,000	−3,464	−1,383	+60	+1,324	+2,332	+3,100	+3,695	+4,105	+4,329	+4,375	+4,394
95,000	−3,464	−1,298	+215	+1,512	+2,532	+3,300	+3,860	+4,210	+4,349	+4,394	+4,394
100,000	−3,464	−1,213	+360	+1,692	+2,700	+3,474	+4,015	+4,315	+4,369	+4,395	+4,395

Plus (+) figures show additional tax imposed if couple married, i.e., the amount of tax saved if couple not married.   Minus (−) figures show tax cost of not being married.

Table V UNMARRIED COUPLES AND THE LAW

TABLE V
Tax Cost of Marriage Exacerbated by Filing Separate Returns

Couple's total taxable income (before personal exemptions)	Tax when couple is married and files joint return	\multicolumn{11}{c}{Tax when couple married and filing separate returns, and share of income earned by lower-earning spouse is:}
		0%	5%	10%	15%	20%	25%	30%	35%	40%	45%	50%
$ 5,000	$ 0	$ 350	$ 306	$ 266	$ 226	$ 186	$ 147	$ 111	$ 76	$ 41	$ 7	$ 0
10,000	702	1,373	1,252	1,132	1,027	922	817	754	732	717	707	701
15,000	1,635	2,797	2,556	2,316	2,098	1,930	1,825	1,759	1,708	1,663	1,640	1,634
20,000	2,745	4,682	4,252	3,859	3,531	3,306	3,147	3,007	2,881	2,811	2,745	2,746
25,000	4,057	6,899	6,295	5,757	5,367	5,033	4,721	4,491	4,291	4,170	4,075	4,057
30,000	5,593	9,349	8,613	7,920	7,410	6,939	6,575	6,245	5,960	5,748	5,621	5,594
35,000	7,348	11,998	11,053	10,220	9,622	9,081	8,591	8,146	7,824	7,589	7,397	7,348
40,000	9,366	14,698	13,618	12,725	11,989	11,301	10,722	10,257	9,865	9,528	9,402	9,365
45,000	11,516	17,458	16,183	15,235	14,419	13,671	13,002	12,425	12,018	11,738	11,566	11,515
50,000	13,798	20,408	18,933	17,809	16,866	16,071	15,377	14,795	14,323	14,031	13,881	13,798
55,000	16,248	23,358	21,743	20,554	19,466	18,481	17,770	17,193	16,764	16,461	16,247	16,248
60,000	18,698	26,524	24,645	23,299	22,131	21,117	20,255	19,638	19,271	18,947	18,798	18,698
65,000	21,178	29,724	27,720	26,184	24,819	23,757	22,883	22,221	21,779	21,547	21,385	21,297
70,000	23,678	32,924	30,795	29,156	27,696	26,440	25,558	24,931	24,407	24,147	23,997	23,997
75,000	26,178	36,124	33,870	32,141	30,602	29,320	28,269	27,641	27,182	26,807	26,697	26,697
80,000	28,678	39,324	36,950	35,126	33,532	32,203	31,206	30,372	29,957	29,607	29,407	29,397
85,000	31,178	42,635	40,030	38,111	36,462	35,133	34,144	33,347	32,732	32,457	32,245	32,097
90,000	33,678	46,035	43,242	41,096	39,400	38,063	37,081	36,322	35,672	35,307	35,082	34,917
95,000	36,178	49,435	46,512	44,228	42,360	41,016	40,019	39,297	38,697	38,222	37,920	37,867
100,000	38,678	52,835	49,786	47,408	45,432	44,006	43,023	42,272	41,722	41,222	40,817	40,817

266

TABLE V-A
Tax Cost of Marriage Exacerbated by Filing Separate Returns

Couple's total taxable income (before personal tax exemptions)	0%	5%	10%	15%	20%	25%	30%	35%	40%	45%	50%
					Dollar cost of filing separate returns rather than joint return when share of income earned by lower-earning spouse is:						
$ 5,000	$ 350	$ 306	$ 266	$ 226	$ 186	$ 147	$ 111	$ 76	$ 41	$ 7	$ 0
10,000	671	550	430	325	220	115	52	30	15	5	0
15,000	1,162	921	681	463	295	190	124	73	28	5	0
20,000	1,937	1,507	1,114	786	561	402	262	136	66	0	1
25,000	2,842	2,238	1,700	1,310	976	664	434	234	113	18	0
30,000	3,756	3,020	2,327	1,817	1,346	982	652	367	155	28	1
35,000	4,650	3,705	2,872	2,274	1,733	1,243	798	476	241	49	1
40,000	5,332	4,252	3,359	2,623	1,935	1,356	891	499	162	36	0
45,000	5,942	4,667	3,719	2,903	2,155	1,486	909	502	222	50	0
50,000	6,610	5,135	4,011	3,068	2,273	1,579	997	525	233	83	0
55,000	7,710	5,495	4,306	3,218	2,233	1,522	945	516	213	1	0
60,000	7,826	5,947	4,601	3,433	2,419	1,557	940	573	249	100	0
65,000	8,546	6,542	5,006	3,641	2,579	1,705	1,043	601	369	207	119
70,000	9,246	7,117	5,478	4,018	2,762	1,880	1,253	729	469	319	319
75,000	9,946	7,692	5,963	4,124	3,142	2,091	1,463	1,004	629	519	519
80,000	10,646	8,272	6,448	4,854	3,525	2,528	1,694	1,279	929	729	719
85,000	11,457	8,852	6,933	5,284	3,955	2,966	2,169	1,554	1,279	1,067	919
90,000	12,357	9,564	7,418	5,722	4,385	3,403	2,644	1,994	1,629	1,404	1,239
95,000	13,257	10,334	8,050	6,182	4,838	3,841	3,119	2,519	2,044	1,742	1,689
100,000	14,157	11,108	8,730	6,754	5,328	4,345	4,094	3,044	2,544	2,139	2,139

267

TABLE VI
Tax Cost of Marriage (Shaded Area) and Nonmarriage

Couple's total taxable income (before personal exemptions)	Tax when couple is married and files joint return	Tax when couple not married to each other or anyone else and higher-earner is taxed as head of household and lower-earner is taxed as unmarried individual, and share of income earned by lower-earner is:					
		0%	10%	20%	30%	40%	50%
$ 5,000	$ 0	$ 237	$ 167	$ 97	$ 27	$ 0	$ 0
10,000	702	1,091	899	719	549	487	487
15,000	1,635	2,236	1,875	1,531	1,371	1,321	1,321
20,000	2,745	3,556	2,995	2,573	3,417	2,318	2,268
25,000	4,051	5,130	4,330	3,805	3,557	3,412	3,364
30,000	5,593	6,942	5,850	5,217	4,842	4,598	4,580
40,000	9,366	11,339	9,596	8,569	7,813	7,401	7,392
50,000	13,798	16,111	13,888	12,515	11,387	10,779	10,692
60,000	18,698	21,111	18,532	16,713	15,463	14,695	14,464
70,000	23,678	26,111	23,212	21,195	19,787	18,991	18,764
80,000	28,678	31,111	27,897	25,715	24,307	23,512	23,506
90,000	33,678	36,111	32,587	30,315	28,952	28,318	28,281
100,000	38,678	41,111	37,287	34,947	33,632	33,278	33,253

Tax is computed on basis of 1979 rates. The taxable income in column 1 is before deductions for personal exemptions. For computation of tax on joint return (column 2), taxable income is reduced by $2,000 for two personal exemptions. For all other columns, each taxpayer's share of the total taxable income is reduced by $1,000 for one personal exemption. The 50% max-tax on personal service income is used where applicable.

TABLE VI-A
Tax Cost of Marriage (Shaded Area) and Nonmarriage

Couple's total taxable income (before personal exemptions)	Dollar amount of marriage penalty tax: comparison of joint return tax to tax when couple not married to each other or anyone else and higher-earner is taxed as head of household and lower-earner is taxed as unmarried individual, and share of income earned by lower-earner is:					
	0%	10%	20%	30%	40%	50%
$ 5,000	−$ 237	−$ 167	−$ 97	−$ 62	−$ 27	$ 0
10,000	− 389	− 197	− 17	+ 152	+ 215	+ 215
15,000	− 601	− 240	+ 103	+ 263	+ 313	+ 313
20,000	− 811	− 250	+ 172	+ 328	+ 427	+ 477
25,000	− 1,073	− 273	+ 251	+ 499	+ 644	+ 692
30,000	− 1,349	− 257	+ 376	+ 751	+ 995	+ 1,013
40,000	− 1,973	− 230	+ 796	+ 1,552	+ 1,964	+ 1,973
50,000	− 2,313	− 90	+ 1,283	+ 2,411	+ 3,019	+ 3,106
60,000	− 2,413	+ 166	+ 1,985	+ 3,235	+ 4,003	+ 4,234
70,000	− 2,433	+ 466	+ 2,483	+ 3,891	+ 4,687	+ 4,914
80,000	− 2,433	+ 781	+ 2,963	+ 4,371	+ 5,166	+ 5,172
90,000	− 2,433	+ 1,091	+ 3,363	+ 4,726	+ 5,360	+ 5,397
100,000	− 2,433	+ 1,391	+ 3,731	+ 5,046	+ 5,400	+ 5,425

Plus (+) figures show additional tax imposed if couple married, i.e., the amount of tax saved if couple not married and if higher-earner qualifies as head of household.
Minus (−) figures show tax cost of not being married.

MARITAL STATUS AND TAXES Table VII-A

TABLE VII
Tax Cost of Marriage (Shaded Area) and Nonmarriage

Couple's total taxable income (before personal exemptions)	Tax when couple is married and files joint return	\multicolumn{6}{c}{Tax when couple not married to each other or anyone else and both are taxed as head of household, and share of income earned by lower-earner is:}
		0%	10%	20%	30%	40%	50%
$ 5,000	$ 0	$ 237	$ 167	$ 97	$ 27	$ 0	$ 0
10,000	702	1,091	899	719	549	487	475
15,000	1,635	2,236	1,875	1,531	1,369	1,289	1,260
20,000	2,745	3,556	2,995	2,573	2,385	2,251	2,183
25,000	4,057	5,130	4,330	3,793	3,495	3,327	3,283
30,000	5,593	6,942	5,850	5,185	4,765	4,527	4,472
40,000	9,366	11,339	9,596	8,502	7,742	7,272	7,112
50,000	13,798	16,111	13,876	12,430	11,278	16,498	10,261
60,000	18,698	21,111	18,500	16,642	15,254	14,295	13,885
70,000	23,678	26,111	23,160	21,106	19,476	18,469	18,085
80,000	28,678	31,111	27,830	25,586	23,906	22,893	22,678
90,000	33,678	36,111	32,510	30,106	28,461	27,610	27,278
100,000	38,678	41,111	37,202	34,666	33,053	32,450	32,222

Tax is computed on basis of 1979 rates. The taxable income in column 1 is before deductions for personal exemptions. For computation of tax on joint return (column 2), taxable income is reduced by $2,000 for two personal exemptions. For all other columns, each taxpayer's share of the total taxable income is reduced by $1,000 for one personal exemption. The 50% max-tax on personal service income is used where applicable.

TABLE VII-A
Tax Cost of Marriage (Shaded Area) and Nonmarriage

Couple's total taxable income (before personal exemptions)	\multicolumn{6}{c}{Dollar amount of marriage penalty tax: comparison of joint return tax to tax when couple not married to each other or anyone else and both are taxed as head of household, and share of income earned by lower-earner is:}
	0%	10%	20%	30%	40%	50%
$ 5,000	$ −237	$ −167	$ −97	$ −27	$ 0	$ 0
10,000	−389	−197	−17	+152	+214	+226
15,000	−601	−240	+103	+265	+345	+374
20,000	−811	−250	+172	+360	+494	+562
25,000	−1,073	−273	+263	+561	+729	+773
30,000	−1,349	−257	+408	+828	+1,066	+1,121
40,000	−1,973	−230	+863	+1,623	+2,093	+2,253
50,000	−2,313	−78	+1,368	+2,520	+3,300	+3,537
60,000	−2,413	+198	+2,056	+3,444	+4,403	+4,813
70,000	−2,433	+518	+2,572	+4,202	+5,209	+5,593
80,000	−2,433	+848	+3,092	+4,772	+5,785	+6,000
90,000	−2,433	+1,168	+3,572	+5,217	+6,068	+6,400
100,000	−2,433	+1,476	+4,012	+5,625	+6,228	+6,456

Plus (+) figures show additional tax imposed if couple married, i.e., the amount of tax saved if couple not married and each qualifies as head of household.
Minus (−) figures show tax cost of not being married.

TABLE VIII
Marriage Status Definitions—Requirements

Taxpayer's status	Tax rate table applicable	Maintenance of household	Member of taxpayer's household	Dependent; required relationship	OR	Nondependent	Other requirements
(1) Married individual	(a) Married individuals filing joint return (IRC § 1(a)) (b) Married individuals filing separate returns (IRC § 1(d))	—	—	—		—	Both spouses must agree to file joint return and to assume joint & several liability for the tax
(2) Surviving spouse (IRC § 2(a))	Married individuals filing joint returns (IRC § 1(a))	Providing over half the cost for the full year of own household	Yes, for the full year	Child, stepchild		—	Not remarried. Deceased spouse died during either of the two preceding years and was not a nonresident alien or, if a nonresident alien, had made an election to subject his worldwide income to US taxation.
(3) Head of household (IRC § 2(b))	Heads of households (IRC § 1(b))	Providing over half the cost for the full year of own household OR Providing over half the cost for the full year of parent's household	Yes, for the full year NO	Child, stepchild, descendant of child, sibling, stepsibling, parent, ancestor of parent, stepparent, sibling's child, parent's sibling, child-in-law, parent-in-law, sibling-in-law Parent		Unmarried child, unmarried stepchild, unmarried descendant of child	

TABLE VIII (continued)
Marriage Status Definitions — Requirements

Taxpayer's status	Tax rate table applicable	Maintenance of household	Member of taxpayer's household	Dependent of taxpayer; required relationship	OR	Nondependent	Other requirements
(4) Married individual "legally separated... under a decree of divorce or of separate maintenance" (IRC § 143(a)(2))	(a) Heads of households (IRC § 1(b))	See line (3) above for head of household requirements					
	(b) Unmarried individuals (IRC § 1(c))	—	—	—		—	—
(5) "Abandoned spouses" — Certain married individuals living apart (IRC § 143(b))	(a) Unmarried individuals (IRC § 1(c))	Providing over half the cost for the full year of own household	Yes, for over half the year	Child, stepchild		—	"Abandoning" spouse must not be a member of household for the entire year
	(b) Heads of households (IRC § 1(b))	Providing over half the cost for the full year of own household	Yes, for the full year	Child, stepchild		—	"Abandoning" spouse must not be a member of household for the entire year
	(c) Married individuals filing separate returns (IRC § 1(d))	—	—	—		—	—
	(d) Married individuals filing joint returns (IRC § 1(a))						Both spouses must agree to file joint return and to assume joint & several liability for the tax

TABLE VIII (continued)
Marriage Status Definitions—Requirements

Taxpayer's status	Tax rate table applicable	Maintenance of household	Member of taxpayer's household	Dependent of taxpayer; required relationship	OR	Nondependent	Other requirements
(6) Married individual whose spouse is a nonresident alien (IRC § 2(b)(2)(c), § 6013(g))	(a) Married individuals filing joint returns (IRC § 1(a))	—	—	—		—	Both spouses must agree to file joint return and to assume joint & several liability for the tax and to subject nonresident alien's worldwide income to US taxation (IRC § 6013(g))
	(b) Heads of households (IRC § 1(b))	Providing over half the cost for the full year of own household	Yes, for the full year	Child, stepchild, descendant of child, sibling, stepsibling, parent, ancestor of parent, stepparent, sibling's child, child-in-law, parent-in-law, sibling-in-law		Unmarried child, unmarried stepchild, unmarried descendant of child	
		OR					
		Providing over half the cost for the full year of parent's household		Parent			
	(c) Married individuals filing separate returns (IRC § 1(d))	—	—	—		—	—

272

CHAPTER 6

STATE-BY-STATE COMMENTARY

Section
6.1 Alabama
6.2 Alaska
6.3 Arizona
6.4 Arkansas
6.5 California
6.6 Colorado
6.7 Connecticut
6.8 Delaware
6.9 District of Columbia
6.10 Florida
6.11 Georgia
6.12 Hawaii
6.13 Idaho
6.14 Illinois
6.15 Indiana
6.16 Iowa
6.17 Kansas
6.18 Kentucky
6.19 Louisiana
6.20 Maine
6.21 Maryland
6.22 Massachusetts
6.23 Michigan
6.24 Minnesota
6.25 Mississippi
6.26 Missouri

Section
6.27 Montana
6.28 Nebraska
6.29 Nevada
6.30 New Hampshire
6.31 New Jersey
6.32 New Mexico
6.33 New York
6.34 North Carolina
6.35 North Dakota
6.36 Ohio
6.37 Oklahoma
6.38 Oregon
6.39 Pennsylvania
6.40 Rhode Island
6.41 South Carolina
6.42 South Dakota
6.43 Tennessee
6.44 Texas
6.45 Utah
6.46 Vermont
6.47 Virginia
6.48 Washington
6.49 West Virginia
6.50 Wisconsin
6.51 Wyoming

> The following sections draw attention to miscellaneous state statutes and decisions which may confirm, add to, or differ from the discussion in the preceding chapters. No attempt has been made to cover the law of each state in its entirety.

6.1. Alabama

Marriage may be contracted in Alabama by parties competent to so contract without ceremony or solemnization. A common-law marriage is effected when such competent parties consent to the marriage relation, permanently and to the exclusion of all others. The agreement must be followed by cohabitation, and they are required openly to mutually assume marital duties and obligations.[1]

In line with the common-law presumption of death after a spouse's unexplained absence of seven years, a subsequent ceremonial marriage can, where the first spouse is in fact alive, result in a common-law marriage, given a cohabitation between the supposed spouses.[2] In other words, Alabama recognizes that a continued cohabitation after the removal of an impediment to what was believed to be a valid marriage results in a common-law marriage.[3] The same recognition is accorded to a cohabitation initially in violation of a statute or judgment forbidding marriage within a stated period after one spouse gets a divorce.[4] The courts further recognize a rebuttable presumption that a prior marriage is dissolved when a subsequent marriage is established.[5]

Noncompliance with a statutory requirement of a physical examination as a precondition of the issuance of a license to marry does not invalidate a common-law marriage.[6]

Adoption

The procedures, where an unwed adult couple wish to adopt a child,[7] require a petition to the appropriate probate court accompanied, inter alia, by information as to the identity of the child's biological parents, with the proviso that, if the child is in the

---

[1] Skipworth v. Skipworth, —— Ala. ——, 360 So. 2d 975 (1978); O'Dell v. O'Dell, 57 Ala. App. 185, 326 So. 2d 747 (1976); Bishop v. Bishop, 57 Ala. App. 619, 330 So. 2d 443 (1976).
[2] Walker v. Walker, 218 Ala. 16, 117 So. 472 (1928).
[3] Hill v. Lindsey, 223 Ala. 550, 137 So. 395 (1931); Hill & Range Songs, Inc. v. Fred Rose Music, Inc., 403 F. Supp. 420 (M.D. Tenn., 1975), affd. 570 F.2d 554 (C.A.-6 Tenn., 1978).
[4] Smith v. Smith, 247 Ala. 213, 23 So. 2d 605 (1945).
[5] Hammond v. Shipp, 292 Ala. 113, 289 So. 2d 802 (1974).
[6] Woodward Iron Co. v. Dean, 217 Ala. 530, 117 So. 52, 60 A.L.R. 536 (1929).
[7] On adoption generally, see section 2.9, herein.

charge of some licensed agency, this information can be dispensed with.[8]

Welfare assistance

As to the eligibility of unmarried cohabitants for aid to families with dependent children,[9] the Supreme Court of the United States invalidated a regulation of the Alabama Department of Pensions and Security denying federally aided assistance for the children of a mother who "cohabits," either on a stable or sporadic basis, with a man other than her husband.[10] Such a regulation, where based on a state interest in discouraging immorality and illegitimacy, conflicts with a federal policy not to visit upon children the "sins" of their parents. The regulation was also objectionable in that it included within the term "father" one who did not owe any state-imposed duty of support of the child. Justice Douglas, concurring, thought that the regulation might truly be unconstitutional in that immorality of the mother has no rational connection with the need of her children for welfare assistance.

Workers' compensation death benefits

Neither a purported widow, nor her illegitimate children,[11] nor one standing in loco parentis[12] to a deceased employee qualifies for workers' compensation benefits under the Alabama statute.

Insurance benefits

If one taking out life insurance names as his beneficiary his "widow," this means his lawful widow and would not cover his co-cohabitant.[13]

---

[8]Ala. Code, § 26–10–1.
[9]See, generally, section 2.11, herein.
[10]King v. Smith, 392 U.S. 309, 20 L. Ed. 2d 1118, 88 Sup. Ct. 2128 (1968).
As to the unconstitutionality of an abortion-controlling ordinance, see Mobile Women's Medical Clinic, Inc. v. Board of Comrs. of City of Mobile, 426 F. Supp. 331 (S.D. Ala., 1977).
[11]Talley v. A & M Constr. Co., 284 Ala. 371, 225 So. 2d 359 (1969), cert. den. 397 U.S. 995, 90 Sup. Ct. 1133 (1970).
[12]Browning v. City of Huntsville, 46 Ala. App. 503, 244 So. 2d 378 (1971).
[13]See Metropolitan Life Ins. Co. v. Spearman, 344 F. Supp. 665 (M.D. Ala., 1972), holding "widow" in Federal Employees Group Life Insurance Act of 1954 to mean "lawful widow."

Tort actions

As to tort liability of cohabitants *inter sese*,[14] punitive damages, as well as mere damages for mental suffering, can be recoverable in an action for fraudulently inducing another to enter into an illegal or void marriage.[15] But civil actions for seduction, criminal conversation, and alienation of affections cannot be brought.[16]

Abortion

Abortion is permitted only to save the life or preserve the health of the mother.[17] The burden of establishing such a necessity is on the defendant, not the state.[18] One challenge to the constitutionality of the abortion statute failed because the defendant, not being a physician, lacked standing to raise the issue, since his act would be criminal regardless of the Supreme Court's abortion decisions.[19]

Possible criminal liability

Living together by any man or woman in adultery or fornication is criminally punishable.[20] If neither is married, the offense is fornication.[21] The statute does not prohibit a single act, or occasional acts, absent a "living together." Nevertheless, a city ordinance which forbade unmarried occupants of a room in a tourist court from having sexual relations in that room has withstood a challenge of unconstitutionality. The argument against the ordinance was that such conduct was not violative of state law and that even if a municipality did have the power to enact such

---

[14]See section 2.23, herein.
[15]See Holcombe v. Whitaker, 294 Ala. 430, 318 So. 2d 289 (1975).
[16]Ala. Code, § 6–5–331.
[17]Id., § 13A–13–7.
[18]Lingle v. State, 51 Ala. App. 210, 283 So. 2d 660 (1973).
[19]State v. Wilkerson, 54 Ala. App. 104, 305 So. 2d 378 (1974).
[20]Ala. Code, § 13A–13–2.
[21]Banks v. State, 96 Ala. 78, 11 So. 404 (1892); Brown v. State, 31 Ala. App. 233, 14 So. 2d 596 (1943), cert. den. 244 Ala. 597, 14 So. 2d 598 (1943) (to establish "living in adultery," there must be proof of intercourse and a continued relation or an intention that it be continued). Since both adultery and fornication fall under the same section it would seem immaterial whether or not a defendant charged thereunder knew of the other's marital status.

an ordinance, it would be discriminatory to single out tourist courts as the target for such restrictions. But the court felt that tourist courts might be more conducive to immorality than other places, and declined to enjoin enforcement of the ordinance.[22]

The relationships which constitute incestuous unions, which are criminal,[23] are spelled out by statute.[24] As to statutory rape,[25] the age of the female's consent being as low as sixteen years,[26] problems are unlikely to be presented to the cohabitants, and there is no criminality if the male involved is under the age of sixteen. If the female is under twelve, the penalty is far more severe.[27]

Status of children

The common-law rule that illegitimate children cannot inherit from either parent,[28] has been partially supplanted by statute. Every illegitimate child is considered the heir of its mother, and inherits her estate in whole or in part, as the case may be, in the same way as if it had been legitimate.[29] It cannot inherit on intestacy from the biological father even if paternity is beyond dispute.[30] However, the legitimate child of an illegitimate can inherit from the illegitimate's mother.[31] And the mother of such a child can inherit, as can kindred of the mother, if the illegitimate leaves no descendants.[32]

The statute does not of course preclude the possibility of a testator intending, by the use of the word "children" in his will, to

---

[22] Allinder v. Homewood, 254 Ala. 525, 49 So. 2d 108, 22 A.L.R.2d 763 (1950).
[23] Ala. Code, § 13A–13–3.
[24] Id.
[25] See section 2.25, herein.
[26] Ala. Code, §§ 13A–6–62, 13A–6–67.
[27] Id., §§ 13A–6–61, 13A–6–66. See Jenkins v. State, —— Ala. ——, 337 So. 2d 72 (1976). For "crimes against nature," see Ala. Code, §§ 13A–6–60, 13A–6–63, 13A–6–64, 13A–11–14.
[28] See section 3.3, herein.
[29] Ala. Code, § 43–3–7.
[30] Moore v. Terry, 220 Ala. 47, 124 So. 80 (1929). As to the constitutionality of such a holding, see Knowles, Legal Status of Women in Alabama: A Crazy Quilt, 29 Ala. L. Rev. 427 (1978).
[31] Foster v. Lee, 172 Ala. 32, 55 So. 125, Ann. Cas. 1913C, 1335 (1911).
[32] Ala. Code, § 43–3–8.

embrace his illegitimate children. Whether or not he so intended is a question of fact.[33]

Detailed provision is made for proceedings to establish the paternity of a child born out of wedlock.[34] Though criminal in nature, the statute does not permit a jury trial. When paternity is adjudicated, the father is subject to all the obligations of any father for the care and education of the child. The authority of the court to modify or vacate a judgment obtained under these proceedings is restricted to situations where substantially changed conditions are shown.[35]

Marriage of the mother and the reputed father renders the child legitimate, if the child is recognized by the father as his.[36] Such a marriage would legitimate the child even if, at the time of its birth, the mother was married to a man other than the biological father.[37]

As to adoption of an illegitimate child, consent of the mother alone is sufficient except where paternity has been established, but if the child is over fourteen the child's consent is also required.[38] Legitimation of the child gives the biological father the rights of a natural father, including a right to veto its adoption and to claim custody. Hence, due process requires that no legitimation proceedings be initiated without notice to the mother. Further, a statute giving such a father preference in the choice of the child's name serves no legitimate state interest and violates equal protection.[39]

---

[33]Walton v. Lindsey, —— Ala. ——, 349 So. 2d 41 (1977).

[34]Ala. Code, §§ 26-12-1 to 26-12-9. See Keener v. State, —— Ala. ——, 347 So. 2d 398 (1977).

[35]State ex rel. Moore v. Strickland, 289 Ala. 488, 268 So. 2d 766 (1972).

[36]Ala. Code, § 26-11-1. It seems that a good faith attempt to marry would legitimate children born before the marriage. See Howard v. Pike, 290 Ala. 213, 275 So. 2d 645 (1973).

[37]See Howard v. Pike, 290 Ala. 213, 275 So. 2d 645 (1973).

[38]Ala. Code, §§ 26-10-3, 26-10-7, 26-11-2. An agreement whereunder the mother surrenders custody of her child to a third person in return for a promise to raise the child is not violative of public policy. Phillips v. Frederick, 257 Ala. 283, 58 So. 2d 584 (1952). As to the irrevocable nature of a mother's consent to adoption, if freely given, see Davis v. Turner, —— Ala. ——, 337 So. 2d 362 (1976). As to her right to due process where custody of the child is involved, see Thorne v. Thorne, —— Ala. App. ——, 344 So. 2d 165 (1977).

[39]Roe v. Conn, 417 F. Supp. 769 (M.D. Ala., 1976).

Property rights of cohabitants

In adjudicating disputes as to the property rights of persons who mistakenly believe in the existence of a valid marriage,[40] much depends on the circumstances of the individual case. Alabama is in harmony with the trend in the country to recognize a need for adjustment of the equities in such a situation.[41] The concept of a resulting trust,[42] where one good faith partner takes title, the other having paid the purchase price, finds its place in this state.[43]

Further, where one partner, mistakenly believing in a valid marriage, has transferred property to the other, the courts will, as long as the property can be traced, order its return to the transferor.[44] The constructive trust[45] would in all likelihood be the remedy used.

6.2. Alaska

Alaska does not recognize common-law marriages.[46]

Adoption

There is provision for the adoption of a child, with the written consent of the child if he is fourteen years of age or older, by any person, married or single.[47] In specifying the persons whose consent need be obtained, the statute dispenses with the necessity of consent of the biological father, or of notice to him, if the child is illegitimate.[48]

---

[40] Discussed in Chapter 4, herein.
[41] See Knowles, Legal Status of Women in Alabama: A Crazy Quilt, 29 Ala. L. Rev. 427 (1978).
[42] See section 4.5, herein.
[43] See Albae v. Harbin, 249 Ala. 201, 30 So. 2d 459 (1947).
[44] See Dorsey v. Dorsey, 259 Ala. 220, 66 So. 2d 135 (1953).
[45] See section 4.8, herein.
[46] Hager v. Hager, 553 P.2d 919 (Alaska, 1976) (though court found prerequisites for a putative marriage).
[47] Alaska Stat., §§ 20.10.010, 20.10.020. As to adoption by unmarried partners generally, see section 2.9, herein.
[48] Id., § 20.10.020(3). As to the possible unconstitutionality of such a provision, see section 3.8, herein.

Workers' compensation death benefits

As to workers' compensation,[49] the death benefit has been extended to a cohabitant who was living with the deceased employee at the time of his death, even though divorced from him.[50] An illegitimate child is also included in the definition of a posthumous child entitled to benefits.[51]

Possible criminal liability

Among an array of crimes "against morality and decency" are concealment of the death of a child,[52] incest (forbidden degrees being computed according to the civil law),[53] cohabiting in a state of adultery or fornication,[54] certain varieties of polygamy,[55] "unnatural crimes," (embracing statutory rape, consent age being sixteen),[56] and taking a female under sixteen years of age for prostitution *or marriage*.[57] If the other participant in a cohabitation is under the age of eighteen the prosecution can be for contributing to the delinquency of a child, to which mistake as to age, no matter how reasonable, is no defense.[58]

Abortion

Parental consent is required for an abortion if the prospective mother is under eighteen years of age.[59]

---

[49] Discussed in section 2.13, herein.
[50] Burgess Constr. Co. v. Lindley, 504 P.2d 1023 (Alaska, 1972).
[51] S.L.W. v. Alaska Workmen's Compensation Bd., 490 P.2d 42 (Alaska, 1971).
[52] Alaska Stat., § 11.40.090.
[53] Id., § 11.40.110.
[54] Id., § 11.40.040. However, if the possession of marijuana for personal consumption in the home is protected by reason of the right of privacy (Ravin v. State, 537 P.2d 494 (Alaska, 1975)), is not fornication logically qualified for the same treatment, where no public harm is involved?
[55] The offense includes bigamy, but does not extend to situations where a spouse has been continuously absent for five consecutive years and is not known to be living, or is believed dead. Alaska Stat., §§ 11.40.050, 11.40.060.
[56] Alaska Stat., § 11.15.120. "Carnal knowledge" includes sodomy and like offenses. It follows that such conduct is denounced only if force is used or the participant is under age sixteen.
[57] Alaska Stat., § 11.40.200.
[58] Id., § 11.40.130. See Anderson v. State, 384 P.2d 669 (Alaska, 1963).
[59] Alaska Stat., § 11.15.060.

Status of children

Legislative provision is made for the legitimation of a child by subsequent marriage of its parents, by written acknowledgment of paternity, and by a judicial finding of paternity. As to legitimation, the Bureau of Vital Statistics is required to place on record a substitute birth certificate.[60]

For the purposes of intestate succession, an illegitimate child who has not been adopted is the child of its mother. It is also the legitimate child of its biological father if the parents have attempted marriage, even if the attempt was ineffective, or if paternity is established by court adjudication.[61] Paternity established by such adjudication does not, however, qualify a father or his kindred to inherit from or through the child unless he has openly treated the child as his, and has not refused to support it.[62]

In proceedings to establish paternity,[63] if the mother is represented by the state, due process requires the appointment of counsel for an indigent defendant.[64]

Property rights of cohabitants

Alaska has abolished the common-law rule, based on the unity of a husband and his wife,[65] that a deed to spouses as such creates a tenancy by the entirety. Unless the deed itself provides otherwise, the grant creates a tenancy in common.[66]

The statute which permits a court to "invade" the property of either spouse acquired before marriage (on a divorce) if the equities require it,[67] has been used to authorize a court to so invade the cohabitant's estate when a putative wife seeks

---

[60] Id., § 25.20.050. As to the requirements and procedures for registration of illegitimate births, see § 18.50.150 et seq.

[61] If the parties to a marriage which is void for failure to comply with statutory requirements subsequently do so comply, the children of the marriage are legitimate. Alaska Stat., § 25.05.311.

[62] Alaska Stat., § 13.11.045. See Calista Corp. v. Mann, 564 P.2d 53 (Alaska, 1977).

[63] Alaska Stat., §§ 11.35.010, 47.23.040, 47.23.050.

[64] Reynolds v. Kimmons, 569 P.2d 799 (Alaska, 1977).

[65] Discussed in section 4.2, herein.

[66] Carver v. Gilbert, 387 P.2d 928, 32 A.L.R.3d 563 (Alaska, 1963).

[67] Alaska Stat., § 09.55.210(6).

compensation for her services during an invalid marriage.[68] The courts have disavowed any sponsorship of the notion that equitable principles will be invoked to adjust the property rights of persons knowingly living in a meretricious relationship;[69] yet, in such a case, there is no reason why, on proof of the precise amount a participant has contributed toward the purchase of an asset held in the name of the other, a prorata division based on a resulting trust[70] cannot be decreed.[71] They do adjust the equities where there has been a putative marriage. In Hager v. Hager,[72] there had been an eight-year-long meretricious relationship prior to the celebration of an invalid marriage in Tijuana, Mexico. In determining the extent to which the putative husband's separate property could be invaded, the reviewing court found that the trial judge had erred in relating back the putative wife's contribution to include the period of meretricious relationship; but, in view of the wife's instrumentality in securing a homestead, assistance in improving it, and her performance of domestic tasks and of bookkeeping work for the husband, the court declined to disturb the award of about eight per cent of the value of the husband's homestead.

In 1972 the Supreme Court of Alaska, in holding a school regulation against long hair unreasonable, offered the following observation: "The United States of America, and Alaska in particular, reflect a pluralistic society, grounded upon such basic values as the preservation of maximum individual choice, protection of minority sentiments, and appreciation for divergent lifestyles."[73] It may well be that the court's aversion to administering equity as between the cohabitants who have no belief in a marriage will erode with the passage of the years.

---

[68]Hager v. Hager, 553 P.2d 919 (Alaska, 1976); Merrill v. Merrill, 368 P.2d 546 (Alaska, 1962); Vanover v. Vanover, 496 P.2d 644 (Alaska, 1972).
[69]Sugg v. Morris, 392 P.2d 313 (Alaska, 1964).
[70]Discussed in section 4.5, herein.
[71]Sugg v. Morris, 392 P.2d 313 (Alaska, 1964).
[72]553 P.2d 919 (Alaska, 1976).
[73]Breese v. Smith, 501 P.2d 159, 169 (Alaska, 1972). Quoted in Carle v. Carle, 503 P.2d 1050 (Alaska, 1972) (child custody case).

6.3. Arizona

The state of Arizona does not recognize common-law marriages.[74]

Workers' compensation death benefits

Arizona workers' compensation law requires that, to qualify as the "widow" of a decedent employee, there must be compliance with the statutory marriage formalities.[75]

Insurance benefits

As to whether a cohabitant qualifies for insurance coverage under a policy covering the insured and his "family," or excluding coverage in respect of family members,[76] a federal court in Arizona has held against a woman who resided with the insured but, unknown to her, was not legally married to him.[77] If this is so, a fortiori an extramarital partner would receive the same treatment.

Adoption

Any adult resident of the state is eligible to adopt a child.[78]

Possible criminal liability

Adultery, which can be committed by a married person or by a single person who has intercourse with a married person,[79] is not prosecuted except on the complaint of the aggrieved spouse.[80] One

---

[74] Ariz. Rev. Stat. Ann., § 25–111.
[75] See Gamez v. Industrial Comm., 114 Ariz. 179, 559 P.2d 1094 (1976). As to the claimant who marries decedent prior to his divorce becoming effective, see Hack v. Industrial Comm., 74 Ariz. 305, 248 P.2d 863 (1952). As to one who marries prior to the one-year waiting period following a divorce, see Davis v. Industrial Comm., 88 Ariz. 117, 353 P.2d 627 (1960).
[76] Discussed in section 2.17, herein.
[77] State Farm Mut. Auto Ins. Co. v. Thompson, 372 F.2d 256 (C.A.-9 Ariz., 1967).
[78] Ariz. Rev. Stat. Ann., § 8–103. As to the prerequisites to an adoption, see §§ 8–106, 8–107.
[79] For other definitions of this crime, see section 2.25, herein.
[80] Ariz. Rev. Stat. Ann., § 13–1408.

who lives in a state of "open and notorious cohabitation" or adultery is guilty of a Class 3 misdemeanor.[81] The gravity of offenses in the nature of statutory rape—the age of consent being at least eighteen—depends on the age of the other participant.[82] However, reasonable mistake of fact as to age in these crimes is a defense.[83] There is an additional crime labeled "public sexual indecency." This includes, inter alia, intentionally or knowingly engaging in an act of sex, if another person is present and the actor is reckless as to whether such other person, as a reasonable person, would be offended or alarmed by the act.[84]

The prevalent ambivalence in the judicial climate in the matter of the constitutionality of statutes denouncing sexual behavior of a deviate nature[85] is shared by the judges of Arizona. In State v. Bateman,[86] the constitutionality of the state's laws proscribing sodomy and lewd and lascivious cohabitation came under attack. The acts complained of took place between two married persons in one case, and between a married person and a single one in another. Justice Hays in summary fashion dismissed the argument that the statutes violate First Amendment rights of freedom of expression. The objection that the statutes were void for vagueness received similar treatment. "The term 'crime against nature' has been in use for centuries. . . . It is no more vague than many other terms used to define criminal conduct and it is, in fact, used in a substantial number of jurisdictions. . . . That term and the term 'lewd and lascivious acts' have been often defined by this court."[87] As to the contention that the statutes were void for

---

[81]Id., § 13–1409.

[82]Id., §§ 13–1404, 13–1405.

[83]Id., § 13–1407.

[84]Id., § 13–1403. (It is assumed that the other person present is not the coparticipant.) As to the unconstitutionality of former §§ 13–651, 13–652 (sodomy and lewdness), see State v. Dale, 25 Ariz. App. 417, 544 P.2d 241 (1975).

[85]Discussed in section 2.25, herein. Sodomy can be committed with the victim's consent and therefore without an assault. State v. Sustaita, 119 Ariz. 583, 583 P.2d 239 (1978).

[86]113 Ariz. 107, 547 P.2d 6 (1976), cert. den. 429 U.S. 864, 97 Sup. Ct. 170 (1976).

[87]Id., 547 P.2d at 9. Since the infamous crime against nature can be committed without force (Ariz. Rev. Stat. Ann., § 13–1411), consensual activity between adults falls within the ban of the statute. State v. Sims, 114 Ariz. 292, 560 P.2d 810 (1977). As to seduction, see Ariz. Rev. Stat. Ann., § 13–3602; incest, § 13–3608; marrying the spouse of another, § 13–3607.

overbreadth, as reaching, on their face, both married and unmarried persons and both consenting and unconsenting adults, the court observed that statutes do not stand alone. Judicial interpretation adds meaning to a statute as certainly as if the words were placed there by the legislature.

As to objections based on privacy: whatever the Supreme Court of the United States may have had to say about the private sexual behavior of two adults, it has not said that the state cannot regulate sexual misconduct. Sodomy, said the court, has been considered wrong since early times in our civilization. The lewd and lascivious acts prohibited have also been traditionally prohibited.

As is to be expected, a dissenting judge expressed "bafflement" as to how the majority could acknowledge a right of privacy to protect conduct in the context of intimate sexual relations between consenting adults in private, whether single or married, and yet conclude that the legislature can separate certain of those relations it finds distasteful, label them as misconduct, and make the participants subject to a prison term of up to twenty years in the state penitentiary.

Abortion

Abortion is proscribed unless necessary to preserve the life of the prospective mother.[88]

Status of children

At one time Arizona had eradicated the status of illegitimacy.[89] Today, however, the statute provides that a child born out of wedlock is the child of the mother. It is also a child of the father if the parents have participated in a marriage ceremony, before or after the birth of the child, even though the attempted marriage is void. Paternity can also be established by adjudication; but paternity so established is ineffective to qualify the father or his kindred to inherit from or through the child unless the father has openly treated the child as his, and has not refused to support it.[90]

---

[88] Ariz. Rev. Stat. Ann., § 13–3603.
[89] See Anonymous v. Anonymous, 10 Ariz. App. 496, 460 P.2d 32 (1969).
[90] Ariz. Rev. Stat. Ann., § 14–2109. As to the effect of a class gift as including illegitimate children, see § 14–2611.

6.3 UNMARRIED COUPLES AND THE LAW

Any rights such a male parent enjoys in regard to his child can be lost if, on a severance proceeding, it is found that he has abandoned the child, for example by refusing to acknowledge or support it.[91]

Primarily to fix a father's obligation to support his child, provision is made to facilitate the establishment of a person's identity and parentage.[92] Proceedings to establish paternity are civil in nature (although provision exists for the arrest of the "accused" father)[93] and are not designed to punish.[94]

In determining who is to have custody of an illegitimate, the father does not necessarily qualify even if the mother is dead. The best interests of the child are to be considered.[95]

Property rights of cohabitants

Arizona is a community property state.[96] As to property rights of unmarried partners, though not expressly recognizing the status of a putative spouse, the state does recognize that one cohabiting in the good faith belief in a marriage is not bereft of equities. To date, however, Arizona has shown little feeling for the equities of an extramarital cohabitant.

A hard case was presented in Stevens v. Anderson.[97] The woman had lived with a decedent for thirty years. She had performed all the domestic chores traditionally expected of a wife. She had lent him money to help make payments on property he had purchased. He had promised her that she would be cared for after his death, and would receive a fair portion of their joint accumulations. But the court held she was not entitled to share in his estate, stating:

---

[91] See Appeal in Pima County, Juvenile Action, 27 Ariz. App. 424, 555 P.2d 892 (1976).
[92] Ariz. Rev. Stat. Ann., §§ 12–621, 12–622.
[93] Id., § 12–841.
[94] Skaggs v. State, 24 Ariz. 191, 207 Pac. 877 (1922).
[95] See In re Guardianship and Estate of Arias, 21 Ariz. App. 568, 521 P.2d 1146 (1974).
[96] Ariz. Rev. Stat. Ann., §25–211.
[97] 75 Ariz. 331, 256 P.2d 712 (1953). See also Cross v. Cross, 94 Ariz. 28, 381 P.2d 573 (1963).

Generally the conscience of the court is not aroused to invoke equitable powers to rescue those from the results of their illegal practices when that is the only basis for granting relief. The parties here not only violated the permanent established public policy of all society but also violated the expressed criminal statutes of the state of Arizona. ... We cannot establish the precedent of assisting those who deliberately choose to substitute illegal cohabitation for lawful wedlock, especially when the only basis for such assistance is the mere fact that they have chosen such a status.[98]

There is authority, however, where a joint venture or an agreement to pool earnings can be established,[99] warranting a separation of the immoral sexual activity from an agreement regarding property rights. For example, in Garza v. Fernandez,[1] summary judgment for the defendant was reversed when a woman sought an accounting, on allegations that, subsequent to the agreement of the parties to live together, they agreed to work together to acquire property for their mutual benefit. Recovery was had on a theory of partnership, although no actual business was involved. The partners just "lent their mutual efforts toward earning a livelihood."[2]

6.4. Arkansas

Arkansas does not recognize common-law marriages.[3]

Adoption

Any adult, single or married, may adopt a child.[4] Since, however, the consent of the spouse is ordinarily required if the petitioner is married,[5] it is unlikely that judicial approval of an adoption by extramarital cohabitants would be secured (if then) without consent of the extramarital partner.

---

[98]Id., 256 P.2d at 715.
[99]Discussed in sections 4.3, 4.4, herein.
[1]74 Ariz. 312, 248 P.2d 869 (1952).
[2]Fernandez v. Garza, 88 Ariz. 214, 354 P.2d 260 (1960).
[3]United States v. White, 545 F.2d 1129 (C.A.-8 Ark., 1976).
[4]Ark. Stat. Ann., § 56–101.
[5]Id.

Discrimination in housing

As to discrimination in housing,[6] a district court of Arkansas has held that a city housing authority could not constitutionally exclude from low-rent subsidized housing facilities an otherwise qualified family solely because there were illegitimate children in the family.[7]

Workers' compensation death benefits

The controlling statute defines a "widow" to include only the legal wife, living with or dependent on the decedent workman for support at the time of his death;[8] a "child" includes an *acknowledged* illegitimate child.[9] Thus even a lawful wife, if not living with the decedent nor dependent on him for support, cannot qualify for death benefits.[10]

Possible criminal liability

There is no statutory denunciation of cohabitation as such, nor of fornication. Public sexual indecency, however, is denounced.[11] Types of sexual misconduct with which the occasional extramarital cohabitant may possibly be concerned are as follows: a "person" commits carnal abuse in the third degree if being twenty years old or older, "he" engages in sexual intercourse or deviate sexual activity with another person not "his" spouse who is less than sixteen years old.[12] In light of the rule that penal statutes must be strictly construed in favor of the defendant, a female charged under statutes worded in this fashion might have a defense. By taking into account the relative ages of the participants as well as the absolute age of the younger party, the provision excludes from its ambit conduct between contemporaries.

---

[6]Discussed in section 2.7, herein.
[7]Thomas v. Housing Authority of City of Little Rock, 282 F. Supp. 575 (E.D. Ark., 1967).
[8]Ark. Stat. Ann., §81–1302.
[9]Id. Acknowledged illegitimate children of a spouse of a deceased employee are also entitled to benefits.
[10]Stephens & Stephens v. Logan, 260 Ark. 78, 538 S.W.2d 516 (1976). See also Holland Constr. Co. v. Sullivan, 220 Ark. 895, 251 S.W.2d 120 (1952).
[11]Ark. Stat. Ann., § 41–1811.
[12]Id., § 41–1806.

A variety of sexual activities between unmarried persons, not classified as rape, is also denounced. One commits "carnal abuse in the first degree" if, being eighteen years or older, he engages in sex or deviate sexual activity with another not his spouse who is less than fourteen years old.[13] Such conduct is punishable to a lesser extent if the other participant is incapable of consent by reason of mental incapacity.[14] Sex or deviate sexual activity with another person not a spouse is separately proscribed,[15] if the other is less than sixteen years old. Reasonable mistake as to the age of the other participant can be a defense to some of these charges,[16] but the actor can always be convicted of another offense based on the age the victim was believed to be.

Consensual deviate sexual activity, as such, is not denounced as criminal. It is the absence of effective consent, rather than the act itself, that constitutes the gravaman of this offense.[17]

Abortion

Abortion, unless to save the mother's life, is proscribed, as is advertising means of producing abortion, or induction of abortion.[18] The statute, however, forbids abortion unless performed by a licensed physician where there is substantial risk to the life or health of the mother, or where the child is substantially likely to have some grave defect, or pregnancy resulted from rape or incest.[19] In the case of a minor, parental consent is required, and if the woman is married, that of her husband is required.[20] These latter provisions are of dubious constitutionality.[21]

---

[13]Id., § 41-1804.
[14]Id., § 41-1805.
[15]Id., § 41-1807.
[16]Id., § 41-1802.
[17]See commentary to Ark. Stat. Ann., § 41-1803, wherein it is pointed out that deviate sexual activity is now punishable in nonconsensual situations only. However, § 41-1811 prohibits deviate sex acts in public and § 41-2914 forbids lingering in a public place with the purpose of engaging in deviate sex.
[18]Ark. Stat. Ann., §§ 41-2551 to 41-2554.
[19]Id., §§ 41-2551 to 41-2554.
[20]Id., § 41-2555. See also §§ 41-2556 to 41-2560. Generally, see May v. State, 254 Ark. 194, 492 S.W.2d 888 (1973), cert. den. 414 U.S. 1024, 38 L. Ed. 2d 315, 94 Sup. Ct. 448 (1973).
[21]See section 2.19, herein.

Status of children

For purposes of intestate succession, a marriage of the biological parents, or a void attempted marriage, qualifies an illegitimate child to inherit from his father.[22] The statutes make detailed provision for the establishment of the paternity of such a child.[23] For the purposes of the statute which requires a jury trial for actions at law for the recovery of money, unless waived, a proceeding to establish paternity is essentially a jury proceeding.[24] Although brought in the name of the state, a paternity action is a civil proceeding.[25] Indemnity and protection of the authorities against the burden of supporting an illegitimate child, and not punishment of the father, are the aims of such an action.[26]

As to custody, an agreement on the part of the mother to permit another to raise the child, without any statutory authority, is freely revocable.[27] A fortiori this is so where the mother is a minor and can disaffirm at any time before reaching majority.[28]

In addition to provisions for legitimation, inter alia by subsequent marriage of the parents,[29] statutes provide for the issuance of new birth certificates following adoption, legitimation, and establishment of paternity. A change of the child's name is authorized.[30]

---

[22] Ark. Stat. Ann., § 61–141. Absent such marriage and recognition, a father cannot inherit from his illegitimate child. See Wright, New Arkansas Inheritance Laws: A Step into the Present with an Eye to the Future, 23 Ark. L. Rev. 313 (1969); Trimble v. Gordon: Expanding the Illegitimate's Right to Inherit, 32 Ark. L. Rev. 120 (1978).
[23] Ark. Stat. Ann., § 34–702 et seq. As to the admission of blood tests, see §§ 34–705.1 to 34–705.3. See also Walker, Legitimacy and Paternity, 14 Ark. L. Rev. 55 (1959–60).
[24] Waddell v. State ex rel. Meeks, 235 Ark. 293, 357 S.W.2d 651, 94 A.L.R.2d 1126 (1962).
[25] Swaim v. State, 184 Ark. 1107, 44 S.W.2d 1098 (1932).
[26] Chambers v. State, 45 Ark. 56 (1886). See Constitutional Law: Defining the Rights of the Father of an Illegitimate Child, 32 Ark. L. Rev. 178 (1978).
[27] See section 3.6, herein.
[28] Rainer v. Rowlett, 255 Ark. 794, 502 S.W.2d 617 (1973).
[29] Ark. Stat. Ann., § 61–141.
[30] Id., § 82–519.

Property rights of cohabitants

Arkansas is not a community property state.[31]

The traditional reluctance of the Arkansas courts to adjust the equities between unmarried cohabitants, even if one or both acted in the good faith belief in a marriage,[32] is not inflexible. In Mitchell v. Fish,[33] there was no pretense of a marriage. The woman had abandoned her husband to live with the man until she had obtained a divorce. They agreed that she was to manage their affairs as a partnership, sharing the profits and losses. When they sold their assets and agreed on a division of the proceeds, the woman sued for an accounting. The court took the view that such a profit-sharing agreement was collateral to, and not contaminated by, the original contract. In other words, though the partnership itself may have been illegal as based on an immoral consideration, that was no concern of the courts because it had already been executed, and the agreement, after the assets had been sold, did not have any taint of immorality. The same thinking finds articulation in Karoley v. Reid.[34] There, the relationship was illicit in its inception. But a contract entered into when the parties decided to separate, that the man would take the property accumulated in consideration of his promise to pay the woman an allowance for the rest of her life, was held enforceable. One writer suggests that, if the courts of Arkansas can thus far overlook the initial immorality of the relationship, it ought not to be a gargantuan task to persuade them that the innocent victim of a voidable marriage merits a degree of protection.[35]

6.5. California

Common-law marriage cannot be contracted in California.[36]

---

[31] Id., § 55–401 et seq.
[32] See Bruno v. Bruno, 221 Ark. 759, 256 S.W.2d 341 (1953); Cooper v. McCoy, 116 Ark. 501, 173 S.W. 412 (1915).
[33] 97 Ark. 444, 134 S.W. 940 (1911).
[34] 223 Ark. 737, 269 S.W.2d 322 (1954).
[35] Effect of Void and Voidable Marriages in Arkansas, 10 Ark. L. Rev. 188 (1956).
[36] Cal. Civ. Code, § 4100.

Schoolteachers

Sexual immorality as such is no ground for termination of a public schoolteacher.[37] If the conduct involves criminal misconduct, however, it can afford grounds for termination on the basis of unfitness to teach.[38]

Adoption

Any adult may adopt any unmarried minor. There are restrictions as to the adoption of an adult or married minor.[39] With some qualifications in the case of stepparents, close relatives and the like, the person adopting should be at least ten years older than the person to be adopted.[40]

In addition to the consent of the biological parents (unless parental rights have been terminated), the consent of the child is required if over the age of twelve.[41] When parental rights are terminated, or the child has been relinquished for adoption, consent of the appropriate state department or of a licensed adoption agency ordinarily[42] is a prerequisite.[43]

To discourage those who would acquire an infant from the "black" or "gray" market,[44] it is forbidden to pay or receive money for the placement of, or consent to the adoption of, a child.[45]

Discrimination in housing

A regulation prohibiting low-income public housing tenants from living with anyone of the opposite sex to whom a tenant is

---

[37]See Morrison v. State Bd. of Education, 1 Cal. 3d 214, 82 Cal. Rptr. 175, 461 P.2d 375 (1969) (homosexual).

[38]See Board of Education of Long Beach Unified School Dist. of Los Angeles County v. Jack M., 19 Cal. 3d 691, 139 Cal. Rptr. 700, 566 P.2d 602 (1977) (soliciting in public restroom); Pettit v. State Bd. of Education, 10 Cal. 3d 29, 109 Cal. Rptr. 665, 513 P.2d 889, 78 A.L.R.3d 1 (1973). See also Siniscalco, Homosexual Discrimination in Employment, 16 Santa Clara L. Rev. 495 (1976); Note, Unfitness to Teach: Credential Revocation and Dismissal for Sexual Conduct, 61 Calif. L. Rev. 1442 (1973).

[39]Generally, as to adoptions, see Cal. Civ. Code, § 221 et seq.
[40]Id., § 222.
[41]Id., § 225.
[42]Id., § 224n.
[43]Id., §§ 224m, 224n, 226.3.
[44]Discussed in section 2.9, herein.
[45]Cal. Penal Code, §§ 266b, 273.

unrelated (which amounted to a total ban on unmarried cohabiting adults) has been held to be an invalid infringement of the right of privacy.[46] As worded, it could have operated to prevent a cohabitant from living with his or her own children if someone of the opposite sex lived in the same house.[47]

Workers' compensation death benefits

The California Labor Code invests the official responsible for the allocation of benefits in respect of a decedent with a very wide discretion; he has been held entitled to award all benefits to dependent children of a woman with whom the worker was living at the time of his death, even if he has a surviving spouse presumptively wholly dependent on him.[48] Though a putative wife can qualify for benefits,[49] an unmarried cohabitant does not.[50] It is not inconceivable, however, that today, on a showing of total dependency predicated on a cohabitation contract of a Marvin type, the responsible state official might exercise his discretion in favor of a surviving cohabitant, especially if there are no other legal dependents of the decedent.

Recovery for wrongful death

Since a parent can recover for damage tortiously caused to an illegitimate child, the right to recover for wrongful causing of death cannot be disputed. The illegitimate, too, can recover for the wrongful death of a parent.[51] An unmarried cohabitant does not qualify to sue under the statute.[52]

---

[46] Atkisson v. Kern County Housing Authority, 59 Cal. App. 3d 89, 130 Cal. Rptr. 375 (1976).
[47] Id.
[48] See Perry v. Industrial Accident Comm., 176 Cal. 706, 169 Pac. 353 (1917).
[49] Brennfleck v. Workmen's Compensation Appeals Bd., 265 Cal. 2d 738, 71 Cal. Rptr. 525 (1968).
[50] Taylor v. Industrial Accident Comm., 131 Cal. App. 468, 21 P.2d 619 (1933).
[51] Cal. Civ. Proc. Code, § 376. Juarez v. System Leasing Corp., 15 Cal. App. 3d 730, 93 Cal. Rptr. 411 (1971) (recovery permitted independently of whether child is qualified to inherit on intestacy).
[52] Vogel v. Pan American Airways, Inc., 450 F. Supp. 224 (S.D. N.Y., 1978) (applying California law).

Abortion, sterilization, and contraception

Therapeutic abortions have long been permissible where reasonably necessary to preserve the life or health of the mother. Prior to the rulings of the Supreme Court of the United States[53] in this matter, the need for parental consent in the case of a minor had been dispensed with.[54] Voluntary sterilization, however, cannot be performed without the consent of those properly concerned.[55]

The federal statute designed to prevent the use of the mails for the corruption of public morals,[56] and the provision declaring unsolicited advertisement of matter intended for preventing conception to be nonmailable matter,[57] have been ruled unconstitutional if construed to apply to persons who furnish or seek birth control information without having any commercial interest therein.[58]

Tort actions

The tort actions for alienation of affections, criminal conversation, seduction of a person over the age of consent, and the action for breach of promise to marry, have been abolished.[59]

Effect of cohabitation on right to alimony

Except as otherwise agreed to by the parties in writing, there is a rebuttable presumption, affecting the burden of proof, of decreased need for support when the recipient is cohabiting with a

---

[53]Discussed in section 2.19, herein.

[54]As to criminal abortion, see Cal. Penal Code, § 274 et seq. See also Cal. Health & Safety Code, § 25950 et seq.; Cal. Civ. Code, § 34.5; Ballard v. Anderson, 4 Cal. 3d 873, 95 Cal. Rptr. 1, 484 P.2d 1345, 42 A.L.R.3d 1392 (1971); Butler, Right to Medicaid Payment for Abortion, 28 Hastings L. J. 931 (1977).

[55]Jessin v. County of Shasta, 274 Cal. App. 2d 737, 79 Cal. Rptr. 359, 35 A.L.R.3d 1433 (1969).

[56]18 U.S.C. § 1461.

[57]39 U.S.C. § 3001.

[58]Associated Students for University of California v. Attorney General of United States, 368 F. Supp. 11 (C.D. Cal., 1973), wherein the court stated that to so construe the statute would be an infringement on free speech and right to privacy and personal choice in matters of sex and family planning.

[59]Cal. Civ. Code, § 43.5. A fraudulent promise to marry or to cohabit after marriage is also not actionable. Id., § 43.4.

person of the opposite sex.[60] On such a finding of changed circumstances the court may modify the payment of support.[61] In reducing an award of spousal support from $500 to $10 a month, a court has noted that, under this statute, a male and a female, each divorced and each receiving spousal support, would be free to cohabit, publicly or secretly, and yet continue to receive spousal support *if* they are able to overcome the presumption of decreased need.[62] It also suggests that the legislature does not respect the fiction that sex outside of marriage has no value as legal consideration, but it made no attempt to place a money value on the woman's sexual favors. It also observed that, while a cohabitant is free to make a gift of such favors, she cannot bring this value into the picture as affecting the question of whether her need for alimony has decreased.[63]

Possible criminal liability

Willful infliction of corporal injury on a cohabitant by the other is felony, and a holding-out as husband and wife is not necessary to constitute cohabitation for this purpose.[64] Marriage prior to indictment bars a prosecution for seduction under promise of marriage.[65] Deviate sexual behavior between consenting adults is no longer criminal.[66] Incest,[67] bigamy[68] and knowingly marrying the spouse of another[69] are punishable. Of relatively recent origin is the crime of abduction to live in illicit relations.[70]

The age of consent for statutory rape is eighteen.[71] The decision

---

[60] Id., § 4801.5(a).
[61] Id.
[62] In re Marriage of Leib, 80 Cal. App. 3d 629, 145 Cal. Rptr. 763 (1978).
[63] Id.
[64] Cal. Penal Code, § 273.5. See Truninger, Marital Violence: The Legal Solutions, 23 Hastings L. J. 259 (1971).
[65] Cal. Penal Code, §§ 268, 269.
[66] See id., §§ 286, 288a (unless victim is in prison. Id., § 286(e)). See also Rape and Rape Laws: Sexism in Society and Law, 61 Calif. L. Rev. 919 (1973); Sexual Freedom for Consenting Adults—Why Not?, 2 Pacific L. J. 206 (1971); Extending the Right to Sexual Privacy, 2 West. St. U. L. Rev. 281 (1975).
[67] Cal. Penal Code, § 285.
[68] Id., §§ 281, 283.
[69] Id., § 284.
[70] Id., § 266b.
[71] Id., § 261.5.

in People v. Hernandez,[72] recognizing good faith mistake as to age as a defense, does not convert the various statutes prohibiting sexual misconduct with persons below the age of consent into "specific intent" crimes.[73]

Status of children

Every illegitimate child is heir of the mother.[74] To qualify for succession on the father's death intestate, the statute requires at least that the decedent have acknowledged his paternity.[75] An adjudication of paternity has been held not to qualify a child for heirship where the putative father consistently disavowed paternity;[76] however, in the light of Trimble v. Gordon,[77] such a holding may well be subject to reconsideration.

The Uniform Parentage Act[78] has been substantially enacted in California.[79] Blood tests, in line with the guidelines furnished by the Uniform Act on Blood Tests,[80] are admissible. There is provision for a new birth certificate when paternity is judicially established,[81] as also for an adjudication of paternity when defendant, in an action for support, denies paternity.[82] It is procedurally possible for an alleged father himself to initiate proceedings to establish that he is not the father.[83] The Uniform Parentage

---

[72]61 Cal. 2d 529, 39 Cal. Rptr. 361, 393 P.2d 673, 8 A.L.R.3d 1092 (1964).
[73]People v. Atchison, 69 Cal. App. 3d 859, 138 Cal. Rptr. 393 (1977).
[74]Cal. Prob. Code, § 255.
[75]Id.
[76]In re Estate of Ginochio, 43 Cal. App. 3d 412, 117 Cal. Rptr. 565 (1974).
[77]430 U. S. 762, 52 L. Ed. 2d 31, 97 Sup. Ct. 1459 (1977), discussed at section 3.3, herein.
[78]Cal. Civ. Code, § 7000 et seq.
[79]See Note, Uniform Parentage Act: What It Will Mean for the Putative Father in California, 28 Hastings L. J. 191 (1976).
[80]See Notes, California's Conclusive Presumption of Legitimacy: Jackson v. Jackson and Evidence Code Section 621, 19 Hastings L. J. 963 (1968); California's Conclusive Presumption of Legitimacy—Its Legal Effect and Its Questionable Constitutionality, 35 So. Calif. L. Rev. 437 (1962). See also California's Tangled Web: Blood Tests and the Conclusive Presumption of Legitimacy, 20 Stan. L. Rev. 754 (1968).
[81]Cal. Health & Safety Code, §10450.
[82]Cal. Civ. Proc. Code, § 1695, which ensures all parties their day in court. For a situation where a minor, not represented in paternity proceedings, had the order vacated, see Jeffrey S., II v. Jeffrey S., 76 Cal. App. 3d 65, 142 Cal. Rptr. 625 (1977).
[83]See Cal. Civ. Code, § 7006 et seq.

Act is supplemented by a variety of other code provisions controlling the rights of a putative father in respect to the child;[84] his right to notice and a hearing in these matters is well ensured.

Property rights of cohabitants

When a marriage is found to be void or voidable, and the court finds that either or both parties believed that it was valid, the court is required to accord to each party the status of a putative spouse. The property is divided as if it had been community property.[85] As such, on dissolution of the union, it would be divided equally.[86] On death intestate, it is possible, there being no other qualifiers, for the survivor to take the entire estate.[87]

Applying these rules mechanically, the result would be that, on the dissolution of a putative marriage (whether or not one of the parties is a conscious bigamist), the property accumulations acquired during the relationship would be divided equally between the putative spouses. On its dissolution by death intestate, the survivor, even if a bigamist, could take the entire estate. However, these rules are not designed to cope with the extraordinary circumstance of purposeful bigamy at the expense of two innocent parties. In a 1974 case, a court affirmed an equal division between the two innocent "spouses" of the assets accumulated during the active phase of the bigamy.[88] It has been well illustrated that the problems which can be presented by this legislative recognition of the bigamist as a putative spouse are manifold in their ramifications.[89]

---

[84] See Custody Rights of Unwed Father, 4 Pacific L. J. 922 (1973); Recent Trends in California Law Concerning the Best Interests of the Child, 1 Pepperdine L. Rev. 89 (1973); Plight of the Putative Father in California Child Custody Proceedings: A Problem of Equal Protection, 6 U.C.D. L. Rev. 1 (1973); Legitimation: The Liberal Judicial Trend in California, 19 Hastings L. J. 232 (1967); Putative Father—The Evolving Constitutional Concepts of Due Process and Equal Protection, 2 West. St. U. L. Rev. 261 (1975).

[85] Cal. Civ. Code, §4452.

[86] Id., § 4800.

[87] Cal. Prob. Code, §§ 201, 220 et seq.

[88] In re Estate of Vargas, 36 Cal. App. 3d 714, 111 Cal. Rptr. 779, 81 A.L.R.3d 1 (1974).

[89] See Laughran and Laughran, Property and Inheritance Rights of Putative Spouses in California: Selected Problems and Suggested Solutions, 11 Loyola U. L. Rev. (L.A.) 45 (1977); Annotation, Rights in decedent's estate as between lawful and putative spouses, 81 A.L.R.3d 6 (1977).

6.5 UNMARRIED COUPLES AND THE LAW

For this reason it is, to say the least, improbable that the courts will apply the statutory provisions controlling the adjustment of property rights between putative spouses to the situation where neither of the parties had any belief in the existence of a valid marriage.[90] In Marvin v. Marvin,[91] where the Supreme Court of California recognized the validity of express contracts between nonmarital partners, it concluded that the statutory provisions above considered do not control the distribution of property acquired during a nonmarital relationship.

In that landmark decision, the court cited plentiful California authority to support an adjustment of the property rights of the cohabitants, even absent express agreement, via the various traditional theories of partnership, joint ventures, agreements to pool earnings, resulting or constructive trusts, etc.[92] Just how is the adjustment to be effected?

It can be predicted that the suggestion of the commissioners who framed the Uniform Marriage and Divorce Act[93] affords the only possible guidelines. The suggestion of the optional provision of that Uniform Act, designed to control where the respective rights of legal and of putative spouses fall for adjudication, is that property, maintenance and support rights be apportioned as appropriate in the circumstances and in the interests of justice.

The burden which such a doctrine seems to place on the courts is not as heavy as would at first appear. Where the theory underlying the distribution rests on an analogy of partnership, joint venture or an agreement to pool earnings, the distribution would, absent other considerations, be an equal division of the assets. Where the theory is one of a resulting trust, proof of the contributions which each made toward the acquisition of assets to which

---

[90]See In re Marriage of Baragry, 73 Cal. App. 3d 444, 140 Cal. Rptr. 779 (1977), wherein a married man cohabited with woman for four years, during which he still vacationed with his wife, ate dinner at her home, and filed joint returns. The court held that property accumulated during those four years fell into the community. "One who enjoys the benefit of a polygamous lifestyle must be prepared to accept its accompanying financial burdens."

[91]18 Cal. 3d 660, 134 Cal. Rptr. 815, 557 P.2d 106 (1976), discussed also in sections 1.1, 4.10, herein.

[92]Discussed in Chapter 4, herein. See Willemsen, Justice Tobriner and the Tolerance of Evolving Lifestyles: Adapting the Law to Social Change, 29 Hastings L. J. 73 (1977).

[93]See section 1.6, herein.

one alone took title should not present insuperable difficulties. Where the theory is one of a constructive trust, the title holder would naturally hold title for the partner who was the reposant of confidence or the victim of fraud. Where, however, the theory underlying the distribution is one of contract implied in fact, the "shared expectations" may indeed present problems. As often as not, no expectations were "shared." Perhaps here the courts could have recourse to an objective test: what can the partners reasonably be deemed to have expected as to the division of these accumulations in the event of a termination of their relationship? Similarly, where the underlying theory is one of restitutionary relief in the nature of quasi-contract, the question, if any, as to the extent the fair value of one partner's contribution exceeds the fair value of that of the other can only be answered by recourse to objective evaluations.

6.6. Colorado

Recognizing that marriage, although it has contractual implications, is a status, the courts of Colorado do not permit an attack on the exercise of legislative power over the relationship based on the constitutional prohibition of the impairment of contracts.[94] The state has adopted, with some variations, the Uniform Marriage Act.[95]

Common-law marriage is recognized.[96] Whether a common-law marriage exists is a question of fact.[97] The fact that the parties were mistaken as to the law, one of the parties believing that a ceremony was necessary to a valid marriage, does not affect its validity if the prerequisites of a common-law marriage are present.[98] Further, a general reputation in the community of the relationship of husband and wife is not a sine qua non of such a marriage.[99] The Colorado courts have also held that a continued

---

[94]In re Marriage of Franks, —— Colo. ——, 542 P.2d 845 (1975).
[95]Colo. Rev. Stat., §§ 14–2–101 to 14–2–113.
[96]See Taylor v. Taylor, 10 Colo. App. 303, 50 Pac. 1049 (1897); In re Peters' Estate, 73 Colo. 271, 215 Pac. 128, 33 A.L.R. 24 (1923).
[97]Valencia v. Northland Ins. Co., —— Colo. App. ——, 514 P.2d 789 (1973) (dispute involving insurance policy covering insured and "wife" against injury by uninsured motorist).
[98]See Moffat Coal Co. v. Industrial Comm., 108 Colo. 388, 118 P.2d 769 (1941).
[99]In re Peters' Estate, 73 Colo. 271, 215 Pac. 128, 33 A.L.R. 24 (1923).

cohabitation after discovery and removal of an impediment to a marriage is sufficient for a common-law marriage.[1]

In line with the Uniform Marriage Act, the status of a putative spouse receives recognition.[2] The children of such a union are legitimate, as are the children of a prohibited marriage,[3] and the party who mistakenly believes in the existence of a valid marriage acquires the rights of a legal spouse, including a right, where the law allows it, to maintenance following a termination of the status. If there is a legal spouse, or there is a contest between two or more putative spouses, the Colorado legislature is content to allow their respective rights to be apportioned in the interest of justice.[4]

Colorado is not a community property state.[5] However, a Disposition of Community Property Rights at Death Act is aimed to ensure that, as to personal property, the rights of a surviving spouse who falls under the laws of a community property state are preserved.[6] On the death of such a person, one-half of the property becomes the property of the surviving spouse. It is not subject to testamentary disposition by the decedent or to distribution as on intestacy.[7] The rights of a purchaser for value, or of a lender taking a security interest in such property, either from the surviving spouse or from the representatives or heirs of the decedent spouse, are, however, preserved.[8]

Schoolteachers

Regarding the impact of the unwed status on schoolteachers,[9] a statute[10] confers on the Board of Education specific powers, and provides that the practices of employment, promotion and dismissal shall be unaffected by an employee's religious beliefs, marital status, and the like.

---

[1]Davis v. People, 83 Colo. 295, 264 Pac. 658 (1928).
[2]Colo. Rev. Stat., § 14–2–111.
[3]Id., § 14–2–110.
[4]Id., § 14–2–111.
[5]Id., § 14–2–201 et seq.
[6]Id., § 15–20–101 et seq.
[7]Id., § 15–20–104.
[8]Id., § 15–20–107.
[9]Discussed in section 2.3, herein.
[10]Colo. Rev. Stat., § 22–32–110(1)(k).

Recovery of gift made on promise of marriage

The statute barring actions for breach of promise of marriage[11] does not operate to preclude recovery, on common-law principles, of a conditional gift when the recipient breaches the promise of marriage.[12]

Adoption

In Colorado, as in most states,[13] any person, including a minor on the approval of the appropriate court, may petition to adopt a child.[14] One having a living spouse from whom he is not legally separated must join the spouse in his petition, unless such spouse is a natural parent of the child or has previously adopted it.[15]

Workers' compensation death benefits

The controlling statute includes, as a dependent of a deceased workman, his wife, unless they are separated, and his minor children.[16] A mere extramarital cohabitant does not so qualify.[17] An illegitimate child, if acknowledged and in fact dependent on the decedent, does so qualify.[18]

Possible criminal liability

Colorado's consensual sodomy laws have been repealed;[19] as has the criminal action for seduction.[20] It is a crime (akin to rape by fraud) to have sexual relations with a victim who erroneously

---

[11]Id., §§ 13-20-202, 13-20-203.
[12]Marriage of Heinzman, —— Colo. App. ——, 579 P.2d 638 (1977).
[13]See section 2.9, herein.
[14]Colo. Rev. Stat., § 19-4-106.
[15]Id. See Gilliam, Adoption of Children in Colorado, 37 Dicta 100 (1960). As to the preconditions for adoption, see Colo. Rev. Stat., § 19-4-107. As to a provision enabling the adoption of adults solely to acquire an heir at law, see § 14-1-101.
[16]Colo. Rev. Stat., § 8-50-109.
[17]Employers Mut. Liability Ins. Co. v. Industrial Comm., 124 Colo. 68, 234 P.2d 901 (1951).
[18]Colo. Rev. Stat., § 8-50-109.
[19]See Hefner, Legal Enforcement of Morality, Symposium on Sex and the Law in Contemporary Perspective, 40 U. Colo. L. Rev. 178 (1968).
[20]Colo. Rev. Stat., § 13-20-202.

believes the actor to be his or her spouse;[21] or if, at the time of the act, the victim is less than eighteen years of age and the actor is the victim's guardian or is responsible for the general supervision of the victim's welfare.[22] As to other variations of sexual assault involving victims under the age of eighteen, it would suffice to say that an age differential between the actor and the victim can affect the gravity of the offense.

Colorado exempts from the operation of its Equal Rights Amendment[23] only those cases in which classification of the sexes is based on physiological differences. Hence, a rape statute punishing only male offenders is not unconstitutional. The amendment, the court reasoned in People v. Salinas,[24] "prohibits unequal treatment based exclusively on the circumstance of sex, social stereotypes connected with gender, and culturally induced dissimilarities. However, it does not prohibit differential treatment among the sexes when, as here, that treatment is reasonably and genuinely based on physical characteristics unique to just one sex. ... In such a case, the sexes are not similarly situated and thus, equal treatment is not required."[25]

Abortion

The constitutional right, even of a minor under the age of eighteen, to terminate a pregnancy through abortion,[26] particularly where she is away from home and has made an informed decision in the matter, receives recognition.[27] Many provisions of the Colorado abortion statutes[28] have been ruled unconstitutional.[29]

---

[21]Id., § 18-3-403(d). As to bigamy, see § 18-6-201; cohabitation as a spouse with a bigamist, § 18-6-202; incest, §§ 18-6-301, 18-6-302; adultery, § 18-6-501.
[22]Colo. Rev. Stat., § 18-3-407(e).
[23]Colo. Const. Art. 2, § 29.
[24]—— Colo. ——, 551 P.2d 703 (1976).
[25]Id., 551 P.2d at 706.
[26]Colo. Rev. Stat., § 18-6-101(1).
[27]Foe v. Vanderhoof, 389 F. Supp. 947 (D. Colo., 1975).
[28]Colo. Rev. Stat., § 18-6-101 et seq.
[29]People v. Norton, 181 Colo. 47, 507 P.2d 862 (1973).

Status of children

The statute which defines a "child" for the purposes of intestate succession[30] clearly indicates a legislative intent to afford adopted children equal inheritance rights with natural children.[31] It no longer permits the adopted child to take by intestate succession from his natural parent; it does not, however, provide that the child is no longer a child of, nor a lineal descendant of, its natural parent.[32] Adoption by the spouse of a natural parent has no effect on the relationship between the child and that natural parent.

In the case of an illegitimate child, it is a child of the mother. It is also a child of the father if (1) the natural parents have participated in a marriage ceremony before or after the birth of the child, even though the attempted marriage is void, or (2) the paternity is established by an adjudication before the death of the father or is established thereafter by a preponderance of the evidence; except that paternity so established is ineffective to qualify the father or his kindred to inherit from or through the child unless the father has openly treated the child as his, and has not refused to support the child.[33]

The Levy and Glona decisions handed down by the Supreme Court of the United States in 1968[34] which go far to eliminate any distinction between legitimate and illegitimate children, has had repercussions in Colorado. Thus, a statute which made provision for a fixed assessment of damages to cover the support of an illegitimate child was, in Munn v. Munn,[35] held to constitute an unconstitutional denial both to the father and to the child of equal protection, since support decrees in the case of a legitimate child are always modifiable with a change in the financial situation of

---

[30] Colo. Rev. Stat., § 15–11–109(a).
[31] See Quintrall v. Goldsmith, 134 Colo. 410, 306 P.2d 246 (1957).
[32] People v. Estate of Murphy, 29 Colo. App. 195, 481 P.2d 420 (1971).
[33] Colo. Rev. Stat., § 15–11–109(b). See Wright v. Wusowatcky, 147 Colo. 317, 363 P.2d 1046 (1961).
[34] Levy v. Louisiana, 391 U.S. 68, 20 L. Ed. 2d 436, 88 Sup. Ct. 1509 (1968), reh. den. 393 U.S. 898, 21 L. Ed. 2d 185, 89 Sup. Ct. 65 (1968) and Glona v. American Guarantee & Liability Ins. Co., 391 U.S. 73, 20 L. Ed. 2d 441, 88 Sup. Ct. 1515 (1968), reh. den. 393 U.S. 898, 21 L. Ed. 2d 185, 89 Sup. Ct. 66 (1968), discussed in sections 3.2, 3.3, herein.
[35] 168 Colo. 76, 450 P.2d 68 (1969).

6.6 UNMARRIED COUPLES AND THE LAW

the father, which would not be the case with an award of a fixed money payment.

Support and custody

Colorado has not enacted the Uniform Civil Liability for Support Act, whereunder support obligations can be enforced long after the time has gone by for an action to establish paternity.[36] Hence, even though proceedings to enforce support obligations can be instituted at any time prior to the eighteenth birthday of the child,[37] the issue of paternity cannot be adjudicated as an adjunct of support proceedings.[38] An argument that different periods control the time for suing to establish paternity and the time to enforce support obligations, and that this violates equal protection, has been rejected.[39] It may well be that the legislature has consciously determined that, after the five-year period from the birth of the child has elapsed without any proceedings to establish paternity or written acknowledgment of paternity or any support furnished,[40] it would impose an unfair burden on an alleged father to have to disprove his paternity. Nonsupport of illegitimates, once the obligation is established, is a crime.[41]

The state has adopted the Uniform Child Custody Jurisdiction Act.[42] Noteworthy is a provision that custody cannot be terminated without notice and an opportunity to be heard to any parent

---

[36] See section 3.5, note 12, herein.

[37] Colo. Rev. Stat., § 19-7-101.

[38] In re People in Interest of D.R.B., 30 Colo. App. 603, 498 P.2d 1166 (1972), affd. 180 Colo. 439, 507 P.2d 468 (1973).

[39] In re People in Interest of L.B., 179 Colo. 11, 498 P.2d 1157 (1972), appeal dismissed 410 U.S. 976, 36 L. Ed. 2d 173, 93 Sup. Ct. 1497 (1973). See Enforcement of Support Duties in Colorado, 33 Rocky Mt. L. Rev. 70 (1960).

[40] As to paternity proceedings, see Colo. Rev. Stat., §§ 19-6-101 to 19-6-107. As to proceedings to compel support of children, see §§ 19-7-101 to 19-7-104. As to the right to blood grouping tests, see § 19-6-101(1) and Franklin v. District Court of Tenth Judicial Dist. in and for County of Pueblo, —— Colo. ——, 571 P.2d 1072 (1977).

[41] Colo. Rev. Stat., § 14-6-101.

[42] Id., §§ 14-13-101 to 14-13-126. See Bodenheimer, Rights of Children and the Crisis in Custody Litigation: Modification of Custody in and out of State, 46 U. Colo. L. Rev. 495 (1975).

(legitimate or not) whose parental rights have not been previously terminated.[43]

Property rights of cohabitants

As indicated above, on the termination of a putative marriage the courts are given wide discretion as to the distribution of the partnership accumulations, between legal and putative spouses.[44] As between two putative spouses, on a declaration of the invalidity of the marriage the courts enjoy the same discretion as that which can be exercised on the dissolution of a lawful marriage.[45] Thus, when a marriage was annulled for fraud (the fraud apparently resting in the fact that he married her for her money and not for love) a Colorado court held that, though title was taken in joint tenancy, it was proper to award all property acquired with the woman's funds to the woman. Title to land in joint tenancy was not determinative of the status as marital property.[46]

Early law, however, suggests that a contract in contemplation of sexual relations is void.[47]

6.7. Connecticut

The common-law marriage is not recognized as a way of entering the marital status in Connecticut.[48] It is not a community property state.[49] As to the effect of a change of domicile of partners to a marriage invalid in Connecticut but valid where celebrated,[50] it would seem that this state would only decline to recognize the union if it goes contrary to a strong public policy.[51]

---

[43]Colo. Rev. Stat., § 14–13–105. See People in Interest of S.S.T., —— Colo. App. ——, 553 P.2d 82 (1976).

[44]Note 4, supra and related text.

[45]In re Marriage of Blietz, —— Colo. App. ——, 538 P.2d 114 (1975). (See Colo. Rev. Stat., § 14–10–111(1)(d).)

[46]Id.

[47]See Baker v. Couch, 74 Colo. 380, 221 Pac. 1089 (1923).

[48]Hames v. Hames, 163 Conn. 588, 316 A.2d 379 (1972); State ex rel. Felson v. Allen, 129 Conn. 427, 29 A.2d 306 (1942).

[49]Conn. Gen. Stat. Ann., § 46–9 et seq.

[50]See section 1.7, herein.

[51]See Catalano v. Catalano, 148 Conn. 288, 170 A.2d 726 (1961), holding an incestuous marriage between persons so closely related as to render the marriage contrary to a strong public policy of the domicile to be invalid, even though valid where celebrated.

Housing

A Connecticut statute forbids those responsible for low-rental municipal housing projects to refuse accommodation to otherwise qualified applicants on the ground that the proposed occupants include illegitimate children.[52]

Welfare assistance

The validity of a Connecticut welfare statute which compelled an unwed mother, under pain of foregoing benefits, to disclose the name of the child's putative father and to institute paternity proceedings, came before the Supreme Court in 1977.[53] The result is inconclusive. That Court held that, in view of a new Connecticut statute which became effective the day after a federal district court had issued its opinion, and which obviously was intended to have some effect in this general area, the case would have to be remanded for clarification as to whether the State Commissioner of Social Services is free to make his own "good cause" and "best interests of the child" determinations in the absence of effective HEW regulations. (One might have thought that this was a question for the Supreme Court's own determination.)[54]

In a similar matter, the Supreme Court has held a Medicaid regulation requiring the written consent by an indigent pregnant woman and prior authorization by the Department of Social Services for the funding of an abortion not to be an unconstitutional denial of equal protection.[55] The Court noted a basic difference between direct state interference with a protected activity[56] and

---

[52]Conn. Gen. Stat. Ann., § 8–45. Housing problems of unmarried partners are discussed in section 2.7, herein.

[53]Maher v. Doe, 432 U.S. 526, 53 L. Ed. 2d 534, 97 Sup. Ct. 2474 (1977). Generally, as to welfare benefits and the unmarried mother, see section 2.11, herein.

[54]In Doe v. Shapiro, 302 F. Supp. 761 (D. Conn., 1969), appeal dismissed 396 U.S. 488, 90 Sup. Ct. 641 (1970), reh. den. 397 U.S. 970, 90 Sup. Ct. 991 (1970), a similar regulation was held not invalid as an invidious distinction based on illegitimacy, but invalid in that it imposed a condition of eligibility for federal aid to families with dependent children which was not required by the Social Security Act, under which a child is eligible if he is both needy and dependent.

[55]Maher v. Roe, 432 U.S. 464, 53 L. Ed. 2d 484, 97 Sup. Ct. 2376 (1977), holding that financial need alone does not indicate a suspect class for equal protection purposes.

[56]As to state interference with the freedom to have an abortion, see section 2.19, herein.

state encouragement of an alternative activity consonant with legislative policy. The state interest in encouraging normal childbirth exceeds the "minimal level of scrutiny" (that the classification must have a rational basis), it not being unreasonable for a state to insist on a showing of medical necessity to ensure that its money is being spent only for authorized purposes.

Adoption

There is no objection to an unmarried couple adopting a child, but the "gray market" appears to be nonexistent.[57] Since, unless good reason is shown, the consent of both spouses seeking to adopt is required,[58] a court hearing the petition would almost surely require both partners to join in such a petition. The consent of the mother, and of the putative father if his parental rights have not been terminated, must be obtained.[59]

Workers' compensation death benefits

An extramarital cohabitant does not qualify as the wife of a decedent workman.[60] Neither do his illegitimate children (at least prior to Weber v. Aetna Casualty and Surety Company)[61] unless he is regularly contributing to their support.[62]

Sexual freedom

From the seed of a Connecticut statute imposing punishment on persons using contraceptives,[63] sprung the multitudinous doctrines wherein the Supreme Court (and, no doubt, lower courts throughout the country) have aided the cause of those who do not wish to marry by upholding statutory interference with their conduct as invasions of their rights to privacy.[64]

---

[57]If the applicant is not related to the minor, the child must have been placed for adoption by an approved agency. Conn. Gen. Stat. Ann., § 45–63.
[58]Conn. Gen. Stat. Ann., § 45–62.
[59]Id., § 45–61. If the child is fourteen or over, its consent is also required.
[60]Wheat v. Red Star Express Lines, 156 Conn. 245, 240 A.2d 859 (1968).
[61]See section 3.2, herein.
[62]Wheat v. Red Star Express Lines, 156 Conn. 245, 240 A.2d 859 (1968).
[63]See section 2.19, herein.
[64]Griswold v. Connecticut, 381 U.S. 479, 14 L. Ed. 2d 510, 85 Sup. Ct. 1678 (1965). As to attempted abortions by nonphysicians, see Connecticut v. Menillo, 423 U.S. 9, 46 L. Ed. 2d 152, 96 Sup. Ct. 170 (1975).

Effect of cohabitation on right to alimony

As indicated earlier,[65] the fact that a divorcee is cohabiting with a new lover does not ordinarily relieve her ex-husband of his obligations under a divorce decree.[66]

Possible criminal liability

The trend of Connecticut's penal legislation has been to eliminate from criminality sexual practices that do not involve force, adult corruption of the young, or public offenses.[67] Mistake of fact is a good defense to a charge of bigamy.[68] The legislature has explicitly provided that, in prosecutions for sexual offenses, proof that the defendant and the alleged victim were at the time living together by mutual consent in a relationship of cohabitation is a defense.[69] The statutes criminalizing adultery, fornication, cohabitation and seduction were repealed in 1971.

Sodomy has had a checkered history in Connecticut. Repealed as a crime in 1971, it was replaced by a provision that an act of deviate sexual conduct in a public place is punishable as "public indecency."[70] But a 1976 amendment to the criminal code omits this.

The only types of sexual assault with which an unwed cohabitant might ordinarily find it helpful to be aware of are where the consensual capacity of the other participant is in some way defective. For example, a crime exists when the participant is (1) under fifteen years of age, or (2) mentally defective, mentally incapacitated or physically helpless, or (3) less than eighteen years old and the actor is the victim's guardian or otherwise responsible for the general supervision of the victim's welfare.[71]

---

[65]See section 2.21, herein.
[66]McAnerney v. McAnerney, 165 Conn. 277, 334 A.2d 437 (1973).
[67]Conn. Gen. Stat. Ann., § 53a–1 et seq.
[68]Id., § 53a–190.
[69]Id., § 53a–67(c).
[70]Id., § 53a–186(2).
[71]Id., § 53a–70a. See Bard, Connecticut's Child Abuse Law, 48 Conn. B. J. 260 (1974).

Abortion

The Connecticut abortion statute[72] has been amended to conform to the right to privacy mandate of Roe v. Wade.[73] The United States Supreme Court has ruled that a statute prohibiting attempted abortion by any person is not unconstitutional as applied to an attempted abortion performed by a nonphysician.[74]

Status of children

Detailed statutory provision is made for the commitment of children to public agencies when their parents are unable to take care of them properly.[75] The mother of an illegitimate child under the age of eighteen is the sole guardian of the child.[76]

As to inheritance rights, the law provides that children born before marriage whose parents afterwards intermarry shall be deemed legitimate and inherit equally with other children. A child born out of wedlock shall inherit from his or her mother and his or her father, provided the father has been adjudicated the father by a court of competent jurisdiction, or has acknowledged under oath in writing to be the father.[77]

---

[72]Conn. Gen. Stat. Ann., §§ 53–29 to 53–31.
[73]410 U.S. 113, 35 L. Ed. 2d 147, 93 Sup. Ct. 705 (1973), reh. den. 410 U.S. 959, 35 L. Ed. 2d 694, 93 Sup. Ct. 1409 (1973). See section 2.19, herein.
As to the right of the authorities to distinguish, for the purposes of Medicaid, abortions which are voluntary and those which are medically necessary, see Lady Jane v. Maher, 420 F. Supp. 318 (D. Conn., 1976), affd. 431 U.S. 926, 53 L. Ed. 2d 242, 97 Sup. Ct. 2628 (1977).
[74]Connecticut v. Menillo, 423 U.S. 9, 46 L. Ed. 2d 152, 96 Sup. Ct. 170 (1975).
[75]Conn. Gen. Stat. Ann., § 17–61. See Soifer, Parental Autonomy, Family Rights and the Illegitimate: A Constitutional Commentary, 7 Conn. L. Rev. 1 (1974).
[76]Conn. Gen. Stat. Ann., § 45–43. See Sullivan v. Bonafonte, 172 Conn. 612, 376 A.2d 69 (1977), holding there to be no abuse of discretion in a denial of visitation rights to a putative father who had refused to marry the mother, urging an abortion, notwithstanding that he had offered a trial marriage after the child's birth, spent money for child's support and gifts at Christmas, and had visited it occasionally when a few months old, but had not developed a meaningful relationship with it.
[77]Conn. Gen. Stat. Ann., § 45–274. As to inheritance by and from adopted children, see § 45–65.

Support and custody

Detailed statutory provision is made for proceedings to establish paternity.[78] If the mother neglects to bring such an action, the welfare authorities can do so, and can compel the mother, under penalty of contempt, to divulge the identity of the putative father.[79] Paternity actions are civil, not criminal.[80] Thus, a court is not required to advise defendant as to his constitutional rights.[81] (However, if he is without counsel, it would certainly be appropriate to acquaint him of his right to refuse to take the stand.) In proceedings of this nature, unlike other actions, when a defendant fails to appear at the hearing the court may take any action it could take if he were present, without resorting to proceedings in default.[82] However, if he had no notice, actual or constructive, of the proceedings, a judgment for the plaintiff can of course be set aside.[83]

An agreement on the part of the putative father, even without an adjudication of paternity, will be enforced.[84] Since he is legally bound to do so, consideration is not required. Any presumption of legitimacy due to the mother's marriage to another at the time of the child's birth does not render such an agreement unenforceable.[85]

If the father has acknowledged paternity, he can seek judicial aid to enforce a claim to visit the child.[86] The court's decision will be controlled largely by the interests of the child itself. For example, if the friction likely to be engendered between the parents by such visits is not offset by any prospective benefit to the child, as for example where a meaningful relationship exists between father and child, the court's discretion to deny such rights is quite proper.[87]

---

[78]Conn. Gen. Stat. Ann., § 52–435a et seq.
[79]Id., § 52–440a.
[80]Robertson v. Apuzzo, 170 Conn. 367, 365 A.2d 824 (1976).
[81]Fulmore v. Deveaux, 3 Conn. Cir. 553, 220 A.2d 462 (1966).
[82]Conn. Gen. Stat. Ann., § 52–435a.
[83]Collins v. Scholz, 34 Conn. Supp. 501, 373 A.2d 200 (1976).
[84]Franklin v. Congelosi, 6 Conn. Cir. 357, 273 A.2d 291 (1970).
[85]Id.
[86]Forestiere v. Doyle, 30 Conn. Supp. 284, 310 A.2d 607 (1973) ("unclean hands" as to a collateral matter did not bar relief).
[87]See Sullivan v. Bonafonte, 172 Conn. 612, 376 A.2d 69 (1977).

No birth certificate shall contain any specific statement or reference to the illegitimacy of the child; the name of a putative father cannot be entered thereon without his written consent.[88]

Property rights of cohabitants

The state has recognized the enforceability of agreements between cohabitants as to the distribution of their accumulations on termination of the relationship. In so holding, a trial court, relying heavily on the California decision of Marvin v. Marvin[88a] for its ruling that a cause of action for some form of relief is stated, said that any other result would bar the courthouse doors to such claimants for no valid policy reason; that since the state policy imposes no criminal sanction for noncommercial sexual relations between consenting adults in private, and requires the father of a child born out of wedlock to contribute to its support and that of the caretaker mother, there is no reason not to require him to honor his agreement to share assets with the mother should they separate.[88b] The court was careful to observe that it was not according legal consequence to the extramarital relationship as such. The relationship does not confer marital status on them. The court simply recognizes the validity of any agreement they have reached and that appropriate remedies, legal as well as equitable, can be harnessed to give effect to it.

6.8. Delaware

Delaware is not a community property state.[89]

Although this state does not allow common-law marriage,[90] it does recognize as valid such marriages when contracted in states

---

[88]Conn. Gen. Stat. Ann., § 7–50. As to correction of birth certificate when parents marry, see § 19–16.

[88a]See section 4.10, herein.

[88b]Dosek v. Dosek (Docket No. 218977, Conn. Sup. Ct., Hartford-New Britain Dist., Sept. 29, 1978).

[89]The philosophy of the Married Woman's Act has led to an evolutionary departure from the common-law concept of the absolute rights and liabilities of the husband and a broadening recognition of the independent rights and liabilities of the wife. Hyland v. Southwell, 320 A.2d 767 (Del. Super., 1974).

[90]Del. Code Ann., Tit. 13, § 126.

6.8 UNMARRIED COUPLES AND THE LAW

which do so recognize their validity.[91] A provision prohibiting and avoiding a marriage between a white person and a negro or mulatto is, of course, unconstitutional.[92] Though the statute requires a ceremonial wedding,[93] and the procurement of a license,[94] marriages are not rendered invalid merely by reason of a failure to take out such license,[95] provided all other formalities are complied with. Further, the courts do give limited recognition to a presumption, readily rebuttable, of marriage arising from marital cohabitation and repute.[96] Such a presumption is rebutted by proof that no marriage ever existed between the parties, or that the cohabitation was from the beginning illicit and not of a marital nature, or that at its commencement either party had a spouse living and undivorced. If the parties separated, and one of them married a stranger, the presumption—if it really merits such a label—would not be as strong as the presumption that the second marriage is valid and not bigamous.[97]

A marriage can be annulled on the ground of fraud.[98] But the fraud must go to the very essentials of the marriage relationship; fraud as to a prior marriage and divorce does not furnish a ground for annulment under the general annulment statute.[99] Though a marriage valid by the law of the place of celebration is valid in Delaware, it does not necessarily follow that a marriage which is voidable by the law of the place of celebration is voidable by a court of Delaware. In Anonymous v. Anonymous[1] a husband sought to annul a marriage he had entered into in New York. In New York it would be a voidable marriage on proof of the wife's misrepresentations as to her marital status, but in Delaware marriage is more than a mere contract; it creates a status, and

---

[91]Cook v. Carolina Freight Carriers Corp., 299 F. Supp. 192 (D. Del., 1969).
[92]Davis v. Gately, 269 F. Supp. 996 (D. Del., 1967).
[93]Del. Code Ann., Tit. 13. §§ 125, 128. See Berdikas v. Berdikas, 54 Del. 297, 178 A.2d 468 (1962).
[94]Del. Code Ann., Tit. 13, § 119 et seq.
[95]Id., § 126. See Wilmington Trust Co. v. Hendrixson, 31 Del. 303, 114 Atl. 215 (1921).
[96]See Owens v. Bentley, 40 Del. 512, 14 A.2d 391 (1940).
[97]Id.
[98]Del. Code Ann., Tit. 13, § 1551.
[99]Saunders v. Saunders, 49 Del. 515, 120 A.2d 160 (1956).
[1]46 Del. 458, 85 A.2d 706 (1951), affd. Du Pont v. Du Pont, 47 Del. 231, 90 A.2d 468 (1952).

such misrepresentation would not furnish grounds for annulment. Hence, applying the law of the forum (because the parties were domiciled in Delaware) the court declined an annulment.

Adoption

The right of unmarried persons to adopt is conditioned on their being resident in the state at the time of filing the petition (unless the child has been placed with them for adoption). They must be over 21 years of age.[2] If the child is fourteen years of age or over, he or she ordinarily must consent.[3] If the child is illegitimate, the consent of both biological parents is required, but the consent of the male parent can be dispensed with if he disclaims paternity, or if they are not living together or married, and the appropriate welfare authorities so recommend.[4] The adoptive parent or parents do not have to be citizens.[5] Unless the adopter is a stepparent or a blood relative, the child must have been placed for adoption by an authorized agency or by the Department of Health and Social Services.[6] At least one of the prospective adopting parents ordinarily must be of the same religion as that of the natural mother, or of the religion in which she has raised the child.[7] It is not impossible to adopt a person over the age of eighteen.[8]

Workers' compensation death benefits

A spouse, and a child under the age of sixteen, are presumed to be dependents of a decedent workman.[9] As to an extramarital cohabitant, the test is dependency, which is a question of fact. One who is sustained by or relies on the decedent for his or her reasonable necessities of life qualifies for the benefits.[10]

---

[2]Del. Code Ann., Tit. 13, § 903.
[3]Id., § 907.
[4]Id., § 908.
[5]Irwin v. State Dept. of Public Welfare, 50 Del. 144, 125 A.2d 505 (1956).
[6]Del. Code Ann., Tit. 13, § 904.
[7]Id., § 911.
[8]Generally, see Del. Code Ann., Tit. 13, § 951 et seq.
[9]Del. Code Ann., Tit. 19, § 2330. See Wilson v. Hill, 45 Del. 251, 71 A.2d 425 (1950).
[10]See Koeppel v. E. I. Du Pont DeNemours, 37 Del. 369, 183 Atl. 516 (1936), affd. 39 Del. 542, 194 Atl. 847 (1937).

6.8 UNMARRIED COUPLES AND THE LAW

Tort actions

Tort actions for alienation of affections, criminal conversation, seduction, enticement and breach of contract to marry have been abolished in Delaware.[11]

Possible criminal liability

Whenever, in the definition of a sexual offense, the criminality of conduct depends on a child's being below the age of sixteen, it is no defense that the actor did not know the child's age, or reasonably believed the child to be older than sixteen. When criminality depends on the child's being below an age other than sixteen, it is a defense that the actor reasonably believed the child to be above the critical age.[12]

Further, whenever the definition of a sexual offense excludes conduct with a spouse, the exclusion is deemed to extend to persons living as man and wife, regardless of the legal status of their relationship. But when the definition excludes conduct with a spouse or conduct by a woman, this does not preclude conviction of a spouse or woman as accomplice in a sexual offense which he or she causes another person not within the exclusion to perform.[13]

A person is guilty of sexual assault when he has sexual contact with another person not his spouse, if the contact occurs with the consent of the victim, but defendant knows the victim is less than sixteen years old and defendant is at least four years older.[14] When the actor is a male, the grade of this offense is raised from misdemeanor to felony.[15] Deviate sexual intercourse with a person less than sixteen when the actor is at least four years older is also a felony.[16] For the more serious crime of rape, and other unconsented-to crimes of similar nature, knowledge that the victim mistakenly believes the parties to be married is sufficient to show want of consent.[17]

---

[11] Id., Tit. 10, § 3924.
[12] Id., Tit. 11, § 772.
[13] Id. The statute adds that, unless a contrary meaning is clearly required, the male pronoun is deemed to refer to both male and female.
[14] Del. Code Ann., Tit. 11, § 761.
[15] Id., § 762.
[16] Id.
[17] Id., § 767(4).

DELAWARE 6.8

Sodomy is restricted to situations where the other participant does not consent.[18] In denouncing incest, the statute spells out the prohibited degrees of relationship, and provides that these relationships include, as well as blood relationships without regard to legitimacy, relationships by adoption.[19]

Abortion

The provision denouncing abortion[20] is of dubious constitutionality in view of the decisions of the Supreme Court of the United States relating to this matter.[21]

Status of children

The child of a void or voidable marriage is deemed legitimate.[22]

For purposes of intestate succession, an illegitimate child, as well as being a child of its mother,[23] is a child of the father if the parents have married before or after its birth, even though the marriage is void; or if paternity is judicially established before the death of the father; but such judicial decree does not qualify the father or his kindred to inherit from or through the child unless the father has openly treated the child as his, and has not refused to support the child.[24] The intestate heir to an illegitimate child is its mother or her heirs.[25] It inherits the same rights as a legitimate in respect of the father if it has been legitimated.[26]

---

[18] Id., §§ 765, 766. Consent is absent where the coparticipant is less than sixteen years of age. Id., § 767.
[19] Id., § 771.
[20] Id., §§ 651 to 653. It was at one time held that a statute providing that a pregnant female over twelve years of age could give her own consent to abortion controlled over a therapeutic abortion statute (Del. Code Ann., Tit. 24, § 1790) which required parental consent. In re Diane, 318 A.2d 629 (Del. Ch., 1974). But Title 13, § 708 now excludes abortions from the dispensation of parental consent in respect of a minor's operations. Parental consent is thus required if she is under eighteen (Tit. 24, § 1790(f)(3)). As to the situations in which a termination of pregnancy is permitted, see id., §§ 1790 to 1793. Title 24, § 1791 immunizes those who refuse to operate for conscientious reasons.
[21] See section 2.19, herein.
[22] Del. Code Ann., Tit. 13, § 105.
[23] Id., § 1303.
[24] Id., Tit. 12, § 508.
[25] Id., Tit. 13, § 1302.
[26] Id., § 1304.

6.8 UNMARRIED COUPLES AND THE LAW

Legitimation is effected by marriage of the parents before the birth of the child, or marriage after adjudication or acknowledgement of paternity after the birth of the child, or upon written acknowledgment of paternity by both parents, or by the father if the mother is not living. Such notice must be filed in the Prothonotary's office of any county.[27]

The public policy of the state, as reflected in its statutes,[28] is that adopted children are to be considered under the law as natural children.[29] Thus, the term "issue" when used in a will includes an "adopted person" and makes such person, whatever his or her age at the time of the adoption, the child of the adoptive parent.[30]

Support and custody

As to the parental duty of support, a provision[31] sets up priorities, listing, in order of their priority, claims regarding (1) the minor child, (2) the spouse, (3) the woman pregnant with his illegitimate child,[32] (4) a stepchild, or the child of a person with whom the obligor cohabits as a husband, and (5) a poor person being a spouse, parent or child, in that order. The state has adopted the Uniform Reciprocal Enforcement of Support Act.[33] A civil action can be brought in the family court when paternity is not in issue. When it is in issue, the proceeding is quasi-criminal in nature and proof beyond a reasonable doubt is required.[34]

---

[27]Id., § 1301.
[28]Id., §§ 919, 920.
[29]Jackson v. Riggs Nat. Bank of Washington, D.C., 314 A.2d 178 (Del., 1973). As to the construction of a statute which would have permitted a legitimate brother to inherit from his illegitimate sister without permitting the latter to inherit from the brother, see In re Klingaman's Estate, 36 Del. Ch. 200, 128 A.2d 311, 60 A.L.R.2d 1175 (1957).
[30]See Wilmington Trust Co. v. Chichester, 369 A.2d 701 (Del. Ch., 1976)., affd. 377 A.2d 11 (Del., 1977).
[31]Del. Code Ann., Tit. 13, § 505.
[32]Delaware imposes on the biological father a duty to support the woman whose child he has begotten. This may include her necessary prenatal and postnatal medical, hospital and lying-in expenses. Del. Code Ann., Tit. 13, § 504.
[33]Del. Code Ann., Tit. 13, §§ 602 to 639.
[34]See G. L. v. S. D., 382 A.2d 252 (Del. Super., 1977). Nonsupport is punishable criminally. Del. Code Ann., Tit. 13, § 521. As to the father's duty to reimburse the state for support furnished, see § 1305.

Delaware has enacted the Uniform Child Custody Jurisdiction Act.[35] Hence, parental custody rights, if not already terminated, cannot be adjudicated without notice and an opportunity to be heard by all involved.

The procedures for termination and transfer of parental rights in adoption proceedings[36] now make it possible for the mother, or the biological father, or both, to petition for termination of parental rights. One of them alone can petition if the other has demonstrated unfitness to be a parent.[37] The consent of both mother and putative father ordinarily is required.[38]

Property rights of cohabitants

In adjusting the rights to accumulations between partners to a nonexistent "marriage," the value of such might depend on whether the court applies a "relation-back" theory of an annulment. In other words, if the marriage is declared *void ab initio,* the likelihood of an equitable distribution of these accumulations is less than if it is decreed void as from the date of the decree. In this light, whatever view the courts may take as to the rights of couples who live together without any pretense of marriage, it seems likely that they would favor the equities of one who mistakenly believed in a valid marriage by not applying a "relation-back" theory.[39]

6.9. District of Columbia

The District of Columbia is not a community property jurisdiction.[40]

Common-law marriages are recognized.[41] There must be an express, mutual, present intent to be husband and wife followed by

---

[35]Del. Code Ann., Tit. 13, §§ 1901 to 1925.
[36]Id., §§ 1101 to 1113.
[37]Id., § 1101.
[38]Id., § 1106.
[39]See R. L. G. v. J. G., 387 A.2d 200 (Del., 1977) and Del. Code Ann., Tit. 13, § 1506(c).
[40]D.C. Code Ann., § 30–201.
[41]Johnson v. Young, 372 A.2d 992 (D.C. App., 1977) (where there is more than one marriage the presumption favors the most recent).

good faith cohabitation.[42] Mere cohabitation, without this expression of intent, to enter into a permanent married state in praesenti, would lead to the conclusion that the relation is a meretricious one, irrespective of the reputation the parties enjoy in the community as spouses.[43] The rule generally adhered to is that, when there was an initial impediment to a valid marriage, a continued cohabitation after the impediment has been removed results in a common-law marriage.[44] A marriage subsequent to a common-law marriage to another is bigamous and void in the District of Columbia, even if the attempted second marriage is celebrated in a foreign state wherein common-law marriages are not recognized, where the parties are domiciliaries of the District of Columbia.[45] However, where a woman had not heard from her first husband for over ten years before a ceremonial marriage to another, and for over thirty years by the time an action was brought, there being no presumption that the first husband was alive, a common-law marriage would result from the removal of the impediment by his death and continued cohabitation between the woman and the second spouse.[46]

Discriminatory practices

A statute entitled the "Human Rights Act of 1977"[47] includes, in its listing of discriminatory practices in the area of employment, housing and educational opportunities, *marital status* as a basis of unfair discrimination. This is defined as the state of being married, single, divorced, separated, widowed and the usual conditions associated therewith, including pregnancy or parenthood. It would seem that unmarried couples who are singled out for

---

[42]Marcus v. Director, Office of Workers' Compensation Programs, 179 App. D.C. 89, 548 F.2d 1044 (1976).
[43]See National Union Fire Ins. Co. v. Britton, 187 F. Supp. 359 (D. D.C., 1960), affd. 110 App. D.C. 77, 289 F.2d 454 (1961).
[44]McVicker v. McVicker, 76 App. D.C. 208, 130 F.2d 837 (1942); Parrella v. Parrella, 74 App. D.C. 161, 120 F.2d 728 (1941); Thomas v. Murphy, 71 App. D.C. 69, 107 F.2d 268 (1939). Compare Friedenwald v. Friedenwald, 57 App. D.C. 13, 16 F.2d 509 (1926).
[45]D.C. Code Ann., § 30–101. See Lee v. Lee, 201 A.2d 873 (D.C. App., 1964).
[46]Williams v. Williams, 33 F. Supp. 612 (D. D.C., 1940), affd. 74 App. D.C. 396, 121 F.2d 737 (1941).
[47]D.C. Laws—1977, No. 2–38.

discriminatory treatment on such a basis would have a cause of action under this statute.

Adoption

Any person may petition to adopt a child. The spouse, if the petitioner has one, must, unless he or she is a natural parent of the adoptee, join in the petition.[48] If the qualification controls, the consent of the natural parent is required.[49] As a prerequisite for either a licensed child placement agency, commissioner, or guardian of the person of a minor to exercise power to consent to an adoption, the parental rights of the biological parents must have been judicially terminated.[50]

The statutes ensure that the interests of the child, of the natural parents, and of all other properly interested parties are fully represented before a child can be adopted.[51]

Workers' compensation death benefits

The Longshoremen's and Harbor Workers' Compensation Act[52] is made applicable to every employer in the District of Columbia.[53] Ambiguities in its wording are resolved in favor of the employee or his dependents.[54] The term "widow" as used in the Act includes only a wife living with or dependent on the decedent workman at the time of his death, and there must be this "conjugal nexus." Once this is present, and a common-law marriage would suffice, the fact that a decedent knowingly accepted his common-law wife's relationship with another man, but contributed to her support and continued to have sexual relations with her, and she helped to care for him in illness, justified a court in finding her his "widow" for this purpose.[55] It seems likely, however,

---

[48]D.C. Code Ann., § 16–302.
[49]Id.
[50]In re C.A.P., 356 A.2d 335 (D.C. App., 1976).
[51]D.C. Code Ann., §§ 16–301, 16–302.
[52]See section 2.13, herein.
[53]D.C. Code Ann., § 36–501. In the District of Columbia it is known as the Employees' Compensation Act.
[54]J. V. Vozzolo, Inc. v. Britton, 126 App. D.C. 259, 377 F.2d 144 (1967).
[55]Matthews v. Walter, 168 App. D.C. 27, 512 F.2d 941 (1975).

6.9 UNMARRIED COUPLES AND THE LAW

that an extramarital partner, even if she qualified as a common-law wife, who deserts the decedent to live with another man would have severed this "conjugal nexus," and would not qualify for death benefits.[56]

Social security benefits

Illegitimate children can inherit from their mother, and likewise from their father if parenthood has been established by judicial process, or if he has acknowledged them.[57] The constitutionality of this statute was upheld in a proceeding relating to the qualification of such a child for benefits under the Social Security Act.[58] However, in the light of Trimble v. Gordon,[59] the question cannot yet be regarded as conclusively adjudicated.

Insurance benefits

Illegitimates are within the term "children" as used in the substitute beneficiary clause of the Federal Employees Group Life Insurance Act.[60]

Cohabitation between "colored persons"

A relic of the past, a statute validating cohabitation between "colored persons" and legitimating their issue,[61] has been repealed.

Breach of promise

In the District of Columbia, the tort action for breach of promise of marriage still lies.[62]

Abortion

Under the statute[63] prohibiting abortions unless "necessary for the preservation of the mother's life or health," this operation is

---

[56] See Weeks v. Behrend, 77 App. D.C. 341, 135 F.2d 258 (1943).
[57] D.C. Code Ann., § 19–316.
[58] Watts v. Veneman, 155 App. D.C. 84, 476 F.2d 529 (1973).
[59] See section 3.3, herein.
[60] Green v. Green, 365 A.2d 610 (D.C. App., 1976). See also section 2.13, herein.
[61] D.C. Code Ann., § 30–117. The children of such unions are, if not for all purposes, legitimate for purposes of intestate succession.
[62] Worthy v. Major, 275 A.2d 244 (D.C. App., 1971).
[63] D.C. Code Ann., § 22–201.

permitted for mental health reasons whether or not the patient has a previous history of mental defects.[64] A decision that anticipated Roe v. Wade[65] denied an eighteen year old's petition for the appointment of a special guardian to obtain consent to a therapeutic abortion, stating that the applicant alone had power over her person and was entitled to consent for herself to any form of medical treatment.[66]

Possible criminal liability

Fornication is a criminal offense in the District of Columbia,[67] as is sodomy.[68] The sodomy provision does not single out any particular group of persons; it applies to acts between men, between women, and between a man and a woman, and makes no distinction between acts committed by homosexuals or bisexuals. Thus, it does not deny equal protection on its face.[69] The statute has also withstood an attack on First Amendment grounds, in which it was argued that such a prohibition is a direct and unbroken legacy of the Christian church. Rejecting this argument, the court labeled the statute a reasonable exercise of the right of the legislature to maintain a decent society, and that any objection that the statute is overbroad in that it could be applied in a private domestic context cannot be brought by one who clearly did not act in private.[70] A court has explicitly stated that the individual's right to privacy does not extend to homosexual conduct even in private between consenting adults.[71] And members of a "health club" (membership of which could be obtained with minimum formality and for a modest fee) were held not to have the right to or reasonable expectation of privacy which could render their sodomitic activity outside the proscription of the statute.[72]

---

[64]United States v. Vuitch, 402 U.S. 62, 28 L. Ed. 2d 601, 91 Sup. Ct. 1294 (1971).
[65]Discussed in section 2.19, herein.
[66]In re Guardianship of Boe, 322 F. Supp. 872 (D. D.C., 1971).
[67]D.C. Code Ann., § 22-1002.
[68]Id., § 22-3502.
[69]Stewart v. United States, 364 A.2d 1205 (D.C. App., 1976).
[70]Harris v. United States, 315 A.2d 569 (D.C. App., 1974).
[71]Berg v. Claytor, 436 F. Supp. 76 (D. D.C., 1977).
[72]United States v. McKean, 338 A.2d 439 (D.C. App., 1975). As to the crime of solicitation for the purpose of sodomy (D.C. Code Ann., § 22-2701), see United States v. Cozart, 321 A.2d 342 (D.C. App., 1974).

Adultery is so defined[73] that it cannot be committed by a woman who is unmarried, but in such a case the man, if married, would be guilty.[74]

The bigamy statute[75] has a proviso designed to protect one whose spouse has been continually absent for five successive years before the allegedly bigamous marriage. If the marriage took place with an honest and reasonable belief, based on a thorough investigation, that the defendant was free to remarry, this is a defense.[76]

For the crime of incest, the relationship of the participants (in marriage or in sexual intercourse outside of marriage) must be within and not including the fourth degree of consanguinity, computed according to the rules of the Roman or civil law.[77]

For the crime of seduction, the female must have been of previously chaste character and between the ages of sixteen and twenty-one years.[78] Though the statute makes no mention of a promise to marry as an ingredient of the crime, an early court held that, if such a promise was made conditioned on the female becoming pregnant, the statute is not violated.[79] The reasoning was that the object of the enactment was to protect a chaste virgin against betrayal from an honest belief in the betrayer's protestation of love, or an existing promise of marriage, or a present unqualified promise of marriage as an inducement. A more recent court has also violated the rules of construction by stating that chastity is "not an issue."[80]

Nonsupport of an illegitimate child is also a crime.[81]

The age of consent, for statutory rape, is sixteen.[82]

---

[73] D.C. Code Ann., § 22–301.
[74] O'Neil v. O'Neil, 55 App. D.C. 40, 299 Fed. 914 (1924).
[75] D.C. Code Ann., § 22–601.
[76] Alexander v. United States, 78 App. D.C. 34, 136 F.2d 783 (1943).
[77] D.C. Code Ann., § 22–1901. As to the prohibited degrees of relationship in relation to the validity of a marriage, see § 30–101.
[78] D.C. Code Ann., § 22–3001.
[79] Hamilton v. United States, 41 App. D.C. 359, 51 L.R.A. (N.S.) 809 (1914). The court implied that the bargain of chastity for sex was not indicative of "honest belief" in the defendant's promise to marry the woman.
[80] United States v. Dildy, 39 F.R.D. 340 (D. D.C., 1966) (obiter dictum).
[81] D.C. Code Ann., § 16–2355.
[82] Id., § 22–2801. See In re J. W. Y., 363 A.2d 674 (D.C. App., 1976), holding penetration to be an element of the crime.

Status of children

Illegitimate children and their issue are capable of inheriting from their mother.[83] They can also inherit from their father if parenthood has been established by judicial process, or he has acknowledged them.[84] A decision upholding this statute may, as indicated earlier,[85] be of shaky viability as operating to deprive such a child of welfare benefits.

Paternity proceedings, which are civil in nature, are initiated by or on behalf of the Corporation Counsel.[86] The action must be brought within two years after the birth of the child, or within one year after the putative father ceases to contribute to its support.[87] The court may order the father, on adjudicating his paternity, to furnish security for payments ordered, or place him on probation on the condition that the payments be made as ordered.[88]

Support and custody

The duty to support is owed by both parents as long as the child remains a minor.[89] In addition, the court may order the father to pay prenatal care and maintenance until the child is adopted or reaches the age of sixteen.[90] But it is held that the father's duty of support to his legitimate children, in the event that he is in financial straits, takes precedence over his obligations to his illegitimate child.[91]

---

[83] D.C. Code Ann., § 19–316.
[84] Id., § 19–318.
[85] See section 3.3, herein.
[86] D.C. Code Ann., § 16–2341 et seq. Among statutory precautions designed to preserve the child from the stigma of illegitimacy is a provision for the issuance of a new birth record on a marriage of the child's parents. Id., § 16–2345.
[87] See District of Columbia v. Franklin, 154 A.2d 550 (D.C. Mun. App., 1959); Ford v. District of Columbia, 102 A.2d 838 (D.C. Mun. App., 1954), affd. 95 App. D.C. 87, 219 F.2d 769 (1955).
[88] D.C. Code Ann., § 16–2350.
[89] Id., § 30–320.
[90] Id., § 16–2349.
[91] Mitchell v. Mitchell, 144 App. D.C. 246, 445 F.2d 722 (1971). Though one court has indicated that a differentiation between a husband's duty, after divorce, to support a legitimate stepchild from his duty to support an illegitimate one would present problems of a constitutional nature (Fuller v. Fuller, 135 App. D.C. 353, 418 F.2d 1189 (1969)), it is at any rate held that where a husband did not intend that the in loco parentis relation should continue during separation as to the child of a wife by her former marriage, the husband was not obliged to furnish support for such child. Jackson v. Jackson, 278 A.2d 114 (D.C. App., 1971).

If the father voluntarily agrees to support the child, the agreement may be submitted to the court for ratification and approval.[92] Amounts due and unpaid under a court order at the time of the father's death are a valid claim against his estate.[93] The District of Columbia has enacted the Uniform Reciprocal Enforcement of Support Act.[94]

As to visitation rights, it is recognized that the father's right, fundamental though it may be, is not absolute. The state has the duty to protect minors. In a proper case the welfare of the child may dictate that it should be separated from the parent.[95] Similarly, the child's welfare may not be prejudiced by a parent's misconduct; even if the mother wrongfully impedes the father's visitation rights, this does not justify him in withholding support payments.[96]

Property rights of cohabitants

A mere promise to a cohabitant that he would have the title to land placed in her name does not of itself confer any title to the property; thus in such a situation, although the promisee had sent the promisor some of the monthly payments and had made repairs on the premises, she appears to have acquired no rights.[97] (Perhaps if she had sought relief on the basis of a resulting trust pro tanto in respect of her payments, or a quantum meruit in respect of her services, she might have fared better.[98] But it appears that she occupied the premises, and her contributions could just as well have been regarded as compensation for the use of them.)

The rule that persons not validly married cannot hold as tenants by the entireties is respected in the District of Columbia. But, contrary to the usual view,[99] a joint tenancy and not a

---

[92]D.C. Code Ann., § 16–2351.
[93]Id., § 16–2352.
[94]Id., §§ 30–301 to 30–324.
[95]In re Adoption of J. S. R., 374 A.2d 860 (D.C. App., 1977).
[96]Norton v. Norton, 298 A.2d 514 (D.C. App., 1972).
[97]Franklin v. Phoenix, 294 A.2d 483 (D.C. App., 1972).
[98]See Chapter 4, herein.
[99]See section 4.2, herein.

tenancy in common is favored when the parties intended joint ownership.[1]

On an annulment of marriage, the courts are vested with a discretion to award property held in joint tenancy or in tenancy by the entirety as may seem just.[2]

6.10. Florida

Florida is not a community property state.[3]

Common-law marriages entered into after January 1, 1968 are not valid.[4] The statute, however, does not affect marriages which, though otherwise defective, were entered into by the party asserting their validity in good faith and in substantial compliance with the controlling statutory provisions.[5] Where a husband and wife did not separate until one day after dissolution of their marriage, and then three weeks later cohabited and held themselves out as being husband and wife, bought property in their joint names and filed joint income tax returns, no common-law marriage came into existence.[6] A ceremonial marriage which is invalid by reason of an existing undissolved marriage not known to one party becomes a presumptively valid common-law marriage if the impediment ceased to exist prior to the abolition of common-law marriages and if the parties continued to cohabit after dissolution of the prior marriage.[7] If the marriage is recognized as a valid common-law marriage where performed, even after 1968, the Florida courts should recognize it.[8]

---

[1] See Coleman v. Jackson, 109 App. D.C. 242, 286 F.2d 98, 83 A.L.R.2d 1043 (1960), cert. den. 366 U.S. 933, 6 L. Ed. 2d 391, 81 Sup. Ct. 1656 (1961); see also Snipes v. Douglass, 319 A.2d 326 (D.C. App., 1974).
[2] See Nelson v. Nelson, 84 App. D.C. 167, 171 F.2d 1021 (1948).
[3] Estabrook v. Wise, 348 So. 2d 355 (Fla. App., 1977), holding that Florida is thus not required to recognize an encumbrance predicated on a sister state's community property law.
[4] Fla. Stat., § 741.211.
[5] Id.
[6] Duey v. Duey, 343 So. 2d 896 (Fla. App., 1977).
[7] Day v. Day, 331 So. 2d 335 (Fla. App., 1976). As to the requirements of a common-law marriage prior to 1968, see In re Estate of Marden, 355 So. 2d 121 (Fla. App., 1978); In re Estate of Bragg, 334 So. 2d 271 (Fla. App., 1976); Carter v. Carter, 309 So. 2d 625 (Fla. App., 1975); In re Estate of Litzky, 296 So. 2d 638 (Fla. App., 1974); Williams v. Dade County, 237 So. 2d 776 (Fla. App., 1970).
[8] Ops. Atty. Gen. 068–63 (1968).

Students

The legislature has affirmed the right of unmarried students who are pregnant, or students who have had a child out of wedlock,[9] to attend school.[10]

Adoption

Any adult resident of the state may petition for leave to adopt a minor child. Important among the requirements, which are set forth in detail in the controlling statutes,[11] is one postponing, in certain cases, the hearing on a petition until the child has lived with petitioners under the supervision of the state welfare board not less than ninety days.[12] It is possible to adopt an adult.[13] Here, as is the case with a minor, the consent of the natural father, or proof that he has received notice of the proceedings, is essential[14] unless he has by his conduct disqualified himself.[15] An adopter must be more than ten years older than the adoptee.[16]

Workers' compensation death benefits

For the purposes of workers' compensation benefits, the term "spouse" includes only a spouse substantially dependent for financial support on the decedent and living with him at the time of his injury and death, or substantially dependent on him and living apart for justifiable cause.[17] Hence it would seem that a mere cohabitant would have a slim chance of qualifying. A "child" under the statute includes an acknowledged illegitimate child who is dependent on the deceased.[18] A putative father's acknowledgment is sufficient even if the pregnancy had not yet been

---

[9] See section 2.4, herein.
[10] Fla. Stat., § 232.01(2).
[11] Id., §§ 63.011 to 63.291.
[12] Id., § 63.241.
[13] Id., § 63.112.
[14] Id. In re Adoption of Scott, 344 So. 2d 884 (Fla. App., 1977).
[15] See In re Adoption of Brangley, 122 So. 2d 423 (Fla. App., 1960). See also note 65, infra.
[16] Fla. Stat., § 63.241.
[17] Id., § 440.02(15). "Dependency" is a question of fact. See Paul Spellman, Inc. v. Spellman, 103 So. 2d 661 (Fla. App., 1958).
[18] Fla. Stat., § 440.02(13).

determined as a medical fact at the time of the father's death.[19] But, although a liberal construction of the legitimacy statute is favored, the common-law status, except to the extent it is altered by statute, remains in force.[20]

Recovery for wrongful death

Florida permits an unwed mother to sue for the wrongful death of her children.[21] And the courts have added that to recognize such a right in the mother but to deny it in the father would violate equal protection.[22] By virtue of the Emancipation Act, "minor child" now means any unmarried child under the age of eighteen years.[23]

Tort actions

The statutory abolition of the tort actions for alienation of affections, criminal conversation, seduction or breach of contract to marry,[24] does not affect the rights of parties relative to gifts passing between them.[25]

Abortion

A statute penalizing abortion was repealed in 1972, but advertising drugs and the like for abortion purposes is a misdemeanor.[26] An attempt to convict unlicensed medical practitioners for having procured abortions by charging them with "involuntary sexual battery" proved unsuccessful, because in such a

---

[19] Ezell-Titterton, Inc. v. A. K. F., 234 So. 2d 360 (Fla., 1970).
[20] In re Estate of Caldwell, 247 So. 2d 1 (Fla., 1971).
[21] Fla. Stat., § 768.18. See also Evans v. Atlantic Cement Co., 272 So. 2d 538 (Fla. App., 1973).
[22] Wilcox v. Jones, 346 So. 2d 1037 (Fla. App., 1977).
[23] Hanley v. Liberty Mut. Ins. Co., 323 So. 2d 301 (Fla. App., 1975), affd. 334 So. 2d 11 (Fla., 1976).
[24] Fla. Stat., § 771.01.
[25] Gill v. Shively, 320 So. 2d 415 (Fla. App., 1975). See also Mims v. Mims, 305 So. 2d 787 (Fla. App., 1974), holding that a wife has no action for damages based on allegations that the defendant induced her to marry by false protestations of love.
[26] Fla. Stat., § 797.02. See also § 458.22.

crime the actor must have intended to attain sexual arousal or gratification.[27] It is doubtful whether it could ever be committed involuntarily.

A statute[28] requiring that prior to procuring an abortion the mother must obtain her husband's consent, or if unmarried, her parents' consent, was held unconstitutional.[29] Faithful to the mandate of Roe v. Wade,[30] a Florida court has denied to a putative father a right to enjoin the unmarried mother of his child from terminating her pregnancy. If he did have standing to so prevent the abortion, the court asks, would he also have standing to compel an abortion? Could he restrain the potential mother from the use of contraceptives if he can compel her to bear children? The court dismisses such arguments as ludicrous.[31] In Wright v. State[32] a registered nurse appealed her conviction of feloniously terminating a pregnancy. The reviewing court held that (1) the "approved facility" requirement and "certification" requirement of the statute making it unlawful to terminate a pregnancy unless pregnancy is terminated in an approved facility by a physician who submits written certification of his reasons for termination were unconstitutional in that they were not limited to abortions performed after the first trimester of pregnancy; but that (2) the "physician" requirement of the statute is constitutional standing alone and is enforceable despite the invalid requirements.

---

[27] State v. Alonso, 345 So. 2d 740 (Fla. App., 1977).

[28] Fla. Stat., § 458.22(3).

[29] Poe v. Gerstein, 517 F.2d 787 (C.A.-5 Fla., 1975), affd. 428 U.S. 901, 49 L. Ed. 2d 1205, 96 Sup. Ct. 3202 (1976).

[30] See section 2.19, herein.

[31] Jones v. Smith, 278 So. 2d 339 (Fla. App., 1973), cert. den. 415 U.S. 958, 39 L. Ed. 2d 573, 94 Sup. Ct. 1486 (1974). However, in invalidating a statute requiring consent of the husband of a married woman or the parents of an unmarried minor, the court indicated that such persons might have a right which the state would, by a proper statute, protect even during the first trimester, but that the statute which gave husband or parents an unqualified and unconditional right to withhold consent is invalid. Coe v. Gerstein, 376 F. Supp. 695 (S.D. Fla., 1973), affd. 517 F.2d 769 (C.A.-5 Fla., 1975), 417 U.S. 279, 41 L. Ed. 2d 68, 94 Sup. Ct. 2246 (1974), appeal dismissed.

Abortion referral or counseling agencies must make a good faith effort to inform a child's parents. Fla. Stat., § 458.23. As to approval of the termination of pregnancy in the last trimester, see § 458.225.

[32] 351 So. 2d 708 (Fla., 1977).

Possible criminal liability

Fornication, which must involve an unmarried woman,[33] is a misdemeanor.[34] Punishment can be visited on either participant. Further, if any man and woman, not being married to each other, lewdly and lasciviously associate and cohabit together, or if any man or woman, married or unmarried, engages in open and gross lewdness and lascivious behavior, they likewise can be punished for a misdemeanor.[35] Another statute, denouncing "unnatural and lascivious acts,"[36] has withstood several challenges as to constitutionality. The courts seem satisfied that an ordinary citizen can easily understand what character of act is condemned.[37] (There are many, however, who would disagree. Conduct which is highly offensive to some citizens may pass without question to another. Which is the "ordinary citizen"? It seems fair to insist, as the courts do when lewd, lascivious or indecent assault or act on or in the presence of a child is involved,[38] that the prosecution should in all such cases aver and prove exactly what was the act complained of.)[39]

The "abominable and detestable crime against nature," once denounced,[40] withstood an attack based on unconstitutionality for vagueness in the Supreme Court of the United States,[41] but was repealed as a result of a decision of the Florida Supreme Court.[42]

Living in "open and notorious"[43] adultery is a crime.[44] As is

---

[33]Moore v. State, 339 So. 2d 228 (Fla. App., 1976); DeLaine v. State, 262 So. 2d 655 (Fla., 1972).

[34]Fla. Stat., § 798.03.

[35]Id., § 798.02. Either participant can be punished. But there must be a living together as in a conjugal relation. See Wildman v. State, 157 Fla. 334, 25 So. 2d 808 (1946).

[36]Fla. Stat., § 800.02. See Campbell v. State, 331 So. 2d 289 (Fla., 1976); Johnsen v. State, 332 So. 2d 69 (Fla., 1976); Thomas v. State, 326 So. 2d 413 (Fla., 1975).

[37]See Witherspoon v. State, 278 So. 2d 611 (Fla., 1973).

[38]Fla. Stat., § 800.04. See Brown v. State, 344 So. 2d 641 (Fla. App., 1977).

[39]State ex rel. Swanboro v. Mayo, 155 Fla. 330, 19 So. 2d 883 (1944).

[40]Fla. Stat., § 800.01.

[41]Wainwright v. Stone, 414 U.S. 21, 38 L. Ed. 2d 179, 94 Sup. Ct. 190 (1973). See Sodomy—Crime or Sin?, 12 U. Fla. L. Rev. 83 (1959).

[42]See Zimmerman v. State, 320 So. 2d 41 (Fla. App., 1975).

[43]Moore v. State, 339 So. 2d 228 (Fla. App., 1976).

[44]Fla. Stat., § 798.01. See also Victimless Sex Crimes: To the Devil, Not the Dungeon, 25 U. Fla. L. Rev. 139 (1972).

6.10 UNMARRIED COUPLES AND THE LAW

incest.[45] As to bigamy,[46] mistake is a defense,[47] at any rate to the extent that a defendant must know *the other party* is married.

The age of consent for statutory rape is eighteen years.[48] Among the varieties of misconduct which fall under "sexual battery" is the offense committed where the victim is older than eleven but less than eighteen and the defendant is in a position of familial, custodial or official authority over the victim.[49]

Status of children

The presumption of legitimacy of a child born of parents in lawful wedlock[50] plays a strong part in determining the duties of the father. The statute relating to establishment of paternity itself restricts the right to bring an action to an "unmarried woman who shall be pregnant or delivered of a child."[51] This provision, even though it did not permit a married woman to sue for support from the child's putative father, was held constitutional, perhaps because to permit such a suit would have the result of declaring a presumably legitimate child illegitimate.[52] The presumption is to protect the interests of the child;[53] however, although this limitation on the right to sue for determination of paternity has since been declared a denial of equal protection,[54] and a reputed father

---

[45]Fla. Stat., § 826.04. Where the indictment charged rape and did not allege consanguinity, there was no basis for instructions on incest as a lesser-included offense, although the victims were defendant's daughters. Huckaby v. State, 343 So. 2d 29 (Fla., 1977), cert. den. 434 U.S. 920, 98 Sup. Ct. 393 (1977).
[46]Fla. Stat., § 826.01.
[47]Id., § 826.02.
[48]Id., § 794.05. Criminal Law: Mistake of Age as a Defense to Statutory Rape, 18 U. Fla. L. Rev. 699 (1966).
[49]Fla. Stat., §794.011(4)(e). See Whiteman v. State, 343 So. 2d 1340 (Fla. App., 1977).
[50]See sections 3.1, 3.7, herein.
[51]Fla. Stat., § 742.011.
[52]See Kennelly v. Davis, 221 So. 2d 415 (Fla., 1969), cert. den. 396 U.S. 916, 90 Sup. Ct. 237 (1969).
[53]Sacks v. Sacks, 267 So. 2d 73 (Fla., 1972).
[54]Gammon v. Cobb, 335 So. 2d 261 (Fla., 1976). See also Ladies Center of Clearwater, Inc. v. Reno, 341 So. 2d 543 (Fla. App., 1977), holding a clinic and a physician have no right of indemnification or contribution from an unwed father in respect of damages resulting from an unsuccessful abortion, since the only cause of action against such father is one in bastardy.

has the right to challenge his alleged paternity,[55] it still does not seem that anyone other than the natural mother has standing to initiate a bastardy action.[56] A mother who has had no contact with her legal husband for twenty years, and who has cohabited with the putative father during such period, is not qualified to sue under this provision.[57]

Statutes require that all possible precautions are taken to ensure that the illegitimacy of a child does not appear on its birth record.[58]

For the purposes of intestate succession, an illegitimate child is a lineal descendant of its mother. The child is also a lineal descendant of its father and is one of the natural kindred of all members of the father's family if either the natural parents have married, even though the attempted marriage is void, or paternity has been judicially established, or paternity has been acknowledged in writing by the father.[59] The writing need not assume any particular formality.[60]

A child born in wedlock but conceived by artificial insemination[61] is irrebuttably presumed legitimate provided both husband and wife have consented in writing to the artificial insemination.[62]

Legitimation is effected by marriage of the parents,[63] or by

---

[55]Barnett v. Barnett, 336 So. 2d 1213 (Fla. App., 1976), affd. 360 So. 2d 399 (Fla., 1978).

[56]Public authorities, of course, have unquestioned power to place a dependent child under appropriate care. See Fla. Stat., § 39.11. See Collyer, Due Process for the Unwed Father, 46 Fla. B. J. 508 (1972); Florida Bastardy Act—A Law in Need of Change, 24 U. Miami L. Rev. 713 (1970).

[57]Gammon v. Cobb, 335 So. 2d 261 (Fla., 1976).

An unwed pregnant woman may not enter into an agreement with the putative father to release him from liability. Shinall v. Pergeorelis, 325 So. 2d 431 (Fla. App., 1975).

[58]See Fla. Stat., § 382.16 et seq. See also State Dept. of Health and Rehabilitative Services v. Mullarkey, 340 So. 2d 123 (Fla. App., 1976).

[59]Fla. Stat., § 732.108. See In re Estate of Burris, 361 So. 2d 152 (Fla., 1978), holding that the date of death, rather than the date of the probate court's determination of paternity, is the decisive date in determining whether present or former provisions apply to a claim to succeed on intestacy.

[60]In re Estate of Jerrido, 339 So. 2d 237 (Fla. App., 1976). See also Williams v. Estate of Long, 338 So. 2d 563 (Fla. App., 1976).

[61]See section 3.1, herein.

[62]Fla. Stat., § 742.11. See Human Artificial Insemination: An Analysis and Proposal for Florida, 22 U. Miami L. Rev. 952 (1968).

[63]Fla. Stat., § 742.091.

adoption. As is usual, the adoption statutes[64] make careful provision to ensure that the putative father receives his day in court unless there is a clear showing that he has waived or abandoned this right by showing his unfitness as a parent.[65] Thus, where a biological father never received notice of an adoption proceeding instituted by the child's stepfather, and reconstructive service of process was not utilized even though it appeared that his whereabouts could have been ascertained, the adoption decree was held void.[66]

Support and custody

Contrary to the rule in many states, Florida does not permit a mother to contract away her right to seek support for her illegitimate child from the father.[67]

The state has adopted the Uniform Reciprocal Enforcement of Support Act,[68] as well as the Uniform Child Custody Jurisdiction Act.[69] Hence, to deprive a putative father of his rights to notice and a hearing before his custodial rights are taken away and without, for example, apprising him of the public agency's report

---

[64]Id., § 63.062 et seq. See also section 3.8, herein.

[65]See Lovell v. Mason, 347 So. 2d 144 (Fla. App., 1977); Durden v. Henry, 343 So. 2d 1361 (Fla. App., 1977); Turner v. Adoption of Turner, 352 So. 2d 957 (Fla. App., 1977). The provisions for notice to the natural mother have no application in an adoption proceeding where she appeared and participated. In re Adoption of DeGroot, 335 So. 2d 845 (Fla. App., 1976). See also Constitutional Law—Adoption—Father of an Illegitimate Child Is Not Necessarily Entitled to Notice in Adoption Proceedings, 5 Fla. St. U. L. Rev. 480 (1977). The burden of showing abandonment by natural father is on party seeking to adopt. In re Adoption of Lewis, 340 So. 2d 126 (Fla. App., 1976). As to situations where a putative father's consent to adoption is required, see Fla. Stat., § 63.062. See also In re Adoption of Mullenix, 359 So. 2d 65 (Fla. App., 1978).

[66]Canaday v. Gresham, 362 So. 2d 82 (Fla. App., 1978).

[67]Shinall v. Pergeorelis, 325 So. 2d 431 (Fla. App., 1975). A right-to-life protagonist might well argue that if the mother has the exclusive right to destroy the fetus, why should she not have the lesser right to bargain away her right to claim for its support? An answer might be that such an agreement, releasing a putative father in return for payment by him of medical expenses incident to the child's birth, is invalid only to the extent that it purports to affect *the rights of the child*. See Walker v. Walker, 266 So. 2d 385 (Fla. App., 1972).

[68]Fla. Stat., §§ 88.011 to 88.371.

[69]Id., §§ 61.1302 to 61.20.

as to his fitness as a parent, violates due process.[70] It has also adopted the provision of the Uniform Probate Code[71] which includes illegitimates when a class gift is made to "children."[72]

Property rights of cohabitants

One who transfers property to another in the mistaken belief in the validity of their marriage can, if the property can be traced, obtain a decree ordering its restitution.[73]

Some inconsistency appears in the decisions relating to the nature of the title when persons who are not legally married take a deed as "husband and wife."[74] Some adhere to the traditional view that they hold as tenants in common.[75] But where the deed expressly provided rights of survivorship, one court permitted the survivor to take the entire proceeds as a joint tenant.[76]

As to resulting or constructive trusts[77] a court, confronted with a situation "in which good morals would offer no brief in behalf of either party," held that where a meretricious cohabitant had contributed toward the acquisition of a home, though the court made no secret of its inclination to dismiss the case with a Shakespearian "plague on both your houses," it held that the contributor should be given an opportunity to present more definite evidence at a new trial—presumably evidence on which to predicate a resulting trust.[78]

---

[70]See Fla. Stat., §39.01 et seq. In Interest of Baby Boy S., 349 So. 2d 774 (Fla. App., 1977). However, where the proof did not establish an alleged father's paternity, and established that he was convicted of manslaughter for the shooting of the mother, and the authorities had recommended that custody be awarded to the child's maternal grandparents (who already had custody of the child's only sister) an award of custody to the alleged natural father was set aside. Robinson v. Vance, 357 So. 2d 784 (Fla. App., 1978).

[71]See section 3.1, note 13, herein.

[72]Fla. Stat., § 732.608.

[73]Beidler v. Beidler, 43 So. 2d 329 (Fla., 1949).

[74]See section 4.2, herein. Generally, see Atkins v. Atkins, 326 So. 2d 259 (Fla. App., 1976); Jablonski v. Caputo, 297 So. 2d 310 (Fla. App., 1974).

[75]See Kerivan v. Fogal, 156 Fla. 92, 22 So. 2d 584 (1945); Nottingham v. Denison, 63 So. 2d 269 (Fla., 1953).

[76]Kent v. O'Neil, 53 So. 2d 779 (Fla., 1951).

[77]Discussed in sections 4.5, 4.8, herein.

[78]Smith v. Smith, 108 So. 2d 761 (Fla., 1959).

Over a decade earlier, a resulting trust was decreed in a more dubious situation. There was an illicit relationship. The woman had advanced to the man some money to make up delinquent payments on land they had bought. She claimed there was an "understanding" that she be given a one-half interest in the land. The man had secretly secured a deed in his own name and had conveyed title to a stranger. Reasoning that there was no showing that the illicit relationship had any connection with the land transaction, the court approved a resulting trust in favor of the woman in respect of a half interest in the land.[79] It might be commented that such a decree should be restricted to that proportion of the price which the woman could prove she contributed; also that, if the decree was based on his promise, it should be a constructive trust arising from his breach of a confidential relationship. Further, since title had passed into the hands of the stranger, he would ordinarily be protected as a bona fide purchaser for value without notice, whatever the woman's rights to the proceeds vis-a-vis the man.

A contract in contemplation of sexual relations has been held void in Florida.[80]

6.11. Georgia

This is not a community property state.[81]

There is no specific statute covering common-law marriage in Georgia. Such marriages, however, have long been recognized.[82] Provided that a marriage is deliberately entered into *per verba de praesenti* by competent parties,[83] accompanied by consummation (which only means cohabitation), failure to comply with the

---

[79]Williams v. Bullington, 159 Fla. 618, 32 So. 2d 273 (1947). Generally, see Kulzer, Law and the Housewife: Property, Divorce, and Death, 28 U. Fla. L. Rev. 1 (1975).

[80]Wilson v. Rooney, 101 So. 2d 892 (Fla. App., 1958).

[81]See Ga. Code, § 53–503.

[82]The burden is on the cohabitant asserting the existence of a marriage to prove an agreement that they should be husband and wife. Brown v. Brown, 234 Ga. 300, 215 S.E.2d 671 (1975) (man designating woman as his wife and beneficiary under life insurance policy tends to show such agreement).

[83]See Hiter v. Shelp, 129 Ga. App. 401, 199 S.E.2d 832 (1973).

statutory formalities for a marriage does not invalidate it.[84] Even if a ceremonial marriage is void on account of the disability of one or both of the parties to contract marriage, a continued cohabitation after such impediment is removed, if the parties hold themselves out as husband and wife, will create a common-law marriage.[85]

A mere pretense of a ceremonial marriage is insufficient.[86] But if the parties have been divorced from each other, and continue to cohabit as husband and wife, common-law marriage can be found if there was an agreement between them to this effect.[87]

When a ceremonial marriage has taken place after an alleged common-law marriage, and there is no evidence as to the circumstances under which the latter marriage took place, the presumption favors the validity of the second marriage over the one merely founded on cohabitation and repute.[88] (Thus, it might appear that, though a common-law marriage ordinarily can only be dissolved by a divorce, one who seeks to dissolve it in Georgia can do so by simply going through a marriage ceremony with another. This is not necessarily so.)[89]

A common-law marriage can be clandestine. Whether it exists or not being a question of fact,[90] however, if the parties did not hold themselves out as husband and wife, it would certainly militate against a finding of any such fact.[91] On the other hand, where the parties falsely represented to the world that they had been

---

[84]To establish this agreement it is not essential to show any public or private de facto ceremony. Alberson v. Alberson, 237 Ga. 622, 229 S.E.2d 409 (1976).
[85]Heflinger v. Heflinger, 161 Ga. 867, 132 S.E. 85 (1926); Chance v. Chance, 60 Ga. App. 889, 5 S.E.2d 399 (1939).
[86]Wolverine Ins. Co. v. Leach, 100 Ga. App. 570, 112 S.E.2d 10 (1959).
[87]Alberson v. Alberson, 237 Ga. 622, 229 S.E.2d 409 (1976); Satterfield v. Satterfield, 236 Ga. 155, 223 S.E.2d 136 (1976).
[88]See Edwards v. Edwards, 136 Ga. App. 668, 222 S.E.2d 169 (1975).
[89]See Evans v. Marbut, 140 Ga. App. 329, 231 S.E.2d 94 (1976), holding that where there had been a lengthy cohabitation after a divorce, followed by a separation and then a new ceremonial marriage by the husband to another woman, the common-law marriage resulting from the lengthy cohabitation was the one to be recognized.
[90]See Spivey v. Spivey, 236 Ga. 725, 225 S.E.2d 288 (1976); Lavender v. Wilkins, 237 Ga. 510, 228 S.E.2d 888 (1976); Balasco v. Balasco, 235 Ga. 214, 219 S.E.2d 104 (1975); Shepherd v. Shepherd, 233 Ga. 228, 210 S.E.2d 731 (1974), cert. den. 421 U.S. 932, 44 L. Ed. 2d 91, 95 Sup. Ct. 1662 (1975); Simeonides v. Zervis, 127 Ga. App. 506, 194 S.E.2d 324 (1972).
[91]See Lefkoff v. Sicro, 189 Ga. 554, 6 S.E.2d 687, 133 A.L.R. 738 (1939).

through a marriage ceremony this has, in at least one case, tended to persuade the trier of fact that they were embarked on a meretricious cohabitation and were not common-law spouses.[92]

Adoption

As to the right of unmarried cohabitants to adopt a child,[93] the statutory provisions in Georgia are fairly typical. Any adult may petition the court if at least 25 years of age, or married and living with the spouse. If married, the petition must be filed in the name of both spouses except where the child is a stepchild of the party seeking to adopt it. The petitioner(s) must be at least ten years older than the child, a resident of the state and financially, physically, morally fit and mentally able to have the permanent custody of the child.[94] Ordinarily, unless the natural parents have forfeited their rights in this respect, their consent is required. If they have surrendered their parental rights,[95] the consent of the Department of Human Resources or of a licensed child-placing agency is required.[96] A parent whose parental rights have been terminated is not entitled to notice of the proceedings, nor has he any right to object to the adoption or otherwise participate in the proceedings.[97] Unlawful advertisements and inducements for the adoption of children[98] are punishable as a felony.[99]

Students

The fact that high school students who marry or become parents are normally more precocious than others has been regarded as a rational basis for denial of an unwed teenage mother's readmission to school as a regular daytime student. Such a policy was ruled rationally connected to the legitimate state purpose of maintaining discipline.[1]

---

[92] Wolverine Ins. Co. v. Leach, 100 Ga. App. 570, 112 S.E.2d 10 (1959).
[93] Discussed in section 2.9, herein.
[94] Ga. Code, § 74-402.
[95] See id., §§ 74-403, 74-404.
[96] Id., § 74-403. See further, as to the adoption procedures, § 74-405 et seq.
[97] Ga. Code, § 24A-3203.
[98] Id., § 74-418.
[99] Id., § 74-9903.1.
[1] Houston v. Prosser, 361 F. Supp. 295 (N.D. Ga., 1973). See also section 2.4, herein.

The decision begs many questions. Is extramarital pregnancy an indication of precocity? If so, is precocity a rational basis for such discrimination (which had the effect of requiring the plaintiff, as a night student, to pay tuition and furnish her own textbooks)? Even if precocity is normally present in such situations, would not equal protection require an ad hoc showing of precocity in every situation presented? Does the exclusion of precocious students have any bearing on the maintenance of school discipline?

Workers' compensation death benefits

The Georgia workers' compensation law creates a conclusive presumption of dependency of a stepchild of an employee.[2] This provision has resisted a challenge of unconstitutionality.[3] It has also been held applicable to an illegitimate child of the widow of a decedent employee.[4]

One who qualifies as a common-law wife qualifies for benefits payable under the workers' compensation laws.[5] One who does not so qualify, for example by reason of not having held herself out as his wife,[6] or of having married without divorcing a prior spouse,[7] does not. In Wolverine Insurance Company v. Leach,[8] the workman cohabited with one Gertrude for about five years, falsely letting it be known that they had gone through a church wedding. He then left her and cohabited with one Helen for about 23 years, without uttering any falsehoods about a church ceremony. Helen was held to qualify for benefits as his common-law

---

[2]Ga. Code, §§ 114–413, 114–414.

[3]Flint River Mills v. Henry, 239 Ga. 347, 236 S.E.2d 583 (1977), appeal dismissed 434 U.S. 1003, 54 L. Ed. 2d 746, 98 Sup. Ct. 707 (1978). Acknowledged illegitimates are unquestionably so entitled. See Ga. Code, § 114–414.

[4]United States Fire Ins. Co. v. City of Atlanta, 135 Ga. App. 390, 217 S.E.2d 647 (1975).

[5]American Mut. Liability Ins. Co. v. Copeland, 113 Ga. App. 707, 149 S.E.2d 402 (1966).

[6]Georgia Cas. & Surety Co. v. Bloodworth, 120 Ga. App. 313, 170 S.E.2d 433 (1969). See also Johnson v. New Amsterdam Cas. Co., 109 Ga. App. 800, 137 S.E.2d 485 (1964) (no express agreement to marry).

[7]Insurance Co. of North America v. Jewel, 118 Ga. App. 599, 164 S.E.2d 846 (1968).

[8]100 Ga. App. 570, 112 S.E.2d 10 (1959).

6.11 UNMARRIED COUPLES AND THE LAW

wife. It seems odd that such a lie can convert what would otherwise be a common-law marriage, terminable only by divorce, into a mere meretricious relationship which in no way stood in the way of Helen's claim to a common-law marriage.

Possible criminal liability

Though the Georgia Code does not make cohabitation a crime, the cupboard, in so far as it relates to possible crimes of cohabitants, is far from bare. There are the crimes of willful abandonment of an illegitimate child,[9] bastardy,[10] and seduction (by persuasion and false promise inducing a virtuous unmarried female to engage in sex).[11] An unmarried person commits fornication when he voluntarily has sexual intercourse with another person.[12]

The crime of sodomy embraces performance *or submission to* certain types of deviate sexual conduct, including lesbianism. When the other participant does not consent, it is aggravated sodomy.[13] A married person commits adultery by sexual intercourse with a person other than a spouse.[14]

Reasonable belief in eligibility to marry is a defense to the crime of bigamy,[15] as it is to a prosecution for the crime of marrying a person known to be married to another.[16] Similarly, for incest there must have been knowledge that the relationship of the parties was within the forbidden degree.[17]

A female under fourteen years of age is legally incapable of giving consent to sexual intercourse.[18] No conviction can be had on the unsupported testimony of the victim.[19] The results of

---

[9]Ga. Code, § 74-9902.
[10]Id.
[11]Id., § 26-2005.
[12]Id., § 26-2010.
[13]Id., § 26-2002. The constitutionality of this provision was upheld in Wanzer v. State, 232 Ga. 523, 207 S.E.2d 466 (1974).
[14]Ga. Code, § 26-2009.
[15]Id., § 26-2007.
[16]Id., § 26-2008.
[17]Id., § 26-2006. As to the prohibited degrees for invalidity of a marriage, see § 26-9905.
[18]Drake v. State, 239 Ga. 232, 236 S.E.2d 748 (1977).
[19]Ga. Code, § 26-2018.

polygraph tests admitted on stipulation of the parties, however, are sufficient to corroborate a victim's testimony.[20]

Abortion

The abortion statute, amended in 1973,[21] is now rewritten to conform to the mandates of Roe v. Wade.[22]

Status of children

A "bastard" is defined in Georgia as a child born out of wedlock whose parents do not marry, or the offspring of adulterous intercourse of a wife during wedlock;[23] this definition also includes a child whose reputed father has not married the mother and recognized the child as his.[24] If both husband and wife have consented in writing to artificial insemination, children so conceived are legitimate.[25]

The Code forbids a court, commission or quasi-judicial body to discriminate against any person because of his illegitimate birth.[26] This notwithstanding, it has been held that a child cannot recover social security benefits if he is illegitimate.[27] Limitations of aid to families with dependent children, when illegitimates are involved, such as a provision requiring the mother to swear to the name and address of the putative father as a precondition of eligibility,[28] have been held valid as being established for the purpose of maintaining and strengthening family life.[29]

Illegitimate children have no inheritable blood except that given to them by express law. They may inherit from their mother, from each other, and from children of the same mother, in the same manner as if legitimate. If such a person dies without

---

[20]State v. Chambers, 240 Ga. 76, 239 S.E.2d 324 (1977).
[21]Ga. Code, § 26–1201.
[22]See section 2.19, herein.
[23]Ga. Code, § 74–201.
[24]Id., § 74–101.
[25]Id., § 74–101.1.
[26]Id., § 74–204.
[27]Hobby v. Burke, 227 F.2d 932 (C.A.-5 Ga., 1955).
[28]Ga. Code, § 99–903.
[29]Cheley v. Burson, 324 F. Supp. 678 (N.D. Ga., 1971), appeal dismissed 404 U.S. 878, 30 L. Ed. 2d 159, 92 Sup. Ct. 219 (1971).

issue or widow, his mother, brothers and sisters inherit his estate equally.[30] Unless the father has legitimized the child, there is no provision for its succession to the father.

Notwithstanding the statute forbidding judicial discrimination on account of illegitimacy,[31] an illegitimate child cannot recover damages for the tortious causing of its father's death.[32] Such a child can, however, recover for the homicide of its mother,[33] and the mother can recover for the wrongful causing of death of the child.[34] The provision permitting this action to the mother though silent as to the right of the father has been held not violative of due process.[35] The opinion so holding suggests that one of the reasons could be a state's interest in setting a standard of morality, which would be enhanced by refusing the action to the father. Whether or not the decision, which incidentally involved a situation where the father had acknowledged paternity and had supported the child from birth, is reversed by the Supreme Court of the United States, it seems doubtful whether a state has any compelling interest in the promotion, through oblique sanctions of this nature, of the morality of its citizens.

The father of an illegitimate whose paternity has been judicially established is entitled to notice and a hearing before his parental rights can be terminated.[36] If his paternity is not established, he must first establish this before he is entitled to participate in any proceedings relating to the child.[37] He can, on notice to the mother, petition the court for legitimation of the child. If this is effected, the child can inherit from him as if born in lawful wedlock.[38] He can resort to this procedure even though married to a woman other than the child's mother at the time of its conception.[39]

---

[30]Ga. Code, § 113–904. See also § 113–905. As to the mother's rights, see § 74–203. For inheritance by and from illegitimates, see §§ 113–904, 113–905.
[31]Id., § 74–204.
[32]Brinkley v. Dixie Constr. Co., 205 Ga. 415, 54 S.E.2d 267 (1949), 79 Ga. App. 583, 54 S.E.2d 510 (1949). Ga. Code, § 105–1302.
[33]Ga. Code, § 105–1306.
[34]Id., § 105–1307. See also § 74–205.
[35]Hughes v. Parham, 241 Ga. 198, 243 S.E.2d 867 (1978).
[36]Ga. Code, § 24A–3202.
[37]Id.
[38]Id., § 74–103. As to birth registration of illegitimates, see § 88–1709 et seq.
[39]In re Pickett, 131 Ga. App. 159, 205 S.E.2d 522 (1974).

Support and custody

The obligation of the father to support the child on proof of his paternity[40] continues until the child reaches the age of eighteen, marries or becomes self-supporting. This obligation can be good consideration to support a contract made by him.[41] He can be ordered to furnish security for the performance of these obligations, as for his liability for the mother's confinement expenses, and for failure to do so he can be criminally prosecuted.[42]

Georgia has adopted the Uniform Reciprocal Enforcement of Support Act.[43]

Prima facie, the right to custody of the child is in the mother.[44] On a showing of her unfitness, however, the best interests of the child may dictate a change.[45]

The Georgia Code once deprived a putative father of the right to veto an adoption of his child unless he has legitimated it, either by marrying the mother and acknowledging it as his own, or by a court order declaring the child legitimate.[46] Though provisions enacted in 1977 do not in terms so provide, their constitutionality has been upheld by the Supreme Court. Equal protection does not require that such a father be on all fours with those of the father of a child born in lawful wedlock. Even if the putative father has paid support, if he has never sought custody of the child or had any significant responsibility for its well-being, there is no policy reason why his consent should not be dispensed with if the best interests of the child so dictate.[47]

---

[40]Ga. Code, §§ 74–105, 74–202. As to the mother's rights, see § 74–203. In a prosecution for abandonment of an illegitimate, an issue is paternity. Hunt v. State, 101 Ga. App. 126, 112 S.E.2d 817 (1960). As to mother's eligibility for state assistance, see Ga. Code, § 99–903 et seq.

[41]Ga. Code, § 74–202.

[42]Id., § 74–9901 et seq. See McCullough v. State, 141 Ga. App. 840, 234 S.E.2d 678 (1977).

[43]Ga. Code, §§ 99–901a to 99–932a.

[44]Turner v. Head, 236 Ga. 483, 224 S.E.2d 360 (1976).

[45]See Godfrey v. Godfrey, 239 Ga. 707, 238 S.E.2d 378 (1977).

[46]Ga. Code, § 74.403(3). See Wiles v. Brothers, 138 Ga. App. 616, 226 S.E.2d 805 (1976); Wojciechowski v. Allen, 238 Ga. 556, 234 S.E.2d 325 (1977).

[47]Quilloin v. Walcott, 434 U.S. 246, 54 L. Ed. 2d 511, 98 Sup. Ct. 549 (1978). See also Berry v. Samuels, 145 Ga. App. 687, 244 S.E.2d 593 (1978).

Property rights of cohabitants

Up to now, Georgia has evidenced an uncompromising reluctance to recognize any property rights in accumulations of a meretricious cohabitant. At the turn of the century a court lent a deaf ear to the claim of a woman who alleged that she was induced by fraud to cohabit with a man, to render services to him and to deliver to him her earnings.[48] Nearly sixty years later, a court also declined equitable relief to a woman who had contributed to the price of land and improvements to which the man took title, holding that illicit sex formed part of the contract.[49] More recently, a Georgia court has taken the same line. A woman sued for an award of $100 a month for the eighteen years she had lived with a man. She also sought exclusive title to and possession of the house which was jointly purchased. The trial court's award of summary judgment for the defendant (there being no genuine issue as to any material fact) was affirmed. Both parties having admitted the fact of cohabitation in verified pleadings, it was held to be the woman's duty to come forward and introduce evidence to rebut the conclusion that the immorality of the transaction was such as to deny her any claim to relief.[50]

The courts, however, do recognize that when property has been erroneously awarded to one who was not in fact the lawful widow of a decedent, a constructive trust can be impressed on the holder.[51]

6.12. Hawaii

A modified form of the community property system is in effect in Hawaii.[52]

---

[48]Schmitt v. Schneider, 109 Ga. 628, 35 S.E. 145 (1900). Compare Smith v. Du Bose, 78 Ga. 413, 3 S.E. 309, 6 Am. St. Rep. 260 (1887), upholding a contract in consideration of past illicit cohabitation.

[49]Wellmaker v. Roberts, 213 Ga. 740, 101 S.E.2d 712 (1958).

[50]Rehak v. Mathis, 239 Ga. 541, 238 S.E.2d 81 (1977). See Recent Decisions, Domestic Relations, 12 Ga. L. Rev. 361 (1978), wherein the author expresses doubts as to whether the Georgia courts will follow the lead of Marvin v. Marvin, 18 Cal. 3d 660, 134 Cal. Rptr. 815, 557 P.2d 106 (1976), discussed in sections 1.1 and 4.10, herein.

[51]Patrick v. Simon, 237 Ga. 742, 229 S.E.2d 746 (1976). See Salo, Joint Ownership of Assets in Georgia—The Fiduciary Lawyers' Labyrinth, 14 Ga. S.B. J. 14 (1977). Constructive trusts are discussed in section 4.8, herein.

[52]Hawaii Rev. Stat., §§ 510.1 to 510.30.

Common-law marriages cannot validly be contracted in Hawaii, but the state will recognize that institution if legal in the jurisdiction where contracted.[53]

Adoption

Fairly typical statutory provisions entitle any proper adult resident in the state to petition for the adoption of a child.[54] Under these provisions, the adoption of a Philippine child by Hawaiian petitioners has been sustained as valid though the child was not at the time within the territorial jurisdiction of the court hearing the petition.[55]

Workers' compensation death benefits

The Hawaii Workers' Compensation Act defines a "child," for the purposes of recovery of death benefits, to include an illegitimate child acknowledged by the worker prior to the injury in respect of which compensation is being sought.[56] Under the former statute, on which the present act is based, coverage did not include illegitimate children of others taken into the home and not adopted.[57]

Abortion

Termination of the pregnancy "of a non-viable fetus" [sic] is forbidden in Hawaii except by a licensed physician, in a licensed hospital.[58]

Possible criminal liability

The penal legislation of this state reflects the modern reluctance to criminalize private consensual sexual behavior of adults.

---

[53]Id., § 572–3.
[54]Id., § 572–1 et seq.
[55]Pascual v. O'Shea, 421 F. Supp. 80 (D. Haw., 1976).
[56]Hawaii Rev. Stat., § 386–2.
[57]In re Pioneer Mill Co., 31 Haw. 814 (1931).
[58]Hawaii Rev. Stat., § 453–16. See also MacDougal and Nasser, Abortion Decision and Evolving Limits on State Intervention, 11 Hawaii B. J. 51 (1974).

6.12   UNMARRIED COUPLES AND THE LAW

Prior laws denouncing nonmarital sexual intercourse (fornication) and extramarital sex (adultery),[59] no longer appear on the statute books. Sodomy[60] is restricted to unconsented-to "deviate sexual intercourse."[61] (One less than fourteen years of age is presumably incapable of giving an effective consent.) The grade of the crime, and the degree of severity with which it can be punished, clearly rests on the gravity of the attendant circumstances.

The crime of incest is somewhat broader in scope than is usual in criminal statutes. It extends to intercourse with anyone who is within the degrees of consanguinity or affinity within which marriage is prohibited.[62]

In addition to rape in the second degree, which embraces sexual intercourse with a female who is less than fourteen years old,[63] the legislature has denounced as criminal, conduct which amounts to "sexual abuse." This conduct, though not involving intercourse, involves "sexual contact."[64] Sexual abuse in the first degree is committed if one forcibly has sexual contact with another, or intentionally has such contact with a person less than fourteen years old.[65] Sexual abuse in the second degree involves sexual contact with one who is mentally incapacitated or physically helpless, or one who is under sixteen years old and at least fourteen years old and at least four years younger than the actor.[66] This is a misdemeanor. The rationale of this latter crime and the age differential is that voluntary sexual behavior between contemporaries is not regarded as sufficiently heinous in nature to merit the attention of the criminal law. Further, for the misdemeanor of sexual contact with the fourteen-to-sixteen-year-old, promiscuity of the other participant is a defense.[67]

---

[59] As to the constitutionality of an earlier statute which provided lesser penalties for women offenders than for men, see Territory v. Armstrong, 28 Haw. 88 (1924).
[60] Hawaii Rev. Stat., §§ 707-733 to 707-735.
[61] As to the definition of deviate sexual intercourse, see Hawaii Rev. Stat., § 707-700(8).
[62] Id., § 707-741. As to the prohibited degrees, see § 572-1(1).
[63] Id., § 707-731.
[64] As to the definition of sexual contact, see Hawaii Rev. Stat., § 707-700(9).
[65] Id., § 707-733.
[66] Id., § 707-737(b).
[67] Id.

HAWAII 6.12

Status of children

All illegitimate children must bear their mother's name as the family name.[68] They do not inherit from the father, without an express bequest.[69] If the marriage is annulled for any reason[70] the children are legitimate.[71]

The state has, with a few variations, adopted the Uniform Parentage Act[72] which provides for the establishment of paternity, and the powers of the court relating to the support and custody of illegitimate children.[73] It has also enacted the Uniform Reciprocal Enforcement of Support Act,[74] as well as the Uniform Child Custody Jurisdiction Act.[75]

Legitimation is effected either by marriage of the parents, or by a voluntary acknowledgment of the child supported by affidavit of both parents, or by an adjudication of paternity as a result of proceedings under the Parentage Act, or by adoption.[76] It is recognized that such legitimation can be effected even though the child occupied the unenviable status of an adulterine bastard at time of birth.[77]

The proceedings to have the child adopted out, and the necessity of the consent of both parents unless they have relinquished the child, follow a standard pattern.[78] The consent of "[a] concerned natural father who is not the legal, adjudicated, or presumed father but who has demonstrated a reasonable degree

---

[68]Id., § 574–3. See also § 532–6.
[69]Id., § 577–14.
[70]As to grounds for annulment, see Hawaii Rev. Stat., §580–21.
[71]Id., § 580–27. Thus children of an illegal marriage, where one is deceived into a belief as to its validity, are legitimate for inheritance purposes. Id., § 580–25.
[72]See section 3.4, herein.
[73]Hawaii Rev. Stat., §§584–1 to 584–26. It is held that expert testimony as to the resemblance of a child to the person alleged to be the father is admissible to prove paternity. Almeida v. Correa, 51 Haw. 594, 465 P.2d 564 (1970). See also, as to support obligations, Hawaii Rev. Stat., § 577–14.
[74]Hawaii Rev. Stat., §§ 576–1 to 576–41.
[75]Id., §§ 583–1 to 583–26.
[76]Id., § 338–1(7). As to the birth recordation on legitimation, see § 338–21.
[77]McMillan v. Gleason, 29 Haw. 258 (1926), affd. 16 F.2d 273 (C.A.-9 Haw., 1926).
[78]Hawaii Rev. Stat., §§578–1 to 578–17. As to rights to biological parents generally, see section 3.8, herein.

of interest, concern or responsibility as to the welfare of a child"[79] is a requirement not to be ignored.[80]

Property rights of cohabitants

Prior to becoming a state, Hawaii derived its law from Congress, the territorial legislature, the common law of England, and principles of equity. Though an early case had granted relief to a wife who mistakenly believed in the existence of a valid marriage on a basis of joint venture,[81] two years later, in Fung Dai Kim Ah Leong v. Lau Ah Leong, the Supreme Court of Hawaii declined such relief.[82] After an exhaustive survey of the decisional law of various states of this country (many of which did furnish a remedy) it decided that the common law of England permitted no such relief. The parties, after 35 years of living together, had accumulated what was in those days a fortune. They were of Chinese origins and had solemnized their marriage in Hawaii in accordance with Chinese customs, without obtaining a marriage license. On appeal, the United States Court of Appeals noted that all the state decisions favoring the mistaken spouse in such situations, whether rationalized by a theory of partnership, resulting trust or the like, evinced a purpose "to prevent a result so inherently wrong as to shock our common conception of fundamental justice," and reversed.[83] The federal court thought proper consideration should be given to the relative contributions of property and of services made by the respective parties, as well as local statutes affecting alimony and dower rights of the woman.[84] In adjusting the equities, it would also be proper for the court to bear in mind that the husband had, during their cohabitation, entered into a legal marriage with another.

Notwithstanding this decision, the Hawaii Supreme Court held, a few years later, that a woman beguiled into a "marriage"

---

[79] Hawaii Rev. Stat., § 578–2(5).
[80] An adoption decree will be set aside where rights of alleged father were not recognized. In re Adoption of Male Minor Child, 56 Haw. 543, 544 P.2d 728 (1975).
[81] Ah Leong v. Ah Leong, 28 Haw. 581 (1925).
[82] Fung Dai Kim Ah Leong v. Lau Ah Leong, 29 Haw. 770 (1927).
[83] Fung Dai Kim Ah Leong v. Lau Ah Leong, 27 F.2d 582, 583 (C.A.-9 Haw., 1928), cert. den. 278 U.S. 636, 73 L. Ed. 552, 49 Sup. Ct. 33 (1928).
[84] A court has authority to order an allowance for the support of a spouse and family when a marriage is annulled for fraud. Hawaii Rev. Stat., § 580–24.

by a false assertion that the man had no wife would not qualify for an allowance against the decedent man's estate.[85]

Though early precedent does not allow relief to a cohabitant who knows of the nonexistence of a marriage,[86] it is unlikely that the courts would not heed the claims of one who was merely mistaken, in view of the Ah Leong case. And, since the population of Hawaii comprises so many persons of oriental origin, it seems reasonable to predict that, if asked today, the courts will give effect to the parties' reasonable expectations, whether or not they have complied with traditional Western marriage ceremonies.

6.13. Idaho

Idaho is a community property state.[87]

Since a marriage requires the consent of the parties, plus either a solemnization or a mutual assumption of marital rights and duties,[88] common-law marriage is recognized. The requisite cohabitation must of course be of more than a mere furtive nature.[89] As elsewhere, it is held in Idaho that a continued cohabitation after the removal of some legal impediment to their union in marriage can result in a common-law marriage.[90] If one of the parties is already married, though separated from the legal spouse, no common-law marriage can come into existence.[91]

Adoption

Any adult resident in the state may adopt a child. Persons no longer minors can be adopted where an adoption did not take place during the adoptee's minority by reason of inadvertence, mistake or neglect, and the adopter has sustained the relation of

---

[85] In re Estate of Ching Lum, 31 Haw. 469 (1930), reh. den. 31 Haw. 533 (1930).
[86] Kienitz v. Sager, 40 Haw. 1 (1953).
[87] Idaho Code, § 32.906 et seq.
[88] Id., § 32–201.
[89] In re Koshman's Estate, 77 Idaho 96, 288 P.2d 652 (1955).
[90] Thomey v. Thomey, 67 Idaho 393, 181 P.2d 777 (1947); Morrison v. Sunshine Min. Co., 64 Idaho 6, 127 P.2d 766 (1942); Nicholas v. Idaho Power Co., 63 Idaho 675, 125 P.2d 321 (1942).
[91] In re Reichert, 95 Idaho 647, 516 P.2d 704 (1973) (compensation benefits awarded to worker's lawful widow even though he was living with another woman at the time of his death).

6.13 UNMARRIED COUPLES AND THE LAW

parent to the adoptee.[92] Unless the adopting parent is a spouse of the natural parent, a fifteen-year age differential between adopter and adoptee is required.[93]

Workers' compensation death benefits

For the purposes of the workers' compensation law, a child includes an acknowledged illegitimate child.[94] Any child can qualify for these benefits, if under eighteen or incapable of self-support and unmarried, whether or not actually dependent on a decedent worker.[95] To qualify as a widow, however, the spouse must have been living with the decedent or living apart from him for justifiable cause, or actually dependent, wholly or partially, on him.[96]

Abortion

The Idaho legislature has left little room for doubt as to its stance on the much-debated "right-to-life" issue. Provisions enacted in 1973, in response to the Supreme Court's decisions,[97] begin as follows:

> The Supreme Court of the United States having ruled that the several states lack the power to prohibit the practice of abortion or the commission thereof in the fashion previously prescribed by the criminal code of this state, and having specifically stricken down as violative of the constitutional right of privacy of the pregnant mother, criminal and related abortion statutes of the states of Georgia and Texas but reserving to the state the power to provide some standards and restrictions if they deem

---

[92]Idaho Code, § 16–1501. As to adoption of "hard-to-place" children, see §§ 56–801 to 56–806.

[93]Id., § 16–1502. The age differential is not required if the adopter is 25 or older. Generally, as to the procedures to adopt, see §§ 16–1501 to 16–1512.

[94]Id., § 72–102(7)(c). Generally, as to workers' compensation, see § 72–101 et seq.

[95]Id., § 72–410(1).

[96]Id., § 72–410(2). For the purposes of such benefits, the law will presume morality and not immorality, marriage and not concubinage, and legitimacy and not bastardy. If a marriage is shown, the burden is on defendant employer to show it is not a lawful marriage. Mauldin v. Sunshine Min. Co., 61 Idaho 9, 97 P.2d 608 (1939).

[97]See section 2.19, herein.

it appropriate to do so, and appearing that, in the event of the failure of this state to enact legislation regulating and proscribing abortion under such circumstances as it is within the power of the state so to regulate and proscribe, there is an immediate danger of widespread and undesirable abortion practices within the state, the legislature deems it necessary and in the public interest to provide standards and regulations and to define crimes with respect to the general subject of abortion in the interest of filling the voids and resolving the ambiguities generated by the said recent decisions in the Texas and Georgia cases, and in the furtherance and preservation of the public policy of this state in such matters. Without condoning or approving abortion or the liberalization of abortion laws generally, nonetheless by this act the legislature of the state of Idaho does express the policy of the state to regulate and to prescribe the standards with respect to the type of judgment, practice and conduct that is implicit in the performance of the abortions or the submission thereto.[98]

There follow provisions reflecting the state's compliance with the mandates of the Supreme Court in respect to abortions,[99] plus the following interesting provision:

In the event that the states are again permitted to safeguard the lives of unborn infants before the twenty-fifth week of pregnancy as a result of the Supreme Court of the United States overruling the decisions announced on January 22, 1973, in the cases of Doe et al v. Bolton et al. No. 70–40, and Roe et al v. Wade No. 70–18, or an amendment to the United States Constitution overruling these decisions, the governor shall, upon his determination that such event has occurred, make a proclamation declaring said event to have happened and the date of such event.

The statute goes on to provide that if this should happen, all the current legislation shall be repealed and the prior provisions, criminalizing abortions, "shall be in full force and effect on and after said date."[1]

Three other provisions exempting physicians and hospitals

---

[98] Idaho Code, § 18–604.
[99] Id., §§ 18–604 to 18–611. As to the advertising and distribution of contraceptive information, which is restricted to licensed physicians and registered health care providers who in good faith believe the acquirer is sufficiently intelligent and mature to understand the nature and significance thereof, see § 18–603. Compare section 2.19, herein.
[1] Idaho Code, § 18–613.

6.13 UNMARRIED COUPLES AND THE LAW

from refusing to perform abortions, making criminal the procurement of abortion, and also criminalizing a woman's conduct in submitting to an abortion or soliciting one, are made effective contingent upon governor's proclamation.[2]

Possible criminal liability

The sex crimes with which an unmarried Idaho couple might conceivably be involved include the following: adultery (which is committed whenever one of the parties, regardless of gender, is married);[3] incest (which extends to relationships between all persons within the degrees of consanguinity within which marriages are void, and covers intermarriage as well as fornication or adultery);[4] fornication;[5] abduction against a woman's will for marriage or defilement;[6] the "infamous crime against nature"[7] (which is held to embrace fellatio);[8] lewd conduct with a minor,[9] under which there have been many prosecutions;[10] and bigamy and polygamy,[11] offenses for which knowledge of the fact that one is acting unlawfully is required.[12]

Although lewd cohabitation applies to persons who "live and cohabit together as man and wife" or "lewdly and notoriously associate together," it can be doubted whether, in view of the title

---

[2]Id., §§ 18-612, 18-614, 18-615.
[3]Id., § 18-6601.
[4]Id., § 18-6602. As to the prohibited degrees of consanguinity, see § 32-205. These provisions relating to adultery and incest appear to have been repealed in 1971 but re-enacted as from January, 1972.
[5]Id., § 18-6603. Fornication is not a necessarily included offense in a prosecution for lewd conduct with a minor. State v. Herr, 97 Idaho 783, 554 P.2d 961 (1976).
[6]Idaho Code, § 18-501.
[7]Id., § 18-6605.
[8]State v. Drapeau, 97 Idaho 685, 551 P.2d 972 (1976); State v. Izatt, 96 Idaho 667, 534 P.2d 1107 (1975).
[9]Idaho Code, § 18-6607.
[10]See Gonzales v. Hodsdon, 91 Idaho 330, 420 P.2d 813 (1966); State v. Thurlow, 85 Idaho 96, 375 P.2d 996 (1962); State v. McConville, 82 Idaho 47, 349 P.2d 114 (1960); State v. Madrid, 74 Idaho 200, 259 P.2d 1044 (1953); State v. Petty, 73 Idaho 136, 248 P.2d 218 (1952), appeal dismissed 345 U.S. 938, 97 L. Ed. 1364, 73 Sup. Ct. 834 (1953); State v. Evans, 73 Idaho 50, 245 P.2d 788 (1952).
[11]Idaho Code, §§ 18-1101 to 18-1105.
[12]State v. Sayko, 37 Idaho 430, 216 Pac. 1036 (1923).

IDAHO 6.13

of the provision ("Lewd cohabitation"), a mere cohabitation unaccompanied by any aspect offensive to the community would be prosecuted.[13]

The age of consent for statutory rape is eighteen years.[14] Rape is also committed where the female submits to intercourse in the belief, fraudulently induced, by the male that he is her husband.[15]

Status of children

For the purposes of intestate succession, a child born out of wedlock is a child of the mother. It is also a child of the father if: (1) the natural parents participated in a marriage ceremony before or after the birth of the child, even though the attempted marriage is void; or (2) the paternity is established by an adjudication before the death of the father or is established thereafter by clear and convincing proof.[16] However, paternity so established does not qualify the father or his kindred to inherit from or through the child unless the father has openly treated the child as his, and has not refused to support the child.[17] Thus, if a child can sustain the burden of producing clear and convincing proof of the decedent's paternity, he can inherit from the father even where the mother has died as well; though the proof of paternity would certainly present problems.[18] Proceedings to establish paternity follow the standard pattern.[19] Legitimation of a child can be effected by subsequent marriage of the parents,[20] by acknowledgment of paternity,[21] or by adjudication of paternity. A father can legitimate the child by publicly acknowledging it as his own, receiving it, with the consent of his wife if he is married, into his

---

[13] Idaho Code, § 18-6604.
[14] Id., § 18-6101.1.
[15] Id., § 18-6101.6.
[16] Id., § 15-2109.
[17] Id.
[18] See In re Stone's Estate, 78 Idaho 632, 308 P.2d 597 (1957).
[19] Idaho Code, §§ 7-1101 to 7-1123.
[20] Id., § 32-1006.
[21] Id., § 16-1510. As to legitimacy on annulment of marriage, see § 32-503; as to legitimacy of children born of an adulterous wife, see § 32-711.

family, and adopting it as legitimate.[22] Adoption legitimates the child.[23]

Support and custody

The state has adopted the Uniform Reciprocal Enforcement of Support Act.[24] As usual, the natural parents are entitled to custody unless it is affirmatively shown that the child has been abandoned or that a parent is unfit to hold such responsibility.[25]

Property rights of partners

Neither party to a meretricious relationship acquires rights in the property of the other by reason of their cohabitation.[26] However, the courts do not rule out situations where justice demands that the accumulations of a union, initially meretricious, be divided between the partners, as, for example, where the one asserting title is estopped from asserting the invalidity of a common-law marriage.[27]

6.14. Illinois

This is not a community property state.[28]

A statute which required a different age at which males may marry without parental consent to that required of females,[29] was

---

[22] Provision is made for the issuance of a new birth certificate where an Idaho-born person is legitimated by subsequent marriage of parents or by adjudication. Id., § 39–259.

[23] Id., § 16–1508. As to legitimation by a father accepting the child into his home, see § 16–1510. Generally, as to adoption proceedings, see §§ 16–1501 to 16–1512.

[24] Id., §§ 7–1048 to 7–1089.

[25] See Yearsley v. Yearsley, 94 Idaho 667, 496 P.2d 666 (1972). As to termination of the parent/child relation, see Idaho Code, §§ 16–2001 to 16–2015. As to the Child Custody Jurisdiction Act, see §§ 5–1001 to 5–1025.

[26] Cargill v. Hancock, 92 Idaho 460, 444 P.2d 421 (1968).

[27] See Warner v. Warner, 76 Idaho 399, 283 P.2d 931 (1955), where it is said that equity will protect the property rights of a meretrix "either according to their agreement" or according to principles of equity and justice.

[28] Ill. Rev. Stat., ch. 68, § 1–21.

[29] Id., ch. 89, § 3.

ILLINOIS 6.14

declared unconstitutional.[30] The lesser age limits applicable to females are thus applicable to both sexes.[31]

Common-law marriages entered into after June 30, 1905 are invalid unless the parties have subsequently had their union licensed and solemnized.[32] If this is done, the children are deemed legitimate.[33] If one residing in and intending to continue to reside in the state is disabled or prohibited from marriage by the laws of Illinois and goes to another state to marry, the marriage is void for all purposes in Illinois.[34] Subject to this qualification, however, the state does recognize common-law marriages entered into in a state which recognizes such a marriage.[35]

Schoolteachers

The fact that a teacher had only been married for a month when she required maternity leave on account of her advanced pregnancy was held, absent any evidence of any harm to anyone, not to constitute "cause" for her termination.[36]

Students

As to school pupils, the legislature has made provision for alternative instruction for those who cannot attend school due to pregnancy.[37]

Adoption

To adopt a child, one must be of legal age (unless leave of court on good cause can be obtained), and a resident in the state continuously for at least six months immediately preceding the

---

[30]Phelps v. Bing, 58 Ill. 2d 32, 316 N.E.2d 775 (1974).
[31]Id.
[32]Ill. Rev. Stat., ch. 89, § 4.
[33]Id.
[34]Id., ch. 89, § 19.
[35]Peirce v. Peirce, 379 Ill. 185, 39 N.E.2d 990 (1942). See Weyrauch, Informal and Formal Marriage—An Appraisal of Trends in Family Organization, 28 U. Chi. L. Rev. 88 (1960).
[36]Reinhardt v. Board of Education of Alton Community Unit School Dist. No. 11, Madison and Jersey Counties, 19 Ill. App. 3d 481, 311 N.E.2d 710 (1974), vacated on other grounds 61 Ill. 2d 101, 329 N.E.2d 218 (1975).
[37]Ill. Rev. Stat., ch. 122, § 10–22.6a.

commencement of the adoption proceeding.[38] This residence requirement does not apply if the child is a relative or is placed with an agency. If the adopter is married, his or her spouse must join in the application.[39] In at least one case, the issue as to whether the courts can decree an adoption without heeding the recommendations of the Department of Children and Family Services[40] has been resolved in favor of the court.[41]

Workers' compensation death benefits

Illegitimate children to whom a decedent worker owes a duty of support may recover workers' compensation death benefits.[42]

Abortion

As a result of the abortion decisions of the Supreme Court of the United States,[43] the Illinois abortion statute of 1973 (which had little more to say than that abortions must be performed by licensed physicians)[44] was amended by the legislature in 1975, with articulated reluctance, to conform to the requirements of Roe v. Wade.[45] Written informed consent of the woman prior to the completion of the first trimester is required. Subsequent to that period, abortions are forbidden unless the fetus is certified not to be viable, or certificate is made that the operation is necessary for the life and health of the mother.[46]

---

[38]Id., ch. 4, §§ 9.1–1, 9.1–2. The Public Aid Code has detailed provisions controlling the suitability of a home for illegitimate children. See ch. 4, §§ 4 to 6.
[39]Id.
[40]See section 2.9, herein.
[41]Adoption of Smith, 38 Ill. App. 3d 217, 347 N.E.2d 292 (1976), cert. den. 431 U.S. 939 and 434 U.S. 817. As to the higher payments under the AFDC(FC) plan, see Youakim v. Miller, 431 F. Supp. 40 (N.D. Ill., 1976).
[42]Jones v. Industrial Comm., 64 Ill. 2d 221, 1 Ill. Dec. 1, 356 N.E.2d 1 (1976); Yellow Cab Co. v. Industrial Comm., 42 Ill. 2d 226, 247 N.E.2d 601 (1969).
[43]See section 2.19, herein.
[44]See Illinois Abortion Statutes, 1974 University of Illinois Law Forum 421.
[45]Discussed in section 2.19, herein.
[46]Ill. Rev. Stat., ch. 38, § 81–23 et seq. Despite the legislature's attempt to conform to the Supreme Court's guidelines, in Wynn v. Scott, 449 F. Supp. 1302 (N.D. Ill., 1978), a decision containing many rulings on the constitutionality of the Illinois Abortion Act of 1975, the following provisions were held unconstitutional: (a) a requirement that the mother be informed prior to the abortion of the general

Tort actions

The Illinois courts do not recognize a plaintiff born an "adulterine bastard" as having any cause of action against the father.[47]

The statutes allow an action for damages for alienation of affections[48] and for criminal conversation.[49] In both, however, damages are limited to actual damages. Punitive damages are not recoverable. The courts appear to share the legislature's wan support of such litigation.[50] They insist that a plaintiff must aver and establish love and affection for the spouse (something of a challenge whenever a spouse is faithless), plus actual damages (as required by the statute) and overt acts, conduct or enticement willfully designed by the defendant to cause those affections to depart.[51]

Effect of cohabitation on right to alimony

The courts do not allow a divorcee's cohabitation with another as a ground for modification of alimony due her from her ex-husband. Nor, of course, does the failure of the former husband to conduct himself properly afford ground for increasing her allowance. "Conceding the general duty she owes society, what right does it give the husband to property justly hers, if she violates that duty? The husband owes a like duty to lead a moral and virtuous life. If he fails to perform it, could it be contended that it

---

dangers of abortion, including a possibility of subsequent sterility; (b) a requirement of spousal and parental consent; (c) a requirement that two doctors consult with the attending physician before a postviability abortion is performed; (d) a provision for termination of parental rights where a live birth results from attempted abortion, and for notification to the mother of the possibility of such termination; and (e) a prohibition of saline abortions.

[47]Zepeda v. Zepeda, 41 Ill. App. 2d 240, 190 N.E.2d 849 (1963), cert. den. 379 U.S. 945, 85 Sup. Ct. 444 (1964). See also section 2.20, herein.

[48]Ill. Rev. Stat., ch. 68, §§ 34 to 37.

[49]Id., §§ 41 to 47.

[50]See Heck v. Schupp, 394 Ill. 296, 68 N.E.2d 464, 167 A.L.R. 232 (1946).

[51]See Wheeler v. Fox, 16 Ill. App. 3d 1089, 307 N.E.2d 633 (1974), holding medical expenses and loss of profits allegedly resulting from loss of wife not to be compensable; plaintiff's poor health and unemployment being too remotely related to the tortious act alleged. As to a cause of action for torts against a spouse, see Proehl, Anguish of Mind: Damages for Mental Suffering Under Illinois Law, 56 Nw. U. L. Rev. 477 (1961); A Wife May Have an Action for Negligent Invasion of Consortium, 1951 University of Illinois Law Forum 322. See also section 2.22, herein.

would give her a right of additional property, or that there should be an increase in her allowance in consequence? Manifestly not."[52]

Possible criminal liability

Crimes possibly encountered by cohabitants include deviate sexual assault,[53] concealing the death of an illegitimate child,[54] and abortion.[55] Illinois also denounces fornication; this act being defined as cohabitation or sexual intercourse with another not his spouse if the behavior is open and notorious.[56] Consensual sodomy is not criminally punished.[57] For adultery, the cohabitation or sexual intercourse with a nonspouse must be open and notorious, and if an unmarried person is charged, there must be proof of knowledge that the coparticipant is married.[58] The behavior must be prominent, conspicuous and generally known and recognized by the public. The prohibition is designed to protect the public from conduct which disturbs the peace and openly flouts accepted standards of morality in the community. Notoriety must extend to the fact that the parties are not married. Evidence of a situation of serious family concern, but which does not show any publicity or public scandal which could tend to debase and demoralize the community, is not enough.[59]

That the provision is not designed to proscribe a conventional family relationship between unmarried partners is confirmed in Hewitt v. Hewitt,[60] reversing a trial court's dismissal of a complaint for relief brought by a woman who had cohabited with a man for fifteen years as husband and wife in a conventional family situation resulting in the birth of three children. The court points out that the committee involved in the enactment of the

---

[52]Cole v. Cole, 142 Ill. 19, 31 N.E. 109, 111 (1892).
[53]Ill. Rev. Stat., ch. 38, § 11–3.
[54]Id., § 9–4.
[55]Id., §§ 11 to 35.
[56]Id., § 11–8. There must be proof of an "open state" of living together; an isolated night of misconduct is not enough. See People v. Garcia, 37 Ill. App. 2d 90, 185 N.E.2d 1 (1962).
[57]See Sheedy, Law and Morals, 43 Chi. B. Rec. 373 (1962).
[58]Ill. Rev. Stat., ch. 38, § 11–7.
[59]People v. Cessna, 42 Ill. App. 3d 746, 1 Ill. Dec. 433, 356 N.E.2d 621 (1976).
[60]62 Ill. App. 3d 861, 20 Ill. Dec. 476, 380 N.E.2d 454 (1978).

adultery statute had stated the provision not to be intended to proscribe any sexual conduct between consenting adults unless such conduct adversely affects key interests such as, for example, the institution of marriage and normal family relationships. The court clearly did not consider the institution of marriage to be threatened by a mere family relationship embarked upon without benefit of solemnization of a marriage.

For a conviction of bigamy,[61] as for marrying or cohabiting with a bigamist,[62] guilty knowledge is required.

Sexual intercourse or deviate sexual conduct with one to whom the actor knows he is related as brother or sister, either of the whole or half blood, is incest.[63] If the misconduct is with one known to be the actor's son or daughter, the offense is aggravated incest.[64]

Statutory rape is not, as is usual, classified as a form of rape. One of seventeen years of age or over who performs or submits to sex, deviate sexual conduct or "lewd fondling," the other being a child, commits a felony.[65] This crime being designed primarily to protect those who are immature in sexual matters,[66] a reasonable belief that the child was sixteen or over, or is a prostitute, or has previously been married, is a statutory defense.

If the accused is fourteen or over, and performs any of the above acts or performs a lewd act in the presence of the child with intent to arouse sexual desires, and the other person involved is under eighteen, the crime is contributing to the sexual delinquency of a child.[67] Reasonable mistake as to the other's age is no defense.[68] Nevertheless, mistake as to the other's age can reduce what would otherwise be the felony (indecent liberties with a child) to the misdemeanor (contributing to sexual delinquency).[69] In a

---

[61] Ill. Rev. Stat., ch. 38, § 11–12.
[62] Id., § 11–13.
[63] Id., § 11–11.
[64] Id., § 11–10.
[65] Id., § 11–4.
[66] People v. Plewka, 27 Ill. App. 3d 553, 327 N.E.2d 457 (1975).
[67] Ill. Rev. Stat., ch. 38, § 11–5.
[68] Id.
[69] People v. Plewka, 27 Ill. App. 3d 553, 327 N.E.2d 457 (1975).

proper case, the complainant's testimony alone is sufficient to convict in the latter crime.[70]

Status of children

As is usually provided by statute, in Illinois an illegitimate child is heir of its mother, of any maternal ancestor, and of any person from whom its mother might have inherited, if living. The lawful issue of an illegitimate can take by descent any estate which the parent would have taken, if living.[71] The Illinois statute also provides: "A child who was illegitimate whose parents intermarry and who is acknowledged by the father as the father's child is legitimate."[72] This language resisted an attack on constitutional grounds in the Supreme Court of Illinois,[73] but was condemned by the Supreme Court of the United States, in Trimble v. Gordon,[74] as a discriminatory classification violative of the equal protection guarantees of the Constitution. It seems that an adjudication of paternity ought to be sufficient to qualify an illegitimate to succeed on intestacy to the father. (The courts, with the gymnastics often associated with statutory constructions to achieve the desired result, might well have regarded an adjudication of paternity as an "involuntary acknowledgment"—but they did not.) The Trimble decision has been criticized;[75] in fact, one commentator suggests that "Legislatures would do well to refrain from employing statutory classifications except to the

---

[70]People v. Bavirsha, 51 Ill. App. 3d 85, 9 Ill. Dec. 167, 366 N.E.2d 424 (1977). As to indecent solicitation of a child, see Ill. Rev. Stat., ch. 38, § 11–6; as to public indecency (by persons of seventeen and upwards), § 11–9. As to reasonable belief as to the age of female as affecting liability for statutory rape, see 14 De Paul L. Rev. 445 (1965).

[71]Ill. Rev. Stat., ch. 3, § 2–2.

[72]Id.

[73]In re Estate of Karas, 61 Ill. 2d 40, 329 N.E.2d 234 (1975).

[74]430 U.S. 762, 52 L. Ed. 2d 31, 97 Sup. Ct. 1459 (1977). See also section 3.3, herein.

[75]See Constitutional Law—Equal Protection and the Inheritance Rights of Illegitimates Under Intestate Succession Laws, 43 Mo. L. Rev. 116 (1978); Note, Illegitimate Succession—Illinois Statute Denying the Rights of Illegitimate Children to Inherit from Father's Estates Is Unconstitutional, 13 Tulsa L. J. 178 (1977).

extent that the uncertainty of a child's paternity may be exploited dishonestly."[76]

Substantial provisions of the Uniform Paternity Act[77] have been enacted in Illinois to control procedures for the establishment of paternity.[78] Since it is a civil proceeding for recovery of money, the right to a jury is ordinarily to be respected,[79] and the rules of evidence applicable to civil cases control—there need not be proof beyond a reasonable doubt.[80] Thus, the burden of proof is only to establish that defendant, more probably than not, is the father, and the mother's own testimony can be enough to discharge that burden.[81]

Rights and duties of the natural parents

The support liability of a father of an illegitimate child cannot be enforced unless he has been adjudicated the father or acknowledges paternity in open court or by a verified written statement.[82]

Illinois has adopted the Uniform Reciprocal Enforcement of Support Act.[83]

Stanley v. Illinois, discussed earlier,[84] displaced a judicial attitude which tended to impose on the adjudicated father all the

---

[76]Zarski, Recognizing the Father-Illegitimate Child Relation for Intestate Succession, 27 De Paul L. Rev. 175, 189 (1977).
[77]See section 3.4, herein.
[78]Ill. Rev. Stat., ch. 106 3/4, § 51 et seq. See Feirich, Paternity Act of 1957, Blessing or Blight?, 47 Ill. B. J. 824 (1959); Schatkin, Problem of Defense of a Paternity Proceeding, 21 De Paul L. Rev. 85 (1971).
[79]See Ehorn v. Podraza, 51 Ill. App. 3d 816, 9 Ill. Dec. 866, 367 N.E.2d 300 (1977); Hartsock v. Bress, 40 Ill. App. 2d 66, 189 N.E.2d 673 (1963).
[80]LaLacker v. Stuckey, 40 Ill. App. 2d 341, 189 N.E.2d 676 (1963). The provisions of the Illinois Civil Practice Act are applicable to paternity proceedings unless a specific provision of the Paternity Act requires otherwise. People ex rel. Mathis v. Brown, 44 Ill. App. 3d 783, 3 Ill. Dec. 475, 358 N.E.2d 1160 (1976).
[81]People ex rel. Adams v. Kite, 48 Ill. App. 3d 828, 6 Ill. Dec. 653, 363 N.E.2d 182 (1977). As to blood tests to determine paternity, see Harris, Some Observations on the Un-Uniform Act on Blood Tests to Determine Paternity, 9 Vill. L. Rev. 59 (1963). As to limitations on the time to commence a paternity suit, see Cook v. Askew, 34 Ill. App. 3d 1055, 341 N.E.2d 13 (1975). As to vacating a paternity judgment, see Jordan v. Wesley, 48 Ill. App. 3d 446, 6 Ill. Dec. 548, 363 N.E.2d 77 (1977).
[82]Ill. Rev. Stat., ch. 23, § 10–2.
[83]Id., ch. 68, §§ 101 to 142.
[84]See section 3.6, herein.

obligations of parenthood with no concomitant rights.[85] That landmark decision has firmly established the proposition that no father can be deprived of his say in the custody of or adoption of a child without notice and an opportunity to be heard, unless this is completely impracticable. This does not of course mean that he has any absolute rights either to veto an adoption or to insist on visitation of the child. Illinois is no exception to the generally accepted rule that the primary consideration in such matters is the best interests of the child itself.[86]

The issue of a void ceremonial marriage are legitimate.[87] Thus, a father can acquire heirship rights to the proceeds of his son's life insurance even though the marriage did not qualify as a legal marriage.[88] A statute which legitimates children by the intermarriage of their parents can apply to legitimate an adulterine bastard.[89] If the mother was not married to the father at the time of conception and birth, however, the father's name cannot ordinarily be entered on the birth certificate without the written consent of both parents.[90]

The important message of the Adoption Act[91] is that, since an adoption forever terminates the relation between the child and his natural parents,[92] unless both parents have unequivocally consented to relinquish the child for adoption, the initial enquiry of the court should be directed to the fitness or otherwise of the natural parents to provide a suitable home.[93] If the mother has

---

[85]See In re Stanley, 45 Ill. 2d 132, 256 N.E.2d 814 (1970); revd. 405 U.S. 645, 31 L. Ed. 2d 551, 92 Sup. Ct. 1208 (1972); DePhillips v. DePhillips, 35 Ill. 2d 154, 219 N.E.2d 465 (1966); Wallace v. Wallace, 60 Ill. App. 2d 300, 210 N.E.2d 4 (1965).

[86]See Baehr v. Baehr, 56 Ill. App. 3d 624, 14 Ill. Dec. 401, 372 N.E.2d 412 (1978); People ex rel. Ritchie v. Ritchie, 58 Ill. App. 3d 1045, 16 Ill. Dec. 414, 374 N.E.2d 1292 (1978). See also Hession, Adoptions After "Stanley"—Rights for Fathers of Illegitimate Children, 61 Ill. B. J. 350 (1973); Constitutional Law—Stanley v. Illinois: New Rights for Putative Fathers, 21 De Paul L. Rev. 1036 (1972).

[87]Ill. Rev. Stat., ch. 89, § 17a.

[88]In re Estate of Stewart, 131 Ill. App. 2d 183, 268 N.E.2d 187 (1971). See also Calisoff, Return of Enoch Arden, 50 Ill. B. J. 996 (1962).

[89]Robinson v. Ruprecht, 191 Ill. 424, 61 N.E. 631 (1901) (common-law marriages then recognized).

[90]Ill. Rev. Stat., ch. 111 ½, § 73–12.

[91]Id., ch. 4, §§ 9.1–1 to 9.1–24.

[92]In Interest of Jones, 34 Ill. App. 3d 603, 340 N.E.2d 269 (1975).

[93]People in Interest of Patterson v. Patterson, 36 Ill. App. 3d 484, 344 N.E.2d 226 (1976); In Interest of Massey, 35 Ill. App. 3d 518, 341 N.E.2d 405 (1976); In re Ladewig, 34 Ill. App. 3d 393, 340 N.E.2d 150 (1975).

ILLINOIS 6.14

not consented to the adoption, the court should ensure that some independent agency report on the domestic circumstances before adjudicating her unfitness.[94] Birth of a second illegitimate child is prima facie evidence of her unsuitability.[95] Only when this question of fitness is resolved against the mother should the question of the suitability of the prospective adopters fall for consideration; a premature hearing on this point could result in prejudice to the mother.[96]

Consent of all locatable putative fathers is a statutory prerequisite.[97] But if, within thirty days of a notification of pending adoption proceedings, he does not file a declaration of paternity or request to be kept informed, the proceedings can take place without his presence.[98]

Property rights of cohabitants

There are some early indications that the courts would recognize a resulting trust[99] when title is taken by a person to whom the payor of the price mistakenly believed he or she was married.[1]

In adopting the Uniform Marriage and Dissolution of Marriage Act,[2] the state has included the optional section[3] whereunder a court has authority to adjust the equities as between the putative

---

[94]Donlon v. Miller, 42 Ill. App. 3d 64, 355 N.E.2d 195 (1976).
[95]Ill. Rev. Stat., ch. 23, § 4–6.
[96]In re Adoption of Burton, 43 Ill. App. 3d 294, 1 Ill. Dec. 946, 356 N.E.2d 1279 (1976).
[97]Ill. Rev. Stat., ch. 4, §§ 9.1–7, 9.1–8, 9.1–12a. A prior statute providing that a father of an illegitimate should have no right of custody or control unless he has adopted the child was declared invalid in People ex rel. Slawek v. Covenant Children's Home, 52 Ill. 2d 20, 284 N.E.2d 291 (1972). See also Adoption of Illegitimates, 61 Ill. B. J. 378 (1973); Hession, Adoptions After "Stanley"—Rights for Fathers of Illegitimate Children, 61 Ill. B. J. 350 (1973).
[98]Ill. Rev. Stat., ch. 4, §§ 9.1–1 to 9.1–12a. See also Best Interests of the Child—The Illinois Adoption Act in Perspective, 24 De Paul L. Rev. 100 (1974).
[99]Discussed in section 4.5, herein.
[1]See Metropolitan Trust & Sav. Bank v. Perry, 259 Ill. 183, 102 N.E. 218 (1913); McDonald v. Carr, 150 Ill. 204, 37 N.E. 225 (1894). Where a woman knew of an impediment to the marriage, she was awarded one-half share of the property on a finding that she had contributed substantially to the purchase price, and that the parties had intended a joint tenancy. Dean v. Dean, 401 Ill. 406, 82 N.E.2d 342 (1948).
[2]Ill. Rev. Stat., ch. 40, § 101 et seq.
[3]See section 1.6, herein.

spouse and other putative spouses or the legal spouse, in so far as concerns accumulations during the period of living together, "as appropriate in the circumstances."[4]

In Hewitt v. Hewitt,[5] the Appellate Court reversed a trial judge's dismissal of a complaint brought by a woman who had cohabited with the defendant for fifteen years, assisting him in the completion of a professional education and establishing him in practice. The complaint included an allegation that, in addition to services as a companion, housewife and mother, she had provided financial assistance. Her prayer for relief was based not only on allegations of an express oral contract, but on allegations supporting implied contract, equitable relief for misrepresentation and constructive trust.

The court, in remanding the cause for further proceedings, relies heavily on the decision in Marvin v. Marvin,[6] quoting dicta which, in that case, also suggest recovery based on partnership, joint venture and quasi-contract. In short, the decision indicates that Illinois courts will draw on any of the traditional conceptual avenues of recovery[7] when the equities require it. "It is not realistic," said the Illinois court, "to conclude that this determination will 'discourage' marriage for the rule for which defendant contends [denial of any relief to one guilty of improper conduct] can only encourage a partner with obvious income-producing ability to avoid marriage and to retain all earnings which he may acquire."[8] (This argument, of course, could cut both ways. The partner without income-producing ability might be discouraged from insisting on marriage as a precondition of cohabitation by the certain knowledge that the accumulations will be shared or equitably divided in any event.)

6.15. Indiana

This is not a community property state.[9]

Common-law marriages entered into after January 1, 1958 are

---

[4]Ill. Rev. Stat., ch. 40, § 305.
[5]62 Ill. App. 3d 861, 380 N.E.2d 454 (1978).
[6]18 Cal. 3d 660, 134 Cal. Rptr. 815, 557 P.2d 106 (1976), discussed in sections 1.1 and 4.10, herein.
[7]See Chapter 4, herein.
[8]Hewitt v. Hewitt, 380 N.E.2d at 460.
[9]Ind. Code, § 31–1–9–2 et seq.

not recognized.[10] However, a court has held that where the parties in good faith went through the legal formalities necessary to consummate a valid marriage, not knowing of a legal impediment to such marriage, and thereafter the impediment was removed, a living together of the parties as husband and wife raised a presumption of marriage which is not nullified by the statute abolishing common-law marriage.[11] This statement might be read to mean that a putative marriage (both parties being mistaken as to its validity) does not fall within the statute barring common-law marriage.[12] But where the relationship was meretricious in its inception, there was no question as to a common-law marriage.[13]

Adoption

To qualify to adopt a child, one must be a resident of the state; the child must be under the age of eighteen and, if the petitioner for adoption is married, the spouse must join with the petitioner unless the spouse is a natural or adoptive parent—in which event only the spouse's consent is required.[14] The financial status of the petitioner is important: where a petitioner was in receipt of social security benefits, which would be reduced as her children grew, lack of sufficient ability to raise the adoptee suitably was held a

---

[10]Id., § 31-1-6-1. See Note, Common Law Marriage—A Legal Anachronism, 32 Ind. L. J. 99 (1956); Formalities Essential to a Valid Marriage in Indiana, 34 Ind. L. J. 643, 662-664 (1959).

[11]Reger v. Reger, 242 Ind. 302, 177 N.E.2d 901 (1961). See also Azimow v. Azimow, 146 Ind. App. 341, 255 N.E.2d 667 (1970); Gunter v. Dealer's Transp. Co., 120 Ind. App. 409, 91 N.E.2d 377 (1950). As to the requirements prior to the abolition of common-law marriage, see In re Sutherland's Estate, 246 Ind. 234, 204 N.E.2d 520 (1965).

[12]According to the record of the case, the parties married in 1956. The wife secured a valid divorce in 1957. The husband only learned of the invalidity of the marriage in 1960. Thus, they had cohabited as husband and wife for at least some months before January 1, 1958, the date common-law marriages were abolished. Hence, the court could have simply decided there was a common-law marriage, without volunteering the statement for which the case is cited. See also Eddington v. Eddington, 213 Ind. 347, 12 N.E.2d 758 (1938).

[13]Clayton v. Universal Constr. Co., 110 Ind. App. 322, 38 N.E.2d 887 (1942).

[14]Ind. Code, § 31-3-1-1 et seq.

good reason for declining the petition.[15] The requirement of consent of the child's natural parents can be dispensed with where they have properly been deprived of their parental rights;[16] also where they have been so neglectful of their parental obligations that the court can waive this requirement.[17] Such parental consent, where it is not dispensed with, must be accompanied by the written approval of an agency of the state. If the adoption is through a private placement agency, a blanket consent of the parents is sufficient,[18] if executed as provided by the statute.

Adoption petitions cannot be granted without a period of supervision by some licensed child-placing agency or a county department of public welfare.[19] The period is discretionary with the court, and at least where the petitioner is the child's natural mother with custody, it can be dispensed with altogether.[20] It is possible to have the adoption annulled where the welfare of the child demands such drastic action.[21]

Workers' compensation death benefits

A woman who lived with and was supported by a deceased unmarried workman as his wife did not qualify for benefits under

---

[15]In re Adoption of Graft, 153 Ind. App. 546, 288 N.E.2d 274 (1972). Welfare reports should not be considered by the court as part of the evidence in a contested proceeding. In re Adoption of Jeralds, 152 Ind. App. 538, 284 N.E.2d 99 (1972). They should, however, be available to a contesting party. In re Adoption of Sigman, 159 Ind. App. 618, 41 Ind. Dec. 250, 308 N.E.2d 716 (1974).

[16]Hogg v. Peterson, 245 Ind. 515, 198 N.E.2d 767 (1964).

[17]In re Adoption of Lockmondy, —— Ind. ——, 343 N.E.2d 793 (1976); In re Bryant's Adoption, 134 Ind. App. 480, 189 N.E.2d 593 (1963). A father's promise before the birth of the child, that he would consent to its adoption does not estop him from asserting parental rights even though the mother forewent an abortion in reliance thereon. If his paternity has been judicially established, and he has contributed to the support or care of the child, his written consent to the adoption is required. Unwed Father v. Unwed Mother, —— Ind. App. ——, 379 N.E.2d 467 (1978).

[18]Johnson v. Cupp, 149 Ind. App. 611, 274 N.E.2d 411 (1971). See Note, Dispensing with Parental Consent in Indiana Adoption Proceedings, 40 Ind. L. J. 378 (1965).

[19]Ind. Code, § 31-3-1-3.

[20]Horlock v. Oglesby, 249 Ind. 251, 231 N.E.2d 810 (1967), appeal dismissed 390 U.S. 718, 20 L. Ed. 2d 253, 88 Sup. Ct. 1418 (1968).

[21]County Dept. of Public Welfare of St. Joseph County v. Morningstar, 128 Ind. App. 688, 151 N.E.2d 150 (1958) (annulment where the welfare department defrauded the adoptive parents by misrepresenting the child's background). See also

the state workers' compensation laws[22] where she had a living husband.[23] (There was a time when an extramarital partner did so qualify.)[24] As now amended, the statute requires that one cannot qualify as a common-law spouse, and thus a dependent, unless the relationship was entered into before January 1, 1958.[25] A "child" includes an acknowledged illegitimate child for the purposes of the act.[26] The word "children" is held to extend to a posthumous illegitimate child; the burden, though, is on the claimant, usually the child's mother, to establish that the decedent had acknowledged it as his own.[27]

Abortion

A provision in the abortion law,[28] revised to meet the requirements of the Supreme Court of the United States,[29] which requires the consent of the parent or of one in loco parentis as a prerequisite for the abortion of an unmarried minor during the first twelve weeks of pregnancy, has been held unconstitutional.[30] It is a Class C felony to perform or abet the performance of an abortion not expressly provided for in the statute.[31]

Tort actions

Civil actions for breach of promise of marriage, alienation of affections, criminal conversation, and seduction of a female of

---

Warapius v. Price, 128 Ind. App. 529, 150 N.E.2d 759 (1958) (failure to obtain a minor parent's consent to the adoption).

[22]Ind. Code, § 22–3–2–1 et seq.

[23]Willan v. Spring Hill Coal Corp., 118 Ind. App. 422, 78 N.E.2d 880 (1948).

[24]See Thomas v. Central Engineering Constr. Co., 116 Ind. App. 385, 63 N.E.2d 295 (1945); Russell v. Johnson, 220 Ind. 649, 46 N.E.2d 219 (1943).

[25]Ind. Code, § 22–3–7–13.

[26]Hooley v. Hooley, 141 Ind. App. 101, 226 N.E.2d 344 (1967). See Anonymous Child v. Deceased Father's Employer, —— Ind. App. ——, 377 N.E.2d 407 (1978).

[27]See DeArmond v. Myers Gravel & Sand Corp., 142 Ind. App. 60, 231 N.E.2d 864 (1967), holding that unadopted children could be deemed "dependents."

[28]Ind. Code, § 35–1–58.5–1 et seq.

[29]See section 2.19, herein.

[30]Gary-Northwest Indiana Women's Services, Inc. v. Bowen, 421 F. Supp. 734 (N.D. Ind., 1976), affd. 429 U.S. 1067, 50 L. Ed. 2d 785, 97 Sup. Ct. 799 (1977).

[31]Ind. Code, § 35–1–58.5–4. For a conviction as accessory to the crime of attempting to procure an abortion, see Rhim v. State, 264 Ind. 682, 348 N.E.2d 620 (1976).

eighteen years or over are now, in line with current trends,[32] abolished.[33]

Possible criminal liability

In addition to rape,[34] statutory rape is interdicted under provisions relating to child molesting.[35] Bigamy[36] and incest[37] have withstood the legislative slashing of sexual crimes of a consensual nature.

There has also been a conviction in Indiana of a violation of the Mann Act[38] where the court did not restrict the application of this crime to interstate transportation for commercial vice.[39]

Status of children

In line with the general view, the Indiana courts regard as not illegitimate a child born during the existence of a voidable marriage which is annulled,[40] or even void ab initio.[41] For the purposes of local poor relief, an illegitimate child ordinarily follows the "legal settlement" of its mother at the time of its birth in determining which town or county carries the burden of support.[42]

For purposes of intestate succession, an illegitimate child inherits by and through the mother. It can inherit from the father and his relatives (and they from him) if (1) the father's paternity has been judicially established during his lifetime; or, (2) the putative father marries the mother and acknowledges the child to

---

[32]See section 2.23, herein.
[33]Ind. Code, § 34-4-4-1.
[34]Id., § 35-42-4-1. (The statute does not apply to spouses unless a petition for dissolution is pending and the spouses are living apart.)
[35]Id., § 35-42-4-3. As to the effect of mistake as to the victim's age, see Toliver v. State, —— Ind. ——, 372 N.E.2d 452 (1978).
[36]Ind. Code, § 35-46-1-2.
[37]Id., § 35-46-1-3. Compliance with the old provisions denouncing incest and sodomy was required until October, 1977, the effective date of their repeal. Lohm v. State, —— Ind. App. ——, 380 N.E.2d 561 (1978).
[38]See section 2.25, herein.
[39]United States v. Marks, 274 F.2d 15 (C.A.-7 Ind., 1959).
[40]Henneger v. Lomas, 145 Ind. 287, 44 N.E. 462 (1896).
[41]Light v. Lane, 41 Ind. 539 (1873).
[42]Ind. Code, §§ 12-2-1-5, 12-3-22-1.

INDIANA 6.15

be his own.[43] The testimony of the mother alone is insufficient without corroboration.[44] Thus it was held, on a showing that when a child was born before the parents married, and the putative father had acknowledged it to be his but believed the child to be dead when he left him out of his will, that the child was a pretermitted heir of the decedent.[45] Compliance with these provisions by the father does not, however, mean that the child is legitimate for all purposes.[46] It is said that nothing short of a legislative act can accomplish this.[47] Even adoption does not make the adoptee the legitimate child of its adoptive parents.[48]

Support and custody

Provision is made for proceedings to establish the paternity of a child born out of wedlock, for its custody, and support, education and the like.[49] Ordinarily the action must be brought within two years from the birth of the child; an exception is admitted where support is being furnished by the alleged father or by someone on his behalf, voluntarily or pursuant to an agreement with the mother.[50] If that is or has been the case, the two-year period begins to run from the date of the last furnishing of support.[51] The award can properly include support payments due in respect of a period preceding both the date of the judgment establishing paternity and the date suit was filed.[52] Abundant provision is made to protect the confidentiality of the child's illegitimate origins.[53]

---

[43]Id., § 29–1–2–7.
[44]Burnett v. Camden, 253 Ind. 354, 20 Ind. Dec. 75, 254 N.E.2d 199 (1970), cert. den. 399 U.S. 901, 90 Sup. Ct. 2202 (1970).
[45]Haskett v. Haskett, —— Ind. ——, 327 N.E.2d 612 (1975).
[46]A. —— B. —— v. C. —— D. ——, 150 Ind. App. 535, 277 N.E.2d 599 (1971).
[47]Id. See ABCD's of Indiana Legitimation Law, 48 Ind. L. J. 478 (1973).
[48]Id.
[49]Ind. Code, § 31–4–1–1 et seq. As to matters of proof, see Roe v. Doe, 154 Ind. App. 203, 289 N.E.2d 528 (1972); O.Q. v. L.R., 47 Ind. 49, 328 N.E.2d 233 (1975); Beaman v. Hedrick, 146 Ind. App. 404, 255 N.E.2d 828 (1970).
[50]Ind. Code, § 31–4–1–26. See also Sullivan v. O'Sullivan, 130 Ind. App. 142, 162 N.E.2d 315 (1959).
[51]D.E.F. v. E.M., —— Ind. App. ——, 363 N.E.2d 1030 (1977).
[52]B.G.L. v. C.L.S., —— Ind. App. ——, 369 N.E.2d 1105 (1977).
[53]E.g., Ind. Code, §§ 16–4–1–1, 16–4–1–2, 16–4–1–3, 16–1–16–15, 16–1–16–6, 16–1–19–3, 31–4–2–1.

Both parents share the obligation to support the child.[54] However, the alleged father can fulfill his obligation by complying with a compromise agreement made with the mother, provided the consideration is adequate.[55] Provision exists for the authorities to investigate this point before such a compromise can be raised as a defense.[56]

Property rights of cohabitants

Where land is deeded to grantees as husband and wife, and they are not so related, a tenancy-in-common results.[57]

There is early authority to support the proposition that when a purported marriage is void, the courts will, in adjusting the equities, take into consideration the services of the wife on an annulment.[58] Aside from a hint that the theory of a joint venture could be harnessed to buttress such an adjustment of the equities,[59] Indiana decisions contribute little to a solution of the problem of the extramarital partners' property rights on termination of their relationship.[60]

6.16. Iowa

In Iowa, which is not a community property state,[61] common-law marriages receive recognition.[62] Although they can be proved by circumstantial evidence,[63] claims of common-law marriage are regarded with suspicion and will be closely scrutinized.[64] The

---

[54] Id., § 31-4-1-2 et seq.
[55] Sullivan v. O'Sullivan, 130 Ind. App. 142, 162 N.E.2d 315 (1959).
[56] Ind. Code, § 31-4-1-25. As to criminal liability for nonsupport, see § 35-46-1-5. For the Uniform Reciprocal Enforcement of Support provisions, see §§ 31-2-1-1 to 31-2-1-39.
[57] Spanier v. Spanier, 120 Ind. App. 700, 96 N.E.2d 346 (1951).
[58] Sclamberg v. Sclamberg, 220 Ind. 209, 41 N.E.2d 801 (1942).
[59] See Davis v. Webster, 136 Ind. App. 286, 198 N.E.2d 883 (1964).
[60] See Property Rights Between Unmarried Cohabitants, 50 Ind. L. J. 389 (1975), suggesting that courts should approach illicit cohabitation as an essentially economic venture, and in the disposition of property acquired during the relationship should take into consideration the value of capital contributions, of services rendered, and a fair share of the profits.
[61] See Iowa Code Ann., § 597.1 et seq.
[62] In re Estate of Malli, 260 Iowa 252, 149 N.W.2d 155 (1967).
[63] Coleman v. Graves, 255 Iowa 396, 122 N.W.2d 853 (1963).
[64] In re Estate of Fisher, 176 N.W.2d 801 (Iowa, 1970).

proof must show a mutual intent and agreement *in praesenti* to be married,[65] continuous cohabitation and some public declaration that the parties are husband and wife.[66] There can be no secret common-law marriage.[67] Though a marriage is of course void if either party has a husband or wife living at the time of the inception of the relationship, cohabitation after the death or divorce of the former spouse renders it a valid marriage.[68]

Tort actions

The tort actions for alienation of affections or inducing breach of a contract to marry[69] which are separate causes of action[70] are still available in this state, as is a tort action for breach of promise to marry.[71]

Workers' compensation death benefits

It is held that a woman who cohabited with a man knowing that her husband was alive cannot qualify either as a common-law wife or as a "dependent,"[72] which, under the statute,[73] is the general test of eligibility.

---

[65] See In re Marriage of Winegard, 257 N.W.2d 609 (Iowa, 1977), holding that the fact that the conversation between the parties reflecting present intent to be married took place in the air over a sister state not to affect the validity of the marriage.
[66] In re Marriage of Grother, 242 N.W.2d 1 (Iowa, 1976), holding the evidence to be insufficient to establish a common-law marriage, especially in view of the fact that the cohabitation began before dissolution of the alleged husband's marriage to another.
[67] In re Estate of Dallman, 228 N.W.2d 187 (Iowa, 1975).
[68] Iowa Code Ann., § 595.19. Such rule has no application where the initial cohabitation was not on the basis of an alleged marriage, but illicit. In re Marriage of Grother, 242 N.W.2d 1 (Iowa, 1976).
Generally, see Mazanec and Blackburn, Survey of Iowa Law, 19 Drake L. Rev. 124 (1969).
[69] See section 2.20, herein.
[70] See Giltner v. Stark, 219 N.W.2d 700 (Iowa, 1974).
[71] See Iowa Decisions on Breach of Marriage Promise, 4 Iowa Law Bulletin 166 (1918); Limitation of Actions—Breach of Promise to Marry—Injuries to Persons, 13 Ia. L. Rev. 109 (1927). See also section 2.23, herein.
[72] Baldwin v. Sullivan, 201 Iowa 955, 204 N.W. 420 (1925), mod. 204 N.W. 218 (Iowa, 1926).
[73] Iowa Code Ann., § 85.44.

6.16 UNMARRIED COUPLES AND THE LAW

Abortion

Iowa enacted a new criminal abortion law in 1977 which makes it a felony for any nonphysician to terminate a human pregnancy.[74]

Possible criminal liability

The state must demonstrate an interest which is "compelling and necessary" to accomplishing a permissible state policy before it may interfere in recognized areas of fundamental rights, as, for example, sex in private between consenting adults of the opposite sex.[75] Age, however, is a proper factor for consideration in examining the statutes regulating sexual behavior.[76] Thus, the right to privacy does not protect a defendant against prosecution for sexual misconduct with a minor female in violation of a statute fixing the age of consent.[77] The statutory chapter on sexual abuse[78] is restricted to forcible or nonconsensual misconduct.[79] For the purposes of what is ordinarily known as statutory rape, the age of consent is sixteen.[80] Bigamy,[81] as well as incest,[82] abandonment of a dependent,[83] and nonsupport,[84] are also criminally punishable.

Status of children

Unless he has been adopted, an illegitimate child inherits from his natural father when the paternity is proven during the father's lifetime, or when the child has been recognized by the

---

[74]Id., § 707.7 et seq.
[75]State v. Pilcher, 242 N.W.2d 348 (Iowa, 1976).
[76]State v. Drake, 219 N.W.2d 492 (Iowa, 1974).
[77]State v. Coil, 246 N.W.2d 293 (Iowa, 1978). Iowa Code Ann., § 698.4.
[78]Iowa Code Ann., §§ 709.1 to 709.10.
[79]In State v. Pilcher, 242 N.W.2d 348 (Iowa, 1976), the court struck down a former sodomy statute as applied to consensual activity by adults of the opposite sex. The majority specifically reserved the question regarding homosexuals. See Note, Right of Privacy Protects Consensual Heterosexual Behavior, 1977 Wash. U. L. Q. 337. (The writer questions whether a state court should expand the privacy right to protect activities traditionally subject to regulation for the public welfare.) See also Privacy and Prostitution: Constitutional Implications of State v. Pilcher, 63 Ia. L. Rev. 248 (1977).
[80]Iowa Code Ann., § 709.4.
[81]Id., § 726.1.
[82]Id., § 726.2.
[83]Id., § 726.3.
[84]Id., § 726.5.

father as his child. Such recognition must have been general and notorious, or else in writing. If the recognition has been mutual, and the child has not been adopted, the father may inherit from his illegitimate child.[85] If the parents have married, the child is no longer illegitimate.[86] But there may be some question as to whether this qualification of the child's inheritance rights meets the requirements of Trimble v. Gordon.[87]

Paternity, support and custody

The provisions suggested in the Uniform Illegitimacy Act[88] as to the establishment of paternity and duties of support have been adopted in Iowa.[89] The provision that proceedings to enforce the father's obligation cannot be brought more than two years after the birth of the child unless paternity has been judicially established or has been acknowledged by the father in writing or by furnishing of support[90] has withstood a challenge of unconstitutionality; it may not be circumvented by first bringing an action to establish paternity more than two years after the child's birth and then bringing a second action to enforce the father's support obligation.[91] An ancillary statute[92] makes provision for a child support recovery unit to aid the court in establishing paternity and secure a court order for support. It establishes no new theory of child support recovery.[93]

The state has also adopted the Uniform Reciprocal Enforcement of Support Act[94] and the Uniform Child Custody Jurisdiction Act.[95]

---

[85]Id., § 633.222. As to inheritance from the mother, see § 633.221.
[86]Id., § 595.18. Abundant provision exists to ensure that the illegitimacy of the child's origin is not made public. See, e.g., §§ 144.23 et seq., 675.36.
[87]See section 3.3, herein.
[88]See section 3.5, herein.
[89]Iowa Code Ann., § 675.1.
[90]Id., § 675.33.
[91]State ex rel. Krupke v. Witkowski, 256 N.W.2d 216 (Iowa, 1977).
[92]Iowa Code Ann., §§ 252A.1 et seq., 252B.1 et seq.
[93]State ex rel. Krupke v. Witkowski, 256 N.W.2d 216 (Iowa, 1977).
In the absence of a previous demand in writing not more than two years' support furnished prior to the bringing of the action may be recovered. Iowa Code Ann., § 675.3. As to the effect of the statute on the mother's liability for support, see Wehling v. Rottinghaus, 204 N.W.2d 592 (Iowa, 1973).
[94]Iowa Code Ann., §§ 252A.1 to 252A.12.
[95]Id., §§ 598A.1 to 598A.25.

Adoption

Relatively recent legislation relating to the termination of parental rights and adoption, in addition to the standard requirements of statutes of this nature, provides for both a pre- and post-placement investigation of the prospective petitioner for adoption.[96] The statute also requires that the petitioner make a full disclosure of any amounts paid. It is an offense for a natural parent to take, and for any other person to give, any consideration for such a transaction over and above the consideration which reflects the commensurate value of services rendered in this context.

The word "care" in the adoption statute providing that the parent having care of the child may give consent to adoption,[97] means charge or oversight, implying responsibility for the safety and prosperity of the child.[98]

Property rights of cohabitants

Although the law will not imply a promise on the part of either party to reward the other for services rendered during the course of an illicit cohabitation,[99] when the party rendering domestic services is under a mistaken belief as to the existence of a valid marriage the rule is otherwise.[1] Iowa courts do not presume such services were rendered with gratuitous intent.[2]

6.17. Kansas

For a common-law marriage in Kansas (which is not a community property state),[3] there must be capacity of the parties to marry, a present marriage agreement between them, and a holding out to the public as their being husband and wife.[4] Mere

---

[96] Id., §§ 600.1 to 600.10, 633.233.
[97] Id., § 600.3.
[98] In re Adoption of Ellis, 260 Iowa 508, 149 N.W.2d 804 (1967). See also Orcutt v. State, 173 N.W.2d 66 (Iowa, 1969).
[99] See In re Ballard's Estate, 252 Iowa 548, 107 N.W.2d 436 (1961).
[1] In re Fili's Estate, 241 Iowa 61, 40 N.W.2d 286 (1949).
[2] Id.
[3] Kan. Stat. Ann., § 23-201 et seq.
[4] Fleming v. Fleming, 221 Kan. 290, 559 P.2d 329 (1977); In re Estate of Mazlo, 211 Kan. 217, 505 P.2d 762 (1973).

sporadic cohabitation is not enough.[5] A cohabitant who is aware of a decedent's marriage to another cannot qualify for social security insurance benefits as a common-law wife,[6] but if the parties to such a union continue to live together as husband and wife after a divorce has become final a common-law marriage can result.[7]

Workers' compensation death benefits

Where a couple's marriage was invalid because they married before the expiration of the statutory waiting period following a divorce, the woman was denied survivor's benefits on the death of her partner which also occurred before the expiration of the waiting period.[8] But in a similar case in which the worker's death occurred following the running of the statutory period, the award was granted.[9] Illegitimate children of a worker qualify as dependants.[10]

Effect of cohabitation on right to alimony

Where alimony is conditioned on the wife's not having remarried, cohabitation does not, as a matter of policy, require termination of her right to such payment absent a showing that her cohabitant is either supporting her or qualifies as a common-law spouse.[11]

Abortion

The present abortion statute[12] denounces "purposeful and unjustifiable termination of the pregnancy of any female other than

---

[5]Driscoll v. Driscoll, 220 Kan. 225, 552 P.2d 629 (1976).

Where, on a divorce, alimony payments are conditioned on wife's not remarrying, the fact that she is cohabiting with another man does not afford ground for a discontinuance of such alimony. Fleming v. Fleming, note 4, supra. The more recent decisions are indicative of a strong judicial reluctance to recognize claims of common-law marriage. See Kansas Judicial Survey, 15 Washburn L. J. 311, 367 (1976).

[6]Hawkins v. Weinberger, 368 F. Supp. 896 (D. Kan., 1973).
[7]See Cairns v. Richardson, 457 F.2d 1145 (C.A.-10 Kan., 1972).
[8]Peters v. Peters, 177 Kan. 100, 276 P.2d 302 (1954).
[9]Gillaspie v. E. W. Blair Constr. Corp., 192 Kan. 455, 388 P.2d 647 (1964).
[10]See Green v. Burch, 164 Kan. 348, 189 P.2d 892 (1948).
[11]Fleming v. Fleming, 221 Kan. 290, 559 P.2d 329 (1977).
[12]Kan. Stat. Ann., § 21-3407.

by a live birth." The circumstances of justification (the actor being a licensed practitioner) are a belief in a substantial risk that continued pregnancy would impair the physical or mental health of the mother, or that the child would be born with physical or mental defect, or that the pregnancy resulted from felonious intercourse. A section requiring that three physicians attest to the necessity of a termination has been held unconstitutional.[13] Further challenge to the constitutionality of the statute may well never be presented because any physician prosecuted under it would surely protest a belief that the mental health of the mother was at stake—and what fact trier would disbelieve him?[14]

Possible criminal liability

In Kansas, cohabitation without marriage is a misdemeanor.[15] In addition to the crimes of indecent liberties with a child or a ward,[16] and nonsupport of a child or spouse,[17] there are statutes denouncing sodomy (between persons who are not husband and wife or consenting adult members of the opposite sex);[18] adultery

---

[13]Poe v. Menghini, 339 F. Supp. 986 (D. Kan., 1972).

[14]Generally, see Constitutional Law: Elimination of Spousal and Parental Consent Requirements for Abortion, 16 Washburn L. J. 462 (1977); State Limitations upon the Availability and Accessibility of Abortions After Wade and Bolton, 25 Kan. L. Rev. 87 (1976); Constitutional Law—Abortion—Parental and Spousal Consent Requirements Violate Right to Privacy in Abortion Decision, 24 Kan. L. Rev. 446 (1976).

[15]Kan. Stat. Ann., § 23-118. But the criminality of such conduct does not prevent a common-law marriage from coming into being if the other requirements are met. State v. Walker, 36 Kan. 297, 13 Pac. 279 (1887).

In Smith v. Smith, 161 Kan. 1, 165 P.2d 593 (1946), the parties were divorced in 1939. They resumed cohabitation in 1940, resulting in the birth of another child. The wife sought divorce to terminate the common-law marriage and for support for the additional child. The trial court's rejection of the husband's answer that her cause of action was "without equity" was affirmed. No doubt the policy favoring support obligations outweighed any policy disfavoring judicial aid to a criminal (unclean hands), but decisions of this nature point up the inconsistency of a legislative pattern that permits common-law marriage while denouncing cohabitation as criminal. For a discussion of the phrase "living together as husband and wife," see Estates: "Living Together as Husband and Wife" Interpreted, 14 Washburn L. J. 164 (1975).

[16]Kan. Stat. Ann., §§ 21-3503, 21-3504. The age of consent is sixteen, and it is possible that a female participant in indecent sexual conduct with a child could also be prosecuted. The statute is in lieu of the traditional statutory rape legislation.

[17]Kan. Stat. Ann., § 21-3605.

[18]Id., §§ 21-3505, 21-3506.

(which now applies to extramarital sex committed both by a married person and by a single person who knows the other participant is married);[19] bigamy (which extends to cohabitation within the state after a bigamous marriage elsewhere);[20] and incest.[21] A variety of other offenses, such as lewd and lascivious behavior (involving nonprivate sexual acts) are unlikely to be of concern to most unwed partners.[22]

Status of children

The offspring of a marriage which is void or voidable are legitimate.[23] Provision is made for the legitimation of children by the subsequent marriage of their parents,[24] and for artificial insemination, which, when successful, results in the birth of a legitimate child of the consenting partners.[25]

A statute provides that children shall include illegitimate children for purposes of intestate succession where the father has notoriously or in writing recognized paternity, or when paternity has been judicially determined in his lifetime.[26] The courts have applied the same test of legitimacy to any action or proceeding involving the question of legitimacy.[27]

Support

It has been held that the father of an illegitimate child, too young to care for itself, may be under a nonstatutory obligation to support the child.[28] It is difficult, however, to envisage a criminal

---

[19] Id., § 21-3507.
[20] Id., § 21-3601 (reasonable mistake a defense). One who joins in a common-law marriage and is not divorced can be convicted of bigamy if he marries again. State v. Hughes, 35 Kan. 626, 12 Pac. 28 (1886).
[21] Kan. Stat. Ann., §§ 21-3602, 21-3603.
[22] Generally, see id., § 21-3501 et seq.
[23] Id., § 23-124. See Illegitimacy in Kansas, 14 Kan. L. Rev. 473 (1966).
[24] Kan. Stat. Ann., §§ 23-125 to 23-127. Both parents are required to appear before a court as early as possible after the marriage to execute affidavits attesting to their marriage. As to the compulsory registration of births of illegitimate children, see Kan. Stat. Ann., § 65-2409 et seq.
[25] Id., § 23-128 et seq.
[26] Id., § 59-501.
[27] Estate of McKay v. Davis, 208 Kan. 282, 491 P.2d 932 (1971). See also Brown, Intestate Succession in Kansas, 8 Washburn L. J. 284 (1969).
[28] Lawrence v. Boyd, 207 Kan. 776, 486 P.2d 1394 (1971).

charge of nonsupport under the statute[29] unless paternity has in some way been established. Kansas does not permit a child's right to support to be bargained away or defeated by a settlement between the mother and the putative father.[30]

In adopting the Uniform Reciprocal Enforcement of Support Act,[31] the legislature had added a few provisions designed to improve the enforcement of such duties.[32]

Adoption

Any adult, or a husband and wife jointly, may adopt any minor or adult.[33] If the adoptee is over fourteen years of age, his or her consent is required.[34]

Standard procedures are set forth by statute.[35] The courts are scrupulous with regard to the rights of the natural father (unless his parental unfitness is clearly established)[36] to notice and a hearing in respect of any such proceedings.[37]

Property rights of cohabitants

In a dispute between a lawful wife and one who mistakenly believed in the validity of her marriage to the same man, the constructive trust has been harnessed as a means of adjusting the equities.[38] An even earlier decision supports the award to a common-law wife of a share in property, title to which was taken in the man's name, on the basis of her assistance, pecuniary and otherwise, in securing these accumulations.[39] It seems clear enough that the courts of Kansas would not be deaf to the claims

---

[29] Kan. Stat. Ann., § 21–3605.
[30] Lawrence v. Boyd, 207 Kan. 776, 486 P.2d 1394 (1971).
[31] Kan. Stat. Ann., §§ 23–451 to 23–491.
[32] Id., § 23–492 et seq.
[33] Id., § 59–2101.
[34] Id., § 59–2102.
[35] Generally, see Kan. Stat. Ann., §§ 59–2277 to 59–2280.
[36] See In Interest of Hambelton, 2 Kan. App. 2d 68, 574 P.2d 982 (1978).
[37] See Adoption of Lathrop, 2 Kan. App. 2d 90, 575 P.2d 894 (1978). However, the father cannot execute a valid consent to adoption unless he has been adjudicated the father. Kan. Stat. Ann., § 59–2102. See also Aslin v. Seamon, 2 Kan. App. 2d 265, 578 P.2d 277 (1978).
[38] See Titus v. Titus, 151 Kan. 156, 97 P.2d 1113 (1940).
[39] Reese v. Reese, 132 Kan. 438, 295 Pac. 690, 75 A.L.R. 728 (1931).

of one who acted in the good faith belief in the existence of a marriage.[40] Beyond this, whether these courts would recognize any equities in one who assisted in the accumulation of assets during an extramarital cohabitation not believed to be a marriage can only be a matter of conjecture.

6.18. Kentucky

A marriage is prohibited and void where, inter alia, one of the parties has an undivorced spouse,[41] when not solemnized or contracted in the presence of an authorized person or society,[42] and where (with a qualification in the event of pregnancy) the person is under eighteen,[43] and has not obtained parental consent. Though a mere cohabitation, without any pretense of or belief in marriage, of itself confers no rights,[44] this does not mean that equitable considerations cannot influence an adjustment of property rights where one of the parties in good faith believed in the existence of a marriage.[45]

Kentucky will, however, recognize as valid a common-law marriage which is valid where entered into. This can have the effect of validating as a marriage a union between a Kentucky couple who go to another state for the purpose of contracting a common-law marriage,[46] but such status as common-law spouses is not achieved by a mere overnight trip to a sister state where the couple register as husband and wife at a motel and exchange marriage vows in private.[47]

Of interest, too, is a Kentucky decision that where two women had participated in a marriage ceremony obtained by means of a license secured by concealment of the fact that they were of the same sex, no marriage resulted.[48]

---

[40]See Werner v. Werner, 59 Kan. 399, 53 Pac. 217 (1898).
[41]Ky. Rev. Stat., § 402.020(2).
[42]Id., §402.020(3).
[43]Id., §402.020(4).
[44]Jones v. Jones, 313 Ky. 367, 231 S.W.2d 15 (1950).
[45]See notes 93 to 96 and related text, infra.
[46]Brown's Admr. v. Brown, 308 Ky. 796, 215 S.W.2d 971 (1948).
[47]Vaughn v. Hufnagel, 473 S.W.2d 124 (Ky. App., 1971), cert. den. 405 U.S. 1041, 31 L. Ed. 2d 582, 92 Sup. Ct. 1313 (1972).
[48]Jones v. Hallahan, 501 S.W.2d 588, 63 A.L.R.3d 1195 (Ky. App., 1973). See also section 2.24, herein.

As noted earlier,[49] a school regulation which requires any student, of whatever sex, who marries to withdraw from school for at least one year has been condemned as arbitrary and unreasonable, and therefore void.[50]

Adoption

The state has detailed provisions, mostly of a standard nature, controlling the procedure for adopting a child.[51] Ordinarily the child, if under sixteen, must have lived continuously with the petitioner for at least three months immediately prior to the filing of the petition unless the child has been placed for adoption by the authorities.[52] Petitions, where the child has been placed for adoption by the state department concerned or by a licensed child-placing institution, cannot be denied on religious, ethnic, or racial grounds. The fact that private placements are only possible after the appropriate authorities have investigated the home and background of the prospective adopters[53] could well present difficulties in the case of an unwed couple seeking to adopt a child.

Insurance and workers' compensation death benefits

The fact that an illegitimate child may have no rights in respect of the father's estate does not mean that such children are disqualified as beneficiaries under a group life policy providing for dependents of the insured's family.[54] Similarly, in regard to workers' compensation, there is no dearth of authority to support the right of the children of a woman with whom a deceased employee has been living in an illicit relationship to benefits on his

---

[49]See section 2.4, herein.
[50]Board of Education of Harrodsburg, Kentucky v. Bentley, 383 S.W.2d 677, 11 A.L.R.3d 990 (Ky., 1964).
[51]Ky. Rev. Stat., § 199.470 et seq.
[52]See Commonwealth, Dept. of Child Welfare v. Lorenz, 407 S.W.2d 699 (Ky. App., 1966), wherein the constitutionality of the statute receives consideration.
[53]Ky. Rev. Stat., §199.473. See also Commonwealth, Dept. of Child Welfare v. Jarboe, 464 S.W.2d 287 (Ky. App., 1971); Mitchell, Kentucky Law Relating to the Placement of Children for Adoption, 53 Ky. L. J. 223 (1964–65).
[54]Patton v. Lee, 394 F. Supp. 501 (W.D. Ky., 1975). As to the rights of one designated as beneficiary in contemplation of marriage as a "wife," when the subsequent marriage dissolved, see Denton v. Travelers Ins. Co., 555 S.W.2d 825 (Ky. App., 1977).

death provided the requisite dependency is shown.[55] As regards the unwed partner, however, the decisions do not appear to be in accord.[56]

Abortion

As a result of Roe v. Wade,[57] the Kentucky abortion statute has been rewritten.[58] In Wolfe v. Schroering,[59] the Sixth Circuit Court of Appeals reached important conclusions as to the constitutionality of the new statute. The requirement of the mother's written consent, whatever the stage of viability of the fetus, was upheld; as was the requirement that the physician, prior to a post first-trimester abortion, inform the mother of the possible physical and mental consequences of her decision. However, the provision prohibiting the use of the saline method of abortion after the first trimester of pregnancy was stricken; as was the provision requiring either spousal or parental consent for the operation after the first trimester. It was stated that a state cannot constitutionally authorize spouses, parents or guardians to veto an abortion for no reason or for an impermissible reason, that is, a reason not concerned with the protection of maternal health. The requirement of a 24-hour waiting period between the filing of the mother's written consent and the operation was upheld.

Under a former abortion statute, it was held that one who made contact with an abortionist and transported the woman to the place where the abortion was performed was an accomplice to the crime.[60]

---

[55]See, e.g., Schaab v. Townsend, 301 Ky. 121, 190 S.W.2d 1014 (1945); Jones v. Louisville Gas & Elec. Co., 209 Ky. 642, 273 S.W. 494 (1925) (niece of a woman with whom decedent had illicitly cohabited, who was totally dependent on him, qualified for benefits).

[56]See Combs v. Elk Horn Coal Corp., 281 S.W.2d 424 (Ky., 1955); City of Harlan v. Ford, 252 S.W.2d 684 (Ky., 1952). Compare Norrington v. Charles E. Cannell Co., 383 S.W.2d 137 (Ky. App., 1964) (woman who lived with decedent for seventeen years without obtaining divorce from prior husband not "dependent" under compensation law); Jones v. Campbell County, 353 S.W.2d 208 (Ky., 1962) (woman living in adultery with employee could not recover compensation benefits as dependent). Possibly the thinking of the courts is that a dependent cohabitant qualifies for benefits unless the cohabitation is adulterous.

[57]See section 2.19, herein.

[58]Ky. Rev. Stat., § 311.710 et seq.

[59]541 F.2d 523 (C.A.-6 Ky., 1976).

[60]Richmond v. Commonwealth, 370 S.W.2d 399 (Ky. App., 1963).

Possible criminal liability

Among other crimes of possible special concern to unmarried partners are the detaining of a woman against her will (kidnapping),[61] and concealment of the birth of an infant.[62] Statutes on sexual offenses[63] divide rape into degrees of severity according to the age of the victim. Sodomy is divided into four degrees,[64] and the crime of "sexual abuse" into three degrees.[65] It is noteworthy that for sodomy in the fourth degree (a Class A misdemeanor) consent of the other party is no defense.[66] Although these statutes contain no explicit reference to the marital status of the participants, it is spelled out that for the purposes of the chapter "marriage" is "living together as man and wife regardless of the legal status of their relationship."[67] The inference seems justifiable that prosecutions would not lie under any of the provisions for conduct involving consensual sexual behavior of adults of differing sex. The crimes of fornication and adultery no longer remain on the books. Bigamy, however, is committed by one who either purports to marry knowing he or the other participant has a husband or wife, or who cohabits in Kentucky after a bigamous marriage in another state.[68] Belief in legal eligibility to marry is a defense.[69] For incest, liability can be civil[70] as well as criminal.[71]

---

[61] Ky. Rev. Stat., §§ 509.020, 509.030, 510.040, 510.060, 510.110.
[62] Id., § 530.030.
[63] Id., § 510.010 et seq.
[64] Id., §§ 510.070 to 510.100.
[65] Id., §§ 510.110 to 510.130.

Also inserted is a general provision denouncing as "sexual misconduct" sex or deviate sexual relations with another without the other's consent. Ky. Rev. Stat., § 510.140. Commentary to the statutes suggests this could be a useful plea-bargaining tool and also a means of ensuring that an offender avoid the stigma of being labeled a "rapist" or a "sodomist." Generally, as to the overlapping of these crimes, see Cooper v. Commonwealth, 550 S.W.2d 478 (Ky., 1977). As to the inadmissibility of evidence of prior sexual conduct or habits of the complaining witness, see Ky. Rev. Stat., § 510.145.

[66] Ky. Rev. Stat., § 510.100. See Criminal Law—Consensual Homosexual Behavior—The Need for Legislative Reform, 57 Ky. L. J. 591 (1968–69).
[67] Ky. Rev. Stat., § 510.010(3).
[68] Id., § 530.010. An early case indicates that a conviction of statutory rape could result from intercourse after a bigamous marriage. Fields v. Commonwealth, 301 Ky. 551, 192 S.W.2d 478 (1946).
[69] Id.
[70] Ky. Rev. Stat., § 411.040. As to the prohibited degrees of relationship for marriage, see § 402.010.
[71] Id., § 530.020.

In a prosecution for "white slavery,"[72] a federal judge in Kentucky has indicated that pecuniary gain is not an essential motive;[73] however, the fact remains that unless prostitution is involved, such prosecutions are a rarity.

Status of children

The present statute provides that a bastard shall inherit only from his mother and his mother's kindred, but that if the father marries the mother, the child is deemed legitimate.[74] This provision has not escaped criticism.[75] In Rudolph v. Rudolph,[76] it was ruled that the people of Kentucky have no legitimate interest in prohibiting an illegitimate child, admitted by all to be the child of its father, from inheriting from the father. The interest the state has in promoting legitimate family life and in strengthening family ties, and also in ensuring a prompt and definitive determination of ownership of a decedent's estate, is not of sufficient importance to justify such unjust discrimination. The court added that the problems of proof involved where such claims are presented against a decedent's estate seem more reasonably to be addressed to evidentiary standards than to an outright barring of such claims against the estate of a male. No doubt a new statute, attempting to comply with the vague mandates of Trimble v. Gordon,[77] can be anticipated.

Children of a marriage which a court has (during the lifetime of the parents and either in a civil or criminal proceeding) adjudicated as incestuous are not legitimate.[78] The children of any other illegal or void marriage are legitimate.[79] (The illegitimacy of the issue of a couple who make no attempt to comply with the state's marriage laws would of course be beyond all question.)

The proceedings to establish paternity and support obligations,[80]

---

[72] See section 2.25, herein.
[73] Whitt v. United States, 261 F.2d 907 (C.A.-6 Ky., 1959).
[74] Ky. Rev. Stat., § 391.090.
[75] See Pendleton v. Pendleton: An Equal Right of Inheritance for the Illegitimate? 65 Ky. L. J. 712 (1976–77).
[76] 556 S.W.2d 152 (Ky. App., 1977).
[77] See section 3.3, herein.
[78] Ky. Rev. Stat., § 391.100.
[79] Id. As to prohibited marriages, the children of which are legitimate under this provision, see §§ 402.020, 402.030.
[80] Id., §§ 406.010 to 406.180.

6.18 UNMARRIED COUPLES AND THE LAW

which closely follow the Uniform Act on Paternity,[81] have received, since their enactment, further legislative attention.[82] The state has also enacted the Uniform Reciprocal Enforcement of Support Act.[83] As to the custody of children, though the law has favored the right of the mother,[84] modern indications suggest that the rights of the male parent must not be ignored[85] though the best interests of the child are of course the paramount consideration. The fact of multiple illegitimate births is prima facie evidence of a mother's unfitness to have custody of her children and can be sufficient evidence on which to base a judicial termination of her custody rights.[86]

Though it is recognized that a child is legitimated by a subsequent marriage of its parents,[87] it is held that a child fathered by one who was not the husband of a woman married to another cannot be legitimated in this way since such child's legitimacy is covered by the presumption of legitimacy.[88]

Full statutory provision is made for the procedures for adoption of illegitimate children,[89] and for the termination, voluntary or involuntary, of parental rights.[90]

---

[81] See section 3.4, herein.

[82] See Ky. Rev. Stat., §§ 406.021, 406.035 and 406.051. Provision is also made for public assistance for child support, and provisions exist to aid the state in securing reimbursement for any outlays from the true obligor. Id., § 205.715.

[83] Id., §§ 407.010 to 407.440.

[84] See Casale v. Casale, 549 S.W.2d 805 (Ky., 1977).

[85] In determining the award of custody the best interests of the child and equal consideration to the rights of each parent must be considered. Ky. Rev. Stat., § 403.270. See also Effect of the Equal Rights Amendment on Kentucky's Domestic Relations Laws, 12 J. Family L. 151 (1972–73). In Hill v. Garner, 561 S.W.2d 106 (Ky. App., 1977), a putative father who had petitioned the court for recognition of his inability to furnish proper care and whose parental rights had been terminated had no standing to oppose an adoption petition. But see Phillips v. Horlander, 535 S.W.2d 72 (Ky. App., 1975), holding that the father of an illegitimate was entitled to visit with and support the child notwithstanding the mother's opposition to visitation and refusal to accept support payments, absent a showing that such visits would be detrimental to the child's interests.

[86] Ky. Rev. Stat., § 199.605.

[87] See Dudley's Admr. v. Fidelity & Deposit Co. of Md., 240 S.W.2d 76 (Ky., 1951).

[88] Commonwealth, Dept. of Child Welfare v. Helton, 411 S.W.2d 932 (Ky. App., 1967).

[89] Ky. Rev. Stat., § 199.470 et seq.

[90] Id., §§ 199.601 to 199.617.

Property rights of cohabitants

In adopting the Uniform Marriage and Divorce Act,[91] Kentucky did not include the optional provision whereunder a good faith cohabitant can seek whatever relief seems appropriate in respect to the joint accumulations on a termination of the relationship.[92] However, there are indications that the mere fact of a meretricious relationship does not automatically preclude an unmarried partner from an award of restitutionary relief for benefits conferred on the other. As early as 1851 a Kentucky court held that money lent to a paramour by his mistress, to enable him to acquire land to which he took title, could be recovered, the court indeed imposing an equitable lien on the land to secure her right to reimbursement.[93] More recently, where a man paid his mistress a sum of money in return for her oral promise to give him a deed to the land she had acquired, the illicit nature of their relationship did not bar his claim for restitution.[94] And a putative husband, from whom the wife concealed the fact that she was already married, who had paid the entire price for land and had title placed in their joint names, was able to get restitution in the form of a decree that she convey her half interest in the land to him.[95] In another case, a couple accumulated substantial wealth in the course of a twenty-year "togetherness." Though he was married to another, neither party appeared to have considered the strict legality of their relationship a matter of great concern. Assets acquired by their joint efforts were all put in the woman's name. The court affirmed a holding that he was a half owner of these assets on the basis of a joint venture.[96]

It seems not unlikely, therefore, that Kentucky would recognize

---

[91] Id., §§ 403.010, 403.110. See also § 403.350.
[92] See section 1.6, herein.
[93] McDonald v. Fleming, 12 B. Mon. 285, 51 Ky. 285 (1851). For other early cases involving contracts between cohabitants outside of marriage, see Burgen v. Straughan, 7 J.J. Mar. 583; Clark v. Doke's Admr., 6 Ky. R. 655; Sackstaeder v. Kast, 31 Ky. L. R. 1304, 105 S.W. 435 (1907); Bowling v. Bowling's Admr., 222 Ky. 396, 300 S.W. 876 (1927); Yowell v. Bottom, 175 Ky. 635, 194 S.W. 768 (1917); McMillan v. Massie's Exr., 233 Ky. 808, 27 S.W.2d 416 (1929); Clark's Admr. v. Callahan, 216 Ky. 674, 288 S.W. 301 (1926); Arnz v. Arnz's Admr., 302 Ky. 507, 195 S.W.2d 79 (1946).
[94] Cougler v. Fackler, 510 S.W.2d 16 (Ky. App., 1974).
[95] Jones v. Jones, 313 Ky. 367, 231 S.W.2d 15 (1950).
[96] Akers v. Stamper, 410 S.W.2d 710 (Ky. App., 1966).

a right to relief of an equitable nature, based on the reasonable expectations of the parties, where wealth has been acquired in a nonmarital situation. Especially is this so if an agreement, oral or written, can be established.

6.19. Louisiana

In this community property state,[97] a contracting of common-law marriage not only creates no community of acquets and gains,[98] but, up until 1975, was denounced as criminal.[99] A common-law marriage contracted by domiciliaries of Louisiana outside the state is not recognized in Louisiana.[1]

In Louisiana an unmarried female partner is called a concubine. "Concubinage," at any rate for the purposes of a statutory provision restricting gifts of property between such persons,[2] describes a status, not mere acts of fornication or adultery. It imports the maintenance of a relationship resembling marriage without the parties having gone through the formalities.[3] The provision seems to have been designed to inflict a penalty on persons who flaunt public decency and set a bad example, since it does not apply to secret as distinguished from open concubinage.[4]

A similar provision, designed to discourage illicit relationships, denied to the parent of an illegitimate child the capacity to make any substantial donations to "adulterine" children.[5] If the parents left legitimate descendants, no legacies were permitted to any illegitimate child except to the extent necessary for sustenance or to procure employment. In no case could a "bastard" receive more

---

[97]See La. Civ. Code Ann., art. 2334 et seq.
[98]See Mintz & Mintz, Inc. v. Color, 250 So. 2d 816 (La. App., 1971); Tucker v. Joseph, 292 So. 2d 357 (La. App., 1974), holding there to be no putative community property where both cohabitants knew the woman was married to another.
[99]La. Rev. Stat. Ann., art. 14:791, declaring cohabitation by unmarried persons to be a crime, was repealed by 1975 La. Acts No. 638, § 3.
[1]Consolidated Underwriters v. Kelly, 15 S.W.2d 229 (Tex. Civ. App., 1929) (applying Louisiana law).
[2]La. Civ. Code Ann., art. 1481.
[3]Manning v. Harrell, 59 So. 2d 389 (La. App., 1952).
[4]Succession of Keuhling, 187 So. 2d 520 (La. App., 1966); Succession of Franz, 232 La. 310, 94 So. 2d 270 (1957); Succession of Lannes, 187 La. 17, 174 So. 94 (1936).
[5]La. Civ. Code Ann., arts. 1484 to 1488.

than what was necessary for sustenance from either parent. These provisions, to the extent that they have not been invalidated by the courts,[6] would appear to have little interest outside of Louisiana.

Putative spouses

A marriage which has been declared null nevertheless produces its "civil effects" as it relates to the parties and their children, if it has been contracted in good faith.[7] If only one of the parties acted in good faith, the marriage produces such effects only in his or her favor, and in favor of the children born of the marriage.[8] Where a man married in bad faith, knowing himself to be committing bigamy, alimony was held to be a "civil effect" which could follow an annulment.[9]

Most of the Louisiana courts have required some form of a ceremony before a marriage has been held to have been contracted in good faith.[10] There must be an honest and reasonable belief in the validity of the marriage, but the test is not an objective one. For example, a woman of little education, who could not have known of a statute prohibiting a person divorced for adultery from marrying under certain conditions, was held qualified as a "widow" of her putative husband (who had married her in violation of this statute) for the purposes of a group life insurance policy.[11] Similarly, where a girl of sixteen who had lived a sheltered life had been told by a man that he was single, and did not discover that he was married until after her marriage and conception, the mere showing that there had been unsubstantiated rumors regarding his married status did not deter the court from finding her marriage to have been contracted in good faith.[12] If

---

[6] See Succession of Robins, 349 So. 2d 276 (La., 1977). See also Succession of Captain, 341 So. 2d 1291 (La. App., 1977).
[7] La. Civ. Code Ann., art. 117.
[8] Id., art. 118.
[9] Cortes v. Fleming, 307 So. 2d 611, 81 A.L.R.3d 267 (La., 1973).
[10] See Succession of Rossi, 214 So. 2d 223 (La. App., 1968). There was no "good faith" for putative community property where both parties knew of the undissolved prior marriage of one of them. Tucker v. Joseph, 292 So. 2d 357 (La. App., 1974).
[11] Jones v. Equitable Life Assur. Soc. of U.S., 173 So. 2d 373 (La. App., 1965).
[12] Succession of Barbier, 296 So. 2d 390 (La. App., 1974).

the parties have lived together for many years, the burden of disproving good faith is on the party seeking to contest the putative marriage.[13] Reputation in the community and public records indicating a nonmarital status are a sufficient basis for such reasonable belief.[14] The mere fact that the parties lived together prior to their "marriage" does not of itself mean that good faith was absent.[15]

If both the parties are ignorant of the existence of an impediment to their marriage, on a termination of their relationship, whether by death or otherwise, community property laws control the distribution of their accumulations.[16] And if one or the other party to the marriage was already married, community property laws control the distribution of assets of that party acquired prior to the inception of the putative marriage.[17] As to assets acquired subsequent to a bigamous marriage, it was at one time the rule that the bigamous party acquired nothing, and these accumulations were divided between the putative spouse and the lawful spouse.[18] This remains the rule where the bigamous spouse was acting in bad faith.[19] Whether it is just or unjust, the courts have long recognized that where a man contracts a second marriage which is bigamous, the property acquired during the coexistence of the two marriages goes in equal shares to the lawful wife and the putative wife.[20] Probably designed to penalize the man for his wrong, the effect is to penalize his heirs if he is dead,[21] and such a rule takes no account of the proportionate contributions of the respective women.

---

[13]Succession of Pigg, 228 La. 799, 84 So. 2d 196 (1955).
[14]See Gathright v. Smith, 352 So. 2d 282 (La. App., 1977). However, where a deed purported to convey property to a decedent as grantor's "wife," and she had not obtained a divorce from a former spouse, her child could assert no interest in the land without strict proof that she had purchased it with funds obtained independently of the "concubinage." Id.
[15]Succession of Jene, 173 So. 2d 857 (La. App., 1965); Hondlenk v. John, 178 La. 510, 152 So. 67 (1934).
[16]See Succession of Verrett, 224 La. 461, 70 So. 2d 89 (1953); Tillison v. Tillison, 129 So. 2d 522 (La. App., 1961); Succession of Davis, 142 So. 2d 481 (La. App., 1962).
[17]Houston v. Mondy, 306 So. 2d 91 (La. App., 1974).
[18]See, e.g., Ray v. Knox, 164 La. 193, 113 So. 814 (1927).
[19]Succession of Choyce, 183 So. 2d 457 (La. App., 1966).
[20]See Price v. Price, 326 So. 2d 545 (La. App., 1976); Texas Co. v. Stewart, 101 So. 2d 222 (La. App., 1958).
[21]See Succession of Fields, 222 La. 310, 62 So. 2d 495 (1952).

The application of the code provisions regarding putative marriages[22] has been a source of voluminous litigation, especially in situations where only one of the parties acted in good faith, and the results are not entirely clear.[23] To hold, as modern courts tend, that the putative spouse is entitled to a community share in earnings acquired during the existence of the two marriages,[24] is not always a satisfactory answer.[25] In Prince v. Hopson[26] it was held that one half of the property of a good faith bigamous spouse's estate would, on his death intestate, pass to his intestate successors, and that the other half should be divided equally between his legal wife and his putative wife. Such a rule, though to be preferred to a rule that excludes his intestate successors entirely, would appear to be an oversimplification. Suppose that he was worth virtually nothing at the inception of the good faith putative marriage and, through their joint efforts, he and his putative spouse acquired a fortune. Or suppose, to pose the opposite extreme, he was possessed of a vast estate at the time of the inception of the invalid marriage, which he and his putative wife rapidly dissipated before his death. In the light of such possibilities, the suggestion of the authors of the Uniform Marriage and Divorce Act[27] that a degree of leeway be left to the courts, has much to commend it.

Adoption

A single person over the age of 21, or a married couple jointly, may petition to adopt any child.[28]

---

[22]Notes 7 and 8, supra.

[23]See Annotation, Rights and remedies in respect of property accumulated by man and woman living together in illicit relations or under void marriage, 31 A.L.R.2d 1255 (1953). For a full survey of the Louisiana case law in this area, see Annotation, Rights in decedent's estate as between lawful and putative spouses, 81 A.L.R.3d 6 (1977).

[24]Texas Co. v. Stewart, 101 So. 2d 222 (La. App., 1958); Funderburk v. Funderburk, 214 La. 717, 38 So. 2d 502 (1949).

[25]For example, what is the status of property resulting from a judicious investment of funds forming part of the community property of the initial marriage?

[26]230 La. 575, 89 So. 2d 128 (1956).

[27]See section 1.6, herein. Generally, see Riley, Women's Rights in the Louisiana Matrimonial Regime, 50 Tul. L. Rev. 557 (1976); Massip, Rights of the Wife in the Matrimonial Regime, 50 Tul. L. Rev. 549 (1976).

[28]La. Rev. Stat. Ann., art. 9:422. As to the termination of parental rights in the adoption of illegitimate children, see notes 90 and 91, infra, and related text.

6.19   UNMARRIED COUPLES AND THE LAW

Workers' compensation death benefits

For the purposes of the workers' compensation statute,[29] a denial of equal rights to dependent acknowledged illegitimates was held to be an unconstitutional denial of equal protection;[30] the unacknowledged child cannot be relegated to a lesser status in the priority scheme set up by the act. However, the courts require a clear showing of dependency, which is of course a question of fact.[31] A posthumous child qualifies in the same manner as any other child.[32] A mere legal or moral obligation on the part of the worker to support the child is not, absent a presumption of dependency under the statute, sufficient; there must be a showing that he actually did contribute.[33] Further, whatever the status under the laws of Louisiana of adulterously illegitimate offspring of a decedent, in a suit brought under the Jones Act[34] such a child's claim cannot be rejected on the ground that it is not a "child."[35] Similarly, the word "child" for the purposes of the Federal Employees' Liability Act imposing liability for the benefit of a surviving widow and children, includes illegitimates.[36]

A dependent mother of an illegitimate child killed in a work-related accident can also qualify for survivor's benefits.[37] Though a putative spouse is clearly entitled to recover as a dependent,[38] the courts consistently denied such recovery to dependent marital cohabitants,[39] usually where one partner was at the time married

---

[29]La. Rev. Stat. Ann., arts. 1251, 1252.
[30]Weber v. Aetna Cas. & Surety Co., 406 U.S. 164, 31 L. Ed. 2d 768, 92 Sup. Ct. 1400 (1972).
[31]Perteet v. Atlas Constr. Co., 345 So. 2d 972 (La. App., 1977); Lalonde v. Associated Pipeline Contractors, Inc., 496 F.2d 1175 (C.A.-5 La., 1974).
[32]Affiliated Foods, Inc. v. Blanchard, 266 So. 2d 539 (La. App., 1972).
[33]Fidelity & Cas. Co. of New York v. Masters, 335 So. 2d 722 (La. App., 1976).
[34]See section 2.13, herein.
[35]Hebert v. Petroleum Pipe Inspectors, Inc., 396 F.2d 237 (C.A.-5 La., 1968).
[36]Smith v. Clark Sherwood Oil Field Contractors, 457 F.2d 1339 (C.A.-5 La., 1972), cert. den. 409 U.S. 980, 34 L. Ed. 2d 243, 93 Sup. Ct. 308 (1972). See Providing for Illegitimates—Workmen's Compensation, 19 Loyola L. Rev. 242 (1972-73).
[37]McDermott v. Funel, 258 La. 657, 247 So. 2d 567 (1971). To recover death benefits under workers' compensation, all that is required is that claimant be in the family or household and is as such a dependent. Turner v. Consolidated Underwriters, 170 So. 2d 199 (La. App., 1964), affd. 248 La. 37, 176 So. 2d 420 (1965).
[38]See Jenkins v. Pemberton, 87 So. 2d 775 (La. App., 1956).
[39]See Liberty Mut. Ins. Co. v. Caesar, 345 So. 2d 64 (La. App., 1977); Dickerson

to a third person. However, it has now been held that a dependent concubine who had been living with the decedent workman for eleven years in a stable home relationship, could recover where her doing so did not infringe on any share of compensation benefits to which a statutorily entitled claimant was preferentially entitled.[40]

Abortion

The legislature has not in terms decriminalized abortions performed during the first trimester of pregnancy. Abortion is defined to include the performance of acts with the intent of procuring premature delivery of an embryo or fetus.[41] There are provisions which penalize a physician who performs an abortion when, in his best medical judgment, an abortion is unnecessary; also when he lacks the necessary training and expertise to perform such an operation; and when the operation is performed outside a licensed hospital.[42] These provisions have been held to be an impermissible regulation of first-trimester abortions.[43] For the killing of an infant during delivery, unless to save the life of the mother, life imprisonment at hard labor is the mandatory sentence.[44] Intentional failure to sustain the life and health of an aborted viable infant (viability being that stage of fetal development when the life of the unborn child may be continued indefinitely outside the womb by natural or artificial life-support systems) is also criminal.[45]

In addition to forbidding a denial of governmental assistance to a woman or to an institution for refusing to submit to an abortion, or for declining to permit its facilities to be used for that purpose, a statute requires, as a precondition of an abortion, informed

---

v. Employers Mut. Liability Ins. Co. of Wisconsin, 248 So. 2d 852 (La. App., 1971); King v. McCoy Bros. Lbr. Co., 147 So. 2d 77 (La. App., 1962).

[40]Henderson v. Travelers Ins. Co., 354 So. 2d 1031 (La., 1978), overruling Humphreys v. Marquette Cas. Co., 235 La. 355, 103 So. 2d 895 (1958).

[41]La. Rev. Stat. Ann., art. 14:87.

[42]Id., art. 37:1285(8), (8.1), (9).

[43]Emma G. v. Edwards, 434 F. Supp. 1048 (E.D. La., 1977), also holding that medicaid cannot be withheld for therapeutic abortions performed outside a hospital by qualified persons.

[44]La. Rev. Stat. Ann., art. 14:87.1.

[45]Id., art. 14:87.5.

consent of the potential mother.[46] It also requires that a minor, or, if she is emancipated by marriage, her husband, shall also be informed of their right to refuse an abortion for the minor and that such refusal would not involve any deprivation of governmental assistance. Written consent of all parties, including that of the mother who is to be aborted, must contain an acknowledgment that a full explanation of the abortion procedure to be performed has been given and is understood.[47] In an appeal from an injunction against the enforcement of this entire provision, the Supreme Court of the United States vacated the injunction for a more explicit construction, at the state level, of these requirements.[48]

A statute forbids state employees, or any employee of an agency in receipt of governmental assistance, to require or even recommend abortions.[49] An exception is made for the licensed physician who acts to save or preserve the life of the pregnant woman. Of collateral interest is the fact that (probably due in part to a homicide prosecution for causing the death of an eight-month-old fetus)[50] the definition of a "person" for the purposes of the abortion statutes is now amended to include, inter alia, a human being from the moment of fertilization and implantation.[51]

Recovery for wrongful death

The decisions of the Supreme Court of the United States in Levy v. Louisiana, permitting an illegitimate child to recover for the wrongful death of the mother, and in Glona v. American Guarantee & Liability Insurance Company, permitting a mother to recover for the wrongful death of her illegitimate child, are discussed in Chapter 3.[52] The Supreme Court of Louisiana has construed the Levy decision to mean that "when a *parent* openly and publicly recognizes and accepts an illegitimate to be his or

---

[46]Id., art. 40:1299.33.
[47]Id.
[48]Guste v. Jackson, 429 U.S. 399, 50 L. Ed. 2d 638, 97 Sup. Ct. 657 (1977).
[49]La. Rev. Stat. Ann., art. 40:1299.34.
[50]State v. Gyles, 313 So. 2d 799 (La., 1975).
[51]La. Rev. Stat. Ann., art. 14:2(7).
[52]See section 3.2, herein.

her child and the child is dependent upon the parent, such an illegitimate is a 'child' as expressed in Civil Code Article 2315" (the controlling wrongful death statute).[53] Though the right of such a mother to recover is well recognized,[54] it is not so clear that the biological father shares this right if the child already has, at the time of conception and birth, a legitimate father. In George v. Bertrand,[55] the mother had been openly cohabiting with the coplaintiff though married to another at the time of the child's conception and birth. She subsequently married the coplaintiff. He was held not entitled to recover for the child's wrongful death since he was not the legitimate father. However, it has since been held that the child of an adulterous union can be legitimated by the subsequent marriage and thus become the child of its biological father.[56] The decision, which does not reach any conclusion as to whether the presumption of paternity of the husband at the time of birth is displaced, presents a theoretical possibility that such a child could inherit on intestacy from two fathers. However that may be, it is clear that such a child can recover for the wrongful death of the biological father.[57] Whether both of these two males could recover for the wrongful death of the child is a question unlikely to be presented.

A good faith spouse may maintain a wrongful death action for the death of her putative husband.[58] This follows from the fact that the civil effects of marriage flow in favor of a party who marries in good faith just as though the marriage had been legally consummated. Whatever benefit accrues to the legal spouse also accrues to a woman who married in good faith ignorance of the marriage.[59] If the wrongdoer's funds are restricted, it could

---

[53]Levy v. State, Charity Hosp. of Louisiana at New Orleans Bd. of Administration, 253 La. 73, 216 So. 2d 818, 820 (1968) (emphasis added).
[54]See Miles v. City-Parish Government of East Baton Rouge Parish, 219 So. 2d 320 (La. App., 1969).
[55]217 So. 2d 47 (La. App., 1968), writ refused 253 La. 647, 219 So. 2d 177 (1969), cert. den. 396 U.S. 974, 24 L. Ed. 2d 443, 90 Sup. Ct. 439 (1969).
[56]Succession of Mitchell, 323 So. 2d 451 (La., 1975).
[57]Warren v. Richard, 296 So. 2d 813 (La., 1974).
[58]King v. Cancienne, 316 So. 2d 366 (La., 1975).
[59]La. Civ. Code Ann., arts. 117, 118, 2315.

well be that, as in the case of workers' compensation,[60] the claim of the putative spouse would be subordinated to that of the legal spouse who is dependent on the decedent. A concubine, as would be one who married or cohabited with the decedent with knowledge of an existing marriage, would have no claim.[61]

Possible criminal liability

An extramarital cohabitant is no longer as such exposed to criminal sanctions.[62] Reasonable mistake, of law or of fact, can be a defense to a charge of bigamy.[63] Penalties for incest are graduated according to the degree of prohibited relationship.[64]

For crimes in the nature of statutory rape, the victim must be under the age of seventeen.[65] Rape by fraud (inducing consent by a misrepresentation as to marital status) is denounced.[66] A statute covering the "unnatural carnal copulation by a human being with another of the same sex or opposite sex,"[67] a definition not unconstitutionally vague,[68] also has been ruled not to be an unconstitutional invasion of the right to privacy as applied to consenting adults.[69]

Adultery is not a crime.[70]

---

[60]See Fulton Bag & Cotton Mills v. Fernandez, 159 So. 339 (La. App., 1935). In general, the judicial attitude, where the contest is between a lawful wife and a putative wife for benefits payable to a "widow," for example, under the life insurance policy of a decedent or under the Social Security Act, is to permit the claim of the putative wife unless the lawful wife is actively claiming. See also Jackson v. Lindlom, 84 So. 2d 101 (La. App., 1955), where a putative wife was denied a right to sue for the wrongful death of the decedent.
[61]Babineaux v. Pernie-Bailey Drilling Co., 261 La. 1080, 262 So. 2d 328 (1972).
[62]See note 99, supra, and related text.
[63]La. Rev. Stat. Ann., art. 14:76. As to abetting bigamy, see art. 14:77.
[64]Id., art. 14:78.
[65]Id., art. 14:80. The statute was amended in 1977 to criminalize the carnal knowledge of a juvenile where the defendant is over seventeen and the victim is under seventeen but over twelve, there being an age differential of more than two years.
[66]Id., art. 14:43(3).
[67]Id., arts. 14:89, 14:89.1.
[68]State v. Bluain, 315 So. 2d 749 (La., 1975); State v. Lindsey, 310 So. 2d 89 (La., 1975).
[69]State v. McCoy, 337 So. 2d 192 (La., 1976).
[70]Thomason v. Thomason, 355 So. 2d 908 (La., 1978).

Status of children

In Louisiana children are either legitimate, illegitimate, or legitimated, depending on whether they were born in or outside of marriage. Illegitimates are further classified as those conceived of parents who, at conception, might have legally contracted marriage and those whose parents could not then have intermarried. The latter are either adulterous or incestuous bastards. Adulterous children may be acknowledged by a subsequent marriage of their parents but incestuous bastards cannot be acknowledged. If such illegitimates are acknowledged by either parent they are called "natural" children. Such acknowledgment, however, does not confer on them the same rights as legitimate children to inherit on the intestacy of the parents. If the parent has legitimate descendants, an illegitimate child has no inheritance rights beyond its support needs (called alimony).[71]

In Labine v. Vincent[72] the United States Supreme Court stated:

> [T]he power to make rules to establish, protect, and strengthen family life as well as to regulate the disposition of property left in Louisiana by a man dying there is committed by the Constitution of the United States and the people of Louisiana to the legislature of that State. Absent a specific constitutional guarantee, it is for that legislature, not the life tenured judges of this Court, to select from among possible laws.[73]

It is entirely possible that this statement, and the Court's reluctance to invalidate the Louisiana scheme of intestate succession, is attributable to the fact that the Louisiana classifications of the rights of illegitimates (which are beyond the scope of this commentary) are so different to the classifications commonly accepted in our Anglo-American jurisprudence that a meticulous insistence on the requirements of equal protection would involve a dynamiting of a long established and complex set of principles which owe their origins to a system of jurisprudence alien to

---

[71] Generally, see La. Civ. Code Ann., arts. 202 et seq., 918 et seq. See also Status of Illegitimates in Louisiana, 16 Loyola L. Rev. 87 (1969–70); Pascal, Louisiana Succession and Related Laws and the Illegitimate; Thoughts Prompted by Labine v. Vincent, 46 Tul. L. Rev. 167 (1971).

[72] 401 U.S. 532, 28 L. Ed. 2d 288, 91 Sup. Ct. 1017 (1971), reh. den. 402 U.S. 990, 29 L. Ed. 2d 156, 91 Sup. Ct. 1672 (1971).

[73] Id., 401 U.S. at 538, 91 Sup. Ct. at 1021.

Anglo-American traditions. In Louisiana, for example, a natural child, when duly acknowledged by its mother, can succeed to her if she has no lawful children or descendants, to the exclusion of the mother's ascendants or collaterals of lawful kindred.[74] If the mother has lawful children, the rights of the natural children are reduced to alimony (support). But on the death of the father, the natural child inherits only ahead of the state.[75] In no case may a bastard inherit more than alimony,[76] and a natural child cannot inherit from the legitimate relations of the parents.[77]

Without exploring deeper into this labyrinth of classifications and rights, it is obvious that the Louisiana statutes do discriminate against illegitimates. With the revision of its Constitution in 1974, Louisiana adopted its own equal protection clause which, like that of the United States Constitution, forbids discrimination which is arbitrary, capricious or unreasonable on the basis, inter alia, of birth.[78] This notwithstanding, it can be doubted whether this state will ever be persuaded that its system of succession on intestacy is arbitrary, capricious or unreasonable.[79] In Succession of Matte, for example,[80] it is held that duly acknowledged natural children are called to the succession from their biological father only to the exclusion of the state.

The presumption that a child born during a lawful marriage is the child of the male parent, which has its origins in the Roman

---

[74] La. Civ. Code Ann., arts. 918 to 920.
[75] Id., art. 919.
[76] Id., art. 920.
[77] Id., art. 921. It is noteworthy that under these provisions no illegitimate, whatever his status, is disqualified to receive "alimony" (support needs). This may be a feature justifying the constitutionality of the scheme, notwithstanding Trimble v. Gordon (section 3.3, herein), which involved a statute whereunder an illegitimate might get nothing on the death of the father.
[78] La. Const., art. 1, § 3.
[79] See, e.g., Strahan v. Strahan, 304 F. Supp. 40 (W.D. La., 1969), affd. 444 F.2d 528 (C.A.-5 La., 1971), cert. den. 404 U.S. 949, 30 L. Ed. 2d 265, 92 Sup. Ct. 284 (1971); Succession of Captain, 341 So. 2d 1291 (La. App., 1977); Succession of Bush, 222 So. 2d 642 (La. App., 1969), declining to extend by analogy the holding of Levy v. Louisiana to situations which do not involve the same fact situation. See also Equal Protection of Illegitimates, 24 Loyola L. Rev. 116 (1978); All in the Family: Equal Protection and the Illegitimate Child in Louisiana Succession Law, 38 La. L. Rev. 189 (1977); Lorio, Succession Rights of Illegitimates in Louisiana, 24 Loyola L. Rev. 1 (1978).
[80] 346 So. 2d 1345 (La. App., 1977).

law, is firmly entrenched in this state.[81] A husband who seeks to rebut the presumption may bring statutory proceedings to disavow paternity. If he does not do so, he may be liable for the support of a child not his own.[82] The presumption admits of an exception where the parents are separated at the time conception could have occurred, but the exception is not an inflexible one; there can always be proof that the husband was in fact the father.[83] Failure to disavow the child may also result in a denial to the biological father, on a subsequent marriage to the mother, of his right to be recognized as the father.[84]

The state has adopted the Uniform Statute on Blood Tests to determine paternity,[85] and the Uniform Reciprocal Enforcement of Support Act.[86]

Children may be legitimated by either parent by notarial act where there is, either at the time of conception or at the time of legitimation, no legal impediment to their marriage and the parent has no legitimate descendants at the time of the notarial act.[87] Subsequent marriage of the parents, and formal or informal acknowledgment of the children, has the effect of legitimating children other than those born of an incestuous connection.[88] There was a time when adulterine bastards could not be legitimated by a subsequent marriage of the parents. However, the statute has now removed this bar.[89]

Whether or not the child is legitimate, the rights of the natural parents to withhold consent to its adoption can be lost either by judicial decree on a finding of parental unfitness[90] or by voluntary

---

[81]Spaht and Shaw, Jr., Strongest Presumption Challenged: Speculations on Warren v. Richard and Succession of Mitchell, 37 La. L. Rev. 59 (1976).
[82]See Dorsey v. Williamston, 170 So. 2d 773 (La. App., 1964).
[83]La. Civ. Code Ann., art. 184 et seq.
[84]See Taylor v. Taylor, 295 So. 2d 494 (La. App., 1974).
[85]La. Rev. Stat. Ann., arts. 9:396 to 9:398. See Uniform Act on Blood Tests: Disavowal and Divorce, 33 La. L. Rev. 646 (1973).
[86]La. Rev. Stat. Ann., art. 13:1641 et seq. Both needs of child and ability of father to pay should be considered. Smith v. Stamper, 357 So. 2d 904 (La. App., 1978).
[87]La. Civ. Code Ann., art. 200.
[88]See Henry v. Jean, 238 La. 314, 115 So. 2d 363 (1959).
[89]See Succession of Mitchell, 323 So. 2d 451, 80 A.L.R.3d 209 (La., 1975).
[90]La. Rev. Stat. Ann., art. 9:401 et seq. See also Child Custody: Paternal Authority v. Welfare of the Child, 35 La. L. Rev. 904 (1975).

relinquishment.[91] The mother is the "tutrix" (guardian) of her illegitimate children not acknowledged by the father, or acknowledged by him without her concurrence, but the right of a putative father to visitation privileges, subject always to the paramount interests of the child, cannot be ignored.[92]

Property rights of cohabitants

As to the rights of extramarital cohabitants in respect of property accumulated during their relationship, absent a good faith belief in a marriage there can be no claims based on a putative community property.[93] Thus, where land had been purchased with funds acquired through the joint labors of a man and a woman who knew her marriage to him was invalid, she having contributed nothing beyond her labors, a judgment awarding her one half of the proceeds of the land was set aside. She had no greater rights than does a concubine.[94] A concubine is one who assumes the legal responsibilities of a wife without the privileges which flow from a legal marriage.[95] Her services, therefore, are presumed to be rendered as a gift to her paramour.[96] Since the earliest days, it is recognized that if the primary motive of such a cohabitation is concubinage, she can make no claim to any assets acquired in the name of her paramour.[97]

However, there is early recognition of the proposition that, if concubinage was not their motive for coming together but was merely a consequence of a close union of interest between the parties, such unfair enrichment to the paramour will not be countenanced. For example, where the female partner owned a

---

[91]La. Rev. Stat. Ann., art. 9:401 et seq. Neither parent can voluntarily relinquish these rights without the consent of the other. Id., art. 9:404. See In re Martin, 357 So. 2d 893 (La. App., 1978).

[92]See Firmin v. Miller, 355 So. 2d 977 (La. App., 1977). As to the duty of both parents to support their illegitimate children, see La. Civ. Code Ann., arts. 238, 239, 240.

[93]See Mintz & Mintz, Inc. v. Color, 250 So. 2d 816 (La. App., 1971), holding a wage-earning cohabitant not legally bound to pay the debts of the other cohabitant; Tucker v. Joseph, 292 So. 2d 357 (La. App., 1974), holding there was no putative community where both knew the woman was lawfully married to another. See also Sparrow v. Sparrow, 231 La. 966, 93 So. 2d 232 (1957).

[94]Keller v. Keller, 220 So. 2d 745 (La. App., 1969).

[95]Purvis v. Purvis, 162 So. 239 (La. App., 1935) (no recovery for services).

[96]Jenkins v. Prevost, 140 So. 2d 238 (La. App., 1962).

[97]Sparrow v. Sparrow, 231 La. 966, 93 So. 2d 232 (1957).

boardinghouse, which she permitted her paramour to manage and to pocket the profits, she was held entitled to a recovery for her labor and for the depreciation of the furniture.[98] Again, where a woman acted as a man's nurse before she became his mistress, she was held not without right in respect of his accumulations.[99] Herein lie the roots of a qualification which has considerable recognition in the Louisiana decisions. Concubines are not automatically precluded from asserting claims arising out of business transactions between them and their paramours that are independent of the meretricious relationship.[1] But the courts have placed a rather heavy burden on the claimant to prove the amount due on a claim of this nature.[2] A showing, for example, of a joint venture embarked upon independently of the illicit relationship, of a commercial nature, in the course of which her own money was used for the purchase of assets by the paramour, presents a strong case for the application of the qualification.[3] But, by reason of the requirement of strict proof, the fact that the parties were cohabiting prior to the acquisition of the property in which an interest is claimed, even if a commercial partnership can be said to have come into existence, has gone far to influence a court to decline relief on a theory of partnership or joint venture in the interest of good morals.[4] Where open concubinage was the initial motive behind the acquisition of property, one who contributed to its acquisition and spent money on its preservation during the course of the illicit relationship was unable to assert any interest in such property, though sums disbursed after the relationship had come to an end could be recovered.[5]

---

[98]Viens v. Brickle, 8 Mart. (O.S.) 11 (1820).
[99]Succession of Pereuilhet, 23 La. Ann. 294 (1871).
[1]Jackson v. Hampton, 134 So. 2d 114 (La. App., 1961).
[2]See Keller v. Keller, 220 So. 2d 745 (La. App., 1969); Heatwole v. Stansbury, 212 La. 685, 33 So. 2d 196 (1947).
[3]See Guerin v. Bonaventure, 212 So. 2d 459 (La. App., 1968), holding allegations by a concubine that she had invested in a partnership business, was shown as a part owner on partnership returns, had signed checks on a partnership account jointly with defendant, and performed other services for their various ventures, stated a cause of action for recovery.
[4]See Foshee v. Simkin, 174 So. 2d 915 (La. App., 1965).
[5]Chambers v. Crawford, 150 So. 2d 61 (La. App., 1963). See also Sparrow v. Sparrow, 231 La. 966, 93 So. 2d 232 (1957) (court denied partition of land where purpose of relationship was shown to be meretricious, and statute made null and void any partnership formed for immoral purposes).

At present, however, there appears to be no authority on which to buttress an argument that, absent any existence of a commercial venture of some kind, Louisiana courts can intervene on behalf of a "bad faith" extramarital cohabitant to disturb the legal property rights of the other (equally "bad faith") cohabitant in accumulations acquired through their joint efforts or monetary contributions.[6]

6.20. Maine

The state of Maine does not recognize common-law marriage, and there appear to be no rulings of any significance regarding the rights and duties of good faith or bad faith cohabitants.[7]

Adoption

To adopt a child, the consent of its parents, and of the child itself if of the age of fourteen or over, is ordinarily required.[8] If the child is illegitimate the consent of its parents may be dispensed with in proper circumstances.[9] The mere fact that a child has been with petitioners for adoption under a foster home placement program for as long as four and a half years does not estop the parents from asserting their rights to consent to an adoption in the absence of representations by the authorities that might create an estoppel as against the petitioners.[10] The legislature requires that any child placement agency must be licensed, and no one who places a child can charge more than the reasonable costs of services connected with such placement.[11] Detailed statutory provisions also

---

[6]See Nonmarital Relationships: A Fair Termination Is Possible, 24 Loyola L. Rev. 128 (1978). But see Morse v. J. Ray McDermott & Co., 344 So. 2d 1353 (La., 1976), which holds that an immoral condition only annuls an agreement to the extent the agreement depends on it, and might support an argument for an extramarital contract as to accumulations that contains no reference whatever to their living arrangements.
[7]As to the rights of married persons, see Me. Rev. Stat. Ann., tit. 19, § 61 et seq.
[8]Id., § 531 et seq.
[9]Id., § 132.
[10]See Roussel v. State, 274 A.2d 909 (Me., 1971).
[11]Me. Rev. Stat. Ann., tit. 22, § 8204.

ensure, inter alia, that those seeking to adopt a child can furnish a suitable home.[12]

Workers' compensation death benefits

Dependents, if living with a decedent at the time of his death, can qualify for workers' compensation benefits. But in a very early case, where a workman had deserted his wife and taken up residence with a mistress, by whom he had children, the legal wife could not qualify because she had committed adultery and lost the benefit of any presumption of dependency. The mistress could not qualify, though she was dependent and living with him at the time of his death. The illegitimates, however, did so qualify because he had a moral duty to support them.[13] (The decision as to the legal wife, if not that of the mistress, seems to reflect an outmoded approach.)

Abortion

Notwithstanding Roe v. Wade,[14] the operating on any pregnant woman, "whether such child is quick or not" with intent to destroy the child and resulting in its destruction, unless done to preserve the mother's life, is heavily punishable.[15] If the operation is performed merely to induce a miscarriage the potential punishment is slightly lower. A person consenting to or aiding in the operation is liable to the like punishment.[16] The test of necessity to preserve the mother's life is held to be an objective one; good faith on the part of the actor is not a sufficient defense.[17] However, physicians performing abortions are now required to make a detailed report to the department of human services; and the making of such a report immunizes them from any criminal prosecution.[18]

---

[12]Id., tit. 19, §§ 532, 533. See In re Adoption of E: First Amendment Rights and Religious Inquiry in Adoption Proceedings, 24 Maine L. Rev. 149 (1972).
[13]Scott's Case, 117 Maine 436, 104 Atl. 794 (1918).
[14]See section 2.19, herein.
[15]Me. Rev. Stat. Ann., tit. 17, § 51.
[16]Id.
[17]State v. Rudman, 126 Maine 177, 136 Atl. 817 (1927).
[18]Me. Rev. Stat. Ann., tit. 22, § 1596.

Tort actions

Actions for alienation of affections are prohibited.[19]

Possible criminal liability

The Criminal Code, revised in 1975, no longer penalizes sexual behavior between consenting adults. Cohabitation, fornication and adultery are no longer crimes. The pertinent provisions, which cover rape, gross sexual misconduct, sexual abuse of minors, and unlawful sexual contact,[20] are not of likely applicability to the ordinary extramarital cohabitant.[21] Worthy of mention, however, is that unlawful sexual contact is not now limited to any age group and applies, for example, where the other is mentally incapable of understanding the conduct involved, or where the actor is in a position of authority over the other. The fact that the parties are living as husband and wife is no defense.[22] The crime of abduction has been replaced by a kidnapping statute.[23] Though the prior sodomy statute has been repealed, the definition of "sexual act"[24] is broad enough to permit a conviction upon contact in the case of sodomy, fellatio or cunnilingus.[25] It seems that consensual adult conduct of this nature, where there are no circumstances of imposition, is not then punishable.

One who already has a spouse and intentionally marries or purports to marry another knowing he cannot legally do so commits bigamy.[26] An innocent participant is not punishable. Incest is criminal only when both parties are over the age of eighteen. Ignorance of consanguinity is a defense.[27]

Status of children

A child born out of wedlock is the heir and legitimate child of

---

[19] Id., tit. 19, § 167.
[20] Id., tit. 17A, §§ 252 to 255.
[21] Generally, see Potter, Sex Offenses, 28 Maine L. Rev. 65 (1976).
[22] Me. Rev. Stat. Ann., tit. 17A, § 255.
[23] Id., § 301.
[24] Id., § 251.
[25] See State v. McFarland, 369 A.2d 227 (Me., 1977) (involving charges of sodomy among other sexual offenses).
[26] Me. Rev. Stat. Ann., tit. 17A, § 551.
[27] Id., § 556. As to the prohibited degrees of marriage, see tit. 19, § 31.

his parents who intermarry.[28] Any such child, born at any time, is the heir of his mother. If the father of a child born out of wedlock adopts him or her into his family or in writing acknowledges before some justice of the peace or notary public that he is the father, such child is the heir and legitimate child of his or her father. In each case such child and its issue shall inherit from its parents respectively, and from their lineal and collateral kindred, and these from such child and its issue the same as if legitimate.[29]

Maine has adopted the Uniform Act on Paternity[30] under which the father can be made liable for the support of the child and for expenses of pregnancy and confinement, as well as for the cost of prosecuting paternity proceedings.[31]

An interstate compact on welfare services, designed to eliminate barriers caused by restrictive residence or settlement requirements of the various states in matters such as child welfare and the care of unwed mothers, has also been adopted.[32]

Detailed provisions ensure that notice and an opportunity to be heard are furnished to a putative father of an illegitimate wherever practicable before the child can be taken from him or adopted out, even if the mother has relinquished the child.[33]

6.21. Maryland

Though a common-law marriage cannot be contracted,[34] the state recognizes the general rule that, if such a union is valid

---

[28] Id., tit. 18, § 1003.

[29] Id. Generally, as to descent, see Plimpton, Conflict of Laws and the Disposition of Decedents' Movables, 24 Maine L. Rev. 43 (1972). The father's name cannot be entered on the birth certificate without his consent, unless paternity has been judicially established. Me. Rev. Stat. Ann., tit. 22, § 2761(4).

[30] Me. Rev. Stat. Ann., tit. 19, §§ 271 to 287. Generally, see Cousins v. Hooper, 224 A.2d 836 (Me., 1966).

[31] As to nonsupport of dependents, see Me. Rev. Stat. Ann., tit. 17A, § 552 and tit. 19, § 481 et seq. For the Civil Liability for Support Act, see tit. 19, §§ 441 to 453. For the Uniform Reciprocal Enforcement of Support Act, see tit. 19, §§ 331 to 420. Generally, see Thut v. Grant, 281 A.2d 1 (Me., 1971).

[32] Me. Rev. Stat. Ann., tit. 22, § 4101 et seq.

[33] Id., tit. 19, § 532-C.

The father, to protect his right to inherit from a child if he acknowledges paternity, may seek a declaration of his paternal status while evidence is available to support that conclusion, and to contest adoption and assert any custody rights he may have. See Johannesen v. Pfeiffer, 387 A.2d 1113 (Me., 1978).

[34] Md. Ann. Code, art. 62, § 4.

where entered into, it is valid in Maryland.[35] Continued cohabitation after an impediment to a supposedly valid marriage has been removed would not result in a valid marriage.[36] However, a marriage celebrated after the wrongful procurement of a marriage license is neither void nor voidable, and is valid.[37]

Adoption

Any person over eighteen years of age may petition the court for an adoption.[38] If the petitioner is married, unless living apart for reasons that would warrant a dissolution of the marriage or unless the spouse is a natural parent of the adoptee, the consent of such spouse is required.[39]

Social security and welfare benefits

A provision of the Social Security Act whereunder an illegitimate child's well-recognized[40] qualification for benefits on the death of its father was conditioned on a showing of dependency, while that of a legitimate was not,[41] received further judicial recognition of constitutionality in a case arising from Maryland.[42] The courts, however, recognize that a disqualification for welfare benefits, partial[43] or total,[44] *solely* on the ground of illegitimacy violates the Constitution.

---

[35]Jennings v. Jennings, 20 Md. App. 369, 315 A.2d 816 (1974); Madden v. Cosden, 271 Md. 118, 314 A.2d 128 (1974); Marshall v. Stefanides, 17 Md. App. 364, 302 A.2d 682 (1973).
[36]See Mitchell v. Frederick, 166 Md. 42, 170 Atl. 733, 92 A.L.R. 1412 (1934).
[37]Picarella v. Picarella, 20 Md. App. 499, 316 A.2d 826 (1974).
[38]Md. Ann. Code, art. 16, § 70.
[39]Id. As to whose consent is required, and when parental consent can be dispensed with, see notes 88 to 91, infra.
[40]Massey v. Weinberger, 397 F. Supp. 817 (D. Md., 1975).
[41]See sections 2.12, 3.2, herein.
[42]Norton v. Weinberger, 390 F. Supp. 1084 (D. Md., 1975), affd. 427 U.S. 524, 49 L. Ed. 2d 672, 96 Sup. Ct. 2771 (1976) on a jurisdictional point.
[43]Griffin v. Richardson, 346 F. Supp. 1226 (D. Md., 1972), affd. 409 U.S. 1069, 34 L. Ed. 2d 660, 93 Sup. Ct. 689 (1972) (holding unconstitutional a provision which conditions the qualification of illegitimates to situations where legitimate children had received their maximum benefits without exhausting the fund available.
[44]In re Cager, 251 Md. 473, 248 A.2d 384 (1968).

Workers' compensation death benefits

The sole test of eligibility for survivor's benefits under workers' compensation is dependency.[45] A dependent is one who relies on the worker for the reasonable necessities of life.[46] Thus, an extramarital cohabitant, on a showing of dependency, can recover.[47] It is not necessary that an illegitimate child live in the household of the deceased worker.[48]

Definition of "family" and "household" under automobile insurance policy

When an automobile insurance policy excludes the insurer from liability in respect of injury to members of the insured's family or household, the exclusion is held not to extend to an unmarried cohabitant of the insured.[49] This is in line with the doctrine that ambiguities are construed in favor of the insured. For the same reason, though the courts have held that a policy extending coverage to a spouse does not cover an extramarital cohabitant,[50] it would seem likely that an extension of coverage to persons living in the same household would cover such a person.

Definition of "family" under zoning law

For the purposes of a zoning law, extramarital cohabitants and their children have been regarded as a "family."[51]

Sexual misconduct as grounds for modification of alimony

At least one court has permitted a modification of alimony by reason of a divorced wife's sexual misconduct.[52] Such a discretion, however, was not exercised where the divorcee merely spent a few

---

[45] Md. Ann. Code, art. 101, § 36(8).
[46] Id. See Bituminous Constr. Co. v. Lewis, 253 Md. 1, 251 A.2d 888 (1969); Johnson v. Cole, 245 Md. 515, 226 A.2d 268 (1967).
[47] Kendall v. Housing Authority of Baltimore City, 196 Md. 370, 76 A.2d 767 (1950).
[48] Brooks v. Bethlehem Steel Co., 199 Md. 29, 85 A.2d 471 (1952).
[49] Hicks v. Hatem, 265 Md. 260, 289 A.2d 325 (1972).
[50] See section 2.17, herein.
[51] City of Takoma Park v. County Bd. of Appeals, 259 Md. 619, 270 A.2d 772 (1970).
[52] Courson v. Courson, 213 Md. 183, 129 A.2d 917 (1957).

nights with another man, there being no showing of a flagrant misconduct.[53]

Abortion

An abortion is illegal unless performed in a licensed hospital and is necessary to prevent the mother's death or impairment of health, or there is substantial risk of the infant's deformity or the pregnancy was the result of forcible rape.[54] The statute sets forth the conditions under which a pregnancy can be terminated. It forbids this after 26 weeks of gestation unless the mother's life is at stake.[55] But the courts hold that violations of this provision carry no criminal sanctions.[56] The statutory provision which states, inter alia, that it is an offense for a nonphysician to sell or give abortifacients, or advice in regard to termination of pregnancy,[57] has been held to be constitutional to that extent, but insofar as it criminalizes a termination of pregnancy outside of an accredited hospital it is unconstitutional. A licensed physician may perform abortions without restraint as to reason, time or place.[58] The net result appears to be that, as long as the abortion is performed by a licensed physician, the only sanctions applicable in the case of a "forbidden" abortion would be in the nature of disciplinary action against him.

Tort actions

A statute abolishing the tort action for alienation of affections does not have the effect of also abolishing the tort of criminal conversation.[59]

The mother of an illegitimate has a statutory right to recover for the seduction or wrongful injury to such child, if a minor.[60]

---

[53] Atkinson v. Atkinson, 31 Md. App. 65, 281 A.2d 407 (1971).
[54] Md. Ann. Code, art. 43, § 137.
[55] Id.
[56] See Beverungen v. Briele, 25 Md. App. 233, 333 A.2d 664 (1975).
[57] Md. Ann. Code, art. 43, § 139.
[58] State v. Ingel, 18 Md. App. 514, 308 A.2d 223 (1973). See also Vuitch v. Hardy, 473 F.2d 1370 (C.A.-4 Md., 1973), cert. den. 414 U.S. 824, 38 L. Ed. 2d 57, 94 Sup. Ct. 126 (1973); In re Smith, 16 Md. App. 209, 295 A.2d 238 (1972) (consent of minor, if authorized by statute, is not subject to disaffirmance for minority).
[59] Kromm v. Kromm, 31 Md. App. 635, 358 A.2d 247 (1976). Generally, see section 2.20, herein.
[60] Md. Ann. Code, art. 72A, § 3. See Note, Discrimination on the Basis of Illegitimacy in Maryland's Wrongful Death Statute, 3 U. Balt. L. Rev. 251 (1974).

MARYLAND 6.21

Possible criminal liability

One who entices or persuades a female under eighteen to leave home for the purpose, among other things, of fornication, commits the crime of abduction.[61] In a case involving sodomy with a minor, a judge of the state of Maryland expressed an opinion that the rule of Griswold v. Connecticut, that private consensual marital relations are protected from criminal sanctions,[62] does not extend to private consensual conduct of unmarried adults, and that the rationale of that decision, being based on the inherent nature of marriage, does not extend to heterosexual relations outside of marriage.[63]

Adultery is punishable by a nominal fine,[64] but it is unclear whether the crime embraces intercourse by a married man with a single woman or is restricted to situations where only the female participant is married.[65] The statute denouncing bigamy was rewritten in 1976.[66]

As to the varieties of crime commonly denounced as statutory rape, since the age of consent is fourteen,[67] the crime is unlikely to concern most extramarital cohabitants. Mistake as to age is no defense,[68] but an unsubstantial age differential between actor and victim can be important.

The crime of sodomy remains on the books.[69] And since the consent of the participant is no defense to the related crime of unnatural or perverted sex[70] it can be assumed that private, consensual sodomy is included in this crime.

Of related interest is a holding that, though a teacher's homosexual preference is not sufficient ground to transfer him or

---

[61] Md. Ann. Code, art. 27, § 1.
[62] See section 2.6, herein.
[63] Hughes v. State, 14 Md. App. 497, 287 A.2d 299 (1972), cert. den. 409 U.S. 1025, 34 L. Ed. 2d 317, 93 Sup. Ct. 469 (1972).
[64] Md. Ann. Code, art. 27, § 4.
[65] Payne v. Payne, 33 Md. App. 707, 366 A.2d 405 (1976). See section 2.25, herein.
[66] Md. Ann. Code, art. 27, § 18.
[67] Id., § 463.
[68] Eggleston v. State, 4 Md. App. 124, 241 A.2d 433 (1968).
[69] Md. Ann. Code, art. 27, § 553.
[70] Gooch v. State, 34 Md. App. 331, 367 A.2d 90 (1976). See Fisher, Sex Offender Provisions of the Proposed New Maryland Criminal Code: Should Private, Consenting Adult Homosexual Behavior be Excluded?, 30 Md. L. Rev. 91 (1970).

to terminate his employment, a refusal to renew his contract on the ground that he publicized his attitudes in this regard on radio and television was neither arbitrary nor capricious.[71] The argument that if private consensual adult homosexuality is "protectable" (which itself is at least debatable in Maryland) public speech in support of that activity should also be protected, received the answer that teachers have special responsibilities and that such public promotions may not serve the best purposes of sexual adjustment, maturation and student-parent relationships in the educational context.[72]

Status of children

A child born to parents who have not participated in a marriage ceremony with each other is the child of its mother. It is considered the child of the father only if the father (1) has been judicially determined to be the father in a paternity proceeding, or (2) has acknowledged himself in writing to be the father, or (3) has openly and notoriously recognized the child to be his, or (4) has subsequently married the mother and has acknowledged himself, orally or in writing, to be the father.[73]

The legitimacy of a child so established is not restricted to his inheritance rights. The child is legitimate for all purposes. "If the law provides a means of legitimation for the purposes of inheritance, such a procedure should certainly be of sufficient legal validity to establish other rights, ofttimes inferior to that of inheritance, arising from the relationship existing between parent and legitimate issue."[74] Thus, an "open and notorious" recognition

---

[71] Acanfora v. Board of Education of Montgomery County, 359 F. Supp. 843 (D. Md., 1973), affd. 491 F.2d 498 (C.A.-4 Md., 1974), cert. den. 419 U.S. 836, 42 L. Ed. 2d 63, 95 Sup. Ct. 64 (1974). Generally, see section 2.3, herein.
[72] Id.
[73] Md. Est. & Trusts Code Ann., § 1–208. As to inheritance from the illegitimate, see § 3–108. An illegitimate cannot inherit from a deceased half brother who was a legitimate son of the same mother. Penman v. Ayers, 221 Md. 154, 156 A.2d 638 (1959).

The statute can operate to legitimate, by subsequent marriage of the biological parents, a child whose mother was married to another at the time of its birth. See Shelley v. Smith, 249 Md. 619, 241 A.2d 682 (1968).

[74] Thomas v. Solis, 263 Md. 536, 283 A.2d 777, 780 (1971) (father sought a declaration of his paternity).

qualifies the child for benefits under social security.[75] A child conceived by artificial insemination of a married woman with her husband's consent is legitimate.[76]

Support and custody

The proceedings that can be brought to establish paternity, and to enforce the obligation of an adjudicated father to support his child,[77] are civil in nature, not criminal.[78] The old rule of the common law that neither married partner can testify in such a way as to bastardize the issue of their marriage has been relaxed; the presumption of paternity of the husband is no longer a conclusive presumption.[79]

Contrary to the rule in some states, a putative father, without admitting paternity, can validly compromise any alleged liability for support; such a compromise, if approved, can be incorporated in a judicial decree.[80]

A criminal action for nonsupport of an illegitimate, which obligation does not fall within the constitutional ban on imprisonment for debt,[81] must be predicated on a showing that paternity has been established, either by defendant's admission or by judicial determination.[82] This does not, however, mean that paternity cannot be established in the course of such a criminal proceeding for nonsupport.[83] Though at common law this was primarily a liability of the male parent, following the adoption in Maryland of

---

[75] See Massey v. Weinberger, 397 F. Supp. 817 (D. Md., 1975).
[76] Md. Est. & Trusts Code Ann., § 1–206(b). See section 3.1, herein.
[77] Md. Ann. Code, art. 16, §§ 66A to 66P. The paternity statute is the exclusive basis for enforcing the obligation of a putative father to support the child. Williams v. Williams, 18 Md. App. 353, 306 A.2d 564 (1973). The requirement that proceedings to establish paternity and charge the father with support obligations are to be commenced within two years after birth of the child promotes a legitimate state interest and does not violate the child's right to equal protection. Thompson v. Thompson, —— Md. ——, 390 A.2d 1139 (1978).
[78] Corley v. Moore, 236 Md. 241, 203 A.2d 697 (1964).
[79] See Harris v. Brinkley, 33 Md. App. 508, 365 A.2d 304 (1976); Staley v. Staley, 25 Md. App. 99, 335 A.2d 114 (1975); Shelley v. Smith, 249 Md. 619, 241 A.2d 682 (1968).
[80] Md. Ann. Code, art. 16, § 66L.
[81] Md. Const., art. III, § 38.
[82] State v. Rawlings, 38 Md. App. 479, 381 A.2d 708 (1978).
[83] Id.

6.21   UNMARRIED COUPLES AND THE LAW

the Equal Rights Amendment[84] it is now a liability shared by both parents, depending on the extent of their financial resources.[85] The state has adopted the Uniform Reciprocal Enforcement of Support Act,[86] as well as the Uniform Child Custody Jurisdiction Act.[87]

Termination of parental rights

There are detailed requirements as to whose consent is necessary before a child can be adopted out.[88] That of the child itself, if ten years or older, is required. Minority of the parents is no disability, and a subsequent disaffirmance of consent cannot be based thereon.[89] The consent of both parents is required, unless, on a showing of willful neglect, for example, failure to furnish support or to visit the child,[90] or abandonment,[91] the best interests of the child favor the petitioner for adoption even over the parent's veto.[92] A provision defining a "neglected child," inter alia, as one who is living in a home which fails to provide a stable moral environment does not justify a court in concluding that a mother who repeats her mistakes in mothering more than one illegitimate is necessarily an unfit parent.[93] The courts will not use such children as pawns to punish a mother's past promiscuity,[94]

---

[84] Md. Const., art. 46.

[85] See Rand v. Rand, 280 Md. 508, 374 A.2d 900 (1977). For an ingenious, though unsuccessful, argument that the imposition of equal duties of support on the parents is unconstitutional as failing to treat the father equally in that the nexus between the intercourse and the child's birth is broken by the mother's independent decision to bring the fetus to term, see Dorsey v. English, —— Md. ——, 390 A.2d 1133 (1978).

[86] Md. Ann. Code, art. 89C, §§ 1 to 39.

[87] Id., art. 16, §§ 184 to 207. As to the right to custody, the mother is favored if the child is young, but the father may not be denied his right to seek custody. Marshall v. Stefanides, 17 Md. App. 364, 302 A.2d 682 (1973).

[88] Md. Ann. Code, art. 16, § 74.

[89] Id.

[90] See, e.g., Hicks v. Prince George's County Dept. of Social Services, 281 Md. 93, 375 A.2d 558 (1977).

[91] An unwed mother who resorted to ruses to get the child away from its paternal grandparents and did not appear at a custody hearing because the sheriff had told her it was not necessary, had not "abandoned" the child so as to permit its adoption without her consent. Brendoff v. Titus, 22 Md. App, 412, 323 A.2d 612 (1974).

[92] Generally, see Lloyd v. Schutes, 24 Md. App. 515, 332 A.2d 338 (1975).

[93] In re Cager, 251 Md. 473, 248 A.2d 384 (1968).

[94] Id.

but extramarital cohabitation is a factor the court should take into consideration in determining whether parental rights should be terminated.

Property rights of cohabitants

Where one of the parties mistakenly believed in the existence of a valid marriage, the courts have recognized the right of that party to restitution for benefits conferred if that person's contribution can be traced into the hands of the other party.[95] If the innocent party has furnished the consideration for a deed to land, taken by both as tenants by the entireties, a lien for taxes owed by the nonmistaken grantee cannot be impressed on the land, because the latter holds his or her interest on a resulting trust for the innocent partner who paid for it.[96]

A tenancy by the entireties cannot exist when the parties are not legally spouses.[97] In the case of a deed to husband and wife when the supposed marriage was not legal, the state recognizes, as is usual,[98] that a tenancy in common, and not a joint tenancy, results.[99] (Bigamous marriages, incidentally, though at one time regarded as a nullity,[1] can now support a decree of divorce with alimony to a mistaken spouse.)[2]

Where neither party purports to enter into a valid marriage, the courts adhere to the general view that any contract based on consideration, either past or future, of illicit sexual relations, or in any manner promoting or furnishing consideration for unlawful cohabitation, is void.[3] However, a contract the consideration

---

[95] Hutson v. Hutson, 168 Md. 182, 177 Atl. 177 (1935). Compare Cassell v. Pfaifer, 243 Md. 447, 221 A.2d 668 (1966) (finding of a confidential relationship between paramours so as to impose constructive trust for breach thereof not supported by evidence).

[96] Schwarz v. United States, 191 F.2d 618 (C.A.-4 Md., 1951).

[97] Young v. Young, 37 Md. App. 211, 376 A.2d 1151 (1977).

[98] See section 4.2, herein.

[99] Donnelly v. Donnelly, 198 Md. 341, 84 A.2d 89 (1951). Compare Mitchell v. Frederick, 166 Md. 42, 170 Atl. 733, 92 A.L.R. 1412 (1934), where the court, noting that the statute required plural tenancies be construed as tenancies in common rather than as joint tenancies, held that an intent to provide for joint tenancy could be deduced from a clear manifestation of such intent.

[1] Townsend v. Morgan, 192 Md. 168, 63 A.2d 743 (1949).

[2] Hall v. Hall, 32 Md. App. 363, 362 A.2d 648 (1976).

[3] Lynch v. Rogers, 177 Md. 478, 10 A.2d 619 (1941).

for which is past cohabitation is valid.[4] Further, the mere fact of such cohabitation does not disenable the parties from making an enforceable contract with each other if it has no reference to the continuance of the relation or is only incidentally connected with it and may be supported independently of the relationship.[5] Thus, a loan from a man to his mistress to enable her to buy land not for the furtherance of their illicit relationship would be enforceable.[6] Concededly, such an early obiter statement would be a slender basis on which to predicate rights arising from a contract, express or implied, between unmarried partners.

6.22. Massachusetts

A common-law marriage cannot validly be contracted in Massachusetts, and such a status is not recognized as having been created where the contract and cohabitation was in a state that does not recognize such as a marriage.[7] Further, if a domiciliary of Massachusetts contracts a marriage outside of the state which is void or prohibited by the state law of Massachusetts, and the party intends to remain domiciled in Massachusetts, the marriage is void in Massachusetts.[8]

Where one entered into a marriage contract in good faith ignorance that the other partner had a living spouse at the time, continued living together, even with knowledge of the facts, can result in a valid marriage if the impediment is removed.[9] The phrase "living together" in this context requires merely that the parties have not terminated the marriage to the extent that they

---

[4] Id.
[5] Baxter v. Wilburn, 172 Md. 160, 190 Atl. 773 (1937).
[6] Id.
[7] Peck v. Peck, 155 Mass. 479, 30 N.E. 74 (1892).
[8] Levanosky v. Levanosky, 311 Mass. 638, 42 N.E.2d 561 (1942); Sweeney v. Kennard, 331 Mass. 542, 120 N.W.2d 910 (1954).
[9] Mass. Gen. Laws Ann., ch. 207, §§ 6, 47. Stamper v. Stanwood, 339 Mass. 549, 159 N.E.2d 865 (1959); Hopkins v. Hopkins, 287 Mass. 542, 192 N.E. 145, 95 A.L.R. 1286 (1934). Compare Wright v. Wright, 264 Mass. 453, 162 N.E. 894 (1928), holding the statute not to extend to continued cohabitation where the impediment consisted in one spouse marrying within a prohibited time after a divorce.

consider it dissolved. That they are not actually cohabiting, and are living with their respective parents, but frequently exchange visits, does not mean that a survivor and the issue of such a relation would not qualify for social security benefits.[10]

Students

Unwed pregnancy as such is held not a proper ground for exclusion of a school pupil[11] from regular attendance at day classes, at any rate where there is no showing of any danger to the student's physical or mental health, and the only apparent reason for such exclusion is that younger pupils, flexible in their attitudes, might be led to believe that the school authorities condone premarital relations.[12] Such a reason is an insufficient basis for interference with so important a personal right or liberty as the right to an education.[13]

Workers' compensation death benefits

For the purposes of workers' compensation, a mistress does not ordinarily qualify for death benefits even though in fact dependent upon the workman.[14] Nor do the children of such a mistress, even though the workman has assumed responsibility for their support.[15] An illegitimate child, if living with the workman and in fact dependent on him, is entitled to benefits, though the undivorced mother is not.[16]

Insurance benefits

In harmony with the rule that ambiguities in a contract are construed against the drafters, a life insurance beneficiary designated by name and described as "wife" of the insured qualified for the proceeds even though she was a mere cohabitant.[17]

---

[10] Carr v. Hobby, 125 F. Supp. 545 (D. Mass., 1954).
[11] See section 2.4, herein.
[12] Ordway v. Hargraves, 323 F. Supp. 1155 (D. Mass., 1971).
[13] Id.
[14] See Roney's Case, 316 Mass. 732, 56 N.E.2d 859 (1944); Gritta's Case, 236 Mass. 204, 127 N.E. 889 (1920).
[15] See Moore's Case, 294 Mass. 557, 3 N.E.2d 5 (1936).
[16] Gritta's Case, 236 Mass. 204, 127 N.E. 889 (1920).
[17] Strachan v. Prudential Ins. Co. of America, 321 Mass. 507, 73 N.E.2d 840, 173 A.L.R. 711 (1947).

Adoption

Any person of full age may petition to adopt a child.[18] So also may a minor if the child to be adopted is a natural child of one of the parties.[19] The written consent of the mother of an illegitimate child is required, and such consent must be obtained no sooner than the fourth day after birth.[20] The statutory requirement that the court, when practicable, award custody only to persons of the same religious faith as that of the child[21] has withstood attack based on first amendment grounds.[22] Reports from the department of public welfare are ordinarily required.[23]

Abortion

Post-Roe v. Wade[24] abortion legislation has been before the courts. A provision requiring the written consent, informed and freely given by the mother for an abortion during the first twelve weeks of her pregnancy has been upheld.[25]

Further, in supporting the rule that a husband has no right to veto an abortion, a Massachusetts court went out of its way to observe that nothing in its ruling should be taken as having any possible impact on the rights of the objecting husband to divorce, separation or child custody; that although he has no veto, he surely has a legitimate interest in the matter and, if family life is to prosper, should be entitled to participate in the decision.[26]

The new Massachusetts statute requires that, if the mother is less than eighteen years old and is unmarried, the consent of her parents must be obtained, but if one or both parents refuse,

---

[18] Mass. Gen. Laws Ann., ch. 210, §§ 1, 2.
[19] Id.
[20] Id.
[21] Id., § 5B.
[22] Petitions of Goldman, 331 Mass. 647, 121 N.E.2d 843 (1954), cert. den. 348 U.S. 942, 75 Sup. Ct. 363 (1955), holding that where the child is too young to choose a religion it is deemed to adhere to the faith of the mother and natural father.
[23] Mass. Gen. Laws Ann., ch. 210, § 5A. See In re Adoption of Minor, 367 Mass. 684, 327 N.E.2d 875 (1975); Krakow v. Department of Public Welfare, 326 Mass. 452, 95 N.E.2d 184 (1950). As to the requirements of parental consent in adoption, see notes 65 to 68 and related text, infra.
[24] See section 2.19, herein.
[25] Framingham Clinic, Inc. v. Board of Selectmen of Southborough, —— Mass. ——, 367 N.E.2d 606 (1977).
[26] Doe v. Doe, 365 Mass. 556, 314 N.E.2d 128, 62 A.L.R.3d 1082 (1974).

consent may be obtained by a court "for good cause shown."[27] In Bellotti v. Baird[28] the Supreme Court of the United States indicated, with regard to this statute, that a state may perhaps properly require a type of parental consent in situations such as this as long as the minor's best interests are protected. The outcome of later decisions of the Massachusetts state court[29] and of a federal district court[30] is that a provision for parental input is of little value.[31] Since the provision does not bring home as forcefully as possible the limited scope of the issue confronting parents, informing them that their wishes can freely be overridden by the minor by approaching a court, it casts an undue burden on the minor's rights and is unjustifiable.[32] Neither in Bellotti v. Baird nor in Planned Parenthood v. Danforth[33] did the Supreme Court furnish guidelines as to when a minor, due to immaturity or lack of competent judgment, is unable to give an informed consent.

Possible criminal liability

It is a crime for a parent to conceal the death of a child, which if born alive would be illegitimate.[34] If the charge is murder but the prosecution cannot establish that the child was born alive, a conviction of the concealment, if charged in the same indictment, can follow.[35]

Within the qualifications of the Roe v. Wade decision,[36] procuring a miscarriage,[37] and making available instruments to prevent conception or for abortion,[38] are criminal.[39]

---

[27] Mass. Gen. Laws Ann., ch. 112, § 12S.
[28] 428 U.S. 132, 49 L. Ed. 2d 844, 96 Sup. Ct. 2857 (1976).
[29] Baird v. Attorney General, —— Mass. ——, 36 N.E.2d 288 (1977).
[30] Baird v. Bellotti, 428 F. Supp. 854 (D. Mass., 1977).
[31] See Levitt, Constitutionality of Mandatory Parental Consent in the Abortion Decision of a Minor: Bellotti II in Perspective, 4 N. Ky. L. Rev. 323 (1977).
[32] Baird v. Bellotti, 450 F. Supp. 997 (D. Mass., 1978).
[33] 428 U.S. 52, 49 L. Ed. 2d 788, 96 Sup. Ct. 2831 (1976), discussed in section 2.19, herein.
[34] Mass. Gen. Laws Ann., ch. 272, § 22.
[35] Id., § 23.
[36] See section 2.19, herein.
[37] Mass. Gen. Laws Ann., ch. 272, § 19.
[38] Id., § 21.
[39] See, e.g., Commonwealth v. Edelin, —— Mass. ——, 359 N.E.2d 4 (1976); Commonwealth v. Kudish, 362 Mass. 627, 289 N.E.2d 856 (1972); Commonwealth v. Brunelle, 361 Mass. 6, 277 N.E.2d 826 (1972).

6.22   UNMARRIED COUPLES AND THE LAW

Probably as a result of a holding that a complaint alleging paternity and seeking an award for expenses of pregnancy and confinement do not fall within the general equity jurisdiction of probate courts,[40] the legislature has repealed a provision criminalizing getting a woman pregnant.[41] The statute also provoked constitutional objections as a denial of equal protection.[42]

Other crimes of possible concern to unmarried cohabitants could include the inducing of a person under eighteen of chaste life to have unlawful sexual intercourse,[43] adultery[44] and polygamy.[45] Persons of opposite sex who "lewdly and lasciviously" associate and cohabit together commit a crime.[46] This latter statute, however, is unconstitutional as applied to activity where there is no imposition of the behavior on an unsuspecting or unwilling person.[47] Fornication is also denounced.[48] However, a woman who had sexual intercourse in the good faith belief that she was married to the participant, *though said to be guilty of this crime,* was held not disqualified for naturalization as being without good moral character.[49] The holding here as to fornication is of dubious validity; the legislature surely could not have intended to impose strict liability.

Not only does the "abominable and detestable crime against nature" remain on the statute books;[50] any "unnatural and lascivious act with another" is also punishable.[51] This provision has been held unconstitutionally vague as applied to acts of fellatio and oral-anal contact.[52] But a defendant who cannot or does not

---

[40]Davis v. Misiano, —— Mass. ——, 366 N.E.2d 752 (1977).
[41]Mass. Gen. Laws Ann., ch. 273, § 11. Repealed by Mass. Acts 1977, ch. 848, § 7.
[42]See Commonwealth v. MacKenzie, —— Mass. ——, 334 N.E.2d 613 (1975).
[43]Mass. Gen. Laws Ann., ch. 272, § 4.
[44]Id., § 14.
[45]Id., § 15.
[46]Id., § 16.
[47]City of Revere v. Aucella, —— Mass. ——, 338 N.E.2d 816 (1975), appeal dismissed sub nom. Charger Investments, Inc. v. Corbett, 429 U.S. 877, 50 L. Ed. 2d 159, 97 Sup. Ct. 225 (1976).
[48]Mass. Gen. Laws Ann., ch. 272, § 18.
[49]Petition of R. ——, 56 F. Supp. 969 (D. Mass., 1944).
[50]Mass. Gen. Laws Ann., ch. 272, § 34.
[51]Id., § 35. As to cunnilingus, see Commonwealth v. Brown, —— Mass. App. ——, 373 N.E.2d 982 (1978).
[52]Balthazar v. Superior Court of Commonwealth of Massachusetts, 573 F.2d 698 (C.A.-1 Mass., 1978).

invoke the right to privacy in the home has no standing to challenge the constitutionality of the statute on the ground that criminal sanctions cannot be imposed for private sexual activity between consenting adults.[53]

Status of children

An illegitimate child is the heir of its mother and of any maternal ancestor.[54] The lawful issue of such a child can take by descent any estate the child could have taken if living.[55] The illegitimate child can only inherit by intestacy from the father if the father marries the mother *and* either acknowledges the child as his[56] or is judicially established to be the father.[57] In view of Trimble v. Gordon,[58] it is to be expected that the legislature will expand this unconstitutional restriction on the rights of the illegitimate vis-a-vis the father.

In a review of the rights of a married woman to adopt a name of her choosing and, at least absent an objection from the putative father, a name for her illegitimate child, the courts have already recognized that classifications based on illegitimacy, though not subject to "strictest scrutiny," are subject to scrutiny under equal protection guarantees which is not "a toothless one."[59] They also recognize that, unless strong policies of the forum are involved, the question of legitimacy or otherwise depends on the law of the domicile of birth.[60]

---

[53] Commonwealth v. LaBella, 364 Mass. 550, 306 N.E.2d 813 (1974). See, to the same effect, Commonwealth v. Bucaulis, —— Mass. App. ——, 373 N.E.2d 221 (1978).

[54] Mass. Gen. Laws Ann., ch. 190, § 5.

[55] Id.

[56] Houghton v. Dickinson, 196 Mass. 389, 82 N.E. 481 (1907).

[57] Mass. Gen. Laws Ann., ch. 190, § 7. See also Hanson v. Markham, —— Mass. ——, 356 N.E.2d 702 (1976). See Illegitimate in Massachusetts: Born Equal?, 6 Suffolk U. L. Rev. 58 (1971); Status of Illegitimates in New England, 38 B. U. L. Rev. 299 (1958). As to inheritance from or through illegitimates, see Mass. Gen. Laws Ann., ch. 190, §§ 5, 6. As to the right of an illegitimate to inherit from its adoptive parents, see Cennami v. Department of Public Welfare, —— Mass. App. ——, 363 N.E.2d 539 (1977).

[58] See section 3.3, herein.

[59] Secretary of Commonwealth v. City Clerk of Lowell, —— Mass. ——, 366 N.E.2d 717 (1977).

[60] Fuss v. Fuss, —— Mass. ——, 368 N.E.2d 271 (1977).

The presumption that a child born during a lawful marriage is the legitimate child of the husband, while not conclusive, can only be overcome by proof beyond a reasonable doubt that the husband could not have been the father.[61]

The provisions to establish paternity and enable the enforcement of duties of support which were always regarded as essentially civil in nature,[62] follow a fairly standard form.[63] The provisions for an award of pregnancy and confinement expenses to the mother cover her expenses in caring for the unborn child, though the putative father owes no direct duty to the unborn fetus as such.[64]

As is usual, the written consent of the lawful parents is a prerequisite to adoption of an illegitimate.[65] Such consent, however, is dispensed with if a parent has willfully deserted or neglected to provide proper care for the child for at least one year preceding the date of the petition.[66] In invoking the "best interests of the child" test as to whether parental consent can be dispensed with, it was not the legislative intent to disregard natural family ties or to threaten a satisfactory family with the loss of children because they are placed in foster care by reason of temporary adversity.[67] Consent of a putative father who is not a lawful parent at the time of the proceeding and who does not appear, to object to an adoption, is not required.[68]

---

[61]Commonwealth v. Leary, 345 Mass. 59, 185 N.E.2d 641 (1962).
[62]Commonwealth v. Lanoue, 326 Mass. 559, 95 N.E.2d 925 (1950).
[63]See Mass. Gen. Laws Ann., ch. 273, §§ 1 to 23. For Uniform Reciprocal Enforcement of Support provisions, see, §§ 1 to 17.
[64]Baby X v. Misiano, —— Mass. ——, 366 N.E.2d 755 (1977).
[65]Mass. Gen. Laws Ann., ch. 210, § 2.
[66]Id., § 3.
[67]Petition of New England Home for Little Wanderers, 367 Mass. 631, 328 N.E.2d 854 (1975).
[68]In re Adoption of a Minor, 338 Mass. 635, 156 N.E.2d 801 (1959). Generally, as to when parental consent can be dispensed with, see Adoption of a Minor, 362 Mass. 882, 289 N.E.2d 843 (1972); Petition of Dept. of Public Welfare, —— Mass. ——, 358 N.E.2d 794 (1976); In re Adoption of Minor, 367 Mass. 907, 327 N.E.2d 735 (1975); In re Custody of Minor, 2 Mass. App. 68, 308 N.E.2d 911 (1974). As to the right (rarely permitted) to revoke consent once given, see In re Revocation of Appointment of Guardian, 360 Mass. 81, 271 N.E.2d 621 (1971).

As to the rights of one claiming to be the father in adoption proceedings, see Mass. Gen. Laws Ann., ch. 210, § 4A. Where paternity is established or conceded, in a determination as to the rights of a father to visit his child, whatever the

Property rights of cohabitants

The general rule, that where a conveyance is to a husband and wife as tenants by the entirety and they are not in fact legally married, a tenancy in common results,[69] receives recognition.[70]

There is also early authority to support an award of realty on a theory of resulting trust[71] in favor of one who paid the price of land, title to which was taken in the name of one who had defrauded her into belief in a valid marriage.[72] Where both contributed to the price, the innocent party can be awarded a fractional interest in the property on a similar trust basis.[73] Early authority does not, however, support any right of a mistaken believer in the validity of a marriage to recover for domestic services, though she could have an action in tort for deceit.[74] A fortiori is this so where neither party believed in the existence of a valid marriage.[75]

The early courts declined to assist a person in adjusting the equities in a meretricious relationship.[76] Thus, although one who confers benefits in consideration of an illicit relationship cannot qualify for relief,[77] if future cohabitation forms no part of the consideration therefor, the illicit nature of the relationship does not bar recovery.[78] Further, more recently a court, though recognizing that sexual favors often form an important aspect of property arrangements between extramarital partners, saw this to be a jury question. Though not enforcing a promise to bequeath, it allowed a recovery for the fair value of services rendered in

---

mother's attitude in the matter, the courts will look to the best interests of the child. Gardner v. Rothman, —— Mass. ——, 345 N.E.2d 370 (1976).

[69]See section 4.2, herein.

[70]Gleason v. Galvin, —— Mass. ——, 373 N.E.2d 357 (1978); Fuss v. Fuss, —— Mass. ——, 368 N.E.2d 276 (1977).

A subsequent marriage of tenants in common of realty does not of course affect their status as such tenants. Russo v. Russo, —— Mass. App. ——, 330 N.E.2d 220 (1975).

[71]Discussed in section 4.5, herein.

[72]Morin v. Kirkland, 226 Mass. 345, 115 N.E. 414 (1917).

[73]Batty v. Greene, 206 Mass. 561, 92 N.E. 715 (1910).

[74]Cooper v. Cooper, 147 Mass. 370, 17 N.E. 892 (1888).

[75]Zytka v. Dmochowski, 302 Mass. 63, 18 N.E.2d 332, 120 A.L.R. 470 (1938).

[76]Otis v. Freeman, 199 Mass. 160, 85 N.E. 168 (1908).

[77]See section 4.10, herein.

[78]A woman who gave money to a cohabitant on his representation that the money would be used for their mutual benefit when married would not be deprived of her rights as a creditor if the illicit relations formed no part of the consideration. Zytka v. Dmochowski, 302 Mass. 63, 18 N.E.2d 332, 120 A.L.R. 470 (1938).

performance of such a contract.[79] Thus, it is certainly not beyond the realm of possibility that the Massachusetts courts will, in a proper case, honor contractual obligations between such persons.[80]

6.23. Michigan

Michigan no longer recognizes common-law marriages.[81]

If a marriage was in its inception known to be bigamous, a subsequent cohabitation after its termination does not validate the relationship. A new marriage is necessary.[82] But where the parties were merely mistaken as to the validity of the marriage, a continued cohabitation is held to evidence a continuing consent to their intent to marry, and their relation becomes effective as a marriage.[83] Where the impediment consisted of a disease, a continued cohabitation after cure results in a marriage.[84]

Although the state has no roots in the civil law, the legislature has chosen to enact its own community property laws.[85]

Adoption

Statutory provision is made for procedures whereunder a person (including an adult) may be adopted.[86] Provision is also made for termination of parental rights.[87]

Workers' compensation death benefits

For purposes of workers' compensation, the fact that a surviving cohabitant, having lived with the worker for an extended

---

[79] Green v. Richmond, —— Mass. ——, 337 N.E.2d 691 (1975).
[80] See Domestic Relations—Expansion of the Property Rights of Non-marital Partners, 11 Suffolk U. L. Rev. 1327 (1977).
[81] Mich. Comp. Laws Ann., § 551.2; People v. Stanford, 68 Mich. App. 168, 242 N.W.2d 56 (1976).
[82] Stevenson v. City of Detroit, 42 Mich. App. 294, 201 N.W.2d 688 (1972).
[83] See Jones v. General Motors Corp., 310 Mich. 605, 17 N.W.2d 770 (1945); Ryan v. Randall, 252 Mich. 501, 233 N.W. 394 (1930); Walsh v. Ferguson, 249 Mich. 539, 229 N.W. 424 (1930).
[84] Stratos v. Stratos, 317 Mich. 113, 26 N.W.2d 729 (1947).
[85] Mich. Comp. Laws Ann., § 557.201 et seq.
[86] Id., § 710.21 et seq. As to the allegations of a petition, see § 710.24.
[87] See notes 32 to 38, infra.

period, was married to another and had not obtained a divorce, was held not to preclude her from claiming death benefits.[88] But earlier courts held that public policy does not sanction compensation to one living in meretricious cohabitation.[89] This apparent contradiction would probably be resolved in favor of the unmarried cohabitant where there has been a stable "living-together" plus a showing of dependency, but the conclusive presumption of dependency which exists when a wife is "living with" an injured workman would not apply.[90]

The test being dependency, illegitimate children would qualify if dependent on the workman; if adopted out, even legitimate children would not qualify.[91]

Insurance benefits

A "child" for the purposes of a group life policy was held to encompass illegitimate children raised and cared for by the insured.[92]

Tort actions

Prompted by a realization that civil actions for seduction accomplish no useful social purpose, and tend to cause humiliation to persons guilty of nothing more heinous than a change of heart, and furthermore can open up opportunities for extortion,[93] this form of tort action has been abolished.[94]

Abortion

The willful administration to any pregnant woman of anything intended to procure a miscarriage, unless necessary to preserve

---

[88] West v. Barton-Malow Co., 394 Mich. 334, 230 N.W.2d 545 (1975).

[89] See McDonald v. Kelly Coal Co., 335 Mich. 325, 55 N.W.2d 851 (1952).

[90] See McDonald v. Chrysler Corp., 68 Mich. App. 468, 242 N.W.2d 810 (1976), holding the term "living with" as used in a provision entitling a wife to a conclusive presumption of dependency not to embrace the situation where the spouses are living apart due to the worker's inability to provide adequate support.

[91] Theodore v. Packing Materials, Inc., 396 Mich. 152, 240 N.W.2d 255 (1976).

[92] Samuels v. Aetna Life Ins. Co., 48 Mich. App. 761, 211 N.W.2d 104 (1973).

[93] See Feinsinger, Legislative Attack on "Heart Balm," 33 Mich. L. Rev. 979 (1935).

[94] Mich. Comp. Laws Ann., § 551.301.

the life of such a woman, is forbidden as abortion.[95] This provision, which predates the Supreme Court's abortion decisions,[96] recognizes that all induced miscarriages are not criminal.[97] Although it came under heavy judicial fire,[98] it has not been repealed. Instead, it has simply been held that it does not apply to "miscarriages" authorized by a woman's attending physician in the exercise of his medical judgment, and that a physician may not cause a miscarriage after viability except where necessary in his medical judgment to preserve the life *or health* of the mother.[99] The statute clearly controls abortions performed by a nonphysician.[1]

There can be no conviction, even for the attempt or for conspiracy to commit abortion,[2] where the woman operated on was not pregnant.[3]

A court has held that provisions requiring parental consent for an abortion on an unemancipated minor are unconstitutional.[4]

Possible criminal liability

Early statutes denounce, as "abduction," the taking of a woman and compelling her to marry,[5] the taking of a woman with intent to compel her to marry,[6] and the enticing away (for sex or for

---

[95]Id., § 750.14.
[96]See section 2.19, herein.
[97]People v. Wellman, 6 Mich. App. 573, 149 N.W.2d 908 (1967).
[98]See People v. Nixon, 42 Mich. App. 332, 201 N.W.2d 635 (1972), revd. 50 Mich. App. 38, 212 N.W.2d 797 (1973) (holding, inter alia, that the woman herself cannot be convicted of self-induced abortion).
[99]People v. Bricker, 389 Mich. 524, 208 N.W.2d 172 (1973); see also People v. Nixon, 50 Mich. App. 38, 212 N.W.2d 797 (1973).
[1]People v. Nixon, note 98, supra, wherein this statutory shifting of the burden of proof was held to be "impermissible."
[2]For a conspiracy conviction, see People v. Gillespie, 41 Mich. App. 748, 201 N.W.2d 104 (1972).
[3]People v. Tinskey, 394 Mich. 108, 228 N.W.2d 782 (1975).
[4]Abortion Coalition of Michigan, Inc. v. Michigan Dept. of Public Health, 426 F. Supp. 471 (E.D. Mich., 1977). But see Baird v. Bellotti, 428 F. Supp. 854 (D. Mass., 1977), indicating that a parental consent requirement, if it leaves an opportunity for the child to seek judicial approval over a parent's veto, is not necessarily unconstitutional.
[5]Mich. Comp. Laws Ann., § 750.11.
[6]Id., § 750.12. Illustrative of the social mores of another age is a judicial statement that a "man cannot be suffered to evade the statute by artfully avoiding a direct proposition that she go off with him, when his conduct is equivalent to such

marriage) of a female under sixteen years of age without parental consent.[7] A theoretical possibility of prosecutions for lewd and lascivious cohabitation[8] need arouse little apprehension unless the extramarital conduct of the partners grossly outrages the general public's notions of propriety.[9]

The crime of seduction of an unmarried woman remains on the statute books.[10] Another provision makes it criminal for an unmarried woman to conceal the death of her child, "so that it may not be known" whether the child was born alive or murdered.[11]

A proliferation of provisions, under the rubric of "criminal sexual conduct" now controls the offense more commonly known as statutory rape.[12] Unless force is used or the female is below the age of sixteen these laws also present no cause for agitation.

Gross indecency (in public or in private) between male and male,[13] between female and female,[14] and between male and female persons[15] is subject to prosecution. The last-named provision has withstood a constitutional challenge based on vagueness.[16] The penalty for adultery (sexual intercourse where either participant is married)[17] is expressly extended to persons who cohabit together after they have been divorced.[18] Bigamy and polygamy are forbidden.[19]

As to sodomy ("crime against nature"),[20] notwithstanding

---

a proposition and not only suggests it to the girl, but is calculated and designed to induce her to go." People v. Carrier, 46 Mich. 442, 9 N.W. 487 (1881). Since the masculine gender in a statute includes the feminine (Mich. Comp. Laws Ann., § 750.10), the crime of abduction can be committed by persons of either sex.

[7] Mich. Comp. Laws Ann., § 750.13.

[8] Id., § 750.335. The corpus delicti of the crime must be established before an extrajudicial confession of lewd and lascivious cohabitation can be admissible. People v. June, 294 Mich. 681, 293 N.W. 906 (1940).

[9] See People v. Davis, 294 Mich. 499, 293 N.W. 734 (1940).

[10] Mich. Comp. Laws Ann., § 750.532.

[11] Id., § 750.150.

[12] Id., §§ 750.520a to 750.520e. The constitutionality of these provisions is affirmed in People v. Denmark, 74 Mich. App. 402, 254 N.W.2d 61 (1977), and in People v. Howell, 395 Mich. 16, 238 N.W.2d 148 (1976).

[13] Mich. Comp. Laws Ann., § 750.338.

[14] Id., § 750.338a.

[15] Id., § 750.338b.

[16] People v. Clark, 68 Mich. App. 48, 241 N.W.2d 756 (1976).

[17] Mich. Comp. Laws Ann., § 750.29.

[18] Id., § 750.32.

[19] Id., §§ 750.439, 750.441.

[20] Id., §§ 750.158, 750.159.

numerous challenges,[21] the courts insist that a person has no constitutional right to commit criminal acts, even consensually, in his own home.[22]

Status of children

The children of marriages which are void because of consanguinity or affinity between the parties, bigamy, insanity or idiocy, are deemed legitimate.[23] Further, where a child is born before the mother's divorce and remarriage to the biological father, it is legitimate. If the first husband is not deemed the father by reason of the presumption of legitimacy (which is so strong as to be almost irrebuttable)[24] having been rebutted, then the second husband is the father because a subsequent marriage of the biological parents legitimates the child.[25]

Illegitimates inherit from the mother as if born in lawful wedlock.[26] In view of the decision in Trimble v. Gordon,[27] legislation extending the right of intestate succession to the estate of the male parent would not come as a surprise.[28]

The provisions for the establishment of paternity and the

---

[21] E.g., People v. Penn, 70 Mich. App. 638, 247 N.W.2d 575 (1976); People v. Howell, 395 Mich. 16, 238 N.W.2d 148 (1976); People v. Conville, 55 Mich. App. 251, 222 N.W.2d 312 (1974).

[22] Oakland County Prosecuting Attorney v. 46th Judicial Dist. Judge, 76 Mich. App. 318, 256 N.W.2d 776 (1977). Compare Morgan v. City of Detroit, 389 F. Supp. 922 (E.D. Mich., 1975), holding (obiter) that the right of privacy prohibits the state from proscribing activity conducted in private between consenting adults where no overriding state interest can be shown. See also Constitutionality of Laws Forbidding Private Homosexual Conduct, 72 Mich. L. Rev. 1613 (1974).

[23] Mich. Comp. Laws Ann., §§ 552.29, 552.31.

[24] See People v. Wiseman, 63 Mich. App. 137, 234 N.W.2d 429 (1975). As to an order correcting a birth certificate to name the mother's second husband as father of an adulterine bastard when the presumption was overcome, see Minor Child v. Michigan State Health Comr., 16 Mich. App. 128, 167 N.W.2d 880 (1969).

[25] Minor Child v. Michigan State Health Comr., 16 Mich. App. 128, 167 N.W.2d 880 (1969). As to legitimation by subsequent marriage, or, absent such, by written acknowledgment of both legally competent parents, see Mich. Comp. Laws Ann., § 702.83.

[26] Mich. Comp. Laws Ann., § 702.81.

[27] See section 3.3, herein.

[28] See Krause, Equal Protection for the Illegitimate, 65 Mich. L. Rev. 477 (1967). See also Uniform Probate Code—Illegitimacy—Inheritance and the Illegitimate: A Model for Probate Reform, 69 Mich. L. Rev. 112 (1970). As to the right of an illegitimate to sue for wrongful death of parent, see Mich. Comp. Laws Ann., § 600.1410.

enforcement of parental support obligations follow a fairly standard pattern.[29] The circuit courts have jurisdiction where neither biological parent is able to support the child;[30] filiation proceedings can be initiated by the department of social services where the putative father does not himself seek to acknowledge paternity.[31]

As is usual, a child cannot be put out for adoption until an order terminating parental rights has been entered.[32] Once paternity is established, the father's consent can only be dispensed with if his rights have been formally terminated.[33] All reasonable efforts must be made to identify him, and the court must be satisfied that by reason of his failure to make provision for the mother during pregnancy, or for some other reason,[34] he is unfit to assume the role of a parent.[35]

Some of the difficulties which can result from a literal adherence to the rule requiring notice to the putative father as a prerequisite to adoption are surmounted by a provision to the effect that a release given by the mother alone is sufficient to foreclose the father's rights when he has not filed with the probate court, prior to the birth of the child, notice of his intent to claim paternity.[36]

---

[29] Mich. Comp. Laws Ann., § 722.711 et seq. Abundant provision is made for secrecy in recording illegitimate births. See id., §§ 326.12, 326.16(5), 722.725. Fact of paternity or otherwise is a jury question. Hude v. Vannest, 75 Mich. App. 490, 255 N.W.2d 659 (1977). Even though a defendant in a paternity proceeding can be afforded counsel, the quantum of proof required is a mere preponderance of evidence. Requirement of proof beyond a reasonable doubt would undermine the basic purpose of the statute, which is to make provision for support of an illegitimate. Huggins v. Rahfeldt, 83 Mich. App. 740, 269 N.W.2d 286 (1978).
[30] Mich. Comp. Laws Ann., § 722.714.
[31] Id., § 722.714(h). See Butler v. Cann, 62 Mich. App. 663, 233 N.W.2d 827 (1975). As to Reciprocal Enforcement of Support, see Mich. Comp. Laws Ann., §§ 780.151 to 780.174.
[32] Id., § 710.41.
[33] Id., § 710.31, 710.34.
[34] Id., § 710.37.
[35] See In re Barlow, 78 Mich. App. 707, 260 N.W.2d 896 (1977). For an historical review of the development of the law regarding the putative father and his rights in respect of illegitimates, see In re Mark T., 8 Mich. App. 122, 154 N.W.2d 27 (1967) (award of custody to father following mother's secret release of child to a licensed child placement agency). As to the Uniform Child Custody Jurisdiction Act, see Mich. Comp. Laws Ann., § 600.651 et seq.
[36] Mich. Comp. Laws Ann., § 710.3a.

In short, a court cannot approve a petition for adoption without the consent of the illegitimate's parents or, if such consent is dispensed with by reason of unfitness[37] or release for adoption, then the consent of a licensed public authority entrusted with the care of such child.[38]

Property rights of cohabitants

A deed to a couple as husband and wife, when they are not legally married, cannot create a tenancy by the entireties.[39] Most of the rulings on this point are to the effect that they hold as tenants in common.[40] One early decision, however, favored a joint tenancy (with right of survivorship) where the deed described them as joint tenants by the entireties and as husband and wife, the right of survivorship being very clearly spelled out as their purpose in accepting the deed, and both shared a good faith belief in the validity of the marriage.[41]

In such situations, where there is a good faith belief in a valid marriage, the Michigan courts will adjust the equities so as to ensure that one in good faith is not left without a fair share in joint accumulations.[42] Where a "marriage" was "annulled" because the man was already married at the time of its celebration, a trial court's award of virtually entire reimbursement to a wife of her payments was not permitted to stand where his earnings had relieved her of other obligations.[43] But in another case, where the

---

[37] As to lesbianism as a possible ground for unfitness, see People v. Brown, 49 Mich. App. 358, 212 N.W.2d 55 (1973). As to judicial reluctance to set aside adoption decrees, see In re Baby Girl Fletcher, 76 Mich. App. 219, 256 N.W.2d 444 (1977).

[38] See In re Mark T., 8 Mich. App. 122, 154 N.W.2d 27 (1967). The best interests of the child are always paramount, but in custody determinations the natural parent is favored over a stranger, all else being equal. In re P., 36 Mich. App. 497, 194 N.W.2d 18 (1971).

[39] Beaton v. LaFord, 79 Mich. App. 373, 261 N.W.2d 327 (1977).

[40] See Daniels v. Daniel, 362 Mich. 176, 106 N.W.2d 818 (1961); Spence v. Jones, 359 Mich. 231, 102 N.W.2d 543 (1960); Collins v. Norris, 314 Mich. 145, 22 N.W.2d 249 (1946) (meretricious cohabitants); Wright v. Kayner, 150 Mich. 7, 113 N.W. 779 (1907) (deed did not designate them as husband and wife but used a common surname).

[41] Jackson City Bank & Trust Co. v. Fredrick, 271 Mich. 538, 260 N.W. 908 (1935).

[42] See Hackley Union Nat. Bank & Trust Co. v. Sheneman, 30 Mich. App. 1, 186 N.W.2d 344 (1971).

[43] Mixon v. Mixon, 51 Mich. App. 696, 216 N.W.2d 625 (1974).

wife had been defrauded into her belief in the validity of the marriage, she was given an equitable lien to secure reimbursement of the fair value of her contributions to the joint accumulations.[44]

Lip service is paid to the rule that neither party to a meretricious relationship acquires rights in the property of the other by reason of cohabitation alone, but if an agreement, even implied in fact,[45] can be shown to be arrived at independently of the illicit relationship, such agreement will be honored.[46] It is likely, then, that the hurdle of traditional hostility toward the claims of meretricious cohabitants will not, in a proper case, deter the courts from honoring the reasonable expectations of the parties.

6.24. Minnesota

Only common-law marriages contracted in or before 1941 are recognized.[47] A continued cohabitation of purported spouses after the removal, subsequent to such date, of an impediment to the validity of their marriage cannot result in a marriage of any sort.[48] Marriage does not result in community property.[49] Marriages between persons of the same sex are prohibited.[50]

Adoption

Any person who has resided in the state for one year or more may petition to adopt a child or an adult.[51] Ordinarily, a child sought to be adopted must have been placed by the authorities as

---

[44] Walker v. Walker, 330 Mich. 332, 47 N.W.2d 633, 31 A.L.R.2d 1250 (1951).
[45] Roznowski v. Bozyk, 73 Mich. App. 405, 251 N.W.2d 606 (1977).
[46] Tyranski v. Piggins, 44 Mich. App. 570, 205 N.W.2d 595 (1973). See also Burns v. Stevens, 236 Mich. 447, 210 N.W. 483 (1926) (contract not tainted with the immorality of a cohabitation); Harden v. Widovich, 359 Mich. 566, 103 N.W.2d 478 (1960) (plaintiff lent money to defendant to promote adultery between defendant and plaintiff's wife, and the "collateral" immorality of this transaction did not preclude recovery on the instrument evidencing the loan).
[47] See Carlson v. Olson, —— Minn. ——, 256 N.W.2d 249 (1977).
[48] Baker v. Baker, 222 Minn. 169, 23 N.W.2d 582 (1946).
[49] See Minn. Stat. Ann., § 519.02.
[50] Baker v. Nelson, 291 Minn. 310, 191 N.W.2d 185 (1971), appeal dismissed 409 U.S. 810, 34 L. Ed. 2d 65, 93 Sup. Ct. 37 (1972).
[51] Minn. Stat. Ann., § 259.22.

6.24 UNMARRIED COUPLES AND THE LAW

a precondition.[52] If the adoptee's parent is under eighteen years of age, written consent of the latter's parents may be required.[53]

Workers' compensation death benefits

Illegitimate children would qualify for benefits under workers' compensation if shown to be dependent and their parentage is established.[54]

Insurance benefits

By statute,[55] accident and health insurance policies are required to provide the same coverage for maternity benefits to unmarried women and to minor female dependents as they provide to married women, including wives of employees who choose dependent family coverage. Illegitimate children are covered in the same way as are legitimate children.[56] However, maternity benefits do not include elective induced abortions wherever they are performed.[57]

Abortions

As a result of the Supreme Court's rulings on abortion,[58] a new statute was enacted in 1974.[59] Some of its provisions, insofar as they require the use of methods not necessarily related to the mother's health, have been held constitutionally infirm.[60] Further, a provision for termination of parental rights where the operation is for abortion of a "potential" live fetus and a live birth results, has been held unconstitutional, though had the

---

[52]Id.
[53]Id., § 259.25.
[54]See O'Dell v. Hingeveld, 235 Minn. 223, 50 N.W.2d 476 (1951).
[55]Minn. Stat. Ann., § 62A.041.
[56]Id. Denial to an illegitimate of right to participate in group life policy, if required by contract entered into by state, and due solely to illegitimacy, in circumstances such that insured has no fair opportunity to make his own wishes known, denies equal protection. Unborn Child v. Evans, —— Minn. ——, 245 N.W.2d 600 (1976).
[57]See Minn. Stat. Ann., § 62A.041.
[58]Section 2.19, herein.
[59]Minn. Stat. Ann., § 145.411 et seq.
[60]Hodgson v. Lawson, 542 F.2d 1350 (C.A.-8 Minn., 1976).

426

legislature used the word "viable" instead of "potentially viable" it would have sustained an attack on constitutionality.[61]

Tort actions

The tort of alienation of a spouse's affections, regarded with scant favor in many states,[62] receives recognition in Minnesota.[63]

Possible criminal liability

Adults cohabiting in an ongoing, voluntary sexual relationship are excepted from criminal sexual conduct provisions which are designed for the protection of the immature.[64] However, abduction,[65] fornication, [66] adultery,[67] bigamy[68] and incest,[69] (knowledge of the forbidden degree of relationship is required) are punishable. The sodomy statute includes consensual acts,[70] and personal intimacies between a couple on a private "date" have—and not so very long ago—resulted in a conviction under the Mann Act.[71]

The offense of nonsupport of a child[72] extends to nonsupport of an illegitimate whose paternity is established.[73] Concealment of the birth of a child is also an offense.[74]

---

[61] Id.
[62] See section 2.20, herein.
[63] See Gorder v. Sims, 306 Minn. 275, 237 N.W.2d 67 (1975), holding that evidence of marital difficulties between the spouses, though no defense, may be material on the issue of damages. See also Alienation of Affections, 3 William Mitchell L. Rev. 297 (1977).
[64] Minn. Stat. Ann., § 609.349.
[65] Id., § 609.265.
[66] Id., § 609.34.
[67] Id., § 609.36.
[68] Id., § 609.355.
[69] Id., § 609.365.
[70] Id., § 609.293. The fact that one is homosexual is no crime, though sodomy is. State v. Schweppe, 306 Minn. 395, 237 N.W.2d 609 (1975). See also Glueck, An Evaluation of the Homosexual Offender, 41 Minn. L. Rev. 187 (1957).
[71] Reamer v. United States, 318 F.2d 43 (C.A.-8 Minn., 1963), cert. den. 375 U.S. 869, 11 L. Ed. 2d 95, 84 Sup. Ct. 129 (1963).
[72] Minn. Stat. Ann., § 609.375.
[73] Id., § 609.37.
[74] Id., § 617.22.

Status of children

An illegitimate child can inherit from his intestate mother as if born in lawful wedlock.[75] He also qualifies to inherit from one who in writing and before a competent attesting witness has declared himself to be his father.[76] Such writing must be produced in the proceeding in which it is asserted or from the person who has been determined to be the father of such child in a paternity proceeding.[77] Such a child cannot inherit from the kindred of the father by right of representation.[78] A mere adjudication of paternity is not sufficient.[79]

In In re Estate of Pakarinen,[80] a decedent had pleaded guilty in a paternity suit, yet, because he had not made the written attested declaration of paternity required, his illegitimate child could not inherit from him. The court fully acknowledged that distinctions made solely on the basis of legitimacy are a denial of equal protection, but did not think it constitutionally impermissible to require such a child to furnish virtually unassailable proof that the decedent was in fact his father. It noted that the decedent may have plead guilty to the charge merely to avoid the expense and publicity of a paternity suit. It recognized the fact that proof of maternal origins is far easier to establish than that of paternity. It reasoned that, the purpose of the statute being to effectuate the presumed intent of the intestate, the legislature could properly limit succession rights to situations where it is manifest that the decedent acknowledged the child as his.

Although this statute is not quite as hard on the illegitimate as the provision which was stricken in Trimble v. Gordon (which required a marriage of the parents as well as acknowledgment by the father),[81] it is possible that it may not meet the somewhat vague guidelines as to constitutionality laid down in Trimble. Very likely to avoid a confrontation with this issue, the Supreme

---

[75]Id., § 525.172.
[76]Id.
[77]Id.
[78]Id.
[79]In re Estate of Karger, 253 Minn. 542, 93 N.W.2d 137 (1958). As to inheritance from an illegitimate, see Minn. Stat. Ann., § 525.173.
[80]287 Minn. 330, 178 N.W.2d 714 (1970), appeal dismissed 402 U.S. 903, 28 L. Ed. 2d 644, 91 Sup. Ct. 1384 (1971).
[81]See section 3.3, herein.

Court of Minnesota resorted to a strange ruling to reach its determination that the statute had been complied with. The decedent had allegedly fathered a daughter by his wife's sister. There was evidence that his wife, in his presence and at his request, had signed a letter written by him to a son acknowledging his paternity. In this state of affairs, the court thought, she could be signing the acknowledgment on the decedent's behalf and be an attesting witness at the same time![82] (If these facts are believed, would not the fact that he wrote the letter, but declined to sign it, asking his wife to do so in his presence, tend to indicate some reluctance on his part to acknowledge paternity?)

The procedures controlling the establishment of paternity of an illegitimate[83] and the enforcement of the father's support obligations,[84] follow a standard pattern. Leaving the state to evade paternity proceedings is an offense.[85]

In litigation concerning the custody of such child, the putative father's right to his day in court receives adequate recognition.[86]

Legitimation results from a subsequent marriage of the parents to each other, and children of marriages declared null in law are legitimate.[87] An adjudication of paternity also legitimates the child,[88] though not for purposes of intestate succession. Parental rights are terminable, not only on a showing of abandonment or neglect, but also for "repeated lewd and lascivious behavior," or

---

[82] In re Gollner's Estate, —— Minn. ——, 260 N.W.2d 567 (1977). See also Inheritance Rights of Illegitimate Children Under Equal Protection Clause, 54 Minn. L. Rev. 1336 (1970).

[83] As to the role of the commissioner of public welfare, whose duties can arise on receipt of mere notice that an illegitimate birth is likely (Minn. Stat. Ann., § 257.33), see Minn. Stat. Ann., § 256.01 et seq. For provisions controlling establishment of paternity, see § 257.251 et seq.

A paternity action may be commenced after the death of the putative father, but paternity may be proved only by clear and convincing evidence. Weber v. Anderson, —— Minn. ——, 269 N.W.2d 892 (1978).

[84] As to the Uniform Reciprocal Enforcement of Support Act, see Minn. Stat. Ann., § 518.41 et seq.

[85] Minn. Stat. Ann., § 609.31.

[86] See In re Brennan, 270 Minn. 455, 134 N.W.2d 126 (1965); In re Zink, 269 Minn. 535, 132 N.W.2d 795 (1964). As to the Uniform Child Custody Jurisdiction Act, see Minn. Stat. Ann., § 518A.01 et seq.

[87] Minn. Stat. Ann., § 517.19.

[88] Id., § 525.172.

other conduct found by the court to be likely to be detrimental to the health or morals of the child.[89]

Property rights of cohabitants

Property acquired during a marriage that is later annulled is treated as would be property acquired during a valid marriage.[90] Where, however, neither party acted in a good faith belief in the existence of a marriage, a court of some decades past relegated the parties, on termination of their relationship, to whatever remedies they might have had, had they been unmarried.[91]

A woman has been denied restitution for services rendered.[92] However, where the parties were engaged in a commercial venture, there is early recognition of a right to an accounting notwithstanding an illicit relationship.[93]

More recently, in Carlson v. Olson,[94] the Supreme Court of Minnesota, relying heavily on the Marvin decision in California,[95] allowed an equal division of assets accumulated during a 21-year period of cohabitation as husband and wife. With one trifling exception, the male partner had paid for all these assets. Title to the real estate was in both, as joint tenants. Title to the personal assets, presumably, was in the man, who had bought and paid for them. The court held that a lower court was justified in finding that the parties intended that their accumulations were to be divided equally on the theory of an irrevocable mutual exchange of gifts, he of a half share in the assets, she of her services.

The theory of a gift of this nature has been criticized on the

---

[89]Id., § 260.221. There must be a clear and specific finding conformable to the statute before termination of parental rights can be decreed. In re Welfare of Stangle, —— Minn. ——, 247 N.W.2d 419 (1976). But the "other conduct" need not necessarily be morally wrong. McDonald v. Copperud, 295 Minn. 440, 206 N.W.2d 551 (1973). The aim of the statute is not only to remove a child from an undesirable home environment, but to facilitate adoption procedures. In re Welfare of Alle, 304 Minn. 254, 230 N.W.2d 574 (1975).

[90]Minn. Stat. Ann., § 518.54. Fairness is a major consideration. See §§ 518.58, 518.59. See also Marriage—Quasi Contract—Remedy of Putative Wife, 33 Minn. L. Rev. 321 (1949).

[91]Baker v. Baker, 222 Minn. 169, 23 N.W.2d 582 (1946).

[92]In re Hore's Estate, 220 Minn. 374, 19 N.W.2d 783, 161 A.L.R. 1366 (1945).

[93]Speiss v. Speiss, 149 Minn. 314, 183 N.W. 822 (1921).

[94]—— Minn. ——, 256 N.W.2d 249 (1977).

[95]See section 4.10, herein.

ground that a gift "in consideration for wifely and motherly services" is a contradiction in terms.[96] Though there seems to be no objection to the notion of a valid contract to make a gift in the future, supported by consideration, the court's approval in Carlson of the award seems to rest more strongly on the fact that it enforced what the evidence showed to have been the reasonable expectations of the parties.

A 1978 legislative enactment[97] gives the Minnesota courts significant elasticity in providing for an equitable division of the accumulations of a lawfully married couple on a marriage dissolution. Carlson v. Olson applies the same principle to cohabitants out of wedlock. The decision cannot fairly be read to mean that, whenever there has been a living together, the accumulations are to be equally divided. (For example, to say that any such expectations, after a few weeks of cohabitation where one partner did little and earned nothing, would be "reasonable" would be an absurdity.) The decision, however, reinforces the prediction, noted earlier,[98] that whether or not a contract implied in fact is found, the courts will presume that such parties intended to deal fairly with one another in the event of a termination of the relation.

6.25. Mississippi

Common-law marriages entered into prior to 1956[99] will be recognized if satisfactorily established.[1] However, it has recently been held that a woman who, after five years of common-law marriage, had abandoned her mate to live with another man was estopped from inheriting as his widow on his death intestate.[2] Although there is the proposition that misconduct of a surviving spouse can operate to deprive her of rights in her deceased

---

[96]Family Law: Property Rights of Unmarried Cohabitants, 62 Minn. L. Rev. 449 (1978).
[97]Minn. Stat. Ann., § 518.58.
[98]Section 4.1, herein.
[99]Miss. Code Ann., § 93–1–15.
[1]Stutts v. Estate of Stutts, 194 So. 2d 229 (Miss., 1967). As to the meaning of "cohabitation" for purposes of common-law marriage, see Vetrano v. Gardner, 290 F. Supp. 200 (N.D. Miss., 1968).
[2]Gaston v. Gaston, 358 So. 2d 376 (Miss., 1978).

spouse's estate (a legacy from an early English statute),[3] the use of the doctrine of estoppel, where no one can be shown to have relied to his detriment on this misconduct,[4] is hardly apt.

Schoolteachers

As to the impact of unwed pregnancy on the continued retention of a public schoolteacher,[5] absent a showing that the teacher made any attempt to proselytize students or to influence them in any way into an acceptance of the propriety of extramarital relations, termination has been ruled unconstitutional.[6] The reasoning was that a denunciation of all unmarried parentage as "immoral" would in effect create a conclusive presumption in which the presumed fact (immorality) does not result from the proven fact (unwed parenthood). This violates the due process provisions of the Constitution.

Students

As to school pupils, a court, in ordering an unwed mother readmitted to school, noted that the fact that a girl has one child out of wedlock does not forever brand her as a "scarlet woman" undeserving of any chance for rehabilitation or an opportunity of future education, though it added that exclusion might be justified if her presence would taint the educational progress of other students.[7] A few years later the same court again ruled in favor of reinstatement of a student in similar circumstances.[8]

---

[3]See Annotation, Misconduct of surviving spouse as affecting marital rights in other's estate, 71 A.L.R. 277 (1931), 139 A.L.R. 486 (1942).

[4]Compare Annotation, Estoppel to claim rights in estate of deceased spouse by assent or failure to object to unlawful marriage with third person, 28 A.L.R. 1126 (1924).

[5]See section 2.3, herein.

[6]Andrews v. Drew Municipal Separate School Dist., 507 F.2d 611 (C.A.-5 Miss., 1975). See also Constitutional Law—Civil Rights—Unwed Parenthood Held Not to be Grounds for Teacher Dismissal in Fifth Circuit, 6 Memphis St. U. L. Rev. 129 (1975).

[7]Perry v. Grenada Municipal Separate School Dist., 300 F. Supp. 748 (N.D. Miss., 1969).

[8]Shull v. Columbus Municipal Separate School Dist., 338 F. Supp. 1376 (N.D. Miss., 1972).

Adoption

An unmarried adult who has been at least ninety days resident in the state may petition to adopt any person.[9] If married, the spouse must be joined in the petition.[10]

Workers' compensation death benefits

A "child" for the purposes of workers' compensation death benefits includes an acknowledged, dependent illegitimate child.[11] A woman who has entered into a ceremonial marriage with a decedent worker within at least one year of his death qualifies as a dependent.[12]

Abortion

A statute makes it a felony to procure an abortion, unless by a licensed physician and is either necessary to preserve the life of the mother or to take care of a pregnancy resulting from rape.[13] Perhaps due to lack of prosecutions, its restrictive qualifications do not as yet appear to have received legislative or judicial attention.

Possible criminal liability

Among the possible types of behavior of unmarried cohabitants for which criminal prosecution can lie are adultery and fornication.[14] This crime involves cohabitation, which means a "habitual lying together,"[15] and the statute specifies conduct between a

---

[9]As to proceedings for adoption and change of name, see Miss. Code Ann., § 93–17–1 et seq.

[10]Id., § 93–17–1.

[11]Id., § 71–3–3. See Ingalls Shipbuilding Corp. v. Neuman, 322 F. Supp. 1229 (S.D. Miss., 1970), affd. 448 F.2d 773 (C.A.-5 Miss., 1971).

[12]See United Timber & Lbr. Co. v. Alleged Dependents of Hill, 226 Miss. 540, 84 So. 2d 921 (1956); South Central Heating & Plumbing Co. v. Dependents of Campbell, 219 So. 2d 140 (Miss., 1969). The fact that separate maintenance payments have been adjudicated payable by another state does not affect a widow's eligibility for compensation. Walton v. McLendon, 342 So. 2d 732 (Miss., 1977).

[13]Miss. Code Ann., § 97–3–3.

[14]Id., § 97–29–1 et seq.

[15]Hooks v. State, 197 So. 2d 238 (Miss., 1967) (defendant did not entice a girl for "concubinage" when she came and went at night, since concubinage involves a living together). See also Cutrer v. State, 150 Miss. 80, 121 So. 106 (1929).

6.25 UNMARRIED COUPLES AND THE LAW

teacher and a female pupil,[16] persons forbidden to marry,[17] and a guardian and his female ward.[18] Further, if persons prohibited from marriage go out of state and marry, and then have intercourse within the state, this is a separate offense.[19] Perhaps on the notion that every dog is allowed one bite, becoming the natural parent of a *second* illegitimate child is denounced as misdemeanor.[20] Bigamy[21] and incest[22] are also criminal. In addition to various degrees of statutory rape[23] (the age of consent for the least grave of these being eighteen), seduction of a female under the age of eighteen, of previous chaste character, is separately denounced.[24]

The prohibition of "the detestable and abominable crime against nature"[25] has withstood a challenge of unconstitutionality for vagueness.[26]

Status of children

The provision controlling intestate succession is substantially similar to that ruled unconstitutional in Trimble v. Gordon.[27] Illegitimate children can inherit from their mother's side, as can the mother from them.[28] Inheritance from the father is conditioned on a subsequent marriage of the biological parents plus acknowledgment by the father.[29] The children of such illegitimate cannot inherit from any ancestor (including presumably the

---

[16] Miss. Code Ann., § 97–29–3.
[17] Id., § 97–29–5.
[18] Id., § 97–29–7. See Analysis of Mississippi's Criminal Law Under the Equal Rights Amendment, 47 Miss. L. J. 279 (1976).
[19] Miss. Code Ann., § 97–29–9.
[20] Id., § 97–29–11.
[21] Id., § 97–29–13. Knowledge is required. As to exceptions, see § 97–29–15.
[22] Id., §§ 93–29–27, 93–29–29. As to the degrees of relationship for an incestuous marriage, see § 93–1–1.
[23] Id., §§ 97–3–65, 97–3–67.
[24] Id., § 97–5–21.
[25] Id., § 97–29–59.
[26] See State v. Mays, 329 So. 2d 65 (Miss., 1976), cert. den. 429 U.S. 864, 97 Sup. Ct. 170 (1976). See also Mississippi Gay Alliance v. Goudelock, 536 F.2d 1073 (C.A.-5 Miss., 1976), cert. den. 430 U.S. 982, 97 Sup. Ct. 1678 (1977).
[27] See section 3.3, herein.
[28] Miss. Code Ann., § 91–1–15.
[29] Id.

illegitimate's mother) if there be legitimate heirs of such ancestor.[30]

An illegitimate may recover for the wrongful death of the mother, as may a mother for the wrongful death of the illegitimate.[31]

The state has adopted the Uniform Law on Paternity,[32] with additional provisions which authorize the department of public welfare to establish a separate child support unit to develop and implement the program for the implementation of its nonsupport and establishment of paternity aspects.[33]

The effect of an adoption of an illegitimate child is to vest in the adoptee the status of legitimate.[34] A provision of the statute controlling adoptions expressly dispenses with the need for obtaining the consent of the father of a child born out of wedlock.[35]

Property rights of cohabitants

Not only do the courts recognize their equitable powers to prevent a miscarriage of justice when one party to a "marriage" has in good faith conferred benefits on the other, but in at least one case it may perhaps have penalized the bad faith participant in such a union. In Chrismond v. Chrismond,[36] the parties had worked together to accumulate assets for over eight years. The court, in annulling the marriage as bigamous, affirmed an order that the homestead be awarded to the innocent plaintiff free and clear of any encumbrances. However, since there was other land involved aside from the homestead, the award of the homestead, in lieu of alimony, may well have simply reflected the court's intent to achieve an equitable division of the joint accumulations.

---

[30]Id. But see also § 93–9–29(5) which provides that, on entering an order of paternity, if the father is unmarried and could lawfully have married the mother, the court may adjudicate that the child shall inherit from the father as could any lawful child. See also Akers v. Estate of Johnson, 236 So. 2d 437 (Miss., 1970), holding, under the preceding statute, that an illegitimate cannot inherit from a putative paternal grandfather.
[31]Miss. Code Ann., § 11–7–13.
[32]Id., § 93–9–1 et seq.
[33]Id., § 43–19–31 et seq.
[34]Id., § 93–17–13.
[35]Id., § 93–17–5.
[36]211 Miss. 746, 52 So. 2d 624 (1951).

6.26 UNMARRIED COUPLES AND THE LAW

There is also early authority to support the presumption of a resulting trust[37] where title is taken by one bigamous spouse, the price having been paid by the other.[38]

6.26. Missouri

The state of Missouri outlaws common-law marriages entered into after 1921.[39] Such marriages, however, are recognized in Missouri if valid in the state where they were entered into.[40] Further, evidence of cohabitation and general reputation in the community of the couple as husband and wife gives rise to a cogent, though rebuttable, presumption of marriage.[41]

Married women enjoy separate property rights.[42]

Adoption

To adopt a child, if fourteen or over and competent, the adopting petitioner's spouse, if any, must join in the petition. The child's own written consent is required, as well as that of the parents if the child is under 21. Consent of the mother alone is sufficient if the child is illegitimate. Parental consent can, as is usual throughout the states, be dispensed with where this requirement has been waived or has been forfeited by a dereliction of parental responsibilities.[43] However, time and again the courts have used language indicating that the rights of the child's biological or natural parents are to be fully respected and cannot be ignored.[44]

---

[37]See section 4.5, herein.
[38]Shrader v. Shrader, 119 Miss. 526, 81 So. 227 (1919).
[39]Mo. Rev. Stat., § 451.040(5).
[40]See Pope v. Pope, 520 S.W.2d 634 (Mo. App., 1975).
[41]See In re Estate of Tomlinson, 493 S.W.2d 402 (Mo. App., 1973). The use of the term de facto marriage is more applicable. See Hodge v. Conley, 543 S.W.2d 326 (Mo. App., 1976).
[42]Mo. Rev. Stat., § 451.250 et seq.
[43]Generally, see Mo. Rev. Stat., § 453.010 et seq.
[44]See In re Adoption of Fuller, 544 S.W.2d 345 (Mo. App., 1976); R. F. N. v. G. R., 546 S.W.2d 510 (Mo. App., 1976); In re E. C. N., 517 S.W.2d 709 (Mo. App., 1974); In re Adoption of Hecker, 448 S.W.2d 280 (Mo. App., 1969).

As to procedures to obtain birth data from Division of Health, see Mo. Rev. Stat., § 193.240. See also, generally, Cook, Adoption Revisited, 27 Mo. L. Rev. 391 (1962).

The child must have been in lawful custody of the adoptive parents for at least nine months before a decree can be entered.[45]

Workers' compensation death benefits

Illegitimates are eligible to receive death benefits under the Workers' Compensation Act[46] if in fact a dependent of the deceased worker.[47]

Insurance benefits

In determining who is a "child" for the purposes of benefits under the Federal Employees' Group Life Insurance Act, the courts have preferred to adopt the more liberal federal definition, so as to include illegitimate children, over the Missouri definition which would exclude such persons.[48]

Abortion

The Missouri abortion statute came under heavy attack from the Supreme Court in Planned Parenthood of Central Missouri v. Danforth.[49] Important among the provisions ruled to be unconstitutional was a requirement that the physician performing the operation exercise professional care to preserve the life and health of the fetus, *at whatever stage of pregnancy,* at risk of a

---

[45] Mo. Rev. Stat., § 453.080. See In re Adoption of Fuller, 544 S.W.2d 345 (Mo. App., 1976). The withholding of information during an investigation of the petitioner's home by the county division of family services constitutes misrepresentation, and alone may be sufficient for a finding that the petitioner is not a suitable custodian for the child. In re Baby Girl B——, 545 S.W.2d 696 (Mo. App., 1976).

[46] Mo. Rev. Stat., § 287.240.

[47] See Pittman v. Scullin Steel Co., 289 S.W.2d 57 (Mo., 1956); Culberson v. Daniel Hamm Drayage Co., 286 S.W.2d 813 (Mo., 1956); Henderson v. National Bearing Div. of American Brake Shoe Co., 267 S.W.2d 349 (Mo., 1954).

Adultery of a wife does not bar her claim for eligibility, at any rate where decedent husband had condoned it. Delfelder v. Norton Bros. Constr. Co., 231 Mo. App. 296, 98 S.W.2d 127 (1936).

[48] See Wagner v. Califano, 434 F. Supp. 1222 (E.D. Mo., 1977); Haley v. Metropolitan Life Ins. Co., 434 S.W.2d 7 (Mo. App., 1968). See also Stanley v. Secretary of Health, Education and Welfare, 356 F. Supp. 793 (W.D. Mo., 1973), holding unconstitutional a provision of the Social Security Act that does not distinguish between an illegitimate child and an adopted grandchild.

[49] 428 U.S. 52, 49 L. Ed. 2d 788, 96 Sup. Ct. 2831 (1976). See section 2.19, herein.

conviction of manslaughter;[50] a requirement of the written consent of the parents, or of those *in loco parentis,* in the case of an unmarried girl under the age of eighteen, and of the spouse of a woman seeking abortion within the first twelve weeks of pregnancy unless certified as necessary to preserve the mother's life;[51] and the prohibition, after the first twelve weeks of pregnancy, of the procedure of saline amniocentesis as "deleterious to maternal health."[52]

A provision of the statute that withstood challenge was the requirement that, before submitting to an abortion during the first twelve weeks of pregnancy, the mother must consent in writing to the procedure and certify that her consent was informed and freely given.[53] The recordkeeping requirements, too, were held reasonable as long as they respect the patient's confidentiality and privacy. It has since been held that the requirement that the mother be informed by the physician of the provisions terminating parental rights in cases where a live birth results from the operation not performed to save her life or preserve her health[54] are permissible.[55] The similar requirement that she be informed that the infant would be a ward of the state, and that she certify in writing that she has been so informed, has been held violative of due process and equal protection.[56]

Another statute empowers a minor to consent to some types of medical treatment, but specifically excludes abortion.[57] It seems possible, then, that even though the provision requiring the mother's informed consent is permissible, a physician who

---

[50] Mo. Rev. Stat., § 188.035(1).
[51] Id., § 188.020(3), (4).
[52] Id., § 188.050.
[53] Id., § 188.020(2).
[54] Id., §§ 188.040, 188.045.
[55] Frieman v. Ashcroft, 443 F. Supp. 1390 (E.D. Mo., 1978).
[56] Frieman v. Ashcroft, 584 F.2d 247 (C.A.-8 Mo., 1978).
   Generally, see Meaningful Right to Abortion for Indigent Women?, 24 Loyola L. Rev. 301 (1978); State Protection of the Viable Unborn Child After Roe v. Wade: How Little, How Late?, 37 La. L. Rev. 270 (1976) (critical of the Danforth prohibition of the abortion of a *viable* fetus except where necessary to preserve the life or health of the mother).
[57] Mo. Rev. Stat., § 431.061.

performed this operation on one too young to give an effective informed consent might incur civil liability to her parents.[58]

Tort actions

A civil action for alienation of affections remains a threat to one who cohabits with a married person.[59] And in Breece v. Jett,[60] a Missouri court reluctantly admitted the existence of a cause of action for seduction. "The woman of today," the court said, "is not the woman of yesteryear. She has a new-found freedom. The modern adult woman is sophisticated and mature. The former notion that women belong to the weaker sex has long been abandoned. The modern woman is not 'easily beguiled' and does not easily fall to the 'wiles' of man. Women desire and should be held to a reasonable responsibility. While we believe that an action for seduction is socially unwise in modern society we believe that as an intermediate appellate court we cannot abolish the action."[61] (The court considered that this anachronistic type of lawsuit should be abolished by the legislature.)

The tort action for criminal conversation persists.[62]

Possible criminal liability

Recent legislation has eliminated many of the crimes which are of possible interest to extramarital cohabitants. Bigamy remains,[63] and embraces cohabitation in the state after a bigamous marriage in another state. It is immaterial for guilt which of the participants is married; the other can be convicted. Reasonable mistake is a defense.[64] Incest, too, is punishable.[65] It includes marriage, sexual intercourse, or deviate sexual intercourse.

Absent the use of force, if the coparticipant in sexual

---

[58] See Abortion—Possible Alternatives to Unconstitutional Spousal and Parental Consent Provisions of Missouri's Abortion Law, 42 Mo. L. Rev. 291 (1977).
[59] See Moranz v. Schiller, 525 S.W.2d 785 (Mo. App., 1975).
[60] 556 S.W.2d 696 (Mo. App., 1977).
[61] Id., at 708.
[62] See Sutton v. Sutton, 567 S.W.2d 147 (Mo. App., 1978).
[63] Mo. Rev. Stat., § 568.010.
[64] Id.
[65] Id., § 568.020. As to the degrees of relationship forbidden for marriages, see § 451.020.

intercourse outside of marriage is over sixteen years of age, under the recently enacted provisions there would appear to be no criminal responsibility.[66] Below that age, the relative ages of the participants become very important in determining the degree of gravity of the crime. Age has been ruled to be a legitimate legislative consideration in relation to sex crimes, where an older person is unlikely to sustain as serious an injury as a younger one; hence, this factor is directly and reasonably related to the evil sought to be prevented.[67]

Though the "detestable and abominable crime against nature" has long been a part of the criminal law,[68] under the revised Missouri law the gravity of "sexual misconduct," which embraces deviate sexual behavior, is determined by reference to the age of the coparticipant. If consensual behavior between adults is involved, the offense is a Class A misdemeanor.[69]

Status of children

Illegitimate children can inherit and transmit inheritance on the part of their mother, and a mother may inherit from her illegitimate children, as if they had been lawfully begotten of her.[70] In view of the Supreme Court's decision in Trimble v. Gordon[71] this provision, by reason of its silence as to the rights of such children to inherit from the father, can hardly withstand a challenge of unconstitutionality. Grave doubt, too, is cast on the constitutionality of another provision, the pretermitted heir statute,[72] to the extent that it excludes illegitimates from sharing under the father's will. However, the harsh effect on the illegitimate may to an extent be alleviated by judicial acceptance of the

---

[66]Id., § 566.020 et seq.
[67]In re Interest of J. D. G., 498 S.W.2d 786 (Mo., 1973). See Foster and Freed, Offenses Against the Family, 32 U. Kan. City L. Rev. 33 (1964).
[68]See State v. Crosby, 564 S.W.2d 357 (Mo. App., 1978). As to the constitutionality of a crime so vaguely denounced, see State v. Crawford, 478 S.W.2d 314 (Mo., 1972), appeal dismissed 409 U.S. 811, 34 L. Ed. 2d 66, 93 Sup. Ct. 176 (1972), reh. den. 409 U.S. 1051, 34 L. Ed. 2d 505, 93 Sup. Ct. 536 (1972).
[69]See Mo. Rev. Stat., §§ 566.060 to 566.090.
[70]Id., § 474.060.
[71]See section 3.3, herein.
[72]Mo. Rev. Stat., § 474.240.

MISSOURI 6.26

doctrine of "adoption by estoppel" whereunder an illegitimate taken into the home of its parents has been allowed to inherit.[73]

It was not until 1969 that, probably as a result of the 1968 decision in R——v. R——,[74] the legislature recognized the duty of a father to support his illegitimate child.[75]

Legitimation can be effected by a subsequent marriage of the biological parents coupled with a recognition by the father of the child as his.[76] This applies even if the mother was married to another when the child was born.[77] Adoption has the effect of legitimating the child,[78] the child becoming the child of the adopting parents for every purpose as fully as if born to them in lawful wedlock.[79] However, such a child cannot inherit on intestacy from the adoptive parent and at the same time qualify as a pretermitted heir of its natural parent.[80]

Termination of parental rights

As noted earlier,[81] the requirement of parental consent to an adoption can be forfeited, and parental rights terminated, by a

---

[73]See, e.g., Mize v. Sims, 516 S.W.2d 561 (Mo. App., 1974). Generally, see Constitutional Law—Equal Protection and the Inheritance Rights of Illegitimates Under Intestate Succession Laws, 43 Mo. L. Rev. 116 (1978); Rights of Illegitimate Children in Missouri, 40 Mo. L. Rev. 631 (1975).

[74]431 S.W.2d 152 (Mo., 1968).

[75]Mo. Rev. Stat., § 559.353. See State v. Summers, 489 S.W.2d 225 (Mo. App., 1972). As to nonsupport of illegitimates as an offense, see Mo. Rev. Stat., § 568.040. See also Note, Support of Illegitimate Children in Missouri, 13 St. Louis U. L. J. 311 (1968).

As to the establishment of paternity and enforcement of support under the modern procedures, see C—S— v. J—W—, 514 S.W.2d 848 (Mo. App., 1974); In re L—, 499 S.W.2d 490 (Mo., 1973). For the Reciprocal Enforcement of Support Act, see Mo. Rev. Stat., § 454.010 et seq.

[76]Mo. Rev. Stat., § 474.070.

[77]Simpson v. Blackburn, 414 S.W.2d 795 (Mo. App., 1967).

[78]Mo. Rev. Stat., § 453.090.

[79]Wailes v. Curators of Central College, 363 Mo. 932, 254 S.W.2d 645, 37 A.L.R.2d 326 (1953).

[80]Id. As to the impact of adoption on the right of a child to succeed to property given to "children" of the child's natural parent, see Commerce Trust Co. v. Duden, 523 S.W.2d 97 (Mo. App., 1975).

On legitimation, a new birth certificate is mandatory. Mo. Rev. Stat., § 193.260. As to the secrecy of birth records, see § 193.240. Restrictions on the right of an adopted person to see the files relating to adoption (Mo. Rev. Stat., § 453.120) properly protected privacy rights of the natural parents and deny no constitutional rights. Application of Maples, 563 S.W.2d 760 (Mo., 1978).

[81]See notes 43 and 44 supra, and related text.

parent who is derelict in his or her responsibilities. The neglect or abandonment must, however, be so complete as to display a subtle purpose to forego all parental duties and relinquish all parental claims.[82] The neglect must have occurred during the year immediately preceding the filing of the adoption petition.[83] Only in cases of exceptional hardship will the courts exercise their undoubted jurisdiction to set aside an adoption decree; after one year has elapsed from the date of the decree its validity cannot be attacked by reason of any irregularity in the proceedings.[84]

Property rights of cohabitants

Conveyances to persons as husband and wife when they are not legally married result, not in a joint tenancy, but a tenancy in common.[85] However, in a situation where title to land was taken as tenants by the entireties, the female partner being aware of the nonexistence of any valid marriage, one court, on termination of the relationship, quieted title in the male partner who had paid for the land with an adjustment to the female in recognition of work she had done.[86] Such recognition of the value of a homemaker's services is to be seen in the 1974 reform of the state's divorce laws; thus, it is readily predictable that, in the mistaken marriage situation, this factor will carry weight in adjusting the equities no matter where the legal title to their accumulations.[87]

---

[82] See R. F. N. v. G. R., 546 S.W.2d 510 (Mo. App., 1976).

[83] See In re Adoption of R. A. B. v. R. A. B., 562 S.W.2d 356 (Mo., 1978). As to neglect as warranting termination of parental rights, see Adoption of Mike and Russ, 553 S.W.2d 706 (Mo. App., 1977); In re Kerr, 547 S.W.2d 837 (Mo. App., 1977); Smith v. Benson, 542 S.W.2d 571 (Mo. App., 1976). See, generally, Cook, Adoption Revisited, 27 Mo. L. Rev. 391 (1962).

[84] See In re Kerr, 547 S.W.2d 837 (Mo. App., 1977).

[85] See Richardson v. Kuhlmyer, 250 S.W.2d 355 (Mo., 1952). In Reed v. Reed, 516 S.W.2d 568 (Mo. App., 1974), at the time land was purchased by plaintiff, both believed they were validly married, and plaintiff intended joint ownership. On termination of their relationship, the court ruled the land to have been initially vested by the entireties (a dubious holding), and was converted to a tenancy in common by the decree terminating the "marriage."

[86] Anderson v. Stacker, 317 S.W.2d 417 (Mo., 1958).

[87] See Krauskopf, Marital Property at Marriage Dissolution, 43 Mo. L. Rev. 157 (1978); Krauskopf, Theory for "Just" Division of Marital Property in Missouri, 41 Mo. L. Rev. 165 (1976). As to the imposition of a resulting trust, see Collins v. Link, 562 S.W.2d 131 (Mo. App., 1978).

In a situation where there was no belief in a marriage, there is authority for the recognition and enforcement of agreements between the cohabitants. In Lucas v. Smith,[88] a landowner's agreement that the land should be vested in his extramarital partner on his death in consideration of her agreement to keep house for him was held not void as directly promoting sexual immorality. The court reversed a decree quieting title in the woman's grantees because it was not clear how the trial court achieved this result. The agreement obviously could not constitute a deed as no words of present intent to transfer were there. It equally obviously would fail as a will. But it was held possible that the woman might be able to plead facts which would entitle her to specific performance of a contract to devise, which could in turn entitle her grantees to the land.

6.27. Montana

Not only does this state continue to recognize common-law marriage,[89] but also if the parties are living together, the law presumes morality and not immorality, marriage and not concubinage, and legitimacy and not bastardy.[90] The mere fact that they are unable to produce evidence of a mutual consent to common-law marriage is not sufficient to rebut the presumption of such marriage.[91] But sporadic cohabitations are not enough.[92] The circumstances must be such as to show a mutual consent of persons able to marry, an assumption of the marriage relation as of a time certain, followed by cohabitation and repute.[93] If this is the case, the mere use by the woman of her own name for business purposes does not of itself preclude a finding of common-law marriage.[94]

There is also statutory provision for marriage by means of a

---

[88] 383 S.W.2d 513 (Mo., 1964).
[89] Mont. Rev. Codes Ann., § 48–314.
[90] Estate of Swanson, 160 Mont. 271, 502 P.2d 33 (1972).
[91] Spradlin v. United States, 262 F. Supp. 502 (D. Mont., 1967).
[92] Miller v. Townsend Lumber Co., 152 Mont. 210, 448 P.2d 148 (1968).
[93] In re Estate of McClelland, 168 Mont. 160, 541 P.2d 780 (1975). Living together is only one factor. In re Estate of Slavens, 162 Mont. 123, 509 P.2d 293 (1973).
[94] Estate of Swanson, 160 Mont. 271, 502 P.2d 33 (1972).

written declaration, formally acknowledged before the clerk of the district court of the county involved, in lieu of the usual requirements for the solemnization of a legal marriage.[95]

Adoption

To adopt a child, unless it is a biological child of the adopting party or a married couple join in the petition, the petitioner must be at least eighteen years of age.[96] This age requirement extends to the situation where a married adopter is separated from the spouse. Provision exists for an investigation by the state department of social and rehabilitation services or by a licensed private agency of the situation of the adopting party.[97] A decree of adoption cannot be made final without the report, within six months of the filing of the petition, of such investigator on the adoptive home surroundings.[98]

Workers' compensation death benefits

Though the workers' compensation law only includes as a "child," for purposes of claiming death benefits, a child legitimized prior to the worker's injury,[99] in view of Weber v. Aetna[1] the provision would almost certainly be construed to enable recovery to be had by or on behalf of any child once paternity and dependency on the worker is shown.

Abortion

As a result of a holding that the Montana abortion laws were not tailored to accommodate the conflicting rights of pregnant women and the interests of the state and were thus unconstitutional as a unit,[2] the Abortion Control Act[3] took its place on the

---

[95] Mont. Rev. Codes Ann., § 48–130.
[96] Id., § 61–203.
[97] Id., § 61–209.
[98] Id., § 61–211. A doctor who directed unwed mothers to potential adopters, and an attorney whom the doctor recommended to such persons to initiate proceedings, were acting as an adoption agency without a license. Montana Dept. of Social and Rehabilitation Services v. Angel, —— Mont. ——, 577 P.2d 1223 (1978).
[99] Mont. Rev. Codes Ann., § 92–417.
[1] See section 2.13, herein.
[2] Doe v. Woodahl, 360 F. Supp. 20 (D. Mont., 1973).
[3] Mont. Rev. Codes Ann., § 94–5–613 et seq.

statute books in 1974. In it, the legislature "reaffirms the tradition of the state of Montana to protect every human life, whether unborn or aged, healthy or sick."[4] It requires in addition to the informed consent of the potential mother, written notice to the woman's husband unless he is voluntarily separated from her. It also requires written notice to a parent, if living, or the custodian or legal guardian if the mother is under eighteen and unmarried. These requirements do not apply if the abortion is certified as necessary to preserve the life of the mother.[5]

Purposely or negligently causing the death of a premature infant born alive is (if the infant is viable) criminal homicide.[6] A live premature infant which is the subject of abortion becomes a "dependent and neglected child" unless termination of pregnancy is necessary to preserve the mother's life, or either the mother or her spouse have accepted parental responsibilities.[7]

These provisions require notice only, and not consent of the parents or spouse to the abortion, and in all respects appear to conform to the mandates of the Supreme Court's rulings.[8]

Breach of promise actions

The right of action for breach of promise of marriage receives statutory consideration.[9]

Possible criminal liability

The statutory age of consent, for the crime of sexual intercourse without consent, is sixteen.[10] If the actor is three or more years older than the victim, the potential punishment is more severe; however, provided the victim is at least fourteen, reasonable belief child was sixteen or more years old is a defense.[11] Further, when the definition of a sexual offense excludes conduct with a

---

[4]Id., § 94–5–614.
[5]Id., § 94–5–616.
[6]Id., § 94–5–617(1).
[7]Id., § 94–5–617(2).
[8]See section 2.19, herein.
[9]Mont. Rev. Codes Ann., §§ 17–1202 to 17–1206.
[10]Id., § 94–5–503.
[11]Id.

spouse, the exclusion is deemed to extend to persons living as husband and wife regardless of the actual status of their relationship.[12]

Seduction, and open and notorious adultery and fornication, are no longer denounced as criminal. That consensual adult homosexuality is forbidden is implicit in the provision that one convicted of "deviate sexual conduct" without consent incurs the risk of a greater punishment.[13]

Reasonable mistake (of law or of fact) can be a defense to the crime of bigamy[14] and of marrying a bigamist.[15] For incest, too, knowledge of the forbidden relationship is required.[16]

Status of children

Children born of a bigamous or incestuous union are legitimate.[17]

For the purposes of intestate succession, a child born out of wedlock is a child of the mother. It is also a child of the father if the natural parents have married before or after the birth of the child (even if the attempted marriage is void), or paternity has been adjudicated before the death of the father or has been established thereafter by clear and convincing proof.[18] However, the father or his kindred cannot inherit from or through a child whose paternity is established under this provision unless the father has openly treated the child as his and has not refused to support the child.[19] This requirement, of clear and convincing proof, could be the best solution to the dilemma of balancing the policy frowning on spurious claims and the policy favoring equal rights of illegitimates to inherit.[20]

The procedures controlling the establishment of paternity and the enforcement of support obligations of the father are those of

---

[12] Id., § 94-5-506.
[13] Id., § 94-5-505.
[14] Id., § 94-5-604.
[15] Id., § 94-5-605.
[16] Id., § 94-5-606.
[17] Id., § 48-310.
[18] Id., § 91A-2-109.
[19] Id.
[20] See section 3.3, herein.

the Uniform Parentage Act,[21] which has been adopted in Montana.[22]

The courts are strict in ensuring that statutory requirements as to notice to natural parents are complied with.[23] In cases involving abandonment, nonsupport, or the like, parental consent can be dispensed with.[24] Without compliance with the statutory provisions as to notice, an adoption decree would be void.[25]

That the welfare of the adopted child is the paramount consideration in adoption preceedings is well recognized.[26]

Property rights of cohabitants

In adopting the Uniform Marriage and Divorce Act,[27] Montana has included the optional provision relating to the rights of a putative spouse.[28] Any person who has cohabited with another to whom he is not legally married in the good faith belief that he was married to that person is a putative spouse until knowledge of the fact that he is not legally married *terminates his status and prevents acquisition of further rights*.[29] A putative spouse acquires the rights conferred upon a legal spouse, including the right to maintenance following termination of his status, whether or not the marriage is prohibited or declared invalid. If there is a legal

---

[21] See section 3.4, herein.

[22] Mont. Rev. Codes Ann., § 61–301 et seq. As to the Uniform Child Custody Jurisdiction Act, see § 61–401 et seq. As to the Revised Reciprocal Enforcement of Support Act, see § 93–2601–41 et seq.

Legitimation can be effected by subsequent marriage of the parents. Id., § 61–123. As to legitimation by acknowledgment of paternity, see In re Estate of Dauenhauer, 167 Mont. 83, 535 P.2d 1005 (1975), holding that a father could not legitimize the child merely by signing a hospital form (on the mother's admission) stating himself to be the husband.

As to limitations on the disclosure of illegitimate births, see Mont. Rev. Codes Ann., §§ 69–4422, 69–4423.

[23] In re Adoption of Biery, 164 Mont. 353, 522 P.2d 1377 (1974); In re Adoption of Smigaj, —— Mont. ——, 560 P.2d 141 (1977).

[24] Mont. Rev. Codes Ann., § 61–205(1). See also In re Adoption of Smigaj, supra.

[25] See In re Adoption of Hall, —— Mont. ——, 566 P.2d 401 (1977). See Stanley v. Illinois: What it Portends for Adoptions in Montana, 36 Mont. L. Rev. 137 (1975).

[26] See In re Adoption of Conley v. Walden, —— Mont. ——, 555 P.2d 960 (1976).

[27] Mont. Rev. Codes Ann., §§48–301 to 48–341.

[28] See section 1.6, herein.

[29] Mont. Rev. Codes Ann., § 48–312.

spouse or other putative spouses, rights acquired by a putative spouse do not supersede the rights of the legal spouse or those acquired by other putative spouses, but the court shall apportion property, maintenance, and support rights among the claimants as appropriate in the circumstances and in the interests of justice.[30]

The words "terminates his status and prevents acquisition of further rights" could be construed as an indication that a continued cohabitation after learning of the impediment to the validity of a marriage does not result in a common-law marriage, and that, a fortiori, those who cohabit without any initial belief in a marriage acquire no property rights in the joint accumulations to which title is taken in the name of the other. If so interpreted, however, they would be out of keeping with the generally prevailing rule in states still recognizing common-law marriage.[31] It might be arguable that, though knowledge of the impediment terminates the status of a putative spouse, it does not thereby preclude a court from giving effect to reasonable expectations of the parties based on a continued cohabitation.

6.28. Nebraska

Unless entered into prior to 1923, a common-law marriage entered into in this state is not valid.[32] Where, however, such a marriage is recognized in the state where it was contracted, it will be recognized in Nebraska.[33] When a marriage is void as having been entered into within six months of a divorce of one of the parties, a subsequent cohabitation after the six-month period has elapsed no longer results in a valid marriage.[34]

---

[30]Id.

[31]See section 1.5, herein. For a decree, in an annulment suit, that a husband had no rights in property acquired in the joint names of the spouses on a finding that his name had been put on the deed only to secure a loan made by him for a down payment, see Houser v. Houser, —— Mont. ——, 566 P.2d 73 (1977). See also Uniform Marriage and Divorce Act: New Statutory Solutions to Old Problems, 37 Mont. L. Rev. 119 (1976).

[32]Bourelle v. Soo-Crete, Inc., 165 Neb. 731, 87 N.W.2d 371 (1958).

[33]See section 1.7, herein.

[34]In re Binger's Estate, 158 Neb. 444, 63 N.W.2d 784 (1954). Compare Aldrich v. Steen, 71 Neb. 33, 98 N.W. 445 (1904), mod. 71 Neb. 57, 100 N.W. 311 (1904) (the rule was otherwise when the common-law marriage was recognized).

Adoption

Any adult may adopt a minor child. As is usual, if the petitioner for adoption is married, unless the child is that of the other spouse, the spouse must join in the petition.[35] The placement of or advertising of children for placement requires a license from the department of public welfare.[36]

Workers' compensation death benefits

An "actually dependent illegitimate child" is eligible for death benefits under the workers' compensation law.[37] The court may itself undertake the adjudication of paternity for this purpose.[38] As to extramarital partners, a common-law spouse, to the extent that such unions continue to receive recognition, qualifies as a dependent,[39] but since a participant in a marriage which is invalid cannot so qualify,[40] a fortiori the mere fact of living together would not form a basis for qualification under the statute.

Tort actions

The tort action for criminal conversation, and the overlapping tort of alienation of affections, regarded with disfavor in many states,[41] receives recognition, though damages can only be recovered if strictly a natural and probable consequence of the tort.[42]

Effect of cohabitation on right to alimony

The mere fact that a recipient of alimony is living with a cohabitant affords no ground for modification of the right to

---

[35] Neb. Rev. Stat., § 43–101.
[36] Id., § 43–701.
[37] Id., § 48–124.
[38] Id., § 48–152.
[39] See Copple v. Bowlin, 172 Neb. 467, 110 N.W.2d 117 (1961).
[40] Bourelle v. Soo-Crete, Inc., 165 Neb. 731, 87 N.W.2d 371 (1958), holding a woman not entitled to benefits because marriage entered into prior to waiting period following man's divorce.
[41] See section 2.19, herein.
[42] See Breiner v. Olson, 195 Neb. 120, 237 N.W.2d 118 (1975).
Actions for breach of promise to marry are also recognized. As to compensatory damages in these actions, see Kuhlman v. Cargile, 200 Neb. 150, 262 N.W.2d 454 (1978).

6.28   UNMARRIED COUPLES AND THE LAW

alimony. "The indulgence of living together and cohabiting by an unmarried man and a woman is a criminal offense but this is not a criminal case to protect the interest of society and the state in public morality and virtuous conduct. If it were, the accused would be entitled to all the safeguards of the criminal law. This is a civil proceeding by one who as a result of absolute divorce has no greater interest in the conduct of appellant than any other member of society and is not entitled to rely on any irregularity in her conduct, however grievous, to defeat his contractual and adjudicated obligation. It is not the province of appellee to attempt to protect the interests of society for his financial advantage."[43]

Abortion

In the preamble to the abortion statute enacted as a result of Roe v. Wade,[44] the legislature "expressly deplores the destruction of the unborn human lives which has and will occur in Nebraska as a consequence of the Supreme Court's decision."[45] Not only does the statute immunize persons from liability or from discrimination in any form for refusal to perform this operation,[46] but also it denounces any such discrimination for this reason as criminal.[47] In addition, the victim of such discrimination is given a right to recover damages,[48] and to injunctive relief.[49]

The provisions conform to the mandate of the Supreme Court of the United States,[50] and set up a procedure whereunder abortions are to be reported to the bureau of vital statistics.[51] Probably constitutionally infirm, however, is the flat prohibition of an abortion without the consent of the parent or guardian of a minor.[52]

---

[43] Bowman v. Bowman, 163 Neb. 336, 79 N.W.2d 554, 562 (1956) (at the time of this decision, cohabiting was still a crime).
[44] See section 2.19, herein.
[45] Neb. Rev. Stat., § 28-4-143.
[46] Id., § 28-4-157.
[47] Id., § 28-4-158.
[48] Id., § 28-4-159.
[49] Id., § 28-4-160.
[50] Id., § 28-4-143 et seq.
[51] Id., § 28-4-162 et seq.
[52] Id., § 28-4-151. See Note, Abortion: An Unresolved Issue—Are Parental Consent Statutes Unconstitutional?, 55 Neb. L. Rev. 256 (1976).

Recovery for wrongful death

The mother of an illegitimate child can recover for its wrongful death.[53]

Possible criminal liability

Crimes such as seduction under a promise of marriage and living and cohabiting in a state of fornication have been removed from the penal statutes. Debauching a minor (under the age of seventeen)[54] and adultery[55] remain. Bigamy[56] is still a crime, and incestuous marriages, which are defined, are absolutely void[57] and a felony.[58] There are various sexual assault provisions,[59] which include sodomy.[60]

Status of children

The well-known presumption that a child born during a lawful marriage is the legitimate child of the husband[61] can only be rebutted by clear and convincing evidence to the contrary.[62] The children of a marriage which is subsequently annulled are legitimate.[63]

As to inheritance, a statute under which an illegitimate child's right to inherit from the father was conditioned on a written, witnessed acknowledgment of paternity, and in the event of a claim based on such child as representing one or the other parent, the parents must have intermarried and had other children, and the father must have acknowledged the child or adopted it into his family, was repealed in 1977.

Procedures for the establishment of paternity and adjudication

---

[53] Neb. Rev. Stat., §§ 30–809, 30–810. See Piechota v. Rapp, 148 Neb. 442, 27 N.W.2d 682 (1947).
[54] Neb. Rev. Stat., § 28–805.
[55] Id., § 28–704.
[56] Id., § 28–701.
[57] Id., § 28–702.
[58] Id., § 28–703.
[59] Id., §§ 28–317 to 28–323.
[60] Id., § 28–318.
[61] Id., § 42–377.
[62] Perkins v. Perkins, 198 Neb. 401, 253 N.W.2d 42 (1977); Ford v. Ford, 191 Neb. 548, 216 N.W.2d 176 (1974).
[63] Neb. Rev. Stat., § 42–377.

of support obligations[64] are civil in nature, and a mere preponderance of probabilities will suffice.[65] There is no provision whereunder a father may initiate a proceeding to have his paternity adjudicated.[66] A willful abandonment of an illegitimate child[67] and a willful failure to support such child[68] are criminally punishable.

Termination of parental rights

The rights of the parents to custody of their offspring, though well recognized,[69] are not absolute. The public has a paramount interest in protecting the child's interests.[70] Thus, when adoption is being considered, the mother must be accorded her right to withhold consent, unless by her conduct she has demonstrated her unfitness or has relinquished the child for adoption.[71] Sexual misconduct on her part does not automatically disqualify her from asserting her right to custody of the child.[72] As to the father, unless he has within five days of the birth of the child notified the department of public welfare of his intent to claim paternity, it seems that a mother's relinquishment is sufficient to warrant the court in dispensing with his consent.[73]

Property rights of cohabitants

It is recognized that a party to an illicit relationship can acquire no *marital* rights in the property of the other, but this does

---

[64]Id., § 28–446 et seq.
[65]Snay v. Snarr, 195 Neb. 375, 238 N.W.2d 234 (1976); Farmer v. Farmer, 200 Neb. 308, 263 N.W.2d 664 (1978).
[66]See Paltani v. Creel, 169 Neb. 591, 100 N.W.2d 736 (1960).
[67]Neb. Rev. Stat., § 28–446.
[68]Id., § 13–116. As to the Uniform Reciprocal Enforcement of Support Act, see § 42–762 et seq.
[69]See Ex Parte Schwartzkopf, 149 Neb. 460, 31 N.W.2d 294 (1948), regarding father's right to be heard as to custody.
[70]See Rejda v. Rejda, 198 Neb. 465, 253 N.W.2d 295 (1977); In Interest of D. L. H., 198 Neb. 444, 253 N.W.2d 283 (1977). For provisions designed to secure the welfare and protection of infants born out of wedlock, see Neb. Rev. Stat., § 43–506 et seq.
[71]See Neb. Rev. Stat., § 43–104.
[72]Greenfield v. Greenfield, 199 Neb. 648, 260 N.W.2d 493 (1977). Compare Morrissey v. Morrissey, 182 Neb. 268, 154 N.W.2d 66 (1967).
[73]Neb. Rev. Stat., §§ 43–102, and 43–104. Section 43–104.06 gives the father a right to oppose mother's relinquishment and get a hearing as to his fitness.

not preclude the enforcement of rights acquired under general principles of law or of equity.[74] A divorced man cultivated a "friendship" with a woman (the record mentions no relationship other than friendship). He contributed nearly all the money required for the building of a house to be owned by his friend's son-in-law. On learning that the property had been conveyed to the friend he sought equitable relief. The court awarded him the land on the basis of a constructive trust or a resulting trust; the facts suffice for either concept.[75] It allowed the friend an offset of $9,000. This figure represented her contribution to the price of the house ($6,000) and her share of the appreciation in value since its acquisition ($3,000). Clearly, then, Nebraska courts recognize the role of equity in adjusting property rights in an extramarital relationship. Thus, notwithstanding a holding that a marriage contract entered into between parties one of whom is known to be already married is void as against public policy,[76] it is likely that contracts between unmarried partners in a relationship untainted by strong policy objectionability will be honored and enforced.

6.29. Nevada

No common-law marriage can be entered into after 1943.[77] However, where Indians have lived together after a marriage consummated in accordance with their tribal customs, and one of them was, at the time of consummation, legally married to another, a continued cohabitation as husband and wife after the removal of the impediment of the former marriage is recognized as creating a marriage.[78] From such a holding it can be assumed that Nevada courts will recognize a common-law marriage contracted in a state where such marriages continue to receive recognition.

---

[74] Abramson v. Abramson, 161 Neb. 782, 74 N.W.2d 919 (1956).
[75] Kuhlman v. Cargile, 200 Neb. 150, 262 N.W.2d 454 (1978).
[76] Boersen v. Huffman, 189 Neb. 469, 203 N.W.2d 489 (1973).
[77] Nev. Rev. Stat., § 122.010.
[78] Ponina v. Leland, 85 Nev. 263, 454 P.2d 16 (1969). See Nev. Rev. Stat., § 122.170.

Adoption

To adopt a child, the adopting petitioner must be at least ten years older than the minor to be adopted. Consent of the child, if over the age of fourteen, is required.[79] Consent of the parents, if the child has not been relinquished to the authorities for adoption, is required.[80] If the child is illegitimate, and the father has been adjudicated to be the father, his consent is a necessary prerequisite.[81] Though consent of an adopting petitioner's cohabitant is not a statutory requirement, there is no doubt that an uncooperative attitude of such partner would prejudice the application beyond all hope.[82]

Death benefits

For the purposes of eligibility for benefits under the Industrial Insurance Act, an illegitimate under the age of eighteen, or over that age if incapacitated from earning, is conclusively presumed to be a dependent.[83] An unmarried partner would not so qualify.[84]

Abortion

Shortly after the decision in Roe v. Wade,[85] an act was passed to legalize abortions as mandated by that decision. After the 24th week of pregnancy such operation can only be performed by a licensed physician who has reasonable cause to believe it to be necessary to preserve the life or health of the mother; the operation is required to be performed in a hospital or other licensed facility. The physician is required to certify the reasons on which he bases his judgment as to the risk of grave impairment to the physical or mental health of the mother. Parental consent, if the

---

[79]Nev. Rev. Stat., § 127.120.

[80]Id., § 127.140.

[81]In re Adoption of Scott, 88 Nev. 254, 495 P.2d 610 (1972).

[82]As to the role of the welfare authorities, which is investigatory and advisory only, see State v. ——, 91 Nev. 275, 534 P.2d 1264 (1975). Generally, see Nev. Rev. Stat., § 127.010 et seq.

[83]Nev. Rev. Stat., § 616.510.

[84]See Powell v. Rogers, 496 F.2d 1248 (C.A.-9 Cal., 1974), cert. den. 419 U.S. 1032, 42 L. Ed. 2d 307, 95 Sup. Ct. 514 (1974).

[85]See section 2.19, herein. As to the crime of abortion, see Nev. Rev. Stat., § 201.120.

child was a minor, or spousal consent, if the spouses were not living apart, is a prerequisite.[86]

Tort actions

The tort action for alienation of affections has been abolished.[87] An action for seduction, however, still lies.[88]

Effect of cohabitation on right to alimony

A divorcee's rights to alimony, unless otherwise ordered, cease on her remarriage,[89] but the court may, on a proper showing, order such payments to be made to her minor children.[90] Where a divorce settlement agreement stipulates that alimony responsibilities shall cease if the recipient cohabits with another, the courts will honor such a stipulation.[91]

Possible criminal liability

The arm of the criminal law extends to such conduct as sexual intercourse with one afflicted with venereal disease,[92] contributing to the delinquency of a child under eighteen,[93] and endeavoring to conceal the birth of a child by any disposition of its dead body, whether it died before or after birth.[94] The statutes are silent as to fornication or cohabitation. For bigamy, to which mistake is a defense, it does not matter which defendant is the married one.[95]

To be convicted of sexual assault, one must be eighteen years or over and the consenting victim under sixteen.[96] The "infamous

---

[86] Nev. Rev. Stat., § 442.240 et seq.
[87] Id., § 41.370.
[88] Id., §§ 12.060, 12.070.
[89] Id., § 125.150.
[90] Id., § 125.160.
[91] Jones v. Jones, —— Nev. ——, 571 P.2d 103 (1977).
[92] Nev. Rev. Stat., § 202.140.
[93] Id., § 201.110.
[94] Id., § 201.150.
[95] Id., §§ 201.258, 201.170. As to incest, see § 201.180.
[96] Id., § 200.365.

crime against nature" extends to consenting adults of the same sex.[97]

Status of children

The children of marriages which are void or voidable for nonage or for fraud are legitimate.[98] There can be no annulment based on fraud if the parties voluntarily cohabit as husband and wife after receiving knowledge of such ground for annulment.[99]

An illegitimate can inherit on intestacy from the mother. As to inheritance from the father, the statute requires that the latter shall have acknowledged paternity by signing a declaration to that effect in the presence of one credible witness.[1]

Legitimation is effected by a subsequent intermarriage of the parents.[2]

Provisions relating to the establishment of paternity and the enforcement of support obligations are as set forth in the Uniform Illegitimacy Act,[3] a statute which has been placed on the inactive list of uniform acts.[4] A putative father can himself initiate proceedings to have his paternity determined.[5] Abundant provision exists to ensure that the illegitimacy of a child's origins does not become a matter of public knowledge.[6]

Important among the provisions controlling termination of parental rights as a prerequisite to adoption are those requiring notice to the putative father,[7] supplemented by a provision that he is presumed to have abandoned the child unless he acknowledged it or sought to establish parental rights prior to a hearing on a petition to terminate his parental rights.[8]

---

[97]Id., § 201.190. See McMichael v. State, —— Nev. ——, 577 P.2d 398 (1978).
[98]Nev. Rev. Stat., §§ 125.410, 134.170.
[99]Id., § 125.340.
[1]Id., § 134.170. As to the constitutionality of so restrictive a test, see section 3.3, herein.
[2]Nev. Rev. Stat., § 122.140.
[3]Id., § 126.080 et seq. As to desertion and nonsupport, see § 201.015 et seq. As to reciprocal enforcement of support, see § 130.010 et seq.
[4]Section 3.3, herein.
[5]Turner v. Saka, 90 Nev. 54, 518 P.2d 608 (1974). As to father's rights where the two-year limitation period from the birth of the child has expired, see Smith v. Gabrielli, 80 Nev. 390, 395 P.2d 325 (1964).
[6]Nev. Rev. Stat., §§ 126.370, 440.170, 440.290, 440.210, 440.325.
[7]Id., § 128.035.
[8]Id., § 128.095. As to grounds for termination of parental rights, see § 128.105.

Property rights of cohabitants

At least one decision indicates that the courts of Nevada are not deterred by considerations of meretricious cohabitation from decreeing an equitable adjustment of the property rights of extramarital partners. In Cummings v. Tinkler[9] a wife's services constituted virtually the entire consideration for a grant of land, title to which was taken in the name of the husband. The evidence showed that the grantor (and presumably the wife) had intended it to become a part of their community property. The couple divorced, but the decree appears to have made no disposition of this land. They continued to cohabit until the husband died. On his death, the court held that, since had the land been community property it would have vested entirely in the wife, a resulting trust in favor of the wife would achieve that purpose.

The holding seems sound. The fact of post-divorce cohabitation was not regarded, and should not have been regarded, as having any bearing on the matter.

More recently, a woman sued a man, inter alia, to assert property rights in their accumulations on a basis of constructive trust, resulting trust, partnership or joint venture, or quasi contract. The parties had traveled together for over eight years. They had never held themselves out as married. The trial court found that no pooling of earnings or implied partnership was established. In leaving undisturbed the trial court's findings,[10] the court went to the trouble of observing that those portions of the judgment in Marvin v. Marvin[11] which related to implied contract, joint venture, quantum meruit or equitable remedies, are arguably dictum. Such comment, and such careful consideration of the Marvin decision, would not be expected if the Nevada courts are disposed to ignore the doctrines explored in that decision as inapplicable in that state.

Once a child has been voluntarily relinquished for adoption, the relinquishment becomes irrevocable. Id., § 127.080. See Blanchard v. Nevada State Welfare Dept., 91 Nev. 749, 542 P.2d 737 (1975).

[9] 91 Nev. 548, 539 P.2d 1213 (1975).
[10] Warren v. Warren, —— Nev. ——, 579 P.2d 772 (1978).
[11] See section 6.5, herein.

6.30. New Hampshire

Contrary to the modern trend disfavoring the concept of common-law marriage,[12] the legislature of New Hampshire has in effect revived the concept. In 1968 it provided that "persons cohabiting and acknowledging each other as husband and wife, and generally reputed to be such, for the period of three years, and until the decease of one of them, shall thereafter be deemed to have been legally married."[13] In all civil actions, except actions for criminal conversation, evidence of acknowledgment, cohabitation, and reputation is competent proof of marriage.[14] A woman complying with these requirements qualifies for all the rights of a widow in her cohabitant's estate.[15]

Further, a marriage valid where contracted is recognized in this state if the parties are or become permanent residents of the state.[16]

Adoption

Any individual may be adopted.[17] Ordinarily, if the adopting person is married, the spouse should be joined as a petitioner.[18] Consent of the child to be adopted, if over twelve, is required. Consent of the mother, if unwed and under eighteen, can be supplanted by that of her parents or guardian if the court so orders. Consent of the putative father, if he is known and has not married the mother, or is living with the mother and child, or has filed notice of intent to claim paternity, is also required. If these conditions do not exist, he must, if known, be informed prior to the hearing on the petition that he must file such notice of intent to claim paternity within thirty days and that failure to file such notice will result in a forfeiture of all parental rights.[19] Consent is not required of an unwed father who has not complied with the

---

[12]See section 1.5, herein.
[13]N.H. Rev. Stat. Ann., § 457:39.
[14]Id., § 457:40.
[15]See Gray v. Gray, —— N.H. ——, 379 A.2d 442 (1977).
[16]N.H. Rev. Stat. Ann., § 457:3.
[17]Id., § 170-B:3.
[18]Id., § 170-B:4.
[19]Id., § 170-B:5.

above conditions; nor is it required of any parent whose parental rights have been terminated.[20]

No consent or surrender for adoption shall be taken unless at least 72 hours have elapsed from the time of the child's birth.[21]

Workers' compensation death benefits

A common-law spouse is a dependent for the purposes of the workers' compensation law.[22]

Automobile insurance policy

The word "spouse" was not regarded as including a cohabitant for the purposes of an automobile insurance policy covering the insured and his spouse,[23] but this was decided prior to the 1968 statute re-establishing the concept of common-law marriage.[24]

Abortion

The willful administration of anything to procure a miscarriage is denounced,[25] as is the administration of anything to destroy a quick child, unless to preserve the life of the mother.[26]

Tort actions

The cause of action for breach of promise of marriage has been abolished.[27] But the tort of criminal conversation remains.[28]

---

[20] Id., § 170-B:6.
[21] Id., § 170-B:7. A court has inherent jurisdiction to set aside a decree of adoption if the mother can prove that she had revoked her consent before the decree. See Smith v. Consul General of Spain, 110 N.H. 62, 260 A.2d 95 (1969).
[22] N.H. Rev. Stat. Ann., § 281:2 IX.
[23] See Harleysville Mut. Cas. Ins. Co. v. Carroll, 50 Del. Super. 67, 123 A.2d 128 (1956).
[24] N.H. Rev. Stat. Ann., § 457:39.
[25] Id., § 585:12.
[26] Id., § 585:13.
[27] Id., § 508:11.
[28] Id., § 459:41.

6.30 UNMARRIED COUPLES AND THE LAW

Possible criminal liability

Extramarital cohabitation is punishable only as fornication in situations where the behavior is such as to outrage public decency.[29] However, there are statutes denouncing as criminal adultery (either participant can be the married one),[30] bigamy[31] and incest.[32]

Absent special circumstances, as, for example, where the participants are related or the perpetrator is in some position of authority over the victim, statutory rape is now restricted to situations where the victim (of whatever sex) is less than thirteen years old.[33] In 1977 it was held that a former statute, in that it singled out a male for disparate treatment under the law as opposed to a female, was unconstitutional.[34] The possible repercussions of this ruling on similar statutes in other states has already received attention.[35]

The crime of contributing to the delinquency of a minor remains on the books.[36] Statutes forbidding deviate sexual relations[37] or unnatural and lascivious acts with another person[38] have been superseded insofar as consenting adults are concerned.[39]

Concealing the corpse of a newborn child is also an offense.[40]

Status of children

Children of unwed parents and their issue are heirs of the mother and her kindred.[41] Illegitimate children share equally

---

[29]Id., § 645:1.
[30]Id., § 645:3.
[31]Id., § 639:1.
[32]Id., § 639:2. As to the prohibited degrees of marriage, within which a marriage is not only incestuous but the children are illegitimate, see N.H. Rev. Stat. Ann., §§ 457:1 to 457:3. But see Patey v. Peaslee, 90 N.H. 335, 111 A.2d 194, 47 A.L.R.2d 1388 (1955), holding validity of such marriage not subject to attack after death of incompetent spouse.
[33]N.H. Rev. Stat. Ann., § 632-A:2.
[34]Meloon v. Helgemoe, 436 F. Supp. 528 (D. N.H., 1977), affd. 564 F.2d 602 (C.A.-1 N.H., 1977), cert. den. 98 Sup. Ct. 2858 (1978).
[35]See section 2.25, herein.
[36]N.H. Rev. Stat. Ann., § 169:32.
[37]Id., § 632:2.
[38]Id., § 579:9.
[39]See id., § 632-A.
[40]Id., § 639:5.
[41]Id., § 561:4. Such child can inherit from mother even where adopted. Young v. Bridges, 86 N.H. 135, 165 Atl. 272 (1933).

with legitimate children on the mother's death.[42] Statutory silence as to their rights on the death intestate of the male parent might one day force the courts of this state to lay down the guidelines and fill a gap left by Trimble v. Gordon.[43]

The establishment of paternity and enforcement of support duties is largely covered by the adoption of the Uniform Act on Paternity,[44] the Uniform Civil Liability for Support Act,[45] and of the Uniform Act on Blood Tests to determine paternity.[46] Establishment of paternity is an essential prerequisite to imposing support obligations.[47] Thus, when a defendant forfeits bail, thereby avoiding such an adjudication, the bail cannot be diverted to payment of the mother's confinement expenses and child support.[48] An agreement whereunder a putative father promises to pay support in consideration of the mother's promise not to sue him has been held specifically enforceable.[49]

Subsequent marriage of the parents with each other legitimates the children,[50] provided the parents are legally capable of entering into such a marriage.[51]

A statute now authorizes a putative father to petition that his child be declared legitimate.[52] The mother is, if available, a necessary party. The effect of the decree is to entitle the child to all succession rights of lawful children and to impose on the father all obligations owed to his legitimate children. (In the light of this statute, it might well be argued that an involuntary

---

[42]N.H. Rev. Stat. Ann., § 561:5.
[43]See section 3.3, herein.
[44]N.H. Rev. Stat. Ann., §§ 168-A:1 to 168-A:12.
[45]Id., §§ 546-A:1 to 546-A:12.
[46]Id., §§ 522:1 to 522:10. The well known presumption of legitimacy of a child born in lawful wedlock is rebuttable by clear and convincing evidence such as a blood test. Watts v. Watts, 115 N.H. 186, 337 A.2d 350 (1975). As to the sufficiency of blood tests, see State ex rel. Dalloff v. Sargent, 100 N.H. 29, 118 A.2d 596 (1955).
As to the Uniform Reciprocal Enforcement of Support Act, see N.H. Rev. Stat. Ann., §§ 546:1 to 546:41.
[47]N.H. Rev. Stat. Ann., §§ 168-A:1, 168-A:2.
[48]State ex rel. Patten v. Mitton, 113 N.H. 26, 300 A.2d 521 (1973).
[49]Tuttle v. Palmer, —— N.H. ——, 374 A.2d 661 (1977).
[50]N.H. Rev. Stat. Ann., § 457:42.
[51]Hilliard v. Baldwin, 76 N.H. 142, 80 Atl. 139 (1911).
[52]N.H. Rev. Stat. Ann., § 460:29.

adjudication of paternity would have the same effect on succession rights, notwithstanding the statutory silence on this point.)

Property rights of cohabitants

An early decision holds that a loan by a man to a woman on the consideration of her being his mistress cannot be recovered.[53] Another holds that a mistress has no cause of action on an agreement to pay for her services,[54] even if the services are incidental to the meretricious relationship. Where, however, a marriage is declared void ab initio as bigamous, courts have recognized their discretion to adjust the property rights of the parties and take into account the contributions of each to the accumulations acquired during the supposed marriage.[55]

6.31. New Jersey

The institution of common-law marriage has been abolished in New Jersey since 1939.[56] The abolition reflects a policy of the state to prohibit such unions.[57] Hence, where an insured, a domiciliary of New Jersey, went through a marriage ceremony in a sister state when he was already married, and, seven years later, divorced his wife and continued to cohabit with the other woman until he died, neither woman qualified for the proceeds of his life insurance as his "widow." The second marriage was of course void, and, since the parties remained domiciled in New Jersey throughout, the fact that they may have held themselves out as husband and wife from time to time in the sister state did not warrant a New Jersey court in finding there had been a common-law marriage.[58]

---

[53] Harlow v. Laclair, 82 N.H. 506, 136 Atl. 128, 50 A.L.R. 973 (1927).
[54] Gauthier v. Laing, 96 N.H. 80, 70 A.2d 207 (1950) (illicit relations did take place).
[55] See, e.g., Fowler v. Fowler, 97 N.H. 216, 84 A.2d 836 (1951).
[56] N.J. Stat. Ann., § 37:1–10.
[57] Torres v. Torres, 144 N.J. Super. 540, 366 A.2d 713 (1976).
[58] Metropolitan Life Ins. Co. v. Chase, 189 F. Supp. 326 (D. N.J., 1960), affd. 294 F.2d 500 (C.A.-3 N.J., 1961).

Schoolteachers

Though "deviate" lifestyles may have their impact on the continued retention of an employee as a teacher in the public school system,[59] it is recognized that pregnancy in itself cannot properly constitute a basis for termination of a teacher.[60]

Adoption

An unmarried person may petition to adopt a child,[61] but private direct placement is much disfavored.[62] The approval of an adoptive agency is required; however, on a showing that the agency is withholding its approval for reasons which are arbitrary or capricious, final say is with the court.[63]

As is usual, the courts are solicitous of the rights of the parents of an illegitimate child in considering petitions for adoption. Thus, where the father, on the mother's death, had not forsaken his parental obligations toward the child, a petition by the maternal grandparents for adoption could not be granted without his consent.[64] If the parents have not voluntarily surrendered the child for adoption, their parental rights will not readily be ignored. "Forsaken parental obligations" such as will justify termination of their rights to withhold consent must constitute a course of conduct amounting, if not to intentional abandonment, to a very substantial neglect of duty, with no reasonable expectation of any reversal of that conduct in the near future.[65] The mere fact

---

[59] See In re Grossman, 157 N.J. Super. 165, 384 A.2d 855 (1978) (transsexual teacher properly dismissed due to her potential for psychological harm to students); Gish v. Board of Education of Borough of Paramus, Bergen County, 145 N.J. Super. 96, 366 A.2d 1337 (1976), cert. den. 434 U.S. 879, 98 Sup. Ct. 233 (1977) (affirming school board's order of a psychiatric examination for an alleged homosexual). See also Dressler, Gay Teachers: A Disesteemed Minority in an Overly Esteemed Profession, 9 Rutgers Camden L. J. 399 (1978).

[60] Gilchrist v. Board of Education of Borough of Haddonfield, Camden County, 155 N.J. Super. 358, 382 A.2d 946 (1978).

[61] As to general adoption procedures, see N.J. Stat. Ann., § 9:3–37 et seq.

[62] Sees v. Baber, 74 N.J. 201, 377 A.2d 628 (1977).

[63] In re Estate of Neuwirth, 155 N.J. Super. 410, 382 A.2d 972 (1978); M. v. Family & Children's Service, Inc., 130 N.J. Super. 214, 326 A.2d 74 (1974).

[64] In re Adoption of B., 152 N.J. Super. 546, 378 A.2d 90 (1977).

[65] Sorentino v. Family & Childrens Soc. of Elizabeth, 74 N.J. 313, 378 A.2d 18 (1977). See also In re Adoption of Child by A.R., 152 N.J. Super. 541, 378 A.2d 87 (1977).

that a parent has a criminal record does not justify a cutting-off of this right to veto an adoption.[66]

Welfare assistance

A state statute which provided a program of assistance to families of the working poor, but which limited benefits to families consisting of a household composed of two adults of the opposite sex ceremonially married to each other who have at least one minor child of both, the natural child of one and adopted by the other, or a child adopted by both, was held violative of the equal protection clause of the Constitution.[67] There could be no doubt that the benefits extended under such a program were as indispensable to the health and well-being of illegitimate as of legitimate children.[68]

Workers' compensation death benefits

The decisions relating to eligibility for workers' compensation death benefits seem difficult to reconcile. In 1973 a court held that a denial to dependent illegitimate grandchildren of rights otherwise confirmed in their legitimate counterparts violates equal protection,[69] but three years later a court held that the mere fact that the worker had stood *in loco parentis* to a child is insufficient to give the child status as a dependent for this purpose.[70] And though a widow is defined as a "married woman whose husband is dead,"[71] the test of qualification is not the same as under family

---

[66] See In re Adoption of Children by D., 61 N.J. 89, 293 A.2d 171 (1972).

[67] New Jersey Welfare Rights Organization v. Cahill, 411 U.S. 619, 36 L. Ed. 2d 543, 93 Sup. Ct. 1700 (1973). Of collateral interest is a contest as to the validity of a statute which excluded from eligibility under a county pension fund widows of employees who, after reaching the age of fifty, marry a woman more than fifteen years younger than themselves. The statute was sustained as imposing only an indirect economic burden on the employee's right to marry and not being violative of one's fundamental right to marry. Reiser v. Pension Commission of Employees Retirement System of County of Passaic, 147 N.J. Super. 168, 370 A.2d 902 (1976).

[68] New Jersey Welfare Rights Organization v. Cahill, 411 U.S. 619, 36 L. Ed. 2d 543, 93 Sup. Ct. 1700 (1973).

[69] Carr v. Campbell Soup Co., 124 N.J. Super. 382, 307 A.2d 126 (1973).

[70] Miles v. Theobald Industries, 144 N.J. Super. 535, 366 A.2d 710 (1976).

[71] Petrozzino v. Monroe Calculating Mach. Co., 90 N.J. Super. 64, 216 A.2d 244 (1966), revd. on other grounds 47 N.J. 577, 222 A.2d 73 (1966).

law for questions of property, inheritance and legitimacy of offspring. A claimant qualified for death benefits even though the worker had not been divorced when he married her.[72] A woman who resumed cohabitation with the worker after a divorce was held to qualify as a de facto spouse.[73] Also, one who, after her husband's death, held herself out as the wife of another was not thereby deprived of dependency benefits as his widow.[74]

Zoning laws

Extramarital cohabitants have been considered a "family" for purposes of the zoning laws.[75]

Abortion

In New Jersey, since the year 1898, any person who, maliciously or without lawful justification, with intent to procure the miscarriage of a pregnant woman, administers or prescribes or advises or directs her to take or swallow any poison, drug, medicine or noxious thing, or uses any instrument or means whatever, commits a high misdemeanor.[76] Though this statute remains as written, the courts have consistently recognized, since the Supreme Court decisions on abortion,[77] that a mother's right to abortion during the first trimester of pregnancy is exclusively her prerogative.[78] Despite a United States Court of Appeal's adjudication that the New Jersey statute is unconstitutional on vagueness and privacy grounds[79] the state courts continue to

---

[72] Dawson v. Hatfield Wire & Cable Co., 59 N.J. 190, 280 A.2d 173 (1971).

[73] Parkinson v. J & S Tool Co., 64 N.J. 159, 313 A.2d 609 (1974). Compare Gaudreau v. Eclipse Pioneer Div. of Bendix Sir Corp., 137 N.J.L. 666, 61 A.2d 227 (1948), holding cohabitation insufficient for qualification as a widow.

[74] Leitenberger v. Olt Bros. Inc., 136 N.J. Super. 261, 345 A.2d 803 (1975), affd. 71 N.J. 370, 365 A.2d 713 (1976).

[75] Marino v. Mayor and Council of Borough of Norwood, 77 N.J. Super. 587, 187 A.2d 217 (1963).

[76] N.J. Stat. Ann., § 2A:87-1.

[77] See section 2.19, herein.

[78] Rothenberger v. Doe, 149 N.J. Super. 478, 374 A.2d 57 (1977); Doe v. Bridgeton Hosp. Assn., 71 N.J. 478, 366 A.2d 641 (1976), cert. den. 433 U.S. 914, 97 Sup. Ct. 2987 (1977).

[79] Young Women's Christian Assn. of Princeton, N.J. v. Kugler, 463 F.2d 203 (C.A.-3 N.J., 1972).

recognize its viability[80] but construe it to conform to the mandates of the Supreme Court's decisions.[81] Laymen charged under the statute have no standing to challenge its constitutionality as applied to them.[82]

The courts also recognize that the woman's right to terminate a pregnancy is not an unqualified one, but must be gauged against important state interests, namely, legitimate concern for the health of the mother and its interest in protecting the potentiality of human life.[83] A married woman has, within certain limits, a right to an abortion and a right to be sterilized without her husband's consent.[84]

Recovery for wrongful death

The New Jersey courts have held that an illegitimate child has a constitutional right to recover for the wrongful death of its father.[85] The court rejected a contention that, since at the time an illegitimate could take on intestacy only from its mother, the wrongful death should be construed to restrict the right to recovery in the same way.

Action for interference with right to support

The common-law action for alienation of affections has been abolished,[86] however it remains possible for an aggrieved spouse to recover, in a proper case, for interference with a common-law right to spousal support if a marital partner has been enticed from the domestic hearth.[87]

---

[80] Planned Parenthood of New York City, Inc. v. State, Dept. of Institutions and Agencies, 75 N.J. 49, 379 A.2d 841 (1977); State v. Norflett, 67 N.J. 268, 337 A.2d 609 (1975).

[81] Doe v. Bridgeton Hosp. Assn., 71 N.J. 478, 366 A.2d 641 (1976), cert. den. 433 U.S. 914, 97 Sup. Ct. 2987 (1977).

[82] State v. Haren, 124 N.J. Super. 475, 307 A.2d 644 (1973).

[83] State v. Norflett, 67 N.J. 268, 337 A.2d 609 (1975).

[84] Ponter v. Ponter, 135 N.J. Super. 50, 342 A.2d 574 (1975). Where a woman is legally incapable of abortion there can be no conviction of aiding and abetting. State v. Thompson, 56 N.J. Super. 438, 153 A.2d 364 (1959), revd. on other grounds 31 N.J. 540, 158 A.2d 333 (1960), cert. den. 364 U.S. 848, 81 Sup. Ct. 92 (1960).

[85] Schmoll v. Creecy, 54 N.J. 194, 254 A.2d 525, 38 A.L.R.3d 605 (1969).

[86] N.J. Stat. Ann., § 2A:23-1.

[87] See Hafner v. Hafner, 135 N.J. Super. 328, 343 A.2d 166 (1975).

Effect of cohabitation on right to alimony

Subsequent immoral conduct of a divorcee would not, of itself, afford ground for a termination or modification of an award of alimony.[88]

Possible criminal liability

Worthy of note are such crimes as permitting the carnal abuse of a female under the age of eighteen,[89] abduction of a female for marriage or defilement,[90] and concealment of the birth of an illegitimate child or the death of any child.[91] In addition to open lewdness or a notorious act of public indecency, one who in private commits an act of lewdness or carnal indecency with another is punishable.[92] The New Jersey fornication statute,[93] after surviving a barrage of constitutional assaults,[94] finally received a death blow in State v. Saunders.[95] The defendant, who had been charged with rape and convicted of a "lesser included offense" of fornication, obtained a reversal on the ground that the statute was an unconstitutional outlawing of conduct which the state has no power to prohibit. "[T]he conduct statutorily defined as fornication involves, by its very nature, a fundamental personal choice. Thus, the statute infringes upon the right of privacy. Although persons may differ as to the propriety and morality of such

---

[88] See Suozzo v. Suozzo, 16 N.J. Misc. 475, 1 A.2d 930 (1938). But see also Lynn v. Lynn, 153 N.J. Super. 377, 379 A.2d 1046 (1977) and Garlinger v. Garlinger, 129 N.J. Super. 37, 322 A.2d 190 (1974), mod. 137 N.J. Super. 56, 347 A.2d 799 (1975).
[89] N.J. Stat. Ann., § 2A:133–11.
[90] Id., § 2A:86–1 et seq.
[91] Id., § 2A:96–1.
[92] Id., § 2A:115–1.
[93] Id., § 2A:110–1. As to provision for immediate issuance of a marriage license when an arrestee consents to marry, see § 37:1–5.
[94] E.g., State v. Lutz, 57 N.J. 314, 272 A.2d 753 (1971); State v. Clark, 58 N.J. 72, 275 A.2d 137 (1971) (in response to an argument that the statute is a relic of ancient times and out of keeping with today's moral code, the court observed that it is for the legislature to change the law if it chooses to subscribe to more liberal patterns of sexual behavior, and that courts have no authority to promulgate provisions of the Model Penal Code which recommend the legalization of all private, nonviolent, consensual sexual conduct between adults). For discussion of the development of federal privacy concepts and their impact on prosecutions for fornication in New Jersey, see Right of Privacy—Fornication Statute Held Unconstitutional—State v. Saunders, 27 Buffalo L. Rev. 395 (1978).
[95] 75 N.J. 200, 381 A.2d 333 (1977).

conduct and while we certainly do not condone its particular manifestations in this case, such a decision is necessarily encompassed in the concept of personal autonomy which our Constitution seeks to safeguard."[96] It would, said the court, be "rather anomalous" to hold a decision to fornicate as not protected by considerations of the right to privacy when the decision whether or not to bear children is so protected.

> The last two reasons offered by the State as compelling justifications for the enactment—that it protects the marital relationship and the public morals by preventing illicit sex—offer little additional support for the law. Whether or not abstention is likely to induce persons to marry, this statute can in no way be considered a permissible means of fostering what may otherwise be a socially beneficial institution. If we were to hold that the State could attempt to coerce people into marriage, we would undermine the very independent choice which lies at the core of the right of privacy. We do not doubt the beneficent qualities of marriage, both for individuals as well as for society as a whole. Yet, we can only reiterate that decisions such as whether to marry are of a highly personal nature; they neither lend themselves to official coercion or sanction, nor fall within the regulatory power of those who are elected to govern.[97]

The court was careful to observe that sexual conduct between minors was not involved.

One judge, Justice Schreiber, concurred in the result not on the basis of the right to privacy, but squarely on the Constitution of the state of New Jersey, which guarantees to all persons the right to pursue happiness. Happiness, suggests Justice Schreiber, is best obtained in a climate of free decision where each individual has the choice of consenting or not to acts or events which may affect him. Private consensual sexual conduct represents an exercise of that right. The fact that the Supreme Court of the United States has held the decision whether or not to beget a child or to bear it once conceived is essentially a private choice, one with which a state cannot legitimately interfere,[98] does not necessarily mean that the federal right to privacy prevents a

---

[96]Id., 381 A.2d at 339.
[97]Id., 381 A.2d at 342.
[98]Carey v. Population Services Internat., 431 U.S. 678, 52 L. Ed. 2d 675, 97 Sup. Ct. 2010 (1977) (Brennan, J., and White, J.).

state denouncing fornication. In fact, two of the judges in that case noted that the decision invalidating a statutory ban on the sale of contraceptives did not purport to carry with it any ruling as to the constitutionality of statutes outlawing extramarital relations.

As to the argument that this impingement on the right of privacy was justified by some compelling state interest, Justice Schreiber did not question the state's compelling interest in controlling venereal disease. He did, however, question whether the statute was properly designed with that end in mind, and doubted whether it would achieve any such result. The risk of such disease is at least as great a deterrent in itself as the trifling punishment that could accompany a conviction; and indeed a fear of prosecution might deter victims of such disease from seeking treatment. He also found it hard to see how any compelling state interest in preventing the incidence of illegitimate births could be achieved by denouncing fornication.

A dissent, with reluctance, conceded that a state lacks authority to use the criminal process to regulate private decisions which have merely incidental effects on others. And this, "despite the fact that such decision may be in violation of conventional community standards of morality. And that includes the grubby little exercise in self-gratification involved here."[99] The dissent, however, is based on the fact that the reversal should have been on procedural grounds. Defendant, charged with rape, should not have been convicted of fornication as a "lesser included offense" without his day in court as to this issue.

The bigamy statute[1] spells out a qualification where the defendant, due to a five-year absence, believed his or her spouse to be dead. However, the fact that the statute enumerates one defense does not necessarily mean that other defenses of a more general nature are to be excluded; in holding that one who married on the basis of a Mexican mail-order divorce without taking any steps to ascertain the legal validity of such divorce committed bigamy, the court volunteered a dictum that an honest and reasonable belief that a defendant was free to remarry may be a defense.[2] Hence, it

---

[99] 75 N.J. 200, 381 A.2d 333, 347 (1977).
[1] N.J. Stat. Ann., §§ 2A:92-1, 2A:92-2.
[2] State v. De Meo, 20 N.J. 1, 118 A.2d 1, 56 A.L.R.2d 905 (1955).

6.31 UNMARRIED COUPLES AND THE LAW

is likely that reliance on the advice of, say, his attorney would be a defense in such a situation.

The courts at one time construed the adultery statute[3] to mean sexual relations with a married woman,[4] and not to such behavior by a married man.[5] More recently, however, a male alien's relations with an unmarried woman were held adulterous, raising a conclusive presumption of lack of good moral character for the purposes of the immigration laws; and that his subsequent marriage with the other participant did not have a cleansing effect.[6]

For statutory rape, the defendant must be at least sixteen years of age. The victim must be under sixteen with the gravity of the crime depending upon her actual age.[7]

As to sodomy,[8] rulings that consent is no defense even where adults are involved[9] are no doubt ripe for reconsideration.[10]

Status of children

Until recently, the succession statute provided that an illegitimate child takes on intestacy only from the mother and his maternal kindred, and they from him and his children. It added that a subsequent marriage of the parents coupled with a recognition of the child as theirs had the effect of legitimating the child for the purposes of descent and distribution.[11] However, a 1977 revision, effective August, 1979, provides that such a person is also a child of the father if (1) the natural parents, before or after the birth of the child, participate in a ceremonial marriage or shall have consummated a common-law marriage where such marriage is

---

[3]N.J. Stat. Ann., § 2A:88–1.
[4]Petition of Smith, 71 F. Supp. 968 (D. N.J., 1947).
[5]State v. Lash, 16 N.J.L. 380, 32 Am. Dec. 397 (1838).
[6]Brea-Garcia v. Immigration and Naturalization Service, 531 F.2d 693, 33 A.L.R. Fed. 110 (C.A.-3 N.J., 1976).
[7]N.J. Stat. Ann., § 2A:138–1. As to incest, see §§ 2A:114–1, 2A:114–2.
[8]Id., § 2A:143–1.
[9]See State v. Lair, 62 N.J. 388, 301 A.2d 748, 58 A.L.R.3d 627 (1973). In determining whether a fundamental constitutional right exists, courts must look to the traditions and collective conscience of the people. State v. Nugent, 125 N.J. Super. 528, 312 A.2d 158 (1973).
[10]Private personal acts between two consenting adults are not to be lightly meddled with by the state, for the right of personal autonomy is fundamental to a free society. State v. Saunders, 75 N.J. 200, 381 A.2d 333 (1977).
[11]N.J. Stat. Ann., § 3A:4–7.

recognized as valid in the manner authorized by the law of the place where such marriage took place, even though the attempted marriage is void; or (2) the paternity is established by an adjudication before the death of the father or is established thereafter by clear and convincing proof. Paternity established in this manner, however, is not effective to qualify the father or his kindred to inherit from or through the child unless the father has openly treated the child as his, and has not refused to support the child.[12]

This provision seems, as near as can be expected, to meet the guidelines or requirements dictated by Trimble v. Gordon.[13] Its enactment was doubtless prompted by a ruling that the earlier statute was unconstitutional.[14] The statutes controlling succession on intestacy now substantially follow the Uniform Probate Code.[15]

Responsibility for the welfare of illegitimate children, including placement for adoption, is vested in the State Division of Youth and Family Services. Provisions of a fairly standard nature cover the establishment of paternity,[16] enforcement of support,[17] rights to custody of the child,[18] and legitimation.[19] One feature of interest is that a person can incur responsibility for the support of a child by virtue of a doctrine of equitable estoppel. Thus, where a husband who married the mother of an eighteen-month-old child filed a certificate admitting his paternity, and the child, many years later, believed him to be the father even though the mother had admitted the child not to be that of her husband, both spouses were held estopped to deny their parentage.[20] This seems unique. Another decision of interest—very likely inspired by the unpopularity of prosecutions for fornication—is that when the mother of an illegitimate child seeks public aid, whether or not bastardy

---

[12]Id., § 3A:2A-41.
[13]See section 3.3, herein.
[14]In re Estate of Sharp, 151 N.J. Super. 579, 377 A.2d 730 (1977).
[15]N.J. Stat. Ann., § 3A:2A-33 et seq.
[16]Id., § 9:17-1 et seq.
[17]Id., § 2A:4-30.1 et seq. A parent's obligation for the support of an illegitimate child continues until the child becomes of age. Eisler v. Toms, 160 N.J. Super. 272, 389 A.2d 529 (1978).
[18]N.J. Stat. Ann., § 9:16-1 et seq.
[19]Id., § 9:15-1 et seq.
[20]Ross v. Ross, 126 N.J. Super. 394, 314 A.2d 623 (1973), affd. 135 N.J. Super. 35, 342 A.2d 566 (1975).

proceedings ensue against the putative father, neither can be prosecuted for fornication.[21]

A court has awarded, over the mother's objections, visitation rights to one who donated semen to an unmarried woman, on a showing that he fully intended the responsibilities of parenthood. Along with this right, based on his parentage of the child, flowed the concomitant duties of support and maintenance, including confinement expenses.[22]

Property rights of cohabitants

There is early recognition that, when land has been acquired from the combined contributions of partners, one being ignorant of the invalidity of their marriage and title being taken in the name of the other, the latter can be made accountable to the other for his or her share of the contributions.[23] An equitable mortgage has been decreed to secure such reimbursement.[24] Similarly, it was held that where title was taken by grantees as husband and wife, and the man was aware of the invalidity of their supposed marriage, the title was held as a tenancy in common, and the man, after the woman's death intestate, could be equitably estopped from denying her lawful husband's claims, based on a combination of rights of survivorship and of curtesy rights.[25] However, as between the parties themselves, the fact of illicit cohabitation has not deterred the courts from decreeing a tenancy in common where title is taken by them as husband and wife. "The dissolute associations of the parties might if generally known, have aroused the virtuous indignation of the neighborhood, but they do not evict the individual and vested property rights of the offenders from the recognition and protection of the law."[26]

Notwithstanding the declared opposition on the grounds of

---

[21]State v. Clark, 58 N.J. 72, 275 A.2d 137 (1971). Presumably, since the decision invalidating the fornication statute, the same would extend to a prosecution under the "private lewdness" statute, N.J. Stat. Ann., § 2A:115–1.

[22]C. M. v. C. C., 152 N.J. Super. 160, 377 A.2d 821 (1977).

[23]See Conkling v. Conkling, 126 N.J. Eq. 142, 8 A.2d 298 (1936).

[24]Id.

[25]Flammia v. Maller, 66 N.J. Super. 440, 169 A.2d 488 (1961).

[26]Casini v. Lupone, 8 N.J. Super. 362, 72 A.2d 907, 909 (1950).

public policy to cohabitation without marriage,[27] such conduct does not automatically invalidate contracts between the partners.[28] Past illicit relations which operated to induce the making of a contract do not invalidate it if otherwise supported by valuable consideration.[29] Thus, in a contest involving the validity of reciprocal nonrevocable wills made by extramarital partners, a court found that their relationship was but incidental and actually irrelevant to the agreement in question.

> Perhaps it might be said that the agreement came about because the parties lived together. It is not for a secular court to judge whether this relationship was sinful or not. What the law is interested in, under these circumstances, is whether a relationship illegal or contrary to public policy is so inextricably bound with the engagement under consideration so as to taint it fatally. While it might be said that the agreement here in question arose because of the actual relationships between decedent and plaintiff, I must regard that fact as coincidental and, in any event, irrelevant, since there is nothing to show that the agreement in question looks to that relationship to support its validity or existence.[30]

On the other hand, an oral agreement by an alleged father, who was married to another, to make a testamentary gift for the benefit of future-born illegitimate issue was held tainted by illegal and immoral consideration, namely to engage in illicit intercourse in return for the father's promise, and thus unenforceable as in violation of a penal statute and contrary to public policy.[31]

The two decisions are not irreconcilable. The first involved merely an extramarital cohabitation. The second involved more, namely an act of adultery as the consideration for the promise. Extramarital sexual relations, as indicated earlier, have been judicially decriminalized.

Thus, the policy frowning on extramarital cohabitation should not present a serious obstacle to the recognition and enforcement of contracts, either express or implied from the circumstances, relating to the disposition of the accumulations of unmarried

---

[27] See Weiner v. Weiner, 120 N.J. Super. 36, 293 A.2d 229 (1972), affd. 126 N.J. Super. 155, 313 A.2d 222 (1974).
[28] Phillips v. Pullen, 50 N.J.L. 439, 14 Atl. 222 (1888).
[29] Id.
[30] Zabotinsky v. Conklin, 90 N.J. Super. 530, 218 A.2d 422, 426 (1966).
[31] Naimo v. La Fianza, 146 N.J. Super. 362, 369 A.2d 987 (1976).

partners unless sexual relations form an explicit part of the consideration for such agreements.

Kozlowski v. Kozlowski[32] involved a cohabitation of fifteen years' duration wherein the female partner sued for a share of the accumulations of the couple. She also sought compensation for services rendered during this period, and enforcement of an alleged agreement that the male partner would take care of her for the rest of her life.

There being no showing that the plaintiff exercised any control over the man's business activities or had any expectation of sharing in the gains or losses resulting therefrom, relief on a theory of partnership or joint venture was denied.

As to the claim for services, the evidence showed that after about six years of cohabitation the parties had experienced a serious disagreement. At that time the defendant had had the woman sign a release, for a consideration of $5,000, of all claims she might have against him. Thereafter the cohabitation was resumed for another nine years, as a result of his pleas to her to return. At this time, he made it abundantly clear that he had no intention of marrying her. The court ruled that the claim in respect of the first six years of cohabitation had been taken care of by the release. As to the remaining nine years, however, it ruled that her claim for services was satisfied by the various benefits, including support, he had conferred upon her during this period. Though conceding that the meretricious nature of the relationship would not per se rule out a recovery in quasi-contract, the court could find no basis for a claim of unjust enrichment. Nor could it find any basis that would support a contract, even implied in fact, to reward her for her services beyond the benefits she had already received.

The woman, however, fared better in her claim that her partner had promised, in consideration of their resumption of cohabitation, to take care of her for the rest of her life. As the fact trier, the trial judge believed the plaintiff and disbelieved the defendant's testimony that his promise to support was limited to such period as the parties should live together. The case was thus, in effect, remanded for a computation, based on life expectancy tables, of

---

[32] 164 N.J. Super. 162, 395 A.2d 913 (1978), noted in section 4.10, herein.

the present value of the reasonable annual support payable to the plaintiff. (An objection that the agreement, being oral, was unenforceable was countered by the holding that the controlling statute of frauds, as is usual, related only to contracts which are not contemplated to be performed within a year, and not to contracts which may or may not be performed within a year.)

This decision, then, can be viewed as a substantial adoption by the state of New Jersey, albeit obiter in some respects, of the theories of partnership or joint venture, contract implied-in-fact, quasi-contract, and, of course, express contract, as viable bases on which a claim can be presented after the cessation of a long-term and relatively stable cohabitation.

6.32. New Mexico

The provisions of the statute making it lawful for those who may desire to solemnize their contract of matrimony by means of an ordained clergyman or a civil magistrate[33] have been construed to prescribe the only means in which a valid marriage may be contracted.[34] Thus, common-law, sometimes known as de facto, marriages[35] are impermissible.

To give effect to the Equal Rights Amendment on the community property system in force in New Mexico, these statutes were rewritten in 1973.[36]

Schoolteachers

Contrary to the view taken in many states, the termination of an unwed schoolteacher by reason of pregnancy has been held, under the controlling regulations,[37] arbitrary, unreasonable and unsupported by evidence sufficient to warrant such action.[38]

---

[33]N.M. Stat. Ann., §§ 57-1-1, 57-1-2.
[34]In re Gabaldon's Estate, 38 N.M. 392, 34 P.2d 672, 94 A.L.R. 980 (1934).
[35]Hazelwood v. Hazelwood, 89 N.M. 659, 556 P.2d 345 (1976), holding the existence of such a relationship not as such to be ground for modifying alimony payments based on a divorce decree.
[36]N.M. Stat. Ann., § 57-4A-1.1 et seq.
[37]Id., § 77-8-1 et seq.
[38]New Mexico State Bd. of Education v. Stoudt, 91 N.M. 183, 571 P.2d 1186 (1977).

6.32   UNMARRIED COUPLES AND THE LAW

Adoption

Any individual, minor or adult, may be adopted.[39] The petitioner, if married, must join his spouse in the petition unless the spouse is a parent of the adoptee or there is some other good reason to explain such failure to join the spouse. As is usual, unless parental rights have been terminated,[40] the written consent of the biological parents is required; providing, in the case of the male parent, that paternity has been acknowledged or judicially established.[41] The sale of a child for adoption and consent to adoption given for monetary consideration is void. It constitutes abandonment and confers on the court jurisdiction without the required preliminary of consent.[42] The child, provided it is in custody of a placement agency in the state, need not be living in the state at the time petition is filed.[43]

Workers' compensation death benefits

A "child" for the purposes of the workers' compensation law includes an acknowledged illegitimate child.[44] Whether the child is illegitimate or a stepchild, its dependency is regarded as a matter of law.[45]

Abortion

Before the Supreme Court of the United States' abortion decisions,[46] the New Mexico abortion statute had exempted from its provisions certain types of therapeutic abortions.[47] These provisions, insofar as they required the operation to be performed in an accredited hospital and that the approval of other designated

---

[39] See Adoption Act, N.M. Stat. Ann., § 22–2–20 et seq.
[40] The biological father's consent is not required where the child has been abandoned by him. Adoption of Doe, 89 N.M. 606, 555 P.2d 906 (1976). But clear and convincing proof must be furnished before parental rights will be terminated. Huey v. Lente, 85 N.M. 597, 514 P.2d 1093 (1973).
[41] N.M. Stat. Ann., §§ 22–2–24, 22–2–25.
[42] Barwin v. Reidy, 62 N.M. 183, 307 P.2d 175 (1957).
[43] N.M. Stat. Ann., § 22–2–29(2).
[44] Id., § 59–10–12.11.
[45] Shahan v. Beasley Hot Shot Service, Inc., 91 N.M. 462, 575 P.2d 1347 (1978).
[46] See section 2.19, herein.
[47] N.M. Stat. Ann., § 40A–5–1.

members of the medical staff of such a hospital be a prerequisite, have been declared unconstitutional.[48] As it now stands, it is criminal to abort a nonconsenting patient, or one under eighteen whose parental or guardian's consent has not been obtained, or for a nonlicensed person to procure an abortion.[49] The parental consent prerequisite is of dubious constitutionality.[50]

Recovery for wrongful death

Since recovery for wrongful death can be had on behalf of those entitled under the laws of descent and distribution,[51] there is no reason to question that acknowledged illegitimate children could be so entitled.[52]

Possible criminal liability

Extramarital cohabitants need not be concerned with prosecution for the crimes of seduction, or for "unlawfully compelling marriage."[53] Cohabitation with a person under the age of eighteen may subject one to a prosecution for contributing to the delinquency of a minor.[54] To such a charge, reasonable mistake as to age is no defense.[55]

Whoever commits unlawful cohabitation (namely, unmarrieds cohabiting as man and wife), on the first conviction shall only be

---

[48]State v. Strance, 84 N.M. 670, 506 P.2d 1217 (1973). The decision leaves the term "justified medical termination" unqualified except in the matter of consent, meaning that any licensed physician can, at any stage of viability of the fetus, terminate a pregnancy without any legislative restrictions.

[49]N.M. Stat. Ann., §§ 40A–5–1 to 40A–5–3.

[50]See section 2.19, herein.

[51]N.M. Stat. Ann., § 22–20–1 et seq.

[52]See Varney v. Taylor, 77 N.M. 28, 419 P.2d 234 (1966).

[53]N.M. Stat. Ann., §§ 40A–10–4 and 40A–10–5 were repealed in 1973. See Daniels, Impact of the Equal Rights Amendment on the New Mexico Criminal Code, 3 N.M. L. Rev. 106 (1973).

[54]N.M. Stat. Ann., § 40A–6–3. The traditional statutory rape provision has been replaced by "criminal sexual penetration" and "criminal sexual contact of a minor." Id., §§ 40A–9–21, 40A–9–22.

[55]See State v. Gunter, 87 N.M. 71, 529 P.2d 297 (1974), cert. den. 421 U.S. 951, 44 L. Ed. 2d 106, 95 Sup. Ct. 1686 (1975).

warned to cease and desist. If the conduct is persisted in, conviction of a petty misdemeanor can result.[56]

Bigamy consists of *knowingly* entering into a marriage by *or with* a person who has previously contracted one or more marriages which have not been dissolved.[57] Incest extends to intercourse with brothers and sisters of the half blood.[58]

Since 1975, crimes in the nature of sodomy ("criminal sexual penetration" and "criminal sexual contact") are not applicable to consensual behavior between adults.[59]

Status of children

The children of a marriage annulled as within the prohibited degrees, or for nonage, are legitimate.[60]

As to inheritance rights, the statute provides that, in addition to the person born out of wedlock being a child of its mother, it is also a child of the father if (1) the parents have intermarried before or after its birth, even though the attempted marriage is void, or (2) the reputed father has recognized the child in writing, or (3) paternity is judicially established before the father's death, or is established thereafter by a preponderance of the evidence.[61] Paternity established under (3) above, however, does not qualify the father or his kindred to inherit from or through the child unless the father has openly treated the child as his and has not refused to support it.[62]

The provisions controlling procedures for the establishment of paternity and the enforcement of the duty of support (which is now shared by both parents) were revised and re-enacted in 1973 with a view to removing discrimination based on sex.[63] An

---

[56]N.M. Stat. Ann., § 40A–10–2. (It is hard to resist commenting that sanctions of so innocuous a nature might almost be read as an implicit legislative condonation of such behavior.)

[57]Id., § 40A–10–1.

[58]Id., § 40A–10–3. As to incestuous marriages, see § 57–1–7.

[59]See N.M. Stat. Ann., §§ 40A–9–20 to 40A–9–26.

[60]Id., § 57–1–9.

[61]Id., § 32A–2–109.

[62]Id.

[63]See N.M. Stat. Ann., § 22–4–1 et seq. A provision that proceedings to enforce a father's support obligations shall not be brought after a lapse of more than two years from the birth of the child unless paternity has been judicially established,

NEW YORK   6.33

agreement or compromise made by the mother or child or on their behalf concerning the support of the child binds them only when adequate provision is fully secured by payment or otherwise and judicially approved.[64]

6.33. New York

A common-law marriage is valid if entered into before 1933.[65] A subsequent change of mind, once the relationship is established, does not invalidate it.[66] New York will recognize such a marriage if validly contracted under the laws of another state,[67] but not if entered into in a foreign country where common law does not control.[68]

Same-sex marriages are not permitted,[69] and marriages celebrated in that situation can be annulled.[70]

Unwed status and housing discrimination

A landlord has a right to reject a prospective tenant because of his or her failure to meet any standards of acceptability other than those which concern themselves with standards otherwise

---

or has been acknowledged by the father in writing, or support has been furnished, was held unconstitutional to the extent that it limited the right of an illegitimate child to seek a determination of his paternity and support. Stringer v. Dudoich, 92 N.M. 98, 583 P.2d 462 (1978).
  As to the Reciprocal Enforcement of Support Act, see N.M. Stat. Ann., § 22–19–28 et seq.
  [64]Id., § 22–4–19.
  [65]See Stern v. Stern, 88 Misc. 2d 860, 389 N.Y.S.2d 265 (1976) (common-law marriage not established because couple had not held themselves out as married).
  [66]In re Estate of Benjamin, 34 N.Y.2d 27, 355 N.Y.S.2d 356, 311 N.E.2d 495 (1974).
  [67]See Merritt v. Chevrolet Tonawanda Division, General Motors Corp., 50 App. Div. 2d 1018, 377 N.Y.S.2d 663 (1975).
  [68]In re Kabbe's Estate, 158 N.Y.S.2d 551 (1957).
  As to the power of a court to declare legitimate children of a void or voidable marriage, see Bloch v. Ewing, 105 F. Supp. 25 (S.D. Cal., 1952) (stating New York law); Anonymous v. Anonymous, 174 Misc. 906, 22 N.Y.S.2d 598 (1940).
  [69]Anonymous v. Anonymous, 67 Misc. 2d 982, 325 N.Y.S.2d 499 (1971) (annulment despite a change of sex by one partner since the marriage).
  [70]B v. B, 78 Misc. 2d 112, 355 N.Y.S.2d 712 (1974) (annulment on showing "husband" to be a female).

proscribed by statute.[71] Though the human rights law forbids discrimination based on "marital status,"[72] a refusal to sell or to lease to unwed cohabitants based on a seller's or landlord's personal objections to cohabitation outside of marriage is unlikely to be labeled as unlawful discrimination.

Adoption

Standard adoption statutes control the right of a single adult, or a married person joining the spouse, to adopt another person.[73] A natural parent whose child has been taken for adoption without having been properly counseled as to his or her rights can seek the aid of the courts.[74] A putative father has no right of veto over an adoption,[75] but exhaustive provision is made to ensure that, if at all locatable, he receives procedural due process, that is, an opportunity to be heard as to his views as to what is in the child's best interest.[76]

It is possible, on a showing of sufficient cause, for an order of adoption to be vacated or set aside.[77]

In private-placement adoptions, the Division of Adoption Services of the Bureau of Child Welfare of the Department of Social Services conducts a thorough survey of the home, character, stability and suitability of the adoptive parents. Though the statute does not mandate a court appearance of the natural mother at the hearing, the courts prefer her appearance; they have discretion to

---

[71] See Kramarsky v. Stahl Management, 92 Misc. 2d 1030, 401 N.Y.S.2d 943 (1977); In re State Commission for Human Rights v. Kennelly, 30 App. Div. 2d 310, 291 N.Y.S.2d 686 (1968), affd. 23 N.Y.2d 722, 296 N.Y.S.2d 367, 244 N.E.2d 58 (1968).

[72] N.Y. Exec. Law, § 296.

[73] N.Y. Dom. Rel. Law, § 110.

[74] See In re Adoption of T.W.C., 38 N.Y.2d 128, 379 N.Y.S.2d 1, 341 N.E.2d 526 (1975); In re Anonymous (G.), 89 Misc. 2d 514, 393 N.Y.S.2d 900 (1977).

A contract between the parents of an illegitimate not to offer the child for adoption is against public policy. In re Adoption of Brousal, 66 Misc. 2d 711, 322 N.Y.S.2d 28 (1971).

[75] See In re Adoption of Malpica-Orsini, 36 N.Y.2d 568, 370 N.Y.S.2d 511, 331 N.E.2d 486 (1975), appeal dismissed 423 U.S. 1042, 46 L. Ed. 2d 631, 96 Sup. Ct. 765 (1976). In re Benjamin, 93 Misc. 2d 1084, 403 N.Y.S.2d 877 (1978) (unwed father found to have abandoned parental rights).

[76] N.Y. Dom. Rel. Law, § 111-a.

[77] Id., § 114.

order that, if she is out of state, she be cited and served by mail or publication, or that a guardian ad litem be appointed to represent her interests, if she is a minor. In these cases, it is regarded as important that she have the impartial advice of a judge; a private attorney does not ordinarily have the facilities for affording her the kind of counseling that she would receive at the hands of a regular adoption agency.

One court has indicated that, in future private-placement adoptions, it will require detailed explanation of the conditions under which the mother delivered her child to adoptive parents.[78] It is improper for attorneys or hospital personnel to receive a child for adoption; securing children through personal contacts with doctors and hospitals for the purposes of adoption can put an attorney in violation of the social services law.[79] Though a modest fee for his services is not improper, the attorney will be required to furnish the court with detailed information as to the compensation which has changed hands, the number of adoptions he has handled in the past three years, and as to how the adoptive parents became aware of the availability of the child for adoption.[80]

Unmarrieds not within jurisdiction of family court

For the purposes of the rule that the family court has exclusive jurisdiction over disorderly conduct between members of the same "family" or "household," these terms are held not to include persons living together in an unmarried state.[81]

Effect of cohabitation on right to support from father

A father was not relieved of support payments for his nineteen-year-old unemployed daughter who had left the home of her mother, who had been granted custody, because of lack of room, and was living with her paramour by whom she had an illegitimate child.[82]

---

[78]In re Anonymous (G.), 89 Misc. 2d 514, 393 N.Y.S.2d 900 (1977).
[79]See N.Y. Soc. Serv. Law, § 374.
[80]In re Anonymous (G.), note 78, supra.
[81]People v. Dorns, 88 Misc. 2d 1064, 390 N.Y.S.2d 546 (1976); Potter v. Bennett, 40 App. Div. 2d 546, 334 N.Y.S.2d 511 (1972).
[82]Thompson v. Thompson, 94 Misc. 2d 911, 405 N.Y.S.2d 974 (1978).

Workers' compensation death benefits

For the purposes of workers' compensation death benefits, a "child" includes an acknowledged illegitimate child dependent on the deceased.[83] The fact of its birth after the date of a fatal accident does not preclude a finding of dependency.[84]

A mere participation in a sustained adulterous relationship does not of itself constitute abandonment so as to deprive a widow of death benefits;[85] nor does a separation for which the wife is not to blame.[86] However, unless a cohabitant qualifies as a common-law wife,[87] she would no more qualify than would a participant in a bigamous marriage.[88]

Coverage under insurance policies

A woman who openly lived with an insured, who bore children and named him as the father, but who had not married him, was held not to be a "spouse" for the purposes of a statute specifying that no automobile insurance policy covers injuries to a spouse unless provision relating thereto is specifically included in the policy.[89] Also of interest in the matter of insurance, is an opinion of the attorney general that cancellation of a policy because of the insured's "mode of living," namely living with persons in an unmarried state, is discrimination based on marital status and violates the insurance laws.[90]

---

[83]N.Y. Work. Comp. Law, § 2.

[84]Thompson v. Thomashoff Press, Inc., 31 App. Div. 2d 848, 297 N.Y.S.2d 254 (1969).

[85]Johnson v. Birds Eye Frozen Foods, 32 App. Div. 2d 585, 299 N.Y.S.2d 338 (1969); In re Harge v. Leonard Bell & Son, 12 App. Div. 2d 568, 206 N.Y.S.2d 613 (1960).

[86]See Brezickyj v. Eastern R. Builders, Inc., 59 App. Div. 2d 578, 397 N.Y.S.2d 452 (1977), where, though the initial separation was not such as to constitute abandonment, the claimant was disqualified by reason of its continuance, by apparent mutual consent, after the claimant had begun a new life with another man, by whom she had children.

[87]See Peart v. T. D. Bross Line Constr. Co., 45 App. Div. 2d 801, 357 N.Y.S.2d 53 (1974); Biggie v. Northern Distributing Co., 11 App. Div. 2d 591, 200 N.Y.S.2d 763 (1960).

[88]See Lewis v. I. Shulman & Son Co., 7 App. Div. 2d 677, 179 N.Y.S.2d 318 (1958).

[89]U. S. Fire Ins. Co. v. Cruz, 35 Misc. 2d 272, 230 N.Y.S.2d 779 (1962), affd. 239 N.Y.S.2d 531 (1963).

[90]Op. A. G. Dec. 13, 1976. If this is so, it is conceivable that "marital status" for

Abortion

The abortion statute justifies abortion where the mother consents and the operation is performed by a licensed physician who either reasonably believes it to be necessary to save the mother's life or acts within 24 weeks of the inception of pregnancy.[91] The degree of gravity of the crime—which can be committed by a self-induced miscarriage—depends on the stage of development of the embryo or fetus.[92] The law is silent as to the requirement of parental consent.[93]

Recovery for wrongful death

An illegitimate child can recover for the wrongful death of either parent. A statute restricting the right to recover in respect of the mother's death was ruled unconstitutional in that no rational legislative purposes can justify such discrimination, vis-a-vis legitimate children, in depriving them of a cause of action.[94] Unlike inheritance laws, where recognition of the claims of an illegitimate automatically diminishes the share available to a legitimate child, the damages for wrongful death are controlled by the injuries sustained by each individual affected. Presumably, such a plaintiff would nevertheless be required to produce clear and convincing proof of his paternal origins as a prerequisite to recovery. The father (if he can show damage) can likewise recover for wrongful death of his illegitimate child.[95]

---

the purposes of the human rights law (see note 72, supra) could be similarly construed.

[91] N.Y. Penal Law, § 125.05. See Chapman v. Schultz, 86 Misc. 2d 543, 383 N.Y.S.2d 512 (1976).

[92] N.Y. Penal Law, §§ 125.45, 125.50, 125.55. See Reno v. D'Javid, 85 Misc. 2d 126, 379 N.Y.S.2d 290 (1976), mod. 55 App. Div. 2d 876, 390 N.Y.S.2d 421 (1977), 42 N.Y.2d 1040, 399 N.Y.S.2d 210, 369 N.E.2d 766 (1977).

[93] See Right to an Abortion—Problems with Parental and Spousal Consent, 22 N.Y. L. S. L. Rev. 65 (1976); Byrn, American Tragedy: The Supreme Court on Abortion, 41 Fordham L. Rev. 807 (1973). As to an infant's cause of action for wrongful life, see Park v. Chessin, 88 Misc. 2d 222, 387 N.Y.S.2d 204 (1976), mod. 60 App. Div. 2d 80, 400 N.Y.S.2d 110 (1977).

[94] In re Estate of Ortiz, 60 Misc. 2d 756, 303 N.Y.S.2d 806 (1969). See N.Y. Civ. Rights Law, § 80-a.

[95] N.Y. Est., Powers & Trust Law, § 5-4.5.

Tort actions

Actions for alienation of affections, criminal conversation, seduction and breach of promise to marry have been abolished.[96]

Effect of cohabitation on right to alimony

The law gives the courts a discretion, on proof that a divorced wife is habitually living with another man and holding herself out as his wife, to modify or annul any support or alimony decrees awarded in her favor.[97] In a "Bob and Carol, Ted and Alice" situation, a court held that such discretion would not be exercised in favor of a divorced husband who knew, at the time of their estrangement, that the wife was living with another man and signed a separation agreement without a provision terminating alimony if she lived with another man, though he had requested the insertion of such a provision.[98] Though there was a "holding out" as the man's wife, the court, incidentally describing the provision as a step backward into the dark ages, felt that an exercise of its discretion would be a travesty of justice.[99] This provision, though it can be used as a basis for terminating a support order under a divorce decree, cannot be used to impair the wife's rights under a separation agreement which is incorporated but not merged in such a divorce decree.[1]

---

[96]The purpose of the abolition of these tort actions was to outlaw actions based on broken promises of marriage or interference with the marital relationship and not to outlaw all actions in which sexual intercourse is an element. Roy v. Hartogs, 81 Misc. 2d 350, 366 N.Y.S.2d 297 (1975). As to the enforceability of a promise to make a reasonable allowance for maintenance of one whom promisor had allegedly seduced, see Locke v. Pembroke, 280 N.Y. 430, 21 N.E.2d 495 (1939). See also Aadland v. Flynn, 27 Misc. 2d 833, 211 N.Y.S.2d 221 (1961), affd. 14 App. Div. 2d 837, 218 N.Y.S.2d 527 (1961) dismissing an action by a minor against actor Errol Flynn and rejecting an attempt to distinguish "debauchery" from an isolated act of seduction.

[97]N.Y. Dom. Rel. Law, § 248.
[98]In re Anonymous, 90 Misc. 2d 801, 395 N.Y.S.2d 1000 (1977).
[99]Id.
[1]In re Paul S. v. Roberta S., 91 Misc. 2d 211, 397 N.Y.S.2d 568 (1977). The law now bars a divorce from support only if the misconduct would constitute grounds for separation or divorce. N.Y. Dom. Rel. Law, § 236.

Possible criminal liability

Fornication is not a crime in New York. In prosecutions for adultery,[2] bigamy,[3] and the offense of unlawfully procuring a marriage license,[4] reasonable mistake is a defense.[5] New York has four different classifications of rape, much depending on the ages of the participants.[6]

Following upon a series of unsuccessful attempts to strike down the consensual sodomy statute,[7] a family court judge in In re P.,[8] in the course of a lengthy denunciation of the prostitution laws as being violative of equal protection, declared the statute unconstitutional.

> The court has searched for, but cannot find, a proper governmental objective... in distinguishing between the marital status of persons engaging in so-called "deviate" sexual intercourse. Completely lacking is any evidence that the conduct proscribed is more harmful to unmarried participants or that such conduct between unmarried persons is more harmful to the public. If the consensual sodomy law was designed to prevent sexual relations between unmarried people, then "normal" sexual relations between the unmarried would also be sanctioned by the Criminal Law.... If the purpose of the law is to promote conventional sex it also fails in its objective since married persons are permitted to engage in unconventional or "deviate" sexual conduct. Thus, if morality vis a vis sexual norms or the promotion of marriage are the objectives of the legislation, there is no rational let alone substantial relationship between the law itself and these legislative ends.... Since the classification created by section 130.38 of the Penal Law and section 130.00(2) as incorporated therein has no rational basis, the criminalization of "deviate" sexual intercourse

---

[2] N.Y. Penal Law, § 255.17.
[3] Id., § 255.15. As to incest, see §§ 255.25, 255.30.
[4] Id., § 255.10.
[5] Id., § 255.20.
[6] Id., § 130.25. As to endangering welfare of a minor, see § 260.10. See also Ploscowe, Sex Offenses in the New Penal Law, 32 Brooklyn L. Rev. 274 (1966).
[7] As to deviate sexual intercourse, N.Y. Penal Law, § 130.00 et seq. and consensual sodomy, § 130.38, bills to repeal these laws have constantly been introduced and have as constantly failed. See People v. Reilly, 85 Misc. 2d 702, 381 N.Y.S.2d 732 (1976); People v. Mehr, 87 Misc. 2d 257, 383 N.Y.S.2d 798 (1976), affd. 41 N.Y.2d 1018, 395 N.Y.S.2d 626, 363 N.E.2d 1371 (1977); Raphael v. Hogan, 305 F. Supp. 749 (S.D. N.Y., 1969).
[8] In re P., 92 Misc. 2d 62, 400 N.Y.S.2d 455, 463 (1977).

between persons who are not married to each other is an unconstitutional denial of equal protection of the laws.[9]

The judge in In re P. disposes of the Supreme Court of the United State's affirmation without opinion of Doe v. Commonwealth's Attorney of Richmond[10] as not dispositive of any of the issues in the case at bar and as of minimal precedential value. "It [the affirmation without an opinion] means that the court approves of the *result* as to these parties on the facts presented but does not indicate approval of the lower court's reasoning."[11]

A later court, without so much as mention of In re P., reversed a conviction under the sodomy law for procedural reasons: that the indictment had not stated the exact nature of the deviate sexual intercourse.[12]

Status of children

For the purposes of succession on intestacy, an illegitimate child is the child of its mother. It is also a child of the father when he has been so adjudicated.[13] This statute, requiring proof that a court of competent jurisdiction had made an order of filiation declaring paternity during the father's lifetime, has been held to meet the guidelines articulated in Trimble v. Gordon[14] and to be a constitutional exercise of a legitimate state purpose, namely, to make provision for an orderly settlement of estates and the dependability of titles to property passing under the intestacy laws.[15] There is room for elasticity in its application. For example, where an order of filiation was not rendered during the father's life, the only order being an order confirming a

---

[9]Id., 400 N.Y.S.2d at 463.
[10]See section 2.25, herein, note 95.
[11]In re P., 92 Misc. 2d 62, 400 N.Y.S.2d 455, 465, note 21 (1977).
[12]People v. Harley, 62 App. Div. 2d 1064, 404 N.Y.S.2d 140 (1978). Generally, see Ploscowe, Sex Offenses in the New Penal Law, 32 Brooklyn L. Rev. 274 (1966); Richards, Unnatural Acts and the Constitutional Right to Privacy: A Moral Theory, 45 Fordham L. Rev. 1281 (1977); Wilkinson and White, Constitutional Protection for Personal Lifestyles, 62 Cornell L. Rev. 563 (1977); Constitutionality of Sodomy Statutes, 45 Fordham L. Rev. 553 (1976).
[13]N.Y. Est., Powers & Trusts Law, § 4-1.2.
[14]See section 3.3, herein.
[15]Lalli v. Lalli, ––– U.S. –––, ––– L. Ed. 2d –––, 99 Sup. Ct. 518 (1978). See section 3.3, herein.

compromise agreement between the department of social welfare and the father, with the mother's approval, a court permitted the child to inherit under the provision.[16] However, the requirement that the order of filiation be made in a proceeding commenced within two years of the birth of the child is absolute (an order merely directing support without an order of filiation was, in the same case, held insufficient).[17]

The provisions of the statute which exclude paternal kindred other than the father from inheriting from the illegitimate[18] have also been upheld as constitutional.[19]

In 1968, a court drew attention to at least four areas where the current legislation may have a discriminatory effect on children of illegitimate birth.[20] Since that time, extensive legislative additions to the Family Court Act, the social services law and the domestic relations law appear to ensure that such discrimination no longer persists.[21] The Uniform Support of Dependents Act provisions controlling the support of illegitimate children are interpreted and applied so as to remove, as far as is possible, obstacles to equal treatment of the illegitimate with the legitimate child.[22] For example, an agreement between the child's biological parents providing for judicial review of the support payable if the father's income was reduced, without making provision for such review upwards if the father's income was increased, was not approved; the court indicated that, since the latter procedure would be applicable in the case of a legitimate child, not to

---

[16] In re Estate of Kennedy, 89 Misc. 2d 551, 392 N.Y.S.2d 365 (1977). See also In re Estate of Niles, 81 Misc. 2d 937, 367 N.Y.S.2d 173 (1975), upholding the right of an illegitimate to inherit from the father even though statutory procedures were not followed to the letter.

[17] In re Will of Flemm, 85 Misc. 2d 855, 381 N.Y.S.2d 573 (1975).
The provision that an order of filiation declaring paternity must be entered in a proceeding instituted within two years from the birth of the child applies equally to estates passing by will. Estate of Leventritt, 92 Misc. 2d 598, 400 N.Y.S.2d 298 (1977).

[18] N.Y. Est., Powers & Trusts Law, § 4–1.2(a)(2).

[19] In re Estate of Fay, 44 N.Y.2d 137, 404 N.Y.S.2d 554, 375 N.E.2d 735 (1978).

[20] Storm v. None, 57 Misc. 2d 342, 291 N.Y.S.2d 515 (1968).

[21] See Evans v. Matthews, 87 Misc. 2d 112, 384 N.Y.S.2d 649 (1976), affd. 55 App. Div. 2d 1047, 391 N.Y.S.2d 238 (1977).

[22] See Trent v. Loru, 57 Misc. 2d 382, 292 N.Y.S.2d 524 (1968).

incorporate such a provision in the agreement would amount to an invidious classification.[23]

In accord with the rule that the welfare of the child is the paramount consideration in determining who is to have custody of the illegitimate, custody can in a proper case be awarded to the father,[24] but the mere fact that the mother is living with another man is not regarded as evil or immoral per se, so as to warrant awarding custody to the father.[25] An unwed father, merely alleging his paternity, has standing to petition for custody of the child.[26]

Property rights of cohabitants

Contrary to the general rule,[27] when two persons who are not legally married are described as husband and wife in a deed, they take as joint tenants unless expressly declared to be tenants in common.[28] This has long been so if the deed is such as to make it clear that a tenancy by the entireties or a joint tenancy was intended.[29] But, no matter how the grantees are labeled in the title deed, if one of the spouses has defrauded the other into the belief in a valid marriage, the equities can support a constructive trust whereby the defrauded spouse can be awarded the entire land.[30]

---

[23]Storm v. None, 57 Misc. 2d 342, 291 N.Y.S.2d 515 (1968). Compare Ferrer v. Ferrer, 58 App. Div. 2d 529, 395 N.Y.S.2d 197 (1977), where the family court indicates that provision for support of illegitimates can present a sufficiently different practical problem from support of children born in wedlock so as to justify some difference in statutory treatment.
[24]See Barry W. v. Barbara K., 55 App. Div. 2d 607, 389 N.Y.S.2d 624 (1976); Pierce v. Yerkovich, 80 Misc. 2d 613, 363 N.Y.S.2d 403 (1974) (father who lived with child and mother for two and one-half years had visitation rights).
[25]S. v. J., 81 Misc. 2d 828, 367 N.Y.S.2d 405 (1975).
Prima facie, the mother of an illegitimate child, if a proper and suitable person, is the one entitled to its custody as against the father or anyone else. People ex rel. Meredith v. Meredith, 272 App. Div. 79, 69 N.Y.S.2d 462 (1947), affd. 297 N.Y. 692, 77 N.E.2d 8 (1947).
[26]Boatwright v. Otero, 91 Misc. 2d 653, 398 N.Y.S.2d 391 (1977). As to the Uniform Child Custody Jurisdiction Act, see N.Y. Dom. Rel. Law, §§ 75-a to 75-z.
[27]See section 4.2, herein.
[28]N.Y. Dom. Rel. Law, § 6-2.2(d). The statute is not applied retroactively. In re Estate of Kolodji, 85 Misc. 2d 946, 380 N.Y.S.2d 610 (1976).
[29]In re Will of Imp, 68 Misc. 2d 911, 328 N.Y.S.2d 595 (1972); Clearo v. Cook, 11 Misc. 2d 916, 175 N.Y.S.2d 455 (1958); Giudici v. Lofaso, 199 Misc. 401, 103 N.Y.S.2d 335 (1951).
[30]See Randolph v. Randolph, 28 Misc. 2d 66, 212 N.Y.S.2d 468 (1961).

Where there is no belief on either side in the existence of a marriage, though an early decision favored a tenancy in common of all assets, personal as well as real,[31] various other views have been taken. There is authority to support the proposition that, even where their relationship is adulterous, an oral agreement as to the disposition of their accumulations will be enforced on the basis of a constructive trust arising from the confidential nature of their relationship.[32] Other courts have taken into account the respective contributions of each partner in determining how these accumulations should be distributed on a termination of their relationship.[33] Where the partners pooled their earnings to purchase land taken in the man's name, another court was content to allow the wife an equitable lien, presumably to ensure restitution of her contribution.[34]

The decisions denying relief to a meretricious claimant on the basis of immorality of the consideration[35] are too old to be regarded as representative of modern judicial attitudes.[36] Whether the courts will go so far as to enforce contracts between extramarital cohabitants, the more recent authorities mentioned above

---

Where a Mexican divorce obtained by the wife was invalid and where the husband subsequently cohabited with another woman and the wife remarried, the parties still held the property as tenants by the entirety and no action for partition would lie. DeGolyer v. Schutt, 40 App. Div. 2d 943, 339 N.Y.S.2d 240 (1972).

A man already married who defrauds a woman into a bigamous marriage cannot evade alimony obligations on annulment of the bigamous marriage. Zeitlan v. Zeitlan, 31 App. Div. 2d 955, 298 N.Y.S.2d 816 (1969), affd. 26 N.Y.2d 835, 309 N.Y.S.2d 585, 258 N.E.2d 84 (1970).

[31]In re Meyron's Estate, 6 Misc. 2d 673, 164 N.Y.S.2d 443 (1957).

[32]Muller v. Sobol, 277 App. Div. 884, 97 N.Y.S.2d 905 (1950), appeal den. 277 App. Div. 951, 99 N.Y.S.2d 757 (1950). See also Schoenfeld v. Fontek, 67 Misc. 2d 481, 324 N.Y.S.2d 487 (1971), holding that an unmarried man, framing his complaint in fraud as well as unjust enrichment, may recover property given to a married woman in contemplation of a marriage that never took place.

[33]See McGreggor v. Walters, 133 Misc. 24, 230 N.Y.S. 590 (1928); Perrin v. Harrington, 146 App. Div. 292, 130 N.Y.S. 944 (1911). See also Colwell v. Zolkosky, 29 App. Div. 2d 720, 286 N.Y.S.2d 422 (1968).

[34]Marum v. Marum, 21 Misc. 2d 474, 194 N.Y.S.2d 327 (1959).

[35]E.g., In re Greene, 45 F.2d 428 (C.A.-2 N.Y., 1930); Angresani v. Tozzi, 217 App. Div. 642, 216 N.Y.S. 161 (1926), affd. 245 N.Y. 558, 157 N.E. 856 (1927); Vincent v. Moriarty, 31 App. Div. 484, 52 N.Y.S. 519 (1898).

[36]In Marriage Contracts for Support and Services: Constitutionality Begins at Home, 49 N.Y. U. L. Rev. 1161 (1974), the author criticizes the rule not permitting such contracts.

indicate that the courts are no longer disposed to ignore the equities between such parties. In McCullon v. McCullon,[37] for example, the court, after discussing with approval all of the doctrines that received recognition in the Marvin case, granted, on the basis of an implied promise, alimony and child support to a woman who had lived with a man for 28 years.

6.34. North Carolina

The state does not recognize common-law marriage.[38]

Adoption

Any person over eighteen years of age may adopt a minor child.[39] Consent requirements can be dispensed with where parental rights have been judicially terminated,[40] in which case the consent of the director of social services can be required.[41] The adoptee legally becomes a child of the adoptive parents and a stranger to the bloodline of the natural parents.[42]

Workers' compensation death benefits

Under the workers' compensation law, aside from the widow and children of a decedent, dependency, total or partial, is a question of fact.[43] The right of an illegitimate child has received recognition even where the contributions to the child's support did not extend beyond the period in which decedent was separated from the mother.[44] However, children of a "common-law" wife are

---

[37]410 N.Y.S.2d 226 (1978). The rationale, however, was also based on a finding of an out-of-state common-law marriage.
[38]N.C. Gen. Stat., § 51–6. See Shankle v. Shankle, 26 N.C. App 565, 216 S.E.2d 915 (1975).
[39]Id., §§ 48–5 to 48–7.
[40]"Abandonment," to justify termination of parental rights, must have been for six months immediately prior to the filing of the action. N.C. Gen. Stat., § 48–2(3a). See McIntosh v. McIntosh, 20 N.C. App. 742, 202 S.E.2d 804 (1974).
[41]N.C. Gen. Stat., § 48–9.
[42]Id., §§ 48–6, 48–23. See Acker v. Barnes, 33 N.C. App. 750, 236 S.E.2d 715 (1977).
[43]N.C. Gen. Stat., § 97–39.
[44]See Hewett v. Garrett, 274 N.C. 356, 163 S.E.2d 372 (1968).

not eligible since even if supported by the worker, such support was of a voluntary nature only.[45] An extramarital cohabitant does not qualify for dependency benefits.[46]

Abortion

The statute denouncing abortion[47] has a carefully worded qualification (enacted before the Supreme Court of the United States' ruling in Roe v. Wade)[48] applicable to situations, inter alia, where the physician reasonably believes the abortion necessary for the preservation of the life or health of the mother.[49]

Tort actions

The civil action for seduction is still recognized. There need be no actual promise to marry, but defendant must be shown to have induced sexual intercourse by deception, enticement, or other artifice.[50] The tort of alienation of affections, too, still receives recognition.[51]

Effect of cohabitation on right to alimony

Since alimony decrees are modifiable on a showing of changed circumstances,[52] it is probable that a divorcee who takes up

---

[45]Wilson v. Utah Constr. Co., 243 N.C. 96, 89 S.E.2d 864 (1955).
[46]Fields v. Hollowell, 238 N.C. 614, 78 S.E.2d 740 (1953).
When a subsequent marriage between the workman and his alleged wife is shown, the burden is on the earlier wife to establish the invalidity of the second marriage. Hendrix v. L. G. DeWitt, Inc., 19 N.C. App. 327, 198 S.E.2d 748 (1973).
[47]N.C. Gen. Stat., §§ 14–44 to 14–46.
[48]See section 2.19, herein.
[49]N.C. Gen. Stat., § 14–45.1. As to pregnancy resulting from rape as within the exception, see State v. Lenderman, 20 N.C. App. 687, 202 S.E.2d 787 (1974).
The state's policy of denying medicaid and aid to families with dependent children (AFDC) to needy pregnant women until birth of their child has been upheld despite arguments that such denial is an invasion of the women's constitutional rights as evidenced by legislative recognition of the right to an elective abortion. Taylor v. Hill, 420 F. Supp. 1020 (W.D. N.C., 1976).
[50]Hutchins v. Day, 269 N.C. 607, 153 S.E.2d 132 (1967).
[51]Golding v. Taylor, 23 N.C. App. 171, 208 S.E.2d 422 (1974).
[52]N.C. Gen. Stat., § 50–16.9. See Seaborn v. Seaborn, 32 N.C. App. 556, 233 S.E.2d 67 (1977).

residence with a paramour who looks after her needs would jeopardize her rights to such payments.

Possible criminal liability

Fornication and adultery are combined in a provision denouncing "lewd and lascivious association."[53] An early decision holds that there can be no fornication if the defendant does not know the other to be married,[54] but another is to the effect that adultery is merely an aggravated species of fornication.[55] Whether or not the offense is committed by unwed cohabitants, the association must be habitual and not an isolated act.[56] Provisions condemning the occupation by persons of opposite sex of the same bedroom at a hotel for immoral purposes, or falsely registering at the desk as husband and wife,[57] have been stricken for vagueness.[58] Bigamy[59] and incest[60] are proscribed, as is concealing the birth of a child.[61]

"Virtuous girls" under the age of sixteen fall under the mantle of the law's protection.[62] About a century ago a court held that, even if the girl had at some time departed from the path of virtue, if she satisfied the jury that she had "reformed" she is entitled to the protection of the statute.[63] One swallow, it would seem, does not make a summer. An unusual rider to this provision is that if the derelicts from the path of virtue agree to marry, parental consent is not required.[64]

---

[53] N.C. Gen. Stat., § 14–184. See State v. Robinson, 9 N.C. App. 433, 176 S.E.2d 253 (1970).
[54] State v. Cutshall, 109 N.C. 764, 14 S.E. 107 (1891).
[55] State v. Davis, 229 N.C. 386, 50 S.E.2d 37 (1948). Mistaken belief in divorce was a good defense to adulterous cohabitation. Harmon v. Harmon, 245 N.C. 83, 95 S.E.2d 355, 63 A.L.R.2d 808 (1956).
[56] State v. Kleinman, 241 N.C. 277, 85 S.E.2d 148 (1954); State v. Ivey, 230 N.C. 172, 52 S.E.2d 346 (1949).
[57] N.C. Gen. Stat., § 14–186.
[58] State v. Sanders, 37 N.C. 53, 245 S.E.2d 397 (1978).
[59] N.C. Gen. Stat., § 14–183.
[60] Id., §§ 14–178, 14–179.
[61] Id., § 14–16.
[62] Id., § 14–26. A female who carnally knows any male under sixteen also commits a misdemeanor. Id., § 14.21 et seq.
[63] State v. Grigg, 104 N.C. 882, 10 S.E. 684 (1890).
[64] N.C. Gen. Stat., § 14–27. For a more recent challenge to the constitutionality

NORTH CAROLINA   6.34

The statute denouncing sodomy[65] has withstood constitutional attacks,[66] including one based on the argument that homosexuality is a disease, and as such cannot be made criminal.[67]

Status of children

The offspring of a voidable or bigamous marriage are legitimate;[68] however, the fact that paternity has been established by a civil proceeding does not have the effect of legitimating the child.[69] The presumption that a child born of a woman during her marriage is legitimate, though labeled a conclusive presumption, is not conclusive where the wife is living in open and notorious adultery.[70]

An illegitimate child can take on the death intestate of the mother, and it qualifies as an intestate heir of the father if paternity has been judicially established, or has been acknowledged in writing filed during his life with a court.[71] The further provision, that an illegitimate child cannot take as a successor to the father's estate unless he has given written notice of the basis of his claim to the personal representative of the putative father within six months after first publication of notice to creditors,[72] though it does place an extra burden on the illegitimate as distinguished from the legitimate child, is probably constitutionally defensible.[73]

A child can be legitimated by subsequent marriage of the

---

of the statute defining the crime of taking indecent liberties with a child under sixteen, see State v. Vehaun, 34 N.C. App. 700, 239 S.E.2d 705 (1977).

[65] N.C. Gen. Stat., § 14–177. See State v. Joyner, 295 N.C. 55, 243 S.E.2d 367 (1978), holding the crime not to be limited to penetration by the male organ.

[66] State v. Enslin, 25 N.C. App. 662, 214 S.E.2d 318 (1975), appeal dismissed 288 N.C. 245, 217 S.E.2d 669 (1975), cert. den. 425 U.S. 903, 47 L. Ed. 2d 753, 96 Sup. Ct. 1492 (1976), reh. den. 425 U.S. 985, 48 L. Ed. 2d 810, 96 Sup. Ct. 2193 (1976); State v. Jarrell, 24 N.C. App. 610, 211 S.E.2d 837 (1975).

[67] State v. Stubbs, 266 N.C. 295, 145 S.E.2d 899 (1966).

[68] N.C. Gen. Stat., § 50–11.1.

[69] Id., § 49–14.

[70] See Wake County Child Support Enforcement v. Matthews, 36 N.C. App. 316, 244 S.E.2d 191 (1978).

[71] N.C. Gen. Stat., § 29–19. As to the rights of illegitimates under the will of an acknowledged father, see §§ 29–19(d), 31–5.5.

[72] Id., § 29–19(b).

[73] See section 3.3, herein.

parents.[74] Further, a putative father can petition the court for its legitimation.[75] Once legitimated, the child qualifies for succession as those born in lawful wedlock.[76]

Proceedings for legitimation, establishment of paternity and support of illegitimates[77] are required to be brought within three years of the birth of the child or within three years after a father has defaulted in his support obligations. Blood grouping tests, even when they demonstrate nonpaternity, are not regarded as conclusive of the issue.[78] There is a rebuttable presumption that a child born more than ten lunar months or 280 days after the death of the putative father had not been conceived at the time of such death.[79]

Statutes provide for the investigation by the district attorney of situations of nonsupport of illegitimates.[80] Nonsupport is a continuing offense, not barred by a previous conviction for the same offense,[81] for which either parent may be prosecuted.[82] However, there can be no conviction of the father under the nonsupport statute[83] unless paternity has been established,[84] if necessary by a proceeding initiated by the child itself.[85]

---

[74]N.C. Gen. Stat., § 49–12.

[75]Id., § 49–10.

[76]Id., § 29–18. See also § 49–11. And see Illegitimate Child v. The State of North Carolina: Is There a Justifiable Controversy Under the New Constitutional Standards?, 6 N.C. Central L. J. 207 (1975).

[77]See N.C. Gen. Stat., §§ 49–1 to 49–16.

[78]State v. Fowler, 277 N.C. 305, 177 S.E.2d 385 (1970).

[79]Byerly v. Tolbert, 250 N.C. 27, 108 S.E.2d 29 (1959).

[80]N.C. Gen. Stat., § 15–155.1 et seq.

[81]State v. Smith, 246 N.C. 118, 97 S.E.2d 442 (1957).

Prosecution of alleged father for willful neglect or refusal to support his illegitimate child may be initiated by the mother, but since the purpose of the statute is to protect the child and to protect the state against its becoming a public burden, she need not be joined in the action. Tidwell v. Booker, 290 N.C. 98, 225 S.E.2d 816 (1976).

[82]Tidwell v. Booker, supra. Generally, see N.C. Gen. Stat., §§ 14–325, 14–326 and 49–2.

[83]N.C. Gen. Stat., § 49–2.

[84]State v. Ingle, 20 N.C. App. 50, 200 S.E.2d 427 (1973).

[85]The child can, under N.C. Gen. Stat., § 49–14, initiate the action. Wright v. Gann, 27 N.C. App. 45, 217 S.E.2d 761 (1975).

As to the Uniform Reciprocal Enforcement of Support Act, see N.C. Gen. Stat., § 52A-1 et seq.

Property rights of cohabitants

North Carolina recognizes the well-established view that where the grantees in a deed to land are referred to as husband and wife and they are not married, they hold as tenants in common.[86] On a partition, each is therefore entitled to one half of the income derived from the property.[87]

Support is also to be found for the proposition that a woman who is induced to believe in the legality of a marriage can recover for her services less the value of the support she has received during the relationship.[88]

Contracts in consideration of past cohabitation have been upheld,[89] and at least one early court ruled that a continued cohabitation will not invalidate an agreement for compensation for past cohabitation as long as the continued cohabitation is not the real consideration for the contract.[90] In light of the current view that a married couple are not free to replace the law controlling their mutual rights and obligations by their own agreements,[91] it is probable that the courts would recognize and enforce an extramarital agreement as to the property rights of the partners unless an exchange of sexual favors forms an explicit part of the consideration for such a contract.[92]

The right to custody, absent a showing of unfitness, is in the mother even if she has relinquished the child to relations. In re Jones, 14 N.C. App. 334, 188 S.E.2d 580 (1972). Custody orders are enforceable by civil contempt proceedings, or violations thereof are punishable by criminal contempt proceedings. N.C. Gen. Stat., § 50–13.3.

[86] Grant v. Toatley, 244 N.C. 463, 94 S.E.2d 305 (1956).
[87] Lawrence v. Heavner, 232 N.C. 557, 61 S.E.2d 697 (1950).
[88] Saunders v. Ragan, 172 N.C. 612, 90 S.E. 777 (1916).
[89] Burton v. Belvin, 142 N.C. 151, 55 S.E. 71 (1906).
[90] Brown v. Kinsey, 81 N.C. 245 (1879).
[91] See Merritt, Changing Marital Rights and Duties by Contract: Legal Obstacles in North Carolina, 13 Wake Forest L. Rev. 85 (1977).
[92] In Ross v. Sampson, 4 N.C. App. 270, 166 S.E.2d 499 (1969), during an eighteen-year cohabitation, the defendant bought property with the plaintiff's earnings and took title in her own name. He believed they would each have a one-half interest. The court imposed a trust on the defendant in favor of plaintiff for a one-half interest in the property.

6.35. North Dakota

Common-law marriages have not been recognized since 1890.[93] Of possible interest to extramarital cohabitants, however, is that a marriage which is voidable for nonage or as having been induced by force is not annullable if the victim freely cohabited with the other as husband or wife after receiving knowledge of the voidability of the relationship.[94]

Discrimination in public places

There is a statute designed to protect persons against discrimination in public places on grounds of sex, race, color, religion or national origins.[95] By reason of its wording, it is conceivable that the statute could afford a basis for prosecution of one who refuses to permit cohabitants "to exercise [their] rights to full and equal enjoyment of any facility open to the public."[96]

Schoolteachers

The superintendent of public instruction is required to suspend, revoke or annul a teacher's certificate for immorality.[97] Whether the courts will construe legislation of this nature in a way favorable to, or inimical to, unmarried partners can only be a matter of speculation.

Adoption

It is a felony to place or cause to be placed any child other than one's own child in family homes for adoption without a license from the social services board of the state.[98] Only licensed child-

---

[93] Schumacher v. Great Northern Ry. Co., 23 N.D. 231, 136 N.W. 85 (1912); Woodward v. Blake, 38 N.D. 38, 164 N.W. 156, L.R.A. 1918A, Ann. Cas. 1918E 552 (1917). As to what constitutes marriage, see N.D. Cent. Code, § 14–03–01.
[94] N.D. Cent. Code, § 14–04–01.
[95] Id., § 12.1–14–04.
[96] Id.
[97] Id., § 15–36–15. See Behling, Jr., Legal Gravity of Specific Acts in Cases of Teacher Dismissal, 43 N.D. L. Rev. 753 (1967).
[98] N.D. Cent. Code, § 50–12–17.

placing agencies can place children in a foster home or place them for adoption.[99]

Any adult may adopt a person, as may a married couple, even if one or both are minors. As is standard procedure, a married adopter must ordinarily either join the spouse or obtain spousal consent to the adoption.[1]

It has been held that, where a child has not been legitimized, the mother's consent to the adoption is all that is required.[2] But the Uniform Adoption Act, enacted in North Dakota in 1971, requires notice and an opportunity to be heard to be given to the "parents" of the child.[3] And under the Uniform Parentage Act, enacted in 1975,[4] the parent and child relationship extends equally to every child and to every parent, regardless of the marital status of the parents.[5] A case might well arise where the attitude of a biological father who is willing and able to assume responsibility for the child could carry a lot of weight in the adoption proceedings.[6]

Workers' compensation death benefits

The workers' compensation statute[7] is silent as to the right of illegitimate children to benefits payable on the death of a worker, but under the Uniform Parentage Act[8] if dependency is shown, the nonmarital status of the parents would be disregarded.

---

[99]Id., §§ 50–12–01 to 50–12–17.
[1]See N.D. Cent. Code, § 14–15–03 as to who may adopt.
[2]In re Klundt, 196 N.W.2d 76 (N.D., 1972). As to whose consent is required for adoption, see N.D. Cent. Code, §§ 14–15–03, 14–15–05, 14–15–06.
[3]N.D. Cent. Code, § 14–15–19(6).
[4]Id., §§ 14–17–01 to 14–17–26.
[5]Id., § 14–17–02.
[6]See Kottsick v. Carlson, 241 N.W.2d 842 (N.D., 1976) ("The best interests of the child," as the phrase is used in termination of parental rights in an adoption, takes on another meaning from that given in a custody hearing in divorce proceedings, and includes, among other things, "the total relationship between child and parent pertaining to and involving heterogenous values, rights, duties, and concepts").
[7]N.D. Cent. Code, § 65–05–17 et seq.
[8]Id., § 14–17–02.

6.35   UNMARRIED COUPLES AND THE LAW

Abortion

An abortion statute which excepted from criminal liability only a person who procured an abortion to save the mother's life was held violative of due process.[9] As a result the new Abortion Control Act[10] reflects substantial compliance with the Supreme Court's decisions.[11] One provision that may invite challenge is the requirement of the written consent of the husband, or of the person responsible as parent or guardian of an unwed minor, after the fetus has become viable unless to obviate grave risk to the mother's life or health.[12]

Recovery for wrongful death

The wrongful death statute[13] names only the surviving spouse, or a child, or a parent, or the decedent's personal representative as proper persons to bring suit. But here again the Uniform Parentage Act, in effect equating illegitimate with legitimate children, assumes obvious relevance.[14] It is hardly conceivable that an extramarital cohabitant would have any rights under the Act.

Tort actions

The tort of alienation of affections has judicial recognition.[15] By statute, the torts of breach of promise to marry,[16] and abduction or enticement of a husband or of a wife from the other spouse, or of a parent from its child, or of seduction of a wife or daughter,[17] are still recognized. However, an unmarried female cannot recover in her own right for her seduction; she can only sue for the support of any resultant offspring.[18]

---

[9] Leigh v. Olson, 385 F. Supp. 255 (D. N.D., 1974).
[10] N.D. Cent. Code, §§ 14–02.1–01 to 14–02.1–12.
[11] See section 2.19, herein.
[12] N.D. Cent. Code, § 14–02.1–03.
[13] Id., § 32–21–03.
[14] Id., § 14–17–02.
[15] Rott v. Goehring, 33 N.D. 413, 157 N.W. 294 (1916).
[16] N.D. Cent. Code, § 32–03–19.
[17] Id., § 14–02–06.
[18] Ingwaldson v. Skrivseth, 7 N.D. 388, 75 N.W. 772 (1898). See also Braun v.

Possible criminal liability

The crimes of seduction and abduction have been removed from the statute books, but one who lives "openly and notoriously" with one of the opposite sex without being married to that person commits a misdemeanor.[19] The relationship has to partake of the quality of the living together as a married couple: it must be undisguised, unconcealed and not hidden and secret.[20] It does not appear to make any difference whether the couple announce to the world that they are or are not married.

Among other sex crimes[21] are: fornication, which involves sex in a public place,[22] adultery,[23] bigamy,[24] and incest.[25] The offense in the nature of statutory rape receives attention in a provision denouncing "gross sexual imposition" (victim less than fifteen years old),[26] "corruption of minors" (if the actor is a minor, fifteen years or older),[27] and "sexual assault" (if the victim is a minor, fifteen or over, and the actor is an adult).[28] Mistake as to the age is no defense when the victim is under fifteen.[29] A person who performs a deviate sexual act "with intent to arouse or gratify his sexual desire" commits a misdemeanor.[30]

It is a misdemeanor to conceal the stillbirth of a fetus or to fail to report to a physician or to the county coroner the death of an infant under two years of age.[31]

Status of children

For the purposes of intestate succession, an adopted child is the child of the adopting parent and not of the natural parents. How-

---

Heidrich, 62 N.D. 85, 241 N.W. 599, 79 A.L.R. 1221 (1932) (female who engages in a voluntary sexual act cannot sue the male).

[19] N.D. Cent. Code, § 12.1–20–10.
[20] State v. Hoffman, 68 N.D. 610, 282 N.W. 407 (1938).
[21] N.D. Cent. Code, §§ 12.1–20–01 to 12.1–20–15.
[22] Id., § 12.1–20–08.
[23] Id., § 12.1–20–09.
[24] Id., § 12.1–20–13.
[25] Id., § 12.1–20–11. As to the forbidden degrees of marriage, see § 14–03–03.
[26] Id., § 12.1–20–03(d).
[27] Id., § 12.1–20–05.
[28] Id., § 12.1–20–07.
[29] Id., § 12.1–20–01.
[30] Id., § 12.1–20–12.
[31] Id., § 14–02.1–10.

ever, adoption of a child by the spouse of a natural parent has no effect on the relationship of the child and either natural parent.[32]

Where there has been no adoption, the statute provides that a person is the child of its parents regardless of the marital status of its parents and the parent and child relationship may be established under the Uniform Parentage Act.[33] This resulted from a judgment that the prior statute, requiring intermarriage of the parents and the father's acknowledgment of the child as his as a precondition of inheritance, was unconstitutional.[34]

A provision of the Uniform Parentage Act is to the effect that an action brought by or on behalf of a child to establish paternity is not barred until three years after the child reaches the age of majority, but that this does not extend the time within which a right to succession may be asserted beyond the time provided by law relating to distribution and closing of decedents' estates.[35] This latter clause seems to indicate that where a mother has not sued to establish paternity and is barred by her delay, the child must assert its right to succession within the time provided for the closing of probate. Such a construction would probably be regarded as a legitimate limitation on the right to succession and not an invidious discrimination against illegitimates, by reason of the public interest in the expedition of the settlement of decedents' estates and the elimination of spurious claims long after lapse of time has prevented their validity from being established.

Legitimation of an illegitimate child can be effected by a subsequent marriage of the parents,[36] by an adjudication of paternity,[37] and by adoption.[38] The father can adopt and legitimize a minor simply by a public acknowledgment of the child as his, receiving it into his home with the consent of his wife, if he is married, and otherwise treating it as legitimate.[39]

---

[32]Id., § 30.1-04-09(1).
[33]Id., § 30.1-04-09(2).
[34]In re Estate of Jensen, 162 N.W.2d 861 (N.D., 1968).
[35]N.D. Cent. Code, § 14-17-06. See also § 30.1-04-09 (Probate Code).
Application of the Uniform Parentage Act retroactively, even to the extent of reviving causes of action previously barred, does not violate due process. In re W.M.V., 268 N.W.2d 781 (N.D., 1978).
[36]Id., § 14-09-02.
[37]Id., §§ 14-17-14, 23-02.1-18, 30.1-04-09.
[38]Id., §§ 14-15-01 to 14-15-23.
[39]Id., § 14-15-20.

OHIO 6.36

As to custody of the illegitimate,[40] parental rights can be judicially terminated on proper notice and opportunity for a hearing[41] where evidence of unfitness is presented.[42]

The fact that illegitimate births are to be reported at once to the division of child welfare[43] does not mean that abundant provision is lacking to ensure that the illegitimacy of a person's origin not be made public knowledge.[44]

Property rights of cohabitants

Perhaps because cohabitation is regarded as criminal in North Dakota,[45] any disputes that may have arisen as to the rights of such cohabitants in the accumulations of the partnership have not reached the higher courts of the state. There are dicta indicating a joint venture,[46] if established, would receive recognition.[47]

6.36. Ohio

A common-law marriage, though disfavored by the courts as contravening public policy,[48] will receive recognition on clear and convincing evidence of an agreement to marry *in praesenti*[49] made by parties competent to contract which is followed by cohabitation as husband and wife as a result of which they are treated and reputed in the community as spouses.[50] Adoption by

---

[40]Id., § 14-09-05.
[41]In Interest of R. H., 262 N.W.2d 719 (N.D., 1978).
[42]See Waagen v. R. J. B., 248 N.W.2d 815 (N.D., 1976). As to Uniform Child Custody Jurisdiction Act, see N.D. Cent. Code, §§ 14-14-01 to 14-14-26.
[43]N.D. Cent. Code, § 50-20-01.
[44]See, e.g., N.D. Cent. Code, §§ 23-02.1-25, 23-02.1-27, Chapter 50-20.
[45]Id., § 12.1-20-10.
[46]See section 4.3, herein.
[47]See Marriage—Restitution or Other Disposition of Property and Compensation—Right of Putative Wife to Property Jointly Accumulated, 28 N.D. L. Rev. 322 (1952).
A contract in restraint of marriage is void. N.D. Cent. Code, § 9-08-07.

[48]United States v. Goble, 512 F.2d 458 (C.A.-6 Ky., 1975) cert. den. 423 U.S. 914, 46 L. Ed. 2d 143, 96 Sup. Ct. 221 (1975) (relationship did not require exclusion of witness' testimony in prosecution of cohabitant).
[49]As to the requirement of words of the present tense, see section 1.5, herein.
[50]Jolley v. Jolley, 46 Ohio Misc. 40, 347 N.E.2d 557 (1975). See Ohio Rev. Code Ann., § 3105.12.

the woman of the man's name is not alone sufficient, but failure to do so goes far to disprove that they held themselves out as husband and wife.[51] A continued cohabitation after removal of some impediment to the purported marriage can, if all these requirements are met, result in a common-law marriage.[52]

Housing discrimination

A decision of the Supreme Court of the United States, pronouncing unconstitutional a housing ordinance limiting the occupancy of a dwelling unit to members of a single family, with a highly restrictive definition of the term "family," may have its impact on unmarried couples who may encounter housing obstacles based on their nonfamilial relationship.[53]

Schoolteachers

Of passing interest to cohabitants is a dictum to the effect that heterosexual misconduct is no ground for termination of employment as a teacher.[54]

Welfare assistance

A provision applicable to the program for aid to families with dependent children (AFDC) which requires an unwed mother or a caretaker relative of an illegitimate child to assign all rights to

---

[51]State v. Durham, 49 Ohio App. 2d 231, 360 N.E.2d 743 (1976). See also Respole v. Respole, 34 Ohio Ops. 1, 70 N.E.2d 465, 170 A.L.R. 942 (1946) (proxy marriage, even if construed as a contract to marry *in praesenti,* does not establish a common-law marriage absent cohabitation or other conduct amounting to a consummation or ratification of the purported marriage); Merritt v. Chevrolet Tonawanda Division, General Motors Corp., 50 App. Div. 2d 1018, 377 N.Y.S.2d 663 (1975) (overnight visits to Ohio where friends believed the parties were married did not establish a marital agreement).

[52]See Johnson v. Wolford, 117 Ohio St. 136, 157 N.E. 385 (1927).

[53]The constitutional protection of the sanctity of the family extended to family choice in a situation where descendants lived with a grandmother. It is not confined within an arbitrary boundary drawn at the limits of the "nuclear family" consisting of a couple and their dependent children. Moore v. City of East Cleveland, Ohio, 431 U.S. 494, 52 L. Ed. 2d 531, 97 Sup. Ct. 1932 (1977).

[54]Jarvella v. Willoughby-Eastlake City School Dist. Bd. of Education, 12 Ohio Misc. 288, 233 N.E.2d 143 (1967).

OHIO 6.36

support she may have to the state and to assist the authorities in establishing paternity may be constitutionally vulnerable.[55]

Adoption

Provisions of a standard nature control the right of a single person, or of a married person with the consent or co-operation of the spouse, to adopt a minor.[56] To adopt an adult, the consent of the adoptee is ordinarily essential.[57] Detailed provision is made as to whose consent is required for the adoption of a minor. The statute virtually ensures that any putative father who has evinced any active interest in the child's welfare cannot be ignored in such proceedings.[58] Private placements are possible only if *prior* to placement the parents have the approval of the probate court. Following the application for approval, the department of public welfare investigates the proposed placement. A full account of all value that has been exchanged, in agency as well as in private adoptions, must be approved before any decree will issue.[59] Expenses so allowable are tightly restricted. The statute also provides for an annual review of every child in the care of an agency or individual certified to care for or place children for adoption.[60] Though recommendations of an authorized agency are likely to be accepted, it is the court before which the petition is brought that has the last word.[61]

Workers' compensation death benefits

The word "child" as relating to dependent children's death benefits under the Workers' Compensation Act[62] covers legitimate

---

[55]See Civil Liberties Versus Governmental Interest: A Constitutional Context for the Impact of Title IV-D of the Social Security Act on Ohio Families in the Aid to Families with Dependent Children Program, 5 Capital U. L. Rev. 244 (1976). See also Gotherman, Ohio Privacy Act, 7 Capital U. L. Rev. 177 (1977).

[56]Ohio Rev. Code Ann., § 3107.03.

[57]Id., § 3107.02.

[58]Id., § 3107.06(F).

[59]Id., § 3107.10.

[60]For a detailed survey of the controlling provisions, see Sylvester, Revised Law of Adoption in Ohio, 7 Capital U. L. Rev. 219 (1977).

[61]See In re Haun, 31 Ohio App. 2d 63, 286 N.E.2d 478 (1972). Generally, see Yost, Adoption Laws of Ohio: A Critical and Comparative Study, 21 Clev. St. L. Rev. 1 (1972).

[62]Ohio Rev. Code Ann., § 4123.59.

and adopted children.[63] One early decision excludes illegitimates.[64] A spouse by a bigamous marriage does not qualify;[65] however, a common-law wife qualified where the worker's first wife had not been heard from for over seven years prior to the commencement of the common-law marriage.[66]

Abortion

To be legal, abortions must be performed by a licensed physician.[67] The informed consent of the woman must be obtained.[68] A provision requiring the consent of a minor's parents or guardian[69] has been held unconstitutional on the ground that it authorizes an absolute and possibly arbitrary veto, and is not susceptible to a construction that it merely provides some parental input into the mother's decision-making process.[70]

One who fails to take proper measures to protect the life of an aborted infant commits "abortion manslaughter," a felony of the first degree.[71] And experimentation on or sale of an aborted fetus is denounced as "abortion trafficking."[72]

Life insurance benefits

For the purposes of a substitute beneficiary clause of a group life insurance policy, a court has construed the word "children" to embrace all offspring of the insured (who did not name a beneficiary), regardless of legitimacy.[73]

---

[63] Miller v. Industrial Comm., 165 Ohio St. 584, 138 N.E.2d 672 (1956).
[64] Welsh v. Industrial Comm., 136 Ohio St. 387, 26 N.E.2d 198 (1940).
[65] Evans v. Industrial Comm., 166 Ohio St. 413, 143 N.E.2d 705 (1957).
[66] See White v. Industrial Comm., 102 Ohio App. 236, 142 N.E.2d 549 (1956).
[67] Ohio Rev. Code Ann., § 2919.11.
[68] Id., § 2919.12.
[69] Id., § 2919.12(B).
[70] Hoe v. Brown, 446 F. Supp. 329 (N.D. Ohio, 1976).
[71] Ohio Rev. Code Ann., § 2919.13.
[72] Id., § 2919.14. Generally, see Symposium: Abortion and the Law—George, Jr., The Evolving Law of Abortion, 23 Case W. Res. L. Rev. 705, 708 (1972); Pilpel and Zuckerman, Abortion and the Rights of Minors, 23 Case W. Res. L. Rev. 705, 779 (1972); Swan, Compulsory Abortion: Next Challenge to Liberated Women?, 3 Ohio North. L. Rev. 152 (1975).
[73] Butcher v. Pollard, 32 Ohio App. 2d 1, 288 N.E.2d 204, 62 A.L.R.3d 1316 (1972).

Recovery for wrongful death

For the purposes of the wrongful death statute,[74] the word "children" is held not to extend to posthumous illegitimate children, regardless of whether the decedent had acknowledged his paternity.[75]

Effect of cohabitation on right to alimony

The courts have no difficulty in awarding alimony to a wife divorced on grounds of adultery;[76] however, even absent a stipulation or condition of the award that it is to be terminable in the event of her cohabitation with another,[77] at least one court has terminated a woman's right to alimony (excluding arrearages due by the ex-husband) for this reason.[78]

Tort actions

Civil actions for breach of promise of marriage, alienation of affections, criminal conversation and for seduction of a woman of age and capacity to consent have been abolished.[79]

Possible criminal liability

Many forms of sexual misconduct, once denounced, have been removed from the statute books. These include seduction, adultery and fornication, and consensual sodomy. Provisions criminalizing "sexual imposition"[80] and "felonious sexual penetration"[81] are in effect restricted to situations where force or improper duress is resorted to or where the actor knows the other participant does not consent or is for some reason incapable of giving an effective consent. Whatever consenting adults may choose to do privately, in the area of human sexual relations, is

---

[74] Ohio Rev. Code Ann., § 2125.02 et seq.
[75] Bonewit v. Weber, 95 Ohio App. 428, 120 N.E.2d 738 (1952).
[76] See Rabin v. Rabin, 118 Ohio App. 446, 195 N.E.2d 377 (1962).
[77] See Fahrer v. Fahrer, 36 Ohio App. 2d 208, 304 N.E.2d 411 (1973).
[78] Bishop v. Bishop, 18 Ohio Misc. 177, 248 N.E.2d 641 (1969).
[79] Ohio Rev. Code Ann., § 2305.29.
[80] Id., § 2907.06.
[81] Id., § 2907.12.

legal.[82] An obscenity statute[83] which fails to specify the types of sexual conduct that are forbidden has been held unconstitutionally vague.[84] Any married person who married another, or who continues in cohabitation with such other in the state, commits bigamy,[85] but a five-year continuous absence of the true spouse prior to such marriage, if the spouse was not known to be alive within that time, is a defense.[86]

The gravity of sexual offenses relating to minors depends largely on the relative ages of the defendant and the other participant. Unless the latter is under fifteen years of age, however, none of these provisions would appear applicable.[87]

Status of children

The issue of all void marriages are legitimate.[88]

In addition to provision for the legitimation of a child by a marriage of its parents,[89] an unwed father may initiate a judicial proceeding to have his paternity adjudicated. Consent of the mother or, if she is deceased or incompetent, of the legal custodian, is required.[90] This statute, in order to preserve its constitutionality in the face of a challenge that it denies equal protection to illegitimates whose father chooses not to initiate such a procedure, had been judicially expanded to afford all illegitimate children an opportunity to become legitimated by themselves filing an application for legitimation.[91] Once paternity is established by clear and convincing evidence, acknowledgment by the father and consent of the mother are not required.[92]

The statute relating to intestate succession permits an illegiti-

---

[82]City of Columbus v. Scott, 47 Ohio App. 2d 287, 353 N.E.2d 858 (1975).
[83]Ohio Rev. Code Ann., § 2907.01(F).
[84]Sovereign News Co. v. Falke, 448 F. Supp. 306 (N.D. Ohio, 1977).
[85]Ohio Rev. Code Ann., § 2919.01.
[86]Id.
[87]Id., § 2907.01 et seq. As to rape, see § 2941.25 (A),(B).
[88]Id., § 3105.33.
[89]See Burse v. Burse, 48 Ohio App. 244, 356 N.E.2d 755 (1976); Comer v. Comer, 119 Ohio App. 529, 200 N.E.2d 656 (1962), affd. 175 Ohio St. 313, 194 N.E.2d 572 (1963).
[90]Ohio Rev. Code Ann., § 2105.18. As to registration of legitimation, see § 3705.15.
[91]In re Minor of Martin, 51 Ohio App. 2d 21, 365 N.E.2d 892 (1977).
[92]Id.

mate to inherit from and through its mother, but is silent as to the father.[93] It was once held that the equal protection clause of the Fourteenth Amendment mandates that the word "child" include all illegitimate children, whether or not the father has acknowledged or adopted them.[94] A later decision, however, finds no invidious discrimination in the statute.[95] Since that holding, the ruling in Trimble v. Gordon[96] removes all doubt. The statute is unconstitutional, and whether an expansive judicial construction can correct the infirmity is open to some dispute.[97]

Support and custody

The statute relating to establishment of paternity,[98] though referred to as "quasi-criminal,"[99] uses the language of the criminal law. For example, the proceeding is initiated by a complaint "charging" a person with being the father; whereupon the judge issues a warrant directing the law enforcement authorities to "pursue and arrest the accused person" to have him answer.[1] Provisions for the imprisonment of an indigent adjudicated father for inability to pay support awarded have been stricken as unconstitutional.[2]

---

[93] Ohio Rev. Code Ann., § 2105.17.

[94] Green v. Woodard, 40 Ohio App. 2d 101, 318 N.E.2d 397 (1974). An illegitimate can inherit from his stepfather where the mother, who predeceased him, would have so inherited. Kest v. State, 77 Ohio Abs. 193, 146 N.E.2d 755 (1957), affd. 169 Ohio St. 317, 159 N.E.2d 449 (1959).

[95] Moore v. Dague, 46 Ohio App. 2d 75, 345 N.E.2d 449 (1975).

[96] See section 3.3, herein.

[97] In Moore v. Dague, note 95, supra, the court, while deploring the stigma so often attached to the illegitimate who had no choice in his origin, expressed inability to ignore the doctrine of separation of powers by substituting its own judgment for that of the legislature. See Note, Constitutional Law—Equal Protection—Descent and Distribution—Illegitimates—Statute That Prohibits Inheritance by Illegitimate from Father Denies Equal Protection, 44 U. Cin. L. Rev. 415 (1975).

[98] Ohio Rev. Code Ann., § 3111.01 et seq.

[99] See Walker v. Stokes, 45 Ohio App. 2d 275, 344 N.E.2d 159 (1975), holding, inter alia, that a defendant who cannot afford a blood test has a right to have this test at public expense.

[1] Ohio Rev. Code Ann., § 3111.01.

[2] Walker v. Stokes, 54 Ohio App. 2d 119, 375 N.E.2d 1258 (1977) (also holding that proof that a mother was unmarried when she filed a complaint in bastardy is a necessary element, though a married woman may sue in the court of common pleas for past or future support for the child).

6.36 UNMARRIED COUPLES AND THE LAW

It is now settled that the illegitimate child has a constitutional right to enforce the father's obligations of support, which can be asserted against his estate.[3]

When a man marries knowing his bride to be pregnant by another, the courts have not been in harmony as to whether such a marriage constitutes a consent to stand in loco parentis to the child. The latest holding on this question is to the effect that it does, and that the biological father is relieved from any support obligations.[4] But perhaps it would be unfair to regard this presumption that he assumes such responsibility as conclusive.[5]

As to the rights to custody of the illegitimate child, Ohio courts recognize the existence of a distinction between a "putative" father and one who has been adjudicated the father, but a ruling[6] that the former was not on an equal basis with the mother in respect of rights to custody, notwithstanding Stanley v. Illinois,[7] has been overturned.[8] Since any putative father has the right to initiate proceedings to establish his paternity, any presumption of his unfitness would deny him equal protection as it would deny equal protection to any adjudicated or acknowledged father.[9] He has legal standing to seek custody against the mother, and the determination will rest on the child's best interests.

---

[3] In re Estate of Holley, 44 Ohio Misc. 78, 337 N.E.2d 675 (1975). For the Uniform Reciprocal Enforcement of Support Act, see Ohio Rev. Code Ann., §§ 3115.01 to 3115.34.

[4] See Hall v. Rosen, 50 Ohio St. 2d 135, 363 N.E.2d 725 (1977).

[5] See Belk v. Belk, 13 Ohio App. 2d 212, 235 N.E.2d 530 (1968). Compare Miller v. Anderson, 43 Ohio St. 473, 3 N.E. 605 (1885).

[6] In re H., 37 Ohio Misc. 123, 305 N.E.2d 815 (1973), holding that a mother does not by her interracial marriage forfeit her superior right of custody to that of the putative father.

[7] Discussed in sections 3.6 and 3.8, herein.

[8] In re Wright, 52 Ohio Misc. 4, 367 N.E.2d 931 (1977). See also In re Connolly, 43 Ohio App. 2d 38, 332 N.E.2d 376 (1974); Lauerman, Nonmarital Sexual Conduct and Child Custody, 46 U. Cin. L. Rev. 647 (1977); Schwartz, Rights of a Father with Regard to His Illegitimate Child, 36 Ohio S. L. J. 1 (1975); Uniform Child Custody Jurisdiction Act: Its Provisions and Effects in Ohio, 7 Capital U. L. Rev. 453 (1978).

[9] In re Wright, supra.

Property rights of cohabitants

Beyond a provision that a contract the consideration for which is sexual favors is illegal,[10] problems surrounding the adjustment of property rights between cohabiting couples do not as yet appear to have received legislative or judicial attention.

Restitution of property transferred to one who innocently believed in the validity of the marriage has been denied to the transferor who had knowledge of its invalidity.[11] Further, a knowingly bigamous cohabitant has been denied the status of a putative spouse or of a common-law wife for the purpose of adjusting the equities between them on a dissolution of the relationship.[12] Decisions of this nature, however, do not compel any conclusion that the courts of Ohio would not respect the agreements, express or implicit, made between unmarried persons who decide to take up residence together.

6.37. Oklahoma

Given direct evidence of an agreement "per verba de praesenti"[13] between parties competent to contract common-law marriage, and cohabitation as man and wife,[14] such marriages are recognized.[15]

A remarriage to another, or cohabitation with another within six months of divorce, is punishable as bigamy or adultery,[16] and affords grounds for annulment of any such marriage.[17] However, if a divorced person improperly enters into a common-law marriage before six months have elapsed from the divorce, a continued cohabitation after this inhibition has been removed will ripen

---

[10]Ohio Rev. Code Ann., §§ 2907.01, 2907.24, 2907.25.
[11]Kontner v. Kontner, 103 Ohio App. 360, 139 N.E.2d 366 (1956).
[12]Rakestraw v. City of Cincinnati, 69 Ohio App. 504, 44 N.E.2d 278 (1942). Generally, see Reaching Equal Protection Under Law: Alternative Forms of Family and the Changing Face of Monogamous Marriage, 1975 Det. Coll. L. Rev. 95.
[13]In re Estate of Hornback, 475 P.2d 184 (Okla., 1970).
[14]In re Estate of Rogers, 569 P.2d 536 (Okla. App., 1977).
[15]In re Estate of Bouse, 583 P.2d 514 (Okla. App., 1978); United States v. Eaton, 485 F.2d 102 (C.A.-10 Okla., 1973). As to the status of tribal or Indian-custom marriages, see Deo v. State, 272 P.2d 473 (Okla. App., 1954).
[16]Okla. Stat. Ann., tit. 12, § 1280.
[17]Id., § 1281.

an adulterous relationship into a valid common-law marriage.[18] Further, a divorced couple may remarry each other at any time, if only by compliance with the requisites of a common-law marriage.[19] If this is done, the divorce is a nullity. The obligations of the parties with regard to their children are as if they had never been divorced; thus, a child support order would not be enforceable by contempt proceedings or otherwise.[20] Similarly, a continued cohabitation after an underage party reaches the age to marry can become a common-law marriage.[21]

Once established, a common-law marriage can only be terminated by divorce.[22] The burden of showing the existence of a common-law marriage is on the party asserting it.[23]

Adoption

The following persons are eligible to adopt a child: (1) A husband and wife jointly, or either the husband or wife if the other spouse is a parent of the child; (2) an unmarried person who is at least 21 years old; (3) a married person at least 21 years old who is legally separated from the other spouse; and (4) in the case of a child born out of wedlock, its unmarried father or mother.[24]

Ordinarily, the written consent of both parents of the adoptee is required unless parental rights have been judicially terminated. Detailed provision is made for the obtaining of consent of substitutes in the event of the unavailability of the parents for consent.[25] Though the statute provides that, if the child is born out of wedlock, the mother, if sixteen years of age or older, shall be

---

[18]In re Estate of Dowell, 574 P.2d 1089 (Okla. App., 1978).
[19]Thomas v. Thomas, 565 P.2d 722 (Okla. App., 1976).
[20]Id. As to the rights of one who cohabited with a divorced husband after the six-months period (as a common-law wife) when the man subsequently married and divorced, see In re Estate of Ackers, 541 P.2d 284 (Okla. App., 1975).
[21]McKee v. State, 452 P.2d 169 (Okla. Crim. App., 1969).
[22]State ex rel. Bailey v. Powers, 566 P.2d 454 (Okla., 1977) (admitted common-law wife cannot institute paternity proceedings; her proper forum is divorce court); Thomas v. Thomas, 565 P.2d 722 (Okla. App., 1976).
[23]Reed v. Reed, 456 P.2d 529 (Okla., 1969); In re Estate of Hornback, 475 P.2d 184 (Okla., 1970). Compare Tower v. Towie, 368 P.2d 488 (Okla., 1962) (where a child is seeking to establish legitimacy, a rebuttable presumption of marriage arises from cohabitation).
[24]Okla. Stat. Ann., tit. 10, § 60.3.
[25]Id., § 60.5.

deemed capable of giving consent,[26] it seems evident from later enactment that the rights of the putative father to notice and a hearing on the matter cannot be ignored.[27]

It is primarily the court's function to determine whether the petitioners are eligible to adopt, whether the child is eligible to be adopted, and whether the adoption would promote the child's best interests. Negative recommendations of the Department of Institutions and Social Rehabilitative Services, though they cannot be ignored, are not final.[28] The decisions evidence a considerable breadth of judicial discretion in adjudicating on questions of eligibility and the finality of a consent to adoption once given.[29]

It is a criminal offense ("trafficking in children") to accept value for services of any kind relating to the adoption of a child or placement in a foster home.[30] An exception exists in respect of reasonable attorneys' fees for the adoption proceedings, the fees of a licensed placement agency, and the cost of hospital care for the child's mother, if approved by the court.[31]

Workers' compensation death benefits

For the purposes of death benefits under the Workers' Compensation Act,[32] a common-law wife can qualify.[33] In a case where an illegitimate child had had abundant social relations with the alleged father and, even after an order had been entered terminating the latter's rights, the father had publicly acknowledged the

---

[26]Id.
[27]See notes 87, 88 infra.
[28]See State ex rel. Department of Institutions, Social and Rehabilitative Services v. Griffis, 545 P.2d 763, 83 A.L.R.3d 363 (Okla., 1975).
[29]See, e.g., In re Adoption of Morrison, 560 P.2d 240 (Okla. App., 1976); In re Adoption of Jones, 558 P.2d 422 (Okla. App., 1976); DeGolyer v. Chesney, 527 P.2d 844 (Okla., 1974); Murray v. Vandevander, 522 P.2d 302 (Okla. App., 1974) (spousal consent); In re Baby Boy Fontaine, 516 P.2d 1333 (Okla., 1972), cert. den. sub nom. Fortier v. Project Hope, Inc., 414 U.S. 806, 38 L. Ed. 2d 42, 94 Sup. Ct. 72 (1973). See also Wills: The Effect of the Uniform Abortion Act on the Determination of a Testamentary Class, 29 Okla. L. Rev. 260 (1976). Generally, as to the Uniform Adoption Act, see Okla. Stat. Ann., tit. 10, §§ 60.1 to 60.23.
[30]Okla. Stat. Ann., tit. 21, § 866.
[31]Id.
[32]Id., tit. 85, § 48.
[33]Hawkins v. Oklahoma Scrap Paper Co., 389 P.2d 513 (Okla., 1964).

child as his, and received it into his family, the child was held eligible to recover death benefits under the statute.[34]

Abortion

The statutes criminalizing, without qualification, the procuring of an abortion unless to save the mother's life[35] and the act of submitting to or soliciting an abortion[36] have been declared unconstitutional.[37] There is a mandatory jail sentence for a mother who conceals a stillbirth or the death of an illegitimate child under the age of two years.[38]

Another statute provides that if death results from the abortion of a "quick" child, the actor can be convicted of manslaughter.[39] A physician or surgeon can lose his license for unprofessional conduct,[40] which includes the procuring of an abortion.[41] In Henrie v. Derryberry,[42] a psychologist, a psychiatrist and a minister sought to challenge the constitutionality of these provisions on the basis that they penalize a medical practitioner for involvement in abortion of a "quick" child. Since quickening occurs at an earlier stage than viability of the fetus, the provision relating thereto may be constitutionally vulnerable since the state has no rights to interfere prior to the first trimester of pregnancy.[43] However, the court, though recognizing the unconstitutionality of the blanket abortion provisions,[44] declined to pronounce on the constitutionality of the provisions whereunder the physician's license could be jeopardized because the board of medical examiners was not before it as a party to the controversy. It also declined to rule on the "quick" child provision because the state courts might construe this as relating only to a viable fetus, in which case it

---

[34] In re Swarer, 566 P.2d 126 (Okla., 1977).
[35] Okla. Stat. Ann., tit. 21, § 861.
[36] Id., § 862.
[37] Jobe v. State, 509 P.2d 481 (Okla. Crim. App., 1973).
[38] Okla. Stat. Ann., tit. 21, § 863.
[39] Id., § 714. See also § 713 (willful killing of unborn quick child by injury to the mother).
[40] Id., tit. 59, § 503.
[41] Id., § 509.
[42] 358 F. Supp. 719 (N.D. Okla., 1973).
[43] See section 2.19, herein.
[44] Jobe v. State, 509 P.2d 481 (Okla. Crim. App., 1973).

would not go contra to the mandates of the Supreme Court of the United States.

As it now stands, therefore, a physician in Oklahoma could be convicted of manslaughter if death resulted from an abortion procured prior to the end of the first trimester of pregnancy. He could also lose his license for so acting, whether or not death results. The mother could be jailed for concealing an early miscarriage. Revision seems to be called for.[45]

The Health Services for Minors Act[46] authorizes a pregnant minor to consent to treatment. However it excludes abortion from the services which she may obtain without parental consent.[47]

Tort actions

Civil actions for alienation of affections, and for seduction of a person of sound mind and of legal age, are abolished.[48] The action for breach of promise of marriage, however, remains.[49]

Possible criminal liability

For a conviction of "open and notorious adultery,"[50] a living together as if conjugal relations exist must be shown.[51] The relationship must be such as to justify the community in which the parties live in concluding that they are married.[52] Occasional sexual intercourse is not enough.[53] Although unwed cohabitation is not denounced as such, it is noteworthy that a court, in constru-

---

[45]See Henrie v. Derryberry and the Current Status of the Oklahoma Abortion Laws, 10 Tulsa L. J. 273 (1974).
[46]Okla. Stat. Ann., tit. 63, §§ 2601 to 2606.
[47]Id., § 2602(A)(3). See Domestic Relations: Minors and Abortion—The Requirement of Parental Consent, 29 Okla. L. Rev. 145 (1976).
[48]Okla. Stat. Ann., tit. 76, §§ 8, 8.1. See Torts: Alienation of Affections: A Child's Right to Seek Damages for Alienation of His Parent's Affection, 28 Okla. L. Rev. 198 (1975).
[49]Okla. Stat. Ann., tit. 23, § 40. See Price v. Price, 579 P.2d 843 (Okla. App., 1978) (mere cohabitation does not raise inference of promise to marry).
[50]Okla. Stat. Ann., tit. 21, §§ 871, 872. Voluntary sexual intercourse is no crime. Rachel v. State, 71 Okla. Crim. 33, 107 P.2d 813 (1940).
[51]See Hagan v. State, 73 Okla. Crim. 328, 121 P.2d 315 (1942).
[52]Copeland v. State, 10 Okla. Crim. 1, 133 Pac. 258 (1913).
[53]Burns v. State, 17 Okla. Crim. 26, 182 Pac. 738 (1919).

ing a statute which justifies a slaying in defense of, inter alia, a "mistress" felt that it was not the legislative intent to sanction the taking of a life in defense of an unlawful relation "rising to no higher level than that of paramour and concubine," whatever the word may mean in other contexts.[54]

Bigamy,[55] incest,[56] and seduction,[57] as well as rape by fraud,[58] are punishable; as is the crime of compelling a woman to marry,[59] and of abduction for the purposes of marriage or concubinage.[60] (If the girl is under the age of consent for marriage, it would not matter whether defendant intended marriage or a mere living together.)[61] For a conviction of statutory rape, the female must be under sixteen; [62] however, if she is over that age and under eighteen *and* of previous chaste character, this is also rape.[63]

The "detestable and abominable crime against nature" statute[64] has withstood constitutional challenge.[65] In one such decision (where more that mere consensual deviate sex was involved), the court expressed its opinion that the Supreme Court of the United States did not in Griswold v. Connecticut[66] prohibit the state's regulation of sexual promiscuity or misconduct between nonmarried persons.[67]

---

[54]Haines v. State, 275 P.2d 347 (Okla. Crim. App., 1954). See Criminal Law: An Examination of the Oklahoma Laws Concerning Sexual Behavior, 23 Okla. L. Rev. 459 (1970).
[55]See Criminal Law: Prosecution of Adultery and Bigamy in Oklahoma, 14 Okla. L. Rev. 203 (1961).
[56]Okla. Stat. Ann., tit. 21, § 885.
[57]Id., § 1120 et seq.
[58]Id., § 1111 (8th).
[59]Id., §§ 1117, 1118.
[60]Id., § 1119.
[61]Scott v. State, 85 Okla. Crim. 213, 186 P.2d 336 (1947).
[62]Okla. Stat. Ann., tit. 21, § 1111 (1st).
[63]Id., § 1111 (2nd). See Note, People v. Rincon-Pineda: Rape Trials Depart the Seventeenth Century—Farewell to Lord Hale, 11 Tulsa L. Rev. 279 (1975).
[64]Okla. Stat. Ann., tit. 21, § 886. See also § 887.
[65]See Canfield v. State, 506 P.2d 987 (Okla. Crim. App., 1973), appeal dismissed 414 U.S. 991, 38 L. Ed. 2d 230, 94 Sup. Ct. 342 (1973), reh. den. 414 U.S. 1138, 38 L. Ed. 2d 763, 94 Sup. Ct. 884 (1974); Moore v. State, 501 P.2d 529 (Okla. Crim. App., 1972), cert. den. 410 U.S. 987, 36 L. Ed. 2d 185, 93 Sup. Ct. 1517 (1973).
[66]Discussed in section 2.6, herein.
[67]Warner v. State, 489 P.2d 526 (Okla. Crim. App., 1971).

Status of children.

The legislature has found the terms "illegitimate" and "bastard" to be so offensive that it has required the use of the substitute term "child born out of wedlock" in its statutes[68] and in official or quasi-governmental matters.[69] Further, as from July 1, 1974, all children born within the state are regarded as legitimate.[70] The provision presents a problem as to whether it embraces children born in Oklahoma before the stated date.[71] The children of a bigamous marriage are legitimate.[72]

The constitutionality of a provision which restricts a mother's eligibility for public assistance in respect of one illegitimate child only[73] may be open to question. Children born of an artificial insemination, performed by a licensed physician with the approval of a judge having jurisdiction over adoptions, and with the written consent of both spouses, are legitimate.[74]

As to inheritance rights, the statute[75] provides that, in addition to the child born out of wedlock being the child of the mother, it will be deemed the child of the father when (a) the father in writing, before witnesses, acknowledges paternity, or (b) the biological parents intermarry subsequent to the child's birth and the father, after such marriage, acknowledges the child as his own or adopts him into the family, or (c) the father publicly acknowledged the child as his, receiving it as such, with the consent of the wife if married, or (d) the father has been judicially determined to be the father. The issue of all marriages deemed null in law are legitimate.[76]

---

[68] Okla. Stat. Ann., tit. 10, § 1.1.
[69] Id., § 6.5.
[70] Id., § 1.2. Provisions for adoption by the biological father, by public acknowledgment, remain on the books. Id., § 55.
[71] See Illegitimate Succession—Illinois Statute Denying the Rights of Illegitimate Children to Inherit from Father's Estates Is Unconstitutional, 13 Tulsa L. J. 178 (1977).
[72] Green v. Green. 309 P.2d 276 (Okla., 1957); Brokeshoulder v. Brokeshoulder, 84 Okla. 249, 204 Pac. 284, 34 A.L.R. 441 (1921).
[73] Okla. Stat. Ann., tit. 56, § 164(d)(1).
[74] Id., tit. 10, § 551 et seq.
[75] Id., tit. 84, § 215.
[76] As to the possible impact of Trimble v. Gordon (section 3.3, herein) on this legislation, see 13 Tulsa L. J. 178 (1977). Though decided under the statute prior to its amendment, a holding that mere proof of illegitimacy and of paternity is not sufficient (In re Estate of Johnson, 560 P.2d 962 (Okla., 1977)) is unaffected.

Support and custody

Provisions of a fairly standard nature cover the establishment of paternity[77] and the enforcement of support obligations of the father.[78] It has been held that a contract for support which includes additional provision for the child beyond legal maintenance constitutes a contract for the child as a third-party beneficiary, and as such it cannot be modified downward without the child's legal consent.[79]

Even prior to the 1977 amendment of the statute controlling the illegitimate's rights in regard to intestate succession,[80] there was authority to support the declared[81] policy of the courts to favor legitimacy in cases of doubt.[82]

The mother of an illegitimate child has a statutory right to its custody, services and earnings.[83] This right, however, will be foregone on a showing such as will justify a termination of her parental rights.[84]

Termination of parental rights

The effect of a final decree of adoption, as of a final decree in a proceeding to terminate parental rights, is to deprive the affected

---

[77]Okla. Stat. Ann., tit. 10, § 71 et seq. See also tit. 12, § 1600 et seq. As to blood tests, see tit. 10, § 501 et seq.

[78]See Okla. Stat. Ann., tit. 56, § 237. As to the Uniform Reciprocal Enforcement of Support Act, see tit. 12, § 1600.1 et seq.

[79]Plunkett v. Atkins, 371 P.2d 727 (Okla., 1962).

[80]Okla. Stat. Ann., tit. 84, § 215.

[81]In re Swarer, 566 P.2d 126 (Okla., 1977).

[82]See In re Cravens' Estate, 268 P.2d 236 (Okla., 1954); Standridge v. State, 441 P.2d 417 (Okla., 1968).

[83]Okla. Stat. Ann., tit. 10, § 6. Okla. Stat. Ann., tit. 30, § 11, giving the mother preference in determining right to custody of a child of tender years, is not violative of equal protection. Gordon v. Gordon, 577 P.2d 1271 (Okla., 1978).

[84]E.g., Ilee M. v. State Department of Institutions, Social and Rehabilitation Services, 577 P.2d 908 (Okla., 1978); Brim v. Brim, 532 P.2d 1403 (Okla. App., 1975) (white mother who had been sharing her bed with a black, apparently married, paramour three or four nights a week was held not to have been denied her constitutional rights when her three-year-old child was taken from her and given to the custody of her ex-husband, since, according to the court, she had no constitutional right to subject the child to a home environment considered immoral by society).

parent of all rights,[85] including those of visitation.[86] However, appropriate provision now exists to ensure that, unless the biological father's rights have been judicially terminated for good cause,[87] he must receive notice and an opportunity to be heard before the child can be adopted out against his wishes.[88]

Property rights of cohabitants

The courts of Oklahoma have long recognized that one who contributes, in services or otherwise, to the accumulations acquired during the existence of what such person mistakenly believes to be a valid marriage qualifies for an equitable share in such accumulations. As long ago as 1920, where a woman had so contributed in ignorance of the incestuous character of the marriage, the court, citing authority from California, Kansas, Washington and Texas, permitted an equal division of the accumulations when there was no clear showing as to the value of the contributions of either cohabitant.[89] The court declined to entertain a "harsh and cruel interpretation of the law" that would deprive an innocent party of all benefits from her fifteen years of work and the accumulations thereof, letting the pretended husband reap all the benefits of their joint accumulations. In a similar vein, it was held that parties to an illegal marriage cannot shun burdens resulting from their illegal acts or profit by an illegal contract.[90] Later, the same result—an even distribution of the assets—was achieved where both contributed money and services toward the acquisition and improvement of property although it seemed probable that the innocent spouse had contributed the lion's share of the money.[91]

---

[85] West v. State, Dept. of Public Welfare, 536 P.2d 901 (Okla., 1975); Wade v. Brown, 516 P.2d 526 (Okla., 1973).

[86] In re Fox, 567 P.2d 985 (Okla., 1977). See Okla. Stat. Ann., tit. 10, § 60.16.

[87] See Okla. Stat. Ann., tit. 10, § 60.6; In re Adoption of Michelle N., 577 P.2d 68 (Okla., 1978); Mann v. Garrette, 556 P.2d 1003 (Okla., 1976); DeGolyer v. Chesney, 527 P.2d 844 (Okla., 1974).

[88] See Okla. Stat. Ann., tit. 10, § 1131. See also In re Del Moral Rodriguez, 552 P.2d 397 (Okla., 1976). The Uniform Adoption Act is set out at Okla. Stat. Ann., tit. 10, § 60.1 et seq.

[89] Krauter v. Krauter, 79 Okla. 30, 190 Pac. 1088 (1920).

[90] Eggers v. Olson, 104 Okla. 297, 231 Pac. 483 (1924).

[91] King v. Jackson, 196 Okla. 327, 164 P.2d 974 (1945) (court also impressed a lien on the property to secure reimbursement to the noninnocent party's successor of one half of taxes paid subsequent to the death of the noninnocent "spouse").

As to meretricious cohabitations, there is even earlier authority for the proposition that, as long as an agreement was not made in contemplation of the illicit relationship, a contract to pay for domestic services can be enforced notwithstanding the parties lived in a state of concubinage.[92] Further, in Whitney v. Whitney[93] there is support for the viability of a contract between unmarried cohabitants. The court there recognizes a rule that a contract made between spouses as to their property interests pending divorce proceedings is set at naught by a reconciliation, followed by cohabitation. But the case involved a relation which was bigamous in its inception. No husband and wife relationship, therefore, ever existed. The court held that, assuming both knew at the time of their pre-divorce contract that there was a serious question as to the validity of the marriage, their relationship could be analogized to that of partners and the contract would not be disturbed. Since it was quite possible that, at the time of the contract, the woman was unaware that no marriage existed (in which case the cohabitation could well nullify the contract) the case is not on all fours with the straightforward contract between persons who make no pretense of marriage. But the fact that the holding is based on an assumption should not weaken its authority as a statement of what the courts of Oklahoma will hold where the parties contract with full knowledge that marriage exists.

6.38. Oregon

Common-law marriage cannot be contracted in this state.[94] Further, the rule that a marriage valid in the state where it was celebrated is recognized as valid in Oregon admits of qualification where policy considerations favor a different result.[95] Though a

---

[92]Emmerson v. Botkin, 26 Okla. 218, 109 Pac. 531 (1910).

[93]192 Okla. 174, 134 P.2d 357 (1942). When a marriage is attacked by reason of an undissolved prior marriage, the usual presumption is that the earlier marriage had been dissolved. See Evidence: Rebutting Oklahoma's Presumption of Validity of a Subsequent Marriage, 30 Okla. L. Rev. 433 (1977).

[94]Estate of Wilmarth, 27 Ore. App. 303, 556 P.2d 990 (1976); Huard v. McTeigh, 113 Ore. 279, 232 Pac. 658, 39 A.L.R. 528 (1925).

[95]See Garrett v. Chapman, 252 Ore. 361, 449 P.2d 856 (1969).

proxy marriage is valid in Oregon if valid in the state of celebration,[96] such a ceremony performed in Oregon cannot be sustained,[97] even if the parties subsequently cohabit as husband and wife.[98] Similarly, an Oregon couple who vacation in a state recognizing common-law marriage and who there hold themselves out as husband and wife, will not thereby become validly married in Oregon.[99]

However, when a couple openly cohabit as husband and wife, the law will presume a marriage.[1] Inconsistencies in the testimony and a failure to produce a marriage certificate do not necessarily rebut this presumption,[2] though it is of course rebuttable.[3] By reason of a policy favoring the marriage relation, one seeking to challenge a marriage must present most cogent evidence to disprove its existence.[4]

When the validity of a marriage is attacked for having been entered into while one of the parties was still married to another, the second marriage is presumed valid; the prior marriage being presumed to have been ended either by dissolution or annulment or by death of the other spouse.[5]

Any husband and wife who elected to come under the terms of the Oregon Community Property Laws of 1943 (since repealed), may revoke such election on filing with the Secretary of State a notice of such desire.[6]

Since the statute requires, for a valid marriage, that the parties take each other to be husband and wife,[7] it would seem that same-sex marriages are ruled out.

---

[96]See Marriage of Holemar, 27 Ore. App. 613, 557 P.2d 38 (1976).
[97]Ore. Rev. Stat., § 106.140.
[98]See State v. Anderson, 239 Ore. 200, 396 P.2d 558 (1964).
[99]Walker v. Hildenbrand, 243 Ore. 117, 410 P.2d 244 (1966).
[1]Ore. Rev. Stat., § 41.360(30).
[2]Franklin v. Biggs, 14 Ore. App. 450, 513 P.2d 1216 (1973).
[3]Gorman v. Gorman, 211 Ore. 550, 316 P.2d 543 (1957).
[4]Franklin v. Biggs, 14 Ore. App. 450, 513 P.2d 1216 (1973).
[5]In re Estate of Steinberg, 34 Ore. App. 293, 578 P.2d 487 (1978). As to the distinction between marriages which are void (bigamous or incestuous) and those which are merely voidable (want of legal age or understanding, or obtained through force or fraud), see Ore. Rev. Stat., §§ 106.020, 106.030.
[6]As to the form of notice prescribed, see Ore. Rev. Stat., § 108.510.
[7]Id., § 106.150(1).

Schoolteachers

A permanent public schoolteacher can be dismissed for immorality.[8] Conviction of sex offenses can afford grounds for termination of a teacher in a state school.[9] However, since adult consensual sexual behavior is now decriminalized in Oregon, it is virtually unthinkable that unwed cohabitation *as such* could afford grounds for termination. In 1975, a teacher was able to recover damages for wrongful dismissal based on the fact that she was a lesbian, but was unable to secure her reinstatement as a teacher.[10]

Welfare assistance

A regulation, the motivation for which is difficult to understand, permitting full shelter allowance for aid to families with dependent children when recipients were married or heads of family units of the same sex, but denying it when the units were headed by unmarried persons not of the same sex, has been held violative of equal protection.[11]

Adoption

Any person may petition to adopt another. There is the usual requirement of spousal consent if the petitioner is married.[12] Consent of the child's parents, or, if none, of the child's guardian, or, if none, of the child's next of kin, or, if none, of an appointee by the court of a "next friend" is also required.[13] Where parental rights have been terminated or the child has been relinquished for adoption, though the statutory language is permissive only,[14] the courts regard the consent of the Children's Services Division

---

[8]Id., § 342.865.
[9]Id., § 342.175.
[10]Burton v. Cascade School Dist. Union High School No. 5, 512 F.2d 850 (C.A.-9 Ore., 1975), cert. den. 423 U.S. 839, 46 L. Ed. 2d 59, 96 Sup. Ct. 69 (1975). See Remedial Balancing Decisions and the Rights of Homosexual Teachers: A Pyrrhic Victory, 61 Iowa L. Rev. 1080 (1976).
[11]Sawhney v. Public Welfare Division, 24 Ore. App. 685, 546 P.2d 768 (1976).
[12]As to adoption procedures, see Ore. Rev. Stat., §§ 109.307, 109.310.
[13]Id., § 109.312.
[14]Id., § 109.316.

as a jurisdictional prerequisite.[15] Since the best interests of the child are the paramount consideration in ruling on a petition for adoption,[16] when the parents cannot provide a stable home in the foreseeable future, their own wishes in the matter do not carry the weight they would otherwise carry.[17] Provisions restricting the rights of parents to reconsider a relinquishment for adoption,[18] and a provision that after one year no one may question the validity of an adoption,[19] are aimed to preclude the drastic disruption of an adoptive home after the child has acquired its new status.[20]

Workers' compensation death benefits

Cohabitants as husband and wife for over a year prior to an accident which results in workers' compensation death benefits qualify for such benefits only if there are children.[21] Children who have been released for adoption do not so qualify.[22] A surviving spouse of an out-of-state valid common-law marriage has qualified.[23]

---

[15] See In re Adoption of Greybull, 29 Ore. App. 889, 565 P.2d 773 (1977); In re Troy M., 27 Ore. App. 185, 555 P.2d 933 (1976); Children's Services Division, Dept. of Human Resources v. Zach, 18 Ore. App. 288, 525 P.2d 185 (1974).

[16] In re D., 24 Ore. App. 601, 547 P.2d 175 (1976), cert. den. sub nom. C. v. F.F., 429 U.S. 907, 97 Sup. Ct. 273 (1976).

[17] Generally, as to adoptions, see Ore. Rev. Stat., §§ 109.305 to 109.400, 419.523 and 419.527.

[18] Id., § 418.270(4),(5). See also State ex rel. Tanzer v. Williams, 263 Ore. 394, 502 P.2d 596 (1972).

[19] Ore. Rev. Stat., § 109.381(3).

[20] See Campbell v. Kindred, 26 Ore. App. 771, 554 P.2d 599 (1976).

A consent to adoption may be revoked at any time before the court has issued a decree of adoption unless the circumstances indicate that the parents should be estopped from so revoking. See In re Adoption of D., 28 Ore. App. 887, 561 P.2d 1038 (1977) (no estoppel where revocation was within a few weeks after consent and proof demonstrated parental care for the child).

As to the effect of adoption on the status of the child vis-a-vis parents and adoptive parents, see Ore. Rev. Stat., § 109.041 et seq.

[21] Ore. Rev. Stat., § 656.226; In re Lacey, 34 Ore. App. 877, 580 P.2d 1032 (1978). As to the eligibility of an underage spouse who had contracted a common-law marriage out of state, see Johnston v. Georgia-Pacific Corp., 35 Ore. App. 231, 581 P.2d 108 (1978).

[22] See Thomas v. State Accident Ins. Fund, 8 Ore. App. 414, 495 P.2d 46 (1972).

[23] Boykin v. State Industrial Accident Comm., 224 Ore. 76, 355 P.2d 724 (1960). Such a spouse also qualifies for benefits under the Longshoremen's and Harbor Workers' Act. Albina Engine & Machine Works v. O'Leary, 328 F.2d 877 (C.A.-9 Ore., 1964), cert. den. 379 U.S. 817, 85 Sup. Ct. 35 (1964).

Insurance benefits

A statement by an applicant for insurance that he was married, when in fact he had lived unmarried with a woman for fifteen years and begotten two children by her, was held not a misstatement so material as to avoid the policy;[24] a result to be expected in the light of the presumption, already noted,[25] that arises from open cohabitation as husband and wife.

Abortion

Therapeutic abortions were authorized well before the Supreme Court of the United States' decisions precluding state interference with the decision to have an abortion during the first trimester of pregnancy.[26] The statutes require that the physician have "reasonable grounds" to believe there is a "substantial risk" that continued pregnancy will "greatly impair" the physical and mental health of the mother. Consent of parents or the guardian of a minor mother or of an incompetent is required. Hospitals, physicians and their staffs are immunized from any liability or discrimination for nonparticipation, but this does not apply to public hospitals.[27] No pregnancy can be terminated with impunity after the 150th day of pregnancy except in emergency situations.[28] The fact that an abortion was performed under the provisions of the Medical Practice Act is a defense in a prosecution for manslaughter by abortion.[29]

Among the provisions relating to family planning and birth control,[30] it is provided that refusal to accept such services cannot affect the right of a person to public assistance.[31] The provisions

---

[24] Bunn v. Monarch Life Ins. Co., 257 Ore. 409, 478 P.2d 363 (1970).
[25] Ore. Rev. Stat., § 41.360(30).
[26] Id., §§ 435.405 to 435.495.
[27] Id., § 435.475(3).
[28] Id., § 435.425.
[29] Id., § 677.190(2). See State v. Hawkins, 255 Ore. 39, 463 P.2d 858 (1970). In State v. Schulman, 6 Ore. App. 81, 485 P.2d 1252 (1971), an indictment for "unlawfully" procuring an abortion was held sufficient because, defendant not being a licensed physician, the operation must necessarily have been "unlawful."

As to the crime of concealment of the birth of an infant, see Ore. Rev. Stat., § 167.820.

[30] Ore. Rev. Stat., §§ 435.205 to 435.235.
[31] Id., § 435.215.

are to be so construed as not to affect the right of an individual to self-determination in the matter of procreation.[32] The inference is inescapable that medicaid could not be withheld from those electing abortion.

Tort actions

The civil action for alienation of affections has not yet been relegated to the museum.[33] The action for criminal conversation, however, has been abolished.[34]

Possible criminal liability

Aside from bigamy[35] and incest[36] (offenses "against the family"), the sexual offenses, which are variously labeled "sexual abuse,"[37] "sexual misconduct,"[38] and contributing to the delinquency of a minor,[39] no longer extend to consensual sexual behavior between adults.[40] The gravity of the statutory rape type crimes depends very much on the age of the victim, and on the age differential between actor and victim.[41] Reasonable mistake as to the victim's age is no defense where criminality depends on the child's being under sixteen. Where it depends on an age of more than sixteen, or on incapacity to consent by reason of mental or physical infirmity, mistake can excuse.[42]

Status of children

The legal status and legal relations, and the rights and duties between a person and his descendants, and between a person and

---

[32]Id., § 435.235.
[33]See Shrock v. Goodell, 270 Ore. 504, 528 P.2d 1048 (1974).
[34]Ore. Rev. Stat., § 161.005.
[35]Id., § 163.515.
[36]Id., § 163.525.
[37]See State v. Turner, 33 Ore. App. 157, 575 P.2d 1007 (1978).
[38]See State v. Eggleston, 31 Ore. App. 9, 569 P.2d 1088 (1977); State v. Usher, 26 Ore. App. 489, 552 P.2d 1345 (1976).
[39]Generally, see Ore. Rev. Stat., §§ 163.355 to 163.575 as to sex offenses.
[40]Id., §§ 163.385 to 163.395. As to nonconsensual deviate sexual intercourse, see § 163.385 et seq. See also Yturri, Three Rs of Penal Law Reform, 51 Ore. L. Rev. 427 (1972); Fields, Privacy "Rights" and the New Oregon Criminal Code, 51 Ore. L. Rev. 494 (1972).
[41]See Ore. Rev. Stat., § 163.345 et seq. State v. Elmore, 24 Ore. App. 651, 546 P.2d 1117 (1976).
[42]Ore. Rev. Stat., § 163.325.

6.38 UNMARRIED COUPLES AND THE LAW

his parents and their descendants and kindred, are, if paternity is established, the same for all persons, whether or not the parents are married.[43] It follows that for the purposes of intestate succession, once paternity is established during the father's lifetime, the illegitimate child is in the same position as any other child. The same rights of intestate succession are accorded where the father has acknowledged his paternity in writing signed by him during the lifetime of the child.[44]

As to establishment of paternity,[45] where the child is born during lawful wedlock, the husband is conclusively presumed to be the father.[46] If the marriage is or may be void, the presumption is disputable.[47] A provision that the husband must not have been sterile at the time of possible conception is retroactive in operation.[48] But neither this presumption of paternity nor the rule that paternity may be established by marriage of the parents after the child's birth[49] apply where a man married a woman following the birth of a child whom he denies having fathered.[50]

Paternity may be established in the context of a variety of legal proceedings,[51] for example, in a suit for dissolution of marriage, in addition to the statutory "filiation" proceeding;[52] however, whatever form the action takes, the procedural rules incorporated in the filiation statutes, such as the rules relating to the admissibility of evidence of the mother's opportunity to have intercourse with some person other than the alleged father,[53] are to be adhered to.[54]

---

[43]Id., § 109.060.
[44]Id., § 112.105. See In re Estate of Walker, 2 Ore. App. 322, 468 P.2d 655 (1970).
[45]Ore. Rev. Stat., §§ 109.060 to 109.090, 109.125 et seq. (filiation proceedings).
[46]Id., § 41.350.
[47]Id., § 109.070. See also § 41.360.
[48]State ex rel. Dwight v. Justice, 16 Ore. App. 336, 518 P.2d 668 (1974).
[49]See In re Rowe's Estate, 172 Ore. 293, 141 P.2d 832 (1943). As to issuance of new birth certificate where parents intermarry, see Ore. Rev. Stat., § 432.425.
[50]In re Marriage of Gridley, 28 Ore. App. 145, 558 P.2d 1277 (1977).
[51]See Thom v. Bailey, 257 Ore. 572, 481 P.2d 355 (1971); State ex rel. Sockerson v. Pew, 29 Ore. App. 809, 564 P.2d 1375 (1977). As to the rule that paternity can be determined in proceedings under the Uniform Reciprocal Enforcement of Support Act (Ore. Rev. Stat., § 110.005 et seq.), see Clarkston v. Bridge, 273 Ore. 68, 539 P.2d 1094, 81 A.L.R.3d 1166 (1975).
[52]As to filiation proceedings, see Ore. Rev. Stat., § 109.125 et seq. As to blood tests, see §§ 109.250 to 109.262.
[53]State ex rel. Leonard v. Hogan, 32 Ore. App. 89, 573 P.2d 328 (1978).
[54]In re Marriage of Gridley, 28 Ore. App. 145, 558 P.2d 1277 (1977).

Provided the interests of the state, the mother, and the child are adequately protected by the agreement, there is nothing to prevent a court from merely incorporating into its decree an agreement arrived at between the mother and the father prior to the filiation proceedings.[55] But even absent express statutory authority,[56] such decrees are not final. A mother cannot irrevocably contract away her rights in this respect.[57]

As to the putative father's rights in regard to custody[58] and to a voice in the child's adoption,[59] abundant provision now exists to ensure that he receives procedural due process.[60] As is the case with the mother,[61] the father's parental rights can be terminated only after notice and an opportunity for a hearing.[62]

Property rights of cohabitants

Problems involving the distribution of property acquired by nonmarried persons have come before the courts in a variety of situations.[63]

---

[55] State ex rel. Karr v. Shorey, 281 Ore. 453, 575 P.2d 981 (1978).
[56] See Montgomery v. Ledesma, 12 Ore. App. 535, 507 P.2d 405 (1973).
[57] Fox v. Hohenshelt, 19 Ore. App. 617, 528 P.2d 1376 (1974).
[58] On proof of paternity, an unwed father has right of custody equal to that of the mother. Ore. Rev. Stat., §§ 109.030 to 109.094. Formally established unwed parents have all custodial rights married and divorced parents enjoy. Id., § 109.103. See Snegirev v. Samoilov, 26 Ore. App. 687, 554 P.2d 595 (1976).
[59] Adoption of Bantsari, 29 Ore. App. 747, 564 P.2d 1371 (1977). See Sparks v. Phelps, 22 Ore. App. 570, 540 P.2d 397 (1975); Statutory Change in the Rights of Oregon's Unwed Fathers, 12 Willamette L. J. 569 (1976); Adoption Consent Rights of the Unwed Father in Oregon, 53 Ore. L. Rev. 531 (1974). As to the Uniform Child Custody Jurisdiction Act, see Ore. Rev. Stat., §§ 109.700 to 109.930.
[60] See Ore. Rev. Stat., § 109.096 et seq.
[61] See State ex rel. Juvenile Dept. of Multnomah County v. Prince, 20 Ore. App. 212, 530 P.2d 1251 (1975).
[62] Ore. Rev. Stat., § 109.326. The child has a right to independent counsel in termination proceedings. State ex rel. Juvenile Dept. of Multnomah County v. Wade, 19 Ore. App. 314, 527 P.2d 753 (1974), appeal dismissed 423 U.S. 806, 46 L. Ed. 2d 27, 96 Sup. Ct. 16 (1975).
[63] The fact of a meretricious relationship does not give rise to any presumption of undue influence between a testator and a legatee. See In re Kelly's Estate, 150 Ore. 598, 46 P.2d 84 (1935); Penn v. Barrett, 273 Ore. 471, 541 P.2d 1282 (1975).

Where a marriage was annulled after four days of cohabitation, and the husband had given the wife about $3,000, most of which she had used to pay off an encumbrance on her home, the court, in restoring the status quo, ordered restitution of the amount so used, impressing on the property a lien to secure the husband's claim to restitution. In re Marriage of Hanna, 33 Ore. App. 213, 575 P.2d 1024 (1978).

6.38 UNMARRIED COUPLES AND THE LAW

Where the parties mistakenly believed in the existence of a valid marriage, Oregon courts have had no difficulty, if the supposed husband paid and title was taken as tenants in common, in finding that the husband intended to make a gift of a half interest to the wife.[64] It has long been recognized that, even if the parties are aware of the invalidity of or nonexistence of a marriage, a conveyance to them as husband and wife results in a tenancy in common and not a joint tenancy.[65] However, where the relationship is knowingly illicit, this rule favoring a tenancy in common does not necessarily result in an arbitrary division of the property without any adjustment in respect of their respective contributions. In one case, the down payment for the land was made from funds jointly earned by them. They took title as husband and wife (which they knew they were not). After they parted, the man continued to make all payments due on the contract, and the court, though recognizing that each had an equal interest in the land, allowed the man a right to contribution, to be secured by a lien on the land, in respect of a half share of the payments made by him subsequent to their separation.[66]

The courts of Oregon are not deterred by policies disfavoring judicial aid to a meretricious claimant where the equities demand it. Where two properties had been conveyed to an unwed couple as husband and wife, and there was proof of an oral agreement that the woman would convey her interest in the one lot to the man in return for his conveyance to her of his interest in the other, the court enforced the agreement against the man on a showing of performance of the part of the woman.[67]

In Latham v. Latham,[68] the rule, to which lip-service was paid in an early case,[69] that future cohabitation is a vicious consideration which avoids a contract, was regarded as inapplicable to a

---

[64]Brandt v. Brandt, 215 Ore. 423, 333 P.2d 887 (1958).
[65]Hughes v. Kay, 194 Ore. 519, 242 P.2d 788 (1952); Emmons v. Sanders, 217 Ore. 234, 342 P.2d 125 (1959); Pierce v. Hall, 223 Ore. 563, 355 P.2d 259 (1960).
[66]Merit v. Losey, 194 Ore. 89, 240 P.2d 933 (1952).
[67]Hughes v. Kay, 194 Ore. 519, 242 P.2d 788 (1952). Compare Bridgman v. Stout, 10 Ore. App. 474, 500 P.2d 731 (1972) (oral survivorship agreement in respect of land owned by unweds as husband and wife held to be within the statute of frauds).
[68]274 Ore. 421, 547 P.2d 144 (1976).
[69]Traver v. Naylor, 126 Ore. 193, 268 Pac. 75 (1928). See also Olson v. Saxton, 86 Ore. 670, 169 Pac. 119 (1917).

situation where the cohabitation aspects formed no part of the consideration for the agreement to divide the couple's joint accumulations. The court, also relying on an early holding that past cohabitation does not in itself invalidate a contract,[70] honored the agreement though the consideration allegedly to be furnished by the plaintiff was "living with defendant, caring for and keeping after him, and furnishing and providing him all the amenities of married life." The court, however, did make reference to an earlier decision to the effect that no agreement to compensate a woman for her services in such a situation would be implied.[71]

More recently, however, the courts, though not using the language of implied in fact contract, gave effect to the "shared expectations" of an unwed couple in this respect. A divorced couple jointly contracted to buy land as husband and wife. Both made payments on the price from their earnings. They had a joint savings account but separate checking accounts. The court, after discussing modern departures from the older judicial policy of noninterference in the differences between couples embarked on meretricious relations, which so often operated to create injustice, opined that it should look to the intent of the cohabitants, even if not expressed in words. It concluded the facts involved to result in a pooling arrangement and that the property be divided between them. The woman, however, was awarded $500 by reason of her contribution of $1,500 of the $2,000 down payment, and the matter was remanded to the trial court for a determination as to the share of rental value of the property which should be awarded to the nonoccupant from the time their living together had become impossible.[72] The decision explicitly holds that the property distribution should be based on the expressed or implied intent of the parties.

There is, too, recognition that, if a presumption of gratuity can be overcome by competent, satisfactory evidence independent of a claimant's own testimony, recovery for services performed by an

---

[70] Dannells v. United States Nat. Bank of Portland, 172 Ore. 213, 138 P.2d 220 (1943).

[71] York v. Place, 273 Ore. 947, 544 P.2d 572 (1975).

[72] Beal v. Beal, 282 Ore. 115, 577 P.2d 507 (1978). See Family Law Symposium—Folberg and Buren, Domestic Partnership: A Proposal for Dividing the Property of Unmarried Families, 12 Willamette L. J. 413, 453 (1976).

extramarital cohabitant can be predicated on a contract implied in fact.[72a]

6.39. Pennsylvania

Cohabitation between parties capable of contracting marriage, and a reputation in the community as husband and wife, raise a presumption of common-law marriage.[73] Where, however, the cohabitation began while one of the parties was married to a third person, the meretricious nature of their relationship was presumed to continue even after the impediment to their marriage was removed.[74] This latter presumption can be rebutted by statements made by the parties after the removal of the impediment, which, though perhaps not technically a mutual exchange of promises, are indicative of a present intent to marry; for example, a statement "Now we're legally married" responded to with the words "It's about time. That's just what we were waiting for," was sufficient.[75] Similarly (after removal of the impediment by a divorce), a statement "Now you have the ring and you are my wife," receiving the reply "That is fine. I love it," was held to create a common-law marriage.[76]

Both of the above examples are readily construable as "words in the present tense," an essential prerequisite of a common-law marriage in Pennsylvania.[77] A woman who had cohabited with a deceased workman for twelve years and had borne his child, the parties holding themselves out as spouses, failed to qualify for workers' compensation benefits due to her inability to show that there had ever been an exchange of the all-important *verbae de*

[72a] Lawrence v. Ladd, 280 Ore. 181, 570 P.2d 638 (1977).

[73] In re Estate of Garges, 474 Pa. 237, 378 A.2d 307 (1977); Harris v. Weinberger, 377 F. Supp. 141 (W.D. Pa., 1974).

[74] Earley v. Commonwealth, Dept. of Public Welfare, 13 Pa. Cmwlth. 17, 317 A.2d 677 (1974); Mellon v. Richardson, 466 F.2d 524 (C.A.-3 Pa., 1972).

[75] In re Estate of Garges, 474 Pa. 237, 378 A.2d 307 (1977).

[76] In re Rosenberger's Estate, 362 Pa. 153, 155, 65 A.2d 377, 379 (1949).

[77] Mellon v. Richardson, 466 F.2d 524 (C.A.-3 Pa., 1972); Commonwealth ex rel. McDermott v. McDermott, 236 Pa. Super. 541, 345 A.2d 914 (1975) (words of present tense established marriage between couple recently divorced); Commonwealth v. Jones, 224 Pa. Super. 352, 307 A.2d 397 (1973); In re Blecher's Estate, 381 Pa. 138, 112 A.2d 129 (1955).

praesenti.[78] Whatever one may think of such a result, the point is clear: any such magical exchange of words should not go unwitnessed. Such claims of marriage being regarded as a fruitful source of perjury and fraud, they are not encouraged, but merely tolerated by the courts.[79] The claimant has a heavy burden to discharge.[80]

Schoolteachers and other public employees

Since the adoption by the state of the Equal Rights Amendment, of interest is a decision that a school cannot restrict maternity leaves to married teachers only without a showing that it has a mandatory termination policy for unwed males who have children to take care of.[81] The logic of this is appealing: if an unwed mother is forced to quit her employment by reason of pregnancy, the same should apply to the unwed father; antagonists of equal rights could point to this as an illustration of the absurdity of placing both sexes on an absolutely equal footing.

In another way, a public employee's extramarital activities may lead to his dismissal where they can become a matter of legitimate concern to the public employer. It was held that a police officer's right of privacy was not violated by reason of his dismissal for off-duty adultery where this conduct led to rumors and eventual discovery of his relationship and a complaint by his father-in-law.[82]

Adoption

Any person may adopt another,[83] and any person, regardless of age or residence, may be adopted.[84] Consent of the person to be

---

[78]Bowden v. Workmen's Compensation Appeal Bd., 31 Pa. Cmwlth. 476, 376 A.2d 1033 (1977).

[79]In re Wagner's Estate, 398 Pa. 531, 159 A.2d 495, 82 A.L.R.2d 681 (1960).

[80]In re Stauffer's Estate, 372 Pa. 537, 94 A.2d 726 (1953). See also Pennsylvania Common Law Marriage and Annulment: Present Law and Proposals for Reform, 15 Vill. L. Rev. 134 (1969).

[81]Leechburg Area School Dist. v. Commonwealth Human Relations Comm., 19 Pa. Cmwlth. 614, 339 A.2d 850 (1975).

[82]Fabio v. Civil Service Comm. of City of Philadelphia, 30 Pa. Cmwlth. 203, 373 A.2d 751 (1977).

[83]1 Pa. Cons. Stat., § 212.

[84]Id., § 211.

adopted, if over the age of twelve, is an obvious prerequisite. If the adoptive parent is married, spousal consent must be obtained. If the adoptee is not yet eighteen, parental consent is required.[85]

Among the provisions controlling the procedures where the adoptee is in the care of a licensed adoption agency[86] is one which permits such an agency to seek termination of parental rights independently of adoption.[87] One practical advantage could be that it ensures that the adoptive parents never know the identity of the natural parents.[88]

Workers' compensation death benefits

It is well settled that an illegitimate child is entitled to workers' compensation benefits on the death of the father.[89] As to a cohabiting partner, if she qualifies as a common-law spouse she is also so entitled,[90] even if their initial relationship was meretricious[91] or subsequent to a marriage which was invalid.[92] If she cannot establish such a common-law marriage, she is not entitled to these benefits.[93] Extramarital cohabitation, whether or not criminal, can result in a termination of a widow's benefits.[94]

---

[85]Id., § 411.
[86]See id., § 301.
[87]Id., § 311.
[88]See In re Burns, 474 Pa. 615, 379 A.2d 535 (1977). As to the respective rights and functions of the child's parents, the placement agencies and the courts, see Child Care Service of Delaware County Institution Dist. v. Commonwealth, Department of Public Welfare, —— Pa. ——, 385 A.2d 593 (1978); Lee v. Child Care Service Delaware County Institution Dist., 461 Pa. 641, 337 A.2d 586 (1975), appeal dismissed 423 U.S. 919, 46 L. Ed. 2d 245, 96 Sup. Ct. 258 (1975).
[89]Brown v. Workmen's Compensation Appeal Bd., 20 Pa. Cmwlth. 330, 342 A.2d 134 (1975); Penn Sanitation Co. v. Hoskins, 10 Pa. Cmwlth. 528, 312 A.2d 458 (1973) (illegitimate child of employee's wife); Irby Constr. Co. v. Workmen's Compensation Appeal Bd., 9 Pa. Cmwlth. 591, 308 A.2d 924 (1973) (child of bigamous marriage).
[90]Kennedy v. Rossi, 182 Pa. Super. 176, 126 A.2d 531 (1956).
[91]Donaldson v. P. J. Oesterling & Sons, Inc., 199 Pa. Super. 637, 186 A.2d 653 (1962).
[92]Leroy Roofing Co. v. Workmen's Compensation Appeal Bd., 15 Pa. Cmwlth. 396, 327 A.2d 876 (1974).
[93]Bowden v. Workmen's Compensation Appeal Bd., 31 Pa. Cmwlth. 476, 376 A.2d 1033 (1977). In Workmen's Compensation Appeal Bd. v. Jones & Laughlin Steel Corp., 23 Pa. Cmwlth. 87, 351 A.2d 333 (1976), a woman was held entitled even though divorce proceedings had been initiated at time of death.
[94]See Workmen's Compensation Appeal Bd. v. Worley, 23 Pa. Cmwlth. 357, 352

Abortion

The following provisions of the Abortion Control Act of 1974[95] have been pronounced unconstitutional: (1) A provision requiring written consent of the spouse, or parental consent in the case of a minor (though the court recognizes the desirability of some parental involvement wherever this is feasible); (2) an overbroad definition of "viability" which could enable the state to prohibit abortions when to do so would be inconsistent with the Supreme Court of the United States' mandate; (3) a provision which prohibits the advertising of abortion facilities; and (4) a provision requiring record keeping by abortion facilities in respect of abortions that the Commonwealth may not regulate.[96]

Recovery for wrongful death

The right to recover damages for the wrongful death of a child's father[97] is restricted to those children who would qualify to succeed on the death intestate of the putative father.[98]

Effect of cohabitation on right to alimony

Whatever may be the rights to alimony of a wife who is divorced for her adultery,[99] such a decree can, in the exercise of the court's discretion, be vacated on the ground of her sexual misconduct after divorce.[1]

Tort actions

The tort action for criminal conversation has been abolished. It is stated, not only that it was an anachronism, but that it would

---

A.2d 240 (1976), holding that the purpose of the provision is not to punish, but to establish equality of treatment to persons disqualified by remarriage and persons who cohabit without marriage.

[95] 35 Pa. Cons. Stat., § 6601 et seq.
[96] Doe v. Zimmerman, 405 F. Supp. 534 (M.D. Pa., 1975); Planned Parenthood Assn. v. Fitzpatrick, 401 F. Supp. 554 (E.D. Pa., 1975).
[97] 20 Pa. Cons. Stat., § 3371 et seq.
[98] Frazier v. Oil Chemical Co., 407 Pa. 78, 179 A.2d 202 (1962).
[99] See Commonwealth v. Callen, 165 Pa. Super. 163, 67 A.2d 610 (1949).
[1] See Commonwealth v. Hull, 9 Adams Co. L. J. 104 (1967); Commonwealth v. Levitz, 75 Montg. Co. L. R. 174 (1958).

be unreasonable to impose such harsh results on a defendant who has no real opportunity to interject logically valid defenses such as the role of plaintiff's spouse in the matter or the quality of the marriage prior to the occurrence of acts constituting the tort.[2] An action for alienation of affections no longer lies unless the defendant is a parent, or one *in loco parentis,* or a brother or sister of the plaintiff's spouse.[3] Even such close relatives of the spouse would in all likelihood enjoy a limited privilege, only an abuse of which would entail tort liability.

Possible criminal liability

The Pennsylvania joint council on the criminal justice system has recommended repeal of all laws regulating private sex behavior between consenting adults.[4] And the present statutes provide that, when the definition of sex offenses excludes conduct with a spouse, this term extends to persons living as man and wife, regardless of the legal status of their relationship.[5]

The statute proscribing fornication was repealed in 1972.[6] Adultery is no longer criminally punishable,[7] and the conduct labeled adultery has no application to a participant who is not the married one.[8] Bigamy, however, remains a crime,[9] and the "wife" of one validly married to another cannot claim support from the "husband."[10] For statutory rape, the defendant must be at least eighteen years old and the victim below the age of fourteen.[11] Reasonable mistake is a defense only if the criminality of the conduct depends on the child's being below an age older than fourteen.[12] The crime of incest is still on the books.[13]

---

[2] Fadgen v. Lenkner, 469 Pa. 272, 365 A.2d 147 (1976).
[3] 48 Pa. Cons. Stat., § 170.
[4] See Constitutional Law—Right of Privacy—Sodomy Statutes—Supreme Court Summary Affirmance, 15 Duquesne L. Rev. 123 (1976).
[5] 18 Pa. Cons. Stat., § 3103.
[6] See Commonwealth v. Smith, 238 Pa. Super. 422, 357 A.2d 583 (1976).
[7] 18 Pa. Cons. Stat., § 4505 was repealed in 1972.
[8] Hollenbaugh v. Carnegie Free Library, 436 F. Supp. 1328 (W.D. Pa., 1977), affd. without published opinion 578 F.2d 1374 (C.A.-3 Pa., 1978).
[9] 18 Pa. Cons. Stat., § 4301.
[10] Commonwealth ex rel. Alexander v. Alexander, 446 Pa. 511, 284 A.2d 721 (1971).
[11] 18 Pa. Cons. Stat., § 3122.
[12] Id., § 3102.
[13] Id., § 4507.

In holding the sodomy statute constitutional as applied to consenting adults in prison, a court has indicated doubts as to its constitutionality as applied to consenting adults other than prisoners.[14]

Concealment of the death of an illegitimate child, "so that it may not come to light, whether it was born dead or alive or whether it was murdered or not" is a criminal offense.[15]

Status of children

Provisions controlling the status of an illegitimate vis-a-vis the putative father seem clearly in need of revision. For example, the only situation in which it can succeed on intestacy is where the parents have intermarried.[16] Again, in construing a will making reference to "children," the term is to refer only to legitimate children unless the parents have married.[17] Further, for the purposes of a conveyance to one described by relationship to the grantor or to another, an illegitimate child is regarded as a child of the mother but not of the father.[18]

Paternity can be established by civil proceedings, for example, where the father seeks a judicial determination of his paternity,[19] or by proceedings of a criminal nature.[20] If a civil proceeding to obtain a support order is brought, and the father disputes paternity, he must appeal from the support order; if he does not,

---

[14]United States v. Brewer, 363 F. Supp. 606 (M.D. Pa., 1973), affd. without published opinion 491 F.2d 751 (C.A.-3 Pa., 1973), cert. den. 416 U.S. 990, 40 L. Ed. 2d 768, 94 Sup. Ct. 2399 (1974). Voluntary deviate sexual intercourse is a misdemeanor. 18 Pa. Cons. Stat., § 3124.

[15]18 Pa. Cons. Stat., § 4303.

[16]20 Pa. Cons. Stat., § 2107. Compare section 3.3, herein.

[17]Id., § 2514. As to the nonapplicability of the provisions controlling lapsed and void devises and legacies to illegitimate children of the father, see § 2514(8) et seq.

[18]Id., § 6114(5). Illegitimacy in Pennsylvania, 78 Dick. L. Rev. 684 (1974).

[19]18 Pa. Cons. Stat., § 4323. See Commonwealth ex rel. Valentine v. Strongel, 246 Pa. Super. 466, 371 A.2d 931 (1977). As to the invalidity of regulations whereunder mothers are required to co-operate with the Department of Public Welfare as a condition of receiving public assistance, see Williams v. Commissioner, Dept. of Public Welfare, —— Pa. ——, 392 A.2d 340 (1978).

[20]62 Pa. Cons. Stat., § 2043.31 et seq. A classification in a bastardy statute which imposed greater sanctions on a male offender than a female was unconstitutional. Commonwealth v. Staub, 461 Pa. 486, 337 A.2d 258 (1975).

6.39 UNMARRIED COUPLES AND THE LAW

paternity is established as a matter of law.[21] If he is criminally charged with neglect to support a bastard,[22] and the charge is dismissed for want of prosecution within the statutory time limit, in any subsequent civil action to obtain support he is entitled to all the procedural rights of one accused of crime.[23] A conviction for nonsupport does not authorize a court to order continuance of support after the child has reached the age of eighteen years.[24]

Contrary to a rule once regarded as traditional, the mother of an illegitimate has no superior rights to that of the father in respect of custody;[25] there is no presumption that visitation privileges would be detrimental to the child.[26]

The children of a void or voidable marriage are legitimate.[27] There is, however, no provision for legitimation of a child otherwise than by subsequent intermarriage of the parents.[28] A statute enacted in 1971 forbidding the intermarriage of partners in adultery during the life of the "former" wife or husband states that nothing therein contained affects the legitimacy of a child born of the body of the wife during coverture.[29] Though adultery is no longer criminal, this can only mean that the child of such a forbidden marriage is the legitimate child of that later marriage.

A statute providing that the consent of the mother alone is

---

[21]Commonwealth ex rel. Palchinski v. Palchinski, —— Pa. Super. ——, 384 A.2d 1285 (1978). See also Commonwealth ex rel. Gonzalez v. Andreas, 245 Pa. Super. 307, 369 A.2d 416 (1976).

[22]18 Pa. Cons. Stat., § 4323. See Commonwealth v. Parrish, 250 Pa. Super. 176, 378 A.2d 884 (1977).

[23]See Matthews v. Cuff, —— Pa. Super. ——, 385 A.2d 526 (1978). As to the Uniform Act on Blood Tests to determine paternity, see 28 Pa. Cons. Stat., §§ 307.1 to 307.10.

[24]Simpson v. Saponara, 248 Pa. Super. 376, 375 A.2d 146 (1977). As to the Uniform Reciprocal Enforcement of Support Act, see 62 Pa. Cons. Stat., §§ 2043.1 to 2043.42.

[25]Commonwealth ex rel. Scott v. Martin, —— Pa. Super. ——, 381 A.2d 173 (1977).

[26]Commonwealth v. Rozanski, 206 Pa. Super. 397, 213 A.2d 155, 15 A.L.R.3d 880 (1965). As to the Uniform Child Custody Jurisdiction Act, see 11 Pa. Cons. Stat., §§ 2301 to 2325.

[27]48 Pa. Cons. Stat., § 169.1.

[28]Id., § 167.

[29]Id., § 169. Compare Johnson v. J. H. Terry Co., 182 Pa. Super. 258, 126 A.2d 793 (1956), affd. 389 Pa. 586, 133 A.2d 234 (1957), holding that a laudable inclination to legitimate children wherever possible cannot validate a marriage where it is void ab initio.

necessary for the adoption of an illegitimate[30] has been held unconstitutional.[31] If, failing an involuntary termination of her parental rights,[32] the consent of the mother is required, so must be required that of the father.[33] Such a holding goes further than the ordinary requirement that the father is entitled to his day in court[34] on the matter of the child's adoption.[35] But the difficulty may be more apparent than real. If the mother has relinquished her parental rights involuntarily, or voluntarily by surrendering the child to an adoption agency, there is nothing in the Adoption Act which requires it to establish grounds for the involuntary termination of the father's rights.[36] Provided he is afforded all possible notice and opportunity for a hearing on the matter, a court can, if it is in the child's best interests, terminate his rights even though he has not technically "abandoned" the child.[37]

Property rights of cohabitants

When a conveyance is made to an unmarried couple as husband and wife, Pennsylvania deviates from the usual rule[38] that a tenancy in common, and not a joint tenancy with rights of survivorship, results.[39] The courts recognize that, whatever the wording of the deed may be, if there is no valid marriage there can be no tenancy by the entireties.[40] Whether, however, a joint tenancy will result is dependent on the intent of the grantees.[41] If the

---

[30] 1 Pa. Cons. Stat., § 411.
[31] Adoption of M. T. T., 24 Ches. Co. Rep. 221 (1975).
[32] See In re Custody of Hernandez, 249 Pa. Super. 274, 376 A.2d 648 (1977).
[33] Adoption of Walker, 468 Pa. 165, 360 A.2d 603 (1976).
[34] See section 3.8, herein.
[35] See In re Adoption of Young, 469 Pa. 141, 364 A.2d 1307 (1976).
[36] In re Burns, 474 Pa. 615, 379 A.2d 535 (1977).
[37] But compare In re Adoption of M. T. T., 467 Pa. 88, 354 A.2d 564 (1976), where, the father having done all he could to preserve his parental relationship, the court declined to terminate his parental rights so that adoption proceedings could be begun. This points up the dilemma: a biological father's right to withhold consent to an adoption where, with the best will in the world, he cannot furnish the child's needs ought not to be allowed to block an adoption. See Child Custody: Best Interests of Children vs. Constitutional Rights of Parents, 81 Dick. L. Rev. 733 (1977).
[38] See section 4.2, herein.
[39] Masgai v. Masgai, 460 Pa. 453, 333 A.2d 861 (1975).
[40] Id.
[41] See Wosche v. Kraning, 353 Pa. 481, 46 A.2d 220 (1946) (joint bank account).

magic words "tenants by the entireties" are used, whether the living arrangements are in the mistaken belief on the part of one or both in a marriage[42] or simply meretricious,[43] the courts hold for the survivor on a basis of joint tenancy.[44] If the magic words are not present, as, for example, where the deed is to "husband and wife,"[45] a tenancy in common results and the true spouse, if any, qualifies for the decedent's share of the property.[46]

Where the relationship is meretricious, and title is taken in the name of one cohabitant only, there is authority to support an adjustment of their interests on a theory of resulting trust,[47] as well as constructive trust[48] and joint venture,[49] provided always that the proof does not evidence an intended gift to the partner resisting such a claim.[50]

It is long settled that a contract based on, or in contemplation of, present or future illicit cohabitation is void.[51] It is possible, however, that instead of harnessing these analogies to transactions of the nature of joint ventures or resulting or constructive trusts, the courts, where there has been no express agreement between cohabitants as to their property rights, will utilize the common-law marriage institution to obviate injustices, perhaps with a less rigid insistence on the oftentimes impossible requirement of establishing "words of the present tense" as a prerequisite to the creation of such a status.[52]

---

[42]See Frederick v. Southwick, 165 Pa. Super. 78, 67 A.2d 802 (1949).

[43]Maxwell v. Saylor, 359 Pa. 94, 58 A.2d 355 (1948); County Capital Bldg. & Loan Assn. v. Cummings, 55 York Leg. Rec. (1941).

[44]See Estate of Whiteman v. Whiteman, 466 Pa. 343, 353 A.2d 386 (1976); Bove v. Bove, 394 Pa. 627, 149 A.2d 67 (1959); Thornton v. Pierce, 328 Pa. 11, 194 Atl. 897 (1937).

[45]Teacher v. Kijurina, 365 Pa. 480, 76 A.2d 197 (1950). Compare Chambers v. Chambers, 406 Pa. 50, 176 A.2d 673 (1962), where, though the grantees took title as "husband and wife," they were treated as joint tenants for the purposes of enabling the man, who had conveyed the land to the woman to protect it against his creditors, to recover his one-half interest as beneficiary of a constructive trust.

[46]First Federal Sav. & Loan Assn. of Greene County v. Porter, 408 Pa. 236, 183 A.2d 318 (1962).

[47]See Orth v. Wood, 354 Pa. 121, 47 A.2d 140 (1946).

[48]Chambers v. Chambers, 406 Pa. 50, 176 A.2d 673 (1962).

[49]See Wosche v. Kraning, 353 Pa. 481, 46 A.2d 220 (1946).

[50]See Masgai v. Masgai, 460 Pa. 453, 333 A.2d 861 (1975); In re Klemow's Estate, 411 Pa. 136, 191 A.2d 365 (1963).

[51]Schrecengost v. Gallagher, 36 Erie Co. L. J. 50 (1952).

[52]See Common law Marriage and Unmarried Cohabitation: An Old Solution to a New Problem, 39 U. Pitt. L. Rev. 579 (1978).

6.40. Rhode Island

After careful consideration, based mainly on the fact that the statutes prescribing the formalities for a marriage do not state that noncompliance renders a marriage void, a court decided some years ago that common-law marriage can be entered into in Rhode Island.[53]

Welfare benefits

It is from this state that one of the landmark decisions of the United States Supreme Court on the constitutionality of the Social Security Act provisions regarding illegitimates originated. One Cuffee had for many years cohabited, without marriage, with Ruby Lucas. They had two children. When Cuffee died, he had separated from Ruby and was not contributing to their support. They were denied children's benefits under the Act. On their behalf, the Act was challenged as unconstitutional because it presumed dependency in the case of certain classes of illegitimates and conditioned eligibility on proof of dependency as to other classes, into which latter class the children fell.[54] The challenge failed.[55] It does seem harsh to permit such children's eligibility to rest on circumstances beyond their control, but given the fact that Cuffee, the insured, had no legal obligation to support them and was not contributing to their support, and that the Act withstands constitutional challenge, it is at the offspring of this type of liaison that the line is drawn. The decision, however, does not mean that a needy unwed mother is foreclosed from securing welfare benefits for herself and her children because a noncontributing male lives in the home.[56]

Adoption

Any resident of the state may adopt a child younger than himself and under eighteen. If the child is not a resident of Rhode

---

[53]Holgate v. United Elec. Ry. Co., 47 R.I. 337, 133 Atl. 243 (1926).
[54]See sections 3.2, 3.3, herein.
[55]Mathews v. Lucas, 427 U.S. 495, 49 L. Ed. 2d 651, 96 Sup. Ct. 2755 (1976), holding the legislative discrimination was reasonably related to a legitimate end.
[56]See Lund v. Affleck, 442 F. Supp. 1109 (D. R.I., 1977).

Island it must, at the time petition is filed, be in the care of a governmental or licensed child-placing agency. The spouse, if any, of the adopting party must join in the petition. Petitions to adopt persons over eighteen are heard by the probate court of the city or county in which the petitioners live.[57] No one may place a child for adoption without a license.[58] If the adoptee is not a child of one of the parties seeking to adopt it, the court is required to procure the recommendations as to suitability of the state department of social and rehabilitative services or of a licensed child placement agency.[59] Ordinarily, a six-month trial residence in the adoptive home precedes the grant of an adoption petition.[60] Adopted children, if legitimate, retain the right to inherit on the intestacy of the lawful parents. As the law presently stands, an illegitimate inherits only from the mother unless the parents have married.[61]

Workers' compensation death benefits

In many of the states that recognize a common-law marriage, a continued cohabitation, after removal of some impediment to a valid marriage, results in a common-law marriage.[62] Years ago, a Rhode Island court declined to extend this rule in favor of a woman who, while cohabiting with one Silva, filed for divorce of her husband alleging her marital fidelity and then, after the divorce, continued to cohabit with Silva. The court, seemingly outraged by her "fraud" on the court, denied her the status of a common-law wife for the purposes of workers' compensation death benefits.[63]

Abortion

Legislation which forbade the procuring of an abortion,[64] and the advertising or selling of services or drugs to procure miscar-

---

[57]R.I. Gen. Laws, § 15-7-4. As to procedures for adoptions, see §§ 15-7-1 to 15-7-26.
[58]Id., § 15-7-1.
[59]Id., § 15-7-11. As to child placement agencies, see §§ 40-13-1 to 40-13-14.
[60]Id., § 15-7-12.
[61]Id., § 15-7-17.
[62]See section 1.5, herein.
[63]Silva v. Merrit Chapman & Scott Corp., 52 R.I. 30, 156 Atl. 512 (1931).
[64]R.I. Gen. Laws, § 11-3-1.

riage,[65] was in 1973 stricken as unconstitutional in that it established a presumption that life begins at conception and that a fetus is a person.[66] The court said that Rhode Island can choose to assert or not to assert its interest in fetal life, but it cannot by enacting a presumption make its interest any more constitutionally robust and bind the Supreme Court to accord it more constitutional significance.[67] This resulted in an enactment in 1975 to the effect that the willful killing of an unborn "quick" child, unless necessary to preserve the life of the mother, is manslaughter.[68]

The problem was relegated to the state department of health, which promulgated regulations governing medical procedures to be used in the performance of abortions. These regulations reflect an attempt to alleviate inherent potential harm in abortions by ensuring that only skilled physicians, operating in medically acceptable conditions, can terminate pregnancies. In reviewing these regulations, a court has stated that even if the evidence is conclusive that life begins at conception, during the first two trimesters of pregnancy the mother has a constitutional right to terminate her pregnancy; that the Supreme Court of the United States has taken this aspect out of the state's hands, leaving to the state the sole task of ensuring that procedures for terminating pregnancy at this stage are medically safe.[69]

Tort actions

The tort actions for alienation of affections and criminal conversation remain very much alive.[70]

---

[65]Id., §§ 11-3-4, 11-3-5.
[66]Doe v. Israel, 482 F.2d 156 (C.A.-1 R.I., 1973), cert. den. 416 U.S. 993, 40 L. Ed. 2d 772, 94 Sup. Ct. 2406 (1974).
[67]Id.
[68]R.I. Gen. Laws, § 11-23-5.
[69]Constitutional Right to Life Committee v. Cannon, 117 R.I. 152, 363 A.2d 215 (1976).
[70]See Bailey v. Huling, —— R.I. ——, 377 A.2d 220 (1977) ($75,000 for alienation of affections, $1,000 for criminal conversation). As to the one-year statute of limitations, see R.I. Gen. Laws, § 9-1-14.

6.40 UNMARRIED COUPLES AND THE LAW

Remarriage and right to alimony

Remarriage of a divorcee, unless otherwise provided in the decree, constitutes an abandonment of the right to alimony.[71]

Possible criminal liability

Fornication is punishable by a maximum fine of $10.[72] Sexual intercourse where either participant is married is adultery as to each participant.[73] Not only is bigamy criminal,[74] but the marriage is void and the children illegitimate.[75] The performance of a bigamous marriage is also punishable as crime.[76] The age of consent for statutory rape is sixteen.[77]

Assault with intent to commit the abominable and detestable crime against nature,[78] as well as the crime itself,[79] are punishable. The provision has been held applicable to all unnatural sexual copulation,[80] and one who forced a victim to participate has no standing to challenge its constitutionality as applied to consenting adults.[81]

A charge for criminal concealment of a birth out of wedlock[82] can be joined with a murder count.[83]

Status of children

An illegitimate child can inherit or transmit inheritance on the part of the mother as if legitimate. Its rights vis-a-vis the father

---

[71] R.I. Gen. Laws, § 15-5-6.
[72] Id., § 11-6-3.
[73] Id., § 11-6-2.
[74] Id., § 11-6-1.
[75] Id., § 15-1-5. Compare § 15-8-21 (issue of marriage declared null in law are legitimate).
[76] Id., § 15-3-11.
[77] Id., § 11-37-2.
[78] Id., § 11-5-1.
[79] Id., § 11-10-1.
[80] State v. Milne, 95 R.I. 315, 187 A.2d 136 (1962), appeal dismissed 373 U.S. 542, 10 L. Ed. 2d 687, 83 Sup. Ct. 1539 (1963).
[81] State v. Levitt, —— R.I. ——, 371 A.2d 596 (1977). As to incest, see R.I. Gen. Laws, § 11-6-4. As to the prohibited degrees of relationship, see §§ 15-1-1 to 15-1-6.
[82] R.I. Gen. Laws, § 11-18-4.
[83] Id., § 11-23-4.

are conditioned on the parents' intermarriage and acknowledgment of the child as theirs.[84] In view of the Supreme Court's decision in Trimble v. Gordon,[85] this statute clearly calls for amendment.

Provisions of a standard nature control the establishment of paternity of an illegitimate and the enforcement of support obligations.[86] Compromise agreements made by or on behalf of the mother do not bar other remedies to establish or enforce the putative father's liability unless they have received judicial approval and are incorporated in a support order.[87]

Termination of parental rights

Careful provision is made to ensure that a putative father, if his identity can be ascertained, receives notice before parental rights can be terminated or an adoption decreed. If there is a reasonable probability that publication of notice will lead to ascertainment of his identity, the court has discretion to so order. In no case can adoption be decreed without an adjudication as to his rights or an order terminating his rights.[88] If the child has been legitimated by marriage of the parents, the father's consent is of course a prerequisite.[89] Notwithstanding a provision that the children of a bigamous marriage are illegitimate,[90] if it was the man who was already married, a bigamous marriage between the biological parents, at least where the woman acted in good faith, legitimates the children.[91] The provision legitimating the issue of a null

---

[84]Id., § 33–1–8. See Scalzi v. Folsom, 156 F. Supp. 838 (D. R.I., 1957), holding a child not qualified to take on the father's intestacy not to qualify for insurance benefits under the Social Security Act.

[85]See section 3.3, herein.

[86]See R.I. Gen. Laws, §§ 15–8–1 et seq., 15–9–1 to 15–9–8. Blood tests, if they exclude the possibility of paternity, are permitted in evidence. Id., § 15–8–13. As to enforcement of support, see §§ 15–11–1 to 15–11–37.

[87]Id., § 15–8–7.

[88]Id., § 15–7–26. A divorced father owes a duty of support even though the divorce decree awarded custody to the mother and was silent as to support duties; hence, such a father, if found to be derelict in his duty in this respect, can forfeit any right to veto an adoption. See In re Adoption of L. & G., —— R.I. ——, 373 A.2d 799 (1977).

[89]Sklaroff v. Stevens, 84 R.I. 1, 120 A.2d 694 (1956).

[90]Note 75, supra.

[91]Bernier v. Bernier, 101 R.I. 697, 227 A.2d 112 (1967).

marriage[92] modifies the earlier provision.[93] (If it was the mother who was already married, there is no reason to suppose that the children would not presumptively be the legitimate children of her husband.)

Property rights of cohabitants

The courts recognize that a void marriage cannot result in a tenancy by the entireties, whatever the wording of a conveyance.[94]

6.41. South Carolina

Not only does this state recognize common-law marriage, but there is a strong presumption favoring marriage by cohabitation if the cohabitation is apparently matrimonial and the parties are accepted as spouses over a long period.[95] The requirement of "words of the present tense," so often rigidly insisted on,[96] is not apparent from the decisions. However, if the cohabitants wish to be assured recognition of their marital status, an official record can be obtained by two or more witnesses who were informed of their status swearing before a marriage officer that they know the cohabitants to have lived as husband and wife.[97]

Removal of an impediment to marriage does not convert a bigamous marriage into a common-law marriage. There must be a new mutual agreement to enter into a common-law marriage. In Byers v. Mount Vernon Mills, Inc.,[98] a contest arose between two competitors for the status of a "widow" for workers' compensation death benefits. Byers had married one Martha in 1950,

---

[92]R.I. Gen. Laws, § 15-8-21.
[93]Bernier v. Bernier, note 91, supra. Generally, see Status of Illegitimates in New England, 38 B. U. L. Rev. 299 (1958).
[94]Cavanagh v. Cavanagh, —— R.I. ——, 375 A.2d 911 (1977).
[95]Jeanes v. Jeanes, 255 S.C. 161, 177 S.E.2d 537 (1970). Validity of marriage is controlled by law of place of the contract. Zwerling v. Zwerling, —— S.C. ——, 244 S.E.2d 311 (1978).
[96]See section 1.5, herein. See also Common-Law Marriage: What It Is and How to Prove It, 12 S.C. L. Q. 355 (1960).
[97]S.C. Code, § 20-1-570.
[98]268 S.C. 68, 231 S.E.2d 699 (1977).

while he was already married to another. His wife divorced him in 1956, and he continued to live with Martha until 1967. He then married Dorothy in 1968 and lived with her until his death in 1973. Had a common-law marriage resulted from the cohabitation with Martha between 1957 and 1967, his marriage to Dorothy could have been bigamous and void. But the court held for Dorothy. Where, on the other hand, it can be shown by a preponderance of the evidence that, after termination of the marriage which rendered the relationship bigamous, the parties consistently represent themselves as husband and wife in the community, the presumption that the illicit relationship continues is rebutted,[99] and a common-law marriage results.

There is statutory provision for the issuance of a marriage license to persons under eighteen if the female is either pregnant or has borne a child.[1]

Schoolteachers

Worthy of note in passing is that "just cause" for the revocation or suspension of a teacher's credentials can consist of conviction of any crime, or for immorality, or for conduct involving moral turpitude.[2] Whether living together without marriage would qualify as "just cause" remains to be seen.

Adoption

The following persons are eligible to adopt a child: (a) a husband and wife jointly, or either the husband or wife if the other spouse is a parent of the child; (b) an unmarried person who is at least of legal age; (c) a married person at least of legal age who is legally separated from the other spouse; and (d) the unmarried father or mother, regardless of his or her age, of his or her illegitimate child.[3]

Traditionally, consent to an adoption may be revoked at any time before the decree. Today, however, the courts are reluctant to

---

[99] Kirby v. Kirby, —— S.C. ——, 241 S.E.2d 415 (1978).
[1] S.C. Code, § 20–1–300. As to the age of consent for marriage, see § 20–1–250.
[2] Id., § 59–250–160.
[3] Id., § 15–45–30.

permit such consent to be withdrawn, particularly where the child has been taken into the home of the adoptive parents, unless a strong showing is made that the adoption sought would not be in the best interests of the child.[4]

Workers' compensation death benefits

Under workers' compensation, acknowledged illegitimate children qualify for death benefits even if they were not actually supported by the decedent parent.[5] Since a bigamous cohabitant would not qualify as a "widow,"[6] it can be assumed that the qualification of an unwed cohabitant would rest on whether a common-law marriage can be established.

Abortion

South Carolina's abortion statutes were ruled unconstitutional in 1973,[7] and have been supplanted by legislation[8] which recognizes that until a child is viable, the mother's constitutionally protected right to terminate her pregnancy must prevail over any interest the state may have in the preservation of fetal life.[9] The statute requires spousal consent if the mother has reached the third trimester of pregnancy,[10] and parental consent, or the consent of those *in loco parentis,* if the mother is unmarried and under sixteen or incompetent, unless life is endangered.[11]

Recovery for wrongful death

An illegitimate child can recover for the wrongful death of its mother, and the mother, or a brother or sister of the illegitimate, can recover for the wrongful death of the illegitimate.[12] It has

---

[4]See Ellison v. Camby, 269 S.C. 48, 236 S.E.2d 197 (1977).
[5]Flemon v. Dickert-Keowee, Inc., 259 S.C. 99, 190 S.E.2d 751 (1972).
[6]Byers v. Mount Vernon Mills, Inc., 268 S.C. 68, 231 S.E.2d 699 (1977).
[7]State v. Lawrence, 261 S.C. 18, 198 S.E.2d 253 (1973).
[8]S.C. Code, § 44–41–10 et seq.
[9]Floyd v. Anders, 440 F. Supp. 535 (D. S.C., 1977).
[10]S.C. Code, § 44–41–20.
[11]Id., § 44–41–30.
[12]Id., § 15–51–30.

been held that a woman living in adultery is not a "widow" of her decedent partner for the purposes of a wrongful death action.[13]

Effect of cohabitation on right to alimony

By statute,[14] an adulterous wife cannot be awarded alimony.[15] If, by the terms of the divorce decree, alimony is to terminate on a remarriage of the wife, the effect of post-divorce cohabitation will depend on whether it constitutes a common-law marriage.[16] Absent a provision as to remarriage in the decree, remarriage does not automatically require a termination or modification of the right to alimony.[17] No doubt, if the alimony was intended to ensure continued support for the divorced wife and was not intended as a part of the judicial adjustment of the property rights of the spouses, a divorced husband would have a strong case for modification of the decree if he can show a cohabitant is caring for his ex-wife's needs.

Tort actions

Statutory limitations on costs in an action for criminal conversation or for seduction, indicate the continued viability of such causes of action.[18]

Possible criminal liability

Overlapping statutes cover the crimes of living together and carnal intercourse with each other or habitual carnal intercourse without living together of a man and woman, both being unmarried (fornication),[19] and adultery or fornication.[20] In addition to

---

[13] See Folk v. United States, 102 F. Supp. 736 (W.D. S.C., 1952), revd. on other grounds 199 F.2d 889 (C.A.-4 S.C., 1952).
[14] S.C. Code, § 20–3–130.
[15] Nienow v. Nienow, 268 S.C. 161, 232 S.E.2d 504 (1977); Page v. Page, 260 S.C. 298, 195 S.E.2d 613 (1973); Johnson v. Johnson, 251 S.C. 420, 163 S.E.2d 229 (1968).
[16] See Rogers v. Rogers, 260 S.C. 613, 197 S.E.2d 921 (1973); Jeanes v. Jeanes, 255 S.C. 161, 177 S.E.2d 537 (1970).
[17] Darden v. Witham, 258 S.C. 380, 188 S.E.2d 776 (1972).
[18] S.C. Code, § 15–37–50.
[19] Id., § 16–15–80.
[20] Id., § 16–15–60.

denouncing bigamy,[21] it is provided that such marriages are void, with a qualification protecting, inter alia, one whose spouse has been absent for seven years and is not known to be living during that time.[22]

A "maid" under sixteen is protected from abduction by criminal sanctions,[23] and, for the deflowering or the contracting of marriage with such a maid, the "parties grieved" by such conduct can receive a moiety of the fine imposed.[24] Seduction under promise of marriage is also within the ban of the criminal law.[25] With this proliferation of sanctions, it is readily understandable that the criminal sexual conduct with minors provision restricts itself to very young children victims. If the victim is over fourteen but less than sixteen, this statute is violated only when the actor is older than the victim, or in a position of familial, custodial or official authority to coerce the victim to submit.[26] "The abominable crime of buggery, whether with mankind or with beast"[27] does not as yet appear to have encountered constitutional challenge.

Status of children

South Carolina has provisions, rarely present in state statutes, which restrict the amount in which gifts, testamentary[28] or otherwise,[29] can be made to an illegitimate child.

The right to inherit on intestacy by or from illegitimates is on the mother's side only.[30] A contention that denial of the right to inherit from the putative father constituted a denial of equal

---

[21] Id., § 16–15–10.
[22] Id., § 20–1–80.
[23] Id., § 16–15–30.
[24] Id., § 16–15–40.
[25] Id., § 16–15–50.
[26] Id., § 16–3–655. As to incest, see § 16–15–20.
[27] Id., § 16–15–120.
[28] Id., § 21–7–480.
[29] Id., § 27–23–100. The statute restricting an illegitimate's testamentary share of the father's estate does not relate to property the decedent held out of state. Humphries v. Settlemeyer, 91 S.C. 389, 74 S.E. 892 (1912). Nor do the proceeds of a life insurance policy payable to a named beneficiary fall within the reach of these provisions. Bynum v. Prudential Ins. Co. of America, 77 F. Supp. 56 (E.D. S.C., 1948).

These restrictions also apply to gifts to a paramour.
[30] S.C. Code, § 21–3–30.

protection received curt and peremptory dismissal in 1960,[31] but the times have changed.[32]

The children of marriages contracted after the seven-year absence of a spouse, such spouse not known to be living during that period, are legitimate and the legal heirs of their parents.[33] Marriage of the parents also legitimizes the children who then qualify to succeed on intestacy.[34]

Though a proceeding to establish paternity is required to be brought within three years of the birth of the child, this does not preclude an action brought by the department of social services, as assignee of support rights the mother enjoys, from enforcing support obligations when paternity was not so established within the statutory period.[35]

In addition to the usual requirement of parental consent as a prerequisite to the adoption of a child unless parental rights have been judicially terminated, provision now exists in respect to the putative father of an illegitimate. If he has consistently on a continuing basis exercised rights and performed duties as a parent his consent must be secured.[36] Such consent, however, is not required if he is a party to the adoption proceedings (and duly served) or when parental rights have been judicially terminated.[37] This provision, though it does not have the effect of giving him a veto, goes far to ensure that, if his identity is known, he will receive his day in court when the adoption is under consideration.

Property rights of cohabitants

The courts have long been loyal to the concept that a promise in consideration of future illicit cohabitation is void as against pub-

---

[31] Walker v. Walker, 274 F.2d 425 (C.A.-4 S.C., 1960).
[32] See section 3.3, herein.
[33] S.C. Code, § 20-1-50.
[34] Id., § 20-1-60.
[35] South Carolina Dept. of Social Services v. Lowman, 269 S.C. 41, 236 S.E.2d 194 (1977). As to nonsupport of an illegitimate by the father, see S.C. Code, § 20-7-40. Such nonsupport can form the basis for a criminal prosecution. See State v. Bailey, 253 S.C. 304, 170 S.E.2d 376 (1969).
As to enforcement of support, see S.C. Code, § 20-7-110 et seq.
[36] S.C. Code, § 15-45-70(b).
[37] Id.

lic policy.[38] Further, where a mistress performed only such services as were incidental to the meretricious relationship, even an express agreement for compensation was unenforceable.[39]

More recent decisions, however, could well indicate that, *on a proper showing,* an equitable division of the accumulations of cohabitants, albeit "meretricious" is not to be ruled out. In Glover v. Glover,[40] the parties had lived together without marriage for twenty years. On termination of their relationship the woman's claim for a half interest in the "family" home on the basis of a resulting trust failed. Although she had paid the man $500 to enable him to pay his outstanding debts in order to qualify for a loan to buy the home, her claim was rejected on ground that she had not contributed any portion of the purchase money at the time of the purchase (a technical requirement for the resulting trust), and testimony that they "pooled" their income to pay family obligations, including the mortgage, was held insufficient. In Kirby v. Kirby,[41] the male cohabitant's effort to assert an equitable interest in the proceeds of property owned by the woman on the basis of his substantial monetary contributions to its improvement failed because the court found that a common-law marriage had come into existence, and therefore such contributions were presumptively intended as gifts.

6.42. South Dakota

Common-law marriages receive recognition only if entered into prior to 1959.[42] Where a couple were married, divorced, and resumed cohabitation without a second marriage prior to 1959, and

---

[38]Prince v. Mathews, 159 S.C. 526, 157 S.E. 836 (1931).

[39]Grant v. Butt, 198 S.C. 298, 17 S.E.2d 689 (1941) (contract whereunder a black woman agreed to live as the concubine of a white man and to refrain from marriage in consideration of the man's promise to leave her half of his estate was held void).

[40]268 S.C. 433, 234 S.E.2d 488 (1977).

[41] —— S.C. ——, 241 S.E.2d 415 (1978). The fact that contractual attempts to impose a support obligation on a wife towards her husband or family are void, being based on totally different rationale (see Towles v. Towles, 256 S.C. 307, 182 S.E.2d 53 (1971)), sheds no light on the possible attitude of South Carolina courts to extramarital cohabitation situations where sexual relations form no part of the consideration.

[42]S.D. Codified Laws Ann., § 25–1–29.

the cohabitation continued until the husband's death, the period of separation having been short in comparison with the period of their cohabitation after divorce, a court regarded them as common-law spouses.[43] And this notwithstanding that their wills made reference to the cohabitants as "divorced husband" and "divorced wife" respectively. The decision seems to contradict any notion that pre-1959 liaisons would require words of the present tense[44] to achieve recognition as common-law marriage.

Adoption

A minor may be adopted by any adult who is at least ten years older than the adoptee.[45]

Schoolteachers

A decision upholding, in the interest of parental rights to control the upbringing of their children, the termination of an unmarried South Dakota schoolteacher who lived openly with a male friend[46] has received earlier mention.[47]

Insurance benefits

There seems little doubt that a cohabitant would have an insurable interest in the life or health of the other;[48] and discrimination in the issuance or renewal of automobile insurance on the basis of marital status (or the lack thereof?) is expressly prohibited.[49]

---

[43]In re Estate of Miller, —— S.D. ——, 243 N.W.2d 788 (1976). Provisions permit the marriage of underage minors in cases of pregnancy or childbirth. See S.D. Codified Laws Ann., § 25–1–12.
[44]See section 1.5, herein.
[45]S.D. Codified Laws Ann., § 25–6–2. Generally, as to adoption of illegitimate children, see § 25–6–1 et seq. As to the rights of the putative father, see notes 84 to 87, infra.
[46]Sullivan v. Meade County Independent School Dist. No. 101, 387 F. Supp. 1237 (D. S.D., 1975), affd. 530 F.2d 799 (C.A.-8 S.D., 1976).
[47]See section 2.3, herein.
[48]See S.D. Codified Laws Ann., § 58–10–4(2).
[49]Id., § 58–11–55.

Workers' compensation death benefits

Even where spouses are not living together, a lawful wife may be presumed dependent for the purposes of the workers' compensation death benefits.[50] A mere cohabitant probably would not qualify.[51] On principle, an illegitimate child, at least if dependency on the decedent is shown, would.[52]

Abortion

The Supreme Court of the United States' abortion rulings[53] have led to a carefully considered statute[54] regulating abortions virtually to the maximum extent permissible with the constraints of those decisions. Eloquent of the legislative attitude is a concluding provision that the chapter "is repealed on that specific date upon which the states are given exclusive authority to regulate abortions."[55] One possibly vulnerable provision is that requiring parental consent if the mother is an unmarried minor, and spousal consent if she is a married minor.[56] Abortions other than those authorized under this chapter are felonious,[57] as is the intentional killing of a fetus by unauthorized injury to the mother.[58]

Tort actions

Provisions "forbidding" the abduction of a spouse, or seduction of a wife or daughter,[59] have been construed as imposing civil liability only.[60] A tort action lies for seduction not only by relatives of the person seduced,[61] but also by the unmarried woman

---

[50] See Demaray v. Mannerud Constr. Co., 80 S.D. 554, 128 N.W.2d 551 (1964).
[51] See section 2.13, herein.
[52] Id.
[53] See section 2.19, herein.
[54] S.D. Codified Laws Ann., § 34–23A–1 et seq.
[55] Id., § 34–23A–21.
[56] Id., § 34–23A–7.
[57] Id., § 22–17–5.
[58] Id., § 22–17–6.
[59] Id., § 20–9–7.
[60] See Vander Linden v. Oster, 37 S.D. 113, 156 N.W. 911 (1916).
[61] S.D. Codified Laws Ann., § 21–4–2.

herself.[62] If the seducer marries her, and then abandons her, she can include in her damages support and education needs of any child of the forbidden union.[63] The existence of a provision for a six-year statute of limitations in an action for criminal conversation indicates that this tort retains recognition.[64]

Possible criminal liability

Compelling a woman to enter into a marriage (which would of course be annullable)[65] is a crime.[66] Adultery is no longer criminally punishable. Only the married participant can be convicted of bigamy.[67] Those who are not legally married and are within the degrees of consanguinity within which a marriage would be void, who have sexual intercourse, commit incest.[68] The age of consent for statutory rape is fifteen.[69]

A judge of many decades past who regretted it necessary "to soil the pages of our reports with a discussion of a subject so loathsome and disgusting"[70] would no doubt have enhanced regrets were he to learn that the sodomy statutes have been repealed.

Status of children

To qualify for succession on a father's intestacy, a child born out of wedlock (the term "illegitimate" receives legislative disapproval)[71] must establish that the father, in writing, before competent witness, acknowledged paternity. If he is legitimated by the subsequent marriage of his parents, the father must have acknowledged him and adopted him into his family.[72] However a

---

[62] Id., § 21-4-3.
[63] Id., § 21-4-4.
[64] Id., § 15-2-13(5).
[65] Id., § 22-22-11.
[66] Id., § 25-3-5.
[67] Id., § 22-22-15.
[68] Id., § 22-22-19.
[69] Id., § 22-22-1.
[70] State v. Whitmarsh, 26 S.D. 426, 429, 128 N.W. 580, 581 (1910).
[71] S.D. Codified Laws Ann., § 25-8-46.
[72] Id., §§ 29-1-15, 29-1-16. As to legitimation by subsequent marriages of parents, see § 25-5-5. As to provision for new birth certificates, see §§ 34-25-15, 34-25-16.4, 34-25-16.5.

court, anticipating the reasoning of the Supreme Court of the United States[73] by about twenty years, held a child not precluded from inheriting from his putative father by reason of noncompliance with this statute where the child was otherwise legitimized by the father's public acknowledgment of paternity and receipt of the child into his family.[74] Such a decision, evidentiary of a strong public policy favoring legitimacy,[75] carries legislative support.[76]

Procedures for the establishment of paternity and the enforcement of support obligations are controlled by the Uniform Illegitimacy Act.[77] The department of social services may sue to establish and enforce these obligations.[78] The proceedings, which can be civil or criminal in nature, are a function of the state's attorney,[79] but they can be initiated either by the mother or her representatives or by those furnishing support for the child,[80] or by public authorities, if the child is likely to become a public charge.[81]

Prima facie, it is the mother who is entitled to the custody of and earnings of her illegitimate child,[82] and her marital misconduct is not in itself sufficient grounds on which custody can be transferred to the father.[83]

The right of a putative father to notice in adoption, dependency, delinquency or termination of parental rights proceedings is restricted, in effect, to situations where he has been identified by

---

[73]See section 3.3, herein.
[74]In re Kessler's Estate, 76 S.D. 158, 74 N.W.2d 599 (1956).
[75]Application of G. K., —— S.D. ——, 248 N.W.2d 380 (1976).
[76]S.D. Codified Laws Ann., § 25-6-1. A child born out of wedlock and subsequently adopted does not, by virtue of adoption, lose the right conferred by the statute to inherit from the natural mother. Harrell v. McDonald, —— S.D. ——, 242 N.W.2d 148 (1976).
[77]S.D. Codified Laws Ann., §§ 25-8-1 to 25-8-48.
[78]Id., § 26-4-8. For criticism of the handicaps with which a putative father can be faced in paternity proceedings, see Requiring an AFDC Applicant to Name Her Child's Father: Are the Rights of the Putative Father Being Protected?, 23 S.D. L. Rev. 379 (1978).
[79]S.D. Codified Laws Ann., §§ 7-16-12, 7-16-13.
[80]Id., § 25-8-6.
[81]Id., § 25-8-10. As to enforcement of support, see §§ 25-9-1 to 25-9-31.
[82]Id., § 25-5-10.
[83]See Kester v. Kester, —— S.D. ——, 257 N.W.2d 731 (1977). As to the Child Custody Jurisdiction Act, see S.D. Codified Laws Ann., § 26-5-5 et seq.

the mother or has in specified ways indicated his interest as a parent.[84] In the light of Quilloin v. Walcott,[85] these qualifications would probably withstand a challenge of unconstitutionality. One court has held that, if he has made every reasonable effort to receive the child into his home but is obstructed by the mother in these efforts, there is "constructive" receipt of the child into his home for the purposes of the statute[86] wherein a child can be legitimated in this way,[87] in which case his right to notice and a hearing is beyond dispute.

Property rights of cohabitants

Tenancy by the entireties is a concept unknown to South Dakota; husband and wife hold either as joint tenants or as tenants in common.[88]

It has long been recognized that where land has been purchased through equal monetary contributions of unmarried cohabitants, both aware of the nonexistence of a valid marriage, the courts will not permit the mere fact that they hold themselves out as married to enable one of them to assert sole title. They will be held joint owners.[89] In the absence of a controlling contract, where title was taken in the name of the woman during their cohabitation and, though the man had contributed little if anything beyond labor to improve the property, it was held erroneous to award the land to the man.[90] The court took the position that the extent of their respective interests should be proportioned to their respective contributions.

Of particular significance is the qualification, articulated in the latter case, relating to the absence of an express contract.

---

[84]S.D. Codified Laws Ann., § 25–6–1.1.
[85]See section 3.8, herein.
[86]S.D. Codified Laws Ann., § 25–6–1.
[87]Application of G. K., —— S.D. ——, 248 N.W.2d 380 (1976). As to consent requirements where the minor adoptee is to be removed from the state, see S.D. Codified Laws Ann., § 25–5A–7.1. See also Adoption of Illegitimate Children, 4 S.D. L. Rev. 192 (1959).
[88]S.D. Codified Laws Ann., § 25–2–3.
[89]Bracken v. Bracken, 45 S.D. 430, 188 N.W. 46 (1922) and 52 S.D. 252, 217 N.W. 192 (1927).
[90]Beuck v. Howe, 71 S.D. 288, 23 N.W.2d 744 (1946).

6.43. Tennessee

Common-law marriages are replaced by statutory or ceremonial marriages.[91] The courts, however, continue to recognize common-law marriages if contracted in a state where valid.[92] Furthermore, over the years the courts of Tennessee have demonstrated a readiness to presume, from the fact of cohabitation as husband and wife over a long period, a valid marriage based on a theory of estoppel.[93] "Through the use of the presumptions of marriage, continuance of marriage, death or divorce, and legitimacy, in addition to a myriad of lesser presumptions which support them, the courts have developed a flexible system which gives great weight to those factors which protect the integrity of the family unit, the legitimacy of children and the capacity of inheritance."[94] This estoppel rationale, however, seems to be favored only when the rights or status of innocent persons require it. It has been rejected as a basis for claims by surviving females to be de facto widows of decedents.[95]

Adoption

Any person over the age of eighteen may petition to adopt a minor. This age restriction however, does not apply where the mother of an illegitimate seeks to adopt it. If they are spouses, one of them must ordinarily be a citizen of the United States; though if the child is not a citizen, the petitioner is not required to be a citizen.[96] A statutory framework is provided for the monitoring and planning for children in the care of foster parents. It is aimed at either returning the child to its natural parents, or its place-

---

[91] King v. Clinchfield R. Co., 131 F. Supp. 218 (E.D. Tenn., 1955).
[92] See Shelby County v. Williams, 510 S.W.2d 73 (Tenn., 1974); Troxel v. Jones, 45 Tenn. App. 264, 322 S.W.2d 251 (1959); Hill & Range Songs, Inc. v. Fred Rose Music, Inc., 403 F. Supp. 420 (M.D. Tenn., 1975), affd. 570 F.2d 554 (C.A.-6 Tenn., 1978).
[93] See Common-Law Marriage in Tennessee, 21 Tenn. L. Rev. 197 (1952); Informal Marriage in Tennessee—Marriage by Estoppel, by Prescription and by Ratification, 3 Vand. L. Rev. 610 (1950).
[94] Use of Presumptions in Providing the Existence of Marriage Relationships in Tennessee, 5 Memphis St. U. L. Rev. 409, 419 (1975).
[95] See Crawford v. Crawford, 198 Tenn. 9, 277 S.W.2d 389 (1955); Rambeau v. Faris, 186 Tenn. 503, 212 S.W.2d 359 (1948).
[96] Tenn. Code Ann., § 36–105.

ment for adoption, or the ensuring of proper arrangements for its further foster care.[97]

Workers' compensation death benefits

Under workers' compensation, the child of an unwed cohabitation, if the requirement of dependency can be shown, qualifies for benefits on the death of the father.[98] Such a child, if under sixteen, is conclusively presumed a dependent,[99] assuming the claimant is able to establish paternity.[1] The same extends to a posthumous illegitimate child on establishment of paternity.[2] Adoption of the illegitimate, since it puts an end to any duty of the natural father to support the child, disqualifies the child for such benefits.[3]

Unless living apart from the worker at the time of his death, a wife, too, is conclusively presumed to be dependent.[4] One who claims on the basis of an out of state common-law marriage would have to establish the validity of such a marriage.[5] As to a bigamous spouse, there is some reluctance to harness the presumption favoring the later of two successive marriages where the later spouse knew of the impediment, even if she was in fact dependent on the worker.[6] If she was ignorant of the impediment, the reluctance is less apparent.[7]

Insurance benefits

As is so often the case,[8] a cohabitant is not regarded as a member of an insured's "family" when the effect would be to ex-

---

[97]Id., §§ 37–1501 to 37–1510.
[98]Memphis Fertilizer Co. v. Small, 160 Tenn. 235, 22 S.W.2d 1037 (1930).
[99]Williams v. Travelers Ins. Co., 530 S.W.2d 283 (Tenn., 1975).
[1]Terry v. Burlington Industries, Inc., 220 Tenn. 668, 423 S.W.2d 476 (1968).
[2]Shelley v. Central Woodwork, Inc., 207 Tenn. 411, 340 S.W.2d 896 (1960). See also Workmen's Compensation—Dependency—Posthumous Illegitimate Child, 29 Tenn. L. Rev. 600 (1962).
[3]Wilder v. Aetna Cas. & Surety Co., 477 S.W.2d 1 (Tenn., 1972).
[4]Tenn. Code Ann., § 50–1013(a).
[5]Andrews v. Signal Auto Parts, Inc., 492 S.W.2d 222 (Tenn., 1972).
[6]See Floyd v. Indemnity Ins. Co., 184 Tenn. 381, 199 S.W.2d 106 (1947).
[7]See Perry v. Sun Coal Co., 183 Tenn. 141, 191 S.W.2d 181 (1945); Summers v. Tennessee Eastman Corp., 169 Tenn. 335, 87 S.W.2d 1005 (1935). See Dependents Under the Tennessee Workmen's Compensation Act, 7 Memphis St. U. L. Rev. 667 (1977).
[8]See section 2.17, herein.

clude the insured from liability.[9] The ambiguity would probably work the other way when its effect would be to extend the insurer's liability.

Abortion

The abortion statute[10] enacted after the Supreme Court of the United States' controversial rulings[11] has so far attracted little judicial attention. Abortions and fetal deaths are to be reported to the department of public health.[12] Physicians cannot be required to perform such an operation.[13]

Recovery for wrongful death

Recovery can be had by or on behalf of an illegitimate child for the wrongful death of its parents,[14] and, on principle, there can be little doubt that a parent who can show damage can recover for the death of the child.[15]

Tort actions

Courts recognize a distinction between the tort action for criminal conversation and that for alienation of affections. The gist of the former is adulterous intercourse, the alienation of affections resulting therefrom being merely matter of aggravation.[16] The distinction can affect the controlling statute of limitations.[17] A new cause of action for alienation of affections can be stated if one interferes with a marriage after the spouses, once divorced or even merely estranged, have reconciled.[18]

---

[9]State Farm Mut. Auto Ins. Co. v. Oliver, 406 F.2d 409 (C.A.-6 Tenn., 1969).
[10]Tenn. Code Ann., §§ 39–301 to 39–307.
[11]See section 2.19, herein.
[12]Tenn. Code Ann., §§ 53–402(d), 53–473 to 53–475. The mother need not actually be identified by name in the report. Id., § 53–474(b).
[13]Id., § 39–304. See Olson v. Molzen, 558 S.W.2d 429 (Tenn., 1977).
[14]See Federal Employers' Liability Act—Recovery for Wrongful Death by Illegitimate Child, 31 Tenn. L. Rev. 521 (1963).
[15]See section 3.2, herein.
[16]Roberts v. Berry, 541 F.2d 607 (C.A.-6 Tenn., 1976).
[17]Id.
[18]Stone v. Hinds, 541 S.W.2d 598 (Tenn. App., 1976).

Possible criminal liability

Although abduction is a crime,[19] intercourse between consenting adults in private is not. To make it a crime it must be attended with circumstances of publicity and notoriety, that is, it must amount to open and notorious lewdness.[20] Bigamy,[21] as also knowingly marrying the husband or wife of another,[22] as well as incest,[23] are criminal. For some reason the legislature has also gone to the trouble of denouncing as a felony "begetting an illegitimate child on the body of his wife's sister."[24]

Criminal sexual conduct, by virtue of a 1978 statute, is now divided into four degrees, the first being a felony and the fourth, a misdemeanor.[25] Excluded as a victim is a defendant's legal spouse.[26]

Despite judicial opinion that a legislative re-evaluation of the crime against nature statute[27] would be in the public interest and of substantial assistance to the administration of criminal justice,[28] the Supreme Court of the United States has sustained the constitutionality of the statute.[29] The courts have avoided deciding if the statute could be enforced against consenting adults.[30]

Status of children

To deprive a "person born to a union out of wedlock" (the term "illegitimate" being forbidden)[31] of any civil benefit by reason thereof is a misdemeanor.[32] The children of a marriage which has

---

[19] See Jones v. State, 553 S.W.2d 920 (Tenn. Crim. App., 1977).
[20] Wilkerson v. Benson, 542 S.W.2d 811 (Tenn., 1976). Compare Manahan v. State, 188 Tenn. 398, 219 S.W.2d 901 (1949).
[21] Tenn. Code Ann., §§ 39–701, 39–702.
[22] Id., § 39–704.
[23] Id., § 39–705. As to the prohibited degrees of relationship, see § 36–401.
[24] Id., § 39–706.
[25] Id., §§ 39–3701 to 39–3706.
[26] Id., § 39–3707.
[27] Id., § 39–707.
[28] Young v. State, 531 S.W.2d 560 (Tenn., 1975).
[29] Rose v. Locke, 423 U.S. 48, 46 L. Ed. 2d 185, 96 Sup. Ct. 243 (1975).
[30] See Young v. State, 531 S.W.2d 560 (Tenn., 1975).
[31] Tenn. Code Ann., § 36–308.
[32] Id., § 36–309.

6.43 UNMARRIED COUPLES AND THE LAW

been annulled are legitimate,[33] as is a child conceived, with the husband's consent, by artificial insemination.[34]

For purposes of intestate succession an adopted person is the child of the adopting parent and not of the natural parents; however, adoption of a child by the spouse of a natural parent has no effect on the relationship between the child and either natural parent.[35] In cases not covered by this provision, a child born out of wedlock is a child of the mother. It is also a child of the father if the natural parents have participated in a marriage ceremony before or after the birth of the child (even though the attempted marriage is void) or paternity has been judicially established.[36] Furthermore, it has been held that a child who has lived with his father and mother can inherit through his father if the latter has openly acknowledged and claimed the child as his and has supported it.[37]

Procedures for the establishment of paternity[38] and enforcement of a father's support obligations[39] follow a familiar pattern. A release by the mother, whatever the consideration, does not discharge the child's right to receive support from the father.[40]

In addition to marriage of the parents, which legitimizes the offspring,[41] legitimation can result from the mother's action for a

---

[33] Id., § 36–832.
[34] Id., § 53–446.
[35] Id., § 31–206(1). See, to the same effect, § 36–234, which requires the court to notify the state department of health when an order of paternity and support has been entered. As to the right of adopted children to share the rights of the natural children of adoptive parents, see also § 36–126.
[36] Id., § 31–206(2).
[37] Allen v. Harvey, 568 S.W.2d 829 (Tenn., 1978).
[38] Tenn. Code Ann., §§ 36–222 to 36–236. Interrogatories to the putative father do not violate any Fifth Amendment rights since fornication or siring a child out of wedlock is no crime. Wilkerson v. Benson, 542 S.W.2d 811 (Tenn., 1976).
[39] Tenn. Code Ann., § 14–1501 et seq. As to procedures where the mother wants the birth certificate to show the father's identity, see § 53–445.
[40] Reynolds v. Richardson, 483 S.W.2d 747 (Tenn. App., 1971), cert. den. 410 U.S. 944, 35 L. Ed. 2d 611, 93 Sup. Ct. 1381 (1973). As to the Uniform Reciprocal Enforcement of Support Act, see Tenn. Code Ann., §§ 36–901 to 36–929.
[41] Tenn. Code Ann., § 36–307. See Southern Ry. Co. v. Sanders, 193 Tenn. 409, 246 S.W.2d 65 (1952).

determination of paternity[42] or from the father's action to have this question adjudicated.[43]

Provision is made, as a prerequisite to the child being adopted, for the written consent of the mother.[44] If the child has not been legitimated, consent of the father is not required; however, he must receive an opportunity to present proof as to the best interests of the child.[45] Notice to him is only dispensed with where he has consented to the adoption or is found to have abandoned the child.[46] Abandonment, for this purpose, imports any conduct which evinces a settled purpose to forego all parental duties and relinquish all parental claims. It has been held possible for a father, though derelict in his obligations, to reacquire his rights to a hearing in the adoption proceeding.[47]

Property rights of cohabitants

In view of the judicial tendency to harness doctrines of the nature of estoppel or ratification to support claims arising out of a nonexistent marriage, where policy considerations favor such an attitude,[48] it seems likely that such doctrines will come into play where the interests of cohabitants in the acquisitions of the extramarital partnership are to be adjudicated. Estoppel, for example, has been harnessed to preclude the heirs of a grantee of land from asserting, against an innocent purchaser from the surviving grantee, that the land was not held as a tenancy by the

---

[42] Tenn. Code Ann., § 36–224.

[43] Id., §§ 36–301 to 36–309. As to new birth certificates on adoption or legitimation, see §§ 53–449 to 53–453.

[44] Id., § 36–111.

[45] Id.

[46] Id. For a provision authorizing service by publication when the father's address or identity cannot be ascertained, using the name of the child (which may not be likely to achieve any useful purpose), see § 36–108.

[47] Ex parte Wolfenden, 48 Tenn. App. 433, 348 S.W.2d 751 (1961); Fancher v. Mann, 58 Tenn. App. 471, 432 S.W.2d 63 (1968).

As to the due process rights of the father in neglect proceedings, see Smith v. Edmiston, 431 F. Supp. 941 (W.D. Tenn., 1977) (right to counsel if he cannot afford a lawyer).

The authority of the juvenile courts to terminate parental rights and free the child for adoption was substantially enlarged in 1977. See Tenn. Code Ann., § 37–246.

[48] See notes 93 to 95, supra.

entireties though in fact there was no marriage on which such a tenancy could be predicated.[49]

Where the parties operate a business with the use of their common funds, there is early recognition that the fact of their illicit relations will not deter the courts from decreeing an adjustment of their interests on the basis of an oral partnership.[50]

Though contracts for an immoral purpose are not enforceable in Tennessee,[51] an early court has held that a deed, the consideration for which was past, and not future cohabitation, would not be set aside.[52]

6.44. Texas

A 1978 Texas decision merits consideration as illustrative of the ramifications that can result from judicial recognition of a common-law marriage resulting from a continuance of cohabitation when a relationship, initially illicit by reason of a prior marriage, is continued after removal of the impediment. One Enrique Avalos married his first wife in 1918. He remained so married until 1965, when she died. However, from 1946 on he had actually been living with one Margarita, who bore his children. (Margarita was married at the time cohabitation began, but divorced her husband shortly thereafter.)

Beginning in 1965, Avalos led the classic double life. Not only did he continue cohabitation with Margarita, but he also lived with one Enedina. She also bore him children. Enedina, too, was a married woman, but divorced her husband in 1975.

In 1976 Avalos entered into a ceremonial marriage with Enedina. Six months later, he died. In a contest between the two women as to which was the common-law widow of Avalos, the court held for Margarita.[53] The reasoning was that she could es-

---

[49] Duke v. Hopper, 486 S.W.2d 744 (Tenn. App., 1972). Compare Knight v. Knight, 62 Tenn. App. 70, 458 S.W.2d 803 (1970) (where the husband's divorce from his first wife was invalid, his subsequent marriage to another was held invalid ab initio, and a deed purporting to convey land to him and his alleged wife as tenants by the entireties did not create such an estate).
[50] Johnson v. Graves, 15 Tenn. App. 466 (1932).
[51] Fair v. Hartman, 55 Tenn. App. 682, 404 S.W.2d 535 (1965).
[52] Bivins v. Jarnigan, 62 Tenn. 282 (1873).
[53] Rodriguez v. Avalos, 567 S.W.2d 85 (Tex. Civ. App., 1978).

tablish the essentials for a common-law marriage in Texas;[54] that, the impediment of decedent's first marriage having been removed by death of the first wife, the continued cohabitation resulted in a common-law marriage,[55] and that, even though the Code provides that when two or more marriages are alleged, the most recent marriage is presumed valid until the one who asserts the validity of a prior marriage proves its validity,[56] Margarita had proved the validity of her common-law marriage. In effect then, in Texas a cohabitant who has been able to "make an honest man" of one who has virtually deserted his common-law spouse in her favor ends up the loser, even though she, too, has borne him children.

This result seems to pay scant respect to the spirit of the maxim that where the equities are equal, the one who has the legal right prevails. Perhaps the thinking of the trial court, whose findings were affirmed, was that Enedina did not really think decedent's common-law marriage had been dissolved (and there is no reason to believe that it was) and that her ceremonial marriage to him was therefore bigamous. A resolution of the problem by decreeing each woman to qualify for some relief as "widow" would be a logical monstrosity, but decisions of this nature cannot but point up the drawbacks of the doctrine the court applied.

Courts consistently recognize that an agreement to become husband and wife, coupled with cohabitation pursuant to the agreement and a holding out of each other to the public as spouses creates a common-law marriage.[57] If there has been compliance with these requirements, no new agreement need be shown and the period of cohabitation can be short indeed.[58] However, a mere

---

[54]Tex. Fam. Code Ann., § 1.91(a)(2).

[55]Id., § 2.22. See also Caddel v. Caddel, 486 S.W.2d 141 (Tex. Civ. App., 1972) (validity does not relate back to date cohabitation began). The facts must exclude the inference that a prior illicit arrangement was to continue. Howard v. Howard, 459 S.W.2d 901 (Tex. Civ. App., 1970).

[56]Tex. Fam. Code Ann., § 2.01. As to the strength of this presumption, especially where the later marriage is a ceremonial one, see Wood v. Paulus, 524 S.W.2d 749 (Tex. Civ. App., 1975); Rosetta v. Rosetta, 525 S.W.2d 255 (Tex. Civ. App., 1975).

[57]E.g., Bodde v. State, 568 S.W.2d 344 (Tex. Crim. App., 1978); Navarro v. Collora, 566 S.W.2d 304 (Tex. Civ. App., 1978); Warren v. Kyle, 565 S.W.2d 313 (Tex. Civ. App., 1978); Till v. Till, 539 S.W.2d 381 (Tex. Civ. App., 1976); Reilly v. Jacobs, 536 S.W.2d 406 (Tex. Civ. App., 1976); Chatman v. State, 513 S.W.2d 854 (Tex. Crim. App., 1974); Gary v. Gary, 490 S.W.2d 929 (Tex. Civ. App., 1973).

[58]Durr v. Newman, 537 S.W.2d 323 (Tex. Civ. App., 1976) (three days' cohabitation after a divorce).

private exchange of marital vows in Texas between out-of-state residents is not enough.[59] Nor does an agreement between a divorced couple that if things work out and the wife were to get help and counseling they might remarry suffice.[60]

Cohabitants who intend what is essentially a relation of convenience and a status terminable at the will of either will not be regarded as common-law spouses.[61] But a definite understanding that they will marry after one has obtained a divorce can lead to a common-law marriage if cohabitation continues after the divorce is secured.[62]

Adoption

Any adult is eligible to adopt a child who may be adopted.[63] If parental consent cannot be obtained, a petition for termination of parental rights, if not already decreed, can be included in the adoption petition.[64] The court may order a study into the circumstances of the child and the home of the adopting parents.[65] In agency adoptions, a state official (managing conservator) is invested with broad discretion to withhold his consent where he in good faith believes that an adoptive placement is not working out satisfactorily.[66] The burden of showing this official's want of good cause for withholding or revoking consent rests on the party seeking waiver of the consent requirement.[67]

It is held that an adoptive parent can be estopped, when there has been a detrimental reliance by the child on representations that he is adopted, from denying the adoption. The doctrine was applied where an unwed mother agreed to marry on condition

---

[59]In re Estate of Stahl, 13 Ill. App. 3d 680, 301 N.E.2d 82 (1973).
[60]Rosetta v. Rosetta, 525 S.W.2d 255 (Tex. Civ. App., 1975).
[61]Ferrell v. Celebrezze, 232 F. Supp. 281 (S.D. Tex., 1964).
[62]Esparza v. Esparza, 382 S.W.2d 162 (Tex. Civ. App., 1964). Generally, see Baade, Form of Marriage in Spanish North America, 61 Cornell L. Rev. 1 (1975); Common-Law Marriage in Texas, 21 Sw. L. J. 647 (1967); Marriage and Divorce Under the Texas Family Code, 8 Houston L. Rev. 101 (1970); Presumption of the Validity of a Second Marriage, 20 Baylor L. Rev. 206 (1968).
[63]Tex. Fam. Code Ann., § 16.02.
[64]Id., § 16.03. As to the contents of a petition to adopt, see § 11.08. As to whom notice must be given, see § 11.09.
[65]Id., § 11.12.
[66]Id., § 16.05.
[67]Chapman v. Home, 561 S.W.2d 265 (Tex. Civ. App., 1978).

that the husband would adopt the child, to enable the adopted child to qualify as an heir of the decedent husband.[68]

Subject to qualifications relating to lawful fees for attorneys, physicians and child placement agencies and to rights to reimbursement of disbursements incurred on behalf of the child, the sale or purchase of a child for adoption is an offense.[69]

Workers' compensation death benefits

A good faith putative spouse has been held not entitled to compensation benefits on the death of a workman.[70] An illegitimate child stands on the same footing as a legitimate child.[71] If he has been adopted out, however, he does not so qualify.[72]

Abortion

As a result of the review by the Supreme Court of the United States of the Texas abortion statute in Roe v. Wade,[73] the criminal sanctions once visited on physicians who performed nontherapeutic abortions have been removed. There remains, however, a provision mandating jail for the destruction, during parturition, of the life of a child who would otherwise have been born alive.[74]

There are now also provisions safeguarding the rights of medical personnel and private health care facilities not to perform

---

[68]Deveroex v. Nelson, 517 S.W.2d 658 (Tex. Civ. App., 1974), affd. 529 S.W.2d 510 (Tex., 1975). As to "equitable adoption," see Bowden v. Caldron, 554 S.W.2d 25 (Tex., 1977).

[69]Tex. Fam. Code Ann., § 25.06. Unauthorized child-placement is a misdemeanor. Ops. A. G. 1974, H-221.

[70]Travelers Ins. Co. v. Price, 111 F.2d 776 (C.A.-5 Tex., 1940).

[71]Gonzalez v. Texas Employers' Ins. Assn., 509 S.W.2d 423 (Tex. Civ. App., 1974); Texas Employers' Ins. Assn. v. Shea, 410 F.2d 56 (C.A.-5 Tex., 1969) (posthumous illegitimate under Longshoremen's and Harbor Workers' Compensation Act).

[72]Griffith v. Christian, 564 S.W.2d 170 (Tex. Civ. App., 1978). As to the right of the posthumous illegitimate to social security benefits, see Wagner v. Finch, 413 F.2d 267 (C.A.-5 Tex., 1969).

[73]See section 2.19, herein.

[74]Tex. Civ. Stat., art. 4512.5.

6.44   UNMARRIED COUPLES AND THE LAW

abortions, and protecting others against any form of discrimination as a result of their anti-abortion attitudes.[75]

Tort actions

Very likely as a result of a forceful dissent in a decision prior to the legislation,[76] the civil action for criminal conversation, though not for alienation of affections, has been abolished.[77]

Possible criminal liability

The legislature has provided that the exclusion of conduct with a spouse from most of the sex crimes involving those over fourteen years of age extends to persons cohabiting, whether or not they hold themselves out as husband and wife.[78]

Abduction,[79] bigamy[80] and incest[81] are punishable. It is a defense to a charge of statutory rape, for which the age of consent is seventeen, that the female was at the time fourteen or older and had previously engaged in sexual intercourse or deviate sexual intercourse, and that the actor was not more than two years older than the victim.[82]

Unconsented-to deviate sexual intercourse is denounced in several provisions of the Penal Code.[83] The provision forbidding sodomy[84] has faced many challenges on constitutional grounds. The Texas Court of Criminal Appeals expressed disagreement with a federal court that it was void as constitutionally overbroad because it reached the private consensual acts of married persons. It reasoned that, though courts had at times stated that convic-

---

[75]Id., art. 4512.7. As to regulation of contraceptives, see art. 4504. See Rice, Dred Scott Case of the Twentieth Century, 10 Houston L. Rev. 1059 (1973); Putative Father's Rights After Roe v. Wade, 6 St. Mary's L. J. 407 (1974); Father's Rights in the Abortion Decision, 6 Tex. Tech. L. Rev. 1075 (1975).

[76]Felsenthal v. McMillan, 493 S.W.2d 729 (Tex., 1973).

[77]Tex. Fam. Code Ann., § 4.05. See Lueg v. Tewell, 572 S.W.2d 97 (Tex. Civ. App., 1978).

[78]Tex. Penal Code Ann., tit. 5, § 21.12.

[79]Tex. Penal Code Ann., tit. 5, §§ 20.01(2)(A),(B), 20.04. See also Pollard v. State, 567 S.W.2d 11 (Tex. Crim. App., 1978).

[80]Tex. Penal Code Ann., § 25.01.

[81]Id., § 25.02 (includes deviate sex).

[82]Id., § 21.09.

[83]See Id., §§ 21.04, 21.10.

[84]Id., § 21.06 (Class C misdemeanor).

tions under the statute for conduct in a marital situation were "conceivable," in fact there had been no such convictions; if the conduct was in private, there would be no witnesses; and if the acts were consensual, neither spouse would be competent to testify against the other—and if they could, such testimony would require corroboration.[85] A subsequent decision confirmed that the overly broad provisions do not invalidate the statute as an abridgement of the right of privacy and the fundamental personal liberties protected under the First Amendment.[86] A federal court has now also confirmed this view of the statute.[87]

A defendant charged with the former offense of sodomy, who elected to be punished under the existing Penal Code, is held properly punishable for the graver misdemeanor of public lewdness (knowingly engaging in deviate sex in a public place)[88] if the proof shows such behavior.[89] For conviction of this latter offense, it need not be shown that the defendant knew it was a public place,[90] but the indictment must contain an allegation to this effect.[91]

Status of children

For the purposes of rules controlling the parent-child relationship, a child is the legitimate child of its father if it is either born or conceived during the marriage of the father and the mother,[92] or if the parents attempt marriage (even if the attempted marriage is void or voidable) and the child is born or conceived during the attempted marriage.[93] Thus, the children of a putative mar-

---

[85]Pruett v. State, 463 S.W.2d 191 (Tex. Crim. App., 1970), appeal dismissed 402 U.S. 902, 28 L. Ed. 2d 643, 91 Sup. Ct. 1379 (1971), reh. den. 403 U.S. 912, 91 Sup. Ct. 2203 (1971).

[86]Everette v. State, 465 S.W.2d 162 (Tex. Crim. App., 1971). See also Lee v. State, 505 S.W.2d 816 (Tex. Crim. App., 1974).

[87]Cyr v. Walls, 439 F. Supp. 697 (N.D. Tex., 1977).

[88]Tex. Penal Code Ann., § 21.07 (Class A misdemeanor).

[89]Bishoff v. State, 531 S.W.2d 346 (Tex. Crim. App., 1976).

[90]Green v. State, 566 S.W.2d 578 (Tex. Crim. App., 1978).

[91]Brown v. State, 558 S.W.2d 471 (Tex. Crim. App., 1977).

[92]Tex. Fam. Code Ann., § 12.02. This provision is not construed so literally as to mean that the presumption of legitimacy when the parents are married is a conclusive one. Napier v. Napier, 555 S.W.2d 186 (Tex. Civ. App., 1977). See Presumption of Legitimacy in Texas, 27 Baylor L. Rev. 340 (1975).

[93]See Texas Family Law and the Rights of Illegitimate Children, 13 Houston L. Rev. 1062 (1976).

riage are legitimate.[94] However, for the purpose of inheritance from or through the father, a statute which conditioned the child's status as legitimate on intermarriage of the parents, without more, was stricken as unconstitutional.[95]

In a landmark case out of Texas, the Supreme Court of the United States ruled that once a state posits a judicially enforceable right of children to support from their natural fathers there is no constitutionally sufficient justification for denying such right to a child because the natural father has not married the mother.[96] Texas has detailed provisions controlling the establishment of paternity,[97] legitimation,[98] and the enforcement of support obligations.[99]

Provision is made for voluntary legitimation of a child, by obtaining a court decree, on the initiative of the father or the mother or the department of public welfare, if the father has executed a statement of paternity.[1] As to the father, however, it has been ruled that he enjoys no absolute right to such a decree. In Interest of K.,[2] a trial court had refused to accede to father's petition to legitimate his child. It was important to the father to have this status because he wanted his voice heard as to the

---

[94]See Davis v. Davis, 521 S.W.2d 603 (Tex., 1975).

[95]Lovejoy v. Lillie, 569 S.W.2d 501 (Tex. Civ. App., 1978).

A note in 9 Tex. Tech. L. Rev. 113 (1977) points out that in Trimble v. Gordon, 430 U.S. 762, 52 L. Ed. 2d 31, 97 Sup. Ct. 1459 (1977), the Supreme Court of the United States, in striking down an Illinois statute denying an illegitimate the right to inherit from its father (see section 3.3, herein), indicated that its decision would have been otherwise if the statute had provided for inheritance rights where paternity had been adjudicated or the child had been acknowledged and taken into the father's home.

As to inheritance for the adoptive parent, see Inheritance Rights of Parties to the Adoption of a Child: Conflicts Between the Texas Family Code and the Texas Probate Code, 28 Baylor L. Rev. 432 (1976).

[96]Gomez v. Perez, 409 U.S. 535, 35 L. Ed. 2d 56, 93 Sup. Ct. 872 (1973). See section 3.5, herein.

[97]Tex. Fam. Code Ann., §§ 13.01 to 13.09. See State Dept. of Public Welfare v. Martin, 562 S.W.2d 9 (Tex. Civ. App., 1978). The constitutionality of the provisions controlling determination of paternity are affirmed in In re B— M— N—, 570 S.W.2d 493 (Tex. Civ. App., 1978).

[98]Tex. Fam. Code Ann., §§ 13.21 to 13.24.

[99]Tex. Fam. Code Ann., §§ 21.01 to 21.66. See also Alvarado v. Gonzales, 552 S.W.2d 539 (Tex. Civ. App., 1977); Texas Family Law and the Rights of Illegitimate Children, 13 Houston L. Rev. 1062 (1976).

[1]Tex. Fam. Code Ann., §§ 13.21 to 13.24.

[2]535 S.W.2d 168 (Tex., 1976), cert. den. 429 U.S. 907, 97 Sup. Ct. 273 (1976).

child's future. The Supreme Court of Texas upheld the trial court, saying that the petitioner was a father "only in the sense of that relationship which is the biological consequence of erotic ecstacy on a summer night," and that he had engaged in a single hit-and-run sexual adventure.[3] Though the statutes recognize a father's right to due process in proceedings affecting a parent-child relation, as an unwed father he was not a "parent" and the court declined to adjudicate him as such. Stanley v. Illinois,[4] the court opined, does not mandate that all unwed fathers have fundamental rights to full parental status and that every statutory discrimination against the unwed father is suspect. A wiser decision could well have been to permit the legitimation petition, and then, on the ground of his unfitness,[5] terminated his parental rights, as it could,[6] without depriving him of his due process rights in the matter, which Texas of course respects.[7]

Property rights of cohabitants

By reason of the retention in Texas of the civil law doctrine of putative wife,[8] Texas accords to an innocent woman involved in an illegal marriage the rights of a lawful wife in respect of assets acquired by the parties during the period of cohabitation.[9] If the man is dead, she is entitled to a half interest in the post-putative acquisitions of the partnership, the legal spouse's intestate share being dependent on the existence of other lawful heirs of the

---

[3]Id.

[4]405 U.S. 645, 31 L. Ed. 2d 551, 92 Sup. Ct. 1208 (1972), discussed in section 3.8, herein.

[5]See In Interest of Jones, 566 S.W.2d 702 (Tex. Civ. App., 1978); Brokerleg v. Butts, 559 S.W.2d 853 (Tex. Civ. App., 1977).

[6]Tex. Fam. Code Ann., tit. 2, §§ 13.21(d), 15.02. See Smitheal v. Smitheal, 518 S.W.2d 842 (Tex. Civ. App., 1975), cert. den. 423 U.S. 928, 46 L. Ed. 2d 256, 96 Sup. Ct. 277 (1975).

[7]Rogers v. Lowry, 546 S.W.2d 881 (Tex. Civ. App., 1977). See also Nixon v. Humphrey, 565 S.W.2d 365 (Tex. Civ. App., 1978); Due Process for Parents in Emergency Protection Proceedings Under the Texas Family Code—Suggestions for Improving the System, 15 Houston L. Rev. 709 (1978); Child Custody Modification and the Family Code, 27 Baylor L. Rev. 725 (1975).

[8]See Dean v. Goldwire, 480 S.W.2d 494 (Tex. Civ. App., 1972) (on dissolution of a putative marriage, or until discovery of an impediment to the marriage, a putative spouse is entitled to share equally in community property).

[9]See Timmons v. Timmons, 222 S.W.2d 339 (Tex., 1949).

decedent.[10] Thus, in Davis v. Davis,[11] where the post-putative marital assets consisted of back wages and the proceeds of an accident insurance policy payable to the decedent's estate, the court awarded one-half to the putative wife. The other half was distributed in equal shares between his lawful wife, on the one hand, and the children of his various marriages on the other. The court disposed of the presumption of the validity cf the second of two ceremonial marriages[12] by simply holding that the absence of any record of divorce proceedings in any place where the decedent could reasonably have been expected to file for divorce rebutted such presumption, and that therefore the participant in the later marriage was only a putative spouse, and not a lawful widow.

This putative marriage status, however, terminates as soon as the putative spouse learns of the invalidity of her marriage.[13] It may arise either out of a ceremonial marriage or by reason of a common-law marriage.[14]

In a proper case, a lawful wife can be estopped or barred by her laches from asserting the invalidity of her divorce as a basis of her claim for an interest in the decedent husband's estate.[15]

The judicial attitudes in respect of the rights of a "meretricious" cohabitant on a termination of the relationship have not been entirely consistent. Taking the ostrich-like stance toward an "adulteress and lawbreaker," a court has conceded, obiter, that the relationship could be analogized to that of a partnership when she has contributed something to the acquisition of the assets.[16] But any share in the assets on a basis of community property doctrines would be out of the question.[17] Nevertheless, other courts confirm recognition that she can recover a share, even if

---

[10]Caruso v. Lucius, 448 S.W.2d 711 (Tex. Civ. App., 1969); Hupp v. Hupp, 235 S.W.2d 753 (Tex., 1950); Woods v. Hardware Mut. Cas. Co., 141 S.W.2d 972 (Tex., 1940).
[11]521 S.W.2d 603 (Tex., 1975).
[12]Tex. Fam. Code Ann., § 2.01.
[13]Dean v. Goldwire, 480 S.W.2d 494 (Tex. Civ. App., 1972); Curtin v. State, 155 Tex. Crim. 625, 238 S.W.2d 187 (1951).
[14]Rey v. Rey, 487 S.W.2d 245 (Tex. Civ. App., 1972).
[15]Moorehouse v. Moorehouse, 111 S.W.2d 831 (Tex., 1937).
[16]Meador v. Ivy, 390 S.W.2d 391 (Tex. Civ. App., 1965).
[17]Timmons v. Timmons, 222 S.W.2d 339 (Tex., 1949).

her contribution consisted merely of services,[18] if she can state a cause of action without relying on any immoral agreement.[19] Services have been held to constitute value for the purposes of a resulting trust,[20] and the one taking title has been held to the obligations of an express oral trust on proof of an agreement that title was to be taken for their joint benefit.[21]

Agreements in which the consideration is future illicit cohabitation have been held unenforceable.[22] In fact one early outraged court described such a liaison as "an unholy and adulterous companionship. Such unorthodox arrangement, conceived in iniquity and shorn of all the elements of common decency, was wholly immoral, against public policy and violated all the finer impulses of the marriage relationship."[23]

The courts have construed as mandatory the provisions of the Family Code[24] for an equitable division of accumulations of the parties on the annulment of a marriage, and, as observed earlier, the rights of a common-law spouse have been held to prevail over those of one who has later entered into a ceremonial marriage with another.[25] This notwithstanding, the courts hold that, absent proof of an express trust, or of contributions on the part of a cohabitant that warrant the imposition of a resulting trust, or the existence of a partnership, no property rights flow from a meretricious relationship. Outside of such situations, the courts have so far been of mind to leave the parties as they find them, just as they refuse to enforce any contract which by reason of its objects, or the nature of the consideration on which it rests, is violative of law or against public policy.[26]

---

[18] Hyman v. Hyman, 275 S.W.2d 149 (Tex. Civ. App., 1954) (implied pooling agreement).

[19] McClelland v. Cowden, 175 F.2d 601 (C.A.-5 Tex., 1949).

[20] See Dean v. Goldwire, 480 S.W.2d 494 (Tex. Civ. App., 1972).

[21] Cluck v. Sheets, 141 Tex. 219, 171 S.W.2d 860 (1943). See also Mathews v. Mathews, 310 S.W.2d 629 (Tex. Civ. App., 1958) (constructive trust).

[22] McClelland v. Cowden, 175 F.2d 601 (C.A.-5 Tex., 1949).

[23] Groves v. Whittenberg, 120 S.W.2d 870, 871 (Tex., 1938).

[24] Tex. Fam. Code Ann., § 3.63. See Garrison v. Texas Commerce Bank, 560 S.W.2d 451 (Tex. Civ. App., 1977).

[25] Rodriguez v. Avalos, 567 S.W.2d 85 (Tex. Civ. App., 1978). A putative marriage can spring from belief in the existence of a common-law marriage. Rey v. Rey, 487 S.W.2d 245 (Tex. Civ. App., 1972).

[26] Faglie v. Williams, 569 S.W.2d 557 (Tex. Civ. App., 1978) (to establish a resulting trust in her favor, a woman cohabitating meretriciously with a man at

6.45. Utah

De facto marriage is not recognized. The statutory provisions for ceremonial marriages preclude it as a means of contracting marriage.[27] Plural or polygamous marriages are prohibited by the Constitution.[28] Where there are successive marriages by the same person, the traditional presumption favoring the validity of the later marriage controls.[29]

Schoolteachers and public employees

A teacher can be terminated for immoral or unprofessional conduct or unfitness.[30]

Adoption

Any adult may adopt a minor. Parental consent is required unless the parent's rights have been judicially terminated. The adopting parent must be at least ten years older than the child to be adopted.[31]

Agreements to adopt[32] are enforceable as any other contract except insofar as the child's welfare might otherwise require.[33]

Although the buying and selling of an unborn child is a

---

the time land was purchased in his name had to prove that she contributed to the purchase price, which is done by proving that they worked together to a common purpose, that the proceeds of their labor became joint property, and that such proceeds, a specified part to which the woman contributed, was used to purchase the land; however, no such trust will arise out of dealings between the parties after the title has vested).

[27] Utah Code Ann., § 30-1-6(3). See In re Vetas' Estate, 110 Utah 187, 170 P.2d 183 (1946); Schurler v. Industrial Comm., 86 Utah 284, 43 P.2d 696, 100 A.L.R. 1085 (1935).
[28] Utah Const. Art. III, § 1.
[29] Martin v. Martin, 29 Utah 2d 413, 510 P.2d 1102 (1973).
[30] Utah Code Ann., § 53-2-24.
[31] As to procedures for adoption, see Utah Code Ann., § 78-30-1 et seq. As to adoption by acknowledgment (§ 78-30-12), see Carter v. Carter, 19 Utah 2d 183, 429 P.2d 35 (1967), holding a child reared by its parents and acknowledged as theirs to be legitimate even though the parents had been divorced prior to its conception and birth.
[32] Utah Code Ann., § 78-30-8.
[33] In re Adoption of K ——, 24 Utah 2d 59, 465 P.2d 541 (1970).

felony,[34] as is sale of any child, it is not unlawful to pay reasonable expenses of the mother during her confinement as an act of charity, if not made to induce one qualified to consent to an adoption to co-operate.[35]

Workers' compensation death benefits

Under the controlling statute,[36] as also under the occupational diseases statute,[37] the term "dependents" includes only relatives enumerated and members of the family. But since the latter term is construed to extend to those persons as to whom the decedent has assumed a moral obligation to support,[38] it undoubtedly embraces illegitimate children to whom decedent owed a legal duty of support.[39]

The courts have thus far denied that membership of the family can arise out of cohabitation in a nonmarital relationship.[40] If, however, at some future date cohabitation contracts receive judicial recognition, and such a contract carries with it an obligation of this nature, the possibility of a revision of this attitude cannot be ignored. The purpose of these statutes being to create a right additional to any common-law right in persons deprived of maintenance by industrial accidents, and to that extent to relieve society from the support of those left dependent by industrial accidents,[41] such a revision is not illogical.

---

[34] Utah Code Ann., § 76-7-311.
[35] Id., § 76-7-203. The licensing of adoption agencies does not prohibit private placements and adoptions. In re S., —— Utah 2d ——, 572 P.2d 1370 (1977).
[36] Id., § 35-1-71.
[37] Id., § 35-2-30.
[38] Utah Fuel Co. v. Industrial Comm. of Utah, 64 Utah 328, 230 Pac. 681 (1924).
[39] See Campton v. Industrial Comm., 106 Utah 571, 151 P.2d 189, 154 A.L.R. 691 (1944) (the question of whether children of mother living with decedent in meretricious relationship were "members of the family," where real father of children was living, could be determined by considering evidence of father's liability under Federal Soldiers' Allotment Act).
[40] Schurler v. Industrial Comm., 86 Utah 284, 43 P.2d 696, 100 A.L.R. 1085 (1935).
[41] Utah Fuel Co. v. Industrial Comm. of Utah, 64 Utah 328, 230 Pac. 681 (1924).

Abortion

In 1973 a provision of the abortion statute[42] requiring the consent of the parent or gardian of a pregnant minor as a precondition to abortion was stricken as an unconstitutional violation of the mother's right of privacy.[43] As a result, the statute now provides only for notice to be given to the parents or guardian, or the husband if the mother is married.[44] A federal court has affirmed a declination to rule as to whether this notice requirement extends to require notice to the "husband" where the father was one other than the woman's husband.[45] The provision was also held ambiguous as to whether such notice may be given after the decision to abort has been made; in which case, the court thought, no constitutional issues would be involved.[46] (However, even if the provision were so construed, the requirement would in all likelihood have its impact on the mother's decision. Hence this observation is open to question.)

The statute also provides that the consent of the mother must be preceded by information as to the location of at least two licensed adoption agencies, and as to the possible complications and risks of the operation.[47] No procedure designed to kill or injure an unborn child is permitted unless necessary to save the mother's life or prevent serious and permanent damage to health.[48]

Sexual freedom

Regulations controlling the access of minors to contraceptives and to birth control information have attracted judicial attention on at least two occasions. In 1973 a plaintiff sought to require a

---

[42] Utah Code Ann., §§ 76-7-301 to 76-7-317.
[43] Doe v. Rampton, 366 F. Supp. 189 (D. Utah, 1973), vacated 410 U.S. 950, 35 L. Ed. 2d 683, 93 Sup. Ct. 1423 (1973).
[44] Utah Code Ann., § 76-7-304(2).
[45] Roe v. Rampton, 535 F.2d 1219 (C.A.-10 Utah, 1976).
[46] Id.
[47] Utah Code Ann., § 76-7-305.
[48] Id., § 76-7-307.

planned parenthood association to make available contraceptive information without parental consent. She lost. The Supreme Court of Utah, basing its reasoning entirely on the equal protection provisions of the Constitution, said:

> The law which makes sexual relations lawful between spouses and unlawful between others has never been considered to deny the equal protection of the law to single people who may want to satisfy their lusts on each other. If refusing the requests of this plaintiff here denies to her and her class the equal protection of the law, then the statutes which provide a punishment for fornication and carnal knowledge are such a denial.[49]

However, a later federal court took a broader look at the constitutional impact of regulations mandating parental consent in this area. It stated that neither the interest in protecting minor females from evil effects and the unsuspected harm of actions which go against the mores of society, nor the state's interest in enforcing the right of parents to control the family, are so compelling as to override a minor's right of privacy. Nevertheless, it contented itself with striking the challenged regulations on a narrower basis, saying that even if they did not violate a minor's right of privacy as applied to welfare recipients they would violate the equal protection clauses since they do not prohibit affluent minors from access to contraceptives. The court was careful to emphasize that it was not ruling that a nondiscriminatory requirement that legal custodians of minors be *notified* before such services were furnished would be unconstitutional.[50]

---

[49]Doe v. Planned Parenthood Assn. of Utah, 29 Utah 2d 356, 510 P.2d 75, 77 (1973), appeal dismissed 414 U.S. 805, 38 L. Ed. 2d 42, 94 Sup. Ct. 138 (1973), criticized in 88 Harv. L. Rev. 1001 (1975).

[50]T —— H —— v. Jones, 425 F. Supp. 873 (D. Utah, 1975). See Doe v. Planned Parenthood Association of Utah—The Constitutional Right of Minors to Obtain Contraceptives Without Parental Consent, 1974 Utah L. Rev. 433. As to unmarried couples and the right of privacy generally, see section 2.6, herein.

As to voluntary sterilization, see Parker v. Rampton, 28 Utah 2d 36, 497 P.2d 848 (1972) (permissible for a consenting adult). Sherlock and Sherlock, Voluntary Contraceptive Sterilization: The Case for Regulation, 1976 Utah L. Rev. 115.

As to sale of prophylactics, see Utah Code Ann., § 58–19–8 et seq. (wholesale sales restricted to licensed persons; sale by pharmacists only to married persons or those over eighteen, or licensed persons such as physicians).

Right to alimony

It has been held that a divorced wife's right to alimony is not terminated either by entering into a marriage that was void ab initio or by bearing an illegitimate child.[51]

Tort actions

The tort action for interference with a marital relation still has recognition,[52] as does an action for seduction of a minor.[53]

Possible criminal liability

Any unmarried person who voluntarily engages in sex commits fornication.[54] Grave among the various sexual offenses[55] is that of intercourse by a male with a female under sixteen; even graver is this if the male is more than three years older than the female.[56] A married participant in extramarital sex can be convicted of adultery.[57] As to bigamy,[58] a court has held that enumeration in the legislative definition of one exception only (mistake) excludes all other defenses.[59] The provision denouncing incest sets forth the forbidden degrees of relationship.[60]

The "sickening, disgusting and depraved" crime[61] embraces deviate sexual intercourse "regardless of the sex of either participant."[62]

Belief in polygamy affords no defense to a Mann Act charge of

---

[51]Kent v. Kent, 28 Utah 2d 34, 497 P.2d 652 (1972).
[52]Cahoon v. Pelton, 9 Utah 2d 224, 342 P.2d 94 (1959).
[53]Utah Code Ann., §§ 78-11-4, 78-11-5.
[54]Id., § 76-7-104.
[55]Id., §§ 76-5-401 to 76-5-407.
[56]Id., § 76-5-401.
[57]Id., § 76-7-103.
[58]Id., § 76-7-101.
[59]State v. Hendrickson, 67 Utah 15, 245 Pac. 375, 57 A.L.R. 786 (1926). This is an ill-considered statement: suppose, for example, a participant had been forced to go through the ceremony at gun-point.
[60]Utah Code Ann., § 76-7-102. As to marriages avoided for incest, see § 30-1-1.
[61]Salt Lake City v. Piepenburg, 571 P.2d 1299 (Utah, 1977).
[62]Utah Code Ann., § 76-5-403(1). See Constitutional Law—Right of Privacy—State Statute Prohibiting Private Consensual Sodomy Is Constitutional, 1977 Brigham Young U. L. Rev. 170.

transporting a woman interstate for the purpose of having her as a mistress.[63]

Status of children

For the purposes of intestate succession, an adopted child is the child of the adopting parent and not of its natural or any previously adopting parents. However, adoption of a child by the spouse of a natural or previously adopting parent has no effect on the relationship between the child and the natural or previously adopting parent.[64]

As to illegitimates who have not been adopted, such a child, in addition to being a child of the mother, is also a child of the father if the parents have married before or after the birth of the child, even if the attempted marriage is void, or if paternity is judicially established before the father's death or is thereafter established by clear and convincing proof.[65] Establishment of paternity, however, does not qualify the father to inherit from or through the child unless the father has openly treated the child as his and has not refused to support the child.[66] Another enactment provides that the father's public acknowledgment of the child as his, coupled with its receipt, with the consent of his wife, into the family and its treatment as legitimate renders it legally adopted. Such a child is deemed *for all purposes* legitimate from the time of its birth.[67] Whatever may be the "scrutiny" to which qualifying statutes in this area are to be subjected,[68] the present Utah provisions should be invulnerable to constitutional challenge.[69]

The establishment of paternity and the enforcement of support

---

[63]Cleveland v. United States, 329 U.S. 14, 91 L. Ed. 12, 67 Sup. Ct. 13 (1946).
[64]Utah Code Ann., § 75-2-109.
[65]Id.
[66]Id.
[67]Id., § 78-30-12. Illegitimates are included in class gift terminology and terms of relationship for purposes of intestate succession. See § 75-2-611.
[68]See section 3.3, herein.
[69]As to the inheritance rights of children of an illegitimate whose domicile was Illinois and who could not qualify under Illinois law, in respect of relatives in Utah, see In re Estate of Duquesne, 29 Utah 2d 94, 505 P.2d 779 (1973). See also Intestate Succession and Adoption in Utah: A Need for Legislation, 1969 Utah L. Rev. 56; Aaron, Proposals for Truce in the Holy War: Utah Adoption, 1970 Utah L. Rev. 325.

obligations are provided for in two acts, namely, the Uniform Act on Paternity[70] and the Bastardy Act.[71] The one does not repeal the other.[72]

The primary right to the custody of an illegitimate child of tender years is in the mother,[73] but the right is not of course an absolute one.[74]

Marriage of the biological parents has the effect of legitimizing the child, unless consent to its adoption has been properly given.[75] In addition, the issue of a marriage celebrated where a participant's former spouse is believed to be dead or validly divorced are legitimate.[76] However, contrary to the usual rebuttable presumption of legitimacy in such cases, the issue of adulterous intercourse, though conceived and born in lawful wedlock, are declared illegitimate.[77]

Although provision exists for the adoption of an illegitimate without the consent of the putative father when he has abandoned the child,[78] such abandonment is not readily found;[79] his conduct must have been intentional and not due to misfortune or to misconduct of an extrinsic nature.[80] Where this is not found, the statutes carefully ensure that his rights in respect to the child's future cannot be disregarded without his having been afforded all possible opportunity for notice and a hearing.[81]

---

[70]Utah Code Ann., §§ 78-45a-1 to 78-45a-17.
[71]Id., § 77-60-1 et seq.
[72]State v. Judd, 27 Utah 2d 79, 493 P.2d 604 (1972). For examples of the interaction of the statutes, see Astorga v. Julio, 564 P.2d 1385 (Utah, 1977); Nielsen State Dept. of Social Services v. Hansen, 564 P.2d 1113 (Utah, 1977). As to the Uniform Civil Liability for Support Act, see Utah Code Ann., §§ 78-45-1 to 78-45-13. As to the Uniform Reciprocal Enforcement of Support Act, see §§ 77-61a-1 to 77-61a-39.
[73]Utah Code Ann., § 77-60-12.
[74]See Smith v. Smith, 564 P.2d 307 (Utah, 1977); State in Interest of M., 25 Utah 2d 101, 476 P.2d 1013, 45 A.L.R.3d 206 (1970).
[75]Utah Code Ann., § 77-60-14. As to supplementary birth certificates for legitimated or adopted persons, see § 26-15-16.
[76]Id., § 30-1-3.
[77]Id., § 77-60-1. See State v. Hunt, 13 Utah 2d 32, 368 P.2d 261 (1962).
[78]Utah Code Ann., §§ 78-30-4, 78-30-5. Compare § 77-60-1.
[79]See Robertson v. Hutchison, 560 P.2d 1110 (Utah, 1977).
[80]See Hall v. Anderson, 562 P.2d 1250 (Utah, 1977); In re Adoption of Jameson, 20 Utah 2d 53, 432 P.2d 881 (1967).
[81]See, e.g., In re State ex rel. M., 25 Utah 2d 101, 476 P.2d 1013 (1970).
One who claims paternity may register notice of his claim and of his willingness to support the child. If he does not, he cannot thereafter sue to establish his

Property rights of cohabitants

In suits to determine the validity of a marriage, the courts have statutory authority, if there is a genuine need arising from economic change of circumstances due to the marriage, to make such orders as to the property rights and mutual obligations of the parties as may be equitable.[82] The purpose of the enactment is clearly to enable a court to eliminate some of the hardships that can result from a total refusal to recognize any equities as resulting from an invalid marriage.[83] Where only one of the parties was mistaken as to the validity of the marriage, in terminating the relationship the courts strive to treat the innocent party as if the marriage had indeed been valid.[84]

There is authority to support an equitable distribution of the assets accumulated during an invalid marriage even where, because both parties knew that a party's divorce from a prior spouse had not become absolute, both were wanting in good faith.[85]

More recently, the Supreme Court of Utah seems to have accepted a trial court's resolution of the rights of participants in an invalid marriage on a contract theory. Plaintiff had married defendant knowing he was already married to one Erica. She shared with the operation of a business, at times on her own, without any compensation in the traditional sense. For a period of five months she was paid minimal salary which was required to be "reinvested" in the business. About a year after this "marriage," title to a house was taken by the couple in joint tenancy with a new "wife," one Marinette. All three resided therein for several years. Plaintiff sought, inter alia, a partition of the property. The award to her of a one-third interest in the house was affirmed. Though the Supreme Court regarded the award as a "share of the busi-

---

paternity and such failure constitutes an abandonment and a waiver of any right to notice in any judicial proceeding for adoption. However, absent a showing of his consent, the Bureau of Vital Statistics is required to certify that a diligent search has been made to discover his identity and whereabouts, and that he has not registered as a parent. Utah Code Ann., § 78-30-4(3).

[82]Utah Code Ann., § 30-1-17.2.

[83]Maple v. Maple, 566 P.2d 1229 (Utah, 1977), holding that a court which declared null and void a marriage between a citizen of Thailand and an American serviceman did not abuse its discretion in granting the wife enough to finance her return, and the return of her son by a prior marriage, to her native land.

[84]See Buck v. Buck, 19 Utah 2d 161, 427 P.2d 954 (1967).

[85]See Jenkins v. Jenkins, 107 Utah 239, 153 P.2d 262 (1944).

ness" as somewhat of a misnomer (therein rejecting any notion of a partnership or joint venture theory) and would have preferred to regard it as "merely a restoration of earnings" (therein espousing a restitutionary or quasi-contract theory), it was content to affirm the trial court's contract theory, affirming the award of a one-third interest in the house as supported by basic property law. Not a word was uttered about the meretricious nature of the relationship.[86]

6.46. Vermont

Vermont does not recognize common-law marriage.[87] A statute provides that if a resident of the state, who intends continued residence, is prohibited from contracting marriage under the laws of Vermont and goes out of state and there contracts such a prohibited marriage, it is void in Vermont.[88] To what extent, if any, this provision would apply to the resident who, while temporarily out of state for good reason, enters into a common-law marriage in a state recognizing such a relation, can but be a matter for speculation.

Adoption

A person or spouses may adopt any other person as his or their heir with or without a change of name of the person adopted. Married persons cannot adopt without spousal consent and cooperation.[89]

Abortion

In 1972 a court declined to rule, on behalf of a physician seeking declaratory relief, as to the constitutionality of the abortion

---

[86]Edgar v. Wagner, 572 P.2d 405 (Utah, 1977).
[87]Stahl v. Stahl, —— Vt. ——, 385 A.2d 1091 (1978).
[88]Vt. Stat. Ann., tit. 15, § 5.
[89]Vt. Stat. Ann., tit. 15, § 431. As to the agencies authorized to receive minors who are relinquished for adoption, see § 432. As to the formal requirements of a petition for adoption, see § 436. For provisions as to whose consent is a prerequisite, see § 435. For the Interstate Compact on the Placement of Children, see tit. 33, § 3151 et seq.

statute,[90] reasoning that no justiciable controversy was presented insofar as the physician was concerned.[91] He was under no obligation to accede to the potential mother's request for an abortion and, if he did so, could raise the constitutionality of the statute as defensive matter. As to the pregnant woman who joined in the suit, however, the court considered her dilemma as one justifying declaratory relief. Since the statute specifically exempts her from criminality, she was in effect confronted with a law which simultaneously asserts her right to terminate her pregnancy and denies her professional medical aid in all but cases where the operation is necessary to preserve her life. Hence, it held the provisions invalid as applied to physicians.

Effect of cohabitation on right to alimony

An award of alimony, insofar as it reflects provision for the support needs of a divorcee, is always modifiable.[92] A lump-sum award in lieu of alimony would not be.[93] A court has declined to modify alimony on grounds that the divorcee had cohabited for two years with another, such cohabitation having ceased and the woman having taken good care of her child throughout.[94] Another attempt on the part of a divorced husband to have alimony modified by reason of the wife's extramarital cohabitation failed for more legalistic reasons. He contended that the New York law, which he argued was applicable to his situation, gave the court a discretion to modify or annul an alimony decree on proof that the wife was habitually living with another man and holding herself out as his wife. From the evidence before the court, it held that the wife could only, at worst, be deemed to have admitted "habitually living with another man" without the other required element of "holding herself out as his wife"[95]

---

[90]Id., tit. 13, § 101 et seq., which criminalize abortions except to save the life of the mother.
[91]Beecham v. Leahy, 130 Vt. 164, 287 A.2d 836 (1972). The decision provokes the observation that the statute was not necessarily designed to assert the woman's *right* to have an abortion. The judicial trend has been not to punish the woman's participation. Perkins, *Criminal Law*, ch. 2, § 4 (2d ed., 1969). Further clarification of the position of physicians seems to be called for.
[92]vanLoon v. vanLoon, 132 Vt. 236, 315 A.2d 866 (1974).
[93]See Ellis v. Ellis, 135 Vt. 83, 370 A.2d 200 (1977).
[94]Stahl v. Stahl, —— Vt. ——, 385 A.2d 1091 (1978).
[95]DeWolfe v. DeWolfe, 134 Vt. 581, 367 A.2d 662 (1976).

6.46 UNMARRIED COUPLES AND THE LAW

Though neither of these decisions are conclusive on the point, they tend to indicate that the courts of Vermont would be reluctant to modify an alimony decree solely by reason of the recipient's post-divorce extramarital cohabitation, without any showing of decreased need.

Tort actions

The tort actions for alienation of affections, criminal conversation, seduction and breach of contract to marry have been abolished.[96]

Possible criminal liability

Perhaps to take care of the ambiguity in the statutory lack of definition in denouncing adultery,[97] or perhaps only to take care of the difficulties of proof, a statute makes it a crime for a man to be found with another man's wife, or a woman with another woman's husband, "in bed together, under circumstances affording presumption of an illicit relation."[98] Cohabitation or sexual intercourse between spouses who have been divorced or whose marriage has been annulled is also criminal.[99]

Bigamy[1] and incest[2] are crimes, as is a neutral gender-wise provision forbidding sex with a participant under sixteen.[3]

Status of children

In addition to mutual inheritance rights from or through the mother, an illegitimate child can inherit on intestacy from or through the father if the father's paternity has been judicially

---

[96] Vt. Stat. Ann., tit. 15, § 11.
[97] Id., tit. 13, §§ 201, 202.
[98] Vt. Stat. Ann., tit. 13, § 203. It is held no defense to a prosecution under this so-called Blanket Act that defendant mistakenly believed in the validity of a divorce; though mistake of fact has been accepted as a defense in adultery prosecutions. State v. Woods, 107 Vt. 354, 179 Atl. 1 (1935).
[99] Vt. Stat. Ann., tit. 13, § 204.
[1] Id., § 206. Situations where, for example, a previous spouse was believed dead, or a partner was believed to be divorced, are excluded.
[2] Id., § 205.
[3] Id., tit. 16, § 3252 ("sexual assault").

established or the father has openly and notoriously claimed the child to be his own.[4]

Bastardy proceedings,[5] although criminal in form, are civil in nature. Hence proof by a mere preponderance of evidence can suffice.[6] They can be initiated by the mother, and her marriage after the birth of the child does not bar a suit.[7] If she does not charge a person with being the father within thirty days after the birth of the child, she may herself be compelled to be examined in an effort to discover the child's paternity.[8] The legislature has now furnished additional remedies to enable the authorities responsible for dependent children to reach the assets of responsible parents for reimbursement.[9]

Legitimation (with capacity to inherit) can be effected by marriage of the parents coupled with recognition by the father of the child as his.[10]

The mother is the guardian of the child until another is appointed.[11] In making judicial determinations as to custody, however, the best welfare of the child must yield to the opposing wishes of the child itself.[12] An Attorney General Opinion[13] confirms the laws of Vermont as conforming to the letter the mandate of the Supreme Court in Stanley v. Illinois.[14] In this regard, however, a decision permitting the temporary placement of an illegitimate pending final adoption without furnishing to the putative father an opportunity to claim custody because his appeal was not "ripe" for determination, the mother's rights not yet having been extinguished,[15] has been criticized: by the time these paternal rights "ripen," the best interests of the child would probably favor the adoptive or foster parents; in which case the

---

[4] Id., tit. 14, § 553.
[5] Generally, see Vt. Stat. Ann., tit. 15, § 331 et seq.
[6] Montgomery v. Watts, —— Vt. ——, 380 A.2d 75 (1977).
[7] DeCoster v. Chandler, —— Vt. ——, 385 A.2d 1079 (1978).
[8] Vt. Stat. Ann., tit. 15, § 373.
[9] Id., tit. 33, § 2711 et seq. As to the enforcement of support, see tit. 15, §§ 385 to 428.
[10] Id., tit. 14, § 554. As to new birth certificate, see tit. 18, § 5077 et seq.
[11] Id., tit. 14, § 2644.
[12] Valeo v. Valeo, 132 Vt. 526, 322 A.2d 306 (1974).
[13] 1974 Op. Atty. Gen. 230.
[14] See section 3.8, herein.
[15] In re M & G, 132 Vt. 410, 321 A.2d 19 (1974).

putative father would have been, in an oblique manner, robbed of his day in court on the matter.[16]

Property rights of cohabitants

A Vermont decision supports the proposition that even a good faith belief in the validity of a marriage will not qualify a conferror of benefits to restitution, on discovery of its invalidity, if the recipient can raise an estoppel. In Lariviere v. Larocque,[17] a "husband" transferred property to his "wife" if she would move elsewhere to live with him. She did so at considerable sacrifice. The court felt it would be inequitable to decree a cancellation of the deed.

An early court, in strong terms, denied any recovery for services rendered by a woman to one with whom she was living in an extramarital situation. "Not only does the relationship as of husband and wife negative that of master and servant, but such cohabitation being in violation of principles of morality and chastity, and so against public policy, the law will not imply a promise to pay for services rendered under such circumstances."[18] Despite this, as long as sex does not form an explicit part of the consideration for an express contract, the door to judicial recognition of the contract rights of the parties remains open.[19]

6.47. Virginia

Common-law marriages are not recognized in Virginia.[20]

Adoption

Any resident of the state or person properly entrusted with the custody of a child may petition for adoption.[21] The petitioner's spouse, if any, must join in the petition. A full disclosure of the

---

[16]See In re M & G: A Misapplication of Stanley v. Illinois, 27 Maine L. Rev. 321 (1975).
[17]105 Vt. 460, 168 Atl. 559, 91 A.L.R. 1514 (1934).
[18]Stewart v. Waterman, 97 Vt. 408, 123 Atl. 524, 526 (1924).
[19]See Beattie v. Traynor, 114 Vt. 238, 42 A.2d 435, 159 A.L.R. 1399 (1945).
[20]Va. Code, § 20–13.
[21]Id., § 63.1–221.

circumstances under which the child came to live with the petitioner is required.[22] Ordinarily, there must be a probationary period to enable the welfare department to satisfy itself as to the suitability of the adoptive parents.[23]

For the adoption of certain classes of persons of eighteen years or over, for example, specified close relatives and persons as to whom the petitioners have stood *in loco parentis* for a substantial time, the consent of the adoptee only, and not that of his or her parents, is required, and investigations by the appropriate authorized agencies[24] are merely discretionary.[25] Special provisions control the adoption of an infant by a new spouse of a natural or adoptive parent.[26]

In addition, there are now provisions designed to afford financial help to agencies and adoptive parents where the person to be adopted has special needs, for example, by reason of physical defects or racial background.[27] Welfare authorities are required, where the legal custody of a child is their responsibility, to prepare a foster care plan for the consideration of the parents and for judicial approval.[28]

Workers' compensation death benefits

Acknowledged illegitimate children are conclusively presumed dependent on the worker.[29] In addition, since the controlling test of eligibility is dependency,[30] it seems entirely possible that an unacknowledged illegitimate, or even a cohabitant in respect of whom there lay a contractual obligation to support, could receive favorable consideration.

---

[22]Id. As to the consent required, see § 63.1–225.
[23]Id., § 63.1–226. See Newton v. Wilson, 199 Va. 864, 102 S.E.2d 299 (1958).
[24]Va. Code, §§ 63.1–223, 63.1–228.
[25]Id., § 63.1–222.
[26]Id., § 63.1–231.
[27]Id., § 63.1–238.1 et seq.
[28]Id., § 16.1–281 et seq.
[29]Va. Code, § 65.1–66. See Workmen's Compensation and Welfare, 61 Va. L. Rev. 1862 (1975).
[30]See Miller & Long Co. of Va., Inc. v. Frye, 215 Va. 591, 212 S.E.2d 258 (1975).

Abortion

The statutory requirement of parental consent to a minor's abortion during all three trimesters of pregnancy may be vulnerable insofar as it relates to the first trimester,[31] but it could be saved by the severability clause[32] in the statute.

A separate statute requires prompt reporting of all fetal deaths on forms prescribed by the department of health.[33]

Termination of alimony on marriage

Alimony ceases on remarriage of a divorced spouse.[34]

Tort actions

The actions for alienation of affections, breach of promise, criminal conversation and seduction have been abolished.[35]

Possible criminal liability

Fornication,[36] as well as lewd and lascivious cohabitation[37] (which means conduct which, by its openness and notoriety, tends to affront the public conscience and debase the community morality)[38] retain their place in the statutes. Adultery,[39] as well as "adultery and fornication by persons forbidden to marry" (incest)[40] and bigamy[41] are forbidden. Although carnal knowledge of

---

[31]See section 2.19, herein.
[32]Va. Code, § 18.2-76.2. See Minor's Right to Abortion and the Requirement of Parental Consent, 60 Va. L. Rev. 305 (1974).
[33]Va. Code, § 32-353.21.
[34]Id., § 20-110. Annulment of the second marriage does not entitle the divorced spouse to reinstatement of alimony. McConkey v. McConkey, 216 Va. 106, 215 S.E.2d 640 (1975). But a decree which merely approves a contract for payments in lieu of alimony without incorporating it does not fall within this provision. Shoosmith v. Scott, 217 Va. 789, 232 S.E.2d 787 (1977).
[35]Va. Code, § 8.01-220.
[36]Id., § 18.2-344.
[37]Id., § 18.2-345.
[38]Everett v. Commonwealth, 214 Va. 325, 200 S.E.2d 564 (1973).
[39]Va. Code, § 18.2-365.
[40]Id., § 18.2-366.
[41]Id., § 18.2-362 et seq. See Wadlington, Sexual Relations After Separation or Divorce: The New Morality and the Old and New Divorce Laws, 63 Va. L. Rev. 249 (1977).

a female under thirteen[42] and between thirteen and fifteen[43] scarcely merit mention, it is also a crime to cause or encourage a child under the age of eighteen to commit misdemeanors.[44]

The sodomy statute,[45] as applied to active and regular homosexual relations between adult males, consensually and in private, has withstood a formidable frontal assault on constitutional grounds. Precision bombing via the First and Ninth Amendment guarantees of privacy, artillery fire of the Fifth and Fourteenth Amendments assuring due process, and sniping via First Amendment rights of freedom of expression and Eighth Amendment prohibitions of cruel and unusual punishment, proved to be fruitless. The state, in the proper exercise of its police power, was held to have a legitimate interest in forbidding this conduct, and was not required to show that moral delinquency actually results; it was held enough to show that such conduct is likely to end in a contribution to moral delinquency.[46]

Although the statute has no application to private conduct between spouses, spectators (if known to be such) can oust such spouses of the protective umbrella afforded by the right of privacy.[47]

Status of children

For the purposes of intestate succession an illegitimate child, in addition to being recognized as a child of its mother, is a child of the father if the biological parents intermarried before or after its birth, even if such marriage was prohibited and is annulled.[48]

Such a child further qualifies as a child of the father if paternity has been judicially established. In addition, it so qualifies if

---

[42]Va. Code, § 18.2-61.
[43]Id., § 18.2-63.
[44]Id., § 18.2-371.
[45]Id., § 18.2-361. Same sex marriages are prohibited. Id., § 20-45.2.
[46]Doe v. Commonwealth's Attorney for City of Richmond, 403 F. Supp. 1199 (E.D. Va., 1975), affd. 425 U.S. 901, 47 L. Ed. 2d 751, 96 Sup. Ct. 1489 (1976), reh. den. 425 U.S. 985, 48 L. Ed. 2d 810, 96 Sup. Ct. 2192 (1976).
[47]Lovisi v. Slayton, 539 F.2d 349 (C.A.-4 Va., 1976), cert. den. 429 U.S. 977, 97 Sup. Ct. 485 (1976), discussed in section 2.19, herein. For a critical discussion of this decision, see Consent Not Morality, as the Proper Limitation on Sexual Privacy, 4 Hastings Const. L. Q. 637 (1977).
[48]Va. Code, § 64.1-5.1.

paternity is established by clear and convincing evidence, limited to the following:[49] (1) That he cohabited openly with the mother during all of the ten months immediately prior to the time the child was born; (2) that he gave consent to someone, other than the mother, charged with responsibility for the preparation of a birth record that his name be used as the father on the birth records; (3) that he allowed by a general course of conduct the common use of his surname by the child; (4) that he claimed the child as his on any statement, tax return or other document filed and signed by him with any local, state or the federal government; (5) that he admitted before any court having jurisdiction to try and dispose of the same that he is the father; or (6) that he voluntarily admitted paternity in writing, under oath.

However, paternity established by means other than marriage of the biological parents does not qualify the father or his kindred to inherit *from or through* the child unless the father has openly treated the child as his and has not refused to support the child.[50]

The provisions for the establishment of paternity and for the enforcement of support duties[51] furnish strict standards of proof. They do not, however, impair the jurisdiction of courts of general equitable jurisdiction, in a proceeding for the support of a child, to determine whether the child is the issue of a null marriage within the meaning of the provision[52] that the issue of a marriage deemed null in law or dissolved are legitimate.[53]

A subsequent marriage of the parents, coupled with recognition by the father of the child as his, legitimates the child.[54] Both this provision and the provision that the issue of a void or dissolved marriage are legitimate[55] are characterized as statutes of inher-

---

[49]Id., §§ 64.1–5.1, 64.1–5.2.
[50]Id.
[51]Id., § 20–61 et seq.
[52]Id., § 20–31.1.
[53]Brown v. Commonwealth ex rel. Custis, 218 Va. 40, 235 S.E.2d 325 (1977). For an order enforcing a husband's promise to treat the wife's illegitimate child as his own, see T —— v. T ——, 216 Va. 867, 224 S.E.2d 148 (1976). See also Helmholz, Support Orders, Church Courts, and the Rule of *Filius Nullius*: A Reassessment of the Common Law, 63 Va. L. Rev. 431 (1977). As to the Revised Uniform Reciprocal Enforcement of Support Act, see Va. Code, §§ 20–88.12 to 20–88.31.
[54]Va. Code, § 20–31.1.
[55]Id.

itance.[56] By reason of the latter provision, the child of a bigamous marriage can participate in a recovery of damages for the wrongful death of a parent,[57] as can an acknowledged illegitimate child.[58]

In custody disputes between the parents, the once popular notion that the mother is to be preferred is today little more than a permissible inference.[59]

Unless the child has been relinquished for adoption,[60] parental rights cannot be terminated without cause.[61] Notice, if at all feasible, and an opportunity to be heard cannot be denied to a putative father.[62]

Property rights of cohabitants

A gift induced by reliance on a fraudulently induced marriage can be recovered.[63] Restitution for the value of services rendered in such a situation, however, has been denied; a tort action for damages being more appropriate.[64] A claim based on a theory of partnership for a share of the fruits of an ostensible marriage has failed for the want of proof beyond the claimant's self-serving conclusory statement that the business was operated as a partnership.[65]

Those criminal provisions directed against extramarital cohabitation may well account for the virtual absence of litigation

---

[56]Withrow v. Edwards, 181 Va. 344, 25 S.E.2d 343 (1943), mod. 181 Va. 592, 25 S.E.2d 899 (1943).

[57]Grove v. Metropolitan Life Ins. Co., 271 F.2d 918 (C.A.-4 Va., 1959).

[58]Carroll v. Sneed, 211 Va. 640, 179 S.E.2d 620 (1971). See also Kasey v. Richardson, 331 F. Supp. 580 (W.D. Va., 1971), affd. 462 F.2d 757 (C.A.-4 Va., 1972), holding that a child born of a cohabitation, during which the mother's lawful husband was in prison, qualified as legitimate for social security purposes.

[59]See Va. Code, § 31-15. See "Tender Years" Doctrine in Virginia, 12 U. Richmond L. Rev. 593 (1978).

[60]See Harry v. Fisher, 216 Va. 530, 221 S.E.2d 118 (1976).

[61]See Carson v. Elrod, 411 F. Supp. 645 (E.D. Va., 1976), affd. without published opinion 562 F.2d 44 (C.A.-4 Va., 1977), cert. den. 434 U.S. 1019, 98 Sup. Ct. 742 (1978).

[62]See Va. Code, § 63.1 225. Commonwealth v. Hayes, 215 Va. 49, 205 S.E.2d 644 (1974).

[63]Pretlow v. Pretlow, 177 Va. 524, 14 S.E.2d 381 (1941).

[64]Alexander v. Kuykendall, 192 Va. 8, 63 S.E.2d 746 (1951).

[65]Cooper v. Spencer, 218 Va. 541, 238 S.E.2d 805 (1977). Both parties had mistakenly believed in the validity of their ceremonial marriage. A farm, taken by

between extramarital partners as to their respective equities or adjustment of property rights.

6.48. Washington

Common-law marriages cannot be contracted in Washington,[66] and it is likely that such a marriage, even if entered into in a state recognizing the institution, would not receive recognition if the participants are domiciliaries of this state.[67]

Schoolteachers

Whether a schoolteacher can be discharged for open cohabitation with a member of the opposite sex is yet to be decided, but proof of known homosexuality has been held sufficient justification.[68]

Adoption

The right of unmarried persons to adopt a child, which is controlled by provisions of a standard nature,[69] is in reality no more than a privilege. It is for the petitioners to satisfy the court as to their suitability to care for the needs of the child. Especially is this so where a licensed placement agency has withheld its consent. Such consent can only be dispensed with on good and sufficient reason.[70]

---

them as tenants by the entireties, had been sold and the proceeds divided between them. It may well be that the plaintiff would have fared better had she addressed her appeal to the inherent jurisdiction of the court to adjust the equities, instead of relying solely on a theory of implied partnership.

[66] Wash. Rev. Code Ann., §§ 26.04.070, 26.04.110. See Lewis v. Department of Labor and Industries, 190 Wash. 620, 70 P.2d 298 (1937).

[67] See State ex rel. Smith v. Superior—Court for King County, 23 Wash. 2d 357, 161 P.2d 188 (1945).

[68] Gaylord v. Tacoma School Dist. No. 10, 88 Wash. 2d 286, 559 P.2d 1340 (1977), cert. den. 434 U.S. 879, 98 Sup. Ct. 234 (1977). See Civil Rights—Homosexual Teacher Dismissal: A Deviant Decision, 53 Wash. L. Rev. 499 (1978).

[69] Wash. Rev. Code Ann., § 26.32.010 et seq.

[70] In re Adoption of Doe, 74 Wash. 2d 396, 444 P.2d 800 (1968). As to when agency consent is required, see State ex rel. Van Cleave v. Frater, 21 Wash. 2d 231, 150 P.2d 391 (1944).

The provisions requiring notice to be given to the parents of an adoptee are strictly abserved. A failure to afford timely notice as required by the statute can render the adoption decree void.[71] The consent requirements, however, are less rigid. The consenting parent need not include the names of the prospective adoptive parents.[72]

Abortion

The Supreme Court of Washington has ruled the requirement of parental consent to a minor's abortion[73] unconstitutional. It was held that the "conclusive presumption" that the parents' judgment is better than the mother's cannot withstand constitutional scrutiny, and is not justified by the state's interest in supporting parental authority, strengthening the family unit and ensuring informed and considered decision-making by minors.[74] A suggestion that the state might properly require notice to the parents, to give them an opportunity to seek a judicial determination as to whether the child's best interest is against the procedure, presents the difficulty that if, as a result of such delays, the pregnancy advances to a stage where the state does have legitimate interests, the mother's decision is obliquely frustrated.

Tort actions

The action for alienation of affections has been abolished by judicial fiat,[75] the court holding that the harm it engenders far outweighs any reasons for its continuance. The action for breach of promise of marriage, however, survives.[76]

---

[71] In re Adoption of Hickey, 18 Wash. App. 259, 567 P.2d 260 (1977).
[72] In re Adoption of Jackson, 89 Wash. 2d 945, 578 P.2d 33 (1978), holding that parental consent may not be revoked after entry of order of relinquishment and approval of consent but prior to decree of adoption.
[73] Wash. Rev. Code Ann., § 9.02.070. Generally, see §§ 9.02.060 to 9.02.090.
[74] State v. Koome, 84 Wash. 2d 901, 530 P.2d 260 (1975). Four justices dissented.
[75] Wyman v. Wallace, 15 Wash. App. 395, 549 P.2d 71 (1976).
[76] See Stanard v. Bolin, 88 Wash. 2d 614, 565 P.2d 94 (1977), holding that damages for loss of expected financial and social position are not recoverable. As to seduction, see Wash. Rev. Code Ann., § 4.24.030.

Possible criminal liability

Bigamy[77] and incest[78] are denounced, as well as the crime of abduction.[79]

Though the age of the defendant is a material factor in the various classifications of statutory rape,[80] noteworthy is the situation where the actor is over eighteen and the participant is fourteen or older but not less than sixteen.[81]

The consensual sodomy laws have been repealed.[82]

It is to Washington that we owe a decision (which may one day be important) that the Mann Act does not violate equal protection by its failure to reach out and protect males from transportation in interstate commerce.[83]

Status of children

With prophetic foresight, weeks before the landmark decisions of the United States Supreme Court,[84] the Washington court ruled that to restrict the protection of the wrongful death statute to legitimate children only would be an unfortunate and ill-advised exercise of its judicial function, there being no valid social reason, in this context, for taking illegitimates out of the broader class of "children."[85]

Similarly, the spirit of Trimble v. Gordon[86] was anticipated in a statute that provides that, for the purposes of inheritance to, through and from any child, the effect and treatment of the parent-child relationship shall not depend upon whether or not the parents have been married.[87]

An adopted child is not an heir of its natural parents.[88] Adoption transfers all rights of inheritance from his natural family to

---

[77]Wash. Rev. Code Ann., § 9A.64.010.
[78]See State v. Clevenger, 69 Wash. 2d 136, 417 P.2d 626 (1966).
[79]Wash. Rev. Code Ann., § 9A.88.060.
[80]Id., §§ 9.79.200, 9.79.210.
[81]Id., § 9.79.220.
[82]Same sex marriages are prohibited. Wash. Rev. Code Ann., § 26.04.010, upheld in Singer v. Hara, 11 Wash. App. 247, 522 P.2d 1187 (1974).
[83]United States v. Green, 554 F.2d 372 (C.A.-9 Wash., 1977).
[84]See section 3.2, herein.
[85]Armijo v. Wesselius, 73 Wash. 2d 716, 440 P.2d 471 (1968).
[86]See section 3.3, herein.
[87]Wash. Rev. Code Ann., § 11.04.081.
[88]Id., § 11.04.085.

his adopted family, and cuts off any rights in respect of the former.[89]

Procedures for the establishment of paternity and the enforcement of support are for the most part furnished in the Uniform Parentage Act.[90] This is supplemented by provisions[91] for more effective procedures for reaching the earnings and property of a responsible parent whose child is receiving public assistance. None of them authorize the department of social and health services to determine paternity in an administrative proceeding.[92]

The Illegitimate Children and Parental Rights Act[93] reflects an effort to implement Stanley v. Illinois,[94] and to respond to holdings that the prior filiation and adoption statutes were unconstitutional insofar as they failed to recognize the constitutional rights of a putative father.[95] Conviction of a crime does not automatically justify a dispensation with parental consent to an adoption,[96] nor does extramarital cohabitation as such affect an otherwise recognized right to custody of a child.[97] To justify dispensation with the requirement of parental consent there must be a showing of a willful and substantial lack of regard for the obligations of the parent involved.[98]

Property rights of cohabitants

Washington courts have long recognized that, where one or both of the parties believed in the existence of a valid marriage,

---

[89] In re Estates of Donnelly, 81 Wash. 2d 430, 502 P.2d 1163, 60 A.L.R.3d 620 (1972).
[90] Wash. Rev. Code Ann., §§ 26.26.010 to 26.26.905. As to the Uniform Reciprocal Enforcement of Support Act, see §§ 26.21.010 to 26.21.910.
[91] Id., §§ 74.20A.010 et seq., 26.26.040 et seq.
[92] Taylor v. Morris, 88 Wash. 2d 586, 564 P.2d 795 (1977). As to the constitutionality of the filiation statute, and to the standing of a father who has custody to seek support from the unwed mother, see State v. Wood, 89 Wash. 2d 97, 569 P.2d 1148 (1977).
[93] Wash. Rev. Code Ann., § 26.24.190.
[94] See section 3.8, herein.
[95] See In re Guardianship of Harp, 6 Wash. App. 701, 495 P.2d 1059 (1972).
[96] Adoption of Kurth, 16 Wash. App. 579, 557 P.2d 349 (1976).
[97] Wildermuth v. Wildermuth, 14 Wash. App. 442, 542 P.2d 463 (1975). See Rights of Putative Fathers in Custody and Adoption Proceedings—Washington's Law in Perspective, 9 Gonzaga L. Rev. 826 (1974).
[98] See In re Adoption of Webb, 14 Wash. App. 651, 544 P.2d 130 (1975). The statute withstood constitutional attack in In re Welfare of Hansen, 15 Wash. App. 231, 548 P.2d 333 (1976).

6.48 UNMARRIED COUPLES AND THE LAW

there must be a fair and equitable division of property accumulated during the existence of the cohabitation.[99] Thus, where a woman had lived with the decedent for many years, not knowing that their marriage had been contracted before the required six-month period following his divorce from his first wife, she was held entitled to one-half of the post-putative marital estate.[1] In a similar case, where a divorce nunc pro tunc had the effect of legalizing their ceremonial marriage, the wife qualified as the decedent spouse's lawful heir.[2]

Where neither party believed in the existence of a marriage, but title has been taken in the names of both, each qualifies for an undivided one-half interest in the property.[3] Where title to the property is taken by one alone, under the so-called Creasman rule, the courts at one time left the parties to a meretricious relationship where they stood; the presumption, in the absence of some trust relation,[4] being that the parties intended to dispose of the property exactly as they did.[5]

This presumption, whereunder the courts washed their hands of disputes between extramarital cohabitants, leaving them where they find themselves, has since come under heavy criticism.

> [S]uch pronouncements seem overly fastidious and a bit fatuous. They are unrealistic and, among other things, ignore the fact that an unannounced (but nevertheless effective and binding) rule of law is inherent in any such terminal statements by a court of law. . . . The rule often operates to the great advantage of the cunning and the shrewd, who wind up with possession of the property, or title to it in their own names, at the end of a so-called meretricious relationship. So, although the courts proclaim that they will have nothing to do with such matters, the proclamation in itself establishes, as to the parties in-

---

[99] See Poole v. Schrichte, 39 Wash. 2d 558, 236 P.2d 1044 (1951) (equal division of assets); Powers v. Powers, 117 Wash. 248, 200 Pac. 1080 (1921); Buckley v. Buckley, 50 Wash. 213, 96 Pac. 1079 (1908) (one-quarter of community property to divorced wife, one-quarter to good faith putative spouse).

[1] In re Brenchley's Estate, 96 Wash. 223, 164 Pac. 913 (1917).

[2] In re Estate of Storer, 14 Wash. App. 687, 544 P.2d 95 (1975).

[3] Hynes v. Hynes, 28 Wash. 2d 660, 184 P.2d 68 (1947).

[4] Stans v. Baitey, 9 Wash. 115, 37 Pac. 316 (1894) (evidence insufficient to show a trust).

[5] Creasman v. Boyle, 31 Wash. 2d 345, 196 P.2d 835 (1948); Engstrom v. Peterson, 107 Wash. 523, 182 Pac. 623 (1919).

volved, an effective and binding rule of law which tends to operate purely by accident or perhaps by reason of the cunning, anticipatory designs of just one of the parties.[6]

The presumption is now so riddled with and undermined by qualifications that it can no longer fairly be said to be a conclusive one.[7] The courts have adjusted the property rights of extramarital cohabitants on a basis of a theory of partnership;[8] agreements to pool earnings are a recognized alternative basis;[9] the constructive trust[10] as well as the resulting trust[11] has been harnessed; and the express or implied contract to make a will is not without recognition.[12] At least one court has suggested that a long-term stable meretricious relationship can result in a community property interest.[13] An additional qualification can lie in the fact that a true spouse can, by failure to make timely objection, be estopped from seeking a share, as against a bigamous spouse, of the decedent spouse's estate.[14]

All this notwithstanding, a 1978 court reverted to the Creasman rule in leaving title to the assets acquired during a meretricious relationship in the party who acquired title. From the evidence it was apparent that the relationship developed from circumstances other than a deep emotional involvement. Said the court: "The whole question of the division of property following a breakup of a meretricious relationship is rife with fictions, presumptions and exceptions."[15]

---

[6]West v. Knowles, 50 Wash. 2d 311, 311 P.2d 689, 692 (1957).
[7]See Humphries v. Riveland, 67 Wash. 2d 376, 407 P.2d 967 (1965); Latham v. Hennessey, 87 Wash. 2d 550, 554 P.2d 1057 (1976) (discussing the qualifications to the Creasman rule).
[8]See Latham v. Hennessey, supra. In re Estate of Thornton, 81 Wash. 2d 72, 499 P.2d 864 (1972); In re Estate of Thorton, 14 Wash. App. 397, 541 P.2d 1243 (1975) (no meretricious relation established); Meretricious Relationships—Property Rights: A Meretricious Relationship May Create an Implied Partnership, 48 Wash. L. Rev. 635 (1973).
[9]Hynes v. Hynes, 28 Wash. 2d 660, 184 P.2d 68 (1947).
[10]Omer v. Omer, 11 Wash. App. 386, 523 P.2d 957 (1974); Humphries v. Riveland, 67 Wash. 2d 376, 407 P.2d 967 (1965).
[11]Walberg v. Mattson, 38 Wash. 2d 808, 232 P.2d 827 (1951).
[12]See In re Estate of Thornton, 81 Wash. 2d 72, 76, 499 P.2d 864 (1972) and 14 Wash. App. 397, 541 P.2d 1243 (1975).
[13]Latham v. Hennessey, 13 Wash. App. 518, 535 P.2d 838 (1975), affd. 87 Wash. 2d 550, 554 P.2d 1057 (1976).
[14]See In re Estate of Grauel, 70 Wash. 2d 870, 425 P.2d 644 (1967).
[15]Hinkle v. McColm, 89 Wash. 2d 769, 575 P.2d 711, 712 (1978). As to the

There is early recognition that, though a contract the consideration for which is illicit cohabitation is not enforceable,[16] an otherwise valid contract is not vitiated by the fact of sexual relations between the parties.[17] However, in view of a recently expressed opinion that the whole question is in need of reevaluation[18] it cannot categorically be stated that extramarital cohabitants can place implicit reliance on the courts to grope for a finding of "reasonable expectations" which never found articulation during their togetherness.[19]

6.49. West Virginia

Though a marriage valid by the laws of the place of its celebration is ordinarily accorded recognition, common-law marriage cannot be contracted in West Virginia.[20] Hence, such a type of cohabitant could not qualify as a "widow" for social security benefits by reason merely of a purported common-law marriage contracted in the state.[21]

Adoption

Any single person, or a married person with spousal consent, may petition to adopt a child. If the child is born out of wedlock

---

nonrecoverability of gifts between persons contemplating marriage with knowledge, at the time of the gift, that the recipient was unable to marry the donor, see Heilman v. Wentworth, 18 Wash. App. 751, 571 P.2d 963 (1977); Adams v. Jensen-Thomas, 18 Wash. App. 757, 571 P.2d 958 (1977).
[16]Armitage v. Hogan, 25 Wash. 2d 672, 171 P.2d 830 (1946).
[17]Anderson v. Petridge, 45 Wash. 2d 299, 274 P.2d 352 (1954).
[18]Hinkle v. McColm, 89 Wash. 2d 769, 575 P.2d 711 (1978).
[19]Cross, Community Property Law in Washington, 49 Wash. L. Rev. 729 (1974), predicts that courts will continue to apply the Creasman presumption where short term meretricious relationships are involved. See also Domestic Relations—Disposition of Property upon Termination of Nonmarital Cohabitation, 53 Wash. L. Rev. 145 (1977).
[20]State v. Bragg, 152 W. Va. 372, 163 S.E.2d 685 (1968). See also State v. Austin, —— W. Va. ——, 234 S.E.2d 657 (1977), holding that a statute (W. Va. Code, § 48-1-17) providing that a marriage contracted in another state by residents of West Virginia with intention of evading the marriage laws will be governed by the law of West Virginia is nothing more than a statutory extension of the common-law rule that a state is not *required* to recognize a marriage performed in another state if it is repugnant to the former state's statutes or public policy.
[21]Pace v. Celebrezze, 243 F. Supp. 317 (S.D. W. Va., 1965).

the consent of the father (if living) is required only if his paternity is "determined."[22] A six-months residence in the adoptive home prior to the petition is required.[23] Out-of-state agencies cannot place a child in a private home in the state without state approval.[24] Any such agency remains responsible for the child's supervision, either by itself or through a licensed child welfare agency in the state.[25]

Provision now exists for subsidized adoption in the case of children for some reason difficult to place.[26]

Workers' compensation death benefits

Since out-of-state common-law marriages receive recognition, if valid where contracted, a woman so married qualifies as a decedent worker's widow. Conversely, if the "marriage" was purportedly entered into in West Virginia, she would not.[27]

A provision that the children of a marriage deemed null in law are legitimate[28] has been held to cover the children of marriages which are bigamous, incestuous, and of invalid common-law marriages.[29] It has been held not to cover the children of a purely meretricious connection.[30] However, in the light of subsequent Supreme Court rulings,[31] it is likely that dependent illegitimate children would qualify for benefits not only here, but also in respect of damages for wrongful death of the putative father.[32]

---

[22]W. Va. Code, § 48-4-1. As to notice to the putative father and termination of parental rights, see In re Adoption of Daft, —— W. Va. ——, 230 S.E.2d 475 (1976).
[23]Id.
[24]W. Va. Code, § 49-2-15.
[25]Id. As to a provision for adoption of adults, see § 48-4-7.
[26]Id., § 49-2-17.
[27]Meade v. State Compensation Comr., 147 W. Va. 72, 125 S.E.2d 771 (1962). See Domestic Relations—The Effect of a Bigamous Marriage in a Workman's Compensation Proceeding, 65 W. Va. L. Rev. 57 (1962).
[28]W. Va. Code, § 42-1-7.
[29]See Kester v. Kester, 106 W. Va. 615, 146 S.E. 625 (1929).
[30]Francis v. Tazewell, 120 W. Va. 319, 91 S.E. 202 (1917).
[31]See section 3.2, herein.
[32]As to equal protection of illegitimate children in wrongful death context, see Constitutional Law—Torts—Equal Protection of Illegitimate Children, 71 W. Va. L. Rev. 52 (1968); Torts—Wrongful Death—Dependent Distributee Need Not be Totally Dependent upon Deceased, 75 W. Va. L. Rev. 88 (1972).

Abortion

The only defense spelled out in the West Virginia abortion law[33] relates to a situation where the operation is necessary to save the life of the mother or child.

Effect of cohabitation on right to alimony

Subsequent cohabitation on the part of an ex-wife has been held not to justify a court in modifying an alimony award.[34]

Tort actions

The actions for alienation of affections and breach of promise to marry have been abolished.[35] The action for seduction remains.[36]

Possible criminal liability

The current trend towards a liberalization of the attitudes relating to the sexual behavior of consenting adults has received but limited recognition in this state. Adultery and fornication,[37] as well as lewd and lascivious cohabitation and conduct,[38] remain at least nominally punishable. As, of course, does bigamy[39] and incest.[40]

Abduction of a female is a crime.[41] The gravity of the various degrees of "sexual abuse" (embracing misconduct with minors)[42] depends largely on the relative ages of the participants. Statutes imposing a heavier penalty on males than on females have withstood challenge as based on an unconstitutional gender-based

---

[33] W. Va. Code, § 61-2-8. Abortion is not an approved method of family planning, see § 16-2B-2. A very old case holds false accusations of a wife of abortion to be grounds for divorce. Maxwell v. Maxwell, 69 W. Va. 414, 71 S.E. 571 (1911).

[34] Cariens v. Cariens, 50 W. Va. 113, 40 S.E. 335 (1901).

[35] W. Va. Code, § 56-3-2A.

[36] Id., § 55-7-1.

[37] Id., § 61-8-3 ($20 maximum fine).

[38] Id., § 61-8-4. The crime requires a living together as husband and wife (State v. Bridgeman, 88 W. Va. 231, 106 S.E. 708 (1921)) and not mere occasional acts of sex. State v. Miller, 42 W. Va. 215, 24 S.E. 882 (1896).

[39] W. Va. Code, § 61-8-1.

[40] Id., § 61-8-12. As to the prohibited relations, see §§ 48-1-2, 48-1-3.

[41] Id., § 61-2-14.

[42] Id., § 61-8B-2 et seq.

classification;[43] however the wording of the present statute, defining "sexual assault in the third degree" in terms of sex by one sixteen years or over with one less than sixteen, or at least four years younger than the actor, indicates a legislative switch to sexual neutrality.[44]

Status of children

The West Virginia statute merely provides that bastards can inherit and transmit inheritance on the part of their mother.[45]

In addition to provisions to enable the mother of a child to obtain a judicial determination of paternity,[46] the procedures for the enforcement of a father's obligations of support[47] permit such an adjudication if nonpaternity is asserted as a defense.[48] Although the fathering of an illegitimate child is no crime, nonsupport of a child is; hence, paternity being an element of this crime, the courts now require proof, where paternity is in issue, beyond a reasonable doubt.[49]

The right of a putative father to visit the children in the custody of the mother is a matter for the court's discretion.[50] Where, however, the mother is dead, the father is ordinarily the person entitled to custody of the child.[51]

Prior to 1976, no particular form of notice to the father of an illegitimate child was required before it could be adopted, and the requirement was held satisfied where actual notice was impossible, by such constructive notice as was reasonably calculated to apprise him of the pendency of the action.[52] Since that date, how-

---

[43]See Hall v. McKenzie, 537 F.2d 1232 (C.A.-4 W. Va., 1976); Moore v. McKenzie, —— W. Va. ——, 236 S.E.2d 342 (1977).

[44]W. Va. Code, § 61–8B–5. A conviction under the Mann Act has been had where the purpose involved merely intercourse, not an exchange of money. Hunter v. United States, 45 F.2d 55, 73 A.L.R. 70 (C.A.-4 W. Va., 1930).

[45]W. Va. Code, § 42–1–5.
[46]Id., § 48–7–1 et seq.
[47]Id., § 48–8–1 et seq.
[48]Id., § 48–9–26.

[49]State v. Clay, —— W. Va. ——, 236 S.E.2d 230 (1977). As to the Uniform Reciprocal Enforcement of Support Act, see W. Va. Code, §§ 48–9–1 to 48–9–42.

[50]J.M.S. v. H.A., —— W. Va. ——, 242 S.E.2d 696 (1978).

[51]W. Va. Code, § 44–10–7. See Hammack v. Wise, —— W. Va. ——, 211 S.E.2d 118 (1975). As to legitimation by marriage, see W. Va. Code, § 42–1–6.

[52]In re Adoption of Daft, —— W. Va. ——, 230 S.E.2d 475 (1976).

6.50 UNMARRIED COUPLES AND THE LAW

ever, the legislature has made far more specific provision to ensure the father's right to be heard is not lightly to be ignored even if he is alleged to have abandoned the child.[53]

Property rights of cohabitants

Eloquent evidence of the moral climate in West Virginia is the fact that, not only has the inadequate statute relating to the inheritance rights of children from their putative father[54] attracted no judicial attention at the higher level, but neither has the question, so hotly debated elsewhere, as to the disposition of the accumulations of an extramarital relationship.[55]

6.50. Wisconsin

Common-law marriages were abolished in 1917.[56]

Though it was at one time held that a marriage illegal in its inception did not become valid by reason of continued cohabitation after removal of the impediment,[57] this is no longer so.[58]

Adoption

Any person, with spousal consent if married, can petition to adopt a child. The adopting petitioner, if practicable, should be of the same religious faith as the child's natural parents.[59] A six-month probationary residence in the prospective adoptive home is ordinarily required.[60] The fact that the petitioner is living with another of the opposite sex does not of itself mean that the peti-

---

[53] W. Va. Code, § 48-4-1. As to revocation of adoption where requisite notice was never afforded, see § 48-4-6.

[54] Id., § 42-1-5.

[55] As to the status of an agreement to make compensation for an injury resulting from past illicit cohabitation, clear of any taint of being in consideration of future cohabitation, see Tearney v. Marmion, 103 W. Va. 394, 137 S.E. 543 (1927).

[56] See In re Van Schaick's Estate, 256 Wis. 214, 40 N.W.2d 588 (1949).

[57] See Hall v. Industrial Comm., 165 Wis. 364, 162 N.W. 312 (1917).

[58] See Davidson v. Davidson, 35 Wis. 2d 401, 151 N.W.2d 53 (1967); Hoffman v. Hoffman, 242 Wis. 83, 7 N.W.2d 428 (1943).

[59] Wis. Stat. Ann., § 48.82. As to whose consent is required, see Wis. Stat. Ann., § 48.84.

[60] Wis. Stat. Ann., § 48.90.

tion will be denied,[61] but since personal qualities of the adoptive parents are of far more importance than age, income and social class,[62] it would no doubt be a factor to be taken into consideration when, as is usual, the recommendation of the department of public welfare is required.[63]

Workers' compensation death benefits

An illegitimate child who was living with the deceased worker and dependent on him at the time of his death could qualify for benefits.[64] The eligibility of a posthumously born illegitimate would seem to be dependent on whether there are benefits available other than the "primary benefits" payable under the controlling statute.[65]

Abortion

The statute criminalizing the intentional destruction of the life of an unborn quick child, unless necessary to save the life of the mother,[66] has been ruled unconstitutional on a number of occasions.[67] Nevertheless, hospitals,[68] nurses[69] and physicians[70] can properly decline to co-operate.

---

[61] See In re Estate of Komarr, 68 Wis. 2d 473, 228 N.W.2d 681 (1975).

[62] See In re Adoption of Tachick, 60 Wis. 2d 540, 210 N.W.2d 865 (1973) (age differential of half a century or more, and ill health of adoptive grandparents, were held not alone sufficient to establish unfitness of grandparents to adopt). See also In re Adoption of Randolph, 68 Wis. 2d 64, 227 N.W.2d 634 (1975).

[63] Wis. Stat. Ann., § 48.89. As to the effect of adoption on rights of inheritance from natural parents, see In re Estate of Komarr, 68 Wis. 2d 473, 228 N.W.2d 681 (1975). See also Re-evaluation of Inheritance and Testamentary Rights with Respect to Adopted Children in Wisconsin, 1956 Wis. L. Rev. 504.

[64] Waunakee Canning Corp. v. Industrial Comm., 268 Wis. 518, 68 N.W.2d 25 (1955).

[65] See Larson v. Wisconsin Dept. of Industry, Labor & Human Relations, 76 Wis. 2d 595, 252 N.W.2d 33 (1977); Wis. Stat. Ann., §§ 102.49(1), 102.51(1), (2)(a).

[66] Wis. Stat. Ann., § 940.04.

[67] Doe v. Bellin Memorial Hosp., 479 F.2d 756 (C.A.-7 Wis., 1973), holding also that a statute which requires the medical profession to observe unnecessary abortion-restricting rules is invalid, and that there is nothing in the Supreme Court of the United States' decisions (see section 2.19, herein) conditioning a woman's right to abortion on the consent of the father of the unborn child. See also Larkin v. McCann, 368 F. Supp. 1352 (E.D. Wis., 1974); Harling v. Department of Health and Social Services, 323 F. Supp. 899 (E.D. Wis., 1971); Babbitz v.

6.50   UNMARRIED COUPLES AND THE LAW

Sexual freedom

A statute imposing controls on the sale and distribution of contraceptives,[71] insofar as it operated to preclude the sale of such to unmarried persons, was held unconstitutional.[72] The state's interest in the absence of, or low incidence of, premarital sexual intercourse was not regarded as sufficiently compelling to warrant denial or impairment of the fundamental interest of an unmarried woman in making her own decision whether to become pregnant.

Recovery for wrongful death

An illegitimate child's eligibility for damages due to a wrongful causing of the death of its father depends on whether that child would qualify under the laws of intestate succession to a share of the father's estate.[73]

Effect of cohabitation on right to alimony

Alimony is not awarded to a wife divorced for adultery,[74] and in the exercise of its discretion to modify such awards,[75] an ex-wife's subsequent cohabitation with another has been held a proper ground for termination of such payments, though it was indicated that a future material change in her circumstances could entitle a court to reinstate the award.[76]

McCann, 310 F. Supp. 293 (E.D. Wis., 1970), appeal dismissed 400 U.S. 1, 27 L. Ed. 2d 1, 91 Sup. Ct. 12 (1970).
[68]Wis. Stat. Ann., § 140.42.
[69]Id., § 441.06.
[70]Id., § 448.06(8). As to suspension of license for abortions by physician, see Withrow v. Larkin, 421 U.S. 35, 43 L. Ed. 2d 712, 95 Sup. Ct. 1456 (1975).
[71]Wis. Stat. Ann., § 450.11.
[72]Baird v. Lynch, 390 F. Supp. 740 (W.D. Wis., 1974).
[73]Robinson v. Kolstad, 84 Wis. 2d 579, 267 N.W.2d 886 (1978); In re Estate of Blumreich, 84 Wis. 2d 545, 267 N.W.2d 870 (1978).
As to an unsuccessful attempt on the part of an illegitimate to recover from the father for "wrongful life" (which is not yet recognized as actionable, see section 2.20, herein), see Slawek v. Stroh, 62 Wis. 2d 295, 215 N.W.2d 9 (1974).
[74]See Molloy v. Molloy, 46 Wis. 2d 682, 176 N.W.2d 292 (1970).
[75]Wis. Stat. Ann., § 247.32.
[76]Taake v. Taake, 75 Wis. 2d 115, 233 N.W.2d 449 (1975). See also 60 Marq. L. Rev. 435 (1977).

Tort actions

The actions for breach of promise of marriage, alienation of affections and criminal conversation have been abolished.[77] This, however, does not bar a recovery of property procured by false representations of intent to marry.[78] Nor do these provisions prevent a conviction of theft by fraud[79] (although proof beyond a reasonable doubt that the promisor, when obtaining his bounty, had no intention of implementing his promise would make such a prosecution a virtual futility in most cases).

Possible criminal liability

Sexual intercourse with a person not the actor's spouse is a Class A misdemeanor.[80] Also forbidden, as lewd and lascivious behavior, is open cohabitation with a person known not to be a spouse under circumstances that imply sexual intercourse.[81] This open cohabitation has no reference to the place or to the number of people who know of it.[82]

Adultery includes the conduct of one who has sexual relations with a married person, as well as the participant.[83] The crime can be proved by circumstantial evidence, if the circumstances afford clear and convincing evidence of an activity which is seldom conducted in the market place.[84]

Of interest in the crime of statutory rape is a rebuttable presumption of incapacity to consent when the victim is between fifteen and seventeen years old: if the victim is under fifteen, the presumption is conclusive.[85]

---

[77]Wis. Stat. Ann., § 248.01 et seq. Such abolition has been criticized as, inter alia, an impairment of contract obligations. See Abolition of Breach of Promise in Wisconsin—Scope and Constitutionality, 43 Marq. L. Rev. 341 (1959–60). Seduction, however, remains a tort. See Slawek v. Stroh, 62 Wis. 2d 295, 215 N.W.2d 9 (1974).

[78]Wis. Stat. Ann., § 248.06.

[79]Lambert v. State, 73 Wis. 2d 590, 243 N.W.2d 524 (1976).

[80]Wis. Stat. Ann., § 944.15.

[81]Id., § 944.20(3).

[82]State v. Juneau, 88 Wis. 180, 59 N.W. 580 (1894). See LaFave, Police and Nonenforcement of the Law, 1962 Wis. L. Rev. 104.

[83]Wis. Stat. Ann., § 944.16.

[84]See Roach v. Keane, 73 Wis. 2d 524, 243 S.W.2d 508 (1976). As to bigamy, see Wis. Stat. Ann., § 944.05. As to incest, see § 944.06.

[85]Wis. Stat. Ann., § 940.225.

6.50   UNMARRIED COUPLES AND THE LAW

"Unless mandated by the Constitution," the application of the sexual perversion statute[86] is not restricted to nonconsensual sexual acts, the only exception being in respect of married persons engaging in such intimacies in a private place.[87] The statute has been held not to be an unconstitutional invasion of the rights of privacy.[88]

Status of children

The illegitimate child inherits from its mother on intestacy as any other child. As to the father, the statute provides that it can inherit if (1) paternity has been adjudicated; (2) the father has admitted in open court his paternity; or (3) the father has in a writing signed by him acknowledged his paternity.[89] These requirements have been held to meet the demands of Trimble v. Gordon.[90] "To permit paternity to be established after the death of the putative father, on the basis of his alleged informal, verbal statements, would be to place his estate at an unreasonable disadvantage in defending against spurious claims."[91] As observed by an earlier court, even though it is not irrational to assume that most decedents would discriminate against persons born out of wedlock, the state may not, for that reason alone, make comparable discriminatory choices by prohibiting persons born out of wedlock from inheriting in all or certain circumstances.[92]

The constitutional right of a putative father to establish his parentage and assert parental rights[93] finds recognition in a provision whereunder he can file a declaration, at any time prior to a termination of his parental rights, which must be sent to the mother.[94] An adjudication of paternity can follow if the matter is disputed.[95] An action to establish paternity must be brought

---

[86]Id., § 944.17.
[87]Gossett v. State, 73 Wis. 2d 135, 242 N.W.2d 899 (1976). See also Mentek v. State, 71 Wis. 2d 799, 238 N.W.2d 752 (1976).
[88]Jones v. State, 55 Wis. 2d 742, 200 N.W.2d 587 (1972).
[89]Wis. Stat. Ann., § 852.05. As to the status of one legitimated by subsequent marriage of his parents, see § 245.25. As to one legally adopted, see § 851.51.
[90]Discussed in section 3.3, herein.
[91]In re Estate of Blumreich, 84 Wis. 2d 545, 267 N.W.2d 870, 877 (1978).
[92]Eskra v. Morton, 524 F.2d 9 (C.A.-7 Wis., 1975).
[93]See Slawek v. Stroh, 62 Wis. 2d 295, 215 N.W.2d 9 (1974).
[94]Wis. Stat. Ann., § 48.025.
[95]Id., § 48.425.

within five years of the birth of the child or, if the parents live together as husband and wife, within five years after their separation.[96]

A scheme is provided whereunder the department of social services is entrusted with the promotion and enforcement of laws for the protection of children born out of wedlock. It enables the department, for example, to co-operate with the juvenile courts and placement agencies and to ensure that paternity is established.[97] Detailed provisions for the care and support of such children[98] supplement the more general provisions for the enforcement of support duties.[99] A section furnishing an exclusive procedure for the creation of an enforceable contract for the support of such a child between its parents[1] has withstood a challenge that it is an unconstitutional impairment of a contract.[2]

Earlier judicial criticism of the inadequacy of the procedures whereunder a putative father's parental rights could be terminated[3] have led to an enactment which now ensures that such a parent is afforded proper notice of any proceedings affecting the future of the child until such time as his parental rights are judicially terminated.[4]

---

[96]Id., § 893.195. The constitutionality of the provisions whereunder paternity can be established has been confirmed. Robinson v. Kolstad, 84 Wis. 2d 579, 267 N.W.2d 886 (1978); In re Estate of Blumreich, 84 Wis. 2d 545, 267 N.W.2d 870 (1978).

[97]Id., § 46.011 et seq. As to the constitutionality of a provision requiring the unwed mother to identify the putative father (§ 52.24), see Burdick v. Miech, 409 F. Supp. 982 (E.D. Wis., 1975).

[98]Wis. Stat. Ann., § 46.001 et seq.

[99]Id., §§ 52.055, 52.10 et seq.

[1]Id., § 52.28.

[2]Smazal v. Dassow's Estate, 23 Wis. 2d 336, 127 N.W.2d 234, 20 A.L.R.3d 493 (1964). For the Uniform Reciprocal Enforcement of Support Act, see Wis. Stat. Ann., § 52.10.

[3]State ex rel. Lewis v. Lutheran Social Services of Wisconsin and Upper Michigan, 59 Wis. 2d 1, 207 N.W.2d 826 (1973), appeal after remand 68 Wis. 2d 36, 227 N.W.2d 643 (1975).

[4]Wis. Stat. Ann., § 48.195. See also §§ 48.42 et seq., 48.425. Generally, see Constitutional Rights of a Putative Father to Establish His Parentage and Assert Parental Rights, 58 Marq. L. Rev. 175 (1975).

As to grounds for termination of parental rights, which include consent, neglect or inability for a prolonged indeterminate period to give necessary care, and repeated lewd behavior, see Wis. Stat. Ann., § 48.40.

As to the Uniform Child Custody Jurisdiction Act (Wis. Stat. Ann., §§ 822.01 to 822.25), see Wisconsin and the Uniform Child Custody Jurisdiction Act: In Whose Hand Soloman's Sword, 61 Marq. L. Rev. 79 (1977).

6.51 UNMARRIED COUPLES AND THE LAW

Property rights of cohabitants

Where title to land is taken by unmarried persons as joint tenants,[5] or the deed uses terms clearly indicative of their intent to provide for survivorship,[6] the right of the survivor receives recognition regardless of the meretricious character of their relationship. Further, where a marriage is annulled, the courts have long countenanced an equitable distribution of the marital accumulations whether or not one or both were aware of the invalidity of their marriage.[7] An early decision also views a good faith wife as entitled to the reasonable value of her services to the extent that they exceed the value of support furnished during the existence of cohabitation in the mistaken belief in a valid marriage.[8]

Where there was no belief on either side in the existence of a marriage, the traditional "hands-off" attitude, which leaves the assets with the party who was so fortunate as to hold the legal title, has judicial acceptance.[9] A woman who lived with a man under a common-law marriage contract, knowing well of the invalidity of such a union, was denied any equitable division of the property. However, the court indicated that a partnership or joint venture agreed on before the relationship began could have dictated a different result.[10]

6.51. Wyoming

Since the common-law marriage is not a way of acquiring the status of legal spouses in this state,[11] a continued cohabitation

---

[5]Neitge v. Severson, 256 Wis. 628, 42 N.W.2d 149 (1950).
[6]Weber v. Nedin, 210 Wis. 39, 246 N.W. 307 (1933). See Concurrent Ownership: Joint Tenancy & Tenancy in Common Under Chapter 700, 55 Marq. L. Rev. 321 (1972); Recent Developments in the Wisconsin Law of Jointly Held Personal Property, 1970 Wis. L. Rev. 1162.
[7]See Siskoy v. Siskoy, 250 Wis. 435, 27 N.W.2d 488 (1947); Wheeler v. Wheeler, 79 Wis. 303, 48 N.W. 260 (1891).
[8]In re Fox's Estate, 178 Wis. 369, 190 N.W. 90, 31 A.L.R. 420 (1922). As to estoppel or laches as barring claim of a lawful wife based on the invalidity of a second marriage, see In re Estate of Gibson, 7 Wis. 2d 506, 96 N.W.2d 859 (1959).
[9]Smith v. Smith, 255 Wis. 96, 38 N.W.2d 12, 14 A.L.R.2d 914 (1949).
[10]Id. See Also Brill v. Salzwedel, 235 Wis. 551, 292 N.W. 908 (1940).
[11]Wyo. Stat., § 20-1-101.

after some impediment to a valid marriage has been removed does not result in any status of husband and wife.[12]

Adoption

Any person may be adopted who is within the state when the petition for adoption is filed.[13] An adult resident, if found fit, may adopt another.[14] When the adoptee is a minor, special provisions control;[15] for example, the court may order the appropriate authorities or a licensed agency to investigate and report on the background of the child and of the petitioners, as well as on that of the consenting parents.[16] Parental consent can be dispensed with in cases of abandonment, mistreatment and the like.[17] Such provisions, however, are strictly construed and every reasonable intendment is made in favor of the claims of a nonconsenting parent.[18]

Workers' compensation death benefits

The controlling statute is now construed to include illegitimate children who are dependent on the decedent worker.[19] A cohabitant, however, does not qualify as a widow.[20]

Recovery for wrongful death

An illegitimate child can recover for the wrongful death of either parent.[21]

---

[12]In re Roberts' Estate, 58 Wyo. 438, 133 P.2d 492 (1943).
[13]Wyo. Stat., § 1–22–102. As to an action for breach of a contract to adopt, see Nichols v. Pangarova, 443 P.2d 756 (Wyo., 1968).
[14]Wyo. Stat., § 1–22–103.
[15]Id., § 1–22–104.
[16]Id., § 1–22–111.
[17]Id., § 1–22–110.
[18]See In re Adoption of Voss, 550 P.2d 481 (Wyo., 1976); In re Adoption of Narragon, 530 P.2d 413 (Wyo., 1975).
[19]Heather v. Delta Drilling Co., 533 P.2d 1211 (Wyo., 1975).
[20]Bowers v. Getter Trucking Co., 514 P.2d 837 (Wyo., 1973).
[21]Jordan v. Delta Drilling Co., 541 P.2d 39, 78 A.L.R. 3d 1215 (Wyo., 1975).

Abortion

The present statutes reflect substantial compliance with the mandates of the Supreme Court of the United States[22] restricting the constitutional right of the state to criminalize abortion to very specific situations.[23]

Tort actions

Tort actions for alienation of affections, criminal conversation, seduction and breach of contract to marry have been abolished.[24] Severe penalties can result merely from the filing of pleadings of this nature.[25]

Possible criminal liability

Assuming an extramarital relationship is neither bigamous[26] nor incestuous,[27] it seems unlikely that the criminal laws would present any serious threat, provided only that the activities do not fall within the purview of the legislation denouncing sexual assault.[28]

Status of children

An illegitimate child can inherit on intestacy from the mother. Succession to the father is conditioned on subsequent intermarriage of the parents and recognition by the father of the child as his.[29]

Proceedings for the establishment of paternity, which substantially follow the Uniform Parentage Act,[30] are not regarded as criminal in nature. Hence, a mere preponderance of evidence is

---

[22]See section 2.19, herein.
[23]Wyo. Stat., § 35–6–101 et seq.
[24]Wyo. Stat., § 1–23–101 et seq.
[25]Id., § 1–23–104. It is not clear whether these penalties would be visited on the attorney who files such pleadings.
[26]Id., § 6–5–101. As to belief in death as a defense, see Belief in Death of Absent Consort as a Defense to a Charge of Bigamy, 10 Wyo. L. J. 158 (1956).
[27]Wyo. Stat., § 6–5–102.
[28]Id., § 6–4–301 et seq.
[29]Id., § 2–3–109.
[30]See section 3.4, herein.

sufficient.[31] An independent provision articulates the interrelating functions of the welfare authorities and of the law enforcement officials in furnishing aid to dependent children, locating parents, establishing paternity and recovery of support.[32]

At one time only the consent of the mother was required for the adoption of an illegitimate child. Today, however, careful provision is made to ensure that the father's right to notice and a hearing, if he is known, is respected.[33]

Property rights of cohabitants

A claim on the part of one who mistakenly believed in the existence of a valid marriage to an equitable share of the marital accumulations will not fall on deaf ears.[34] On the other hand, a claim for the value of services rendered by a meretricious cohabitant, at any rate in earlier days, met with little sympathy. Not only, a court has said, does the relationship of husband and wife negate that of master and servant, but such cohabitation, being in violation of principles of morality and chastity, and so contrary to public policy, cannot furnish the basis of any implied promise to compensate.[35]

---

[31] X v. Y, 482 P.2d 688 (Wyo., 1971).

[32] Wyo. Stat., § 14–3–201 et seq. As to the Uniform Child Custody Jurisdiction Act, see § 20–5–101 et seq.

[33] Id., § 20–4–101 et seq.

[34] See Roberts v. Roberts, 64 Wyo. 433, 196 P.2d 361 (1948).

[35] Willis v. Willis, 48 Wyo. 403, 49 P.2d 670 (1935), reh. den. 49 Wyo. 296, 54 P.2d 814 (1936).

APPENDICES

                                                                                                                             Page

A. Complaint filed by Michelle Marvin against Lee Marvin (February 22, 1972) 609

B. Opinion of Justice Mathew O. Tobriner, Supreme Court of California, in Marvin v. Marvin, 18 Cal. 3d 660, 134 Cal. Rptr. 815, 557 P.2d 106 (December 27, 1976) 617

C. Memorandum Opinion of Judge Arthur K. Marshall, Superior Court of the State of California for the County of Los Angeles, in Marvin v. Marvin (April 18, 1979) 643

APPENDIX A

COMPLAINT FILED BY MICHELLE MARVIN AGAINST LEE MARVIN

Law Offices of Marvin M. Mitchelson
and Donald N. Woldman
1800 Avenue of the Stars
Suite #825
Los Angeles, California 90067

Attorneys for Plaintiff

SUPERIOR COURT OF THE STATE OF CALIFORNIA
FOR THE COUNTY OF LOS ANGELES

Michelle Marvin, aka)
Michelle Triola,) No. C 23303
       Plaintiff,)
) COMPLAINT FOR:
            v.)
) (1) Declaratory Relief
Lee Marvin and Does I through)
X, inclusive,) (2) Constructive Trust
       Defendants.)

COMES NOW plaintiff, Michelle Marvin, aka Michelle Triola, hereinafter referred to as plaintiff, and for causes of action alleges as follows:

FIRST CAUSE OF ACTION

1.

That the Does named herein are sued pursuant to the provisions of Section #474 of the California Code of Civil Procedure. When their true names and capacities are ascertained, plaintiff will ask leave of court to amend this complaint to so state.

2.

That at all times herein mentioned plaintiff and defendant Lee Marvin, hereinafter referred to as

APPENDIX A

defendant Marvin and Does I through X inclusive, were and now are residents of the County of Los Angeles, State of California.

3.

That the above named Doe defendants, and each of them, claim some right, title, estate, lien or interest in the hereinafter described property.

4.

That in or about October, 1964, plaintiff and defendant Marvin entered into an oral agreement wherein each agreed that during the time thereafter that the parties lived together they would combine their efforts and earnings and would share equally any and all property accumulated as a result of their efforts whether individual or combined.

a) That it was further agreed that during the time the parties lived together that plaintiff and defendant would hold themselves out to the general public as husband and wife and plaintiff would further render her services as a companion, homemaker, housekeeper and cook to said defendant.

5.

That shortly after the entering into the said agreement, the agreement was modified in the following respect only:

a) That in order that plaintiff would be able to devote her full time to defendant Marvin as a companion, homemaker, housekeeper and cook, it was further agreed that plaintiff would give up her lucrative career as an entertainer/singer.

b) That in return defendant Marvin would provide for all of plaintiff's financial support and needs for the rest of her life.

6.

That as a further result of the said agreement, plaintiff had her name legally changed from Michelle Triola to Michelle Marvin.

7.

That pursuant to and in reliance upon the said agreement, plaintiff and defendant Marvin lived together continuously from October of 1964, through May of 1970.

8.

That plaintiff has at all times performed each and every covenant and condition by her to be performed and rendered the services as required by the terms of the agreement.

9.

That in or about May of 1970, at defendant Marvin's request and insistence, plaintiff was forced to leave defendant Marvin's household, and the parties have been separated since that date.

10.

That during the time that plaintiff and defendant Marvin lived together, they acquired as a result of their efforts and earnings, personal and real property, hereinafter referred to as ''Equitable Property'', consisting of the following:
a) Real property and residence located at 21404 Pacific Coast Highway, Malibu, California.
b) Furniture, furnishings and personal effects located in the above residence.
c) Motion picture rights, deferred earnings, options, and ancillary rights related thereto presently standing in the name of defendant Marvin having a gross value of not less than $1,000,000.
d) Santana Records, Inc.
3) Plaintiff is informed and believes and on such information and belief alleges that there is additional ''Equitable Property'' accumulated by the parties, through their efforts while living together. Plaintiff will ask leave to amend this complaint to set forth the description and value of said property when that information has been ascertained by her.

11.

That subsequent to the separation of plaintiff and defendant Marvin, defendant Marvin provided monies to plaintiff for her support and maintenance continuously

APPENDIX A

until November of 1971, at which time he refused and now continues to refuse to provide further support and maintenance for plaintiff.

12.

That all of said ''Equitable Property'' is in defendant Marvin's possession and under his control and plaintiff has demanded that defendant Marvin recognize her interest in said ''Equitable Property'', but defendant Marvin has refused to and does now refuse to do so, or to pay to plaintiff a sum equal to one-half of the reasonable value of all of said ''Equitable Property''.

13.

That an actual controversy has arisen between plaintiff and defendants, and each of them, relating to the legal rights, duties and obligations of said parties, to wit:

A. Plaintiff contends:

　1. As a result of said agreement and said acquisition of ''Equitable Property'', plaintiff is the owner of one-half of all of said property as a tenant in common with defendant Marvin.

　2. That defendant Marvin has the duty and obligation to pay to plaintiff a reasonable sum as and for her support and maintenance.

　3. That all of said ''Equitable Property'' was acquired while the parties were living in California and is located in this state and should be treated as would community property if there were a valid marriage entered into between plaintiff and defendant Marvin; and that to not enforce her rights in this regard would constitute a denial of due process and equal protection of the law under the United States and California State Constitutions.

　4. That defendant Marvin is estopped from denying the validity or effectiveness of said agreement by reason of:

　　a) Defendant Marvin's intentional inducement of plaintiff to abandon her career as an entertainer and singer.

　　b) Plaintiff's abandonment of her career in reliance on the agreement and defendant Marvin's continuous representation to her that said agreement was binding and effective.

c) The irreparable financial loss to plaintiff by reason of her having so abandoned her prior career as a singer-entertainer.

5. That in the alternative, should this court not enforce the said agreement, plaintiff by reason of the facts hereinabove alleged, has suffered damages in excess of $100,000.00. The exact amount of said damages have not been presently ascertained by plaintiff who will ask leave to amend this complaint to insert the exact amount upon ascertainment of same or according to proof.

B. That plaintiff is informed and believes and upon such information and belief alleges that defendants deny each and all of plaintiff's contentions and specifically deny that the agreement was entered into between plaintiff and defendant Marvin, and further deny that plaintiff is entitled to one-half of the ''Equitable Property'' or has any right to support and maintenance from defendant Marvin.

14.

That no adequate remedy, other than herein prayed for, exists by which the rights of the parties hereto may be determined.

15.

That plaintiff desires a judicial determination of her and defendant's rights, duties, obligations and interests and a further determination as to the validity of the agreement.

SECOND CAUSE OF ACTION

16.

Plaintiff incorporates paragraphs 1,2,3,4,5,6,7,8,9, 10,11, 12 A-1, 12 A-2, 12 A-3, 12 A-4 and 13 of this complaint, as though again herein set forth in full.

17.

That at all times herein mentioned a confidential and fiduciary relationship existed between plaintiff and defendant Marvin.

APPENDIX A

18.

That by reason of the facts, more particularly hereinabove set forth, and the confidential and fiduciary relationship between plaintiff and defendant Marvin, defendants, and each of them, are involuntary trustees of an individual one-half interest in all ''Equitable Property'' in constructive trust for the benefit of plaintiff with the duty to reconvey the same to plaintiff forthwith.

WHEREFORE, plaintiff prays for judgment against defendants, and each of them, as follows:

FIRST CAUSE OF ACTION

19.

That this court declare that plaintiff has an undivided one-half interest in all ''Equitable Property'' as described within this complaint, as a tenant in common with defendant Marvin.

20.

That this court order a partition of said ''Equitable Property'' according to the respective rights of the parties, or, if it appears that a partition cannot be had without great prejudice to the parties, that a sale of said ''Equitable Property'' be ordered, and the proceeds thereof be divided between the parties according to their respective rights.

21.

That defendant Marvin be ordered to pay to plaintiff a reasonable sum per month as and for the support and maintenance of plaintiff.

22.

In the alternative, for damages according to proof.

SECOND CAUSE OF ACTION

23.

That this court declare that plaintiff has an undivided one-half interest in all ''Equitable Property'' as described within this complaint, as a tenant in common with defendant Marvin.

24.

That this court order a partition of said ''Equitable Property'' according to the respective rights of the parties, or, if it appears that a partition cannot be had without great prejudice to the parties, that a sale of said ''Equitable Property'' be ordered, and the proceeds thereof be divided between the parties according to their respective rights.

25.

That defendant Marvin be ordered to pay to plaintiff a reasonable sum per month as and for the support and maintenance of plaintiff.

26.

For a judicial declaration that defendants, and each of them, hold the ''Equitable Properties'', as described within this complaint, as involuntary trustees of an undivided one-half interest in all ''Equitable Property'' in constructive trust for the benefit of plaintiff with the duty to reconvey the same to plaintiff forthwith.

ALL CAUSES OF ACTION

27.

For all costs of suit.

28.

Defendant Marvin be ordered to pay plaintiff reasonable attorney's fees.

29.

For such other and further relief as the court may deem proper.

Law Offices of Marvin M. Mitchelson

By: *[signature]*

APPENDIX A

(VERIFICATION — 446, 2015.5 C. C. P.)
STATE OF CALIFORNIA } ss.
COUNTY OF Los Angeles

I am the Plaintiff

in the above entitled action; I have read the foregoing COMPLAINT
FOR: (1) Declaratory Relief; (2) Constructive Trust

and know the contents thereof; and I certify that the same is true of my own knowledge, except as to those matters which are therein stated upon my information or belief, and as to those matters I believe it to be true.

I certify (or declare), under penalty of perjury,* that the foregoing is true and correct.

Executed on February 17, 1972 *at* Los Angeles *, California*
                  (date)   (place)

                                        Signature
                                   MICHELLE MARVIN

(PROOF OF SERVICE BY MAIL — 1013a, 2015.5 C. C. P.)
STATE OF CALIFORNIA } ss.
COUNTY OF

* * *

APPENDIX B

Opinion of Justice Mathew O. Tobriner

Michelle MARVIN, Plaintiff and Appellant,
v.
Lee MARVIN, Defendant and Respondent.

L.A. 30520.

Supreme Court of California, In Bank.
Dec. 27, 1976.

TOBRINER, Justice.

During the past 15 years, there has been a substantial increase in the number of couples living together without marrying.[1] Such nonmarital relationships lead to legal controversy when one partner dies or the couple separates. Courts of Appeal, faced with the task of determining property rights in such cases, have arrived at conflicting positions: two cases (*In re Marriage of Cary* (1973) 34 Cal. App. 3d 345, 109 Cal. Rptr. 862; *Estate of Atherley* (1975) 44 Cal. App. 3d 758, 119 Cal. Rptr. 41) have held that the Family Law Act (Civ. Code, § 4000 et seq.) requires division of the property according to community property principles, and one decision (*Beckman v. Mayhew* (1975) 49 Cal. App. 3d 529, 122 Cal. Rptr. 604) has rejected that holding. We take this opportunity to resolve that controversy and to declare the principles which should govern distribution of property acquired in a nonmarital relationship.

We conclude: (1) The provisions of the Family Law Act do not govern the distribution of property acquired during a nonmarital relationship; such a relationship remains subject solely to judicial decision. (2) The courts should enforce express contracts between nonmarital partners except to the extent that the contract is ex-

---

[1] "The 1970 census figures indicate that today perhaps eight times as many couples are living together without being married as cohabited ten years ago." (Comment, *In re Cary: A Judicial Recognition of Illicit Cohabitation* (1974) 25 Hastings L.J. 1226.)

plicitly founded on the consideration of meretricious sexual services. (3) In the absence of an express contract, the courts should inquire into the conduct of the parties to determine whether that conduct demonstrates an implied contract, agreement of partnership or joint venture, or some other tacit understanding between the parties. The courts may also employ the doctrine of quantum meruit, or equitable remedies such as constructive or resulting trusts, when warranted by the facts of the case.

In the instant case plaintiff and defendant lived together for seven years without marrying; all property acquired during this period was taken in defendant's name. When plaintiff sued to enforce a contract under which she was entitled to half the property and to support payments, the trial court granted judgment on the pleadings for defendant, thus leaving him with all property accumulated by the couple during their relationship. Since the trial court denied plaintiff a trial on the merits of her claim, its decision conflicts with the principles stated above, and must be reversed.

1. *The factual setting of this appeal.*

Since the trial court rendered judgment for defendant on the pleadings, we must accept the allegations of plaintiff's complaint as true, determining whether such allegations state, or can be amended to state, a cause of action. (See *Sullivan v. County of Los Angeles* (1974) 12 Cal. 3d 710, 714, 715, fn. 3, 117 Cal. Rptr. 241, 527 P.2d 865; 4 Witkin, Cal. Procedure (2d ed. 1971) pp. 2817, 2818.) We turn therefore to the specific allegations of the complaint.

Plaintiff avers that in October of 1964 she and defendant "entered into an oral agreement" that while "the parties lived together they would combine their efforts and earnings and would share equally any and all property accumulated as a result of their efforts whether individual or combined." Furthermore, they agreed to "hold themselves out to the general public as husband and wife" and that "plaintiff would further render her services as a companion, homemaker, housekeeper and cook to ... defendant."

Shortly thereafter plaintiff agreed to "give up her lucrative career as an entertainer [and] singer" in order to "devote her full time to defendant ... as a companion, homemaker, housekeeper and cook"; in return defendant agreed to "provide for all of plaintiff's financial support and needs for the rest of her life."

Plaintiff alleges that she lived with defendant from October of 1964 through May of 1970 and fulfilled her obligations under the agreement. During this period the parties as a result of their efforts and earnings acquired in defendant's name substantial real and personal property, including motion picture rights worth over $1 million. In May of 1970, however, defendant compelled plaintiff to leave his household. He continued to support plaintiff until November of 1971, but thereafter refused to provide further support.

On the basis of these allegations plaintiff asserts two causes of action. The first, for declaratory relief, asks the court to determine her contract and property rights; the second seeks to impose a constructive trust upon one half of the property acquired during the course of the relationship.

Defendant demurred unsuccessfully, and then answered the complaint. Following extensive discovery and pretrial proceedings, the case came to trial.[2] Defendant renewed his attack on the

---

[2]When the case was called for trial, plaintiff asked leave to file an amended complaint. The proposed complaint added two causes of action for breach of contract against Santa Ana Records, a corporation not a party to the action, asserting that Santa Ana was an alter ego of defendant. The court denied leave to amend, and plaintiff claims that the ruling was an abuse of discretion. We disagree; plaintiff's argument was properly rejected by the Court of Appeal in the portion of its opinion quoted below.

No error was committed in denial of plaintiff's motion, made on the opening day set for trial, seeking leave to file a proposed amended complaint which would have added two counts and a new defendant to the action. As stated by plaintiff's counsel at the hearing, "[T]here is no question about it that we seek to amend the Complaint not on the eve of trial but on the day of trial."

In *Hayutin v. Weintraub,* 207 Cal. App. 2d 497, 24 Cal. Rptr. 761, the court said at pages 508–509, 24 Cal. Rptr. at page 768 in respect to such a motion that had it been granted, it "would have required a long continuance for the purpose of canvassing wholly new factual issues, a redoing of the elaborate discovery procedures previously had, all of which would have imposed upon defendant and his witnesses substantial inconvenience ... and upon defendant needless and substantial additional expense.... The court did not err in denying leave to file the proposed amended complaint." (See also: *Nelson v. Specialty Records, Inc.,* 11 Cal. App. 3d 126, 138–139, 89 Cal. Rptr. 540; *Moss Estate Co. v. Adler,* 41 Cal. 2d 581, 585, 261 P.2d 732; *Bogel v. Thrifty Drug Co.,* 43 Cal. 2d 184, 188, 272 P.2d 1.) "The ruling of the trial judge will not be disturbed upon appeal absent a showing by appellant of a clear abuse of discretion. [Citations.]" (*Nelson v. Specialty Records, Inc., supra,* 11 Cal. App. 3d at p. 139, 89 Cal. Rptr. at p. 548.) No such showing here appears.

APPENDIX B

complaint by a motion to dismiss. Since the parties had stipulated that defendant's marriage to Betty Marvin did not terminate until the filing of a final decree of divorce in January 1967, the trial court treated defendant's motion as one for judgment on the pleadings augmented by the stipulation.

After hearing argument the court granted defendant's motion and entered judgment for defendant. Plaintiff moved to set aside the judgment and asked leave to amend her complaint to allege that she and defendant reaffirmed their agreement after defendant's divorce was final. The trial court denied plaintiff's motion, and she appealed from the judgment.

2. *Plaintiff's complaint states a cause of action for breach of an express contract.*

In *Trutalli v. Meraviglia* (1932) 215 Cal. 698, 12 P.2d 430 we established the principle that nonmarital partners may lawfully contract concerning the ownership of property acquired during the relationship. We reaffirmed this principle in *Vallera v. Vallera* (1943) 21 Cal. 2d 681, 685, 134 P.2d 761, 763, stating that "If a man and woman [who are not married] live together as husband and wife under an agreement to pool their earnings and share equally in their joint accumulations, equity will protect the interests of each in such property."

In the case before us plaintiff, basing her cause of action in contract upon these precedents, maintains that the trial court erred in denying her a trial on the merits of her contention. Although that court did not specify the ground for its conclusion that plaintiff's contractual allegations stated no cause of action,[3] defendant offers some four theories to sustain the ruling; we proceed to examine them.

Defendant first and principally relies on the contention that the alleged contract is so closely related to the supposed "immoral"

---

[3]The colloquy between court and counsel at argument on the motion for judgment on the pleadings suggests that the trial court held the 1964 agreement violated public policy because it derogated the community property rights of Betty Marvin, defendant's lawful wife. Plaintiff, however, offered to amend her complaint to allege that she and defendant reaffirmed their contract after defendant and Betty were divorced. The trial court denied leave to amend, a ruling which suggests that the court's judgment must rest upon some other ground than the assertion that the contract would injure Betty's property rights.

character of the relationship between plaintiff and himself that the enforcement of the contract would violate public policy.[4] He points to cases asserting that a contract between nonmarital partners is unenforceable if it is "involved in" an illicit relationship (see *Shaw v. Shaw* (1964) 227 Cal. App. 2d 159, 164, 38 Cal. Rptr. 520 (dictum); *Garcia v. Venegas* (1951) 106 Cal. App. 2d 364, 368, 235 P.2d 89 (dictum), or made in "contemplation" of such a relationship (*Hill v. Estate of Westbrook* (1950) 95 Cal. App. 2d 599, 602, 213 P.2d 727; see *Hill v. Estate of Westbrook* (1952) 39 Cal. 2d 458, 460, 247 P.2d 19; *Barlow v. Collins* (1958) 166 Cal. App. 2d 274, 277, 333 P.2d 64 (dictum); *Bridges v. Bridges* (1954) 125 Cal. App. 2d 359, 362, 270 P.2d 69 (dictum)). A review of the numerous California decisions concerning contracts between nonmarital partners, however, reveals that the courts have not employed such broad and uncertain standards to strike down contracts. The decisions instead disclose a narrower and more precise standard: a contract between nonmarital partners is unenforceable only *to the extent* that it *explicitly* rests upon the immoral and illicit consideration of meretricious sexual services.

In the first case to address this issue, *Trutalli v. Meraviglia, supra,* 215 Cal. 698, 12 P.2d 430, the parties had lived together without marriage for 11 years and had raised two children. The man sued to quiet title to land he had purchased in his own name during this relationship; the woman defended by asserting an agreement to pool earnings and hold all property jointly. Rejecting the assertion of the illegality of the agreement, the court stated that "The fact that the parties to this action at the time

---

[4]Defendant also contends that the contract was illegal because it contemplated a violation of former Penal Code section 269a, which prohibited living "in a state of cohabitation and adultery." (§ 269a was repealed by Stats. 1975, ch. 71, eff. Jan. 1, 1976.) Defendant's standing to raise the issue is questionable because he alone was married and thus guilty of violating section 269a. Plaintiff, being unmarried could neither be convicted of adulterous cohabitation nor of aiding and abetting defendants's violation. (See *In re Cooper* (1912) 162 Cal. 81, 85– 86, 121 P. 318.)

The numerous cases discussing the contractual rights of unmarried couples have drawn no distinction between illegal relationships and lawful nonmarital relationships. (*Cf. Weak v. Weak* (1962) 202 Cal. App. 2d 632, 639, 21 Cal. Rptr. 9 (bigamous marriage).) Moreover, even if we were to draw such a distinction—a largely academic endeavor in view of the repeal of section 269a—defendant probably would not benefit; his relationship with plaintiff continued long after his divorce became final, and plaintiff sought to amend her complaint to assert that the parties reaffirmed their contract after the divorce.

APPENDIX B

they agreed to invest their earnings in property to be held jointly between them were living together in an unlawful relation did not disqualify them from entering into a lawful agreement with each other, so long as such immoral relation was not made a *consideration* of their agreement." (Emphasis added.) (215 Cal. at pp. 701–702, 12 P.2d 430, 431.)

In *Bridges v. Bridges* (1954) 125 Cal. App. 2d 359, 270 P.2d 69, both parties were in the process of obtaining divorces from their erstwhile respective spouses. The two parties agreed to live together, to share equally in property acquired, and to marry when their divorces became final. The man worked as a salesman and used his savings to purchase properties. The woman kept house, cared for seven children, three from each former marriage and one from the nonmarital relationship, and helped construct improvements on the properties. When they separated, without marrying, the court awarded the woman one-half the value of the property. Rejecting the man's contention that the contract was illegal, the court stated that: "Nowhere is it expressly testified to by anyone that there was anything in the agreement for the pooling of assets and the sharing of accumulations that contemplated meretricious relations as any part of the consideration or as any object of the agreement." (125 Cal. App. 2d at p. 363, 270 P.2d at p. 71.)

Croslin v. Scott (1957) 154 Cal. App. 2d 767, 316 P.2d 755 reiterates the rule established in *Trutalli* and *Bridges*. In *Croslin* the parties separated following a three-year nonmarital relationship. The woman then phoned the man, asked him to return to her, and suggested that he build them a house on a lot she owned. She agreed in return to place the property in joint ownership. The man built the house, and the parties lived there for several more years. When they separated, he sued to establish his interest in the property. Reversing a nonsuit, the Court of Appeal stated that "The mere fact that parties agree to live together in meretricious relationship does not necessarily make an agreement for disposition of property between them invalid. It is only when the property agreement is made in connection with the other agreement, or the illicit relationship is made a consideration of the property agreement, that the latter becomes illegal." (154 Cal. App. 2d at p. 771, 316 P.2d at p. 758.)

Numerous other cases have upheld enforcement of agreements

between nonmarital partners in factual settings essentially indistinguishable from the present case. (*In re Marriage of Foster* (1974) 42 Cal. App. 3d 577, 117 Cal. Rptr. 49; *Weak v. Weak, supra,* 202 Cal. App. 2d 632, 639, 21 Cal. Rptr. 9; *Ferguson v. Schuenemann* (1959) 167 Cal. App. 2d 413, 334 P.2d 668; *Barlow v. Collins, supra,* 166 Cal. App. 2d 274, 277–278, 333 P.2d 64; *Ferraro v. Ferraro* (1956) 146 Cal. App. 2d 849, 304 P.2d 168; *Cline v. Festersen* (1954) 128 Cal. App. 2d 380, 275 P.2d 149; *Profit v. Profit* (1953) 117 Cal. App. 2d 126, 255 P.2d 25; *Garcia v. Venegas, supra,* 106 Cal. App. 2d 364, 235 P.2d 89; *Padilla v. Padilla* (1940) 38 Cal. App. 2d 319, 100 P.2d 1093; *Bacon v. Bacon* (1937) 21 Cal. App. 2d 540, 69 P.2d 884.)[5]

Although the past decisions hover over the issue in the somewhat wispy form of the figures of a Chagall painting, we can abstract from those decisions a clear and simple rule. The fact that a man and woman live together without marriage, and engage in a sexual relationship, does not in itself invalidate agreements between them relating to their earnings, property, or expenses. Neither is such an agreement invalid merely because the parties may have contemplated the creation or continuation of a nonmarital relationship when they entered into it. Agreements between nonmarital partners fail only to the extent that they rest upon a consideration of meretricious sexual services. Thus the rule asserted by defendant, that a contract fails if it is "involved in" or made "in contemplation" of a nonmarital relationship, cannot be reconciled with the decisions.

The three cases cited by defendant which have *declined* to

---

[5]Defendant urges that all of the cited cases, with the possible exception of *In re Marriage of Foster, supra,* 42 Cal. App. 3d 577, 177 Cal. Rptr. 49, and *Bridges v. Bridges, supra,* 125 Cal. App. 2d 359, 270 P.2d 69, can be distinguished on the ground that the partner seeking to enforce the contract contributed either property or services additional to ordinary homemaking services. No case, however, suggests that a pooling agreement in which one partner contributes only homemaking services is invalid, and dictum in *Hill v. Estate of Westbrook* (1950) 95 Cal. App. 2d 599, 603, 213 P.2d 727, states the opposite. A promise to perform homemaking services is, of course, a lawful and adequate consideration for a contract (see *Taylor v. Taylor* (1954) 66 Cal. App. 2d 390, 398, 152 P.2d 480)— otherwise those engaged in domestic employment could not sue for their wages—and defendant advances no reason why his proposed distinction would justify denial of enforcement to contracts supported by such consideration. (See *Tyranski v. Piggins* (1973) 44 Mich. App. 570, 205 N.W.2d 595, 597.)

APPENDIX B

enforce contracts between nonmarital partners involved consideration that *was* expressly founded upon an illicit sexual services. In *Hill v. Estate of Westbrook, supra,* 95 Cal. App. 2d 599, 213 P.2d 727, the woman promised to keep house for the man, to live with him as man and wife, and to bear his children; the man promised to provide for her in his will, but died without doing so. Reversing a judgment for the woman based on the reasonable value of her services, the Court of Appeal stated that "the action is predicated upon a claim which seeks, among other things, the reasonable value of living with decedent in meretricious relationship and bearing him two children. . . . The law does not award compensation for living with a man as a concubine and bearing him children. . . . As the judgment is, at least in part, for the value of the claimed services for which recovery cannot be had, it must be reversed." (95 Cal. App. 2d at p. 603, 213 P.2d at p. 730.) Upon retrial, the trial court found that it could not sever the contract and place an independent value upon the legitimate services performed by claimant. We therefore affirmed a judgment for the estate. (*Hill v. Estate of Westbrook* (1952) 39 Cal. 2d 458, 247 P.2d 19.)

In the only other cited decision refusing to enforce a contract, *Updeck v. Samuel* (1964), 123 Cal. App. 2d 264, 266 P.2d 822, the contract "was based on the consideration that the parties live together as husband and wife." (123 Cal. App. 2d at p. 267, 266 P.2d at p. 824.) Viewing the contract as calling for adultery, the court held it illegal.[6]

The decisions in the *Hill* and *Updeck* cases thus demonstrate

---

[6]Although not cited by defendant, the only California precedent which supports his position is *Heaps v. Toy* (1942) 54 Cal. App. 2d 178, 128 P.2d 813. In that case the woman promised to leave her job, to refrain from marriage, to be a companion to the man, and to make a permanent home for him; he agreed to support the woman and her child for life. The Court of Appeal held the agreement invalid as a contract in restraint of marriage (Civ. Code, § 1676) and, alternatively, as "contrary to good morals" (Civ. Code, § 1607). The opinion does not state that sexual relations formed any part of the consideration for the contract, nor explain how—unless the contract called for sexual relations—the woman's employment as a companion and housekeeper could be contrary to good morals.

The alternative holding in *Heaps v. Toy,* supra, finding the contract in that case contrary to good morals, is consistent with the numerous California decisions upholding contracts between nonmarital partners when such contracts are not founded upon an illicit consideration, and is therefore disapproved.

that a contract between nonmarital partners, even if expressly made in contemplation of a common living arrangement, is invalid only if sexual acts form an inseparable part of the consideration for the agreement. In sum, a court will not enforce a contract for the pooling of property and earnings if it is explicitly and inseparably based upon services as a paramour. The Court of Appeal opinion in *Hill*, however, indicates that even if sexual services are part of the contractual consideration, any *severable* portion of the contract supported by independent consideration will still be enforced.

The principle that a contract between nonmarital partners will be enforced unless expressly and inseparably based upon an illicit consideration of sexual services not only represents the distillation of the decisional law, but also offers a far more precise and workable standard than that advocated by defendant. Our recent decision in *In re Marriage of Dawley* (1976) 17 Cal. 3d 342, 551 P.2d 323, offers a close analogy. Rejecting the contention that an antenuptial agreement is invalid if the parties contemplated a marriage of short duration, we pointed out in *Dawley* that a standard based upon the subjective contemplation of the parties is uncertain and unworkable; such a test, we stated, "might invalidate virtually all antenuptial agreements on the ground that the parties contemplated dissolution . . . but it provides no principled basis for determining which antenuptial agreements offend public policy and which do not." (17 Cal. 3d 342, 352, 551 P.2d 323, 329.)

Similarly, in the present case a standard which inquires whether an agreement is "involved" in or "contemplates" a nonmarital relationship is vague and unworkable. Virtually all agreements between nonmarital partners can be said to be "involved" in some sense in the fact of their mutual sexual relationship, or to "contemplate" the existence of that relationship. Thus defendant's proposed standards, if taken literally, might invalidate all agreements between nonmarital partners, a result no one favors. Moreover, those standards offer no basis to distinguish between valid and invalid agreements. By looking not to such uncertain tests, but only to the consideration underlying the agreement, we provide the parties and the courts with a practical guide to determine when an agreement between nonmarital partners should be enforced.

APPENDIX B

Defendant secondly relies upon the ground suggested by the trial court: that the 1964 contract violated public policy because it impaired the community property rights of Betty Marvin, defendant's lawful wife. Defendant points out that his earnings while living apart from his wife before rendition of the interlocutory decree were community property under 1964 statutory law (former Civ. Code, §§ 169, 169.2)[7] and that defendant's agreement with plaintiff purported to transfer to her a half interest in that community property. But whether or not defendant's contract with plaintiff exceeded his authority as manager of the community property (see former Civ. Code, § 172), defendant's argument fails for the reason that an improper transfer of community property is not void *ad initio,* but merely voidable at the instance of the aggrieved spouse. (See *Ballinger v. Ballinger* (1937) 9 Cal. 2d 330, 334, 70 P.2d 629; *Trimble v. Trimble* (1933) 219 Cal. 340, 344, 26 P.2d 477.)

In the present case Betty Marvin, the aggrieved spouse, had the opportunity to assert her community property rights in the divorce action. (See *Babbitt v. Babbitt* (1955) 44 Cal. 2d 289, 293, 282 P.2d 1.) The interlocutory and final decrees in that action fix and limit her interest. Enforcement of the contract between plaintiff and defendant against property awarded to defendant by the divorce decree will not impair any right of Betty's, and thus is not on that account violative of public policy.[8]

Defendant's third contention is noteworthy for the lack of authority advanced in its support. He contends that enforcement of the oral agreement between plaintiff and himself is barred by

---

[7]Sections 169 and 169.2 were replaced in 1970 by Civil Code section 5118. In 1972 section 5118 was amended to provide that the earnings and accumulations of *both* spouses "while living separate and apart from the other spouse, are the separate property of the spouse."

[8]Defendant also contends that the contract is invalid as an agreement to promote or encourage divorce. (See 1 Witkin, Summary of Cal. Law (8th ed.) pp. 390–392 and cases there cited.) The contract between plaintiff and defendant did not, however, by its terms require defendant to divorce Betty, nor reward him for so doing. Moreover, the principle on which defendant relies does not apply when the marriage in question is beyond redemption (*Glickman v. Collins* (1975) 13 Cal. 3d 852, 858–859, 120 Cal. Rptr. 76, 533 P.2d 204); whether or not defendant's marriage to Betty was beyond redemption when defendant contracted with plaintiff is obviously a question of fact which cannot be resolved by judgment on the pleadings.

Civil Code section 5134, which provides that "All contracts for marriage settlements must be in writing. . . ." A marriage settlement, however, is an agreement in contemplation of marriage in which each party agrees to release or modify the property rights which would otherwise arise from the marriage. (See *Corker v. Corker* (1891) 87 Cal. 643, 648, 25 P. 922.) The contract at issue here does not conceivably fall within that definition, and thus is beyond the compass of section 5134.[9]

Defendant finally argues that enforcement of the contract is barred by Civil Code section 43.5, subdivision (d), which provides that "No cause of action arises for . . . [b]reach of a promise of marriage." This rather strained contention proceeds from the premise that a promise of marriage impliedly includes a promise to support and to pool property acquired after marriage (see *Boyd v. Boyd* (1964) 228 Cal. App. 2d 374, 39 Cal. Rptr. 400) to the conclusion that pooling and support agreements not part of or accompanied by promise of marriage are barred by the section. We conclude that section 43.5 is not reasonably susceptible to the interpretation advanced by defendant, a conclusion demonstrated by the fact that since section 43.5 was enacted in 1939, numerous cases have enforced pooling agreements between nonmarital partners, and in none did court or counsel refer to section 43.5.

In summary, we base our opinion on the principle that adults who voluntarily live together and engage in sexual relations are nonetheless as competent as any other persons to contract respecting their earnings and property rights. Of course, they cannot lawfully contract to pay for the performance of sexual services, for such a contract is, in essence, an agreement for prostitution and unlawful for that reason. But they may agree to pool their earnings and to hold all property acquired during the relationship in accord with the law governing community property; conversely they may agree that each partner's earnings and the property acquired from those earnings remains the separate property of

---

[9]Our review of the many cases enforcing agreements between nonmarital partners reveals that the majority of such agreements were oral. In two cases (*Ferguson v. Schuenemann, supra*, 167 Cal. App. 2d 413, 334 P.2d 668; *Cline v. Festersen, supra*, 128 Cal. App. 2d 380, 275 P.2d 149), the court expressly rejected defenses grounded upon the statute of frauds.

the earning partner.[10] So long as the agreement does not rest upon illicit meretricious consideration, the parties may order their economic affairs as they choose, and no policy precludes the courts from enforcing such agreements.

In the present instance, plaintiff alleges that the parties agreed to pool their earnings, that they contracted to share equally in all property acquired, and that defendant agreed to support plaintiff. The terms of the contract as alleged do not rest upon any unlawful consideration. We therefore conclude that the complaint furnishes a suitable basis upon which the trial court can render declaratory relief. (See 3 Witkin, Cal. Procedure (2d ed.) pp. 2335–2336.) The trial court consequently erred in granting defendant's motion for judgment on the pleadings.

3. *Plaintiff's complaint can be amended to state a cause of action founded upon theories of implied contract or equitable relief.*

As we have noted, both causes of action in plaintiff's complaint allege an express contract; neither assert any basis for relief independent from the contract. In *In re Marriage of Cary, supra,* 34 Cal. App. 3d 345, 109 Cal. Rptr. 862, however, the Court of Appeal held that, in view of the policy of the Family Law Act, property accumulated by nonmarital partners in an actual family relationship should be divided equally. Upon examining the *Cary* opinion, the parties to the present case realized that plaintiff's alleged relationship with defendant might arguably support a cause of action independent of any express contract between the parties. The parties have therefore briefed and discussed the issue of the property rights of a nonmarital partner in the absence of an express contract. Although our conclusion that plaintiff's complaint states a cause of action based on an express contract alone compels us to reverse the judgment for defendant, resolution of the *Cary* issue will serve both to guide the parties upon retrial

---

[10] A great variety of other arrangements are possible. The parties might keep their earnings and property separate, but agree to compensate one party for services which benefit the other. They may choose to pool only part of their earnings and property, to form a partnership or joint venture, or to hold property acquired as joint tenants or tenants in common, or agree to any other such arrangement. (See generally Weitzman, *Legal Regulation of Marriage: Tradition and Change* (1974) 62 Cal. L. Rev. 1169.)

and to resolve a conflict presently manifest in published Court of Appeal decisions.

Both plaintiff and defendant stand in broad agreement that the law should be fashioned to carry out the reasonable expectations of the parties. Plaintiff, however, presents the following contentions: that the decisions prior to *Cary* rest upon implicit and erroneous notions of punishing a party for his or her guilt in entering into a nonmarital relationship, that such decisions result in an inequitable distribution of property accumulated during the relationship, and that *Cary* correctly held that the enactment of the Family Law Act in 1970 overturned those prior decisions. Defendant in response maintains that the prior decisions merely applied common law principles of contract and property to persons who have deliberately elected to remain outside the bounds of the community property system.[11] *Cary*, defendant contends, erred in holding that the Family Law Act vitiated the force of the prior precedents.

As we shall see from examination of the pre-*Cary* decisions, the truth lies somewhere between the positions of plaintiff and defendant. The classic opinion on this subject is *Vallera v. Vallera, supra,* 21 Cal. 2d 681, 134 P.2d 761. Speaking for a four-member majority, Justice Traynor posed the question: "whether a woman living with a man as his wife but with no genuine belief that she is legally married to him acquires by reason of cohabitation alone the rights of a co-tenant in his earnings and accumulations during the period of their relationship." (21 Cal. 2d at p. 684, 134 P.2d

---

[11] We note that a deliberate decision to avoid the strictures of the community property system is not the only reason that couples live together without marriage. Some couples may wish to avoid the permanent commitment that marriage implies, yet be willing to share equally any property acquired during the relationship; others may fear the loss of pension, welfare, or tax benefits resulting from marriage (see *Beckman v. Mayhew, supra,* 49 Cal. App. 3d 529, 122 Cal. Rptr. 604). Others may engage in the relationship as a possible prelude to marriage. In lower socio-economic groups the difficulty and expense of dissolving a former marriage often leads couples to choose a nonmarital relationship; many unmarried couples may also incorrectly believe that the doctrine of common law marriage prevails in California, and thus that they are in fact married. Consequently we conclude that the mere fact that a couple have not participated in a valid marriage ceremony cannot serve as a basis for a court's inference that the couple intend to keep their earnings and property separate and independent; the parties' intention can only be ascertained by a more searching inquiry into the nature of their relationship.

APPENDIX B

at p. 762.) Citing *Flanagan v. Capital Nat. Bank* (1931) 213 Cal. 664, 3 P.2d 307, which held that a nonmarital "wife" could not claim that her husband's estate was community property, the majority answered that question "in the negative." (21 Cal. 2d pp. 684–685, 134 P.2d 761.) *Vallera* explains that "Equitable considerations arising from the reasonable expectation of the continuation of benefits attending the status of marriage entered into in good faith are not present in such a case." (21 Cal. 2d at p. 685, 134 P.2d p. 763.) In the absence of express contract, *Vallera* concluded, the woman is entitled to share in property jointly accumulated only "in the proportion that her funds contributed toward its acquisition." (21 Cal. 2d at p. 685, 134 P.2d p. 763.) Justice Curtis, dissenting, argued that the evidence showed an implied contract under which each party owned an equal interest in property acquired during the relationship.

The majority opinion in *Vallera* did not expressly bar recovery based upon an implied contract, nor preclude resort to equitable remedies. But Vallera's broad assertion that equitable considerations "are not present" in the case of a nonmarital relationship (21 Cal. 2d at p. 685, 134 P.2d 761) led the Courts of Appeal to interpret the language to preclude recovery based on such theories. (See *Lazzarevich v. Lazzarevich* (1948) 88 Cal. App. 2d 708, 719, 200 P.2d 49; *Oakley v. Oakley* (1947) 82 Cal. App. 2d 188, 191–192, 185 P.2d 848.)[12]

Consequently, when the issue of the rights of a nonmarital partner reached this court in *Keene v. Keene* (1962) 57 Cal. 2d 657, 21 Cal. Rptr. 593, 371 P.2d 329, the claimant forwent reliance upon theories of contract implied in law or fact. Asserting that she had worked on her partner's ranch and that her labor had enhanced its value, she confined her cause of action to the claim that the court should impress a resulting trust on the property derived from the sale of the ranch. The court limited its opinion

---

[12]The cases did not clearly determine whether a nonmarital partner could recover in quantum meruit for the reasonable value of services rendered. But when we affirmed a trial court ruling denying recovery in *Hill v. Estate of Westbrook, supra,* 39 Cal. 2d 458, 247 P.2d 19, we did so in part on the ground that whether the partner "rendered her services because of expectation of monetary reward" (p. 462, 247 P.2d p. 21) was a question of fact resolved against her by the trial court—thus implying that in a proper case the court would allow recovery based on quantum meruit.

accordingly, rejecting her argument on the ground that the rendition of services gives rise to a resulting trust only when the services aid in acquisition of the property, not in its subsequent improvement. (57 Cal. 2d at p. 668, 21 Cal. Rptr. 593, 371 P.2d 329.) Justice Peters, dissenting, attacked the majority's distinction between the rendition of services and the contribution of funds or property; he maintained that both property and services furnished valuable consideration, and potentially afforded the ground for a resulting trust.

This failure of the courts to recognize an action by a nonmarital partner based upon implied contract, or to grant an equitable remedy, contrasts with the judicial treatment of the putative spouse. Prior to the enactment of the Family Law Act, no statute granted rights to a putative spouse.[13] The courts accordingly fashioned a variety of remedies by judicial decision. Some cases permitted the putative spouse to recover half the property on a theory that the conduct of the parties implied an agreement of partnership or joint venture. (See *Estate of Vargas* (1974) 36 Cal. App. 3d 714, 717–718, 111 Cal. Rptr. 779; *Sousa v. Freitas* (1970) 10 Cal. App. 3d 660, 666, 89 Cal. Rptr. 485.) Others permitted the spouse to recover the reasonable value of rendered services, less the value of support received. (See *Sanguinetti v. Sanguinetti* (1937) 9 Cal. 2d 95, 100–102, 69 P.2d 845.)[14] Finally, decisions affirmed the power of a court to employ equitable principles to achieve a fair division of property acquired during putative marriage. (*Coats v. Coats* (1911) 160 Cal. 671, 677–678, 118 P. 441; *Caldwell v. Odisio* (1956) 142 Cal. App. 2d 732, 735, 299 P.2d 14.)[15]

Thus in summary, the cases prior to *Cary* exhibited a schizophrenic inconsistency. By enforcing an express contract between

---

[13]The Family Law Act, in Civil Code section 4452, classifies property acquired during a putative marriage as "quasi-marital property," and requires that such property be divided upon dissolution of the marriage in accord with Civil Code section 4800.

[14]The putative spouse need not prove that he rendered services in expectation of monetary reward in order to recover the reasonable value of those services. (*Sanguinetti v. Sanguinetti, supra,* 9 Cal. 3d 95, 100, 69 P.2d 845.)

[15]The contrast between principles governing nonmarital and putative relationships appears most strikingly in *Lazzarevich v. Lazzarevich, supra,* 88 Cal. App. 2d 708, 200 P.2d 49. When Mrs. Lazzarevich sued her husband for divorce in 1945,

APPENDIX B

nonmarital partners unless it rested upon an unlawful consideration, the courts applied a common law principle as to contracts. Yet the courts disregarded the common law principle that holds that implied contracts can arise from the conduct of the parties.[16] Refusing to enforce such contracts, the courts spoke of leaving the parties "in the position in which they had placed themselves" (*Oakley v. Oakley, supra,* 82 Cal. App. 2d 188, 192, 185 P.2d 848, 850), just as if they were guilty parties "in pari delicto."

Justice Curtis noted this inconsistency in his dissenting opinion in *Vallera,* pointing out that "if an express agreement will be enforced, there is no legal or just reason why an implied agreement to share the property cannot be enforced." (21 Cal. 2d 681, 686, 134 P.2d 761, 764; see Bruch, *Property Rights of De Facto Spouses Including Thoughts on the Value of Homemakers' Services* (1976) 10 Family L.Q. 101, 117–121.) And in *Keene v. Keene, supra,* 57 Cal. 2d 657, 21 Cal. Rptr. 593, 371 P.2d 329, Justice Peters observed that if the man and woman "were not illegally living together . . . it would be a plain business relationship and a contract would be implied." (Diss. opn. at p. 672, 21 Cal. Rptr. at p. 602, 371 P.2d at p. 338.)

Still another inconsistency in the prior cases arises from their treatment of property accumulated through joint effort. To the

---

she discovered to her surprise that she was not lawfully married to him. She nevertheless reconciled with him, and the Lazzareviches lived together for another year before they finally separated. The court awarded her recovery for the reasonable value of services rendered, less the value of support received, until she discovered the invalidity of the marriage, but denied recovery for the same services rendered after that date.

[16]"Contracts may be express or implied. These terms, however, do not denote different kinds of contracts, but have reference to the evidence by which the agreement between the parties is shown. If the agreement is shown by the direct words of the parties, spoken or written, the contract is said to be an express one. But if such agreement can only be shown by the acts and conduct of the parties, interpreted in the light of the subject matter and of the surrounding circumstances, then the contract is an implied one." (*Skelly v. Bristol Sav. Bank* (1893) 63 Conn. 83, 26 A. 474, 475, quoted in 1 Corbin, Contracts (1963) p. 41.) Thus, as Justice Schauer observed in *Desny v. Wilder* (1956) 46 Cal. 2d 715, 299 P.2d 257, in a sense all contracts made in fact, as distinguished from quasi-contractual obligations, are express contracts, differing only in the manner in which the assent of the parties is expressed and proved. (See 46 Cal. 2d at pp. 735–736, 299 P.2d 257.)

extent that a partner had contributed *funds* or *property*, the cases held that the partner obtains a proportionate share in the acquisition, despite the lack of legal standing of the relationship. (*Vallera v. Vallera, supra,* 21 Cal. 2d at p. 685, 134 P.2d at 761; see *Weak v. Weak, supra,* 202 Cal. App. 2d 632, 639, 21 Cal. Rptr. 9.) Yet courts have refused to recognize just such an interest based upon the contribution of *services*. As Justice Curtis points out "Unless it can be argued that a woman's services as cook, housekeeper, and homemaker are valueless, it would seem logical that if, when she contributes money to the purchase of property, her interest will be protected, then when she contributes her services in the home, her interest in property accumulated should be protected." (*Vallera v. Vallera, supra,* 21 Cal. 2d 681, 686–687, 134 P.2d 761, 764 (diss. opn.); see Bruch, op. cit. *supra,* 10 Family L.Q. 101, 110–114; Article, *Illicit Cohabitation: The Impact of the Vallera and Keene Cases on the Rights of the Meretricious Spouse* (1973) 6 U.C. Davis L. Rev. 354, 369–370; Comment (1972) 48 Wash. L. Rev. 635, 641.)

Thus as of 1973, the time of the filing of *In re Marriage of Cary, supra,* 34 Cal. App. 3d 345, 109 Cal. Rptr. 862, the cases apparently held that a nonmarital partner who rendered services in the absence of express contract could assert no right to property acquired during the relationship. The facts of *Cary* demonstrated the unfairness of that rule.

Janet and Paul Cary had lived together, unmarried, for more than eight years. They held themselves out to friends and family as husband and wife, reared four children, purchased a home and other property, obtained credit, filed joint income tax returns, and otherwise conducted themselves as though they were married. Paul worked outside the home, and Janet generally cared for the house and children.

In 1971 Paul petitioned for "nullity of the marriage."[17] Follow-

---

[17] The Court of Appeal opinion in *In re Marriage of Cary, supra,* does not explain why Paul Cary filed his action as a petition for nullity. Briefs filed with this court, however, suggest that Paul may have been seeking to assert rights as a putative spouse. In the present case, on the other hand, neither party claims the status of an actual or putative spouse. Under such circumstances an action to adjudge "the marriage" in the instant case a nullity would be pointless and could not serve as a device to adjudicate contract and property rights arising from the parties' nonmarital relationship. Accordingly, plaintiff here correctly chose to assert her rights by means of an ordinary civil action.

APPENDIX B

ing a hearing on that petition, the trial court awarded Janet half the property acquired during the relationship, although all such property was traceable to Paul's earnings. The Court of Appeal affirmed the award.

Reviewing the prior decisions which had denied relief to the homemaking partner, the Court of Appeal reasoned that those decisions rested upon a policy of punishing persons guilty of cohabitation without marriage. The Family Law Act, the court observed, aimed to eliminate fault or guilt as a basis for dividing marital property. But once fault or guilt is excluded, the court reasoned, nothing distinguishes the property rights of a nonmarital "spouse" from those of a putative spouse. Since the latter is entitled to half the "quasi marital property" (Civ. Code, § 4452), the Court of Appeal concluded that, giving effect to the policy of the Family Law Act, a nonmarital cohabitor should also be entitled to half the property accumulated during an "actual family relationship." (34 Cal. App. 3d at p. 353, 109 Cal. Rptr. 862.)[18]

Cary met with a mixed reception in other appellate districts. In *Estate of Atherley, supra,* 44 Cal. App. 3d 758, 119 Cal. Rptr. 41, the Fourth District agreed with *Cary* that under the Family Law Act a nonmarital partner in an actual family relationship enjoys the same right to an equal division of property as a putative spouse. In *Beckman v. Mayhew, supra,* 49 Cal. App. 3d 529, 122 Cal. Rptr. 604, however, the Third District rejected *Cary* on the ground that the Family Law Act was not intended to change California law dealing with nonmarital relationships.

---

[18]The court in *Cary* also based its decision upon an analysis of Civil Code section 4452, which specifies the property rights of a putative spouse. Section 4452 states that if the "court finds that either party or both parties believed in good faith that the marriage was valid, the court should declare such party or parties to have the status of a putative spouse, and shall divide, in accordance with Section 4800, that property acquired during the union. . . ." Since section 4800 requires an equal division of community property, *Cary* interpreted section 4452 to require an equal division of the property of a putative marriage, so long as one spouse believed in good faith that the marriage was valid. Thus under section 4452, *Cary* concluded, the "guilty spouse" (the spouse who knows the marriage is invalid) has the same right to half the property as does the "innocent" spouse.

Cary then reasoned that if the "guilty" spouse to a putative marriage is entitled to one-half the marital property, the "guilty" partner in a nonmarital relationship should also receive one-half of the property. Otherwise, the court stated, "We should be obliged to presume a legislative intent that a person, who by deceit leads another to believe a valid marriage exists between them, shall be legally guaran-

634

If *Cary* is interpreted as holding that the Family Law Act requires an equal division of property accumulated in nonmarital "actual family relationships," then we agree with *Beckman v. Mayhew* that *Cary* distends the act. No language in the Family Law Act addresses the property rights of nonmarital partners, and nothing in the legislative history of the act suggests that the Legislature considered that subject.[19] The delineation of the rights of nonmarital partners before 1970 had been fixed entirely by judicial decision; we see no reason to believe that the Legislature, by enacting the Family Law Act, intended to change that state of affairs.

But although we reject the reasoning of *Cary* and *Atherley*, we share the perception of the *Cary* and *Atherley* courts that the application of former precedent in the factual setting of those cases would work an unfair distribution of the property accumulated by the couple. Justice Freidman in *Beckman v. Mayhew*,

---

teed half of the property they acquire even though most, or all, may have resulted from the earnings of the blameless partner. At the same time we must infer an inconsistent legislative intent that two persons who, candidly with each other, enter upon an unmarried family relationship, shall be denied any judicial aid whatever in the assertion of otherwise valid property rights." (34 Cal. App. 3d at p. 352, 109 Cal. Rptr. at p. 866.)

This reasoning in *Cary* has been criticized by commentators. (See Note, op. cit., supra, 25 Hastings L.J. 1226, 1234–1235; Comment, *In re Marriage of Carey* [sic]: *The End of the Putative-Meretricious Spouse Distinction in California* (1975) 12 San Diego L. Rev. 436, 444–446.) The Commentators note that Civil Code section 4455 provides that an "innocent" party to a putative marriage can recover spousal support, from which they infer that the Legislature intended to give only the "innocent" spouse a right to one-half of the quasi-marital property under section 4452.

We need not now resolve this dispute concerning the interpretation of section 4452. Even if *Cary* is correct in holding that a "guilty" putative spouse has a right to one-half of the marital property, it does not necessarily follow that a nonmarital partner has an identical right. In a putative marriage the parties will arrange their economic affairs with the expectation that upon dissolution the property will be divided equally. If a "guilty" putative spouse receives one-half of the property under section 4452, no expectation of the "innocent" spouse has been frustrated. In a nonmarital relationship, on the other hand, the parties may expressly or tacitly determine to order their economic relationship in some other manner, and to impose community property principles regardless of such understanding may frustrate the parties' expectations.

[19]Despite the extensive material available on the legislative history of the Family Law Act neither *Cary* nor plaintiff cites any reference which suggests that the Legislature ever considered the issue of the property rights of nonmarital partners, and our independent examination has uncovered no such reference.

APPENDIX B

supra, 49 Cal. App. 3d 529, 535, 122 Cal. Rptr. 604, also questioned the continued viability of our decisions in *Vallera* and *Keene;* commentators have argued the need to reconsider those precedents.[20] We should not, therefore, reject the authority of *Cary* and *Atherley* without also examining the deficiencies in the former law which led to those decisions.

The principal reason why the pre-*Cary* decisions result in an unfair distribution of property inheres in the court's refusal to permit a nonmarital partner to assert rights based upon accepted principles of implied contract or equity. We have examined the reasons advanced to justify this denial of relief, and find that none have merit.

First, we note that the cases denying relief do not rest their refusal upon any theory of "punishing" a "guilty" partner. Indeed, to the extent that denial of relief "punishes" one partner, it necessarily rewards the other by permitting him to retain a disproportionate amount of the property. Concepts of "guilt" thus cannot justify an unequal division of property between two equally "guilty" persons.[21]

Other reasons advanced in the decisions fare no better. The principal argument seems to be that "[e]quitable considerations

---

[20]See *Bruch,* op. cit., *supra,* 10 Family L.Q. 101, 113; Article, op. cit., *supra,* 6 U.C. Davis L. Rev. 354; Comment (1975) 6 Golden Gate L. Rev. 179, 197–201; Comment, op. cit., *supra,* 12 San Diego L. Rev. 4356; Note, op. cit., *supra,* 25 Hastings L.J. 1226, 1246.

[21]Justice Finley of the Washington Supreme Court explains: "Under such circumstances [the dissolution of a nonmarital relationship], this court and the courts of other jurisdictions have, in effect, sometimes said, 'We will wash our hands of such disputes. The parties should and must be left to their own devices, just where they find themselves.' To me, such pronouncements seem overly fastidious and a bit fatuous. They are unrealistic and, among other things, ignore the fact that an unannounced (but nevertheless effective and binding) rule of law is inherent in any such terminal statements by a court of law. The unannounced but inherent rule is simply that the party who has title, or in some instances who is in possession, will enjoy the rights of ownership of the property concerned. The rule often operates to the great advantage of the cunning and the shrewd, who wind up with possession of the property, or title to it in their names, at the end of a so-called meretricious relationship. So, although the courts proclaim that they will have nothing to do with such matters, the proclamation in itself establishes, as to the parties involved, an effective and binding rule of law which tends to operate purely by accident or perhaps by reason of the cunning, anticipatory designs of just one of the parties." (*West v. Knowles* (1957) 50 Wash. 2d 311, 311 P.2d 689, 692 (conc. opn.).)

arising from the reasonable expectation of . . . benefits attending the status of marriage . . . are not present [in a nonmarital relationship]." (*Vallera v. Vallera, supra,* 21 Cal. 2d at p. 685, 134 P.2d 761, 763.) But, although parties to a nonmarital relationship obviously cannot have based any expectations upon the belief that they were married, other expectations and equitable considerations remain. The parties may well expect that the property will be divided in accord with the parties' own tacit understanding and that in the absence of such understanding the courts will fairly apportion property accumulated through mutual effort. We need not treat nonmarital partners as putatively married persons in order to apply principles of implied contract, or extend equitable remedies; we need to treat them only as we do any other unmarried persons.[22]

The remaining arguments advanced from time to time to deny remedies to the nonmarital partners are of less moment. There is no more reason to presume that services are contributed as a gift than to presume that funds are contributed as a gift; in any event the better approach is to presume, as Justice Peters suggested, "that the parties intend to deal fairly with each other." (*Keene v. Keene, supra,* 57 Cal. 2d 657, 674, 21 Cal. Rptr. 593, 603, 371 P.2d 329, 339 (dissenting opn.); see *Bruch,* op. cit., *supra,* 10 Family L.Q. 101, 113.)

The argument that granting remedies to the nonmarital partners would discourage marriage must fail; as *Cary* pointed out, "with equal or greater force the point might be made that the pre-1970 rule was calculated to cause the income producing partner to avoid marriage and thus retain the benefit of all of his or her accumulated earnings." (34 Cal. App. 3d at p. 353, 109 Cal. Rptr. at p. 866.) Although we recognize the well-established public policy to foster and promote the institution of marriage (see *Deyoe v. Superior Court* (1903) 140 Cal. 476, 482, 74 P. 28), perpetuation of judicial rules which result in an inequitable distribution of property accumulated during a nonmarital relationship is neither a just nor an effective way of carrying out that policy.

In summary, we believe that the prevalence of nonmarital re-

---

[22] In some instances a confidential relationship may arise between nonmarital partners, and economic transactions between them should be governed by the principles applicable to such relationships.

APPENDIX B

lationships in modern society and the social acceptance of them, marks this as a time when our courts should by no means apply the doctrine of the unlawfulness of the so-called meretricious relationship to the instant case. As we have explained, the nonenforceability of agreements expressly providing for meretricious conduct rested upon the fact that such conduct, as the word suggests, pertained to and encompassed prostitution. To equate the nonmarital relationship of today to such a subject matter is to do violence to an accepted and wholly different practice.

We are aware that many young couples live together without the solemnization of marriage, in order to make sure that they can successfully later undertake marriage. This trial period,[23] preliminary to marriage, serves as some assurance that the marriage will not subsequently end in dissolution to the harm of both parties. We are aware, as we have stated, of the pervasiveness of nonmarital relationships in other situations.

The mores of the society have indeed changed so radically in regard to cohabitation that we cannot impose a standard based on alleged moral considerations that have apparently been so widely abandoned by so many. Lest we be misunderstood, however, we take this occasion to point out that the structure of society itself largely depends upon the institution of marriage, and nothing we have said in this opinion should be taken to derogate from that institution. The joining of the man and woman in marriage is at once the most socially productive and individually fulfilling relationship that one can enjoy in the course of a lifetime.

We conclude that the judicial barriers that may stand in the way of a policy based upon the fulfillment of the reasonable expectations of the parties to a nonmarital relationship should be removed. As we have explained, the courts now hold that express agreements will be enforced unless they rest on an unlawful meretricious consideration. We add that in the absence of an express agreement, the courts may look to a variety of other remedies in order to protect the parties' lawful expectations.[24]

---

[23]Toffler, Future Shock (Bantam Books, 1971) page 253.

[24]We do not seek to resurrect the doctrine of common law marriage, which was abolished in California by statute in 1895. (See *Norman v. Thomson* (1898) 121 Cal. 620, 628, 54 P. 143; *Estate of Abate* (1958) 166 Cal. App. 2d 282, 292, 333 P.2d 200.) Thus we do not hold that plaintiff and defendant were "married," nor do we

The courts may inquire into the conduct of the parties to determine whether that conduct demonstrates an implied contract or implied agreement of partnership or joint venture (see *Estate of Thornton* (1972) 81 Wash. 2d 72, 499 P.2d 864), or some other tacit understanding between the parties. The courts may, when appropriate, employ principles of constructive trust (see *Omer v. Omer* (1974) 11 Wash. App. 386, 523 P.2d 957) or resulting trust (see *Hyman v. Hyman* (Tex. Civ. App. 1954) 275 S.W.2d 149). Finally, a nonmarital partner may recover in quantum meruit for the reasonable value of household services rendered less the reasonable value of support received if he can show that he rendered services with the expectation of monetary reward. (See *Hill v. Estate of Westbrook, supra,* 39 Cal. 2d 458, 462, 247 P.2d 19.)[25]

Since we have determined that plaintiff's complaint states a cause of action for breach of an express contract, and, as we have explained, can be amended to state a cause of action independent of allegations of express contract,[26] we must conclude that the trial court erred in granting defendant a judgment on the pleadings.

The judgment is reversed and the cause remanded for further proceedings consistent with the views expressed herein.[27]

WRIGHT, C. J., and McCOMB, MOSK, SULLIVAN and RICHARDSON, JJ., concur.

CLARK, Justice (concurring and dissenting).

The majority opinion properly permits recovery on the basis of either express or implied in fact agreement between the parties. These being the issues presented, their resolution requires reversal of the judgment. Here, the opinion should stop.

---

extend to plaintiff the rights which the Family Law Act grants valid or putative spouses; we hold only that she has the same rights to enforce contracts and to assert her equitable interest in property acquired through her effort as does any other unmarried person.

[25] Our opinion does not preclude the evolution of additional equitable remedies to protect the expectations of the parties to a nonmarital relationship in cases in which existing remedies prove inadequate; the suitability of such remedies may be determined in later cases in light of the factual setting in which they arise.

[26] We do not pass upon the question whether, in the absence of an express or implied contractual obligation, a party to a nonmarital relationship is entitled to support payments from the other party after the relationship terminates.

[27] We wish to commend the parties and amici for the exceptional quality of the briefs and argument in this case.

APPENDIX B

This court should not attempt to determine all anticipated rights, duties and remedies within every meretricious relationship—particularly in vague terms. Rather, these complex issues should be determined as each arises in a concrete case.

The majority broadly indicates that a party to a meretricious relationship may recover on the basis of equitable principles and in quantum meruit. However, the majority fails to advise us of the circumstances permitting recovery, limitations on recovery, or whether their numerous remedies are cumulative or exclusive. Conceivably, under the majority opinion a party may recover half of the property acquired during the relationship on the basis of general equitable principles, recover a bonus based on specific equitable considerations, and recover a second bonus in quantum meruit.

The general sweep of the majority opinion raises but fails to answer several questions. First, because the Legislature specifically excluded some parties to a meretricious relationship from the equal division rule of Civil Code section 4452, is this court now free to create an equal division rule? Second, upon termination of the relationship, is it equitable to impose the economic obligations of lawful spouses on meretricious parties when the latter may have rejected matrimony to avoid such obligations? Third, does not application of equitable principles—necessitating examination of the conduct of the parties—violate the spirit of the Family Law Act of 1969, designed to eliminate the bitterness and acrimony resulting from the former fault system in divorce? Fourth, will not application of equitable principles reimpose upon trial courts the unmanageable burden of arbitrating domestic disputes? Fifth, will not a quantum meruit system of compensation for services—discounted by benefits received—place meretricious spouses in a better position than lawful spouses? Sixth, if a quantum meruit system is to be allowed, does fairness not require inclusion of all services and all benefits regardless of how difficult the evaluation?

When the parties to a meretricious relationship show by express or implied in fact agreement they intend to create mutual obligations, the courts should enforce the agreement. However, in the absence of agreement, we should stop and consider the ramifications before creating economic obligations which may violate legislative intent, contravene the intention of the parties, and surely generate undue burdens on our trial courts.

By judicial overreach, the majority perform a nunc pro tunc marriage, dissolve it, and distribute its property on terms never contemplated by the parties, case law or the Legislature.

APPENDIX C

Memorandum Opinion of
Judge Arthur K. Marshall, Superior Court of the State of California for the County of Los Angeles*

MICHELLE MARVIN, aka
MICHELLE TRIOLA,
  Plaintiff,

vs.

LEE MARVIN,
  Defendant.

LEE MARVIN,
  Cross-Complainant,

vs.

MICHELLE MARVIN, aka
MICHELLE TRIOLA,
  Cross-Defendant.

CASE NO. C 23303

April 18, 1979

The Supreme Court in *Marvin v. Marvin* (1976) 18 C.3d 660, 665, 134 Cal. Rptr. 815, 557 P.2d 106, decided that an unmarried person may recover from a person, with whom the former had lived, in accordance with any written contract between them unless the agreement "rest(s) on an unlawful meretricious consideration." That court also determined that a nonmarital partner may recover if the conduct of the couple was such that a trial court could imply therefrom either "an implied contract, agreement of partnership or joint venture, or some other tacit understanding between the parties." Lacking evidence which would support any such finding, "(T)he courts may also employ the doctrine of quantum meruit, or equitable remedies such as constructive or resulting trusts, when warranted by the facts of the case."

---

*Reprinted by permission of The Bureau of National Affairs, Inc., from **Family Law Reporter, Vol. 5, No. 24, April 24, 1979.** Footnote references to pages of the transcript are omitted.

APPENDIX C

Finally, the Supreme Court declared that a nonmarital partner may recover in quantum meruit for the reasonable value of household services less the reasonable value of support received. The action was remanded to the Superior Court where evidence has been taken in implementation of the above described decision. The last mentioned remedy, quantum meruit, need not be considered here inasmuch as the plaintiff has dismissed her fourth and fifth causes of action based on such ground.

The first three causes of action, amended to reflect the remedies described by the Supreme Court, allege contractual, express and implied and equitable bases for judgment in favor of plaintiff.

In order to comply with the Supreme Court mandate, the trial court collected all available evidence which might bear on the relationship established after defendant allegedly promised plaintiff half of his property or which might serve as a basis for a tacit agreement or for equitable relief.

FACTS

In June, 1964, the parties met while they both were working on a picture called "Ship of Fools," he as a star and she as a stand-in. (She also was employed as a singer at the "Little Club" in Los Angeles.) A few days after their first meeting, they lunched together, then dined together. In a short time they saw each other on a daily basis after work. Sexual intimacy commenced about two weeks after their first date. During these early meetings, there was much conversation about their respective marital problems. The defendant said that, although he loved his wife and children, communication between him and his spouse had failed and he was unhappy. Plaintiff said that her marriage had been dissolved but her husband sought reconciliation.

Plaintiff testified that defendant told her that as soon as two people sign "a piece of paper," (meaning a marriage certificate) they waved that paper at each other whenever any problem arose instead of attempting to settle the problem. Defendant allegedly said that a license is a woman's insurance policy and he did not like that. Defendant further stated to plaintiff that when two people loved each other, there is no need for a license. Plaintiff declared that she told him that she did not necessarily agree with him.

Plaintiff testified that she hoped to secure a part in "Flower Drum Song" and was to journey to New York City for that purpose, but defendant did not want her to go as, he said, it was hard to conduct a romance at long distance. She did not go to New York. She rented an apartment for approximately one month. Defendant stayed with her from time to time.

In October, 1964, the plaintiff rented and moved into a house. The defendant moved in with her although he also maintained a room at a nearby hotel and occasionally stayed at the home where he had lived with his wife and children. Plaintiff told defendant that they were not "living together." His response was, "What does it mean when your blouse and my suit come back (from) to the cleaners together?" He inquired, "Does it mean that I live here?" She testified that she replied, "Well, I guess it does."

Defendant allegedly repeated again and again, his opinion that a piece of paper, a marriage certificate, is not needed by people in love. Plaintiff testified that at first she thought he was crazy and asked him to explain. She did not think it would work without the "paper." Defendant responded that marriage was lacking in communication and that he was unhappy about it.

The defendant went to San Blas, Mexico in November or December of 1964 for sport fishing. He later invited plaintiff to join him, which she did. There, the defendant allegedly told her that he was unhappily married, that he might be terminating his marriage, and that he and plaintiff could be together. She testified that she doubted his words. He declared again that a woman does not need a piece of paper, a marriage certificate, for security. He repeated his belief that whenever there was a misunderstanding, each waved the paper at each other instead of working hard at clearing up the misunderstanding. He allegedly said that he would never marry again because he did not like that kind of arrangement. He declared that he was almost positive that his marriage was not going to mend and asked whether plaintiff and defendant could share their lives. She inquired as to his meaning. He replied that after the divorce he would be left with only "the shirt on his back (and alimony)" but would she like to live on the beach. She initially responded she was going to New York. Two days later she asked defendant if he really thought living together without marriage would work out. He said that it would and she agreed to live with him.

APPENDIX C

Then defendant allegedly uttered the words which plaintiff contends constitute a contractual offer. He said, "what I have is yours and what you have is mine." She then accepted the alleged offer but declared that she had her own career and she did not want to depend on anyone. Defendant said that he had no objection to her career, but they still could share and build their lives. She told him that she loved him, that she would care for him and their home, and that she would cook and be his companion. She offered to learn how to fish, a sport of which he was quite fond, although she got seasick. He said that she would get over her seasickness.

The defendant was intoxicated in San Blas a "few times" to the point of losing control. She said that in subsequent years, 1965 and 1966, he lost control whenever he drank. She testified that she asked him to stop drinking and that he did not do so.

Defendant vigorously denies telling plaintiff, "what I have is yours and what you have is mine;" he declared that he never said he would support her for life and that he never stated "I'll take care of you always." He further denies saying that a marriage license is a piece of paper which stood in the way of working out problems. He testified that he decided to get a divorce from his wife after he arrived at his beach house, many months after his return from San Blas. During the examination of defendant under Evidence Code, Section 776, counsel for plaintiff read from defendant's deposition wherein defendant declared that he wanted a relationship of no responsibility and that the plaintiff agreed thereto.

The defendant rented and later purchased a house on the Malibu beach. Plaintiff moved in, bringing a bed, stereo equipment and kitchen utensils. A refrigerator and washing machine were purchased. She bought food, cooked meals for defendant, cleaned house (after the first year, she had the periodic help of a cleaning woman). On occasion, the couple had visitors and they in turn went together to the homes of friends. In the circle of their friends and their acquaintances in the theatrical world, the plaintiff was reputed not to be defendant's wife.

In the six years of their relationship, they did considerable traveling, over 30 months away from the beach house, for the most part on various film locations. Plaintiff usually accompanied the defendant except for the seven months devoted to the filming of "Dirty Dozen" in England (she visited him for about a month) and an exploratory trip to Micronesia preliminary to filming "Hell in the Pacific."

Plaintiff testified that her acquaintance with the theatre began in 1957 as a dancer. She danced with several troupes. She states that she was a featured dancer in a group organized by Barry Ashton, who produced shows in Las Vegas. She further alleges that she was also a singer from about 1957 and appeared in nightclubs in several states and abroad. Her compensation was usually "scale," ranging from $285 to $400 a week. As to motion pictures, she served as a "stand-in" or in background groupings until her appearance in "Synanon" (shortly after working in "Ship of Fools" where she met defendant) in which she spoke some lines but was not a featured performer.

After the parties moved into the beach house, plaintiff continued to have singing engagements, encouraged by the defendant who would frequently attend, bringing friends and buying drinks for them to lengthen their stay and thereby increase plaintiff's audience.

A decorator was hired to work on the beach house and, after some structural changes, a substantial amount of furniture was purchased. Plaintiff worked with the decorator; both consulted defendant on occasion as to the purchases and alterations.

In 1966, defendant contacted a friend in Hawaii and secured a singing engagement for plaintiff. Before she left for Hawaii Santana Records, Inc., was organized by defendant and defendant paid for the recordation of four songs by plaintiff under the Santana label. With the assistance of her manager, Mimi Marleaux, plaintiff visited disc jockeys in Hawaii and promoted the record.

In that same year, 1966, defendant went to London to make a picture entitled, "Dirty Dozen." During his stay in England he wrote eight letters to plaintiff wherein he expressed affection for the plaintiff and looked forward to her coming to London. In one letter, Exhibit 13, he portrays an imaginary scene wherein he was "found guilty of robbing a 33-year-old cradle" and he answers the judge, "absolutely guilty, your honor. . . . Yes sir, I accept life with her, thank you your honor and the court. Will the jury please get out of that cradle!"

After the filming of "Dirty Dozen" and the parties' return to Malibu, Miss Marleaux allegedly was present in the Malibu house when defendant said, after plaintiff told Marleaux she was sorry she let her (Marleaux) down (by the slump in her career), "I don't know what you're worrying about. I'll always take care of you. . . ."

While in Hawaii, plaintiff alleges that there was a ninth letter wherein defendant demanded that she give up her career, cut short her promotion of her record in Hawaii and come to London and if she did not, the relationship would be ended. At one point in the suit, plaintiff declared that she could not locate the letter. She now contends that it was destroyed by defendant. Miss Marleaux recollects a telephone call by defendant to the same effect but defendant introduced bills which indicate he made no such call.

In March of 1967, defendant testified that he told plaintiff that she would have to prepare for separation and that she should learn a trade. The plaintiff responded that if he left her, she would reveal his fears, his worries to the public and his career would be destroyed. She also threatened suicide.

In 1967, the plaintiff accompanied defendant to Baker, Oregon, where the latter made a film called "Paint Your Wagon." The parties rented a house in Baker and established a joint bank account. Plaintiff signed most of the checks drawn on that account.

The plaintiff returned to Los Angeles while "Paint Your Wagon" was still being filmed in Oregon in order to confer with one of the defendant's attorneys, Louis L. Goldman. She asked him whether it would be any trouble to change her name to "Marvin" as their different names were embarrassing to her as well as defendant in a place like Baker. Goldman said if the change was approved by defendant, it was agreeable with him. She then requested him to arrange with defendant for the placement of some property or a lump sum in her name. She declared to him that she did not know whether the relationship would last forever, that she had talked to defendant about conveying the house to her but that he had [said] absolutely no. She requested Goldman to persuade defendant to do something for her. Goldman later telephoned plaintiff to inform her that defendant had refused to agree to any of her requests.

Goldman testified that plaintiff told him that neither she nor defendant wanted to get married, that each wanted to be free to come and go as they please and to terminate the relationship if they wished. The subject of defendant's frequent intoxication was discussed.

On cross-examination, plaintiff testified that they were "always very proud of the fact that nothing held us. We weren't—we weren't legally married." After the breakup she declared to an interviewer: "We used to laugh and feel a great warmth about the fact that either of us could walk out at anytime."

Following the completion of "Paint Your Wagon" (after additional work in Los Angeles), defendant made a picture entitled, "Hell in the Pacific" on the island of Palau in Micronesia. The parties again opened a joint account on location and drew funds therefrom for payment of food, clothing, etc. The plaintiff issued the greater number of checks.

She alleges that defendant introduced her as "Mrs. Marvin" although most of the American community on the island knew that they were not married, including the crew filming the picture and the cast. The defendant denies that he so introduced her.

The parties returned to Palau for a second sojourn. The parties enjoyed the fishing and the defendant supervised and assisted in the completion of a fishing boat which he hoped would vitalize the Palauan fishing industry. The parties talked to an architect about building a house, part of which they could occupy and part of which could be rented to visitors of Palau for the fishing.

Marriage was far from the thoughts of the parties. On the second visit to Palau plaintiff testified that defendant asked her to marry him but she thought he was joking and laughed. A few weeks later plaintiff allegedly asked defendant to marry her and *he* laughed.

On Palau, the parties met Richard Doughty, a member of the Peace Corps fishery department. Doughty testified that he had sexual relations with plaintiff approximately twenty times, on the island, and additional times later in Los Angeles and Tucson. Plaintiff vigorously denied this and claimed that Doughty was a homosexual, offering supporting witnesses. This in turn was vigorously denied by Doughty who also offered witnesses who would rebut such a charge. Doughty's testimony was corroborated by Carol Clark who testified that plaintiff admitted to her that she (plaintiff) had "an affair" with him.

Doughty's testimony is weakened by his denial of such relationship when defendant's counsel, A. David Kagon, first questioned him prior to the trial. He explained that he decided to tell the truth at the trial because he did not wish defendant to be railroaded and because he now was more willing to accept responsibility after he had recovered from a serious illness.

La Verna Hogan, wife of the production manager of "Hell in the Pacific," accompanied plaintiff on a trip from Palau to Hawaii. They stayed overnight in Guam where plaintiff told Mrs. Hogan that she was to meet two men in Hawaii. Mrs. Hogan asked plaintiff why she was going to meet them in view of her relationship with defendant and plaintiff responded, "We (plaintiff and defendant) have an understanding. He does his thing and I do mine." Plaintiff denies any such Hawaiian meeting.

In 1969, defendant filmed "Monte Walsh" on locations approximately two hours from Tucson. He rented a house in Tucson for the ten to twelve weeks of shooting. Doughty secured employment in "Monte Walsh" as a dialogue coach and lived with the parties. A joint bank account was again opened and funded by Edward Silver, defendant's business manager. Plaintiff signed most of the checks.

At the end of the shooting of the pictures, "Hell in the Pacific," "Paint Your Wagon" and "Monte Walsh," the Palau, Baker and Tucson joint bank accounts were closed and the balances transferred to defendant's account.

Plaintiff had a separate account in Malibu in which defendant's business manager deposited $400 per month for her personal use.

The plaintiff testified that in May, 1970, defendant left the Malibu beach house upon her request. Later, she was told by defendant's agent, Mishkin, that defendant wished that they separate (Mishkin had referred to a "divorce" but testified that he was mistaken in his use of the term). The plaintiff later sought and found defendant in La Jolla. There he told her, plaintiff alleges, that he would not give up drinking, that it was part of his life and that his relationship with plaintiff was no longer enjoyable because of her frequent admonitions as to his drinking.

In May, 1970, plaintiff went to the office of defendant's attorney, Goldman. He informed her that defendant wanted her out of the house and out of his life and that defendant would pay her $833 per month (net after deduction of taxes from a gross of $1050) for five years. Plaintiff testified that she told Goldman she could not exist on such a stipend. Goldman responded that defendant could not afford to pay more because of the alimony which he paid to his former wife. Plaintiff testified that she replied that defendant had promised to take care of her for life. Goldman, however, testified that she had simply thanked him for the arrangement and said that $833 would be enough for her needs.

She returned to the beach house but finally departed after an emotional confrontation with defendant and his attorneys, Goldman and Kagon. Checks for $833 each began to arrive. According to defendant, the payments were made on condition that she removed herself from his life and not discuss with anyone anything she learned about defendant during their relationship. Defendant said that plaintiff thought this was fair. According to the plaintiff, the checks were stopped when defendant saw an item about him in one of the Hollywood columns. Defendant did send one more check but again stopped payment because, plaintiff declares, defendant was angered by her suit against Roberts. She told her attorney (then Howard I. Rosoff) to dismiss the action but, when no more checks came, she reversed her instructions. According to Goldman, plaintiff said she had nothing to do with the item in the column (re defendant's marriage to Pamela breaking up). He testified that she also said that she would not do it again and to give her another chance. Goldman replied that defendant "was at the end of the road."

The plaintiff filed an application dated March 26, 1970 to change her name to Michelle Triola Marvin. The verified application declared that she had been known professionally as "Marvin" and that she used the name in her acting and singing career.

Plaintiff stated in her deposition that she never used the name "Marvin" professionally. She now declares that she meant (in her application) that she used "Marvin" *during* her career but only socially.

The plaintiff also declared in her deposition that she had asked for a written agreement as to property shortly after moving into the beach house. Defendant allegedly said an agreement was being prepared but they did not need any papers. The plaintiff said they did. Plaintiff said nothing further about the nonappearance of an agreement during 1968, 1969 and 1970.

The defendant stated in his deposition that he wanted a relationship of no responsibility and that the plaintiff agreed with him.

On trips out of town, plaintiff was introduced on occasion as Michelle Marvin to avoid embarrassment in hotels, but defendant contends he never introduced her as *Mrs*. Marvin. Bills were rarely addressed to Mrs. Lee Marvin, but rather to Michelle Marvin. In the Malibu community and the actor-producer circles in which they moved, the couple's relationship was known not to be that of husband and wife.

The plaintiff testified that she never told the defendant that she would hold herself out as his wife, that the parties never used the terms "husband and wife," those words were not in their vocabulary and that they never used the word "homemaker."

Defendant testified that in the winter of 1969 plaintiff wanted him to finance a European trip at $10,000–$15,000 per month as the price for separation. Later, she offered to "get out of your (his) life for $50,000" and he would never hear from her again. Still later, she requested $100,000. Plaintiff denies that she made any such offer.

Rather than review the great number of allegations by plaintiff as to defendant's drinking to excess, it is enough to observe that defendant admits that he was frequently intoxicated. It is a reasonable inference therefrom that in such condition he needed care and that plaintiff provided it.

TESTIMONIAL INCONSISTENCIES

The weight of the testimony of the plaintiff is lessened by several inconsistencies.

Plaintiff claims to have had considerable help from Gene Kelly in the procurement of employment in "Flower Drum Song" in New York City. He however, denied that he hired plaintiff. He further testified that he never talked to plaintiff about "Flower Drum Song" in 1963 or 1964 and that at that time the play was not being performed in New York City. In later testimony plaintiff altered her allegation of employment by Kelly to an offer of letters of introduction by him. She also modified her declaration that she was going to New York City to appear in "Flower Drum Song" to say that she did not know whether it was then being performed on Broadway.

Plaintiff's contention of many weeks of employment of Playboy clubs in Chicago, Phoenix, Miami, New York City, San Francisco and three other clubs and repeated in Chicago, Phoenix and San Francisco is countered by evidence from Playboy records of only one engagement in Phoenix, and then for only two weeks. In fact, Noel Stein testified that the San Francisco club did not open until years after plaintiff's alleged engagement there. As for her allegation of employment by "Dino's Lodge" for 24 weeks in 1961 and 1962, its manager from 1958 on, Paul Wexler, declares that he recollects no employment of her by "Dino's Lodge" before 1965.

The testimony of plaintiff as to her right to compensation from Bobby Roberts, the producer of Monte Walsh, contains three variations as to the type of compensation sought. At first she was to receive a Rolls Royce, then a 10% finders fee and lastly 50% of the producer's fee in return for informing Roberts as to the availability of the Monte Walsh script. Also, she testified that she met Roberts and Landers in their offices on or about March 15, 1968 whereas she was in Palau from Christmas of 1967 to April or May of 1968.

According to the records of Sears Roebuck, an account had been opened in the name of Lee Marvin (Exhibit 117; the application was signed by Betty Marvin, defendant's former wife). Plaintiff testified, however, that an account was opened by her with defendant present in the name of "Mr. and Mrs. Marvin" or Lee Marvin. Sears records do not list her on any application nor as an authorized signator (Exhibit 119).

Plaintiff testified that she "never had an apartment while I was with Lee." However, Exhibit 151 dated May 1, 1965 and signed by plaintiff is a lease of an apartment at 8633 West Knoll Drive, West Hollywood. Plaintiff contends she signed the lease on behalf of her manager, Mimi Marleaux, and that she, the plaintiff, had no belongings there nor did she make any rent payments. Yet, testimony by Marleaux reveals that plaintiff did have some clothes in the apartment and that she, Marleaux, had only stayed a month or two in the apartment. On cross-examination, plaintiff admitted that she may have paid the rent and on direct rebuttal she testified that she did pay the rent two or three times. Exhibit 186 indicates that a Continental Bank signature card signed on December 28, 1965 bore the West Knoll address as plaintiff's

APPENDIX C

residence. At a later time, that address was crossed off and that of the Malibu Beach house was inserted.

Plaintiff testified that she asked defendant for a written agreement to protect her rights. The defendant responded that it was not necessary and she believed him. In her deposition, however, she stated that she continued to request such agreement.

LAW

Is There An Express Contract?

An express contract must be founded on a promise directly or indirectly enforceable at law. (1 Corbin on Contracts, § 11.) Every contract requires, *inter alia* the mutual consent of the parties. (Civil Code §§ 1550, 1565.)

A review of the extensive testimony clearly leads this court to the conclusion that no express contract was negotiated between the parties. Neither party entertained any expectations that the property was to be divided between them.

Further, before mutual consent can exist, an intent to contract must be present. Also, the meaning of the agreement must be ascertainable and both parties must have the same understanding of its meaning. *Merrit & Co.* (1959) 176 C.A. 2d 719, 1 Cal. Rptr. 500. The basic statement on which plaintiff relies is the one which she says (and defendant denies) was made by defendant at San Blas—"What I have is yours and what you have is mine."

Considering the circumstances from which it allegedly sprung, the lack of intent to make a contract is immediately apparent. In 1964–1965 defendant was married; he had considerable unresolved financial problems; he had repeatedly informed plaintiff that he did not believe in marriage because of the property rights which a wife thereby acquires. Plaintiff could not have understood that phrase to accord the same rights to one who was *not* defendant's wife. If those words had been spoken, they were not spoken under circumstances in which either party would be entitled to believe that an offer of a contract was intended. (See *Fowler v. Security Pacific Bank* (1956) 146 C.A. 2d 37, 47, 303 P.2d 565.)

In addition, the meaning of the phrase is difficult to ascertain. Does it mean a sharing of future as well as presently owned property? Does it mean a sharing of the *use* of property or is title to be extended to both parties? Does it mean that all property is shared even though the relationship may be terminated in a week or weekend? These are all unanswered questions. It is more reasonable to conclude that the declaration is simply hyperbole typical of persons who live and work in the entertainment field. It was defendant's way of expressing his affection for the plaintiff. As the defendant testified, in his business terms of affection are bandied about freely; one "loves" everyone and calls everybody "sweetheart."

Also, after hearing defendant's views on marriage and noting his antagonism against a person acquiring any rights by means of a certificate of marriage, it is not reasonable to believe that plaintiff understood that defendant intended to give her such rights even without a certificate. Without intent to contract and with no clearly ascertainable meaning of the contractual phrase, no express contract exists.

During a meeting with Marleaux in the fall of 1966 and in the presence of the defendant, the plaintiff told Marleaux that she (plaintiff) was sorry she had let Marleaux down by not pursuing her career. Defendant then allegedly stated, "I don't know what you're worrying about. I'll always take care of you."

Corbin has this to say about remarks of that sort: "The law does not attempt the realization of every expectation that has been induced by a promise; the expectation must be a reasonable one. Under no system of law that has ever existed are all promises enforceable. The expectation must be one that most people would have, and the promise must be one that most people would perform." (Corbin on Contracts, p. 2 [West Pub. Co. 1852].) Surely plaintiff had no expectation that defendant would extend such care to her after separation, remembering defendant's antagonism to such automatic rights in a wife if the relationship failed (and to which she testified).

In addition, the phrase "I'll always take care of you" leaves many questions unanswered: Does defendant mean that plaintiff has the right to care even if separation is caused by plaintiff? What level of care? What if plaintiff marries, does the care continue? An offer as indefinite as this cannot be the basis of an enforceable contract (*Apablasa, supra,* at 723).

Further, the alleged promise lacks mutuality; the plaintiff made no enforceable promise in response. Even if, *arguendo,* she

APPENDIX C

had promised to forego her career, defendant could not have legally enforced such promise. (See *Mattei v. Hopper* (1959) 51 C.2d 119, 122, 330 P.2d 625.) Actually, plaintiff's career, never very brisk-paced, was sputtering and not because of any act of defendant; it came to an end unmourned and unattended by plaintiff who made no attempt to breathe life into it.

Doubt is cast upon the Marleaux testimony as to the alleged promise. The statement was allegedly made in the presence of Marleaux. The plaintiff testified that she remembers the event very clearly and that it was very important in her life. Yet in plaintiff's deposition of October, 1978, she was asked whether anyone other than the defendant was present and she responded, "I can't recall if anyone was present." (Deposition, p. 66, lines 19–23, read into the trial record at Vol. 30, p. 5490, lines 25–28, p. 5491, lines 1–3.)

The phrase, "Yes sir, I accept life with her, thank you, Your Honor, and the court" contained in Exhibit 13 (a letter written from London in 1966) adds no legal basis for a contract. It was a letter protraying an imaginary court scene from which one can infer the affection of defendant for plaintiff but from which one certainly cannot believe an offer of a contract was intended. (See *Fowler v. Security Pacific Bank, supra.*)

IS THERE AN IMPLIED CONTRACT?

The conduct of the parties after the San Blas conversation certainly does not reveal any implementation of any contract nor does such conduct give rise to an implied contract. No joint bank accounts were established and no real property was placed in joint tenancy or tenancy in common. Plaintiff used a separate bank account for her allowance of $400 per month, her earnings from the Hawaii engagement and her settlement of the Roberts suit. When defendant bought real property, he placed it in his own name. Their tax returns were separate.

In plaintiff's letter to defendant dated November 2, 1971, (Ex. 67) she describes her activities after their separation, thanks defendant for his "financial help" (monthly payments for five years) and says nothing about any contract or agreement. In Ex. 155, a page from a book by plaintiff's counsel, he declares that plaintiff only asked him how to enforce defendant's promise to make payments pursuant to the five-year arrangement. Nothing was said then to counsel about any agreement to divide property. Plaintiff's attorney sent a letter to defendant's attorney, demanding recommencement of the payments for the five-year period. Plaintiff was quoted in an interview recorded in the Brenda Shaw article (Ex. 37) as follows: "We were always very proud of the fact that nothing really held us. We both agreed, and we were really pleased with the fact that you work harder at a relationship when you know that there is nothing really holding you." This evidence bars the finding of any contract.

The very fact that plaintiff pursued a claim for compensation from Roberts makes it plain that she expected no part of any earnings of defendant from the picture. Otherwise, why would she commence a lawsuit to recover a finder's fee or half of a producer's fee when she would have rights to half of the million dollars paid to defendant for the picture?[1]

The evidence does not support plaintiff's contention that she gave up her career in order to care for defendant and on his demand that she do so.

She claimed that defendant demanded that plaintiff give up her career and join him in London or else the relationship would end. Looking at the facts, she did go to London but remained only a few weeks. She declares that she returned because defendant was drinking heavily, and it was then too late to resume promotion of her record. Yet in her 1978 deposition she stated that she returned because her manager wanted her to come home to promote her record and in fact she did attempt to do so, but discovered that the radio stations were not interested. As for loss of momentum, in the promotion of her record by reason of her London trip, witnesses for defendant as well as one for plaintiff testified that no loss occurred. Contrary to any ultimatum, a witness for defendant declared that the latter expressed hope that she would have a successful career.

---

[1] After plaintiffs and defendants separated, plaintiff testified she heard from Roberts many times. In her deposition *** she said she never heard from Roberts after separation. Another inconsistency.

APPENDIX C

Plaintiff testified that the ultimatum was delivered to her by letter.[2]

However, her witness, Marleaux, declared that it came by way of telephone. One must doubt that the defendant issued an ultimatum (allegedly in the missing letter) demanding that plaintiff come to London when he writes in Ex. 12, "only a month and a half to go, w(h)oopee," indicating that plans for her coming to London had already been made by the parties.

The plaintiff's testimony as to defendant's drinking habits would indicate that he was virtually awash with alcohol. Yet during this same period, defendant starred in several major films, all demanding of him physical stamina, a high degree of alertness and verbal as well as physical concentration. Her portrayal of large-scale and all pervasive inebriation raises doubt as to her accuracy of observation.

An implied as well as an express agreement must be founded upon mutual consent. Such consent may be inferred from the conduct of the parties. Proof of introductions of plaintiff as Mrs. Marvin, and the occasional registrations at hotels as Mrs. Marvin and evidence of a relationship wherein plaintiff furnishes companionship, cooking and home care do not establish that defendant agreed to give plaintiff half of his property. Those services may be rendered out of love or affection and are indeed so rendered in a myriad of relationships between man and woman which are not contractual in nature. They may be consideration for a contract to receive property but the other elements of such contract remain to be established. Discussion of an equitable basis for an award because of homemaking services is to be found in a later portion of this opinion.

The change of name to Marvin appears to have had one motivation to avoid embarrassment when traveling. It ended the awkwardness occurring when, for example, plaintiff's passport was examined in customs. Coming at a time so close to the date of separation and after some indication of difficulties between the parties, the change of name does raise a question whether plaintiff sought relief from embarrassment or whether she

---

[2]The letter has been allegedly destroyed by defendant although at first the plaintiff declared that it was missing.

wished to acquire the right to use defendant's name after separation.

The evidence of a contract as to property may be imputed from a change in the manner of holding, such as joint tenancy bank accounts, but not such joint accounts as were set up on the various filming locations (Tucson, Baker, Palau). These accounts were transient, employed solely for the convenience of attending to current needs away from California. The disposition of funds remaining after the film was completed underlined the single purpose of the accounts: upon completion the funds were placed not in a joint account in Los Angeles but in defendant's separate account.

Plaintiff's use of charge accounts certainly does not establish that defendant by his alleged consent to such use intended that half of his property be given to plaintiff.

Registering at hotels as Mr. and Mrs. Marvin does not indicate that defendant intended to give plaintiff one-half of the property. Such evidence may assist in proving a relationship which on its surface resembles marriage in areas away from home, but relationships resembling marriage may exist without any property arrangements. Hence more must be proved by a preponderance of evidence, that is, that plaintiff used the charge accounts *because defendant had agreed to give her half of the property.*

Plaintiff proved that she acted as companion and homemaker, that she prepared a number of defendant's meals and that she cleaned house or supervised a cleaning woman. That she did so in consideration of a contract, express, implied, or tacit, with respect to disposing of property, remains unproven. The existence of such property agreement has not been established by the requisite preponderance of the evidence. The decision of *In re Marriage of Cary* (1973) 34 Cal. App. 3d 345, 109 Cal. Rptr. 862 and *Estate of Atherley* (1975) 44 Cal. App. 3d 758, 119 Cal. Rptr. 41 afford no comfort to the plaintiff as their facts distinguish them from the instant case. In *Cary,* the disputed property was placed in the joint names of both parties, joint income tax returns were filed, money was borrowed and business was conducted as husband and wife. In *Atherley,* both parties pooled earnings accumulated for 13 years and bought property as joint tenants. Both worked and contributed funds to the construction of improvements on land bought with such earnings. None of

APPENDIX C

these facts were established in this case; there was no pooling of earnings, no property was purchased in joint names, and no joint income tax returns were executed. Joint accounts set up on filming locations were only used as convenient and transient methods of payment of bills with the balance returned to the separate account of the defendant when the film was completed.

As for pooling of earnings, the bulk of plaintiff's compensation for singing was used to pay her musician and arrangers. When she did achieve a net income in the Hawaiian engagement, she placed the money in her separate account. Defendant's income was deposited in his own bank account and used to buy property in his own name. This case therefore bears little resemblance either to *Cary* or *Atherley*.

Finding no contract, the testimony of Doughty is not evaluated as that relates to an alleged breach of contract.

It is clear that the parties came together because of mutual affection and not because of mutual consent to a contract. Nothing else, certainly no contract, kept them together and, when that affection diminished, they separated.

EQUITABLE REMEDIES

If no contract, express or implied, is to be found, the Supreme Court adjures the trial court to ascertain whether any equitable remedies are applicable. The high court suggests constructive and resulting trusts as well as quantum meruit. The court also declares: "Our opinion does not preclude the evolution of additional equitable remedies to protect the expectations of the parties to a nonmarital relationship in cases in which existing remedies prove inadequate; the suitability of such remedies may be determined in later cases in light of the factual setting in which they arise."[3]

The plaintiff has, by her dismissal of her fourth and fifth causes of action—both for quantum meruit—removed that remedy from the court's consideration.

If a resulting trust is to be established, it must be shown that property was intended by the parties to be held by one party in

---

[3]Marvin v. Marvin, supra, footnote 25.

trust for the other and that consideration was provided by the one not holding title to purchase the property. As Witkin puts it, there must be "circumstances showing that the transferee (holder of title) was not intended to take the beneficial interest."[4]

No evidence has been adduced to show such consideration having been provided by the plaintiff to buy property.[5] It may be contended that as the defendant did not need to expend funds to secure homemaking services elsewhere, she thereby enhanced the financial base of the defendant and enabled him to increase his property purchases. (See Bruch, *supra,* p. 123.) Such alleged enhancement, however, would appear to be offset by the considerable flow of economic benefits in the other direction. Those benefits include payments for goods and services for plaintiff up to $72,900 for the period from 1967-1970 alone (Ex. 194). Exhibit 196 indicates that living expenses for the parties were $221,400 for the period from 1965 to 1970. Among such benefits were a Mercedes Benz automobile for plaintiff, fur coats, travel to London, Hawaii, Japan, Micronesia, and the pleasures of life on the California beach in frequent contact with many film and stage notables. Further, defendant made a substantial financial effort to launch plaintiff's career as a recording singer. No equitable basis for an expansion of the resulting trust theory is afforded in view of this evidence.

A constructive trust, pleaded in the second cause of action, is "equity's version of implied-in-law recovery" (see Bruch, *supra,* 125) based on unjust enrichment. This is a trust imposed to force restitution of something that in fairness and good conscience does not belong to its owner. (See Bruch, *supra,* p. 125). However, the defendant earned the money by means of his own effort, skill and reputation. The money was then invested in the properties now held by him. It cannot be said in good conscience that such properties do not belong to him.

As Witkin points out, such a trust is an equitable remedy imposed where a person obtains property by fraudulent misrepre-

---

[4] 7 Witkin, Summary of Calif. Law, § 123, p. 5481.
[5] Such establishment must be made by clear and convincing proof. (J. G. Bogert and G. T. Bogert, Handbook of the Law of Trusts, § 74 at p. 279 (5th Edition 1973); Moulton v. Moulton (1920) 182 Cal. 185, 187 p. 421; Bruch, Property Rights of De Facto Spouses, 10 Family Law Quarterly, p. 101.)

APPENDIX C

sentation or concealment or by some wrongful act.[6] No such wrongdoing can be elicited from the facts of this case.

Plaintiff contends that the Supreme Court by its opinion in *Marvin v. Marvin, supra,* requires that plaintiff receive a reasonable proportion of the property in defendant's name because of her performance of the homemaker-companion-cook and other wife-like functions even though no contract, express or implied, exists and even though no basis for a constructive or resulting trust can be found. To accede to such a contention would mean that the court would recognize each unmarried person living together to be automatically entitled by such living together, and performing spouse-like functions, to half of the property bought with the earnings of the other nonmarital partner. This is tantamount to recognition of common law marriages in California. As they were abolished in 1895, the Supreme Court surely does not mean to resurrect them by its opinion in *Marvin v. Marvin.*[7] The trial court's understanding of *Marvin v. Marvin* is that if there is mutual consent or proof of the mutual intent of the parties, by reason of their conduct or because of surrounding circumstances, to share the property or if the plaintiff directly participated in the procurement of or the nurturing of investments, or if there has been mutual effort (which will be discussed later) the property should be divided. None of these conditions pertains here.

While the Supreme Court directs under certain circumstances a fair apportionment of property even though there is no express or implied contract, it has imposed a condition, that such property be "accumulated through mutual effort." (p. 682.) Plaintiff declares that her work as homemaker, cook and companion constituted "mutual effort."

---

[6]Civil Code, §§ 2223, 2224; 7 Witkin, Summary of Calif. Law, §§ 131, 132, pp. 5487, 5488.

[7]Footnote 24 of Marvin v. Marvin *** expressly denies any intent to revive the relationship: "We do not seek to resurrect the doctrine of commonlaw marriage, which was abolished in California by statute in 1895. (See Norman v. Thompson (1898) 121 Cal. 620, 628, [54 F. 143]; Estate of Abate (1958) 166 Cal. App. 2d 282, 292 [333 P.2d 200].) Thus we do not hold that plaintiff and defendant were 'married,' nor do we extend to plaintiff the rights which the Family Law Act grants valid or putative spouses; we hold only that she has the same rights to enforce contracts and to assert her equitable interest in property acquired *through her effort* as does any other unmarried person." (Emphasis added)

The two cases cited as examples of mutual effort, *In re Marriage of Cary* (1973) 34 Cal. App. 3d 345, 109 Cal. Rptr. 862 and *Estate of Atherley* (1975) 44 Cal. App. 3d 758, 119 Cal. Rptr. 41, reveal considerably more involvement on the part of the woman in the accumulation of property. In the first place, Paul Cary and Janet Forbes (in *Cary, supra*) held themselves out to be husband and wife. That is not the case here. The reputation of the parties in the community in which they settled was not that they were a married couple. Not only did Cary and Forbes purchase a home, but they also borrowed money, obtained credit, and filed joint income tax returns. Four children were born to the couple. The children's birth certificates and school registration recorded them as Paul and Janet Cary. None of these facts are present in the instant case.

In *Atherley*, the parties, Harold and Annette, lived together for 22 years; after 14 years Harold divorced a prior wife *ex parte* in Juarez, Mexico and then married Annette in Reno, Nevada. Both were employed and pooled their earnings in various bank accounts. They had been advised by a Los Angeles attorney that the Mexican divorce was valid. Both contributed services to the construction of improvements on land purchased by them. Funds used to purchase both land and materials can be traced to their accumulated earnings. Two bank accounts were established with funds accumulated by Harold and Annette. Upon the sale of an improved parcel, a promissory note representing part of the sales price was held in joint tenancy. None of these facts is present in the instant case.[8]

In this case we have all assets bought solely with the earnings of the defendant. The plaintiff had no net earnings except from the Hawaiian engagement and those funds went into her own account. Plaintiff secured $750 from the settlement of her suit against Roberts and those funds also did not go into defendant's account. There were, on the other hand, funds that were expended by defendant to further plaintiff's career. The defendant also persuaded a friend to employ plaintiff in Hawaii. He brought people to hear her sing and bought drinks to keep them

---

[8] Mere possession of property or the holding of title is not a determinant if standing alone. See Marvin v. Marvin, footnote 21.

in attendance. It was the plaintiff who stopped trying to sell her record and get singing engagements. The evidence does not establish that such cessation was caused by defendant.

It would be difficult to deem the singing career of plaintiff to be the "mutual effort" required by the Supreme Court. Certainly, where both wanted to be free to come and go without obligation, the basis of any division of property surely cannot be her "giving up" her career for him. It then can only be her work as cook, homemaker and companion that can be considered as plaintiff's contribution to the requisite "mutual effort." Yet, where $72,000 has been disbursed by defendant on behalf of plaintiff in less than six years, where she has enjoyed a fine home and travel throughout the world for about 30 months, where she acquired whatever clothes, furs and cars she wished and engaged in a social life amongst screen and stage luminaries, such services as she has rendered would appear to have been compensated. Surely one cannot glean from such services her participation in a "mutual effort" between the parties to earn funds to buy property as occurred in *Cary* and *Atherley, supra*.

The Supreme Court doubtless intended by the phrase "mutual effort" to mean the relationship of a man and woman who have joined together to make a home, who act together to earn and deposit such earnings in joint accounts, who pay taxes together, who make no effort to gain an advantage by reason of the association, (such as informing a producer of a script for a fee and taking defendant's name without his consent), who have children if possible and bring them up together. *Cary* and *Atherley* in fact demands more of the partners: they require participation in money-earning activities. Plaintiff's fund-raising put money in her own account.

To construe "mutual effort" to mean services as homemaker, cook and companion and nothing else[9] would be tantamount to the grant of the benefits of the Family Law Act to the nonmarital partner as well as to the married person. This the Supreme Court has refused to do. Therefore, one must seek and find in each case those additional factors which indicate the expendi-

---

[9]This is not to gainsay that an express or implied contract may be valid and enforceable where the consideration is ordinary homemaking services. (Marvin v. Marvin, supra, footnote 5.

ture of "mutual effort," such as those present in *Cary* and *Atherley*. Such factors are not present in this case.

The court is aware that footnote 25, *Marvin v. Marvin, supra,* urges the trial court to employ whatever equitable remedy may be proper under the circumstances. The court is also aware of the recent resort of plaintiff to unemployment insurance benefits to support herself and of the fact that a return of plaintiff to a career as a singer is doubtful. Additionally, the court knows that the market value of defendant's property at time of separation exceeded $1,000,000.

In view of these circumstances, the court in equity awards plaintiff $104,000[10] for rehabilitation purposes so that she may have the economic means to re-educate herself and to learn new, employable skills or to refurbish those utilized, for example, during her most recent employment[11] and so that she may return from her status as companion of a motion picture star to a separate, independent but perhaps more prosaic existence.

DATED: April 17, 1979
s ARTHUR K. MARSHALL
JUDGE OF THE SUPERIOR COURT

---

[10]Plaintiff should be able to accomplish rehabilitation in less than two years. The sum awarded would be approximately equivalent to the highest scale she ever earned as a singer, $1,000 per week, for two years.

[11]While part of the funds may be used for living expenses, the primary intent is that they be employed for retraining purposes.

INDEX

References are to Pages

B

Bastards—See Children, illegitimate
Bigamy, 102–103
Blood grouping tests to determine paternity, 130
Birth control, unmarried female's right to practice, 78–79
Birth, wrongful, as cause of action, 84–85
Breach of promise to marry
    abolition of actions constitutional, 81
    seduction under promise of marriage, action against cohabitant, 90–92

C

California
    abortions, 73, 294
    adoption, 292
    alienation of affections actions abolished, 294
    alimony, effect of cohabitation on payments, 294–295
    breach of promise to marry actions abolished, 294
    common-law marriages, 291
    consortium denied for injury prior to marriage, 88
    criminal conversation actions abolished, 294
    criminal statutes, 96, 295–296
    housing discrimination against unmarried cohabitants, 42–43, 292
    illegitimate children, 53, 117 n, 121, 124, 134, 141, 143, 146, 293, 296
    insurance
        cohabitant under automobile policy, 68–69
        insured cohabiting at time of application, 67
    Marvin v. Marvin—See Marvin v. Marvin
    parental rights, termination, 149
    paternity actions, 129 n, 130 n, 296
    probation, noncohabitation as condition, 108
    property rights of cohabitants, 154 n, 160–161, 162, 164 n, 165 n, 168, 170, 171, 173, 177, 178, 183, 297–299
    putative marriages, 14 n, 15 n, 297–298
    schoolteachers, grounds for dismissal, 30, 292
    seduction actions abolished, 294
    services contributed to household, claim for, 158
        improvement on property, 171
    termination of nonmarital relationship, 154 n, 160–161, 162, 164 n, 165 n, 168, 170, 171, 173, 177, 178, 183, 297–299
    workers' compensation death benefits, 60, 293
    wrongful death actions, 293
Children
    adoption of child by unmarried couple, 45–48—See also Adoption
    aid to families with dependent children, 53–55
    foster parents, unmarried couple as, 46–47
    illegitimate children—See also individual states
        acknowledgment as legitimizing child, statutory provisions, 146
        adoption, termination of parental rights, 146–151—See also Adoption

INDEX

References are to Pages

Children (continued)
- illegitimate children (continued)
    - aid to families with dependent children, eligibility, 53–55
    - bastardy statutes as not discriminatory against males, 129 n
    - "children" as term used in instruments and statutes, inclusion of illegitimates, 112–117
    - common-law approach to illegitimates, 111–121
        - constitutionality of, 112–115, 117–121
    - Copyright Act, rights under, 58
    - custody, 138–142
    - death of child, concealment, 94
    - death of cohabitant
        - posthumous child, 59, 121
        - social security benefits, 50–53
        - workers' compensation benefits, 56–61
        - wrongful death actions, 89
    - Dependents' Medical Care Act, care under, 117 n
    - equal protection for, 112–129
        - support, 132–138
    - Glona v. American Guarantee & Liability Insurance Company, 120–121
    - housing regulation prohibiting, 41
    - inheritance and intestacy, 122–129
    - insurance policies, inclusion under, 58, 113
    - Labine v. Vincent, 123
    - legitimation, 143–146
    - Levy v. Louisiana, 120
    - Mathews v. Lucas, 123
    - name used by child, preference to father unconstitutional, 144 n
    - paternity actions, 129–132
    - presumption of legitimacy, 115–116
    - Social Security Act, benefits under, 118–119
    - Stanley v. Illinois, 141–142, 148, 150
    - "strictest scrutiny" test, 117–118
    - support, 132–137
    - Trimble v. Gordon, 125–128
    - visitation rights, 142–143
    - welfare benefits, eligibility, 50–55
    - wrongful death statutes, 119–121
- wrongful birth action against parents, 84–85

Choice of law—See Conflict of laws

Civil Rights Act of 1964, discrimination under Title VII
- airlines industry, 25
- employment generally, 22, 24–27, 30–31—See Employment
- homosexuals, 26
- marital status as grounds, 22, 24–27, 30
- maternity leave policy, 26–27
- schoolteachers, pregnant and unmarried or cohabiting, 30

Coercion of married woman, doctrine inapplicable to cohabitants, 2

Cohabitation as alternative to marriage
- accumulated property or income—See Termination of nonmarital relationship
- adoption rights, 45–48—See also Adoption

INDEX

References are to Pages

Cohabitation as alternative to marriage (continued)
    advantages over marriage, generally, 7-9
    alimony, effect of cohabitation on right to payments, 85-88
    children—See Children
    common-law marriage as result of cohabitation, 45—See also Common-law marriages
    credit of partner, authority to pledge, 80
    crime, cohabitation as, 95, 97
        risk of criminal liability generally, 94-107
    death of cohabitant—See Death of unmarried cohabitant
    disadvantages generally, 6-8
    discrimination against unmarried couples—See Constitutional law; Employment; Housing; Insurance; Privacy
    "head of family," cohabitant as, 48
    "head of household," cohabitant as, 48-49
        for income tax purposes—See Income tax
    homestead laws, unmarried couples under, 48-49
    income accumulated during cohabitation—See Termination of nonmarital relationship
    insurance policies, coverage under, 63-72—See also Insurance
    privacy rights, 95-97—See Privacy
    property accumulated during cohabitation—See Termination of nonmarital relationship
    property conveyed to cohabitants as husband and wife, 161-165—See also Termination of nonmarital relationship
    resumption of cohabitation after termination of marriage, 13
    services contributed to household, value, 157-161—See also Termination of nonmarital relationship
    sexual conduct, risk of criminal liability, 94-107
    social security benefits, 50-53
    tax consequences—See Estate tax; Gift tax; Income tax
    termination of relationship—See Termination of nonmarital relationship
    tort actions between cohabitants, 89-92
Colleges and universities—See Educational opportunities
Colorado
    abortions, 302
    adoption, 301
    breach of promise of marriage actions abolished, 301
        recovery of gifts, 301
    common-law marriages, 299
    community property law, 300
    criminal statutes, 301-302
    illegitimate children, 133, 301, 303-304
    parental rights, termination, 304-305
    paternity actions, 304
    property rights of cohabitants, 305
    putative marriages, 299-300, 305
    schoolteachers' marital status not to affect employment, 300
    termination of nonmarital relationship, 305
    workers' compensation death benefits, 301
Common-law marriages—See also individual states
    bigamy and common-law marriage, 102

INDEX

References are to Pages

Common-law marriages (continued)
 change of residence, 13-14, 16-19
 cohabitation as creating common-law marriage, 44-45
 conflict of laws problems, 16-19
 death of spouse, survivor's rights under compensation statutes, 56-61
 historical considerations, 10
 income tax law, status of common-law spouse, 210
 marriage to another during common-law relationship, 13
 name of spouse, adoption of, 12, 44-45
 place of cohabitation, effect on validity of relationship, 13-14
 requirements for common-law marriage, 11-14
 social security benefits, common-law spouse and, 51
 states recognizing common-law marriages, 11
 termination of common-law marriage, cohabitation following, 13
 Uniform Marriage and Divorce Act, effect, 11
 visits to other states, 12-13
Communes, food stamp regulation discouraging, 55
Community property laws, 6
Comstock Act, 78
Confinement of unwed mother
 liability of putative father for, 136
 payment for by adoptive parents, 47
Conflict of laws, common-law and nonmarital relationships, 16-19
Connecticut
 abortions, 306, 309
 adoption, 307
 alimony, effect of cohabitation on right to, 308
 common-law marriages, 305
 criminal statutes, 99, 308
 illegitimate children, 142, 306, 307, 309, 310
 insurance, cohabitant as "member of family" under automobile policy, 69
 paternity actions, 134, 306, 310
 privacy rights, 37, 78, 307
 property rights of cohabitants, 311
 termination of nonmarital relationship, 311
 workers' compensation death benefits, 307
Consideration, illicit sex as invalidating cohabitation contract, 2, 157, 179
Consortium action, of dubious viability without marriage, 7, 88
Conspiracy as basis of liability for misconduct of other cohabitant, 97
Constitutional law
 civil rights, denial of—See Civil Rights Act of 1964, discrimination under Title VII
 due process of law, denial of
  armed services, unwed pregnancies in, 35-37
  employment generally, 21-24, 28-34—See Employment
  housing, 40-43
  illegitimate children, 117
   rights of biological parents, 138-143, 146-151
  schoolteachers, pregnant and unmarried or cohabiting, 28-34
  students, pregnant and unmarried or cohabiting, 34-35
 equal protection of the laws, denial of
  armed services, unwed pregnancies in, 35-37

INDEX

References are to Pages

Constitutional law (continued)
    equal protection of the laws, denial of (continued)
        employment generally, 21–24, 28–34—See Employment
        housing, 40–43
        illegitimate children, 112–128
            support, 132–138
        schoolteachers, pregnant and unmarried or cohabiting, 28–34
        students, pregnant and unmarried or cohabiting, 34–35
    right of privacy, denial of—See Privacy
Constructive trust theory in adjusting rights of cohabitants, 174–176—See also Termination of nonmarital relationship
Contraceptives, unmarried female's right to use, 37, 78–79
Contracts between cohabitants to divide accumulated property or income, 177–187—See Termination of nonmarital relationship
Contracts between cohabitants to reduce income taxes—See Income tax
Contracts between married persons, 183
Contracts, liability of cohabitant for partner's, 80
Conveyances, cohabitants' rights under, 161–165
Copyright Act, rights of illegitimate children under, 58
Coverture, as status of woman under old marriage laws, 8
Credit, married woman's difficulties regarding, 9
Criminal conversation actions, 80–84—See also individual states
Criminal statutes, cohabitants' conduct as possible violation, 94–107—See also individual states
Curtesy, as advantage of marriage, 3, 6
Custody of illegitimate children, 138–142

D

Death of unmarried cohabitant
    survivors and dependents, rights of
        federal compensation statutes, 56–58
        illegitimate children, inheritance, 122–129—See also individual states
        insurance benefits, 63–67—See also Insurance
        social security benefits, 50–53
        workers' compensation benefits, 56–61—See also individual states
        wrongful death actions, 89—See also individual states
Death on the High Seas Act
    bigamous marriage, denial of compensation to innocent spouse, 58
    common-law spouse eligible for survivor's benefits, 58
Declaratory relief, as to existence of common-law marriage, 11
Deeds and conveyances to cohabitants as husband and wife, 161–165—See also Termination of nonmarital relationship
Delaware
    abortions, 315
    adoption, 313, 316, 317
    alienation of affections actions abolished, 314
    breach of contract to marry actions abolished, 314
    common-law marriages, 311–312
    criminal conversation actions abolished, 314
    criminal statutes, 314

INDEX

References are to Pages

Delaware (continued)
    enticement actions abolished, 314
    illegitimate children, 142, 313, 315–317
    marriage requirements, 312
    parental rights, termination, 317
    paternity actions, 134–135 n, 315
    property rights of cohabitants, 317
    termination of nonmarital relationship, 317
    workers' compensation death benefits, 313
Demerits of cohabitation, 6–8—See also Cohabitation as alternative to marriage
Dependents—See Children; Income tax
District of Columbia
    abortions, 320–321
    adoption, 319
    breach of promise of marriage actions, 91, 320
    common-law marriages, 317
    criminal statutes, 321–322
    discrimination on basis of marital status prohibited, 318
    illegitimate children, 113 n, 134, 320, 322, 323–324
    insurance policy, inclusion of illegitimates, 113 n, 320
    parental rights, termination, 147, 319
    paternity actions, 323
    property rights of cohabitants, 162, 175, 324
    termination of nonmarital relationship, 162, 175
    workers' compensation death benefits, 319
Division of accumulated property or income—See Termination of nonmarital relationship
Divorce
    cohabitation as affecting alimony payments, 85–88—See also Alimony
    proof of fault in divorce proceedings, 7
    tax considerations—See Income tax
Dower and curtesy, 3, 6
Due process of law, denial of—See Constitutional law

E

Earnings of cohabitants—See Income tax; Termination of nonmarital relationship
Educational opportunities, impact of cohabitation on, 34–35
Employment
    Civil Rights Act of 1964, discrimination under, 22, 24–27, 30–31
    immorality as breach of employment contract, 21–24
        schoolteachers, 28–33
    maternity leave policy, discrimination against unmarried employees, 26–27
        sex discrimination, 26–27
    termination or refusal to hire
        apartment managers, requirement that applicants be married, 26
        cohabitation or extramarital relationship as grounds, 23–24, 28–33, 37–38
        generally, as denial of constitutional or civil rights, 21–28

INDEX

References are to Pages

Employment (continued)
    termination or refusal to hire (continued)
        Hollenbaugh v. Carnegie Free Library, 23
        homosexuality as grounds, 22, 26, 29 n, 30 n
        marriage or marital status as grounds, 24–27, 31–32
        pregnancy as grounds, 22, 26, 27, 28–33, 56
            unemployment benefits, 56
            unwed pregnancy, 22, 26, 27, 28–33
        schoolteachers, 22, 26, 28–33
        sex discrimination, 24–27
        unmarried status as grounds, 21–24, 26–27
Entireties, tenancy by the, conveyances to cohabitants, 161
Equal protection of the laws, denial of—See Constitutional law
Equal Rights Amendment as affecting support obligations, 134
Equitable lien, use in adjusting rights of cohabitants, 176–177—See also Termination of nonmarital relationship
Estate tax
    cohabitation versus marriage, 243–246
    decedent's earlier divorce invalid, status of surviving spouse, 214
    joint property owned by cohabitants, 245–246
    percentage of persons taxed, 191 n
    state death taxes, 191 n

F

Family
    definition of family, 5
        term ambiguous, 68
    "head of family," who qualifies, 48
    status of family encouraged by law, 4
    unmarried cohabitant as "member of family" for insurance purposes, 67–72
"Family car doctrine," status of cohabitant under automobile insurance policy, 70–72
"Family purpose doctrine," status of cohabitant under automobile insurance policy, 70–72
Federal Employees Compensation Act, benefits on death of unmarried cohabitant, 56–57
Federal Employers' Liability Act, benefits on death of unmarried cohabitant, 56–57, 114
Federal estate taxes—See Estate tax
Federal gift tax—See Gift tax
Federal income taxes—See Income tax
Federal welfare benefits for children of unmarried cohabitants, 50–55
Feticide, 94
Filiation orders, 129
Fire insurance—See Insurance
Florida
    abortions, 76, 327–328
    adoption, 147, 148, 151, 326
    alienation of affections actions abolished, 327
    breach of contract to marry actions abolished, 327

INDEX

References are to Pages

Florida (continued)
- common-law marriages, 325
- criminal conversation actions abolished, 327
- criminal statutes, 92, 329–330
- illegitimate children, 113 n, 121, 133, 137, 138, 147, 148, 151, 326, 327, 330–332
- insurance policy, inclusion of illegitimates, 113 n
- parental rights, termination, 147, 148, 151, 332
- paternity actions, 330
- pregnant and unmarried students, 326
- probation, noncohabitation as condition, 108
- property rights of cohabitants, 162, 170, 183 n, 333–334
- seduction actions abolished, 327
- termination of nonmarital relationship, 162, 170, 183 n, 333–334
- workers' compensation death benefits, 326
- wrongful death actions, 121, 327

Food stamp regulation discouraging communes, 55

Fornication, 97

Foster parent
- alternative to adoption, 47–48
- *loco parentis* to child, 48

Fraud
- actions against cohabitant, 90
- marriage induced by fraud, property rights, 154
- rape by fraud, 94
- statute of frauds, impact on cohabitation contracts, 182

G

Gays—See Homosexuals

Georgia
- abortions, 339
- adoption, 150–151, 336, 341
- alienation of affections actions, 81 n, 83
- common-law marriages, 13, 334–336
- criminal statutes, 338
- illegitimate children, 19 n, 113 n, 114 n, 337, 339–341
- parental rights, termination, 150–151, 336, 340
- pregnant and unmarried students, 35 n, 336
- property rights of cohabitants, 155, 166 n, 176, 182, 342
- termination of nonmarital relationship, 155, 166 n, 176, 182, 342
- workers' compensation death benefits, 337
- wrongful death action, 340

Gift tax
- cohabitation and gift tax, 198–199, 201, 245–246, 250–251
  - joint property, 245–246
  - property settlement on break-up, 198–199, 201
  - transfer of assets between cohabitants, 250–251
  - trusts created by cohabitants, 250–251
- credits and exclusions, 243–245
- definition of taxable gift, 242–243

INDEX

References are to Pages

Gift tax (continued)
    marital deduction, 244-246
    rate, 243-244
    state gift tax, 191 n
Good faith spouse—See Putative marriage
Goods, household, accumulated by cohabitants, 159-161—See also Termination of nonmarital relationship
Guest statute, passenger cohabitant of driver, 92

H

Hawaii
    abortions, 343
    adoption, 343, 345
    common-law marriages, 343
    community property state, 342
    criminal statutes, 343-344
    illegitimate children, 143, 343, 345
    parental rights, termination, 345
    paternity actions, 345
    property rights of cohabitants, 154, 173, 346-347
    termination of nonmarital relationship, 154, 173, 346-347
    workers' compensation death benefits, 343
Head of family under homestead laws, unmarried cohabitant as, 48-49
Head of household
    homestead laws, unmarried cohabitants, 48-49
    income tax law—See Income tax
Heart balm statutes, 90-92
Hiring, discrimination in—See Employment
Homestead laws, unmarried cohabitants under homestead laws, 48-49
Homosexuals
    attitude of society generally, 4
    cohabitations, homosexual, 92-94
        not recognized as "marriages" for tax purposes, 211
    custody of children, lesbianism as affecting right, 140
    employment discrimination, 22, 26, 29 n, 30 n
    privacy rights, 40
    sodomy statutes, 98-100
Hotels, discrimination against unmarried couples, 41
Household
    "head of household," who qualifies, 48-49
        for income tax purposes—See Income tax
    term ambiguous, 5
    insurance policies, cohabitant as "member of household," 67-70
Housing
    discrimination against unmarried couples, 40-43
        as invasion of privacy, 39
    Fair Housing Act, 41
    illegitimate children, housing regulation prohibiting, 41
Husband and wife, conveyances to cohabitants as, 161-165—See also Termination of nonmarital relationship

677

INDEX

References are to Pages

I

Idaho
    abortions, 348–350
    adoption, 347, 352
    common-law marriages, 347
    community property state, 347
    criminal statutes, 350–351
    illegitimate children, 348, 351–352
    paternity actions, 351
    property rights of cohabitants, 155 n, 352
    termination of nonmarital relationship, 155 n, 352
    workers' compensation death benefits, 348

Illegitimate children—See Children

Illinois
    abortions, 354
    adoption, 146, 147, 148, 353, 360–361
    alienation of affections actions, 83, 84, 355
    alimony, effect of cohabitation on right to, 355
    common-law marriages, 353
    criminal conversation actions, 355
    criminal statutes, 356–358
    illegitimate children, 125–126, 127, 338, 354, 355, 358, 359–361
    parental rights, termination, 146, 147, 148, 360–361
    paternity actions, 129, 361
    property rights of cohabitants, 170 n, 183 n, 361–362
    schoolteacher's unwed pregnancy, 353
    student pregnancies, 353
    termination of nonmarital relationship, 170 n, 183 n, 361–362
    workers' compensation death benefits, 354

Immigration
    extramarital cohabitation as affecting right to enter or remain in country, 61–63
    illegitimate child under "parent or child" preference clause of Act, 63

Immorality
    custody rights, effect of mother's immorality on, 139
    employment rights, effect of immorality on, 21–24
    welfare benefits, effect of mother's immorality on, 51–55

Implied-in-fact contract between cohabitants, 171–173—See also Termination of nonmarital relationship

Incest, 103–104

Income tax
    "abandoned spouse," 223–225
    alien spouse, nonresident, 225–227
    alimony, 197, 217
    alternative minimum tax, 205
    annulment of marriage, effect on tax status, 211–212
    classification of taxpayers, 202–203
    cohabitation as alternative to marriage
        case history, 191–202
        dependents
            cohabitant as dependent, 236–238
            cohabitant's child or parent as dependent, 239

INDEX

References are to Pages

Income tax (continued)
    cohabitation as alternative to marriage (continued)
        generally, 191–202, 206–209, 257–259
        income splitting, 247–251
        Marvin v. Marvin-type awards, 200–202
        partnerships formed by cohabitants, 248
        property settlements on break-up, 197–202
        services rendered cohabitant, 195–198
        share-and-share-alike agreements, 248–249, 251–252
        sharing of expenses, 252–254
        tax consequences generally, 190–208, 257–260, 261–272
        transfer of assets between cohabitants, 249–251
        trusts created by one cohabitant for other, 249–251
    common-law marriages, marital status, 210
    credits
        child and dependent care credit, 207, 225
        elderly, credit for, marital status as affecting, 225
        earned income credit, 207
    deductions
        alimony, 197, 217
        capital loss deduction, effect of filing separate return, 208
        investment indebtedness, ceiling on deduction for excess interest affected by marital status, 208
        personal exemption deduction, 232–233
        services rendered cohabitant, 195–196
        small business stock loss, effect of filing joint return, 208
        termination of nonmarital relationship, payments to cohabitant, property settlements, 197–202
    dependents
        cohabitant as dependent, 236–238
        cohabitant's children or parent as dependent, 239
        definition, 233–241
        "member of household test," 235–236, 240
    divorce
        a mensa et thoro, marital status of parties, 217
        a vinculo matrimonii, marital status of parties, 217
        invalid divorce and subsequent marriage, marital status, 213–215
        reduction of taxes through divorce, 215, 257–259
            divorce and remarriage, IRS view on, 215, 257
        support *pendente lite* order, marital status, 217
        year-end divorces, 215, 257
    exemptions, personal, 232–233
    head of household
        definition, 229–232
        two households in one, cohabitants' claiming, 254–255
    income splitting, 195–196
        cohabitants, 247–251
    joint returns
        community property states, 192
        consent of spouse, 192
        credits and deductions, 207–208
        husband separated and cohabiting, 192
        "unfriendly wife" situation, 192

INDEX

References are to Pages

Income tax (continued)
    "married" as defined under state and federal law, 209–225
    "marriage penalty tax," 206–209
    Marvin v. Marvin-type award, how taxed, 200–202
    "max-tax" on earned income, 193, 204
    partnerships by cohabitants, 248
    reform of income tax law needed, 259–260
    separated but not divorced, 191–194
        deduction for children as dependents, 233–236
        "living apart a full taxable year," 223
        marital status of parties, 216–222
    services rendered cohabitant, 195–198
    "share-and-share-alike" agreements by cohabitants, 248–249, 251–252
        sharing of expenses, 252–254
    state income taxes, 191 n
    support *pendente lite* order, marital status of parties, 217
    surviving spouse
        deceased spouse's prior divorce invalid, 213–214
        definition, 227–228
        lower tax rate, requirements, 227–228
        marital status, 209
            date determining, 222–223
    tax preference items, additional tax, 205
    tax rates, 203, 261–269
    termination of nonmarital relationship, property settlement between cohabitants, 197–202
    transfer of assets between cohabitants, reduction of taxes, 249–251
    trust created by cohabitants, reduction of taxes, 249–251
    void or voidable marriages, marital status of parties, 211–213
    working wife, effect on tax rate, 206, 208
    "zero bracket amount" (ZBA), 190 n, 203, 206
Indebitatus assumpsit theory in adjusting rights of cohabitants, 173–174—See also Termination of nonmarital relationship
Indiana
    abortions, 365
    adoption, 363
    alienation of affections actions abolished, 365
    breach of promise of marriage actions abolished, 365
    common-law marriages, 362
    criminal conversation actions abolished, 365
    criminal statutes, 366
    illegitimate children, 59–60, 125 n, 365, 366–368
    parental rights, termination, 363–364
    paternity actions, 129, 367
    property rights of cohabitants, 368
    seduction actions abolished, 365
    termination of nonmarital relationship, 368
    workers' compensation death benefits, 59–60, 364–365
Infanticide, 94
Informal marriage—See Common-law marriage
Inheritance rights of illegitimate children, 122–129

INDEX

References are to Pages

Insurance—See also individual states
    beneficiary changed from spouse to cohabitant, 65–66
    cohabitant as named beneficiary, 65
    cohabitant erroneously designated spouse, 66
    extramarital cohabitation as grounds for refusal to insure, 63–64, 67
    "family car doctrine," status of cohabitant under, 70–72
    "family," cohabitant as member of, 67–72
    "family purpose doctrine," status of cohabitant under, 70–72
    "household," cohabitant as member of, 67–70
    "husband" or "wife" designated beneficiary, cohabitant as claimant, 66
    illegitimate children as claimants, 113
        National Service Life Insurance, 58
    "immoral relations" as reason to deny payment, 65
    insurable interest requirement, 64
    marital status misrepresented, 66–67
    omnibus clause in automobile policy, effect of consent of cohabitant, 69
Intestacy, rights of illegitimate children, 122–129
Iowa
    abortions, 370
    adoption, 372
    alienation of affections actions, 369
    breach of promise to marry actions, 369
    common-law marriages, 12, 16 n, 368–369
    criminal statutes, 102 n, 370
    illegitimate children, 370–371
    paternity actions, 131, 371
    property rights of cohabitants, 372
    schoolteacher's extramarital cohabitation, 30
    services rendered during cohabitation, compensation, 372
    workers' compensation death benefits, 369

J

Joint tenancy, property held by cohabitants in, 161–165
Joint venture theory in adjusting rights of cohabitants, 165–167—See also Termination of nonmarital relationship

K

Kansas
    abortions, 373–374
    adoption, 376
    alimony, cohabitation as affecting right to, 86, 373
    common-law marriages, 372
    criminal statutes, 374
    illegitimate children, 373, 375–376
    property rights of cohabitants, 177, 376
    termination of nonmarital relationship, 177, 376
    workers' compensation death benefits, 373

INDEX

References are to Pages

Kentucky
    abortions, 379
    adoption, 147, 378
    alimony, cohabitation as affecting right to, 85
    criminal statutes, 380
    illegitimate children, 139, 143 n, 378, 381–382
    marriage requirements, 377
    parental rights, termination, 147, 382
    property rights of cohabitants, 169 n, 171 n, 383
    termination of nonmarital relationship, 169 n, 171 n, 383
    workers' compensation death benefits, 378, 379

L

Landowners' refusal to sell or lease to cohabitants, 40–43
Lesbians—See Homosexuals
Lessors' discrimination against cohabitants, 40–43
Life insurance—See Insurance
Longshoremens' and Harbor Workers' Compensation Act, benefits on death of unmarried cohabitant, 57
Louisiana
    abortions, 389–390
    adoption, 387, 395
    alimony, cohabitation as affecting right to, 87 n
    community property state, 384
    criminal statutes, 392
    illegitimate children, 59, 115, 118, 122, 123, 124, 133, 144–145, 393–396
    mistake as to valid marriage, 14 n, 15 n, 385–387
    parental rights, termination, 395
    paternity actions, 115 n, 394
    property rights of cohabitants, 154, 396–398
    putative marriages, 14 n, 15 n, 385–387
    services contributed to household, compensation, 157, 396
    termination of nonmarital relationship, 154, 157, 396–398
    workers' compensation death benefits, 59, 388–389
    wrongful death actions, 113, 120–121, 390–392

M

Maine
    abortions, 399
    adoption, 398
    alienation of affections actions prohibited, 400
    criminal statutes, 400
    common-law marriages, 398
    illegitimate children, 400–401
    workers' compensation death benefits, 399
Maintenance—See Alimony; Support of illegitimate children
Mann Act violations, 106–107

INDEX

References are to Pages

Marriage
    advantages over unmarried cohabitation, 6–8—See also Cohabitation as alternative to marriage
    breach of promise of marriage actions, 90–92—See also individual states
    common-law marriages, 10–14—See Common-law marriages; See also individual states
    conflict of laws problems, 16–19
    definition of marriage, 4 n
    income taxes, discrimination against married couples—See Income tax
    license defective or not obtained, 14
    mistake as to validity of marriage, good faith party as "putative spouse," 14–15
    putative marriages, 14–15
    seduction under promise of marriage actions, 90–92—See also individual states
    subsequent marriage of biological parents as legitimizing child, 145

Married women
    disabilities at common-law, 7–8
    inequities remain, 8
    maiden name, use of, 43–44
    Married Women's Property Acts, 8
    services, compensation for, 8

Marvin v. Marvin, 1–2, 177–184, 200–202, 298–299
    complaint, App. A
    opinion of Supreme Court of California, App. B
    trial decision, App. C

Maryland
    abortions, 404
    adoption, 402, 408
    alienation of affections actions abolished, 404
    alimony, sexual misconduct as affecting, 403
    common-law marriages, 401–402
    criminal conversation actions, 404
    criminal statutes, 405
    illegitimate children, 134, 139 n, 402, 403, 404, 406–409
    insurance policies, status of cohabitant, 68, 403
    parental rights, termination, 148, 408
    paternity actions, 129, 407
    property rights of cohabitants, 162, 163 n, 164, 175, 178, 409–410
    termination of nonmarital relationship, 162, 163 n, 164, 175, 178, 409–410
    zoning laws, status of cohabitants and their children, 403

Massachusetts
    abortions, 76, 77, 412
    adoption, 412
    common-law marriages, 410
    criminal statutes, 413–415
    illegitimate children, 112 n, 117, 415–416
    insurance policy, cohabitant described as "wife," 411
    mistake as to validity of marriage, 410
    parental rights, termination, 416
    paternity actions, 130, 416

INDEX

References are to Pages

Massachusetts (continued)
    property rights of cohabitants, 162, 174 n, 180, 417
    student pregnancies, 411
    termination of nonmarital relationship, 162, 174 n, 180, 417
    workers' compensation death benefits, 411

Maternity leave for pregnant, unmarried employees, 26—See also Employment

Michigan
    abortions, 419–420
    adoption, 418, 423–424
    common-law marriages, 418
    community property law, 418
    criminal statutes, 420–422
    illegitimate children, 113 n, 139, 140, 419, 422–424
    insurance policies, illegitimate children under, 113 n, 419
    parental rights, termination, 423
    paternity actions, 422–423
    property rights of cohabitants, 162, 164 n, 171 n, 172, 177, 181, 424–425
    seduction actions abolished, 419
    termination of nonmarital relationship, 162, 164 n, 171 n, 172, 177, 181, 424–425
    workers' compensation death benefits, 418–419

Military service, impact of unwed pregnancy, 35–37

Minnesota
    abortions, 426–427
    adoption, 425–426
    alienation of affections actions, 82, 84, 427
    common-law marriages, 425
    criminal statutes, 427
    illegitimate children, 113 n, 124, 125 n, 141, 426, 427, 428–430
    insurance benefits
        illegitimate children as claimants, 113 n, 426
        maternity benefits for unmarried women, 426
    paternity actions, 428–429
    property rights of cohabitants, 154, 155, 160, 171 n, 181, 430–431
    termination of nonmarital relationship, 154, 155, 160, 171 n, 181, 430–431
    workers' compensation death benefits, 426

Miscegenation statutes, 95
    disregarded for tax purposes, 210

Mississippi
    abortions, 433
    adoption, 433, 435
    common-law marriages, 431
    criminal statutes, 433–434
    illegitimate children, 433, 434–435
    paternity actions, 435
    property rights of cohabitants, 435–436
    schoolteachers, unwed pregnancy as grounds for dismissal, 432
    student pregnancies, 432
    termination of nonmarital relationship, 435–436
    workers' compensation death benefits, 433

INDEX

References are to Pages

Missouri
    abortions, 76, 77, 437–439
    adoption, 149, 436
    alienation of affections actions, 84, 439
    common-law marriages, 436
    criminal conversation actions, 439
    criminal statutes, 439–440
    illegitimate children, 136, 437, 440–442
    insurance benefits
        cohabitant as "member of family," 70
        illegitimate children as claimants, 113 n, 437
    parental rights, termination, 149, 441–442
    property rights of cohabitants, 162 n, 164 n, 170, 442–443
    seduction under promise of marriage, 91, 92, 439
    termination of nonmarital relationship, 162 n, 164 n, 170 n, 442–443
    workers' compensation death benefits, 437
Mistake, in belief of a marriage, 153–161—See also Putative marriages
Montana
    abortions, 444–445
    adoption, 444, 447
    breach of promise of marriage actions, 445
    common-law marriages, 12, 17 n, 443
        marriage by written declaration, 443–444
    criminal statutes, 445–446
    illegitimate children, 139 n, 444, 446–447
    parental rights, termination, 447
    paternity actions, 446–447
    property rights of cohabitants, 447–448
    termination of nonmarital relationship, 447–448
    workers' compensation death benefits, 444
Motels, discrimination against unmarried couples, 41

N

Names
    common-law marriages, adoption of spouse's surname, 12, 44–45
    illegitimate children, statute giving father preference as to name, 144 n
    unmarried cohabitants, adoption of male's surname, 44–45
        as evidence of common-law marriage, 44–45
National Service Life Insurance Act, rights of illegitimates under, 58—See also Insurance
Naturalization, impact of cohabitation on petition for, 62
Nature, crime against, 98–101
Nebraska
    abortions, 450
    adoption, 449
    alimony, effect of cohabitation on right to, 449–450
    common-law marriages, 448
    criminal conversation actions, 449
    criminal statutes, 451
    illegitimate children, 140, 451–452

INDEX

References are to Pages

Nebraska (continued)
    parental rights, termination, 452
    paternity actions, 452
    property rights of cohabitants, 155, 175, 452–453
    schoolteachers, life style as grounds for dismissal, 28, 29
    termination of nonmarital relationship, 155, 175, 452–453
    workers' compensation death benefits, 449
    wrongful death, mother of illegitimate as claimant, 41

Nevada
    abortions, 454
    adoption, 454
    alienation of affections actions abolished, 455
    alimony, effect of cohabitation on right to, 86 n, 455
    common-law marriages, 453
    criminal statutes, 455–456
    illegitimate children, 454, 456
    parental rights, termination, 146, 456
    paternity actions, 456
    property rights of cohabitants, 162, 183 n, 457
    seduction, civil action for, 455
    termination of nonmarital relationship, 162, 183 n, 457
    workers' compensation death benefits, 454

New Hampshire
    abortions, 459
    adoption, 458
    breach of promise of marriage actions abolished, 459
    common-law marriages, 458
    criminal conversation actions, 459
    criminal statutes, 105, 460
    illegitimate children, 135 n, 460–462
    insurance coverage, cohabitant not "spouse" under automobile policy, 459
    paternity actions, 461
    property rights of cohabitants, 462
    termination of nonmarital relationship, 462
    workers' compensation death benefits, 459

New Jersey
    abortions, 465–466
    adoption, 463
    alienation of affections actions, 81, 466
    alimony, effect of divorcee's conduct on right to, 467
    common-law marriages, 462
    criminal statutes, 467–470
    illegitimate children, 121, 138, 141, 142, 145 n, 463, 464, 466, 470–472
    parental rights, termination, 147, 150 n, 463
    property rights of cohabitants, 163, 164, 170 n, 184, 472–475
    schoolteachers, life style as grounds for dismissal, 463
    termination of nonmarital relationship, 163, 164, 170 n, 184, 472–475
    workers' compensation death benefits, 464–465
    wrongful death actions, 466
    zoning laws, cohabitants considered "family," 465

New Mexico
    abortions, 476

INDEX

References are to Pages

New Mexico (continued)
    adoption, 149, 476
    alimony, effect of cohabitation on right to, 86
    common-law marriages, 475
    community property state, 475
    criminal statutes, 477–478
    illegitimate children, 476, 477
    parental rights, termination, 149, 476
    paternity actions, 478
    schoolteacher's termination for unwed pregnancy, 32 n, 475
    workers' compensation death benefits, 476
    wrongful death actions, 477

New York
    abortions, 483
    adoption, 146, 147, 149, 150, 480–481
    alienation of affections actions abolished, 484
    alimony, effect of cohabitation on right to, 85, 86, 484
        husband's right to alimony, 9 n, 85
    breach of promise of marriage actions abolished, 484
    common-law marriages, 479
    criminal conversation actions abolished, 484
    criminal statutes, 485–486
    family court, disputes between cohabitants not within jurisdiction, 481
    housing discrimination against unmarried cohabitants, 43 n, 479–480
    illegitimate children, 125, 127, 128, 137, 138 n, 139 n, 140, 145 n, 482, 483, 486–488
    insurance
        cancellation because of mode of living prohibited, 63, 482
        cohabitant not "spouse" under automobile policy, 68, 482
    parental rights, termination, 146, 147, 149, 150, 480
    paternity actions, 115, 137, 487
    property rights of cohabitants, 162, 164 n, 165 n, 166, 171 n, 175 n, 176, 177, 488–490
    schoolteachers, question of fitness, 28
    support obligations of father not relieved by daughter's cohabitation, 481
    termination of nonmarital relationship, 162, 164 n, 165 n, 166, 171 n, 175 n, 176, 177, 488–490
    workers' compensation death benefits, 482
    wrongful death actions, 483

North Carolina
    abortions, 491
    adoption, 490
    alienation of affections actions, 491
    alimony, effect of cohabitation on right to, 491
    common-law marriages, 490
    criminal statutes, 492–493
    illegitimate children, 490, 493–494
    property rights of cohabitants, 170, 495
    seduction, civil action for, 491
    termination of nonmarital relationship, 170, 495
    workers' compensation death benefits, 490–491

INDEX

References are to Pages

North Dakota
    abduction or enticement of husband or wife, civil actions for, 498
    abortions, 498
    adoption, 496-497
    alienation of affections actions, 498
    breach of promise of marriage actions, 498
    common-law marriages, 496
    criminal statutes, 499
    discrimination in public places statute, cohabitant's and, 496
    illegitimate children, 134, 497, 498, 499-501
    paternity actions, 500
    property rights of cohabitants, 501
    schoolteachers, "immorality" as grounds for dismissal, 496
    seduction, civil actions for, 498
    termination of nonmarital relationship, 501
    workers' compensation death benefits, 497
    wrongful death actions, 498

O

Ohio
    abortions, 504
    adoption, 503
    alienation of affections actions abolished, 505
    alimony, effect of cohabitation on right to, 505
    breach of promise of marriage actions abolished, 505
    common-law marriages, 12, 501
    criminal conversation actions abolished, 505
    criminal statutes, 505-506
    housing ordinance limiting occupancy to single "family," 502
    illegitimate children, 118 n, 133, 134, 140, 144, 502, 504, 505, 506-508
    insurance benefits
        cohabitant's insurable interest, 64
        illegitimate children as claimants, 504
    paternity actions, 130, 502-503, 506
    property rights of cohabitants, 509
    putative marriages, 15
    schoolteachers' heterosexual misconduct, 502
    seduction actions abolished, 505
    termination of nonmarital relationship, 509
    workers' compensation death benefits, 503-504
    wrongful death actions, 505

Oklahoma
    abortions, 512-513
    adoption, 510-511, 516-517
    alienation of affections actions abolished, 513
    breach of promise of marriage actions, 513
    cohabitation following divorce, 509
    common-law marriages, 509-510
    criminal statutes, 513-514
    illegitimate children, 146 n, 511, 515-517

INDEX

References are to Pages

Oklahoma (continued)
    parental rights, termination, 516-517
    property rights of cohabitants, 160, 176, 517-518
    seduction actions abolished, 513
    services contributed to household, compensation, 157, 517
    termination of nonmarital relationship, 160, 176, 517-518
    workers' compensation death benefits, 511-512
Oregon
    abortions, 522
    adoption, 147, 148, 149, 520-521
    alienation of affections actions, 523
    common-law marriages, 518-519
    criminal conversation actions abolished, 523
    criminal statutes, 523
    illegitimate children, 137, 140, 521, 523-525
    insurance benefits, cohabitant as claimant, 66, 522
    marriage presumed from open cohabitation, 519
    marriage requirements, 518-519
    parental rights, termination, 147, 148, 149, 520, 525
    property rights of cohabitants, 164, 169, 177, 181, 182, 183 n, 525-527
    schoolteachers and cohabitation, 520
    termination of nonmarital relationship, 164, 169, 177, 181, 182, 183 n, 525-527
    welfare assistance, denial to cohabitants unconstitutional, 55, 520
    workers' compensation death benefits, 521-522

P

Partnership theory in adjusting rights of cohabitants, 165-167—See also Termination of nonmarital relationship
Paternity actions, 129-132—See also individual states
Pennsylvania
    abortions, 531
    adoption, 149, 529-530, 534-535
    adultery as grounds for dismissal of public employee, 529
    alienation of affections actions, 532
    alimony, sexual misconduct as affecting right to, 531
    common-law marriages, 12 n, 528-529
    criminal conversation actions abolished, 82, 83, 531-532
    criminal statutes, 532-533
    illegitimate children, 134, 138, 143, 149, 530, 531, 533-535
    parental rights, termination, 149, 534-535
    paternity actions, 533-534
    property rights of cohabitants, 159, 163 n, 164, 170, 535-536
    schoolteachers' maternity leave policy, discrimination against unmarrieds, 529
    termination of nonmarital relationship, 159, 163 n, 164, 170, 535-536
    workers' compensation death benefits, 12 n, 530
    wrongful death actions, 531
Pooling of earnings theory in adjusting rights of cohabitants, 167-168—See also Termination of nonmarital relationship

INDEX

References are to Pages

Posthumous child, death benefits, 59
    wrongful death actions, 121
Pregnancy
    employers' discrimination against pregnant employees—See Employment
    student pregnancies, 34–35
Privacy
    abortion, denial as invasion of privacy, 38, 72–78
    contraceptives, law prohibiting use as invasion of privacy, 37, 78–80
    housing discrimination against unmarried couples, 39—See also Housing
    right of privacy generally, constitutional basis, 37–40
    sexual conduct of consenting adults, 92–102
        marital versus nonmarital relationships, 37–40
Probation, noncohabitation as condition of, 107–109
Promise to marry, breach of, 81, 90–92
Property insurance—See Insurance
Property rights of cohabitants—See Termination of nonmarital relationship
Purchase money resulting trust, use in adjusting rights of cohabitants, 168–171—See also Termination of nonmarital relationship
Putative fathers—See Children, illegitimate
Putative marriages
    generally, 14–16
    property rights of putative spouse—See Termination of nonmarital relationship
    putative spouse defined, 15
    workers' compensation death benefits, putative spouse as claimant, 60—See also individual states

Q

Quantum meruit theory in adjusting rights of cohabitants, 172—See also Termination of nonmarital relationship
Quasi-contract theory in adjusting rights of cohabitants, 173–174—See also Termination of nonmarital relationship

R

Rape
    fraud, rape by, 94
    statutory rape, 104–106
Real estate—See also Termination of nonmarital relationship
    conveyances to cohabitants as husband and wife, 161–165
    housing discrimination against cohabitants—See Housing
Residence
    change of residence as affecting status of relationship, 16–19
    execution against property of unmarried cohabitants, 48–49
    "head of household," unmarried cohabitant as, 48–49
        income tax purposes—See Income tax
    homestead laws, unmarried cohabitants under, 48–49
    sale of residence, taxable gain affected by marital status, 207

INDEX

References are to Pages

Resulting trust theory in adjusting rights of cohabitants, 168–171—See also Termination of nonmarital relationship
Rhode Island
    abortions, 538–539
    adoption, 537–538, 541–542
    alienation of affections actions, 81, 83, 539
    alimony, effect of remarriage, 540
    common-law marriages, 537
    criminal conversation actions, 81, 539
    criminal statutes, 540
    illegitimate children, 537, 540–542
    parental rights, termination, 541–542
    paternity actions, 541
    property conveyed to parties of void marriage, 542
    workers' compensation death benefits, 538

S

Schools
    students, exclusion or expulsion for marriage, cohabitation or pregnancy, 34–35
    teachers, termination or refusal to hire because of marriage, cohabitation or pregnancy, 28–33—See also Employment
Seduction under promise of marriage, actions for, 81, 90–92, 95, 104—See also individual states
Services contributed by cohabitant, claim for, 157–161—See also Termination of nonmarital relationship
Sexual conduct of cohabitants
    criminal statutes, cohabitants as possible violators, 94–107—See also individual states
    privacy, cohabitants' right to, 37–40, 95–97
Social security
    children of unmarried cohabitants, eligibility for dependents' benefits, 50–53
    cohabitation versus marriage, discrimination in benefits, 256
    tax rate, 190, 255
    unmarried cohabitant not eligible for survivor's benefits, 51
Sodomy, 98–101
South Carolina
    abortions, 544
    adoption, 543, 547
    alimony, remarriage or cohabitation as affecting right to, 545
    common-law marriages, 12, 542
    criminal conversation actions, 545
    criminal statutes, 545–546
    illegitimate children, 544, 546–547
    parental rights, termination, 547
    paternity actions, 547
    property rights of cohabitants, 170, 547–548
    schoolteachers, immorality as grounds for dismissal, 543
    seduction, civil actions for, 545

INDEX

References are to Pages

South Carolina (continued)
    termination of nonmarital relationship, 170, 547–548
    workers' compensation death benefits, 542, 544
    wrongful death actions, 544

South Dakota
    abortions, 550
    adoption, 549
    common-law marriages, 548–549
    criminal conversation actions, 551
    criminal statutes, 551
    illegitimate children, 550, 551–553
    insurance
        discrimination on basis of marital status forbidden, 63–64, 549
        insurable interest of cohabitant, 549
    parental rights, termination, 552–553
    paternity actions, 552
    property rights of cohabitants, 168, 553
    schoolteacher's cohabitation as grounds for dismissal, 29, 549
    seduction, civil action for, 550–551
    termination of nonmarital relationship, 168, 553
    workers' compensation death benefits, 550

Statute of frauds, impact on cohabitation contracts, 182

Statutory rape, 104–106

Students, exclusion or expulsion for marriage, cohabitation or pregnancy, 34–35

Support
    illegitimate children, 132–137
    obligation of father not relieved by daughter's cohabitation, 481

Surname, effect of adoption of cohabitant's, 44–45—See also Names

T

Taxes—See Estate tax; Gift tax; Income tax; Social security

Tenants in common, property held by cohabitants as, 161–165

Tennessee
    abortions, 556
    adoption, 554, 559
    alienation of affections actions, 81, 82, 556
    common-law marriages, 554
    criminal conversation actions, 556
    criminal statutes, 557
    illegitimate children, 137, 555, 556, 557–559
    insurance, cohabitant as "spouse" or "member of family," 68, 555
    parental rights, termination, 559
    paternity actions, 558
    property rights of cohabitants, 162, 163 n, 559–560
    termination of nonmarital relationship, 559–560
    workers' compensation death benefits, 555
    wrongful death actions, 556

Termination of nonmarital relationship
    death of cohabitant, claims for benefits—See Death of unmarried cohabitant

INDEX

References are to Pages

Termination of nonmarital relationship (continued)
    division of accumulated property or income—See also individual states
        equitable lien theory, 176–177
        express contract between parties, 157, 177–187
            suggested provisions, 184–186
        generally, 6, 153–187
        gift tax liability—See Gift tax
        household goods, 159–161
        implied contract between parties, 171–173
        indebitatus assumpsit, theory of, 173
        joint tenants, property held as, 163–164
        joint venture theory, 165–167
        land conveyed to cohabitants as husband and wife, 161–165
        Marvin case—See Marvin v. Marvin
        mistaken belief in valid marriage
            equitable division required, 153, 155–156
            judicial attitude generally, 153–154
            services contributed to household, value of, 157–159
            theories traditionally applied, 154–155, 165–177
        partnership theory, 165–167
        pooling of earnings theory, 167–168
        purchase money resulting trust, 168–171
        putative marriages—See mistaken belief in valid marriage, above
        quantum meruit theory, 172
        quasi-contract theory, 173–174
        resulting trust theory, 168–171
        services contributed to household, 157–161, 171
        tax consequences—See Estate tax; Gift tax; Income tax
        tenants in common, property held as, 163–164

Texas
    abortions, 563
    adoption, 149, 562
    alienation of affections actions, 564
    common-law marriages, 10, 560–562
    criminal conversation actions, 564
    criminal statutes, 564–565
    illegitimate children, 130 n, 133, 145 n, 563, 565–567
    parental rights, termination, 149, 567
    paternity actions, 130 n, 566
    property rights of cohabitants, 154, 155, 156 n, 164 n, 166, 171, 176, 567–569
    putative marriages, 15, 567–568
    termination of nonmarital relationship, 154, 155, 156 n, 164 n, 166, 171, 176, 567–569
    workers' compensation death benefits, 563

Tort liability of cohabitants, 80–84
    actions by cohabitant against partner, 89–92

Trusts
    constructive, 174–176
    resulting, 169–171
    splitting income through trust, 249–251

INDEX

References are to Pages

U

Unemployment, effect of unwed pregnancy on right to payments, 56
Uniform Child Custody Jurisdiction Act, 138
Uniform Illegitimacy Act, 135
Uniform Marriage and Divorce Act, 15, 165
Uniform Parentage Act, 131
Uniform Paternity Act, 129
Uniform Reciprocal Enforcement of Support Act, 135
Utah
    abortions, 572
    adoption, 147, 570
    alimony, effect of remarriage or birth of illegitimate child, 574
    common-law marriages, 16 n, 570
    criminal statutes, 574
    illegitimate children, 139 n, 147, 571, 575–577
    interference with marital relation, civil action for, 574
    minor's right of privacy, 572–573
    parental rights, termination, 147
    paternity actions, 575–576
    polygamous marriages, 570, 574
    property rights of cohabitants, 154, 177, 577–578
    schoolteachers, termination for immoral or unprofessional conduct, 570
    seduction of a minor, civil action for, 574
    termination of nonmarital relationship, 154, 177, 577–578
    workers' compensation death benefits, 60, 571

V

Vermont
    abortions, 578–579
    adoption, 578
    alienation of affections actions abolished, 580
    alimony, effect of cohabitation on right to, 579–580
    breach of contract of marriage actions abolished, 580
    common-law marriages, 578
    criminal conversation actions abolished, 580
    criminal statutes, 580
    illegitimate children, 140, 580–582
    parental rights, termination, 581
    paternity actions, 581
    property rights of cohabitants, 582
    termination of nonmarital relationship, 582
Veteran's Administration Act
    illegitimate children, eligibility for benefits, 58
    "widow" defined, 58
Virginia
    abortions, 584
    adoption, 582–583
    alienation of affections actions abolished, 584
    alimony, effect of remarriage on right to, 584

INDEX

References are to Pages

Virginia (continued)
 common-law marriages, 582
 criminal conversation actions abolished, 584
 criminal statutes, 99, 584–585
 illegitimate children, 116, 134, 583, 585–587
 insurance, cohabitant as undesirable risk, 67
 miscegenation statute, 17 n, 77
 paternity actions, 586
 property rights of cohabitants, 587–588
 seduction actions abolished, 584
 workers' compensation death benefits, 583
Visitation rights of putative father of illegitimate child, 138

W

Washington
 abortions, 76, 589
 adoption, 588
 alienation of affections actions abolished, 589
 breach of promise of marriage actions, 91, 589
 common-law marriages, 588
 criminal statutes, 590
 illegitimate children, 120, 134 n, 136, 590–591
 parental rights, termination, 149, 591
 property rights of cohabitants, 154, 155, 157 n, 160, 163 n, 166 n, 167, 169, 170, 171, 591–594
 schoolteacher's life style as grounds for dismissal, 588
 termination of nonmarital relationship, 154, 155, 157 n, 160, 163 n, 166 n, 167, 169, 170, 171, 591–594
Welfare benefits for children of unmarried cohabitants, 50–55—See also individual states
West Virginia
 abortions, 596
 adoption, 594–595
 agreement to compensate for injury resulting from illicit cohabitation, 598 n
 alienation of affections actions abolished, 596
 alimony, effect of cohabitation on right to, 596
 breach of promise of marriage actions abolished, 596
 common-law marriages, 17 n, 594
 criminal statutes, 596
 illegitimate children, 135 n, 145 n, 595, 597
 parental rights, termination, 597–598
 paternity actions, 135 n, 597
 property rights of cohabitants, 598
 seduction, civil action for, 596
 workers' compensation death benefits, 595
 wrongful death action, illegitimate child as claimant, 595
Wisconsin
 abortions, 599
 adoption, 598

INDEX

References are to Pages

Wisconsin (continued)
    alienation of affections actions abolished, 601
    alimony, effect of cohabitation on right to, 600
    breach of promise of marriage actions abolished, 601
    common-law marriages, 598
    contraceptives, unmarried persons' right to use, 79, 600
    criminal conversation actions abolished, 601
    criminal statutes, 92, 601–602
    illegitimate children 124 n, 127, 136, 599, 602–603
    parental rights, termination, 603
    paternity actions, 127, 602–603
    property rights of cohabitants, 171 n, 604
    termination of nonmarital relationship, 171 n, 604
    workers' compensation death benefits, 599
    wrongful death actions, 600
Witness for or against spouse, competency, 3
    common-law spouse, 3 n
    unmarried cohabitant, 3 n
Workers' compensation death benefits under federal and state acts—See also individual states
    cohabitant as claimant, 56–61
    common-law spouse as claimant, 56–61
    illegitimate child as claimant, 56–61
Wrongful birth actions by children, 84–85
Wrongful death actions—See also individual states
    cohabitant or child of cohabitant as claimant, 89
    illegitimate child as claimant, 119–121
    parent of illegitimate child as claimant, 121
Wyoming
    abortions, 606
    adoption, 605
    alienation of affections actions abolished, 606
    breach of promise of marriage actions abolished, 606
    common-law marriages, 604
    criminal conversation actions abolished, 606
    criminal statutes, 606
    illegitimate children, 605, 606–607
    parental rights, termination, 607
    paternity actions, 606–607
    property rights of cohabitants, 157 n, 607
    seduction actions abolished, 606
    termination of nonmarital relationship, 157 n, 607
    workers' compensation death benefits, 605
    wrongful death actions, 605